JavaScript

Fourth Edition

Don Gosselin

COURSE TECHNOLOGY
CENGAGE Learning

Australia • Brazil • Japan • Korea • Mexico • Singapore • Spain • United Kingdom • United States

COURSE TECHNOLOGY
CENGAGE Learning

JavaScript, Fourth Edition
by Don Gosselin

Vice President, Technology and Trades
ABU: Dave Garza

Director of Learning Solutions:
Sandy Clark

Acquisitions Editor: Amy Jollymore

Managing Editor: Tricia Coia

Development Editor: Ann Shaffer

Content Project Manager: Jill Klaffky

Product Marketing Manager:
Bryant Chrzan

Editorial Assistant: Patrick Frank

Cover Designer: Marissa Falco

Compositor: Value Chain International Ltd.

Manufacturing Coordinator: Julio Esperas

Copy Editor: Harry Johnson

Proofreader: Vicki Zimmer

Indexer: Rich Carlson

For product information and technology assistance, contact us at
Cengage Learning Customer & Sales Support, 1-800-354-9706

For permission to use material from this text or product,
submit all requests online at **cengage.com/permissions**
Further permissions questions can be emailed to
permissionrequest@cengage.com

ISBN: 1-4239-0150-9

ISBN-13: 978-1-4239-0150-1

Course Technology
25 Thomson Place
Boston, MA 02210
USA

Disclaimer
Course Technology Cengage Learning reserves the right to revise this publication and make changes from time to time in its content without notice.

Cengage Learning is a leading provider of customized learning solutions with office locations around the globe, including Singapore, the United Kingdom, Australia, Mexico, Brazil, and Japan. Locate your local office at:
international.cengage.com/region

Cengage Learning products are represented in Canada by Nelson Education, Ltd.

To learn more about Course Technology, visit
www.cengage.com/coursetechnology
To learn more about Cengage Learning, visit
www.cengage.com
Purchase any of our products at your local college store or at our preferred online store **www.ichapters.com**

Printed in the United States of America.
2 3 4 5 6 7 8 9 10 09

Brief Contents

Contents

Preface

JavaScript is a client-side scripting language that allows Web page authors to develop interactive Web pages and sites. Although JavaScript is considered a programming language, it is also a critical part of Web page design and authoring. This is because the JavaScript language "lives" within a Web page's elements. The language is relatively easy to learn, allowing non-programmers to quickly incorporate JavaScript functionality into a Web page. In fact, because it is used extensively in the countless Web pages that are available on the World Wide Web, JavaScript is arguably the most widely used programming language in the world.

JavaScript, 4th Edition teaches Web page development with JavaScript for students with little programming or database experience. Although no prior programming experience is required, knowledge of HTML and Web page design is helpful, but not required. This book covers the basics of ECMAScript Edition 3, which is compatible with recent Web browsers including Microsoft Internet Explorer 4.0 and later and Netscape 6.0 and later, along with advanced topics including object-oriented programming, the Document Object Model (DOM), and AJAX. Further, this book presents JavaScript techniques using XHTML-compatible Web pages. After you complete this course, you will be able to use JavaScript to build professional quality, dynamic Web sites.

The Approach

This book introduces a variety of techniques, focusing on what you need to know to start writing JavaScript programs. In each chapter, you perform tasks that let you use a particular technique to build and create JavaScript programs. In addition to step-by-step tasks, each chapter includes a Chapter Summary, Review Questions, Hands-On Projects, and Case Projects that highlight major concepts and let you practice the techniques you learn. The Hands-On Projects are guided activities that reinforce the skills you learn in the chapter and build on your learning experience by providing additional ways to apply your knowledge in new situations. At the end of each chapter, you will also complete Case Projects that let you use the skills you learned in the chapter to write JavaScript programs on your own.

As with the last edition of this book, Web page examples and exercises are written in XHTML. Although you need to have a solid understanding of HTML to be successful with this book, you do not necessarily need to be an expert with XHTML. Because XHTML is almost identical to HTML, you can easily adapt any of your existing HTML skills to XHTML, and vice versa.

Overview of This Book

The examples and exercises in this book will help you achieve the following objectives:

- Use JavaScript with well-formed Web pages
- Work with JavaScript variables and data types and learn how to use the operations that can be performed on them.
- Add functions, events, and control structures to your JavaScript programs
- Write JavaScript code that controls the Web browser through the browser object model

- Use JavaScript to make sure data was entered properly into form fields and to perform other types of preprocessing before form data is sent to a server

- Include object-oriented programming techniques in your JavaScript programs

- Manipulate data in strings and arrays

- Trace and resolve errors in JavaScript programs

- Save state information using hidden form fields, query strings, and cookies

- Add animation and interactivity to your Web pages using the Document Object Model (DOM) and Dynamic HTML (DHTML)

- Dynamically update Web pages with AJAX

This book presents 12 chapters that cover specific aspects of JavaScript programming. **Chapter 1** discusses basic concepts of the World Wide Web, introduces XHTML documents, and covers the basics of how to add JavaScript to well-formed Web pages. Variables, data types, expressions, and operators are discussed in **Chapter 2**. This early introduction of key JavaScript concepts gives students a framework for better understanding more advanced concepts and techniques later in this book, and allows them to work on more comprehensive projects from the start. **Chapter 3** covers functions and events, and introduces structured logic using control structures and statements. **Chapter 4** teaches how to use JavaScript to manipulate the Web browser via the `Window`, `History`, `Location`, and `Navigator` objects. **Chapter 5** explains how to use JavaScript to make sure data was entered properly into form fields and how to perform other types of preprocessing before form data is sent to a server. **Chapter 6** presents object-oriented programming concepts, including how to use JavaScript's built-in `Array`, `Date`, `Number`, and `Math` classes. **Chapter 7** explains how to manipulate data in strings and arrays. **Chapter 8** provides a thorough discussion of debugging techniques, including how to use Script Debugger for Internet Explorer. **Chapter 9** explains how to save state information using hidden form fields, query strings, and cookies, and also briefly discusses JavaScript security issues. **Chapter 10** and **Chapter 11** teach how to add animation and interactivity to your Web pages using the Document Object Model (DOM) and Dynamic HTML (DHTML). **Chapter 12** introduces the basics of how to use AJAX to dynamically update portions of a Web page with server-side data.

What's New in this Edition?

Enhancements to this edition include:

- The book is now printed in two colors, with keywords, new terms, and other important elements formatted in blue for easier identification.

- Significant revisions and improvements to the chapter projects and examples.

- Completely revised end-of-chapter Hands-On Projects and Case Projects.

- A new chapter has been added (Chapter 7) that explains how to manipulate data in strings and arrays.

- The debugging chapter (now Chapter 8) includes coverage of Mozilla JavaScript Debugger and error handling techniques.

- The cookies and security chapter (now Chapter 9) has been expanded to include secure coding techniques.

- Previous versions of this book included chapters on server-side scripting with ASP. To allow this book to focus solely JavaScript techniques, the ASP chapters have been removed from the printed version of the book. However, the original versions of these chapters are available at *www.course.com*.

- A new chapter (Chapter 12) has been added that introduces the basics of how to use AJAX to dynamically update portions of a Web page with server-side data.

- The following new appendices have been added:

  - Appendix A, "Building a Web Development Environment," which explains how to build a Web development environment consisting of a Web server and PHP.

  - Appendix B, "Introduction to PHP," which introduces the basics of server-side scripting with PHP.

  - Appendix C, "Processing XML," which discusses the basics of XML.

Features

JavaScript, 4th Edition is a superior textbook because it also includes the following features:

- **Chapter Objectives**: Each chapter in this book begins with a list of the important concepts to be mastered within the chapter. This list provides you with a quick reference to the contents of the chapter as well as a useful study aid.

- **Illustrations and Tables**: Illustrations help you visualize common components and relationships. Tables list conceptual items and examples in a visual and readable format.

- **Tips**: These helpful asides provide you with practical advice and proven strategies related to the concept being discussed.

- **Notes**: Notes provide additional helpful information on specific techniques and concepts.

- **Cautions**: These short warnings point out troublesome issues that you need to watch out for when writing JavaScript programs.

- **Chapter Summaries**: These brief overviews of chapter content provide a helpful way to recap and revisit the ideas covered in each chapter.

- **Review Questions**: This set of 20 review questions reinforces the main ideas introduced in each chapter. These questions help determine whether or not you have mastered the concepts covered in the chapter.

- **Hands-On Projects**: Although it is important to understand the concepts behind JavaScript programming, no amount of theory can improve on real-world experience. To this end, along with conceptual explanations, each chapter provides Hands-On Projects related to each major topic aimed at providing you with practical experience. Because the Hands-On Projects ask you to go beyond the boundaries of the text itself, they provide you with practice using JavaScript skills in real-world situations.

- **Case Projects**: The Case Projects at the end of each chapter are designed to help you apply what you have learned to business situations much like those you can expect to encounter as a JavaScript programmer. They give you the opportunity to independently synthesize and evaluate information, examine potential solutions, and make recommendations, much as you would in an actual programming situation.

Teaching Tools

The following supplemental materials are available when this book is used in a classroom setting. All of the teaching tools available with this book are provided to the instructor on a single CD-ROM.

- **Electronic Instructor's Manual**. The Instructor's Manual that accompanies this textbook includes: Additional instructional material to assist in class preparation, such as Sample Syllabi, Chapter Outlines, Technical Notes, Lecture Notes, Quick Quizzes, Teaching Tips, Discussion Topics, and Additional Case Projects.

- **ExamView®**. This textbook is accompanied by ExamView, a powerful testing software package that allows instructors to create and administer printed, computer (LAN-based), and Internet exams. ExamView includes hundreds of questions that correspond to the topics covered in this text, enabling students to generate detailed study guides that include page references for further review. The computer-based and Internet testing components allow students to take exams at their computers, and also save the instructor time by grading each exam automatically.

- **PowerPoint Presentations**. This book comes with Microsoft PowerPoint slides for each chapter. These are included as a teaching aid for classroom presentation, to make available to students on the network for chapter review, or to be printed for classroom distribution. Instructors can add their own slides for additional topics they introduce to the class.

- **Data Files**. Files that contain all of the data necessary for the Hands-On Projects and Case Projects are provided through the Course Technology Web site at *www.course.com*, and are also available on the Teaching Tools CD-ROM.

- **Solution Files**. Solutions to end-of-chapter Review Questions, Hands-On Projects, and Case Projects are provided on the Teaching Tools CD-ROM and may also be found on the Course Technology Web site at *www.course.com*. The solutions are password protected.

- **Distance Learning**. Course Technology is proud to present online test banks in WebCT and Blackboard, as well as MyCourse 2.0, Course Technology's own course enhancement tool, to provide the most complete and dynamic learning experience possible. Instructors are encouraged to make the most of the course, both online and offline. For more information on how to access your online test bank, contact your local Course Technology sales representative.

Read This Before You Begin

The following information will help you as you prepare to use this textbook.

To the User of the Data Files

To complete the steps and projects in this book, you will need data files that have been created specifically for this book. The data files are located on the CD-ROM that came with this book. You also can obtain the files electronically from the Course Technology Web site by connecting to *www.course.com* and then searching for this book title. Note that you can use a computer in your school lab or your own computer to complete the steps and Hands-On Projects in this book.

Using Your Own Computer

You can use a computer in your school lab or your own computer to complete the chapters, Hands-On Projects, and Case Projects in this book. To use your own computer, you will need the following:

- **A Web browser**. You can use any browser you like to view the solutions to this exercises in this text, as long as it is compatible with the standardized version of the DOM that is recommended by the World Wide Web Consortium (W3C). At the time of this writing, Internet Explorer 5.0 and higher and Netscape 6 and higher are compatible with the W3C DOM, although other browsers are also compatible.

- **A code-based HTML editor**, such as Macromedia Dreamweaver, or a text editor such as Notepad on Windows, GNU Emacs on UNIX/Linux, or SimpleText on the Macintosh.

- **A Web server** (for Chapter 12) such as Apache HTTP Server or Microsoft Internet Information Services and **PHP**. Appendix A contains detailed instructions on how to install a Web server and PHP.

To the Instructor

To complete all the exercises and chapters in this book, your students must work with a set of user files, called data files, and download software from Web sites. The data files are located on the CD-ROM that came with this book and are also included in the Instructor's Resource Kit. They may also be obtained electronically through the Course Technology Web site at *www.course.com*. Have students follow the instructions in Chapter 1 to install the data files.

Course Technology Data Files

You are granted a license to copy the data files to any computer or computer network used by individuals who have purchased this book.

Visit Our World Wide Web Site

Additional materials designed especially for this book might be available for your course. Periodically search *www.course.com* for more information and materials to accompany this text.

Acknowledgements

A text such as this represents the hard work of many people, not just the author. I would like to thank all the people who helped make this book a reality. First and foremost, I would like to thank Ann Shaffer, Development Editor, Tricia Coia, Managing Editor, and Amy Jollymore, Acquisitions Editor, for helping me get the job done. I would also like to thank Jill Klaffky, Content Project Manager, for all her hard work on the Production side of things, and Nicole Ashton of Green Pen Quality Assurance for her meticulous review of the technical material in the book.

Many, many thanks to the reviewers who provided plenty of comments and positive direction during the development of this book, including: Wendy Ceccucci, Quinnipiac University; Doug Hulsey, Limestone College, and Judy Scholl, Austin Community College.

On the personal side, I would like to thank my family and friends for supporting me in my career; I don't see many of you nearly as often as I'd like, but you are always in my thoughts. My most important thanks always goes to my wonderful wife Kathy for her never ending support and encouragement, and to Noah the wonder dog.

I dedicate this book to my mother, Pamela Rurka, for fighting the good fight. Keep fighting, Mama. Keep fighting.

1

Introduction to JavaScript

In this chapter you will:

- Study the history of the World Wide Web
- Work with well-formed Web pages
- Learn about Web development
- Learn about the JavaScript programming language
- Add structure to your JavaScript programs
- Learn about logic and debugging

The original purpose of the World Wide Web (WWW) was to locate and display information. However, once the Web grew beyond a small academic and scientific community, people began to recognize that greater interactivity would make the Web more useful. As commercial applications of the Web grew, the demand for more interactive and visually appealing Web sites also grew.

To respond to the demand for greater interactivity, an entirely new Web programming language was needed. Netscape filled this need by developing the JavaScript programming language. Originally designed for use in the Navigator Web browser, JavaScript is now also used in most Web browsers including Internet Explorer.

Although JavaScript is considered a programming language, it is also a critical part of Web page design and authoring. This is because the JavaScript language "lives" within a Web page's elements. In other words, the JavaScript code you write is usually placed within the elements that make up a Web page. JavaScript can turn static documents into applications such as games or calculators. JavaScript code can change the contents of a Web page after a browser has rendered it. It can also create visual effects such as animation, and it can control the Web browser window itself. None of this was possible before the creation of JavaScript.

In this chapter, you will learn the skills required to create basic JavaScript programs. In order to be successful in your JavaScript studies, you should already possess a strong knowledge of HTML and Web page-authoring techniques. The first part of this chapter provides a quick refresher on the history of the World Wide Web and the basics on how to create Web pages with HTML and its successor, XHTML. If you are extremely comfortable with how to create Web pages, then feel free to skip this material. However, be sure that you understand key terms, such as "document" and "element," because they are used frequently throughout this book.

TIP

For the most current Web page-authoring techniques, see Don Gosselin's *XHTML*, also published by Course Technology.

The World Wide Web

The Internet is a vast network that connects computers all over the world. The original plans for the Internet grew out of a series of memos written by J. C. R. Licklider of Massachusetts Institute of Technology (MIT), in August 1962, discussing his concept of a "Galactic Network." Licklider envisioned a global computer network through which users could access data and programs from any site on the network. The Internet was actually developed in the 1960s by the Advanced Research Projects Agency (or ARPA) of the U.S. Department of Defense, which later changed its name to Defense Advanced Research Projects Agency (or DARPA). The goal of the early Internet was to connect the main computer systems of various universities and research institutions that were funded by this agency. This first implementation of the Internet was referred to as the ARPANET. More computers were connected to the ARPANET in the years following its initial development in the 1960s, although access to the ARPANET was still restricted by the U.S. government primarily to academic researchers, scientists, and the military.

The 1980s saw the widespread development of local area networks (LANs) and the personal computer. Although at one time restricted to academia and the military, computers and networks soon became common in business and everyday life. By the end of the 1980s, businesses and individual computer users began to recognize the global communications capabilities and potential of the Internet, and convinced the U.S. government to allow commercial access to the Internet.

In 1990 and 1991, Tim Berners-Lee created what would become the World Wide Web, or the Web, at the European Laboratory for Particle Physics (CERN) in Geneva, Switzerland, as a way to easily access cross-referenced documents that existed on the CERN computer network. When other academics and scientists saw the usefulness of being able to easily access cross-referenced documents using Berners-Lee's system, the Web as we know it today was born. In fact, this method of accessing cross-referenced documents, known as hypertext linking, is probably the most important aspect of the Web because it allows you to open other Web pages quickly. A hypertext link, or hyperlink, contains a reference to a specific Web page that you can click to open that Web page.

TIP

If you want to learn more about the history of the Internet, the Internet Society (ISOC) maintains a list of links to Internet histories at *http://www.isoc.org/internet/history/*.

A common misconception is that the words "Web" and "Internet" are synonymous. The Web is only one *part* of the Internet, and is a means of communicating on the Internet. The Internet is also composed of other communication methods such as e-mail systems that send and receive messages. However, due to its enormous influence on computing, communications, and the economy, the World Wide Web is arguably the most important part of the Internet today and is the primary focus of this book.

A document on the Web is called a Web page and is identified by a unique address called the Uniform Resource Locator, or URL. A URL is also commonly referred to as a Web address. A URL is a type of Uniform Resource Identifier (URI), which is a generic term for many types of names and addresses on the World Wide Web. The term Web site refers to the location on the Internet of the Web pages and related files (such as graphic and video files) that belong to a company, organization, or individual. You display a Web page on your computer screen using a program called a Web browser. A person can retrieve and open a Web page in a Web browser either by entering a URL in the Web browser's Address box or by clicking a hypertext link. When a user wants to access a Web page, either by entering its URL in a browser's Address box or by clicking a link, the user's Web browser asks a Web server for the Web page in what is referred to as a request. A Web server is a computer that delivers Web pages. What the Web server returns to the user is called the response.

Web Browsers

You can choose from a number of different browsers, but at the time of this writing, Microsoft Internet Explorer is the most popular browser on the market. Although Internet Explorer is the most popular browser, it was not the first. NCSA Mosaic was created in 1993 at the University of Illinois and was the first program to allow users to navigate the Web using a graphical user interface (GUI). In 1994, Netscape released Navigator, which soon controlled 75% of the market. Netscape maintained its control of the browser market until 1996, when Microsoft entered the market with the release of Internet Explorer, and the so-called browser wars began, in which Microsoft and Netscape fought for control of the browser market.

NOTE

Prior to version 6, the Netscape Web browser was called Navigator or Netscape Navigator. With the release of version 6, however, Netscape dropped "Navigator" from the browser name, and now simply refers to its browser as "Netscape." For this reason, in this book "Navigator Web browser" refers to versions older than version 6, and "Netscape Web browser" refers to version 6 and later.

The browser wars began over DHTML, a combination of various technologies including HTML and JavaScript that allows a Web page to change after it has been rendered by a browser. Examples of DHTML include the ability to position text and elements, change document background color, and create effects such as animation.

Earlier versions of Internet Explorer and Navigator included DHTML elements that were incompatible. Furthermore, Microsoft and Netscape each wanted its version of DHTML to become the industry standard. To settle the argument, the World Wide Web Consortium set out to create a platform-independent and browser-neutral version of DHTML. The World Wide Web

Consortium, or W3C, was established in 1994 at MIT to oversee the development of Web technology standards. While the W3C was drafting a recommendation for DHTML, versions 4 of both Internet Explorer and Navigator added a number of proprietary DHTML elements that were completely incompatible with the other browser. As a result, when working with advanced DHTML techniques such as animation, a programmer had to write a different set of HTML code for each browser type. Unfortunately for Netscape, the W3C adopted as the formal standard the version of DHTML found in version 4 of Internet Explorer, which prompted many loyal Netscape followers to defect to Microsoft.

TIP

DHTML is actually a combination of HTML, Cascading Style Sheets, and JavaScript. The term Cascading Style Sheets (CSS), or style sheets, refers to a standard set by the W3C for managing Web page formatting.

NOTE

The W3C does not actually release a version of a particular technology. Instead, it issues a formal recommendation for a technology, which essentially means that the technology is (or will be) a recognized industry standard.

One great benefit of the browser wars is that it has forced the Web industry to rapidly develop and adopt advanced Web page standards (including JavaScript, CSS, and DHTML) that are consistent across browser types. When the third edition of this book was published in 2004, Internet Explorer appeared to be winning the browser wars as it controlled 95% of the browser market. Yet, in the past few years, Internet Explorer has lost significant market share to a contentious newcomer, Mozilla Firefox. The Firefox Web browser is open source software that is developed by the Mozilla organization (*http://www.mozilla.org*). Open source refers to software for which the source code can be freely used and modified. At the time of this writing, Internet Explorer usage has slipped to approximately 60%, while Firefox now controls approximately 30% of the market (according to W3 Schools browser statistics page at *http://www.w3schools.com/browsers/browsers_stats.asp*). One of the most fascinating aspects of Firefox is that it's essentially an open source version of the Netscape browser. So in a figurative sense, the original Netscape browser has risen from the ashes to resume battle with its arch nemesis, Internet Explorer. Healthy competition is good for any market, so hopefully the renewed hostilities in the browser wars will encourage vendors to continue improving browser quality and capabilities, and to adopt and adhere to Web page standards.

HTML Documents

Originally, people created Web pages using Hypertext Markup Language. Hypertext Markup Language, or HTML, is a markup language used to create the Web pages that appear on the World Wide Web. Web pages are also commonly referred to as HTML pages or documents. A markup language is a set of characters or symbols that define a document's logical structure—that is, it specifies how a document should be printed or displayed. HTML is based on an older language called Standard Generalized Markup Language, or SGML, which defines the data in a document independent of how the data will be displayed. In other words, SGML separates the data in a document from the way that data is formatted. Each element in an SGML document is marked according to its type, such as paragraphs, headings, and so on. Like SGML, HTML was originally designed as a way of defining the elements in a document independent of how they would appear. HTML was not intended to be used as a method of designing the actual appearance of the pages in a Web browser. However, HTML gradually evolved into a language that is capable of defining how elements should appear in a Web browser.

NOTE
This textbook uses the terms "Web pages" and "HTML documents" interchangeably.

Basic HTML Syntax

HTML documents are text documents that contain formatting instructions, called tags, which determine how data is displayed on a Web page. HTML tags range from formatting commands that make text appear in boldface or italic, to controls that allow user input, such as option buttons and check boxes. Other HTML tags allow you to display graphic images and other objects in a document or Web page. Tags are enclosed in brackets (< >), and most consist of an opening tag and a closing tag that surround the text or other items they format or control. The closing tag must include a forward slash (/) immediately after the opening bracket to define it as a closing tag. For example, to make a line of text appear in boldface, you use the opening tag <b> and the closing tag </b>. Any text contained between this pair of tags appears in boldface when you open the HTML document in a Web browser.

A tag pair and any data it contains are referred to as an element. The information contained within an element's opening and closing tags is referred to as its content. Some elements do not require a closing tag. Elements that do not require a closing tag are called empty elements because you cannot use a tag pair to enclose text or other elements. For instance, the <hr> element, which inserts a horizontal rule on a Web page, does not include a closing tag. You simply place the <hr> element anywhere in an HTML document where you want the horizontal rule to appear.

TIP
HTML documents must have a file extension of .html or .htm.

There are literally hundreds of HTML elements. Table 1-1 lists some of the more common elements.

HTML element	Description
`<b></b>`	Formats enclosed text in a bold typeface
`<body></body>`	Encloses the body of the HTML document
` `	Inserts a line break
`<center>`	Centers a paragraph in the middle of a Web page
`<head></head>`	Encloses the page header and contains information about the entire page
`<hn></hn>`	Indicates heading level elements, where n represents a number from 1 to 6
`<hr>`	Inserts a horizontal rule
`<html></html>`	Begins and ends an HTML document; these are required elements
`<i></i>`	Formats enclosed text in an italic typeface
`<img src="…" alt="…">`	Inserts an image file
`<p></p>`	Identifies enclosed text as a paragraph
`<u></u>`	Formats enclosed text as underlined

Table 1-1   Common HTML elements

All HTML documents must use the `<html>` element as the root element. A root element contains all the other elements in a document. This element tells a Web browser to assemble any instructions between the tags into a Web page. The opening and closing `<html>`...`</html>` tags are required and contain all the text and other elements that make up the HTML document.

Two other important HTML elements are the `<head>` element and the `<body>` element. The `<head>` element contains information that is used by the Web browser, and you place it at the beginning of an HTML document, after the opening `<html>` tag. You place several elements within the `<head>` element to help manage a document's content, including the `<title>` element, which contains text that appears in a browser's title bar. A `<head>` element must contain a `<title>` element. With the exception of the `<title>` element, elements contained in the `<head>` element do not affect the display of the HTML document. The `<head>` element and the elements it contains are referred to as the document head.

Following the document head is the `<body>` element. The `<body>` element and the text and elements it contains are referred to as the document body.

When you open an HTML document in a Web browser, the document is assembled and formatted according to the instructions contained in its elements. The process by which a Web browser assembles or formats an HTML document is called parsing or rendering. The following example shows how to make a paragraph appear in boldface in an HTML document:

```
<p><b>This paragraph will appear in boldface in a Web
browser.</b></p>
```

HTML is not case sensitive, so you can use <B> in place of <b>. However, the next generation of HTML, a language called XHTML, is case sensitive, and you must use lowercase letters for elements. For this reason, this book uses lowercase letters for all elements. (You will learn about XHTML shortly.)

You use various parameters, called attributes, to configure many HTML elements. You place an attribute before the closing bracket of the opening tag, and separate it from the tag name or other attributes with a space. You assign a value to an attribute using the syntax *attribute="value"*. For example, you can configure the <img> element, which embeds an image in an HTML document, with a number of attributes, including the src attribute. The src attribute specifies the filename of an image file or video clip. To include the src attribute within the <img> element, you type <img src="mygraphic.gif">.

When a Web browser parses or renders an HTML document, it ignores nonprinting characters such as tabs and line breaks; the final document that appears in the Web browser includes only recognized HTML elements and text. You cannot use line breaks in the body of an HTML document to insert spaces before and after a paragraph; the browser recognizes only paragraph <p> and line break <br> elements for this purpose. In addition, most Web browsers ignore multiple, contiguous spaces on a Web page and replace them with a single space. The following code shows a simple HTML document, and Figure 1-1 shows how it appears in a Web browser.

```
<html>
<head>
<title>Canada</title>
</head>
<body>
<h1>Canada</h1>
<img src="Canada.gif" alt="Image of the Canadian flag.">
<h2>Statistics</h2>
<p><b>Capital</b>: Ottawa<br>
<b>Largest City</b>: Toronto</p>
<p><b>Official Languages</b>: English, French</p>
<p><b>National Anthem</b>: "O Canada"<br>
<b>Royal Anthem</b>: "God Save the Queen"</p>
</body>
</html>
```

The majority of the screen captures of Web pages shown in this book were taken in the Mozilla Firefox Web browser, version 2.0, running on the Windows XP operating system. Different Web browsers may render the parts of a Web page slightly differently from other browsers. The appearance of a Web browser itself can also vary across platforms. If you are using a Web browser other than Firefox and an operating system other than Windows XP, your Web pages and Web browser might not match the figures in this book.

Figure 1-1
A simple HTML document in a Web browser

Creating an HTML Document

Because HTML documents are text files, you can create them in any text editor, such as Notepad or WordPad, or any word-processing application capable of creating simple text files. If you use a text editor to create an HTML document, you cannot view the final result until you open the document in a Web browser. Instead of a text editor or word processor, you could choose to use an HTML editor, which is an application designed specifically for creating HTML documents. Some popular HTML editors, such as Macromedia Dreamweaver and Microsoft FrontPage, have graphical interfaces that allow you to create Web pages and immediately view the results, similar to the WYSIWYG (what-you-see-is-what-you-get) interface in word-processing programs. In addition, many current word-processing applications, including Microsoft Word and WordPerfect, allow you to save files as HTML documents.

Like text editors, HTML editors create simple text files, but they automate the process of applying elements. For example, suppose you are creating a document in Word. You can add boldface to a heading in the document simply by clicking a toolbar button. Then, when you save the document as an HTML document, Word automatically adds the <b> element to the text in the HTML document.

TIP
Many people who are new to creating Web pages are surprised by the fact that you cannot use a Web browser to create an HTML document.

CHAPTER 1

Any HTML editor can greatly simplify the task of creating Web pages. However, HTML editors automatically add many unfamiliar elements and attributes to documents that might confuse you and distract from the learning process. For this reason, in this book you create Web pages using a simple text editor.

Now you are ready to start creating an HTML document that displays the home page for Forestville Funding. The document will contain some of the elements you have seen in this section. You can use any text editor, such as Notepad or WordPad.

Before you begin the first exercise, be certain to extract the data files, located on the CD-ROM that came with this book. Use the 0150-9d.exe file to install the data files on Windows operating systems and the 0150-9d.jar file to install the data files on UNIX/Linux operating systems. You can also download the files from Course Technology's Web site at *http://www.course.com*. The 0150-9d.exe and 0150-9d.jar files automatically create directories where you can store the exercises and projects you create in this book and install any necessary data files that you will need. By default, the directories and data files are installed for Windows platforms in C:\Course Technology\0150-9 and for UNIX/Linux platforms in usr/local/course/0150-9. The 0150-9 directory contains separate directories for each chapter, which, in turn, contain the Chapter, Projects, and Cases directories. Figure 1-2 illustrates the Windows directory structure for Chapter 1.

Figure 1-2

Windows directory structure for data files

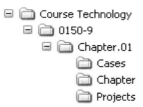

NOTE

The Course Technology directory might also contain data files for other books you have used from Course Technology.

Exercises and projects you create in the main body of each chapter should be saved within the Chapter directory. Save the Hands-on Projects and Case Projects you create at the end of each chapter in the Projects and Cases directories, respectively.

To create a simple HTML document:

1. Start your text editor and create a new document, if necessary.

2. Type the following elements to begin the HTML document. Remember that all HTML documents must begin and end with the <html> element.

```
<html>
</html>
```

3. Next, add the following <head> and <title> elements between the <html>...</html> tag pair. The title appears in your Web browser's title bar.

Remember that the <head> element must include the <title> element. The <title> element cannot exist outside the <head> element.

```
<head>
<title>Forestville Funding</title>
</head>
```

4. Next, add the following elements above the closing </html> tag. The <body> element contains all of the elements that are rendered in a Web browser.

```
<body>
</body>
```

5. Add the following elements and text above the closing </body> element. The code contains standard HTML elements along with the text that is displayed in the Web browser.

```
<font face="Arial" color="olive">
<h1>Forestville Funding</h1><hr>
<h2>Fixed Rates</h2></font>
<font face="Arial" color="blue">
<ul>
<li>30-year: 6.25%</li>
<li>15-year: 6.00%</li>
</ul></font>
<font face="Arial" color="olive"><h2>Adjustable Rates</h2></font>
<font face="Arial" color="blue">
<ul>
<li>1/1 ARM: 5.26%</li>
<li>3/1 ARM: 5.51%</li>
<li>5/1 ARM: 5.60%</li>
</ul></font>
<font face="Arial" color="olive"><h2>Popular Mortgage
Programs</h2></font>
<font face="Arial" color="blue">
<ul>
<li>No money down</li>
<li>No income or asset verification</li>
<li>Interest only loans</li>
<li>Home equity loans</li>
</ul>
<hr>
<p>Forestville Funding. Member FDIC. Equal Housing Lender.<br>
&copy; 2008 Forestville Funding. All rights reserved.</p></font>
```

6. Save the document as **ForestvilleFunding.html** in the Chapter folder for Chapter 1. Some text editors automatically add their own extensions to a document. Notepad, for instance, adds an extension of .txt. Be sure your document is saved with an extension of .html. Keep the document open in your text editor.

Some Web servers do not correctly interpret spaces within the name of HTML files. For example, some Web servers may not correctly interpret a filename of Forestville Funding.html, with a space between Forestville and Funding. For this reason, filenames in this book do not include spaces.

7. Open the **ForestvilleFunding.html** document in your Web browser. (You open a local document in most Web browsers by selecting Open or Open File from the File menu.) Figure 1-3 displays the ForestvilleFunding.html document as it appears in Firefox.

Figure 1-3

ForestvilleFunding.html in Firefox

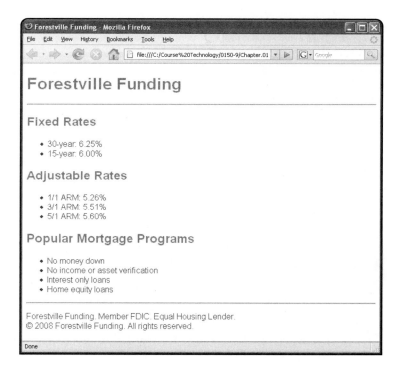

8. Close your Web browser window.

Working with Well-Formed Web Pages

HTML first became an Internet standard in 1993 with the release of version 1.0. The next version of HTML, 2.0, was released in 1994 and included many core HTML features such as forms and the ability to bold and italicize text. However, many of the standard features that are widely used today, such as using tables to organize text and graphics on a page, were not available until the release of HTML 3.2 in 1996. The current version of HTML, 4.01, was released in 1999. HTML 4.01, however, is the last version of the HTML language; it has been replaced with Extensible Hypertext Markup Language, or XHTML, which is the next generation markup language for creating the Web pages that appear on the World Wide Web.

HTML has been replaced because it is useful only for rendering documents in traditional Web browsers like Firefox or Internet Explorer. That worked well as long as browsers running on computers were the main source of requests for files over the Web. These days, however, many types of devices besides computers use the Web. For example, mobile phones and PDAs are commonly used to browse the Web. An application that is capable of retrieving and processing HTML and XHTML documents is called a user agent. A user agent can be a traditional Web browser or a device such as a mobile phone or PDA, or even an application such as a crawler for a search engine that simply collects and processes data instead of displaying it.

Although user agents other than browsers can process HTML, they are not ideally suited to the task, primarily because HTML is more concerned with how data appears than with the data itself. As Web browsers have evolved over the years, they have added extensions (elements and attributes) to HTML to provide functionality for displaying and formatting Web pages. For instance, one extension to the original HTML language is the `<font>` element, which allows you to specify the font for data in an HTML document. The `<font>` element has nothing to do with the type of data in an HTML document. Instead, its sole purpose is to display data in a specific typeface within a Web browser. There is nothing wrong with continuing to author your Web pages using HTML and design elements such as the `<font>` element—provided your Web pages will be opened only in a Web browser. However, many user agents (such as mobile phones and PDAs) display only black and white or grayscale text and are incapable of processing HTML elements that handle the display and formatting of data. User agents such as these require a language that truly defines data (such as a paragraph or heading) independently of the way it is displayed.

NOTE

XHTML is based on Extensible Markup Language, or XML, which is used for creating Web pages and for defining and transmitting data between applications.

The Web page examples and exercises in this book are written in XHTML. Although you need to have a solid understanding of HTML to be successful with this book, you do not necessarily need to be an expert with XHTML. Because XHTML is almost identical to HTML, you can easily adapt any of your existing HTML skills to XHTML, and vice versa.

TIP

To ensure backward compatibility with older browsers, you should save XHTML documents with an extension of .html or .htm, just like HTML documents.

XHTML Document Type Definitions (DTDs)

When a document conforms to the rules and requirements of XHTML, it is said to be well formed. Among other things, a well-formed document must include a `<!DOCTYPE>` declaration and the `<html>`, `<head>`, and `<body>` elements. The `<!DOCTYPE>` declaration belongs in the first line of an XHTML document and determines the Document Type Definition with which the document complies. A Document Type Definition, or DTD, defines the elements and attributes that can be used in a document, along with the rules that a document must follow when it includes them. You can use three types of DTDs with XHTML documents: transitional, strict, and frameset.

To understand the differences among the three types of DTDs, you need to understand the concept of deprecated HTML elements. One of the goals of XHTML is to separate the way HTML is structured from the way the parsed Web page is displayed in the browser. To accomplish this goal, the W3C decided that several commonly used HTML elements and attributes for display and formatting would not be used in XHTML 1.0. Instead of using HTML elements and attributes for displaying and formatting Web pages, the W3C recommends you use Cascading Style Sheets (CSS), which are discussed later in this chapter.

Elements and attributes that are considered obsolete and that will eventually be eliminated are said to be deprecated. Table 1-2 lists the HTML elements that are deprecated in XHTML 1.0.

Element	Description
`<applet>`	Executes Java applets
`<basefont>`	Specifies the base font size
`<center>`	Centers text
`<dir>`	Defines a directory list
`<font>`	Specifies a font name, size, and color
`<isindex>`	Creates automatic document indexing forms
`<menu>`	Defines a menu list
`<s>` or `<strike>`	Formats strikethrough text
`<u>`	Formats underlined text

Table 1-2   HTML elements that are deprecated in XHTML 1.0

The three DTDs are distinguished in part by the degree to which they accept or do not accept deprecated HTML elements. This is explained in more detail in the following sections.

Transitional DTD

The transitional DTD allows you to use deprecated style elements in your XHTML documents. The `<!DOCTYPE>` declaration for the transitional DTD is as follows:

```
<!DOCTYPE html PUBLIC
"-//W3C//DTD XHTML 1.0 Transitional//EN"
"http://www.w3.org/TR/xhtml1/DTD/xhtml1-transitional.dtd">
```

You should use the transitional DTD only if you need to create Web pages that use the deprecated elements listed in Table 1-2.

Frameset DTD

The frameset DTD is identical to the transitional DTD, except that it includes the `<frameset>` and `<frame>` elements, which allow you to split the browser window into two or more frames. The `<!DOCTYPE>` declaration for the frameset DTD is as follows:

```
<!DOCTYPE html PUBLIC
"-//W3C//DTD XHTML 1.0 Frameset//EN"
"http://www.w3.org/TR/xhtml1/DTD/xhtml1-frameset.dtd">
```

You should understand that frames have been deprecated in favor of tables. However, frameset documents are still widely used, and you need to be able to recognize and work with them in the event that you need to modify an existing Web page that was created with frames.

Strict DTD

The strict DTD eliminates the elements that were deprecated in the transitional DTD and frameset DTD. The `<!DOCTYPE>` declaration for the strict DTD is as follows:

```
<!DOCTYPE html PUBLIC
"-//W3C//DTD XHTML 1.0 Strict//EN"
"http://www.w3.org/TR/xhtml1/DTD/xhtml1-strict.dtd">
```

As a rule, you should always try to use the strict DTD. This ensures that your Web pages conform to the most current Web page authoring techniques. Next, you add a `<!DOCTYPE>` declaration for the strict DTD to the Forestville Funding page.

To add a `<!DOCTYPE>` declaration for the strict DTD to the Forestville Funding page:

1. Return to the **ForestvilleFunding.html** document in your text editor.
2. Add the following `<!DOCTYPE>` declaration for the strict DTD as the first line in the document (above the opening `<html>` tag):

   ```
   <!DOCTYPE html PUBLIC
   "-//W3C//DTD XHTML 1.0 Strict//EN"
   "http://www.w3.org/TR/xhtml1/DTD/xhtml1-strict.dtd">
   ```

3. Save your changes to the document.

Writing Well-Formed Documents

As you learned earlier, a well-formed document must include a `<!DOCTYPE>` declaration and the `<html>`, `<head>`, and `<body>` elements. The following list describes some other important components of a well-formed document:

- All XHTML documents must use `<html>` as the root element. The xmlns attribute is required in the `<html>` element and must be assigned the *http://www.w3.org/1999/xhtml* URI.
- XHTML is case sensitive.
- All XHTML elements must have a closing tag.
- Attribute values must appear within quotation marks.
- Empty elements must be closed.
- XHTML elements must be properly nested.

Most of the preceding rules are self-explanatory. However, the last rule requires further explanation. Nesting refers to how elements are placed inside other elements. For example, in the following code, the `<i>` element is nested within the `<b>` element, while the `<b>` element is nested within a `<p>` element.

```
<p><b><i>Call for a free estimate!</i></b></p>
```

In an HTML document, it makes no difference how the elements are nested. Examine the following modified version of the preceding statement:

```
<p><b><i>Call for a free estimate!</b></p></i>
```

In this version, the opening `<i>` element is nested within the `<b>` element, which, in turn, is nested within the `<p>` element. Notice, however, that the closing `</i>` tag is outside the closing `</p>` tag. The `<i>` is the innermost element. In XHTML, the innermost element in a statement must be closed before another element is closed. In the preceding statement, the `<b>` and `<p>` elements are closed before the `<i>` element. Although the order in which elements are closed makes no difference in HTML, the preceding code would prevent an XHTML document from being well formed.

The second-to-last rule in the list ("Empty elements must be closed.") also requires further explanation. Three of the most common empty elements in HTML are the `<hr>` element, which inserts a horizontal rule into the document, the `<br>` element, which inserts a line break, and the `<img>` element, which adds an image to the document. You close an empty element in XHTML by adding a space and a slash before the element's closing bracket. For example, the following code shows how to use the `<hr>` and `<br>` elements in an XHTML document. Figure 1-4 shows how the code appears in a Web browser.

```
<hr />
<p>In 2005, <b>ESPN</b> had 89.9 million subscribers, <br />
<b>A&E Network</b> had 89.0 million subscribers, <br />
and <b>The History Channel</b> had 88.2 million subscribers.</p>
<hr />
```

Figure 1-4
XHTML document with closed empty elements

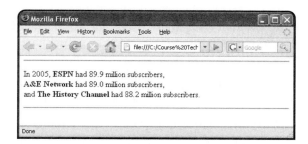

NOTE
You might be wondering why XHTML documents do not use a root element of `<xhtml>`. The `<html>` element is necessary for backward compatibility with older browsers that do not recognize the `<!DOCTYPE>` element, which declares the DTD used by an XHTML element.

Next, you modify the Forestville Funding page so it is well formed. As you complete the following steps, note that, in this book, boldface is used to indicate code that you need to insert within other code. For example, in Step 2 in the following steps, you should type the boldface code after `<html` in the `<html>` element.

To modify the Forestville Funding page so it is well formed:

1. Return to the **ForestvilleFunding.html** document in your text editor.
2. Modify the opening `<html>` element so it includes the `xmlns` attribute. Insert the boldface code into the `<html>` element as follows:

   `<html `**`xmlns="http://www.w3.org/1999/xhtml"`**`>`

3. Delete the six `<font>` elements. Be certain to also delete the closing `</font>` tags. (You need to do this because the `<font>` element has been deprecated in XHTML in favor of CSS.)
4. Add a space and a slash before the closing bracket of the two `<hr>` elements. Also add a space and a slash before the closing bracket of the `<br>` element in the last paragraph.
5. Save the **ForestvilleFunding.html** document and open it in your Web browser. The document should appear similar to the way it did before you made it well formed, although it will not contain any formatting. You learn how to add formatting when you study CSS in the next section.
6. Close your Web browser window.

Using Phrase Elements

Recall that early on, Web browser makers began to add their own extensions to HTML in order to provide functionality for displaying and formatting Web pages. These extensions (such as the bold and font elements) did nothing to describe the type of data being presented, but only served to instruct a Web browser how to display and format it. At the time, these extensions were considered a useful improvement. But as user agents become more complex, more nuanced elements became necessary. For example, consider the bold element. Visually, it's a great way to emphasize a word or phrase. However, it's not so useful for a user agent for the visually impaired that reads the contents of a Web page out loud. The Web developer needs some way of telling this type of user agent which text should receive extra, audible emphasis.

To address this type of issue, XHTML uses two types of inline elements for managing the formatting of text in an XHTML document: formatting elements and phrase elements. Formatting elements provide specific instructions about how their contents should be displayed. Two of the most commonly used formatting elements are the `<b>` element (for boldface) and the `<i>` element (for italics). Phrase elements, on the other hand, primarily identify or describe their contents. For instance, the `<em>` element is an emphasized piece of data, similar to a quotation. How the `<em>` element is rendered is up to each user agent, although most current Web browsers display the contents of the `<em>` element using italics. However, a user agent for the vision impaired may use the `<em>` element to pronounce the text or phrase it contains with more emphasis, in order to get the meaning across to the vision-impaired visitor to the Web site. Although text-formatting elements are commonly used and work perfectly well for displaying text with a specific style of formatting, it's better to format the text on your Web pages using a phrase element that describes its content. Using phrase elements helps ensure that your Web pages are compatible with user agents that may not be capable of handling formatting elements. Generally, you should strive not to use formatting elements at all and use only CSS to manage the display of elements on your Web pages. However, because several of the basic formatting elements are so commonly used, they are not deprecated in XHTML Strict.

Table 1-3 lists the phrase elements that are available in XHTML, along with how each element is rendered by most Web browsers.

Element	Description	Renders as
`<abbr>`	Specifies abbreviated text	Default text
`<acronym>`	Identifies an acronym	Default text
`<cite>`	Defines a citation	Italics
`<code>`	Identifies computer code	Monospace font
`<dfn>`	Marks a definition	Italics
`<em>`	Defines emphasized text	Italics
`<kbd>`	Indicates text that is to be entered by a visitor to a Web site	Monospace font
`<q>`	Defines a quotation	Italics
`<samp>`	Identifies sample computer code	Monospace font
`<strong>`	Defines strongly emphasized text	Bold
`<var>`	Defines a variable	Italics

Table 1-3   Phrase elements

Cascading Style Sheets (CSS)

Although you should always strive to create Web pages that are compatible with all user agents, you can also design and format them so they are visually pleasing when rendered in a traditional Web browser. To design and format Web pages for traditional Web browsers, you use CSS, a standard set by the W3C for managing the design and formatting of Web pages in a Web browser. A single piece of CSS formatting information, such as text alignment or font size, is referred to as a style. Some of the style capabilities of CSS include the ability to change fonts, backgrounds, and colors, and to modify the layout of elements as they appear in a Web browser.

CSS information can be added directly to documents or stored in separate documents and shared among multiple Web pages. The term "cascading" refers to the ability of Web pages to use CSS information from more than one source. When a Web page has access to multiple CSS sources, the styles "cascade," or "fall together." Keep in mind that CSS design and formatting techniques are truly independent of the content of a Web page, unlike text-formatting elements, such as the `<b>` and `<i>` elements. CSS allows you to provide design and formatting specifications for well-formed documents that are compatible with all user agents.

NOTE

Entire books are devoted to CSS. This chapter provides only enough information to get you started. To learn more about CSS techniques, refer to Don Gosselin's *XHTML*, also published by Course Technology. For other books that cover CSS more fully, search for "css" on the Course Technology Web site at *http://www.course.com*. You can also find the latest information on CSS at the W3C's Web site: *http://www.w3.org/style/css/*.

CSS Properties

CSS styles are created with two parts separated by a colon: the property, which refers to a specific CSS style, and the value assigned to it, which determines the style's visual characteristics. Together, a CSS property and the value assigned to it are referred to as a declaration or style declaration. Figure 1-5 shows a simple style declaration for the `color` property that changes the color of an element's text to blue.

Figure 1-5
Style declaration

Inline Styles

When you design a Web page, you often want the elements on your page to share the same formatting. For example, you might want all of the headings to be formatted in a specific font and color. Later in this section, you will learn how to use internal and external style sheets to apply the same formatting to multiple elements on a Web page. However, there might be times when you want to change the style of a single element on a Web page. The most basic method of applying styles is to use inline styles, which allow you to add style information to a single element in a document. You use the `style` attribute to assign inline style information to an element. You assign to the `style` attribute a property declaration enclosed in quotation marks.

Suppose you want to modify a single paragraph in a document so it uses the Verdana font instead of the browser's default font. You can modify the default font using the following statement, which uses an inline style declaration for the `font-family` property. Figure 1-6 shows how the paragraph appears in a Web browser.

```
<p>This paragraph does not use CSS.</p>
<p style="font-family: Verdana">Paragraph formatted with inline
styles.</p>
```

Figure 1-6
Paragraph formatted with an inline style declaration

NOTE
The styles you assign to an element are automatically passed to any nested elements it contains. For example, if you use the `font-family` style to assign a font to a paragraph, that font is automatically assigned to any nested elements the paragraph contains, such as `<strong>` or `<em>` elements.

You can include multiple style declarations in an inline style by separating each declaration with a semicolon. The following statement shows the same paragraph element shown earlier, but this time with two additional style declarations: one for the `color` property, which sets an element's text color to blue, and one for the `text-align` property, which centers the paragraph in the middle of the page. Notice that the `<strong>` element, which is nested in the paragraph element, automatically takes on the paragraph element's style elements. Figure 1-7 shows how the paragraph appears in a Web browser.

```
<p style="font-family: Verdana; color: blue;
text-align: center">Paragraph formatted with <strong>inline
styles</strong>.</p>
```

Figure 1-7

Paragraph formatted with multiple inline style declarations

Next, you modify the Forestville Funding page so it includes inline styles. You add some simple CSS formatting instructions that format the Web page in the Arial font, the headings in the color olive, and the body text in the color blue.

To modify the Forestville Funding page so it includes inline styles:

1. Return to the **ForestvilleFunding.html** document in your text editor.
2. Modify the opening `<body>` tag, so it includes inline styles that modify the `font-family`, `color`, and `background-color` properties, as follows:

   ```
   <body style="font-family: Arial; color: blue;
       background-color: transparent">
   ```

3. Modify the opening `<h1>` tag, so it includes inline styles that modify the `font-family` and `color` properties, as follows:

   ```
   <h1 style="font-family: Arial; color: olive">
   ```

4. Finally, modify the three opening `<h2>` tags, so they include the same styles as the `<h1>` tag. Each opening `<h2>` tag should appear as follows:

   ```
   <h2 style="font-family: Arial; color: olive">
   ```

5. Save the **ForestvilleFunding.html** document and open it in your Web browser. The Web page should appear the same as the HTML version you created with deprecated formatting elements, but this time the font face appears in Arial.
6. Close your Web browser window.

One of the great advantages to using CSS is that you can share styles among multiple Web pages, making it easier to create and maintain a common look and feel for an entire Web site. Inline styles, however, cannot be shared by other Web pages or even by other elements on the same page (except by elements that are nested within other elements). Plus, it is extremely time consuming to add inline styles to each and every element on a Web page. Inline styles are only useful if you need to make a one-time change to a single element on a page. If you want to apply the same formatting to multiple elements on a page or share styles with other Web pages, then you need to use internal or external style sheets.

Internal Style Sheets

You use an internal style sheet to create styles that apply to an entire document. You create an internal style sheet within a `<style>` element placed within the document head. The `<style>` element must include a `type` attribute, which is assigned a value of `"text/css"`, as follows:

```
<style type="text/css">
style declarations
</style>
```

TIP
You can also use an optional `media` attribute with the `<style>` element, which you use to select the destination medium for the style information. Valid values you can assign to the `media` attribute are `screen`, `tty`, `tv`, `projection`, `hand-held`, `print`, `braille`, `aural`, and `all`.

Within the `<style>` element, you create any style instructions for a specific element that are applied to all instances of that element contained in the body of the document. The element to which specific style rules in a style sheet apply is called a selector. You create a style declaration for a selector in an internal style sheet by placing a list of declarations within a pair of braces { } following the name of the selector. Figure 1-8 shows some style declarations for the <p> element (which is the selector), which change the `color` property to `blue`.

Figure 1-8
Selector style declaration

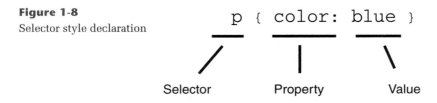

As with inline styles, you separate multiple properties for a selector by semicolons. The following code shows a portion of the Canada Statistics page you saw earlier, but this time it includes an internal style sheet for the h1, h2, and p selectors. A pair of braces containing style instructions follows each selector. All instances of the associated elements in the body of the document are formatted using these style instructions. Figure 1-9 shows how the document appears in a Web browser.

```
<html>
<head>
<title>Canada</title>
```

```
<style type="text/css">
h1 {color: navy; font-size: 2em; font-family: Arial}
h2 {color: red; font-size: 1.5em; font-family: Arial}
body {color: blue; font-family: Arial;
      font-size: .8em; font-weight: normal}
</style>
</head>
<body>
<h1>Canada</h1>
<img src="Canada.gif" alt="Image of the Canadian flag.">
<h2>Statistics</h2>
<p><b>Capital</b>: Ottawa<br>
...
```

Figure 1-9

Document with an
internal style sheet

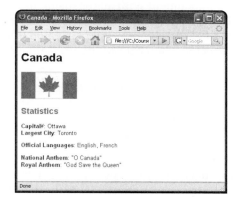

You can also group selectors so they share the same style declarations by separating each selector with a comma. For example, you use the following single declaration to format all of a document's <h1>, <h2>, and <h3> elements to use the same color:

```
<style type="text/css">
h1, h2, h3 {color: navy}
</style>
```

Next, you modify the Forestville Funding page so it contains an internal style sheet.

To modify the the Forestville Funding page so it contains an internal style sheet:

1. Return to the **ForestvilleFunding.html** document in your text editor.

2. Delete the inline styles in the <body>, <h1>, and <h2> tags.

3. Add the following internal style sheet above the closing </head> tag:

```
<style type="text/css">
body {font-family: Arial; color: blue;
    background-color: transparent}
h1, h2 {font-family: Arial; color: olive}
</style>
```

4. Save the **ForestvilleFunding.html** document and open it in your Web browser. The Web page should format the same as it did with the inline styles.

5. Close your Web browser window.

External Style Sheets

Inline styles are useful if you need to format only a single element; internal style sheets are useful for creating styles that apply to an entire document. However, most companies want all of the documents on a Web site to have the same look and feel. For this reason, it's preferable to use external style sheets, which are separate text documents containing style declarations that are used by multiple documents on a Web site. You should create an external style sheet whenever you need to use the same styles on multiple Web pages in the same site.

You create an external style sheet in a text editor, the same as when you create XHTML documents. However, you should save the document with an extension of .css. The style sheet document should not contain XHTML elements, only style declarations. Use the same rules for creating style declarations in an external style sheet as you use in an internal style sheet. The contents of a typical external style sheet may appear as follows. Notice that the code contains no XHTML elements.

```
h1 {color: navy; font-size: 2em; font-family: serif}
h2 {color: red; font-size: 1.5em; font-family: Arial}
body {color: blue; font-family: Arial;
      font-size: .8em; font-weight: normal}
```

The most popular way to access the styles in an external style sheet is to use the empty <link> element to link a document to a style sheet. You place the <link> element in the document head. You include three attributes in the <link> element: an href attribute that is assigned the URL of the style sheet, the rel attribute that is assigned a value of "stylesheet" to specify that the referenced file is a style sheet, and the type attribute, which is assigned the same "text/css" value as the type attribute used in the <style> element. For example, to link a document to a style sheet named company_branding.css, you include a link element in the document head, as follows:

```
<head>
...
<link rel="stylesheet" href="company_branding.css"
    type="text/css" />
</head>
```

Next, you modify the Forestville Funding page so it is formatted with an external style sheet.

To modify the Forestville Funding page so it is formatted with an external style sheet:

1. Return to the **ForestvilleFunding.html** document in your text editor.

2. Copy the style declarations within the <style> element and create a new document in your text editor. Be certain not to copy the <style> tags.

3. Paste the contents into the new file.

4. Save the file as **forestvillefunding_styles.css** in your Chapter folder for Chapter 1.

5. Close the **forestvillefunding_styles.css** file and return to the **ForestvilleFunding.html** file in your text editor.

6. Replace the `<style>` element and the style declarations it contains with the following `<link>` element that links to the forestvillefunding_styles.css external style sheet:

```
<link rel="stylesheet" href="forestvillefunding_styles.css"
type="text/css" />
```

7. Save the **ForestvilleFunding.html** document and open it in your Web browser. The file should appear the same as it did before you linked it to the external style sheet.

8. Close your Web browser window.

Next, you will learn about `content-type` `<meta>` elements, which the W3C strongly encourages you to use to specify an XHTML document's character set.

The Content-Type `<meta>` Element

When a user enters a URL for a Web page in a browser's Address box or clicks a link to a Web page, the user's Web browser asks the Web server for the Web page. One part of the response from the Web server is the requested Web page. Another important part of the response is the response header, which is sent to the Web browser before the Web page is sent to provide information that the browser needs to render the page. One of the most important pieces of information in the response header is the type of data, or content type, that the server is sending. For Web pages, you create a content-type `<meta>` element to specify a content type that the document uses. The term metadata means information about information. In a Web page, you use the `<meta>` element to provide information about the information in a Web page. You must place the `<meta>` element within the `<head>` element. You can use three primary attributes with the `<meta>` element: `name`, `content`, and `http-equiv`.

Another important use of the content-type `<meta>` element is to specify a document's character encoding. This allows a Web server to construct a response header in the appropriate character set. To create a content-type `<meta>` element, you assign a value of *content-type* to the `http-equiv` attribute in a `<meta>` element. You then assign to the `<meta>` element's `content` attribute a value of *text/html; charset=iso-8859-1*. This specifies that the document's MIME type is "text/html" and that the document uses the iso-8859-1 character set, which represents English and many western European languages. The following statement shows how to construct the content-type `<meta>` elements:

```
<meta http-equiv="content-type"
    content="text/html; charset=iso-8859-1" />
```

NOTE
MIME is a protocol that was originally developed to allow different file types to be transmitted as attachments to e-mail messages. Now, MIME has become a standard method of exchanging files over the Internet. You specify MIME types with two-part codes separated by a forward slash (/). The first part specifies the MIME type, and the second part specifies the MIME subtype.

The W3C strongly encourages the use of content-type <meta> elements to specify an XHTML document's character set. However, a content-type <meta> element is not required because most current Web browsers can determine on their own the character set of an XHTML document. For XHTML documents you create in this book, you include the content-type <meta> element in order to comply with the W3C's recommendation.

The content-type <meta> element is just one of many response headers that you can construct with the http-equiv attribute. Go to *http://vancouver-webpages.com/META/* for a complete list of other response header <meta> elements to use with the http-equiv attribute.

Next, you add the content-type <meta> element to the Forestville Funding page.

To add the content-type <meta> element:

1. Return to the **ForestvilleFunding.html** document in your text editor.
2. Add the following content type <meta> element above the closing </head> tag:

```
<meta http-equiv="content-type"
      content="text/html; charset=iso-8859-1" />
```

3. Save the **ForestvilleFunding.html** document.

Validating Web Pages

When you open an XHTML document that is not well formed in a Web browser, the browser simply ignores the errors, as it would with an HTML document with errors, and renders the Web page as best it can. The Web browser cannot tell whether the XHTML document is well formed. To ensure that a Web page is well formed and that its elements are valid, you need to use a validating parser. A validating parser is a program that checks whether a Web page is well formed and whether the document conforms to a specific DTD. The term validation refers to the process of verifying that your document is well formed and checking that the elements in your document are correctly written according to the element definitions in a specific DTD. If you do not validate a document and it contains errors, most Web browsers will probably treat it as an HTML document, ignore the errors, and render the page anyway. However, validation can help you spot errors in your code. Even the most experienced Web page authors frequently introduce typos or some other error into a document that prevent the document from being well formed.

Various Web development tools, including Macromedia Dreamweaver, offer validation capabilities. In addition, several validating services can be found online. One of the best available is W3C

Markup Validation Service, a free service that validates both HTML and XHTML. The W3C Markup Validation Service is located at *http://validator.w3.org/*. The main Web page for the service, shown in Figure 1-10, allows you to validate a Web page by entering its URL or by uploading a document from your computer.

Figure 1-10
W3C Markup Validation
Service

Next, you validate the Forestville Funding page using the W3C Markup Validation Service.

To validate the Forestville Funding page using the W3C Markup Validation Service:

1. Start your Web browser, and enter the Web address for the W3C Markup Validation Service: **http://validator.w3.org/**.

2. In the Validate by File Upload section, click the **Browse** button to display the File Upload dialog box. In the File Upload dialog box, locate the **ForestvilleFunding.html** document in the Chapter folder for Chapter 1. Once you locate the document, double-click it or click it once and select the **Open** button. The drive, folder path, and file name should appear in the File text box on the upload page. Click the **Check** button. The W3C Markup Validation Service validates the document and returns the results displayed in Figure 1-11. If you receive any errors, fix them, resave the document, and then revalidate the page.

3. Close your Web browser window.

Figure 1-11

Validation results for the
Forestville Funding page

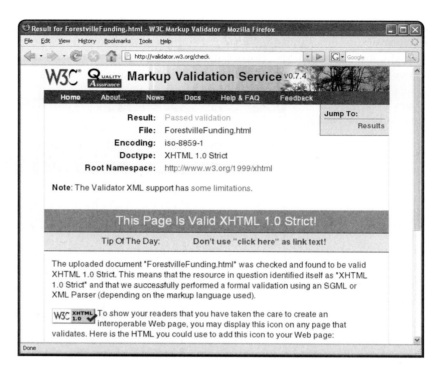

Understanding Web Development

Web page design, or Web design, refers to the visual design and creation of the documents that appear on the World Wide Web. Most businesses today—both prominent and small—have Web sites. To attract and retain visitors, and to stand out from the crowd, Web sites must be exciting and visually stimulating. Quality Web design plays an important role in attracting first-time and repeat visitors. However, the visual aspect of a Web site is only one part of the story. Equally important is the content of the Web site and how that content is structured.

Web design is an extremely important topic. However, this book is *not* about Web design, even though you will certainly learn many Web design concepts and techniques as you work through the chapters ahead. Instead, this book touches on both Web page authoring and Web development. Web page authoring (or Web authoring) refers to the creation and assembly of the tags, attributes, and data that make up a Web page. There is a subtle, but important distinction between Web design and Web page authoring: Web design refers to the visual and graphical design aspects of creating Web pages, whereas a book on Web page authoring refers to the physical task of assembling the Web page tags and attributes. Web development, or Web programming, refers to the design of software applications for a Web site. Generally, a Web developer works "behind the scenes" to develop software applications that access databases and file systems, communicate with other applications, and perform other advanced tasks. The programs created by a Web developer will not necessarily be seen by a visitor to a Web site, although the visitor will certainly use a Web developer's programs, particularly if the Web site writes and reads data to and from a database. Although JavaScript lives more in the realm of Web page authoring, there is certainly some overlap between Web authoring and Web development, especially when it comes to sending and receiving data to and from a Web server.

NOTE
Another term that you might often see in relation to Web development is "Webmaster." Although there is some dispute over exactly what the term means, typically Webmaster refers to a person who is responsible for the day-to-day maintenance of a Web site including the monitoring of Web site traffic and ensuring that the Web site's hardware and software are running properly. The duties of a Webmaster often require knowledge of Web page design, authoring, and development.

TIP
If you would like to study the topic of Web page design itself, refer to Joel Sklar's excellent book, *Web Design*, published by Course Technology.

There are countless ways of combining the hundreds of HTML tags to create interesting Web pages. One technique that professional Web authors use to increase their HTML skill is examining the underlying HTML tags of a Web page that they admire. All Web browsers contain commands that allow you to view the underlying HTML code for a Web page that appears in the browser; in Firefox you select Page Source from the View menu and in Internet Explorer you select the Source command from the View menu.

The open nature of HTML makes it possible for anyone to easily see how another Web author created a Web page. However, you should *never* copy another Web page author's work and attempt to pass it off as your own. As a responsible member of the Web community, you should examine the HTML code behind a Web page only to improve your own skills. The potential theft of another Web page author's hard work and intellectual property is no small concern. Not only is stealing another Web page author's code and Web page designs unscrupulous, but in many cases it is illegal, especially if the work is copyrighted. Throughout this book you will examine the underlying HTML code from various published Web sites. However, remember that your reasons for examining existing HTML code should be to understand the techniques used to create specific elements on an a Web page in order to improve your own skills, not to hijack someone else's hard work.

Client/Server Architecture

To be successful in Web development, you need to understand the basics of client/server architecture. There are many definitions of the terms "client" and "server." In traditional client/server architecture, the server is usually some sort of database from which a client requests information. A server fulfills a request for information by managing the request or serving the requested information to the client—hence the term, client/server. A system consisting of a client and a server is known as a two-tier system.

One of the primary roles of the client, or front end, in a two-tier system is the presentation of an interface to the user. The user interface gathers information from the user, submits it to a server, or back end, then receives, formats, and presents the results returned from the server. The main responsibility of a server is usually data storage and management. On client/server systems, heavy processing, such as calculations, usually takes place on the server. As desktop computers become increasingly powerful, however, many client/server systems have begun placing at least some of the processing responsibilities on the client. In a typical client/server system, a client computer may contain a front end that is used for requesting information from a database on a server. The server locates records that meet the client request, performs some sort of processing, such as calculations on the data, and then returns the information to the client. The client computer can also perform some processing, such as building the queries that are sent to the server or formatting and presenting the returned data. Figure 1-12 illustrates the design of a two-tier client/server system.

Figure 1-12
The design of a two-tier
client/server system

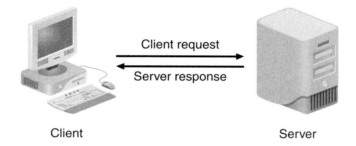

The Web is built on a two-tier client/server system, in which a Web browser (the client) requests documents from a Web server. The Web browser is the client user interface. You can think of the Web server as a repository for Web pages. After a Web server returns the requested document, the Web browser (as the client user interface) is responsible for formatting and presenting the document to the user. The requests and responses through which a Web browser and Web server communicate happen with HTTP. For example, if a Web browser requests the URL *http:// www.course.com*, the request is made with HTTP because the URL includes the HTTP protocol. The Web server then returns to the Web browser an HTTP response containing the response header and the HTML (or XHTML) for Course Technology's home page.

After you start adding databases and other types of applications to a Web server, the client/server system evolves into what is known as a three-tier client architecture. A three-tier, or multitier, client/server system consists of three distinct pieces: the client tier, the processing tier, and the data storage tier. The client tier, or user interface tier, is still the Web browser. However, the database portion of the two-tier client/server system is split into a processing tier and the data storage tier. The processing tier, or middle tier, handles the interaction between the Web browser client and the data storage tier. (The processing tier is also sometimes called the processing bridge.) Essentially, the client tier makes a request of a database on a Web server. The processing tier performs any necessary processing or calculations based on the request from the client tier, and then reads information from or writes information to the data storage tier. The processing tier also handles the return of any information to the client tier. Note that the processing tier is not the only place where processing can occur. The Web browser (client tier) still renders Web page documents (which requires processing), and the database or application in the data storage tier might also perform some processing. Figure 1-13 illustrates the design of a three-tier client/server system.

Figure 1-13

The design of a three-tier client/server system

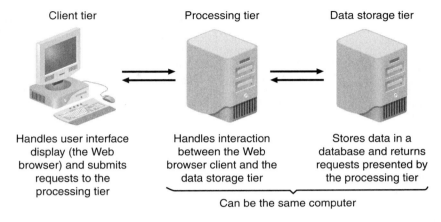

Client tier

Handles user interface display (the Web browser) and submits requests to the processing tier

Processing tier

Handles interaction between the Web browser client and the data storage tier

Data storage tier

Stores data in a database and returns requests presented by the processing tier

Can be the same computer

TIP
Two-tier client/server architecture is a physical arrangement in which the client and server are two separate computers. Three-tier client/server architecture is more conceptual than physical, because the storage tier can be located on the same server.

NOTE
Multitier client/server architecture is also referred to as *n*-tier architecture.

JavaScript and Client-Side Scripting

As mentioned earlier, HTML was not originally intended to control the appearance of pages in a Web browser. When HTML was first developed, Web pages were static—that is, they couldn't change after the browser rendered them. However, after the Web grew beyond a small academic and scientific community, people began to recognize that greater interactivity and better visual design would make the Web more useful. As commercial applications of the Web grew, the demand for more interactive and visually appealing Web sites also grew.

HTML and XHTML could only be used to produce static documents. You can think of a static Web page written in HTML or XHTML as being approximately equivalent to a document created in a word-processing or desktop publishing program; the only thing you can do with it is view it or print it. Thus, to respond to the demand for greater interactivity, an entirely new Web programming language was needed. Netscape filled this need by developing JavaScript.

JavaScript is a client-side scripting language that allows Web page authors to develop interactive Web pages and sites. Client-side scripting refers to a scripting language that runs on a local browser (on the client tier) instead of on a Web server (on the processing tier). Originally designed for use in Navigator Web browsers, JavaScript is now also used in most other Web browsers, including Firefox and Internet Explorer.

The term scripting language is a general term that originally referred to fairly simple programming languages that did not contain the advanced programming capabilities of languages such as Java or C++. When it comes to Web development, the term scripting language refers to any type of language that is capable of programmatically controlling a Web page or returning some sort of response to a Web browser. It's important to note that although the term scripting language originally referred to simple programming languages, today's Web-based scripting languages are anything but simple. The part of a browser that executes scripting language code is called the browser's scripting engine. A scripting engine is just one kind of interpreter, with the term interpreter referring generally to any program that executes scripting language code. When a scripting engine loads a Web page, it interprets any programs written in scripting languages, such as JavaScript. A Web browser that contains a scripting engine is called a scripting host. Firefox and Internet Explorer are examples of scripting hosts that can run JavaScript programs.

JavaScript was first introduced in Navigator and was originally called LiveScript. With the release of Navigator 2.0, the name was changed to JavaScript 1.0. Subsequently, Microsoft released its own version of JavaScript in Internet Explorer 4.0 and named it JScript.

When Microsoft released JScript, several major problems occurred. For example, the Netscape and Microsoft versions of the JavaScript language differed so greatly that programmers were required to write almost completely different JavaScript programs for Navigator and Internet Explorer. To avoid similar problems in the future, an international, standardized version of JavaScript, called ECMAScript, was created. The most recent version of ECMAScript is edition 3. Both Netscape JavaScript and Microsoft JScript conform to ECMAScript edition 3. Nevertheless, Netscape JavaScript and Microsoft JScript each include unique programming features that are not supported by the other language. In this book, you will learn to create JavaScript programs with ECMAScript edition 3, which is supported by all current Web browsers including Firefox, Netscape 6 and higher, and Internet Explorer 4 and higher.

TIP

The next major edition of the JavaScript language is ECMAScript Edition 4. At the time of this writing, the developers of the language have not made a great deal of progress on the new version and it is not known when it will be complete.

NOTE

Many people think that JavaScript is related to or is a simplified version of the Java programming language. However, the languages are entirely different. Java is an advanced programming language that was created by Sun Microsystems and is considerably more difficult to master than JavaScript. Although Java can be used to create programs that can run from a Web page, Java programs are usually external programs that execute independently of a browser. In contrast, JavaScript programs always run within a Web page and control the browser.

Although JavaScript is considered a programming language, it is also a critical part of Web page authoring. This is because the JavaScript language "lives" within a Web page's elements. JavaScript gives you the ability to:

- Turn static Web pages into applications such as games or calculators.
- Change the contents of a Web page after a browser has rendered it.
- Create visual effects such as animation.
- Control the Web browser window itself.

For security reasons, the JavaScript programming language cannot be used outside of the Web browser. For example, to prevent mischievous scripts from stealing information, such as your e-mail address or credit card information you use for an online transaction, or from causing damage by changing or deleting files, JavaScript does not allow any file manipulation whatsoever. Similarly, JavaScript does not include any sort of mechanism for creating a network connection or accessing a database. This limitation prevents JavaScript programs from infiltrating a private network or intranet from which information might be stolen or damaged. Another helpful limitation is the fact that JavaScript cannot run system commands or execute programs on a client. The ability to read and write cookies is the only type of access to a client that JavaScript has. Web browsers, however, strictly govern cookies and do not allow access to cookies from outside the domain that created them. This security also means that you cannot use JavaScript to interact directly with Web servers that operate at the processing tier. Although the programmer can employ a few tricks (such as forms and query strings) to allow JavaScript to interact indirectly with a Web server, if you want true control over what's happening on the server, you need to use a server-side scripting language.

Server-Side Scripting and PHP

Server-side scripting refers to a scripting language that is executed from a Web server. Some of the more popular server-side scripting languages are PHP, ASP, and JSP. One of the primary reasons for using a server-side scripting language is to develop interactive Web sites that communicate with a database. Server-side scripting languages work in the processing tier and have the ability to handle communication between the client tier and the data storage tier. At the processing tier, a server-side scripting language usually prepares and processes the data in some way before submitting it to the data storage tier. Some of the more common uses of server-side scripting language that you have probably already seen on the Web include the following:

- Shopping carts
- Search engines
- Mailing lists and message boards
- Web-based e-mail systems
- Authentication and security mechanisms
- Web logs (blogs)
- Games and entertainment

Unlike JavaScript, a server-side scripting language can't access or manipulate a Web browser. In fact, a server-side scripting language cannot run on a client tier at all. Instead, a server-side scripting language exists and executes solely on a Web server, where it performs various types of processing or accesses databases. When a client requests a server-side script, the script is interpreted and executed by the scripting engine within the Web server software. After the script finishes executing, the Web server software then translates the results of the script (such as the result of a calculation or the records returned from a database) into HTML or XHTML, which it then returns to the client. In other words, a client will never see the server-side script, only the HTML or XHTML that the Web server software returns from the script. Figure 1-14 illustrates how a Web server processes a PHP script.

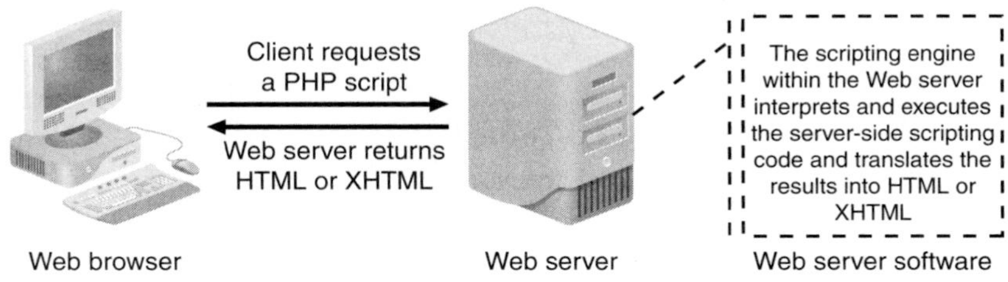

Figure 1-14

How a Web server processes a server-side script

Client requests a PHP script

Web server returns HTML or XHTML

The scripting engine within the Web server interprets and executes the server-side scripting code and translates the results into HTML or XHTML

Web browser   Web server   Web server software

Should You Use Client-Side or Server-Side Scripting?

An important question in the design of any client/server system is deciding how much processing to place on the client or server. In the context of Web site development, you must decide whether to use client-side JavaScript or a server-side script. This is an important consideration because the choice you make can greatly affect the performance of your program. In some cases, the decision is simple. For example, if you want to control the Web browser, you must use JavaScript. If you want to access a database on a Web server, you must use a server-side script. However, there are tasks that both languages can accomplish, such as validating forms and manipulating cookies. Further, both languages can perform the same types of calculations and data processing.

A general rule of thumb is to allow the client to handle the user interface processing and light processing, such as data validation, but have the Web server perform intensive calculations and data storage. This division of labor is especially important when dealing with clients and servers over the Web. Unlike with clients on a private network, it's not possible to know in advance the computing capabilities of each client on the Web. You cannot assume that each client (browser) that accesses your client/server application (Web site) has the necessary power to perform the processing required by the application. For this reason, intensive processing should be placed on the server.

Because servers are usually much more powerful than client computers, your first instinct might be to let the server handle all processing and only use the client to display a user interface. Although you do not want to overwhelm clients with processing they cannot handle, it is important to perform as much processing as possible on the client for several reasons:

- Distributing processing among multiple clients creates applications that are more powerful, because the processing power is not limited to the capabilities of a single computer. Client computers become more powerful every day, and advanced capabilities such as JavaScript are now available in local Web browsers. Thus, it makes sense to use a Web application to harness some of this power and capability. A Web application is a program that executes on a server but that clients access through a Web page loaded in a browser.

- Local processing on client computers minimizes transfer times across the Internet and creates faster applications. If a client had to wait for all processing to be performed on the server, a Web application could be painfully slow over a busy Internet connection.

- Performing processing on client computers lightens the processing load on the server. If all processing in a three-tier client/server system is on the server, the server for a popular Web site could become overwhelmed trying to process requests from numerous clients.

NOTE

The term "distributed application" is used to describe multiple computers sharing the computing responsibility for a single application.

The JavaScript Programming Language

The following sections introduce basic procedures for adding JavaScript to your Web pages.

The <script> Element

JavaScript programs run from within a Web page (either an HTML or XHTML document). That is, you type the code directly into the Web page code as a separate section. JavaScript programs contained within a Web page are often referred to as scripts. The <script> element tells the Web browser that the scripting engine must interpret the commands it contains. The type attribute of the <script> element tells the browser which scripting language and which version of the scripting language is being used. You assign a value of "text/javascript" to the type attribute to indicate that the script is written with JavaScript. You need to include the following code in a document to tell the Web browser that the statements that follow must be interpreted by the JavaScript scripting engine:

```
<script type="text/javascript">
statements
</script>
```

Next, you will add a script section to the Forestville Funding page.

To add a script section to the Forestville Funding page:

1. Return to the **ForestvilleFunding.html** document in your text editor.

2. Add the following script section immediately after the <h2> element for the Fixed Rates heading:

   ```
   <script type="text/javascript">
   </script>
   ```

3. Save the **ForestvilleFunding.html** document.

The individual lines of code, or statements, that make up a JavaScript program in a document are contained within the <script> element. The following script contains a single statement that writes the text "Bienvenue au Canada!" to a Web browser window, using the write() method of the Document object, which you will study shortly:

```
document.write("<p>Bienvenue au Canada!</p>");
```

Notice that the preceding statement ends in a semicolon. Many programming languages, including C++ and Java, require you to end all statements with a semicolon. JavaScript statements are not required to end in semicolons. Semicolons are strictly necessary only when you want to separate statements that are placed on a single line. For example, the following script contains two statements on the same line, with each statement ending in a semicolon:

```
<script type="text/javascript">
document.write("<p>Bienvenue "); document.write ("au Canada!</p>");
</script>
```

As long as you place each statement on its own line, separated from other lines with line breaks, you are not required to end statements with semicolons. The following code shows another example of the preceding script, but this time, each statement is placed on its own line, without an ending semicolon.

```
<script type="text/javascript">
document.write("<p>Bienvenue ")
document.write("au Canada!</p>")
</script>
```

Even though the statements do not end in semicolons, the preceding script is legal. However, that's not the end of the story. Programmers often adopt conventions in their code that make the code easier for the programmer to read in a text editor. In the case of semicolons, it is considered good JavaScript programming practice to end any statement with a semicolon. The semicolon serves to identify the end of each statement, making it easier for the programmer to read his or her own code (and for other programmers to read the code later on). Therefore, be sure to end all of your JavaScript statements with semicolons.

NOTE

Although this book covers JavaScript, you can also use other scripting languages with Web pages. To use VBScript in your Web pages, you would use the following code: <script type="text/vbscript">VBScript code </script>. Do not confuse JScript with VBScript. JScript is Microsoft's version of the JavaScript scripting language. To specify the JScript language, you specify JavaScript as the type attribute.

If you anticipate that your JavaScript programs will run only in Internet Explorer, then you can specify "JScript" as your scripting language by using the statement <script type="JScript">. However, few browsers other than Internet Explorer will recognize "JScript" as a valid type attribute for the <script> element; it is safer always to use "JavaScript."

HTML documents use the `language` attribute to tell the browser which scripting language and which version of the scripting language is being used. However, the `language` attribute is deprecated, so be sure to use the `type` attribute with your XHTML documents.

Understanding JavaScript Objects

Before you can use `<script>` elements to create a JavaScript program, you need to learn some basic terminology that is commonly used in JavaScript programming and in other kinds of programming languages. In addition to being an interpreted scripting language, JavaScript is considered an object-based programming language. An object is programming code and data that can be treated as an individual unit or component. For example, you might create a `Loan` object that calculates the number of payments required to pay off a loan. The `Loan` object may also store information such as the principal loan amount and the interest rate. Individual statements used in a computer program are often grouped into logical units called procedures, which are used to perform specific tasks. For example, a procedure may contain a group of statements that calculate the sales tax based on sales total. The procedures associated with an object are called methods. A property is a piece of data, such as a color or a name, that is associated with an object. In the `Loan` object example, the programming code that calculates the number of payments required to pay off the loan is a method. The principal loan amount and the interest rate are properties of the `Loan` object.

To incorporate an object and an associated method in JavaScript code, you type the object's name, followed by a period, followed by the method. For example, the following code shows the `Loan` object, followed by a period, followed by a method named `calcPayments()`, which calculates the number of payments required to pay off the loan:

```
loan.calcPayments();
```

For many methods, you also need to provide some more specific information, called an argument, between the parentheses. Some methods require numerous arguments, while others don't require any. Providing an argument for a method is referred to as passing arguments. For example, the `calcPayments()` method may require an argument that specifies the amount paid each month toward the loan. In that case, the JavaScript statement would look like this:

```
loan.calcPayments(800);
```

You use an object's properties in much the same way you use a method, by appending the property name to the object with a period. However, a property name is not followed by parentheses. One of the biggest differences between methods and properties is that a property does not actually do anything; you only use properties to store data. You assign a value to a property using an equal sign, as in the following example:

```
loan.interest = .08;
```

The next part of this chapter focuses on the `write()` and `writeln()` methods as a way of helping you understand how to program with JavaScript.

Using the `write()` and `writeln()` Methods

JavaScript treats many things as objects. One of the most commonly used objects in JavaScript programming is the `Document` object. The `Document` object represents the content of a browser's window. Any text, graphics, or other information displayed in a Web page is part of the `Document` object. One of the most common uses of the `Document` object is to add new text to a Web page. You create new text on a Web page with the `write()` method or the `writeln()` method of the `Document` object. For example, you could use the `write()` method to render a Web page containing custom information such as a user's name or the result of a calculation.

You should understand that the only reason to use the `write()` and `writeln()` methods is to add new text to a Web page while it is being rendered. For example, you may want to display a new Web page based on information a user enters into a form. A user may enter, say, sales information into a form for an online transaction. Using the entered information, you can create a new Web page that displays their sales total, order confirmation, and so on. If you simply want to display text in a Web browser when the document is first rendered, there is no need to use anything but standard XHTML elements. The procedures for dynamically gathering information are a little too complicated for this introductory chapter. However, in this chapter you will use the `write()` and `writeln()` methods to display text in a Web browser when the document is first rendered in order to learn the basics of creating JavaScript programs.

Different methods require different kinds of arguments. For example, the `write()` and `writeln()` methods of the `Document` object require a text string as an argument. A text string, or literal string, is text that is contained within double or single quotation marks. The text string argument of the `write()` and `writeln()` methods specifies the text that the `Document` object uses to create new text on a Web page. For example, `document.write("Bienvenue au Canada!");` displays the text "Bienvenue au Canada!" in the Web browser window (without the quotation marks). Note that you must place literal strings on a single line. If you include a line break within a literal string, you receive an error message.

If you are using a version of Internet Explorer higher than 4, you need to turn on error notification by selecting Internet Options from the Tools menu and clicking the Advanced tab. In the Browsing category on the Advanced tab, make sure the Display a notification about every script error check box is selected, and click the OK button to close the dialog box. To view errors in Firefox, you must select Error Console from the Tools menu.

TIP

Programmers often talk about code that "writes to" or "prints to" a Web browser window. For example, you might say that a piece of code writes a text string to the Web browser window. This is just another way of saying that the code displays the text string in the Web browser window.

The `write()` and `writeln()` methods perform essentially the same function that you perform when you manually add text to the body of a standard Web page document. Whether you add text to a document by using standard elements such as the <p> element or by using the `write()` or `writeln()` methods, the text is added according to the order in which the statement appears in the document.

The only difference between the write() and writeln() methods is that the writeln() method adds a line break after the line of text. Line breaks, however, are only recognized inside the <pre> element. In other words, in order to use line breaks with the writeln() method, you must place the method within a <pre> element. The following code contains a script that prints some text in a Web browser using the writeln() method of the Document object. Notice that the <script> element is enclosed within a <pre> element. Figure 1-15 shows the output.

```
<pre style="color: blue; font-family: Arial; font-size: .8em;
font-weight: normal">
<script type="text/javascript">
document.writeln("Abraham Lincoln once said:");
document.writeln("<em>Tact is the ability to describe others as
they see themselves.</em>");
</script>
</pre>
```

Note the use of semicolons at the end of each statement. Remember that it is considered good JavaScript programming practice to end any statement with a semicolon.

Figure 1-15

Output of a script that uses the writeln() method of the Document object

Notice that the second writeln() statement includes the XHTML element <em>. You can include any elements you like as part of an argument for the write() or writeln() methods, including elements such as the <p> and <br> elements. This means that you can use write() statements to add line breaks to the text you create with a script instead of using writeln() statements within a <pre> element. The following code shows a modified version of the previous script, but this time it uses write() statements and does not include a <pre> element. The line break in the text is created by adding a <br /> element to the end of the first line of text.

```
<script type="text/javascript">
document.write("Abraham Lincoln once said:<br />");
document.write("<em>Tact is the ability to describe others as
they see themselves.</em>");
</script>
```

Next, you will modify the elements and text in the Fixed Rates heading so they are added using write() methods of the Document object.

To modify the elements and text in the Fixed Rates heading so they are added using `write()` methods of the `Document` object:

1. Return to the **ForestvilleFunding.html** document in your text editor.

2. Add to the script section the following `document.write()` statements which print the text and elements that should appear beneath the Fixed Rates heading:

```
document.write("<ul>");
document.write("<li>30-year: 6.25%</li>");
document.write("<li>15-year: 6.00%</li>");
document.write("</ul>");
```

   Remember that the only reason you are using `write()` statements to add text to a Web page when it is first rendered is to learn the basics of JavaScript.

3. Now delete the original text elements located between the closing `</script>` tag and the `<h2>` element containing "Adjustable Rates".

4. Save the **ForestvilleFunding.html** document and open it in your Web browser. The document should appear the same as it did before you added the script section.

5. Close your Web browser window.

Case Sensitivity in JavaScript

Like XHTML, JavaScript is case sensitive, and within JavaScript code, object names must always be all lower case. This can be a source of some confusion, because in written explanations about JavaScript, the names of objects are usually referred to with an initial capital letter. For example, throughout this book, the `Document` object is referred to with an uppercase D. However, you must use a lowercase d when referring to the `Document` object in a script. The statement `Document.write("Bienvenue au Canada!");` causes an error message because the JavaScript interpreter cannot recognize an object named `Document` with an uppercase D.

Similarly, the following statements will also cause errors:

```
DOCUMENT.write("Bienvenue au Canada!");
Document.Write("Bienvenue au Canada!");
document.WRITE("Bienvenue au Canada!");
```

Adding Comments to a JavaScript Program

When you create a program, whether in JavaScript or any other programming language, it is considered good programming practice to add comments to your code. In this section, you will learn how to create JavaScript comments. Comments are nonprinting lines that you place in your code to contain various types of remarks, including the name of the program, your name and the date you created the program, notes to yourself, or instructions to future programmers who may need to modify your work. When you are working with long scripts, comments make it easier to decipher how a program is structured.

JavaScript supports two kinds of comments: line comments and block comments. A line comment hides a single line of code. To create a line comment, add two slashes // before the text you want to use as a comment. The // characters instruct the JavaScript interpreter to ignore all text immediately following the slashes to the end of the line. You can place a line comment either at the end of a line of code or on its own line. Block comments hide multiple lines of code. You create a block comment by adding /* to the first line that you want included in the block, and you close a comment block by typing */ after the last character in the block. Any text or lines between the opening /* characters and the closing */ characters are ignored by the JavaScript interpreter. The following code shows a <script> element containing line and block comments. If you open a document that contains the following script in a Web browser, the browser does not render the text marked with comments.

```
<script type="text/javascript">
/*
This line is part of the block comment.
This line is also part of the block comment.
*/
document.writeln("<h1>Comments Example</h1>");   // Line
comments can follow code statements
// This line comment takes up an entire line.
/* This is another way of creating a block comment. */
</script>
```

TIP

Comments in JavaScript use the same syntax as comments created in C++, Java, and other programming languages.

Next, you will add comments to the Forestville Funding page.

To add comments to the Forestville Funding page:

1. Return to the **ForestvilleFunding.html** document in your text editor.

2. Add the following block comment immediately after the opening <script> tag:

    ```
    /*
    JavaScript code for Chapter 1.
    The purpose of this code is simply to demonstrate
    how to add a script section to a Web page.
    */
    ```

3. Next, add the following line comments immediately after the block comment, taking care to replace "your name" with your first and last name and "today's date" with the current date:

    ```
    // your name
    // today's date
    ```

4. Save the **ForestvilleFunding.html** document, and then open it in your Web browser to confirm that the comments are not displayed.

5. Close your Web browser window.

Structuring JavaScript Code

When you add JavaScript code to a document, you need to follow certain rules regarding the placement and organization of that code. The following sections describe some important rules to keep in mind when structuring your JavaScript code.

Including a `<script>` Element for Each Code Section

You can include as many script sections as you like within a document. However, when you include multiple script sections in a document, you must include a `<script>` element for each section. The following document includes two separate script sections. The script sections create the information that is displayed beneath the `<h2>` heading elements. Figure 1-16 shows the output.

```
<h1>Multiple Script Sections</h1>
<h2>First Script Section</h2>
<script type="text/javascript">
document.write("<p>Output from the first script section.</p>");
</script>
<h2>Second Script Section</h2>
<script type="text/javascript">
document.write("<p>Output from the second script section.</p>");
</script>
```

Figure 1-16

Output of a document with two JavaScript sections

Next, you will modify the text and comments beneath the "Adjustable Rates" and "Popular Mortage Programs" headings so they are added to the page from a script section.

To modify the text and comments beneath the "Adjustable Rates" and "Popular Mortage Programs" headings so they are added to the page from a script section:

1. Return to the **ForestvilleFunding.html** document in your text editor.

2. Modify the text and elements beneath the "Adjustable Rates" heading so they are added to the page from a script section, as follows:

```
<script type="text/javascript">
document.write("<ul>");
```

```
document.write("<li>1/1 ARM: 5.26%</li>");
document.write("<li>3/1 ARM: 5.51%</li>");
document.write("<li>5/1 ARM: 5.60%</li>");
document.write("</ul>");
</script>
```

3. Modify the text and elements beneath the "Popular Mortgage Programs" heading so they are added to the page from a script section, as follows.

```
<script type="text/javascript">
document.write("<ul>");
document.write("<li>No money down</li>");
document.write("<li>No income or asset verification</li>");
document.write("<li>Interest only loans</li>");
document.write("<li>Home equity loans</li>");
document.write("</ul>");
</script>
```

4. Save the **ForestvilleFunding.html** document and open it in your Web browser. The document should appear the same as it did before you added the new script sections.

5. Close your Web browser window.

Placing JavaScript in the Document Head or Document Body

You can place <script> elements in either the document head or document body. Where you place your <script> elements varies, depending on the program you are writing. The statements in a script are rendered in the order in which they appear in the document. As a general rule, then, it is a good idea to place as much of your JavaScript code as possible in the document head, because the head of a document is rendered before the document body. When placed in the document head, JavaScript code is processed before the main body of the document is displayed. It is especially important to place JavaScript code in the document head when your code performs behind-the-scenes tasks that are required by script sections located in the document body.

Next, you will modify the <h1> element and the <hr> element that follows it so they are added to the page from a script section in the document head.

To modify the <h1> element and the <hr> element that follows it so they are added to the page from a script section in the document head:

1. Return to the **ForestvilleFunding.html** document in your text editor.

2. Create a new script section immediately above the closing </head> tag, as follows:

```
<script type="text/javascript">
</script>
```

3. Add the following document.write() statement to the new script section, which prints the <h1> and <hr> elements:

```
document.write("<h1>Forestville Funding</h1><hr />");
```

4. Delete the <h1> and <hr> elements that follow the opening <body> tag.

5. Save the **ForestvilleFunding.html** document and open it in your Web browser. The document should appear the same as it did before you added the new script sections.

6. Close your Web browser window.

Creating a JavaScript Source File

JavaScript is often incorporated directly into a Web page. However, you can also save JavaScript code in an external file called a JavaScript source file. You can then write a statement in the document that executes (or "calls") the code saved in the source file. When a browser encounters a line calling a JavaScript source file, it looks in the JavaScript source file and executes it.

A JavaScript source file is usually designated by the file extension .js and contains only JavaScript statements; it does not contain a <script> element. Instead, the <script> element is located within the document that calls the source file. To access JavaScript code that is saved in an external file, you use the src attribute of the <script> element. You assign to the src attribute the Uniform Resource Locator (URL) of a JavaScript source file. For example, to call a JavaScript source file named scripts.js, you would include the following code in a document:

```
<script type="text/javascript" src="scripts.js">
</script>
```

JavaScript source files cannot include XHTML elements. If you include XHTML elements in a JavaScript source file, your Web page generates an error message. Also, when you specify a source file in your document using the src attribute, the browser ignores any other JavaScript code located within the <script> element. For example, consider the following JavaScript code. In this case, the JavaScript source file specified by the src attribute of the <script> element executes properly, but the write() statement is ignored.

```
<script type="text/javascript" src="scripts.js">
document.write("<p>This statement will be ignored.</p>");
</script>
```

If the JavaScript code you intend to use in a document is fairly short, then it is usually easier to include JavaScript code in a <script> element within the document itself. However, for longer JavaScript code, it is easier to include the code in a .js source file. There are several reasons you may want to use a .js source file instead of adding the code directly to a document:

- Your document will be neater. Lengthy JavaScript code in a document can be confusing. You may not be able to tell at a glance where the XHTML code ends and the JavaScript code begins.

- The JavaScript code can be shared among multiple Web pages. For example, your Web site may contain pages that allow users to order an item. Each Web page displays a different item but uses the same JavaScript code to gather order information. Instead of recreating the JavaScript order information code within each document, the Web pages can share a central JavaScript source file. Sharing a single source file among multiple documents reduces disk space. In addition, when you share a source file among multiple documents, a Web browser needs to keep only one copy of the file in memory, which reduces system overhead.

- JavaScript source files hide JavaScript code from incompatible browsers. If your document contains JavaScript code, an incompatible browser displays that code as if it were standard text. By contrast, if you put your code in a source file, incompatible browsers simply ignore it.

You can use a combination of embedded JavaScript code and JavaScript source files in your documents. The ability to combine embedded JavaScript code and JavaScript source files in a single Web page is advantageous if you have multiple Web pages, each of which requires individual JavaScript code statements, but all of which also share a single JavaScript source file.

Suppose you have a Web site with multiple Web pages. Each page displays a product that your company sells. You may have a JavaScript source file that collects order information, such as a person's name and address, that is shared by each of the product Web pages. Each individual product page may also require other kinds of order information that you need to collect using JavaScript code. For example, one of your products may be a shirt, for which you need to collect size and color information. On another Web page, you may sell jellybeans, for which you need to collect quantity and flavor information. Each of these products can share a central JavaScript source file to collect standard information, but each may also include embedded JavaScript code to collect product-specific information.

Next, you will create a JavaScript source file that prints the contents of the "Popular Mortgage Programs" heading.

To create a JavaScript source file that prints the contents of the "Popular Mortgage Programs" heading:

1. Create a new document in your text editor.
2. Add the following statements, which print the text that will be displayed beneath the "Popular Mortgage Programs" heading. These will be the only statements in the document. Remember that you do not include a script section within a source file.

```
document.write("<ul>");
document.write("<li>No money down</li>");
document.write("<li>No income or asset verification</li>");
document.write("<li>Interest only loans</li>");
document.write("<li>Home equity loans</li>");
document.write("</ul>");
```

3. Save the document as **mortgage.js** in the Chapter folder for Chapter 1 and then close it.
4. Now return to the **ForestvilleFunding.html** document in your text editor.
5. Delete the statements that appear within the script section for the "Popular Mortgage Programs" heading.
6. Add an `src` attribute to the opening `<script>` tag for the "Popular Mortgage Programs" heading as follows, so it calls the external JavaScript source file:

```
<script type="text/javascript" src="mortgage.js">
</script>
```

7. Save the **ForestvilleFunding.html** document and open it in your Web browser. The document should appear the same as it did before you added the new script sections.

8. Close your Web browser window.

Writing Valid JavaScript Code

You should always strive to create Web pages that conform to the rules and requirements of XHTML. However, JavaScript can prevent an XHTML document from being well formed because some JavaScript statements contain symbols such as the less-than symbol (<) symbol, the greater-than symbol (>), and the ampersand (&). This is not a problem with HTML documents because the statements in a <script> element are interpreted as character data instead of as markup. A section of a document that is not interpreted as markup is referred to as character data, or CDATA. If you were to validate an HTML document containing a script section, the document would validate successfully because the validator would ignore the script section and not attempt to interpret the text and symbols in the JavaScript statements as HTML elements or attributes. By contrast, with XHTML documents, the statements in a <script> element are treated as parsed character data, or PCDATA, which identifies a section of a document that is interpreted as markup.

JavaScript code in an XHTML document is treated as PCDATA. That means that if you attempt to validate an XHTML document that contains a script section, it will fail the validation. To avoid this problem, you can do one of two things. One option is to move your code into a source file, which prevents the validator from attempting to parse the JavaScript statements. Alternatively, if you prefer to keep the JavaScript code within the document, you can enclose the code within a <script> element within a CDATA section, which marks sections of a document as CDATA. The syntax for including a CDATA section on a Web page is as follows:

```
<![CDATA[
statements to mark as CDATA
]]>
```

The following example contains JavaScript code that is enclosed within a CDATA section.

```
...
<body>
<script type="text/javascript">
<![CDATA[
document.write("<h1>Order Confirmation</h1>");
document.write("<p>Your order has been received.</p>");
document.write("<p>Thank you for your business!</p>");
]]>
</script>
</body>
</html>
```

The CDATA section in the preceding example prevents the validator from attempting to parse the JavaScript statements. However, the JavaScript interpreter will attempt to treat the <![CDATA[and]]> lines as JavaScript statements, which will cause an error. To avoid this problem, you can enclose the opening and closing portions of a CDATA section within block comments, as shown in the following example. Figure 1-17 shows the output.

```
...
<body>
<script type="text/javascript">
/* <![CDATA[ */
document.write("<h1>Order Confirmation</h1>");
document.write("<p>Your order has been received.</p>");
document.write("<p>Thank you for your business!</p>");
/* ]]> */
</script>
</body>
</html>
```

Figure 1-17

Output of Web page with hidden JavaScript code

Next, you will modify the script sections in the Forestville Funding page so they are hidden from incompatible browsers and are well formed.

To modify the script sections in the Forestville Funding page so they are hidden from incompatible browsers and are well formed:

1. Return to the **ForestvilleFunding.html** document in your text editor.

2. Modify the script section in the document head (that prints the <h1> and <hr> elements) as follows so the code is contained with a CDATA section to ensure that the Web page can be validated:

```
<script type="text/javascript">
/* <![CDATA[ */
document.write("<h1>Forestville Funding</h1><hr />");
/* ]]> */
</script>
```

3. Add the same code to the script sections for the Fixed Rates and Adjustable Rates headings. (You do not need to add the statements to the "Popular Mortgage Programs" heading because it calls an external JavaScript source file.)

4. Save the **ForestvilleFunding.html** document, validate it with the W3C Markup Validation Service, and open it in your Web browser. You should be using a browser that supports JavaScript, so the document should be rendered correctly.

5. Close your Web browser window and text editor window.

Logic and Debugging

All programming languages, including JavaScript, have their own syntax, or rules. To write a program, you must understand the syntax of the programming language you are using. You must also understand computer-programming logic. The term logic refers to the order in which various parts of a program run, or execute. The statements in a program must execute in the correct order to produce the desired results. In an analogous situation, although you know how to drive a car well, you may not reach your destination if you do not follow the correct route. Similarly, you might be able to write statements using the correct syntax, but be unable to construct an entire, logically executed program that works the way you want. Similarly, you might be able to use a programming language's syntax correctly, but be unable to execute a logically constructed, workable program. A typical logical error might be multiplying two values when you meant to divide them. Another might be producing output before obtaining the appropriate input (for example, printing an order confirmation on the screen before asking the user to enter the necessary order information).

Any error in a program that causes it to function incorrectly, whether because of incorrect syntax or flaws in logic, is called a bug. The term debugging refers to the act of tracing and resolving errors in a program. Grace Murray Hopper, a mathematician who was instrumental in developing the Common Business-Oriented Language (COBOL) programming language, is said to have first coined the term "debugging." As the story from the 1940s goes, a moth short-circuited a primitive computer that Hopper was using. Removing the moth from the computer "debugged" the system and resolved the problem. Today, a bug refers to any sort of problem in the design and operation of a program.

CAUTION

Do not confuse bugs with computer viruses. Bugs are problems within a program that occur because of syntax errors, design flaws, or run-time errors. Viruses are self-contained programs designed to "infect" a computer system and cause mischievous or malicious damage. Virus programs themselves can contain bugs if they contain syntax errors or do not perform as their creators envisioned.

NOTE

As you work through this book, keep in mind that debugging is not an exact science. Every program you write is different and requires different methods of debugging. While there are some tools available to help you debug your JavaScript code, your own logical and analytical skills are the best debugging resources you have.

Chapter Summary

▶ In 1990 and 1991, Tim Berners-Lee created what would become the World Wide Web, or the Web, at the European Laboratory for Particle Physics (CERN) in Geneva, Switzerland, as a way to easily access cross-referenced documents that existed on the CERN computer network.

▶ The World Wide Web Consortium, or W3C, was established in 1994 at the Massachusetts Institute of Technology (MIT) to oversee the development of Web technology standards.

▶ HTML documents are text documents that contain formatting instructions, called tags, which determine how data is displayed on a Web page. A tag pair and the data it contains are referred to as an element.

▶ Extensible Hypertext Markup Language, or XHTML, is the next generation markup language for creating the Web pages that appear on the World Wide Web.

▶ A document type definition, or DTD, defines the elements and attributes that can be used in a document, along with the rules that a document must follow when it includes them.

▶ To design and format the display of Web pages for traditional Web browsers, you use CSS, a standard set by the W3C for managing the design and formatting of Web pages in a Web browser.

▶ A validating parser is a program that checks whether a document is well formed and whether the document conforms to a specific DTD.

▶ Web page design, or Web design, refers to the visual design and creation of the documents that appear on the World Wide Web.

▶ Web page authoring (or Web authoring) is the process of creating and assembling the tags, attributes, and data that make up a Web page.

▶ The term "Web development" (or "Web programming") refers to the design of software applications for a Web site.

▶ In traditional client/server architecture, the server is usually some sort of database from which a client requests information.

▶ A system consisting of a client and a server is known as a two-tier system. The Web is built on a two-tier client/server system, in which a Web browser (the client) requests documents from a Web server.

▶ A three-tier, or multitier, client/server system consists of three distinct pieces: the client tier, the processing tier, and the data storage tier.

▶ JavaScript is a client-side scripting language that allows Web page authors to develop interactive Web pages and sites.

▶ An object is programming code and data that can be treated as an individual unit or component.

▶ Comments are nonprinting lines that you place in your code to contain various types of remarks, including the name of the program, your name and the date you created the program, notes to yourself, or instructions to future programmers who may need to modify your work.

▶ Character data, or CDATA, refers to a section of a document that is not interpreted as markup.

▶ Parsed character data, or PCDATA, identifies section of a document that should be parsed.

▶ To ensure that you can validate an XHTML document that contains a script section, you can move code into a source file or enclose the code within a `<script>` element within a CDATA section.

▶ The term "logic" refers to the order in which various parts of a program run, or execute.

▶ Any error in a program that causes it to function incorrectly, whether because of incorrect syntax or flaws in logic, is called a bug.

▶ The term "debugging" refers to the act of tracing and resolving errors in a program.

Review Questions

1. Why were the Internet and World Wide Web developed?

2. Hypertext linking was originally developed as a way to easily access cross-referenced documents that were stored on the CERN computer network. True or false?

3. Which of the following is a generic term for many types of names and addresses on the World Wide Web?

    a. URM

    b. URI

    c. URA

    d. URL

4. Which organization created the first program to allow users to navigate the Web using a graphical user interface (GUI)?

    a. Microsoft

    b. Netscape

    c. World Wide Web Consortium (W3C)

    d. University of Illinois

5. Netscape and Firefox are currently the most popular browsers on the market. True or false?

6. What are the basic elements that define the structure of a Web page? What are each of these elements called?

7. The process by which a Web browser assembles or formats an HTML document is called _____. (Choose all that apply.)

    a. parsing

    b. compiling

    c. rendering

    d. interpreting

8. Most of today's Web browsers can be used to create Web pages. True or false?

9. What is a user agent and why should you use XHTML with them?

10. Which XHTML DTD(s) allow you to use deprecated elements? (Choose all that apply.)

    a. XML

    b. transitional

    c. strict

    d. frameset

11. Explain the basic rules for writing well-formed documents.

12. Which element do you use to create an internal style sheet?

    a. `<style>`

    b. `<styles>`

    c. `<css>`

    d. `<link>`

13. Explain when you should use inline styles, internal style sheets, or external style sheets.

14. If you do not validate an XHTML document and it contains errors, most Web browsers will not render the page. True or false?

15. Explain the difference between Web page authoring and Web development.

16. The _____ tier in a three-tier client/server system handles the interaction between the Web browser client and the data storage tier.

    a. client

    b. processing

    c. data storage

    d. rendering

17. Explain the difference between server-side scripting and client-side scripting.

18. JavaScript statements must end in semicolons. True or false?

19. Which of the following statements causes an error? (Choose all that apply.)

    a. `Document.write("There's no business like show business!");`

    b. `document.Write("There's no business like show business!");`

    c. `Document.Write("There's no business like show business!");`

    d. `document.write("There's no business like show business!");`

20. Explain how to ensure that an XHTML document containing JavaScript can be validated.

Hands-On Projects

Project 1-1

In this project, you will create a Web page that displays information about the country of Azerbaijan. The Web page will be an HTML document that does not conform to XHTML.

1. Create a new document in your text editor, and type the `<html>` element, document head, and `<body>` element. Use "Azerbaijan" as the content of the `<title>` element. Your document should appear as follows:

```
<html xmlns="http://www.w3.org/1999/xhtml">
<head>
<title>Azerbaijan</title>
<meta http-equiv="content-type" content="text/html; charset=iso-
8859-1" />
</head>
<body>
</body>
</html>
```

2. Next, add the following text and elements to the document body. Notice that the document includes the deprecated `<center>` and `<font>` elements.

```
<center><font face="arial" color="navy">
<h1>Azerbaijan</h1>
<p><b>Official name</b>: <i>Republic of Azerbaijan</i><br />
<b>Ethnic groups</b>: <i>Azeri 90%, Dagestani 3%, Russian 3%,
Armenian 2%</i><br />
<b>Principal languages</b>: <i>Azeri (official), Russian,
Armenian</i><br /></p>
</font></center>
```

3. Save the document as **Azerbaijan.html** in the Projects folder for Chapter 1, then open it in your Web browser and examine how the elements are rendered.

4. Close your Web browser window and return to the **Azerbaijan.html** document in your text editor.

5. Change the `<i>` and `<b>` elements in the document body to the `<em>` and `<strong>` phrase elements. The document body should appear as follows:

```
<center><font face="arial" color="navy">
<h1>Azerbaijan</h1>
<p><strong>Official name</strong>: <em>Republic of
Azerbaijan</em><br />
<strong>Ethnic groups</strong>: <em>Azeri 90%, Dagestani 3%,
Russian 3%, Armenian 2%</em><br />
```

```
<strong>Principal languages</strong>: <em>Azeri (official),
Russian, Armenian</em><br /></p>
</font></center>
```

6. Save the document as **Azerbaijan.html** document, close it in your text editor, and then open it in your Web browser and examine how the elements are rendered. The document should appear the same as before you changed the `<i>` and `<b>` elements to the `<em>` and `<strong>` phrase elements.

7. Close your Web browser window.

Project 1-2

In this project, you will create a Web page that displays ultraviolet index forecast information. The Web page will conform to the strict DTD.

1. Create a new document in your text editor, and type the `<html>` element, document head, and `<body>` element. Use "Ultraviolet (UV) Index Forecast" as the content of the `<title>` element. Your document should appear as follows:

```
<!DOCTYPE html PUBLIC "-//W3C//DTD XHTML 1.0 Strict//EN"
"http://www.w3.org/TR/xhtml1/DTD/xhtml1-strict.dtd">
<html xmlns="http://www.w3.org/1999/xhtml">
<head>
<title>Ultraviolet (UV) Index Forecast</title>
<meta http-equiv="content-type" content="text/html;
    charset=iso-8859-1" />
</head>
<body>
</body>
</html>
```

2. Add the following text and elements to the document body. The elements build a table that display the ultraviolet index forecast information.

```
<h1>Ultraviolet (UV) Index Forecast</h1>
<table width="100%" border="1">
<tr align="left"><th>UV Index</th><th>Exposure</th><th>Minimum
Precautions</th></tr>
<tr><td>0-2</td><td>Minimal</td><td>SPF 15 sun screen</td></tr>
<tr><td>3-4</td><td>Low</td><td>Sun screen and hat</td></tr>
<tr><td>5-6</td><td>Moderate</td><td>Sun screen, hat, UV
sunglasses</td></tr>
<tr><td>7-9</td><td>High</td><td>Sun screen, hat, UV
sunglasses, avoid sun between 10am and 4am</td></tr>
</table>
```

3. Save the document as **UVIndex.html** in the Projects folder for Chapter 1.

4. Use the W3C Markup Validation Service to validate the **UVIndex.html** document and fix any errors that the document contains. Once the document is valid, close it in your text editor and then open it in your Web browser and examine how the elements are rendered.

5. Close your Web browser window.

Project 1-3

In this project, you will create a Web page that describes the Super Bowl and that contains inline styles. The Web page will conform to the strict DTD.

1. Create a new document in your text editor, and type the `<html>` element, document head, and `<body>` element. Use "Super Bowl" as the content of the `<title>` element. Your document should appear as follows:

```
<!DOCTYPE html PUBLIC "-//W3C//DTD XHTML 1.0 Strict//EN"
"http://www.w3.org/TR/xhtml1/DTD/xhtml1-strict.dtd">
<html xmlns="http://www.w3.org/1999/xhtml">
<head>
<title>Super Bowl</title>
<meta http-equiv="content-type" content="text/html;
    charset=iso-8859-1" />
</head>
<body>
</body>
</html>
```

2. Modify the opening `<body>` tag so it contains inline styles as follows:

```
<body style="color: black; background: white; margin-bottom:
6ex; font-family: Verdana, Arial, Helvetica, sans-serif;
font-size: 12px">
```

3. Add the following heading element to the document body. The `<h1>` element contains a `style` attribute that defines several inline styles for the heading.

```
<h1 style="color: #039; background: white; margin-bottom:
2ex">Super Bowl</h1>
```

4. Add the following paragraph to the document body. The `<p>` element also contains a `style` attribute that defines several inline styles for the heading.

```
<p style="margin-left: 6em;margin-right: 6em">The Super Bowl
is the end-of-season championship game in American football.
This game takes place between the winners of the two major
American leagues: the National Football Conference (NFC) and
the American Football Conference (AFC). The first Super Bowl
took place in 1967 and now takes place in January or February
following the regular season.</p>
```

5. Save the document as **SuperBowlInline.html** in the Projects folder for Chapter 1, and then open it in your Web browser and examine how the elements and styles are rendered.

6. Close your Web browser window, but leave the SuperBowlInline.html document open in your text editor.

Project 1-4

In this project, you will modify the Super Bowl Web page so it uses an internal style sheet instead of inline styles.

1. Return to the **SuperBowlInline.html** document in your text editor and immediately save it as **SuperBowlInternal.html** in the Projects folder for Chapter 1.

2. Add the following internal style sheet to the document head, immediately above the `</head>` tag. This style sheet contains the same inline styles that you added in the last exercise.

```
<style type="text/css">
body {
  color: black;
  background: white;
  margin-bottom: 6ex;
  font-family: Verdana, Arial, Helvetica, sans-serif;
  font-size: 12px;
}
h1 {
  color: #039;
  background: white;
  margin-bottom: 2ex;
}
p {
  margin-left: 6em;
  margin-right: 6em;
}
</style>
```

3. Delete the inline styles from the `<h1>`, `<body>`, and `<p>` tags.

4. Save the **SuperBowlInternal.html** document and open it in your Web browser. The elements should appear the same as they did before you converted the inline styles to an internal style sheet.

5. Close your Web browser window, but leave the SuperbowlInternal.html document open in your text editor.

Project 1-5

In this project, you will modify the Super Bowl Web page so it uses an external style sheet instead of an internal style sheet.

1. Return to the **SuperBowlInternal.html** document in your text editor and immediately save it as **SuperBowlExternal.html** in the Projects folder for Chapter 1.

2. Copy the style declarations to your Clipboard, but be sure not to copy the `<style>` or `</style>` tags.

2. Create a new document in your text editor and paste the style declarations from your Clipboard.

3. Save the document as **superbowl_styles.css** in the Projects folder for Chapter 1, and then close it in your text editor.

4. Return to the **SuperBowlExternal.html** document in your text editor and delete the `<style>` element and the declarations it contains.

5. Add the following `<link>` element to the document head, immediately above the `</head>` tag. This element links to the external superbowl_styles.css style sheet.

    ```
    <link rel="stylesheet" href=" superbowl_styles.css"
        type="text/css" />
    ```

6. Save the **SuperBowlExternal.html** document and open it in your Web browser.

7. Use the W3C Markup Validation Service to validate the **SuperBowlExternal.html** document and fix any errors that the document contains. Once the document is valid, close it in your text editor and then open it in your Web browser and examine how the elements are rendered. The elements should appear the same as they did before you converted the internal style sheet to an external style sheet.

8. Close your Web browser window.

Project 1-6

In this project you will create a Web page that uses document.`write()` statements in a script section to print dietary recommendations for a healthy heart. The Web page will conform to the strict DTD.

1. Create a new document in your text editor, and type the `<html>` element, document head, and `<body>` element. Use "Dietary Recommendations" as the content of the `<title>` element. Your document should appear as follows:

    ```
    <!DOCTYPE html PUBLIC "-//W3C//DTD XHTML 1.0 Strict//EN"
    "http://www.w3.org/TR/xhtml1/DTD/xhtml1-strict.dtd">
    <html xmlns="http://www.w3.org/1999/xhtml">
    <head>
    <title>Dietary Recommendations</title>
    <meta http-equiv="content-type" content="text/html;
        charset=iso-8859-1" />
    </head>
    <body>
    </body>
    </html>
    ```

2. Add the following text and elements to the document body:

```
<h1>Dietary Recommendations</h1>
<p>The American Heart Association recommends the following
dietary guidelines for a healthy heart:</p>
```

3. Add the following script section to the end of the document body. The script section contains a CDATA section to ensure that the Web page is valid and includes block comments that will contain your name, the current date, and "Project 1-6". Be sure to add your name and the current date where indicated.

```
<script type="text/javascript">
/* <![CDATA[ */
/*
your name
current date
Project 1-6
*/
/* ]]> */
</script>
```

4. Add the following document.write() statements to the script section immediately after the statement containing the closing block comment characters (*/). These statements use an unordered list element to print dietary recommendations for a healthy heart.

```
document.write("<ul>");
document.write("<li>Eat less fat</li>")
document.write("<li>Avoid sugary and processed foods</li>")
document.write("<li>Eat plenty of fiber-rich foods</li>")
document.write("<li>Cut down on salt</li>")
document.write("<li>Eat at least 400g of fruit and vegetables
each day</li>")
document.write("<ul>");
```

5. Save the document as **HealthyHeart.html** in the Projects folder for Chapter 1.

6. Use the W3C Markup Validation Service to validate the **HealthyHeart.html** document and fix any errors that the document contains. Once the document is valid, close it in your text editor and then open it in your Web browser and examine how the elements are rendered.

7. Close your Web browser window.

CHAPTER 1

Case Projects

Save your Case Projects files in the Cases folder for Chapter 1. Be sure to validate the files you create with the W3C Markup Validation Service.

Case Project 1-1

Create a Web page for a store that rents computers by the hour. Use the strict DTD and an internal style sheet. Format the heading level styles in olive and the paragraphs in blue. Format the heading and body elements using sans-serif fonts such as Arial and Helvetica. Include headings such as Services Offered, Hours of Operation, Rental Charges, and Accepted Forms of Payment. Within the Rental Charges heading, create a table that lists the cost of different types of computer platforms, such as Windows, Linux, and Macintosh. Format the rows in the table so they alternate from white to gray. Within the gray rows, format the text to be white. Within the white rows, format the text to be black. You will need to set the `color` and `background-color` properties for the table's `<tr>` elements using class selectors. Save the Web page as **ComputerCenter.html**.

Case Project 1-2

Create a Web page for a company that rents horses. Use the strict DTD and an external style sheet. Format the heading elements in navy and the paragraphs in black. Use the body selector to format all of the text in the body using serif fonts such as Garamond and Times New Roman. Use whatever size you like for the heading and paragraph font sizes. Include at least three paragraphs that describe the services the company offers. Format each paragraph so its line height is spaced at 150%. Also, format the first word in every paragraph so it is 30% larger than the surrounding text, formatted in blue, and uses a sans-serif font such as Arial. Save the Web page as **HorseRentals.html** and the style sheet as **horses.css**.

Case Project 1-3

Create a document with an `<h1>` element containing the text "Forestville Funding" and an `<h2>` element containing the text "Auto Loan Rates." Use the strict DTD and link the document to the js_styles.css style sheet, located in your Cases folder for Chapter 1. Add a script section containing a CDATA section to the document body. Within the CDATA section, use the `document.write()` statement to print the following auto loan rate information: 5.85% (24 Month Terms), 6.25% (36 Month Terms), and 7.65% (48 Month Terms). Print each line as an item in an unordered list by using the `<ul>` and `<li>` elements. Use another `document.write()` statement to print a `<p>` element after the unordered list that contains the text "Minimum down payment: 10%". Add JavaScript comments with your name, today's date, and Case Project 1-3. Include code to hide the JavaScript code from incompatible browsers. Save the document as **AutoRates.html**.

Case Project 1-4

Create a document with three script sections: one in the document head and two in the document body. Use the strict DTD and link the document to the js_styles.css style sheet, located in your Cases folder for Chapter 1. Be sure to include CDATA sections within the script sections. In the script section in the document head, include a `document.write()` statement that prints a line that reads `"<h1>Don's Jungle Tours</h1>"`. Be sure to include the heading element. Add `<h2>Adventure</h2>` above the first script section and `<h2>Excellence</h2>` above the second script section. Add JavaScript comments with your name, today's date, and Case Project 1-4. In the first script section in the document body, use five `document.write()` statements to print an unordered list containing the following three lines: "Ecotourism is our specialty", "Get up close and personal with nature", and "Destinations include Africa, South America, and Asia". The second script section in the document body should call a JavaScript source file that prints the following two lines as list items: "Best quality and price" and "Authentic in-country experience". Save the Web page document as **JungleTours.html** and the JavaScript source file as **travel.js**.

Case Project 1-5

The Cases folder for Chapter 1 contains a Web page named HighestWaterfalls.html that uses `document.write()` statements to print a table containing the names, locations, and height of the 10 highest waterfalls in the world. Both the XHTML elements and the JavaScript statements contain errors that prevent the Web page from validating against the strict DTD and the `document.write()` statements from functioning. Identify and fix the problems in the file. Be sure that the document validates against the strict DTD, prints the names, locations, and heights for all 10 waterfalls, and does not generate any JavaScript errors.

2

Working with Data Types and Operators

In this chapter you will:

- Work with variables
- Study data types
- Use expressions and operators
- Work with strings
- Study operator precedence

One of the most important aspects of programming is the ability to store values in computer memory and to manipulate those values. The values stored in computer memory are called variables. The values, or data, contained in variables are classified into categories known as data types. In this chapter, you will learn about JavaScript variables and data types, and the operations that can be performed on them.

Using Variables

The values a program stores in computer memory are commonly called **variables**. Technically speaking, though, a variable is actually a specific location in the computer's memory. Data stored in a specific variable often changes. You can think of a variable as similar to a storage locker—a program can put any value into it, and then retrieve the value later for use in calculations. To use a variable in a program, you first have to write a statement that creates the variable and assigns it a name. For example, you may have a program that creates a variable named curTime and then stores the current time in that variable. Each time the program runs, the current time is different, so the value varies.

Programmers often talk about "assigning a value to a variable," which is the same as storing a value in a variable. For example, a shopping cart program might include variables that store customer names and purchase totals. Each variable will contain different values at different times, depending on the name of the customer and the items they are purchasing.

NOTE

ECMAScript Edition 3 allows you to create constants using the `const` keyword. A constant contains information that does not change during the course of program execution. (You can think of a constant as a variable with a value that does not change.) However, at the time of this writing, few browsers support the `const` keyword, so you will not study it in this chapter.

Naming Variable Names

The name you assign to a variable is called an **identifier**. You must observe the following rules and conventions when naming a variable:

- Identifiers must begin with an uppercase or lowercase ASCII letter, dollar sign ($), or underscore (_).
- You can use numbers in an identifier, but not as the first character.
- You cannot include spaces in an identifier.
- You cannot use reserved words for identifiers.

CAUTION

Some older versions of Web browsers, including Navigator 2.02 and Internet Explorer 3.02, do not recognize the dollar sign in variable names. If you want your scripts to interact seamlessly with older Web browsers, avoid using the dollar sign in variable names.

Reserved words (also called **keywords**) are special words that are part of the JavaScript language syntax. As just noted, reserved words cannot be used for identifiers. Table 2-1 lists the JavaScript reserved words.

abstract	else	instanceof	switch
boolean	enum	int	synchronized
break	export	interface	this
byte	extends	long	throw
case	false	native	throws
catch	final	new	transient
char	finally	null	true
class	float	package	try
const	for	private	typeof
continue	function	protected	var
debugger	goto	public	void
default	if	return	volatile
delete	implements	short	while
do	import	static	with
double	in	super	

Table 2-1   JavaScript reserved words

TIP

It's common practice to use an underscore (_) character to separate individual words within a variable name, as in `my_variable_name`. Another option is to use a lowercase letter for the first letter of the first word in a variable name, with subsequent words starting with an initial cap, as in `myVariableName`.

Variable names, like other JavaScript code, are case sensitive. Therefore, the variable name `myVariable` is a completely different variable than one named `myvariable`, `MyVariable`, or `MYVARIABLE`. If you receive an error when running a script, be sure that you are using the correct case when referring to any variables in your code.

Declaring and Initializing Variables

Before you can use a variable in your code, you have to create it. In JavaScript, you usually use the reserved keyword `var` to create variables. For example, to create a variable named `myVariable`, you use this statement:

```
var myVariable;
```

Using the preceding statement to create a variable is called **declaring** the variable. When you declare a variable, you can also assign a specific value to, or **initialize**, the variable using the following syntax. The equal sign in a variable declaration assigns a value to the variable.

```
var variable_name = value;
```

The equal sign (=) in the preceding statement is called an **assignment operator** because it assigns the value on the right side of the expression to the variable on the left side of the expression. The value you assign to a variable can be a literal string or a numeric value. For example, the following statement assigns the literal string "Don" to the variable `myName`:

```
var myName = "Don";
```

When you assign a literal string value to a variable, you must enclose the text in quotation marks, the same as when you use a literal string with the `document.write()` or `document.writeln()` methods. However, when you assign a numeric value to a variable, do not enclose the value in quotation marks or JavaScript will treat the value as a string instead of a number. The following statement assigns the numeric value 59 to the `retirementAge` variable:

```
var retirementAge = 59;
```

TIP

You are not required to use the `var` keyword to declare a variable. However, omission of the `var` keyword affects where a variable can be used in a script. Regardless of where in your script you intend to use a variable, it is good programming practice always to use the `var` keyword when declaring a variable.

You can declare multiple variables in the statement using a single var keyword followed by a series of variable names and assigned values separated by commas. For example, the following statement creates several variables using a single var keyword:

```
var customerName = "Don Gosselin", orderQuantity = 100,
    salesTax = .05;
```

Notice in the preceding example that each variable is assigned a value. Although you can assign a value when a variable is declared, you are not required to do so. Your script may assign the value later, or you may use a variable to store user input. However, your script will not run correctly if it attempts to use a variable that has not been initialized. Therefore, it is good programming practice always to initialize your variables when you declare them.

In addition to assigning literal strings and numeric values to a variable, you can also assign the value of one variable to another. For instance, in the following code, the first statement creates a variable named salesTotal without assigning it an initial value. The second statement creates another variable named curOrder and assigns to it a numeric value of 40. The third statement then assigns the value of the curOrder variable to the salesTotal variable.

```
var salesTotal;
var curOrder = 40;
salesTotal = curOrder;
```

Displaying Variables

To print a variable (that is, display its value on the screen), you pass the variable name to the document.write() or document.writeln() method, but without enclosing it in quotation marks, as follows:

```
document.write("<p>Your sales total is $"
        + salesTotal + ".</p>");
```

Notice in the preceding code that the document.write() method uses a plus sign (+) to combine a literal string with a variable containing a numeric value. You will learn more about performing similar operations as you progress through this chapter. However, you need to understand that using a plus sign to combine literal strings with variables containing numeric values does not add them together, as in an arithmetic operation. Rather, it combines the values to create a new string, which is then printed to the screen. Figure 2-1 shows how the script appears in a Web browser.

Figure 2-1

Results of script that assigns the value of one variable to another

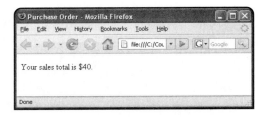

In addition to using a plus sign to combine a literal string with the numeric value of a variable, you can also use a plus sign to perform arithmetic operations involving variables that contain numeric values. For instance, the following code declares two variables and assigns to them

numeric values. The third statement declares another variable and assigns to it the sum of the values stored in the other variables. If you were to print the value of the grandTotal variable after assigning to it the sum of the salesTotal and shipping variables, it would print a value of "50", as shown in Figure 2-2.

```
var salesTotal = 40;
var shipping = 10;
var grandTotal = salesTotal + shipping;
document.write("<p>Your sales total plus shipping is $"
        + grandTotal + ".</p>");
```

Figure 2-2

Results of script that adds the values of two variables

Modifying Variables

Regardless of whether you assign a value to a variable when it is declared, you can change the variable's value at any point in a script by using a statement that includes the variable's name, followed by an equal sign, followed by the value you want to assign to the variable. The following code declares a variable named salesTotal, assigns it an initial value of 40, and prints it using a document.write() method. The fourth statement changes the value of the salesTotal variable by adding its value with the value of another variable named shipping. The fifth statement prints the new value of the salesTotal variable. Notice that it's only necessary to declare the salesTotal variable (using the var keyword) once. Figure 2-3 shows the output in a Web browser.

```
var salesTotal = 40;
document.write("<p>Your sales total is $" + salesTotal
        + ".</p>");
var shipping = 10;
salesTotal = salesTotal + shipping;
document.write("<p>Your sales total plus shipping is $" +
        salesTotal + ".</p>");
```

Figure 2-3

Results of script that includes a changing variable

Next, you create a simple script that prints information about the winners of the Daytona 500 between 2000 and 2005.

To create the Daytona 500 script:

1. Create a new document in your text editor.

2. Type the `<!DOCTYPE>` declaration, `<html>` element, header information, and the `<body>` element. Use the strict DTD and "Daytona 500 Winners, 2000-2005" as the content of the `<title>` element. Include a `<link>` element that links to the js_styles.css style sheet in your Chapter folder. Your document should appear as follows:

```
<!DOCTYPE html PUBLIC "-//W3C//DTD XHTML 1.0 Strict//EN"
"http://www.w3.org/TR/xhtml1/DTD/xhtml1-strict.dtd">
<html xmlns="http://www.w3.org/1999/xhtml">
<head>
<title>Daytona 500 Winners, 2000-2005</title>
<meta http-equiv="content-type" content="text/html;
charset=iso-8859-1" />
<link rel="stylesheet" href="js_styles.css" type="text/css" />
</head>
<body>
</body>
</html>
```

3. Add the following `<h1>` element to the document body:

```
<h1>Daytona 500 Winners, 2000-2005</h1>
```

4. Add the following script section to the end of the document body:

```
<script type="text/javascript">
<!-- HIDE FROM INCOMPATIBLE BROWSERS
// STOP HIDING FROM INCOMPATIBLE BROWSERS -->
</script>
```

5. In the script section, type the following statements that declare variables containing the names, cars, and average miles per hour of the Daytona 500 winners between 2000 and 2005:

```
var driver2000 = "Dale Jarrett";
var driver2001 = "Michael Waltrip";
var driver2002 = "Ward Burton";
var driver2003 = "Michael Waltrip";
var driver2004 = "Dale Earnhardt, Jr.";
var driver2005 = "Jeff Gordon";
var car2000 = "Ford";
var car2001 = "Chevrolet";
var car2002 = "Dodge";
var car2003 = "Chevrolet";
var car2004 = "Chevrolet";
```

```
var car2005 = "Chevrolet";
var avgMPH2000 = 155.669;
var avgMPH2001 = 161.783;
var avgMPH2002 = 142.971;
var avgMPH2003 = 133.870;
var avgMPH2004 = 156.345;
var avgMPH2005 = 135.173;
```

6. Next, add the following statements to the end of the script section that print the values stored in each of the variables you declared and initialized in the last step:

```
document.write("<p><strong>2000</strong>: " + driver2000 +
" won while driving a " + car2000 + " at an average speed of " +
avgMPH2000 + " miles per hour.</p>");
document.write("<p><strong>2001</strong>: " + driver2001 +
" won while driving a " + car2001 + " at an average speed of " +
avgMPH2001 + " miles per hour.</p>");
document.write("<p><strong>2002</strong>: " + driver2002 +
" won while driving a " + car2002 + " at an average speed of " +
avgMPH2002 + " miles per hour.</p>");
document.write("<p><strong>2003</strong>: " + driver2003 +
" won while driving a " + car2003 + " at an average speed of " +
avgMPH2003 + " miles per hour.</p>");
document.write("<p><strong>2004</strong>: " + driver2004 +
" won while driving a " + car2004 + " at an average speed of " +
avgMPH2004 + " miles per hour.</p>");
document.write("<p><strong>2005</strong>: " + driver2005 +
" won while driving a " + car2005 + " at an average speed of " +
avgMPH2005 + " miles per hour.</p>");
```

7. Save the document as **Daytona500.html** in the **Chapter** folder for Chapter 2.

8. Open the **Daytona500.html** document in your Web browser. Figure 2-4 shows how the document looks in a Web browser.

Figure 2-4

Daytona500.html document in a Web browser

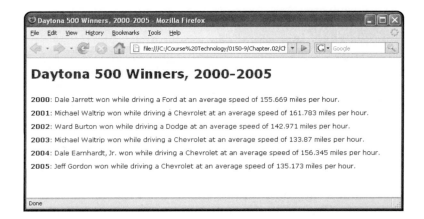

CHAPTER 2

NOTE

If you receive error messages, make sure that you typed all the JavaScript code in the correct case. (Remember that JavaScript is case sensitive.) Also check to see that you have entered all of the opening and closing tags for each element.

9.   Close your Web browser window.

Working with Data Types

Variables can contain many different kinds of values—for example, the time of day, a dollar amount, or a person's name. A **data type** is the specific category of information that a variable contains. The concept of data types is often difficult for beginning programmers to grasp because in real life you don't often distinguish among different types of information. If someone asks you for your name, your age, or the current time, you don't usually stop to consider that your name is a text string and that your age and the current time are numbers. However, a variable's specific data type is very important in programming because the data type helps determine how much memory the computer allocates for the data stored in the variable. The data type also governs the kinds of operations that can be performed on a variable.

Data types that can be assigned only a single value are called **primitive types**. JavaScript supports the six primitive data types described in Table 2-2.

Data type	Description
Number	Positive or negative numbers with or without decimal places, or number written using exponential notation
Boolean	A logical value of true or false
String	Text such as "Hello World"
Undefined	A variable that has never had a value assigned to it, has not been declared, or does not exist
Null	An empty value

Table 2-2   Primitive JavaScript data types

The null value is a data type as well as a value that can be assigned to a variable. Assigning the value "null" to a variable indicates the variable does not contain a usable value. A variable with a value of "null" has a value assigned to it—null is really the value "no value." You assign the "null" value to a variable when you want to ensure that the variable does not contain any data. For instance, with the salesTotal variable you saw earlier, you may want to ensure that the variable does not contain any data before you use it to create another purchase order. In contrast, an undefined variable is a variable that has never had a value assigned to it, has not been declared, or does not exist. The value undefined indicates that the variable has never been assigned a value—not even the null value. One use for an undefined variable is to determine whether a value is being used by another part of your script. As an example of an undefined variable, the following code shows the salesTotal variable declared without a value. When the second statement uses the document.write() method to print the salesTotal variable, a value of "undefined" is printed because the variable has not yet been assigned a value. The variable is then assigned a value of 40, which is printed to the screen, and then a value of "null", which is also printed to the screen. Figure 2-5 shows the output in a Web browser.

```
var salesTotal;
document.write("<p>Your sales total is $"
    + salesTotal + ".</p>");
var salesTotal = 40;
document.write("<p>Your sales total is $"
    + salesTotal + ".</p>");
salesTotal = null;
document.write("<p>Your sales total is $"
    + salesTotal + ".</p>");
```

Figure 2-5

Variable assigned values of "undefined" and "null"

The JavaScript language also supports **reference**, or **composite**, data types, which can contain multiple values or complex types of information, as opposed to the single values stored in primitive data types. The three reference data types supported by the JavaScript language are functions, objects, and arrays. You will learn about arrays later in this section, and functions and objects in later chapters.

Many programming languages require that you declare the type of data that a variable contains. Programming languages that require you to declare the data types of variables are called **strongly typed programming languages**. Strong typing is also known as **static typing**, because data types do not change after they have been declared. Programming languages that do not require you to declare the data types of variables are called **loosely typed programming languages**. Loose typing is also known as **dynamic typing** because data types can change after they have been declared. JavaScript is a loosely typed programming language. In JavaScript you are not required to declare the data type of variables in JavaScript, and in fact are not allowed to do so. Instead, the JavaScript interpreter automatically determines what type of data is stored in a variable and assigns the variable's data type accordingly. The following code demonstrates how a variable's data type changes automatically each time the variable is assigned a new literal value:

```
changingVariable = "Hello World";  // String
changingVariable = 8;              // Integer number
changingVariable = 5.367;          // Floating-point number
changingVariable = true;           // Boolean
changingVariable = null;           // null
```

The next two sections focus on two especially important data types: numeric and Boolean data types.

Numeric Data Types

Numeric data types are an important part of any programming language, and are particularly useful for arithmetic calculations. JavaScript supports two numeric data types: integers and floating-point numbers. An **integer** is a positive or negative number with no decimal places. Integer values in JavaScript can range from -9007199254740990 (-2^{53}) to 9007199254740990 (2^{53}). The numbers -250, -13, 0, 2, 6, 10, 100, and 10000 are examples of integers. The numbers -6.16, -4.4, 3.17, .52, 10.5, and 2.7541 are not integers; they are floating-point numbers because they contain decimal places. A **floating-point number** is a number that contains decimal places or that is written in exponential notation. **Exponential notation**, or **scientific notation**, is a shortened format for writing very large numbers or numbers with many decimal places. Numbers written in exponential notation are represented by a value between 1 and 10 multiplied by 10 raised to some power. The value of 10 is written with an uppercase or lowercase *E*. For example, the number 200,000,000,000 can be written in exponential notation as 2.0e11, which means "two times ten to the eleventh power." Floating-point values in JavaScript range from approximately $\pm 1.7976931348623157 \times 10^{308}$ to $\pm 5 \times 10^{-324}$.

CAUTION

Floating-point values that exceed the largest positive value of $\pm 1.7976931348623157 \times 10^{308}$ result in a special value of `Infinity`. Floating-point values that exceed the smallest negative value of $\pm 5 \times 10^{-324}$ result in a value of `-Infinity`.

Next, you will create a script that uses variables containing integers, floating-point numbers, and exponential numbers to print the 20 prefixes of the metric system. A metric prefix, or SI prefix, is a name that precedes a metric unit of measure. For example, the metric prefix for centimeter is centi, and it denotes a value of 1/100th. In other words, a centimeter is the equivalent of 1/100th of a meter.

To create a script that prints metric prefixes:

1. Create a new document in your text editor.

2. Type the `<!DOCTYPE>` declaration, `<html>` element, header information, and the `<body>` element. Use the strict DTD and "Metric Prefixes" as the content of the `<title>` element. Include a `<link>` element that links to the js_styles.css style sheet in your Chapter folder. Your document should appear as follows:

```
<!DOCTYPE html PUBLIC "-//W3C//DTD XHTML 1.0 Strict//EN"
"http://www.w3.org/TR/xhtml1/DTD/xhtml1-strict.dtd">
<html xmlns="http://www.w3.org/1999/xhtml">
<head>
<title>Metric Prefixes</title>
<meta http-equiv="content-type" content="text/html;
charset=iso-8859-1" />
<link rel="stylesheet" href="js_styles.css" type="text/css" />
</head>
```

```
<body>
</body>
</html>
```

3. Add the following heading element to the document body:

```
<h1>Metric Prefixes</h1>
```

4. Add the following script section to the end of the document body:

```
<script type="text/javascript">
<!-- HIDE FROM INCOMPATIBLE BROWSERS
// STOP HIDING FROM INCOMPATIBLE BROWSERS -->
</script>
```

5. In the script section, add the following variable declarations for the 20 metric prefixes:

```
var yotta = 1e24;
var zetta = 1e21;
var exa = 1e18;
var peta = 1e15;
var tera = 1e12;
var giga = 1e9;
var mega = 1e6;
var kilo = 1000;
var hecto = 100;
var deca = 10;
var deci = .1;
var centi = .01;
var milli = .001;
var micro = 1e-6;
var nano = 1e-9;
var pico = 1e-12;
var femto = 1e-15;
var atto = 1e-18;
var zepto = 1e-21;
var yocto = 1e-24;
```

6. Add to the end of the script section the following statements to print the value of each metric prefix variable as cells in a table:

```
document.write("<table border='1'
width='100%'><tr><th>Prefix</th><th>Decimal Equivalent</th>
</tr>");
document.write("<tr><td>Yotta</td><td>" + yotta + "</td>
</tr>");
document.write("<tr><td>Zetta</td><td>" + zetta + "</td>
</tr>");
document.write("<tr><td>Exa</td><td>" + exa + "</td></tr>");
document.write("<tr><td>Peta</td><td>" + peta + "</td></tr>");
document.write("<tr><td>Tera</td><td>" + tera + "</td></tr>");
```

```
document.write("<tr><td>Giga</td><td>" + giga + "</td></tr>");
document.write("<tr><td>Mega</td><td>" + mega + "</td></tr>");
document.write("<tr><td>Kilo</td><td>" + kilo + "</td></tr>");
document.write("<tr><td>Hecto</td><td>" + hecto + "</td>
</tr>");
document.write("<tr><td>Deca</td><td>" + deca + "</td></tr>");
document.write("<tr><td>Deci</td><td>" + deci + "</td></tr>");
document.write("<tr><td>Centi</td><td>" + centi + "</td>
</tr>");
document.write("<tr><td>Milli</td><td>" + milli + "</td>
</tr>");
document.write("<tr><td>Micro</td><td>" + micro + "</td>
</tr>");
document.write("<tr><td>Nano</td><td>" + nano + "</td></tr>");
document.write("<tr><td>Pico</td><td>" + pico + "</td></tr>");
document.write("<tr><td>Femto</td><td>" + femto + "</td>
</tr>");
document.write("<tr><td>Atto</td><td>" + atto + "</td></tr>");
document.write("<tr><td>Zepto</td><td>" + zepto + "</td>
</tr>");
document.write("<tr><td>Yocto</td><td>" + yocto + "</td>
</tr>");
document.write("</table>");
```

7. Save the document as **MetricPrefixes.html** in the **Chapter** folder for Chapter 2, and then validate it with the W3C Markup Validation Service at **http://validator.w3.org/**. Once the file is valid, close it in your text editor.

8. Open the **MetricPrefixes.html** document in your Web browser. Figure 2-6 shows how the document looks in a Web browser.

Figure 2-6

MetricPrefixes.html document in a Web browser

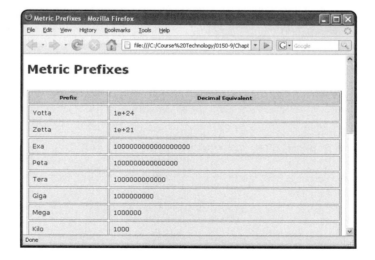

NOTE
Most Web browsers automatically display very large numbers, such as the values represented by the zetta and yotta metric prefixes, in exponential format.

9. Close your Web browser window.

Boolean Values

A **Boolean value** is a logical value of true or false. You can also think of a Boolean value as being yes or no, or on or off. Boolean values are most often used for deciding which parts of a program should execute and for comparing data. In JavaScript programming, you can only use the words true and false to indicate Boolean values. In other programming languages, you can use the integer values of 1 and 0 to indicate Boolean values of true and false—1 indicates true and 0 indicates false. JavaScript converts the values true and false to the integers 1 and 0 when necessary. For example, when you attempt to use a Boolean variable of true in a mathematical operation, JavaScript converts the variable to an integer value of 1. The following shows a simple example of two variables that are assigned Boolean values, one true and the other false. Figure 2-7 shows the output in a Web browser:

```
var repeatCustomer = true;
var corporateDiscount = false;
document.write("<p>Repeat customer: " + repeatCustomer + "</p>");
document.write("<p>Corporate discount: " + corporateDiscount +
"</p>");
```

Figure 2-7
Boolean values

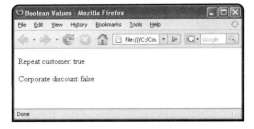

Arrays

An **array** contains a set of data represented by a single variable name. You can think of an array as a collection of variables contained within a single variable. You use arrays when you want to store groups or lists of related information in a single, easily managed location. Lists of names, courses, test scores, and prices are typically stored in arrays. For example, Figure 2-8 shows that you can manage the lengthy and difficult-to-spell names of hospital departments using a single array named `hospitalDepts[]`. You can use the array to refer to each department without having to retype the names and possibly introduce syntax errors through misspellings.

CHAPTER 2

Figure 2-8

Conceptual example of
an array

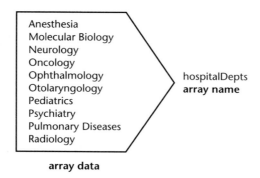

array data

NOTE

The identifiers you use for an array name must follow the same rules as identifiers
for variables: They must begin with an uppercase or lowercase ASCII letter, dollar
sign ($), or underscore (_), can include numbers (but not as the first character),
cannot include spaces, and cannot be reserved words.

Declaring and Initializing Arrays

Arrays are represented in JavaScript by the `Array` object. The `Array` object contains a special
constructor named `Array()` which is used for creating an array. A **constructor** is a special
type of function that is used as the basis for creating reference variables (that is, variables whose
data type is the reference data type). You create new arrays by using the keyword `new` and the
`Array()` constructor with the following syntax:

```
var arrayName = new Array(number of elements);
```

Within the parentheses of the `Array()` construction, you include an integer that represents the
number of elements to be contained in the array. Each piece of data contained in an array is called
an **element**. The following code creates an array named `hospitalDepts[]` that has 10 elements:

```
var hospitalDepts = new Array(10);
```

The numbering of elements within an array starts with an index number of zero (0). (This
numbering scheme can be very confusing for beginners.) An **index** is an element's numeric
position within the array. You refer to a specific element by enclosing its index number in brackets
at the end of the array name. For example, the first element in the `hospitalDepts[]` array is
`hospitalDepts[0]`, the second element is `hospitalDepts[1]`, the third element is
`hospitalDepts[2]`, and so on. This also means that if you have an array consisting of ten elements, then the tenth element in the array would be referred to using an index number of 9. You
assign values to individual array elements in the same fashion as you assign values to a standard
variable, except that you include the index for an individual element of the array. The following
code assigns values to the first three elements within the `hospitalDepts[]` array:

```
hospitalDepts[0] = "Anesthesia";    // first element
hospitalDepts[1] = "Molecular Biology";    // second element
hospitalDepts[2] = "Neurology";    // third element
```

When you create a new array with the `Array()` constructor, declaring the number of array elements is optional. You can create the array without any elements and add new elements to the array as necessary. The size of an array can change dynamically. If you assign a value to an element that has not yet been created, the element is created automatically, along with any elements that might precede it. For example, the first statement in the following code creates the `hospitalDepts[]` array without any elements. The second statement then assigns "Anesthesia" to the third element, which also creates the first two elements (`hospitalDepts[0]` and `hospitalDepts[1]`) in the process. However, note that until you assign values to them, `hospitalDepts[0]` and `hospitalDepts[1]` will both contain `undefined` values.

```
hospitalDepts = new Array();
hospitalDepts[2] = "Anesthesia";
```

You can also assign values to array elements when you first create the array. The following code assigns some values to the `hospitalDepts[]` array when it is created, then prints each of the values, using the array element numbers:

```
hospitalDepts = new Array("Anesthesia", "Molecular Biology",
    "Neurology");
```

Most programming languages require that all of the elements in an array be of the exact same data type. However, in JavaScript the values assigned to array elements can be of different data types. For example, the following code creates an array and stores values with different data types in the array elements:

```
var hotelReservation = new Array(4);
hotelReservation[0] = "Don Gosselin"; // guest name (string)
hotelReservation[1] = 2; // # of nights (integer)
hotelReservation[2] = 89.95; // price per night (floating point)
hotelReservation[3] = true; // non-smoking room (Boolean)
```

NOTE
You will study advanced array techniques in Chapter 7.

Accessing Element Information

You access an element's value just as you access the value of any other variable, except you include brackets and the element index. For example, the following code prints the values contained in the first three elements of the `hospitalDepts[]` array:

```
document.writeln(hospitalDepts[0]); // prints "Anesthesia"
document.writeln(hospitalDepts[1]); // prints "Molecular Biology"
document.writeln(hospitalDepts[2]); // prints "Neurology"
```

Modifying Elements

You modify values in existing array elements in the same fashion as you modify values in a standard variable, except you include brackets and the element index. The following code assigns values to the first three elements in the hospitalDepts[] array:

```
hospitalDepts[0] = "Anesthesia";     // first element
hospitalDepts[1] = "Molecular Biology";    // second element
hospitalDepts[2] = "Neurology";    // third element
```

After you have assigned a value to an array element, you can change it later, just as you can change other variables in a script. To change the first array element in the hospitalDepts[] array from "Anesthesia" to "Anesthesiology," you use the following statement:

```
hospitalDepts[0] = "Anesthesiology";
```

In the following example, you modify the driver name, car, and average miles-per-hour variables in the Daytona 500 script so they are stored in arrays instead of as individual variables.

To add arrays to the Daytona 500 script:

1. Return to the **Daytona500.html** document in your text editor.

2. Replace the driver name variables with the following array declaration and element assignments:

   ```
   var drivers = new Array(6);
   drivers[0] = "Dale Jarrett";
   drivers[1] = "Michael Waltrip";
   drivers[2] = "Ward Burton";
   drivers[3] = "Michael Waltrip";
   drivers[4] = "Dale Earnhardt, Jr.";
   drivers[5] = "Jeff Gordon";
   ```

3. Replace the car variables with the following array declaration and element assignments:

   ```
   var car = new Array(6);
   car [0] = "Ford";
   car [1] = "Chevrolet";
   car [2] = "Dodge";
   car [3] = "Chevrolet";
   car [4] = "Chevrolet";
   car [5] = "Chevrolet";
   ```

4. Replace the average miles-per-hour variables with the following array declaration and element assignments:

   ```
   var avgMPH = new Array(6);
   avgMPH[0] = 155.669;
   avgMPH[1] = 161.783;
   avgMPH[2] = 142.971;
   ```

```
avgMPH[3] = 133.870;
avgMPH[4] = 156.345;
avgMPH[5] = 135.173;
```

5. Finally, modify the `document.write()` statements so they reference the new arrays and elements. The portions of each statement that you need to modify are bolded in the following code:

```
document.write("<p><strong>2000</strong>: " + drivers[0] +
" won while driving a " + car[0] + " at an average speed of " +
avgMPH[0] + " miles per hour.</p>");
document.write("<p><strong>2001</strong>: " + drivers[1] +
" won while driving a " + car[1] + " at an average speed of " +
avgMPH[1] + " miles per hour.</p>");
document.write("<p><strong>2002</strong>: " + drivers[2] +
" won while driving a " + car[2] + " at an average speed of " +
avgMPH[2] + " miles per hour.</p>");
document.write("<p><strong>2003</strong>: " + drivers[3] +
" won while driving a " + car[3] + " at an average speed of " +
avgMPH[3] + " miles per hour.</p>");
document.write("<p><strong>2004</strong>: " + drivers[4] +
" won while driving a " + car[4] + " at an average speed of " +
avgMPH[4] + " miles per hour.</p>");
document.write("<p><strong>2005</strong>: " + drivers[5] +
" won while driving a " + car[5] + " at an average speed of " +
avgMPH[5] + " miles per hour.</p>");
```

6. Save the **Daytona500.html** document, and then validate it with the W3C Markup Validation Service at **http://validator.w3.org/** and fix any errors that the document contains. Once the file is valid, close it in your text editor.

7. Open the **MetricPrefixes.html** document in your Web browser. The document should appear the same as it did in Figure 2-4, before you replaced the variables with arrays.

8. Close your Web browser window.

Determining the Number of Elements in an Array

The `Array` class contains a single property, the **length property**, which returns the number of elements in an array. You append the `length` property to the name of the array whose length you want to determine using the following syntax: *array_name*`.length;`. Remember that property names are not followed by parentheses, as are method names. The following statements illustrate how to use the `length` property to return the number of elements in the `hospitalDepts[]` array:

```
hospitalDepts[0] = "Anesthesia";    // first element
hospitalDepts[1] = "Molecular Biology";    // second element
hospitalDepts[2] = "Neurology";    // third element
document.write("<p>The hospital has " + hospitalDepts.length
+ " departments.</p>");
```

Building Expressions

Variables and data become most useful when you use them in an expression. An **expression** is a literal value or variable or a combination of literal values, variables, operators, and other expressions that can be evaluated by the JavaScript interpreter to produce a result. You use operands and operators to create expressions in JavaScript. **Operands** are variables and literals contained in an expression. A **literal** is a value such as a literal string or a number. **Operators**, such as the addition operator (+) and multiplication operator (*), are symbols used in expressions to manipulate operands. You have worked with several simple expressions so far that combine operators and operands. Consider the following statement:

```
myNumber = 100;
```

This statement is an expression that results in the value "100" being assigned to myNumber. The operands in the expression are the myNumber variable name and the integer value "100". The operator is the equal sign (=). The equal sign operator is a special kind of operator, called an assignment operator, because it assigns the value 100 on the right side of the expression to the variable (myNumber) on the left side of the expression. Table 2-3 lists the main types of JavaScript operators. You'll learn more about specific operators in the following sections.

Operator type	Operators	Description
Arithmetic	addition (+), subtraction (–), multiplication (*), division (/), modulus (%), increment (++), decrement (– –), negation (–)	Used for performing mathematical calculations
Assignment	assignment (=), compound addition assignment (+=), compound subtraction assignment (–=), compound multiplication assignment (*=), compound division assignment (/=), compound modulus assignment (%=)	Assigns values to variables
Comparison	equal (==), strict equal (===), not equal (!=), strict not equal (!==), greater than (>), less than (<), greater than or equal (>=), less than or equal (<=)	Compares operands and returns a Boolean value
Logical	and (&&), or (||), not (!)	Used for performing Boolean operations on Boolean operands
String	concatenation operator (+), compound assignment operator (+=)	Performs operations on strings
Special	property access (.), array index ([ ]), function call (( )), comma (,), conditional expression (?:), delete (delete), property exists (in), object type (instanceof), new object (new), data type (typeof), void (void)	Used for various purposes and do not fit within other operator categories

Table 2-3   JavaScript operator types

NOTE

Another type of JavaScript operator, bitwise operators, operate on integer values and are a fairly complex topic. Bitwise operators and other complex operators are beyond the scope of this book.

JavaScript operators are binary or unary. A **binary operator** requires an operand before and after the operator. The equal sign in the statement `myNumber = 100;` is an example of a binary operator. A **unary operator** requires a single operand either before or after the operator. For example, the increment operator (++), an arithmetic operator, is used for increasing an operand by a value of one. The statement `myNumber++;` changes the value of the `myNumber` variable to "101".

TIP
The operand to the left of an operator is known as the left operand, and the operand to the right of an operator is known as the right operand.

Next, you will learn more about the different types of JavaScript operators.

Arithmetic Operators

Arithmetic operators are used in JavaScript to perform mathematical calculations, such as addition, subtraction, multiplication, and division. You can also use an arithmetic operator to return the modulus of a calculation, which is the remainder left when you divide one number by another number.

Arithmetic Binary Operators

JavaScript binary arithmetic operators and their descriptions are listed in Table 2-4.

Name	Operator	Description
Addition	+	Adds two operands
Subtraction	-	Subtracts one operand from another operand
Multiplication	*	Multiplies one operand by another operand
Division	/	Divides one operand by another operand
Modulus	%	Divides one operand by another operand and returns the remainder

Table 2-4   Arithmetic binary operators

The following code shows examples of expressions that include arithmetic binary operators. Figure 2-9 shows how the expressions appear in a Web browser.

```
var x, y, returnValue;
// ADDITION
x = 100;
y = 200;
returnValue = x + y;   // returnValue changes to 300
document.write("<p>returnValue after addition expression: "
     + returnValue + "</p>");
// SUBTRACTION
x = 10;
```

```
y = 7;
returnValue = x - y;   // returnValue changes to 3
document.write("<p>returnValue after subtraction expression: "
      + returnValue + "</p>");
// MULTIPLICATION
x = 2;
y = 6;
returnValue = x * y;   // returnValue changes to 12
document.write("<p>returnValue after multiplication expression: "
      + returnValue + "</p>");
// DIVISION
x = 24;
y = 3;
returnValue = x / y;   // returnValue changes to 8
document.write("<p>returnValue after division expression: "
      + returnValue + "</p>");
// MODULUS
x = 3;
y = 2;
returnValue = x % y;   // returnValue changes to 1
document.write("<p>returnValue after modulus expression: "
      + returnValue + "</p>");
```

Figure 2-9

Results of arithmetic expressions

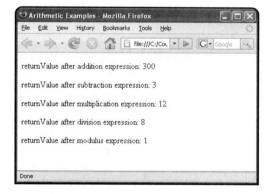

Notice in the preceding code that when JavaScript performs an arithmetic calculation, it performs the operation on the right side of the assignment operator, and then assigns the value to a variable on the left side of the assignment operator. For example, in the statement returnValue = x + y;, the operands x and y are added, then the result is assigned to the returnValue variable on the left side of the assignment operator.

You may be confused by the difference between the division (/) operator and the modulus (%) operator. The division operator performs a standard mathematical division operation. For example, dividing 15 by 6 results in a value of 2.5. By contrast, the modulus operator returns the remainder that results from the division of two integers. The following code, for instance, uses the division and modulus operators to return the result of dividing 15 by 6. The division of 15 by

6 results in a value of 2.5, because 6 goes into 15 exactly 2.5 times. But if you only allow for whole numbers, 6 goes into 15 only 2 times, with a remainder of 3 left over. Thus the modulus of 15 divided by 6 is 3, because 3 is the remainder left over following the division. Figure 2-10 shows the output.

```
var divisionResult = 15 / 6;
var modulusResult = 15 % 6;
document.write("<p>15 divided by 6 is "
    + divisionResult + ".</p>"); // prints '2'
document.write("<p>The whole number 6 goes into 15 twice, with a
remainder of "+ modulusResult + ".</p>"); // prints '3'
```

Figure 2-10

Division and modulus expressions

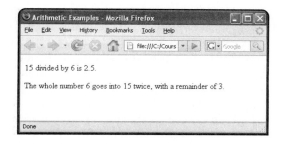

You can include a combination of variables and literal values on the right side of an assignment statement. For example, any of the following addition statements are correct:

```
returnValue = 100 + y;
returnValue = x + 200;
returnValue = 100 + 200;
```

However, you cannot include a literal value as the left operand because the JavaScript interpreter must have a variable to which to assign the returned value. Therefore, the statement 100 = x + y; causes an error.

When performing arithmetic operations on string values, the JavaScript interpreter attempts to convert the string values to numbers. The variables in the following example are assigned as string values instead of numbers because they are contained within quotation marks. Nevertheless, the JavaScript interpreter correctly performs the multiplication operation and returns a value of "6".

```
x = "2";
y = "3";
returnValue = x * y;   // the value returned is 6
```

The JavaScript interpreter does not convert strings to numbers when you use the addition operator. When you use the addition operator with strings, the strings are combined instead of being added together. In the following example, the operation returns a value of "23" because the x and y variables contain strings instead of numbers:

```
x = "2";
y = "3";
returnValue = x + y;   // a string value of 23 is returned
```

CHAPTER 2

Arithmetic Unary Operators

Arithmetic operations can also be performed on a single variable using unary operators. Table 2-5 lists the unary arithmetic operators available in JavaScript.

Name	Operator	Description
Increment	++	Increases an operand by a value of one
Decrement	--	Decreases an operand by a value of one
Negation	-	Returns the opposite value (negative or positive) of an operand

Table 2-5   Arithmetic unary operators

The increment (++) and decrement (--) unary operators can be used as prefix or postfix operators. A **prefix operator** is placed before a variable. A **postfix operator** is placed after a variable. The statements ++myVariable; and myVariable++; both increase myVariable by one. However, the two statements return different values. When you use the increment operator as a prefix operator, the value of the operand is returned *after* it is increased by a value of one. When you use the increment operator as a postfix operator, the value of the operand is returned *before* it is increased by a value of one. Similarly, when you use the decrement operator as a prefix operator, the value of the operand is returned *after* it is decreased by a value of one, and when you use the decrement operator as a postfix operator, the value of the operand is returned *before* it is decreased by a value of one. If you intend to assign the incremented or decremented value to another variable, then whether you use the prefix or postfix operator makes a difference.

You use arithmetic unary operators in any situation in which you want to use a more simplified expression for increasing or decreasing a value by 1. For example, the statement count = count + 1; is identical to the statement ++count;. As you can see, if your goal is only to increase a variable by 1, then it is easier to use the unary increment operator. But remember that with the prefix operator the value of the operand is returned *after* it is increased or decreased by a value of 1, whereas with the postfix operator, the value of the operand is returned *before* it is increased or decreased by a value of 1.

For an example of when you would use the prefix operator or the postfix operator, consider an integer variable named studentID that is used for assigning student IDs in a class registration script. One way of creating a new student ID number is to store the last assigned student ID in the studentID variable. When it's time to assign a new student ID, the script could retrieve the last value stored in the studentID variable and then increase its value by 1. In other words, the last value stored in the studentID variable will be the next number used for a student ID number. In this case, you would use the postfix operator to return the value of the expression *before* it is incremented by using a statement similar to currentID = studentID++;. If you are storing the last assigned student ID in the studentID variable, you would want to increment the value by 1 and use the result as the next student ID. In this scenario, you would use the prefix operator, which returns the value of the expression after it is incremented using a statement similar to currentID = ++studentID;.

Figure 2-11 shows a simple script that uses the prefix increment operator to assign three student IDs to a variable named curStudentID. The initial student ID is stored in the studentID variable and initialized to a starting value of "100". Figure 2-12 shows the output.

Figure 2-11

Script that uses the prefix increment operator

```
var studentID = 100;
var curStudentID;
curStudentID = ++studentID; // assigns '101'
document.write("<p>The first student ID is "
    + curStudentID + "</p>");
curStudentID = ++studentID; // assigns '102'
document.write("<p>The second student ID is "
    + curStudentID + "</p>");
curStudentID = ++studentID; // assigns '103'
document.write("<p>The third student ID is "
    + curStudentID + "</p>");
```

prefix increment operator

Figure 2-12

Output of the prefix version of the student ID script

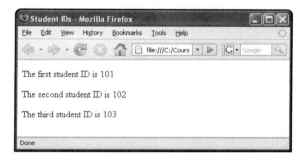

The first student ID is 101

The second student ID is 102

The third student ID is 103

The script in Figure 2-13 performs the same tasks, but using a postfix increment operator. Notice that the output in Figure 2-14 differs from the output in Figure 2-12. Because the first example of the script uses the prefix increment operator, which increments the studentID variable *before* it is assigned to curStudentID, the script does not use the starting value of "100". Rather, it first increments the studentID variable and uses "101" as the first student ID. By contrast, the second example of the script does use the initial value of "100" because the postfix increment operator increments the studentID variable *after* it is assigned to the curStudentID variable.

Figure 2-13

Script that uses a postfix increment operator

```
var studentID = 100;
var curStudentID;
curStudentID = studentID++; // assigns '100'
document.write("<p>The first student ID is "
    + curStudentID + "</p>");
curStudentID = studentID++; // assigns '101'
document.write("<p>The second student ID is "
    + curStudentID + "</p>");
curStudentID = studentID++; // assigns '102'
document.write("<p>The second student ID is "
    + curStudentID + "</p>");
```

postfix increment operator

CHAPTER 2

Figure 2-14

Output of the postfix version of the student ID script

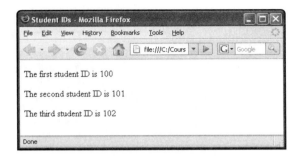

Next, you will create a script that prints scoring statistics for the two highest all-time scorers in the NBA finals. The script uses addition, multiplication, and division to calculate total points and averages per game.

To create a script that prints the all-time NBA finals scoring statistics:

1. Create a new document in your text editor.

2. Type the `<!DOCTYPE>` declaration, `<html>` element, header information, and the `<body>` element. Use the strict DTD and "NBA Finals All-Time Scoring Leaders" as the content of the `<title>` element. Include a `<link>` element that links to the js_styles.css style sheet in your Chapter folder. Your document should appear as follows:

```
<!DOCTYPE html PUBLIC "-//W3C//DTD XHTML 1.0 Strict//EN"
"http://www.w3.org/TR/xhtml1/DTD/xhtml1-strict.dtd">
<html xmlns="http://www.w3.org/1999/xhtml">
<head>
<title>NBA Finals All-Time Scoring Leaders</title>
<meta http-equiv="content-type" content="text/html;
charset=iso-8859-1" />
<link rel="stylesheet" href="js_styles.css" type="text/css" />
</head>
<body>
</body>
</html>
```

3. Add the following heading elements to the document body:

```
<h1>NBA Finals<h1>
<h2>All-Time Scoring Leaders</h2>
```

4. Add the following script section to the end of the document body:

```
<script type="text/javascript">
<!-- HIDE FROM INCOMPATIBLE BROWSERS
// STOP HIDING FROM INCOMPATIBLE BROWSERS -->
</script>
```

5. Add to the script section the following statements, which create an array for the top basketball player, Rick Barry. The first element in each array contains the player's name and the second element contains the number of games played. The third element contains the number of two point baskets and the fourth element contains the number of free throws. Notice that the fifth element, which contains the total number of points, uses multiplication and addition to calculate the total number of points while the sixth element uses division to calculate the average number of points.

```
var leader1 = new Array();
leader1[0] = "Rick Barry";        // player name
leader1[1] = 10;                  // number of games
leader1[2] = 138;                 // two point baskets
leader1[3] = 87;                  // free throws
leader1[4] = leader1[2] * 2
     + leader1[3];                // total points
leader1[5] = leader1[4]
     / leader1[1];                // average points per game
```

6. Add to the end of the script section the following array declaration and assignments for the second scoring leader, Michael Jordan:

```
var leader2 = new Array();
leader2[0] = "Michael Jordan";
leader2[1] = 35;
leader2[2] = 438;
leader2[3] = 258;
leader2[4] = leader2[2] * 2 + leader2[3];
leader2[5] = leader2[4] / leader2[1];
```

7. Add the following statements to print the statistics:

```
document.write("<p><strong>" + leader1[0] + "</strong> scored "
+ leader1[1] + " two point baskets and " + leader1[2] + " free
throws in " + leader1[3] + " games for a total of " + leader1[4]
+ " points and averaging " + leader1[5] + " points per
game.</p>");
document.write("<p><strong>" + leader2[0] + "</strong> scored "
+ leader2[1] + " two point baskets and " + leader2[2] + " free
throws in " + leader2[3] + " games for a total of " + leader2[4]
+ " points and averaging " + leader2[5] + " points per
game.</p>");
```

8. Save the document as **NBAStatLeaders.html** in the **Chapter** folder for Chapter 2.

9. Open the **NBAStatLeaders.html** document in your Web browser. Figure 2-15 shows how the document looks in a Web browser.

10. Close your Web browser window.

CHAPTER 2

Figure 2-15
NBAStatLeaders.html in
a Web browser

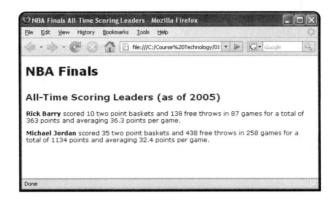

Assignment Operators

Assignment operators are used for assigning a value to a variable. You have already used the most common assignment operator, the equal sign (=), to assign values to variables you declared using the var statement. The equal sign assigns an initial value to a new variable or assigns a new value to an existing variable. For example, the following code creates a variable named myCar, uses the equal sign to assign it an initial value, then uses the equal sign again to assign it a new value:

```
var myCar = "Ford";
myCar = "Chevy";
```

JavaScript includes other assignment operators in addition to the equal sign. These additional assignment operators, called **compound assignment operators**, perform mathematical calculations on variables and literal values in an expression, and then assign a new value to the left operand. Table 2-6 displays a list of the common JavaScript assignment operators.

Name	Operator	Description
Assignment	=	Assigns the value of the right operand to the left operand
Compound addition assignment	+=	Combines the value of the right operand with the value of the left operand or adds the value of the right operand to the value of the left operand and assigns the new value to the left operand
Compound subtraction assignment	-=	Subtracts the value of the right operand from the value of the left operand and assigns the new value to the left operand
Compound multiplication assignment	*=	Multiplies the value of the right operand by the value of the left operand and assigns the new value to the left operand
Compound division assignment	/=	Divides the value of the left operand by the value of the right operand and assigns the new value to the left operand
Compound modulus assignment	%=	Divides the value of the left operand by the value of the right operand and assigns the remainder (the modulus) to the left operand

Table 2-6   Assignment operators

You can use the += compound addition assignment operator to combine two strings as well as to add numbers. In the case of strings, the string on the left side of the operator is combined with the string on the right side of the operator, and the new value is assigned to the left operator.

Before combining operands, the JavaScript interpreter attempts to convert a nonnumeric operand, such as a string, to a number. If a nonnumeric operand cannot be converted to a number, you receive a value of "NaN". The value "NaN" stands for "Not a Number" and is returned when a mathematical operation does not result in a numerical value. The following code shows examples of the different assignment operators:

```
var x, y;
x = "Hello ";
x += "World";     // x changes to "Hello World"
document.write("<p>" + x + "<br />");
x = 100;
y = 200;
x += y;           // x changes to 300
document.write(x + "<br />");
x = 10;
y = 7;
x -= y;           // x changes to 3
document.write(x + "<br />");
x = 2;
y = 6;
x *= y;           // x changes to 12
document.write(x + "<br />");
x = 24;
y = 3;
x /= y;           // x changes to 8
document.write(x + "<br />");
x = 3;
y = 2;
x %= y;           // x changes to 1
document.write(x + "<br />");
x = "100";
y = 5;
x *= y;           // x changes to 500
document.write(x + "<br />");
x = "one hundred";
y = 5;
x *= y;           // x changes to NaN
document.write(x + "</p>");
```

Comparison and Conditional Operators

Comparison operators are used to compare two operands and determine if one numeric value is greater than another. A Boolean value of true or false is returned after two operands are compared. For example, the statement 5 < 3 would return a Boolean value of false, because 5 is not less than 3. Table 2-7 lists the JavaScript comparison operators.

Name	Operator	Description
Equal	==	Returns true if the operands are equal
Strict equal	===	Returns true if the operands are equal and of the same type
Not equal	!=	Returns true if the operands are not equal
Strict not equal	!==	Returns true if the operands are not equal or not of the same type
Greater than	>	Returns true if the left operand is greater than the right operand
Less than	<	Returns true if the left operand is less than the right operand
Greater than or equal	>=	Returns true if the left operand is greater than or equal to the right operand
Less than or equal	<=	Returns true if the left operand is less than or equal to the right operand

Table 2-7   Comparison operators

CAUTION
The comparison operator (==) consists of two equal signs and performs a different function than the one performed by the assignment operator that consists of a single equal sign (=). The comparison operator *compares* values, while the assignment operator *assigns* values.

TIP
Comparison operators are often used with two kinds of special statements: conditional statements and looping statements. You'll learn how to use comparison operators in these statements in Chapter 3.

You can use number or string values as operands with comparison operators. When two numeric values are used as operands, the JavaScript interpreter compares them numerically. For example, the statement returnValue = 5 > 4; results in true because the number 5 is numerically greater than the number 4. When two nonnumeric values are used as operands, the JavaScript interpreter compares them in alphabetical order. The statement returnValue = "b" > "a"; returns true because the letter *b* is alphabetically greater than the letter *a*. When one operand is a number and the other is a string, the JavaScript interpreter attempts to convert the string value to a number. If the string value cannot be converted to a number, a value of false is returned. For example, the statement returnValue = 10 == "ten"; returns a value of false because the JavaScript interpreter cannot convert the string "ten" to a number.

The comparison operator is often used with another kind of operator, the conditional operator. The **conditional operator** executes one of two expressions, based on the results of a conditional expression. The syntax for the conditional operator is *conditional expression ? expression1: expression2;*. If the conditional expression evaluates to true, then expression1 executes. If the conditional expression evaluates to false, then expression2 executes.

The following code shows an example of the conditional operator. In the example, the conditional expression checks to see if the intVariable variable is greater than 100. If intVariable is greater than 100, then the text "intVariable is greater than 100" is assigned to the result variable. If intVariable is not greater than 100, then the text "intVariable is less than or equal to 100" is assigned to the `result` variable. Because `intVariable` is equal to 150, the conditional statement returns a value of true, the first expression executes, and "intVariable is greater than 100" prints to the screen.

```
var intVariable = 150;
var result;
(intVariable > 100) ? result =
      "intVariable is greater than 100" : result =
      "intVariable is less than or equal to 100";
document.write(result);
```

Next, you add a conditional operator to the NBAStatLeaders.html script that determines which player participated in the most NBA final games.

To add a conditional operator to the NBAStatLeaders.html script:

1. Return to the **NBAStatLeaders.html** document in your text editor.

2. Add the following conditional expression to the end of the script section. The conditional expression compares the number of games assigned to the second element in each array, and then assigns an appropriate message to the `mostGames` variable, depending on which player participated in the most games.

```
(leader1[1] > leader1[1]) ? mostGames =
      leader1[0] + " competed in more NBA final games than "
      + leader1[0] : mostGames =
leader2[0] + " competed in more NBA final games than " + leader1[0];
```

3. Add the following statement to the end of the script section to print the value assigned to the `mostGames` variable:

```
document.write("<p>" + mostGames + ".</p>");
```

4. Save the **NBAStatLeaders.html** document, and then open it in your Web browser. Figure 2-16 shows how the document looks in a Web browser.

Figure 2-16
NBAStatLeaders.html document in a Web browser after adding a conditional operator

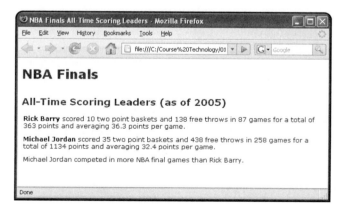

5. Close your Web browser window.

CHAPTER 2

Logical Operators

Logical operators are used for comparing two Boolean operands for equality. For example, a script for an automobile insurance company may need to determine whether a customer is male *and* under 21 in order to determine the correct insurance quote. As with comparison operators, a Boolean value of true or false is returned after two operands are compared. Table 2-8 lists the JavaScript logical operators.

Name	Operator	Description
And	&&	Returns true if both the left operand and right operand return a value of true; otherwise, it returns a value of false
Or	||	Returns true if either the left operand or right operand returns a value of true; if neither operand returns a value of true, then the expression containing the Or || operator returns a value of false
Not	!	Returns true if an expression is false and returns false if an expression is true

Table 2-8   Logical operators

The Or (||) and the And (&&) operators are binary operators (requiring two operands), while the Not (!) operator is a unary operator (requiring a single operand). Logical operators are often used with comparison operators to evaluate expressions, allowing you to combine the results of several expressions into a single statement. For example, the And (&&) operator is used for determining whether two operands return an equivalent value. The operands themselves are often expressions. The following code uses the And operator to compare two separate expressions:

```
var gender = "male";
var age = 17;
var riskFactor = gender=="male" && age<=21;    // returns true
```

In the above example, the gender variable expression evaluates to true because it is equal to "male" and the age variable expression evaluates to true because its value is less than or equal to 21. Because both expressions are true, riskFactor is assigned a value of true. The statement containing the And (&&) operator essentially says, "if variable gender is equal to "male" *and* variable age is less than or equal to 21, then assign a value of true to riskFactor. Otherwise, assign a value of false to riskFactor." In the following code, however, riskFactor is assigned a value of false, because the age variable expression does not evaluate to true:

```
var gender = "male";
var age = 28;
var riskFactor = gender=="male" && age<=21;    // returns false
```

The logical Or (||) operator checks to see if either expression evaluates to true. For example, the statement in the following code says, "if the variable speedingTicket is greater than 0 *or* variable age is less than or equal to 21, then assign a value of true to riskFactor. Otherwise, assign a value of false to riskFactor."

```
var speedingTicket = 2;
var age = 28;
var riskFactor = speedingTicket>0 || age<=21;    // returns true
```

The `riskFactor` variable in the above example is assigned a value of true, because the `speedingTicket` variable expression evaluates to true, even though the `age` variable expression evaluates to false. This result occurs because the Or (`||`) statement returns true if *either* the left *or* right operand evaluates to true.

The following code is an example of the Not (`!`) operator, which returns true if an operand evaluates to false and returns false if an operand evaluates to true. Notice that since the Not operator is unary, it requires only a single operand.

```
var trafficViolations = true;
var safeDriverDiscount = !trafficViolations;    // returns false
```

Logical operators are often used within conditional and looping statements such as the `if...else, for,` and `while` statements. You will learn about conditional and looping statements in Chapter 3.

Working with Strings

As you learned in Chapter 1, a text string is text that is contained within double or single quotation marks. Examples of strings you may use in a script are company names, user names, comments, and other types of text. You can use text strings as literal values or assign them to a variable.

Literal strings can be also be assigned a zero-length string value called an **empty string**. For example, the following statement declares a variable named `customerName` and assigns it an empty string:

```
var customerName = "";
```

Empty strings are valid values for literal strings and are not considered to be `null` or `undefined`. Why would you want to assign an empty string to a literal string? Think for a moment about the `prompt()` method, which displays a dialog box with a message, a text box, an OK button, and a Cancel button. You can pass two string arguments to the `prompt()` method. The first argument displays an instruction to the user, while the second argument is the default text that appears in the prompt dialog box text box. If you do not include the second argument, then the value "undefined" appears as the default text of the prompt dialog box. To prevent "undefined" from displaying as the default text in the prompt dialog text box, you pass an empty string as the second argument of the `prompt()` method.

When you want to include a quoted string within a literal string surrounded by double quotation marks, you surround the quoted string with single quotation marks. When you want to include a quoted string within a literal string surrounded by single quotation marks, you surround the quoted string with double quotation marks. Whichever method you use, a string must begin and end with the same type of quotation marks. For example, `document.write("This is a text string.");` is valid because it starts and ends with double quotation marks, while the statement `document.write("This is a text string.');` is invalid because it starts with a double quotation mark and ends with a single quotation mark. In the second case you would receive an error message because the Web browser cannot tell where the literal strings begin and end. The following code shows an example of a script that prints strings. Figure 2-17 shows the output.

```
<script type="text/javascript">
<!-- HIDE FROM INCOMPATIBLE BROWSERS
document.write("<p>This is a literal string.<br />");
document.write("This string contains a 'quoted' string.<br />");
document.write('This is another example of a "quoted" string.<br />');
var firstString = "This literal string was assigned to a
variable.<br/>";
var secondString = 'This literal string was also assigned to a
variable.</p>';
document.write(firstString);
document.write(secondString);
// STOP HIDING FROM INCOMPATIBLE BROWSERS -->
</script>
```

Figure 2-17

String examples in a Web browser

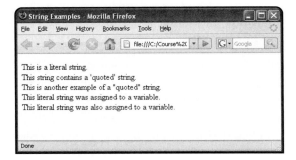

NOTE

Unlike other programming languages, there is no special data type in JavaScript for a single character, such as the `char` data type in the C, C++, and Java programming languages.

String Operators

JavaScript has two operators that can be used with strings: + and +=. When used with strings, the plus sign is known as the concatenation operator. The **concatenation operator** (+) is used to combine two strings. You have already learned how to use the concatenation operator. For example, the following code combines a string variable and a literal string, and assigns the new value to another variable:

```
var destination = "Jakarta";
var location = "Indonesia";
destination = destination + " is in " + location;
```

The combined value of the `location` variable and the string literal that is assigned to the destination variable is "Jakarta is in Indonesia."

You can also use the compound assignment operator (+=) to combine two strings. The following code combines the two text strings, but without using the `location` variable:

```
var destination = "Jakarta";
destination += " is in Indonesia";
```

Note that the same symbol—a plus sign—serves as the concatenation operator and the addition operator. When used with numbers or variables containing numbers, expressions using the concatenation operator return the sum of the two numbers. As you learned earlier in this chapter, if you use the concatenation operator with a string value and a number value, the string value and the number value are combined into a new string value, as in the following example:

```
var textString = "The legal voting age is ";
var votingAge = 18;
newString = textString + votingAge;
```

Escape Characters and Sequences

You need to use extra care when using single quotation marks with possessives and contractions in strings, because the JavaScript interpreter always looks for the first closing single or double quotation mark to match an opening single or double quotation mark. For example, consider the following statement:

```
document.write('<p>My city's zip code is 01562.</p>');
```

This statement causes an error. The JavaScript interpreter assumes that the literal string ends with the apostrophe following "city" and looks for the closing parentheses for the `document.write()` statement immediately following "city's". To get around this problem, you include an escape character before the apostrophe in "city's". An **escape character** tells the compiler or interpreter that the character that follows it has a special purpose. In JavaScript, the escape character is the backslash \. Placing a backslash in front of an apostrophe tells the JavaScript interpreter that the apostrophe is to be treated as a regular keyboard character, such as "a", "b", "1", or "2", and not as part of a single quotation mark pair that encloses a text string. The backslash in the following statement tells the JavaScript interpreter to print the apostrophe following the word "city" as an apostrophe.

```
document.write('<p>My city\'s zip code is 01562.</p>');
```

You can also use the escape character in combination with other characters to insert a special character into a string. When you combine the escape character with other characters, the combination is called an **escape sequence**. The backslash followed by an apostrophe \' and the backslash followed by a double quotation mark \" are both examples of escape sequences. Most escape sequences carry out special functions. For example, the escape sequence \t inserts a tab into a string. Table 2-9 describes the escape sequences that can be added to a string in JavaScript.

NOTE
If you place a backslash before any character other than those listed in Table 2-9, the backslash is ignored.

CHAPTER 2

Escape sequence	Character
\\	Backslash
\b	Backspace
\r	Carriage return
\"	Double quotation mark
\f	Form feed
\t	Horizontal tab
\n	New line
\0	Null character
\'	Single quotation mark
\v	Vertical tab
\XXX	Latin-1 character specified by the *XX* characters, which represent two hexadecimal digits
\XXXXX	Unicode character specified by the *XXXX* characters, which represent four hexadecimal digits

Table 2-9   JavaScript escape sequences

Notice that one of the characters generated by an escape sequence is the backslash. Because the escape character itself is a backslash, you must use the escape sequence \\ to include a backslash as a character in a string. For example, to include the path "C:\JavaScript_Projects\Files\" in a string, you must include two backslashes for every single backslash you want to appear in the string, as in the following statement:

```
document.write("<p>My JavaScript files are located in
C:\\JavaScript_Projects\\Files\\</p>");
```

The following code shows an example of a script containing strings with several escape sequences. Figure 2-18 shows the output.

```
<pre>
<script type="text/javascript">
<!-- HIDE FROM INCOMPATIBLE BROWSERS
document.write("<p>This line is printed \non two lines.</p>");
     // New line
document.write("<p>\tThis line includes a horizontal tab.</p>");
     // Horizontal tab
document.write("<p>My personal files are in c:\\personal.</p>");
     // Backslash
document.write("<p>My dog's name is \"Noah.\"</p>");
     // Double quotation mark
document.write('<p>California\'s capital is Sacramento.</p>');
     // Single quotation mark
// STOP HIDING FROM INCOMPATIBLE BROWSERS -->
</script>
</pre>
```

Figure 2-18

Output of script with
strings containing escape
sequences

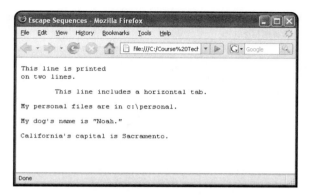

NOTE

Several of the escape sequences, including the new line and horizontal tab escape
sequences, are only recognized inside a container element such as the `<pre>`
element.

Next, you modify the NBAStatLeaders.html script so it contains strings that include single quotes
and escape characters.

To modify the NBAStatLeaders.html script so it contains strings that include single quotes and
escape characters:

1. Return to the **NBAStatLeaders.html** document in your text editor.

2. Add the following array declaration and assignments for the third scoring leader,
   Shaquille O'Neal, immediately above the first `document.write()` statement in
   the script section. Notice that the statement that assigns Shaquille O'Neal's name
   to the array element includes a single quotation mark escape sequence for the
   apostrophe that appears in the last name and double quotation mark escape
   sequences that surround O'Neal's nickname, "Shaq".

```
var leader3 = new Array();
leader3[0] = "Shaquille \"Shaq\" O\'Neal";
leader3[1] = 24;
leader3[2] = 306;
leader3[3] = 171;
leader3[4] = leader3[2] * 2 + leader3[3];
leader3[5] = leader3[4] / leader3[1];
```

3. Replace the remainder of the statements in the script section, including the
   conditional operator statement, with the following statements to print the array
   values in a table. Notice that attribute values within the text strings are surrounded
   by single quotation marks instead of double quotation marks.

```
document.write("<table border='1' width='100%'>
<colgroup span='1' width='30%' /><colgroup span='5'
width='14%' /><tr><th>Player</th><th>Games</th><th>2 Pt.
```

```
Baskets</th><th>Free Throws</th><th>Total Points</th><th>Avg
</th></tr>");
document.write("<tr><td>" + leader1[0] + "</td><td>" +
leader1[1] + "</td><td>" + leader1[2] + "</td><td>" +
leader1[3] + "</td><td>" + leader1[4] + "</td><td>" +
leader1[5] + "</td></tr>");
document.write("<tr><td>" + leader2[0] + "</td><td>" +
leader2[1] + "</td><td>" + leader2[2] + "</td><td>" +
leader2[3] + "</td><td>" + leader2[4] + "</td><td>" +
leader2[5] + "</td></tr>");
document.write("<tr><td>" + leader3[0] + "</td><td>" +
leader3[1] + "</td><td>" + leader3[2] + "</td><td>" +
leader3[3] + "</td><td>" + leader3[4] + "</td><td>" +
leader3[5] + "</td></tr>");
document.write("</table>");
```

4. Save the **NBAStatLeaders.html** document, and then open it in your Web browser. Figure 2-19 shows how the document looks in a Web browser.

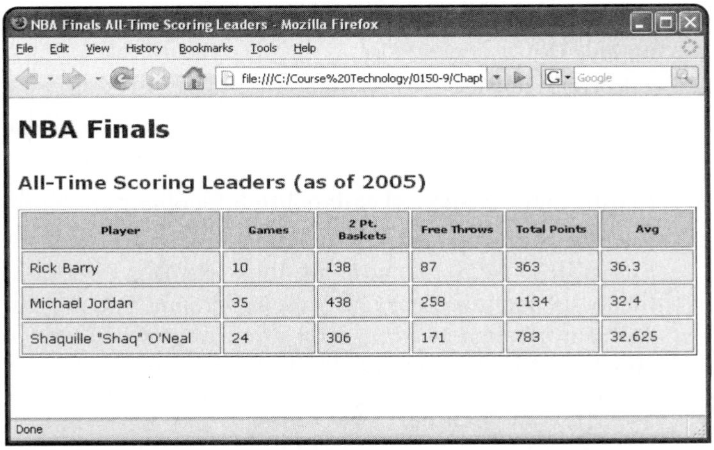

Figure 2-19

NBAStatLeaders.html document in a Web browser after adding strings that contain single quotes and escape characters

5. Close your Web browser window.

Special Operators

JavaScript also includes the special operators that are listed in Table 2-10. These operators are used for various purposes and do not fit within any other category.

You will be introduced to the special JavaScript operators as necessary throughout this book. One special operator that you will use in this section is the typeof operator. This operator is useful because the data type of variables can change during the course of program execution. This can cause problems if you attempt to perform an arithmetic operation and one of the variables is a string or the null value. To avoid such problems, you can use the typeof operator to determine the data type of a variable. The syntax for the typeof operator is typeof(*variablename*);.

You should use the `typeof` operator whenever you need to be sure that a variable is the correct data type. The values that can be returned by the `typeof` operator are listed in Table 2-11.

Name	Operator	Description
Property access	.	Appends an object, method, or property to another object
Array index	[]	Accesses an element of an array
Function call	()	Calls up functions or changes the order in which individual operations in an expression are evaluated
Comma	,	Allows you to include multiple expressions in the same statement
Conditional expression	?:	Executes one of two expressions based on the results of a conditional expression
Delete	delete	Deletes array elements, variables created without the `var` keyword, and properties of custom objects
Property exists	in	Returns a value of true if a specified property is contained within an object
Object type	instanceof	Returns true if an object is of a specified object type
New object	new	Creates a new instance of a user-defined object type or a predefined JavaScript object type
Data type	typeof	Determines the data type of a variable
Void	void	Evaluates an expression without returning a result

Table 2-10   Special operators

Return value	Returned for
Number	Integers and floating-point numbers
String	Text strings
Boolean	True or false
Object	Objects, arrays, and null variables
Function	Functions
Undefined	Undefined variables

Table 2-11   Values returned by `typeof` operator

CHAPTER 2

Understanding Operator Precedence

When using operators to create expressions in JavaScript, you need to be aware of the precedence of an operator. The term **operator precedence** refers to the order in which operations in an expression are evaluated. Table 2-12 shows the order of precedence for JavaScript operators. Operators in the same grouping in Table 2-12 have the same order of precedence. When performing operations with operators in the same precedence group, the order of precedence is determined by the operator's **associativity**—that is, the order in which operators of equal precedence execute. Associativity is evaluated from left-to-right or right-to-left depending on the operators involved, as explained shortly.

Operators	Description	Associativity
.	Objects—highest precedence	Left to right
[]	Array elements—highest precedence	Left to right
()	Functions/evaluation—highest precedence	Left to right
new	New object—highest precedence	Right to left
!	Not	Right to left
-	Unary negation	Right to left
++	Increment	Right to left
--	Decrement	Right to left
typeof	Data type	Right to left
void	Void	Right to left
delete	Delete object	Right to left
* / %	Multiplication/division/modulus	Left to right
+ -	Addition/subtraction/concatenation	Left to right
< <= > >=	Comparison	Left to right
instanceof	Object type	Left to right
in	Object property	Left to right
== != === !==	Equality	Left to right
&&	Logical and	Left to right
||	Logical or	Left to right
?:	Conditional	Right to left
= += -= *= /= %=	Compound assignment	Right to left
,	Comma—lowest precedence	Left to right

Table 2-12   Operator precedence

NOTE

The preceding list does not include bitwise operators. As explained earlier, bitwise operators are beyond the scope of this book.

Operators in a higher grouping have precedence over operators in a lower grouping. For example, the multiplication operator (*) has a higher precedence than the addition operator (+). Therefore, the statement 5 + 2 * 8 evaluates as follows: the numbers 2 and 8 are multiplied first for a total of 16, then the number 5 is added, resulting in a total of 21. If the addition operator had a higher precedence than the multiplication operator, then the statement would evaluate to 56, because 5 would be added to 2 for a total of 7, which would then be multiplied by 8.

As an example of how associativity is evaluated, consider the multiplication and division operators. These operators have an associativity of left to right. Thus the statement 30 / 5 * 2 results in a value of 12. Although the multiplication and division operators have equal precedence, the division operation executes first due to the left to right associativity of both operators. Figure 2-20 conceptually illustrates the left to right associativity of the 30 / 5 * 2 statement.

Figure 2-20

Conceptual illustration of left to right associativity

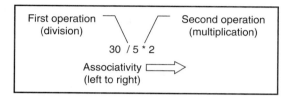

If the multiplication operator had higher precedence than the division operator, then the statement 30 / 5 * 2 would result in a value of 3 because the multiplication operation (5 * 2) would execute first. By contrast, the assignment operator and compound assignment operators—such as the compound multiplication assignment operator (*=)—have an associativity of right to left. Therefore, in the following code, the assignment operations take place from right to left. The variable x is incremented by one *before* it is assigned to the y variable using the compound multiplication assignment operator (*=). Then, the value of variable y is assigned to variable x. The result assigned to both the x and y variables is 8. Figure 2-21 conceptually illustrates the right to left associativity of the x = y *= ++x statement.

```
var x = 3;
var y = 2;
x = y *= ++x;
```

Figure 2-21

Conceptual illustration of right to left associativity

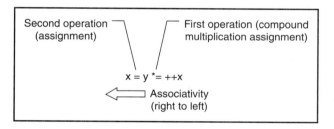

As you can see from the list, parentheses have the highest precedence. Parentheses are used with expressions to change the associativity with which individual operations in an expression are evaluated. For example, the statement 5 + 2 * 8, which evaluates to 21, can be rewritten to (5 + 2) * 8, which evaluates to 56. The parentheses tell the JavaScript interpreter to add the numbers 5 and 2 before multiplying by the number 8. Using parentheses forces the statement to evaluate to 56 instead of 21.

The declaration assignments in the NBAStatLeaders.html script that assign total points and averages per game to the last two elements in each array aren't really necessary. Instead, you can simply perform this calculation in the document.write() statements that print the values.

However, this requires using parentheses to force the statements to calculate correctly, as you will see in the next exercise.

To modify the NBAStatLeaders.html script so the calculations are performed in the `document.write()` statements:

1. Return to the **NBAStatLeaders.html** document in your text editor.

2. Delete the statements that assign values to the fourth and fifth elements of each array. The modified declaration statements should appear as follows:

```
var leader1 = new Array();
leader1[0] = "Rick Barry";           // player
leader1[1] = 10;                     // number of games
leader1[2] = 138;                    // two point baskets
leader1[3] = 87;                     // free throws
var leader2 = new Array();
leader2[0] = "Michael Jordan";
leader2[1] = 35;
leader2[2] = 438;
leader2[3] = 258;
var leader3 = new Array();
leader3[0] = "Shaquille \"Shaq\" O\'Neal";
leader3[1] = 24;
leader3[2] = 306;
leader3[3] = 171;
```

3. Replace the references in the `document.write()` statement to the fourth and fifth elements of each array (that you just deleted) with calculations that calculate each player's total points and average points per game. For example, for Rick Berry, you must replace `leader1[4]` with `leader1[2] * 2 + leader1[3]` to calculate the total points, and `leader1[5]` with `leader1[2] * 2 + leader1[3] / leader1[1]` to calculate the average number of points per game. The portions of each statement that you need to modify are bolded in the following code:

```
document.write("<tr><td>" + leader1[0] + "</td><td>" +
leader1[1] + "</td><td>" + leader1[2] + "</td><td>" +
leader1[3] + "</td><td>" + leader1[2] * 2 + leader1[3] +
"</td><td>" + leader1[2] * 2 + leader1[3] / leader1[1] +
"</td></tr>");
document.write("<tr><td>" + leader2[0] + "</td><td>" +
leader2[1] + "</td><td>" + leader2[2] + "</td><td>" +
leader2[3] + "</td><td>" + leader2[2] * 2 + leader2[3] +
"</td><td>" + leader2[2] * 2 + leader2[3] / leader2[1] +
"</td></tr>");
document.write("<tr><td>" + leader3[0] + "</td><td>" +
leader3[1] + "</td><td>" + leader3[2] + "</td><td>" +
leader3[3] + "</td><td>" + leader3[2] * 2 + leader3[3] +
"</td><td>" + leader3[2] * 2 + leader3[3] / leader3[1] +
"</td></tr>");
```

4. Save the **NBAStatLeaders.html** document and open it in your Web browser. Notice that the total points and averages for each player do not calculate correctly. For example, Rick Barry's total points and average are incorrectly calculated as 27687 and 2768.7 (they should be 363 and 36.3, respectively). This occurs because the JavaScript interpreter is not recognizing the individual pieces of the calculation as being part of the same calculation. In the case of Rick Barry, the interpreter is calculating the first part of the calculation, which multiplies the number of two point baskets by two, but does not recognize the portion of the calculation that adds the number of free throw points. Instead, the JavaScript interpreter is calculating and printing the score from two point baskets (276) and then just printing the number of free throw points (87). Although the result looks like a single number, it is really two separate numbers printed next to each other. To resolve this problem, you must enclose the calculation within parentheses, as shown in the following bolded code. Note that you must add parentheses to the calculation that calculates the total number of points and to the calculation that calculates the average points per game:

```
document.write("<tr><td>" + leader1[0] + "</td><td>" +
leader1[1] + "</td><td>" + leader1[2] + "</td><td>" +
leader1[3] + "</td><td>" + (leader1[2] * 2 + leader1[3]) +
"</td><td>" + (leader1[2] * 2 + leader1[3]) / leader1[1] +
"</td></tr>");
document.write("<tr><td>" + leader2[0] + "</td><td>" +
leader2[1] + "</td><td>" + leader2[2] + "</td><td>" +
leader2[3] + "</td><td>" + (leader2[2] * 2 + leader2[3]) +
"</td><td>" + (leader2[2] * 2 + leader2[3]) / leader2[1] +
"</td></tr>");
document.write("<tr><td>" + leader3[0] + "</td><td>" +
leader3[1] + "</td><td>" + leader3[2] + "</td><td>" +
leader3[3] + "</td><td>" + (leader3[2] * 2 + leader3[3]) +
"</td><td>" + (leader3[2] * 2 + leader3[3]) / leader3[1] +
"</td></tr>");
```

5. Save the **NBAStatLeaders.html** document, validate it with the W3C Markup Validation Service at **http://validator.w3.org/**, and fix any errors that the document contains. Once the file is valid, close it in your text editor.

6. Open the **NBAStatLeaders.html** document in your Web browser. The total points and averages per game should calculate correctly.

7. Close your Web browser window and text editor.

CHAPTER 2

Chapter Summary

▶ The values a program stores in computer memory are commonly called variables.

▶ The name you assign to a variable is called an identifier.

▶ Reserved words, which are also called keywords, are special words that are part of the JavaScript language syntax.

▶ A data type is the specific category of information that a variable contains.

▶ JavaScript is a loosely typed programming language.

▶ An integer is a positive or negative number with no decimal places.

▶ A floating-point number is a number that contains decimal places or that is written in exponential notation.

▶ A Boolean value is a logical value of true or false.

▶ An array contains a set of data represented by a single variable name.

▶ An expression is a single literal value or variable or a combination of literal values, variables, operators, and other expressions that can be evaluated by the JavaScript interpreter to produce a result.

▶ Operands are variables and literals contained in an expression. A literal is a value such as a literal string or a number.

▶ Operators are symbols used in expressions to manipulate operands, such as the addition operator (+) and multiplication operator (*).

▶ A binary operator requires an operand before and after the operator.

▶ A unary operator requires a single operand either before or after the operator.

▶ Arithmetic operators are used in JavaScript to perform mathematical calculations, such as addition, subtraction, multiplication, and division.

▶ Assignment operators are used for assigning a value to a variable.

▶ Comparison operators are used to compare two operands and determine if one numeric value is greater than another.

▶ The conditional operator executes one of two expressions, based on the results of a conditional expression.

▶ Logical operators are used for comparing two Boolean operands for equality.

▶ An escape character tells the compiler or interpreter that the character that follows it has a special purpose.

▶ Operator precedence is the order in which operations in an expression are evaluated.

Review Questions

1. What is a variable and how is it used in JavaScript?

2. Which of the following are valid identifiers? (Choose all that apply.)

   a. `var _copyrightYear = 2008;`

   b. `var 2008Copyright Year = true;`

```
   c.  var $CopyrightYear = 2008;
   d.  var copyrightYear = 2008;
```

3. Variable names are case sensitive. True or false?

4. Which of the following variable declaration statements are valid? (Choose all that apply.)

```
   a.  highwaySpeed;
   b.  var highwaySpeed;
   c.  var highwaySpeed = 65;
   d.  var highwaySpeed(65);
```

5. Variables must be declared on separate lines, regardless of whether they are separated by commas. True or false?

6. Which of the following statements correctly prints the value of a variable named endFiscalYear? (Choose all that apply.)

```
   a.  document.write("<p>The fiscal year ends on" +
       endFiscalYear + "</p>");
   b.  document.write("<p>The fiscal year ends on +
       endFiscalYear + </p>");
   c.  document.write("<p>endfiscalYear</p>");
   d.  document.write("endFiscalYear);
```

7. Explain the concept of data types.

8. JavaScript is a strongly typed programming language. True or false?

9. Explain the purpose of the null data type.

10. Which of the following values are integers? (Choose all that apply.)

```
   a.  1
   b.  1.1
   c.  4e12
   d.  -10
```

11. Which of following values can be assigned to a Boolean variable? (Choose all that apply.)

```
   a.  0
   b.  1
   c.  true
   d.  false
```

12. The identifiers you use for an array name must follow the same rules as identifiers for variables. True or false?

13. What is the correct syntax for creating an array named `taxRules` that contains five elements?

    a. `new Array(taxRules) = 5;`

    b. `Array(taxRules) + 5;`

    c. `var taxRules = Array(5);`

    d. `var taxRules = new Array(5);`

14. An error occurs if you attempt to assign a value to an element that has not yet been created. True or false?

15. Which of the following properties returns the number of elements in an array?

    a. `length`

    b. `size`

    c. `elements`

    d. `indexes`

16. The Or (| |) operator returns true if _____. (Choose all that apply.)

    a. the left operand and right operand both return a value of true

    b. the left operand returns a value of true

    c. the left operand and right operand both return a value of false

    d. the right operand returns a value of true

17. Which of the following characters separates expressions in a conditional expression?

    a. `?`

    b. `:`

    c. `;`

    d. `&&`

18. The concatenation operator (+) is used for _____. (Choose all that apply.)

    a. adding numbers

    b. combining text strings

    c. combining variables

    d. incrementing numeric variables

19. Which of the following is the correct syntax for including double quotation marks within a string that is already surrounded by double quotation marks?

    a. `"Ralph Nader is a \"third party\" presidential candidate."`

    b. `"Ralph Nader is a "third party" presidential candidate."`

    c. `"Ralph Nader is a /"third party/" presidential candidate."`

    d. `"Ralph Nader is a ""third party"" presidential candidate."`

20. Which of the following expressions returns a value of 56?

    a. `7 * (3 + 5)`
    b. `(7 * 3) + 5`
    c. `(7 * 3 + 5)`
    d. `3 + 5 * 7`

Hands-On Projects

 ## Project 2-1

In this project, you will create a Web page that uses variables to display information about the five largest islands in the world.

1. Create a new document in your text editor, and type the `<html>` element, document head, and `<body>` element. Use "Largest Islands" as the content of the `<title>` element.

2. Add the following `<h1>` element to the document body:

    ```
    <h1>Largest Islands</h1>
    ```

3. Add the following script section to the end of the document body:

    ```
    <script type="text/javascript">
    <!-- HIDE FROM INCOMPATIBLE BROWSERS
    // STOP HIDING FROM INCOMPATIBLE BROWSERS -->
    </script>
    ```

4. In the script section, type the following statements, which declare variables containing the names and sizes of the world's five largest islands:

    ```
    var island1Name = "Greenland";
    var island2Name = "New Guinea";
    var island3Name = "Borneo";
    var island4Name = "Madagascar";
    var island5Name = "Baffin";
    var island1Size = 2175600;
    var island2Size = 790000;
    var island3Size = 737000;
    var island4Size = 587000;
    var island5Size = 507000;
    ```

5. Next, add the following statements to the end of the script section that print the values stored in each of the variables you declared and initialized in the last step:

    ```
    document.write("<p>The largest island in the world is "
    + island1Name + " with " + island1Size + " miles.</p>");
    document.write("<p>The second largest island in the world is "
    ```

```
+ island2Name
        + " with " + island2Size + " miles.</p>");
document.write("<p>The third largest island in the world is "
+ island3Name
        + " with " + island3Size + " miles.</p>");
document.write("<p>The fourth largest island in the world is "
+ island4Name
        + " with " + island4Size + " miles.</p>");
document.write("<p>The fifth largest island in the world is "
+ island5Name
        + " with " + island5Size + " miles.</p>");
```

6. Save the document as **LargestIslands.html** in the Projects folder for Chapter 2, and then open it in your Web browser and examine how the elements are rendered.

7. Close your Web browser window, but leave the LargestIslands.html document open in your text editor.

Project 2-2

In this project, you will modify the Largest Islands Web page so the island names and sizes are stored in arrays.

1. Return to the **LargestIslands.html** document in your text editor and immediately save it as **LargestIslands_Arrays.html** in the Projects folder for Chapter 2.

2. Replace the island name variables with the following array declaration and element assignments:

```
var islandNames = new Array(5);
islandNames[0] = "Greenland";
islandNames[1] = "New Guinea";
islandNames[2] = "Borneo";
islandNames[3] = "Madagascar";
islandNames[4] = "Baffin";
```

3. Replace the island size variables with the following array declaration and element assignments:

```
var islandSizes = new Array(5);
islandSizes[0] = 2175600;
islandSizes[1] = 790000;
islandSizes[2] = 737000;
islandSizes[3] = 587000;
islandSizes[4] = 507000;
```

4. Finally, modify the document.write() statements so they reference the new arrays and elements. The portions of each statement that you need to modify are bolded in the following code:

```
document.write("<p>The largest island in the world is "
        + islandNames[0] + " with " + islandSizes[0] +
```

```
                     " miles.</p>");
document.write("<p>The second largest island in the world is "
        + islandNames[1] + " with " + islandSizes[1] +
        " miles.</p>");
document.write("<p>The third largest island in the world is "
        + islandNames[2] + " with " + islandSizes[2] +
        " miles.</p>");
document.write("<p>The fourth largest island in the world is "
        + islandNames[3] + " with " + islandSizes[3] +
        " miles.</p>");
document.write("<p>The fifth largest island in the world is "
        + islandNames[4] + " with " + islandSizes[4] +
        " miles.</p>");
```

5. Save the **LargestIslands_Arrays.html** document.

6. Use the W3C Markup Validation Service to validate the
    LargestIslands_Arrays.html document and fix any errors that the document
    contains. Once the document is valid, close it in your text editor and then open it in
    your Web browser and examine how the elements are rendered. The elements should
    appear the same as they did before you converted the variables to arrays.

7. Close your Web browser window.

 ## Project 2-3

In this project, you will create a script that uses assignment operators.

1. Create a new document in your text editor.

2. Type the `<!DOCTYPE>` declaration, `<html>` element, header information, and the
    `<body>` element. Use the strict DTD and "Assignment Operators" as the content
    of the `<title>` element.

3. Add the following `<h1>` element to the document body:

    ```
    <h1>Assignment Operators</h1>
    ```

4. Add the following script section to the document body:

    ```
    <script type="text/javascript">
    <!-- HIDE FROM INCOMPATIBLE BROWSERS
    // STOP HIDING FROM INCOMPATIBLE BROWSERS -->
    </script>
    ```

5. Type the following statements in the script section. These statements perform several
    compound assignment operations on a variable named `dataVar`. After each
    assignment operation, the result is printed.

    ```
    var dataVar = "Don ";
    dataVar += "Gosselin";
    document.writeln("<p>Variable after addition assignment = "
            + dataVar + "<br />");
    ```

```
dataVar = 70;
dataVar += 30;
document.writeln("Variable after addition assignment = "
        + dataVar + "<br />");
dataVar -= 50;
document.writeln("Variable after subtraction assignment = "
        + dataVar + "<br />");
dataVar /= 10;
document.writeln("Variable after division assignment = "
        + dataVar + "<br />");
dataVar *= 9;
document.writeln("Variable after multiplication assignment = "
        + dataVar + "<br />");
dataVar %= 200;
document.writeln("Variable after modulus assignment = "
        + dataVar + "</p>");
```

6. Save the document as **AssignmentOperators.html** in the Projects folder for Chapter 2.

7. Use the W3C Markup Validation Service to validate the **AssignmentOperators.html** document and fix any errors that the document contains. Once the document is valid, close it in your text editor and then open it in your Web browser and examine how the elements are rendered.

8. Close your Web browser window.

Project 2-4

In this project, you will create a script that uses comparison operators.

1. Create a new document in your text editor.

2. Type the `<!DOCTYPE>` declaration, `<html>` element, header information, and the `<body>` element. Use the strict DTD and "Comparison Operators" as the content of the `<title>` element.

3. Add the following `<h1>` element to the document body:

```
<h1>Comparison Operators</h1>
```

4. Add the following script section and paragraph elements to the document body:

```
<script type="text/javascript">
<!-- HIDE FROM INCOMPATIBLE BROWSERS
// STOP HIDING FROM INCOMPATIBLE BROWSERS -->
</script>
```

5. Add the following statements to the script section that perform various comparison operations on two variables. Notice that the first comparison is performed using the conditional operator.

```
var conditionalValue;
var value1 = "Don";
var value2 = "Dave";
value1 == value2 ?
    document.write("<p>value1 equal to value2: true<br />")
    : document.write("<p>value1 equal to value2: false<br />");
value1 = 37;
value2 = 26;
conditionalValue = value1 == value2;
document.write("value1 equal to value2: "
    + conditionalValue + "<br />");
conditionalValue = value1 != value2;
document.write("value1 not equal to value2: "
    + conditionalValue + "<br />");
conditionalValue = value1 > value2;
document.write("value1 greater than value2: "
    + conditionalValue + "<br />");
conditionalValue = value1 < value2;
document.write("value1 less than value2: "
    + conditionalValue + "<br />");
conditionalValue = value1 >= value2;
document.write(
    "value1 greater than or equal to value2: "
    + conditionalValue + "<br />");
conditionalValue = value1 <= value2;
document.write(
    "value1 less than or equal to value2: "
    + conditionalValue + "<br />");
value1 = 21;
value2 = 21;
conditionalValue = value1 === value2;
document.write(
    "value1 equal to value2 AND the same data type: "
    + conditionalValue + "<br />");
conditionalValue = value1 !== value2;
document.write(
    "value1 not equal to value2 AND not the same data type: "
    + conditionalValue + "</p>");
```

6. Save the document as **ComparisonOperators.html** in the Projects folder for Chapter 2.

7. Use the W3C Markup Validation Service to validate the **ComparisonOperators.html** document and fix any errors that the document contains. Once the document is valid, close it in your text editor and then open it in your Web browser and examine how the elements are rendered.

8. Close your Web browser window.

Project 2-5

In this project, you will create a script that uses logical operators.

1. Create a new document in your text editor.
2. Type the `<!DOCTYPE>` declaration, `<html>` element, header information, and the `<body>` element. Use the strict DTD and "Order Fulfillment" as the content of the `<title>` element.
3. Add the following `<h1>` element to the document body:

    ```
    <h1>Order Fulfillment</h1>
    ```
4. Add the following script section and paragraph elements to the document body:

    ```
    <script type="text/javascript">
    <!-- HIDE FROM INCOMPATIBLE BROWSERS
    // STOP HIDING FROM INCOMPATIBLE BROWSERS -->
    </script>
    ```
5. Add the following statements to the script section that use logical operators on two variables:

    ```
    var orderPlaced = true;
    var orderFilled = false;
    document.write("<p>Order has been placed: " + orderPlaced +
    "<br />");
    document.write("Order has been filled: " + orderFilled +
    "<br />");
    var orderComplete = orderPlaced && orderFilled;
    document.write("Order has been placed and filled: "
        + orderComplete + "</p>");
    ```
6. Save the document as **OrderFulfillment.html** in the Projects folder for Chapter 2.
7. Use the W3C Markup Validation Service to validate the **OrderFulfillment.html** document and fix any errors that the document contains. Once the document is valid, close it in your text editor and then open it in your Web browser and examine how the elements are rendered.
8. Close your Web browser window.

Project 2-6

In this project, you will create a script that displays a portion of a review for a production of the opera *Pagliacci*, performed by an opera company called the Pine Knoll Productions. The review will be rendered using `document.write()` statements that combine text strings with escape characters. Note that you can create the same document more easily using only XHTML elements. The purpose of this exercise is to demonstrate how text strings can be combined with escape characters.

1. Create a new document in your text editor.

2. Type the `<!DOCTYPE>` declaration, `<html>` element, header information, and the `<body>` element. Use the strict DTD and "Pine Knoll Productions" as the content of the `<title>` element.

3. Add the following style section to the document head:

```
<style type="text/css">
body { font-family: 'Trebuchet MS', Arial, Helvetica,
sans-serif }
</style>
```

4. Add the following script section and paragraph elements to the document body:

```
<script type="text/javascript">
<!-- HIDE FROM INCOMPATIBLE BROWSERS
// STOP HIDING FROM INCOMPATIBLE BROWSERS -->
</script>
```

5. Add to the script section the following `document.write()` statements that contain combinations of text, elements, and escape characters:

```
document.write("<p>Pine Knoll Productions presents</p>");
document.write("<h1>Pagliacci</h1>");
document.write("<p><strong>by Ruggero Leoncavallo</strong></p>
<hr />");
document.write("<p>The Pine Knoll Press calls the company\'s
production ");
document.write("of Leoncavallo\'s <em>Pagliacci</em>
a \"spectacular event\" ")
document.write("that will \"astound you\".");
```

CAUTION
Be sure to type the text strings in the preceding code on the same line. They contain line breaks here due to space limitations.

6. Save the document as **Pagliacci.html** in the Projects folder for Chapter 2.

7. Use the W3C Markup Validation Service to validate the **Pagliacci.html** document and fix any errors that the document contains. Once the document is valid, close it in your text editor and then open it in your Web browser and examine how the elements are rendered.

8. Close your Web browser window.

Project 2-7

Next, you will create a script that assigns different data types to a variable and prints the variable's data type. You will use the `typeof` operator to determine the data type of each variable.

1. Create a new document in your text editor.

2. Type the `<!DOCTYPE>` declaration, `<html>` element, header information, and the `<body>` element. Use the strict DTD and "Changing Data Types" as the content of the `<title>` element.

3. Add the following script section to the document body:

```
<script type="text/javascript">
<!-- HIDE FROM INCOMPATIBLE BROWSERS
// STOP HIDING FROM INCOMPATIBLE BROWSERS -->
</script>
```

4. Declare a variable in the script section named `changingType`:

```
var changingType;
```

5. At the end of the script section, type the following line, which prints the data type contained in the `changingType` variable. The data type is currently "undefined," because `changingType` has not yet been assigned a value.

```
document.write("<p>The changingType variable is "
    + typeof(changingType) + "<br />");
```

6. To the end of the script section, add the following two lines, which assign a string to the `changingType` variable and repeat the statement that prints the data type.

```
changingType = "It's a jungle out there.";
document.writeln("The changingType variable is "
    + typeof(changingType) + "<br />");
```

7. To the end of the script section, add the following lines, which change the `changingType` variable to the integer, floating-point, Boolean, and null data types. The statement that prints each data type repeats each time the variable's data type changes.

```
changingType = 250;
document.writeln("The changingType variable is "
    + typeof(changingType) + "<br />");
changingType = 87.346;
document.writeln("The changingType variable is "
    + typeof(changingType) + "<br />");
changingType = true;
document.writeln("The changingType variable is "
    + typeof(changingType) + "<br />");
changingType = null;
document.writeln("The changingType variable is "
    + typeof(changingType) + "</p>");
```

8. Save the document as **ChangingTypes.html** in the Projects folder for Chapter 2.

9. Use the W3C Markup Validation Service to validate the **ChangingTypes.html** document and fix any errors that the document contains. Once the document is valid, close it in your text editor and then open it in your Web browser and examine how the elements are rendered.

10. Close your Web browser window.

Project 2-8

Next, you will create a script that contains the formula for converting Fahrenheit temperatures to Celsius. You will need to modify the formula so it uses the correct order of precedence to convert the temperature.

1. Create a new document in your text editor.

2. Type the `<!DOCTYPE>` declaration, `<html>` element, header information, and the `<body>` element. Use the strict DTD and "Convert to Celsius" as the content of the `<title>` element.

3. Add the following script section to the document body:

```
<script type="text/javascript">
<!-- HIDE FROM INCOMPATIBLE BROWSERS
// STOP HIDING FROM INCOMPATIBLE BROWSERS -->
</script>
```

4. Add to the script section the following declaration for a variable named `fTemp` that represents a Fahrenheit temperature. The variable is assigned a value of 86 degrees.

```
var fTemp = 86;
```

5. Add the following two statements to the end of the script section. The first statement declares a variable named `cTemp` that will store the converted temperature. The right operand includes the formula for converting from Fahrenheit to Celsius. (Remember that the formula as given below is incorrect; later in this exercise you will correct the order of precedence in the formula.) The last statement prints the value assigned to the `cTemp` variable.

```
var cTemp = fTemp - 32 * 5 / 9;
document.write("<p>" + fTemp + " Fahrenheit is equal to "
+ cTemp + "degrees Celsius.</p>");
```

6. Save the document as **ConvertToCelsius.html** in the Projects folder for Chapter 2, and then open it in your Web browser. The temperature 86 degrees Fahrenheit is actually equivalent to 30 degrees Celsius. However, the formula incorrectly calculates that 86 degrees Fahrenheit is equivalent to 68.22222222222223 Celsius.

7. Close your Web browser window and return to the **ConvertToCelsius.html** document in your text editor.

8. Modify the order of precedent in the Fahrenheit-to-Celsius formula by adding parentheses as follows so it correctly calculates a value of 30 degrees Celsius for 86 degrees Fahrenheit:

```
var cTemp = (fTemp - 32) * (5 / 9);
```

9. Save the **ConvertToCelsius.html** document, close it in your text editor, and then open it in your Web browser. The temperature should calculate correctly as 30 degrees Celsius.

10. Close your Web browser window.

Case Projects

Save your Case Projects document in the Cases folder for Chapter 2. Create the documents so they are well formed according to the strict DTD. Be sure to validate each document with the W3C Markup Validation Service.

Case Project 2-1

The formula for calculating body mass index (BMI) is *weight * 703 / height²*. For example, if you weight 200 pounds and are 72 inches tall, then you can calculate your body mass index with this expression: *(200 * 703) / (72 * 72)*. Create a script that declares and assigns two integer variables: one for your weight in pounds and another for your height in inches. Declare another variable and assign to it the results of the body mass calculation. Use `document.write()` statements to print the value of the weight, height, and BMI variables. Include text in the `document.write()` statements that describes each measure, such as "Your weight is 200 pounds". Save the document as **BMI.html**.

Case Project 2-2

Table 2-13 lists the total world carbon dioxide emissions from fossil fuel consumption for various years from 1980 to 2003.

Year	Million Metric Tons
1980	18313.13
1985	19430.24
1990	21402.22
1995	22034.54
2000	23849.00
2002	24464.92
2003	25162.07

Table 2-13   World carbon dioxide emissions from fossil fuel

Create a script that contains two arrays: one for the emission years and one for the amount of emissions in each year. Use `document.write()` statements to print the amount of emissions in each year with statements similar to "In 1980, the world generated 18313.13 million metric tons of carbon dioxide emissions from fossil fuel consumption." Save the document as **CO2Emissions.html**.

Case Project 2-3

Write a script that calculates the cost of an event, such as a wedding. Create a string variable for the name of the event and numeric variables for the number of guests, cost per guest, and number of limousines. Also, create Boolean variables for live music, flowers, and open bar. Assign whatever value you like to the event name, number of guests, cost per guest, and number of limousines variables. Assume that each limousine costs $100 for the event. Assign the total event cost to another variable. Use a conditional expression to determine whether the value assigned to the live music variable is equal to true. If so, add $500 to the total cost of the event. Use another conditional expression to determine whether the value assigned to the flowers variable is equal to true. If so, add $300 to the total cost of the event. Use one more conditional expression to determine whether the value assigned to the open bar is equal to true. If so, add $30 for each of the expected number of guests to the total cost of the event. Use arithmetic operators to determine the cost of each item and for the entire event, and `document.write()` statements to print a breakdown of each cost and the total estimated cost. Assume that the location of the event has a maximum capacity of 500. Use a conditional expression to determine whether the value assigned to the number of guests variable meets or exceeds the location's maximum capacity. If the number of guests exceeds the maximum capacity, print "You have invited too many guests" in parentheses at the end of the statement that prints the number of guests. Save the document as **Event.html**.

3

Functions, Events, and Control Structures

In this chapter you will:

- Learn how to use functions to organize your JavaScript code
- Learn how to work with events
- Use if statements, if...else statements, and switch statements to make decisions
- Nest one if statement in another
- Use while statements, do...while statements, and for statements to execute code repeatedly
- Use continue statements to restart a looping statement

So far, the code you have written has consisted of simple statements placed within script sections. However, almost all programming languages, including JavaScript, allow you to group programming statements in logical units. In JavaScript, groups of statements that you can execute as a single unit are called functions. You'll learn how to use functions in this chapter. One of the primary ways in which JavaScript code, including functions, is executed on a Web page is through the use of events, which you'll also study in this chapter.

The code you have written so far has also been linear in nature. In other words, your programs start at the beginning and end when the last statement in the program executes. Decision-making and flow-control statements allow you to determine the order in which statements execute in a program. Controlling the flow of code and making decisions during program execution are two of the most fundamental skills required in programming. In this chapter you will learn about both decision-making statements and flow-control statements.

Working with Functions

In Chapter 1, you learned that procedures associated with an object are called methods. In JavaScript programming, you can write your own procedures, called **functions**, which are similar to the methods associated with an object. Functions are useful because they make it possible to treat a related group of JavaScript statements as a single unit. Functions, like all JavaScript code, must be contained within a `<script>` element. In the following section you'll learn more about incorporating functions in your scripts.

Defining Functions

Before you can use a function in a JavaScript program, you must first create, or define, it. The lines that make up a function are called the **function definition**. The syntax for defining a function is:

```
function nameOfFunction(parameters) {
    statements;
}
```

Parameters are placed within the parentheses that follow a function name. A **parameter** is a variable that is used within a function. Placing a parameter name within the parentheses of a function definition is the equivalent of declaring a new variable. However, you do not need to include the `var` keyword. For example, suppose you want to write a function named `calculateSquareRoot()` that calculates the square root of a number contained in a parameter named `number`. The function name would then be written as: `calculateSquareRoot(number)`. In this case, the function declaration is declaring a new parameter (which is a variable) named `number`. Functions can contain multiple parameters separated by commas. To add three separate number parameters to the `calculateSquareRoot()` function, you would write the function name as `calculateSquareRoot(number1, number2, number3)`. Note that parameters (such as the `number1`, `number2`, and `number3` parameters) receive their values when you call the function from elsewhere in your program. (You will learn how to call functions in the next section.)

TIP

Functions do not have to contain parameters. Many functions only perform a task and do not require external data. For example, you might create a function that displays the same message each time a user visits your Web site; this type of function only needs to be executed and does not require any other information.

Following the parentheses that contain the function parameters is a set of curly braces (called function braces) that contain the function statements. Function statements are the statements that do the actual work of the function (such as calculating the square root of the parameter, or displaying a message on the screen) and must be contained within the function braces. The following is an example of a function that prints the names of multiple companies using the `write()` methods of the `Document` object. (Recall that functions are very similar to the methods associated with an object.)

```
function printCompanyName(company1, company2, company3) {
    document.write("<p>" + company1 + "</p>");
    document.write("<p>" + company2 + "</p>");
    document.write("<p>" + company3 + "</p>");
}
```

Notice how the preceding function is structured. The opening curly brace is on the same line as the function name, and the closing curly brace is on its own line following the function statements. Each statement between the curly braces is indented one-half inch. This structure is the preferred format among many JavaScript programmers. However, for simple functions it is sometimes easier to include the function name, curly braces, and statements on the same line. (Recall that JavaScript ignores line breaks, spaces, and tabs.) The only syntax requirement for spacing in JavaScript is that semicolons separate statements on the same line. For example, the following simplified version of the `printCompanyName()` function is declared with a single statement:

```
function printCompanyName(company1) { document.write("<p>"
    + company1 + "</p>"); }
```

Calling Functions

A function definition does not execute automatically. Creating a function definition only names the function, specifies its parameters, and organizes the statements it will execute. To execute a function, you must invoke, or **call**, it from elsewhere in your program. The code that calls a function is referred to as a **function call** and consists of the function name followed by parentheses that contain any variables or values to be assigned to the function parameters. The variables or values that you place in the parentheses of the function call statement are called **arguments** or **actual parameters**. Sending arguments to the parameters of a called function is called **passing arguments**. When you pass arguments to a function, the value of each argument is then assigned to the value of the corresponding parameter in the function definition. (Again, remember that parameters are simply variables that are declared within a function definition.)

Always put your functions within the document head, and place calls to a function within the body section. As you recall, the document head is always rendered before the document body. Thus, placing functions in the head section and function calls in the body section ensures that functions are created before they are actually called. If your program does attempt to call a function before it has been created, you will receive an error. The following code shows a script that prints the name of a company. Figure 3-1 shows the output. Notice that the function is defined in the document head and is called from the document body.

```
<!DOCTYPE html PUBLIC "-//W3C//DTD XHTML 1.0 Strict//EN"
"http://www.w3.org/TR/xhtml1/DTD/xhtml1-strict.dtd">
<html xmlns="http://www.w3.org/1999/xhtml">
<head>
<title>Course Technology</title>
<meta http-equiv="content-type" content="text/html;
    charset=iso-8859-1" />
<script type="text/javascript">
/* <![CDATA[ */
function printCompanyName(company_name) {
    document.write("<p>" + company_name + "</p>");
}
/* ]]> */
</script>
</head>
```

```
<body>
<script type="text/javascript">
/* <![CDATA[ */
printCompanyName("Course Technology");
/* ]]> */
</script>
</body>
</html>
```

Figure 3-1

Output of a JavaScript
function being called
from the body section

NOTE

The script that appears in Figure 3-1 contains a statement that calls the function
and passes the literal string "Course Technology" to the function. When the
`printCompanyName()` function receives the literal string, it assigns it to the
`company_name` variable.

A JavaScript program is composed of all the `<script>` sections within a document; each individual `<script>` section is not necessarily its own individual JavaScript program (although it could be if there are no other `<script>` sections in the document).

In many instances, you may want your program to receive the results from a called function and then use those results in other code. For instance, consider a function that calculates the average of a series of numbers that are passed to it as arguments. Such a function would be useless if your program could not print or use the result elsewhere. As another example, suppose you have created a function that simply prints the name of a company. Now suppose that you want to alter the program so that it uses the company name in another section of code. You can return a value from a function to a calling statement by assigning the calling statement to a variable. The following statement calls a function named `averageNumbers()` and assigns the return value to a variable named `returnValue`. The statement also passes three literal values to the function.

```
var returnValue = averageNumbers(1, 2, 3);
```

To actually return a value to a `returnValue` variable, the code must include a return statement within the `averageNumbers()` function. A **return statement** is a statement that returns a value to the statement that called the function. The following script contains the `averageNumbers()` function, which calculates the average of three numbers. The script also includes a return statement that returns the value (contained in the result variable) to the calling statement.

```
function averageNumbers(a, b, c) {
    var sum_of_numbers = a + b + c;
    var result = sum_of_numbers / 3;
    return result;
}
```

TIP

A function does not necessarily have to return a value.

Next, you will create a script that contains two functions. The first function will print a message when it is called, and the second function will return a value that is printed after the calling statement.

To create a script that contains two functions:

1. Open your text editor and create a new document.

2. Type the `<!DOCTYPE>` declaration, `<html>` element, header information, and the `<body>` element. Use the strict DTD and "Two Functions" as the content of the `<title>` element. Include a `<link>` element that links to the js_styles.css style sheet in your Chapter folder. Your document should appear as follows:

```
<!DOCTYPE html PUBLIC "-//W3C//DTD XHTML 1.0 Strict//EN"
"http://www.w3.org/TR/xhtml1/DTD/xhtml1-strict.dtd">
<html xmlns="http://www.w3.org/1999/xhtml">
<head>
<title>Two Functions</title>
<meta http-equiv="content-type" content="text/html;
    charset=iso-8859-1" />
<link rel="stylesheet" href="js_styles.css" type="text/css" />
</head>
<body>
</body>
</html>
```

3. Add the following script section to the document head:

```
<script type="text/javascript">
/* <![CDATA[ */
/* ]]> */
</script>
```

4. Add the first function to the script section as follows. This function writes a message to the screen using an argument that will ultimately be passed to it from the calling statement.

```
function printMessage(first_message) {
    document.write("<p>" + first_message + "</p>");
}
```

5. Add the second function, which displays a second message, to the end of the script section. In this case, the message ("This message was returned from a function.") is defined within the function itself. The only purpose of this function is to return the literal string "This message was returned from a function." to the calling statement.

```
function return_message() {
    return "<p>This message was returned from a function.</p>";
}
```

6. Add the following script section and function to the document body:

```
<script type="text/javascript">
/* <![CDATA[ */
/* ]]> */
</script>
```

7. Add to the script section the following three statements, which call the functions in the document head. The first statement sends the text string "This message was printed from a function." This statement does not receive a return value. The second statement assigns the function call to a variable named return_value, but does not send any arguments to the function. The third statement writes the value of the return_value variable to the screen.

```
printMessage("This message was printed from a function.");
var return_value = return_message();
document.write(return_value);
```

8. Save the document as **TwoFunctions.html** in the **Chapter** folder for Chapter 3, and then validate it with the W3C Markup Validation Service at **http://validator.w3.org/file-upload.html** and fix any errors that it contains. Once the document is valid, close it in your text editor.

9. Open the **TwoFunctions.html** document in your Web browser. Figure 3-2 shows how the TwoFunctions.html document looks in a Web browser.

Figure 3-2

TwoFunctions.html in a Web browser

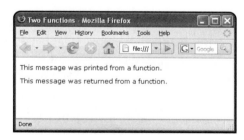

10. Close your Web browser window.

Understanding Variable Scope

When you use a variable in a JavaScript program, particularly a complex JavaScript program, you need to be aware of the **variable's scope**—that is, you need to think about where in your program a declared variable can be used. A variable's scope can be either global or local. A **global variable** is one that is declared outside a function and is available to all parts of your program. A **local variable** is declared inside a function and is only available within the function in which it is declared. Local variables cease to exist when the function ends. If you attempt to use a local variable outside the function in which it is declared, you will receive an error message.

NOTE

The parameters within the parentheses of a function declaration are local variables.

You must use the `var` keyword when you declare a local variable. However, when you declare a global variable, the `var` keyword is optional. For example, you can write the statement `var myVariable = "This is a variable.";` as `myVariable = "This is a variable.";`. If you declare a variable within a function and do not include the `var` keyword, the variable automatically becomes a global variable. However, it is considered good programming technique to always use the `var` keyword when declaring variables because it makes it clear in your code when and where you intend to start using the variable. It is also considered poor programming technique to declare a global variable inside of a function by not using the `var` keyword because it makes it harder to identify the global variables in your scripts. Using the `var` keyword forces you to declare your global variables explicitly outside of any functions and local variables within a function.

The following script includes a global variable named `salesPrice` and a function containing two variable declarations. The first variable declaration in the function, for the `shippingPrice` variable, is a global variable because it does not include the `var` keyword. The second variable declaration in the function, for the `totalPrice` variable, is a local variable because it does include the `var` keyword. Both the global variable and the function are contained in a script section in the document head. When the function is called from the document body, the global variables and the local variable print successfully from within the function. After the call to the function, the global variables again prints successfully from the document body. However, when the script tries to print the local variable (`totalPrice`) from the document body, an error message is generated because the local variable ceases to exist when the function ends.

```
...
<head>
<title>Calculate Sales Price</title>
<meta http-equiv="content-type" content="text/html;
charset=iso-8859-1" />
<script type="text/javascript">
/* <![CDATA[ */
var salesPrice = 100.00;
```

```
function applyShipping() {
     shippingPrice = 8.95;
     var totalPrice = salesPrice + shippingPrice;
     document.write("<p>The sales price is $"
          + salesPrice + "<br />"); // prints successfully
     document.write("The shipping price is $"
          + shippingPrice + "<br />");  // prints successfully
     document.write("The sales price plus shipping is $"
          + totalPrice + "</p>"); // prints successfully
}
/* ]]> */
</script>
</head>
<body>
<script type="text/javascript">
/* <![CDATA[ */
applyShipping();
     document.write("<p>The sales price is $"
          + salesPrice + "<br />"); // prints successfully
     document.write("The shipping price is $"
          + shippingPrice + "<br />"); // prints successfully
     document.write("The sales price plus shipping is $"
          + totalPrice + "</p>");  // error message
/* ]]> */
</script>
</body>
</html>
```

CAUTION

It is considered poor programming practice to intentionally declare a global variable inside of a function by eliminating the var keyword. The only intention of the
shippingPrice variable in the preceding example is to illustrate variable scope.
If the example really needed the shippingPrice variable to be a global variable,
then it should be declared at the global level with the salesPrice variable.

When a program contains a global variable and a local variable with the same name, the local
variable takes precedence when its function is called. The value assigned to a local variable of
the same name is not assigned to a global variable of the same name. In the following code, the
global variable quarterback is assigned a value of "Steve Young" before the function that
contains a local variable of the same name is called. Once the function is called, the local
quarterback variable is assigned a value of "Kurt Warner". After the function ends, "Steve
Young" is still the value of the global quarterback variable. Figure 3-3 shows the output in a
Web browser.

```
var quarterback = "Steve Young";
function duplicateVariableNames() {
    var quarterback = "Kurt Warner";
        document.write("<p>" + quarterback + "</p>");
        // value printed is Kurt Warner
}
duplicateVariableNames();
document.write("<p>" + quarterback + "</p>");
// value printed is Steve Young
```

Figure 3-3

Output of a program that contains a global variable and a local variable with the same name

NOTE

Although the code that displays the output shown in Figure 3-3 is syntactically correct, it is poor programming practice to use the same name for local and global variables because it makes your scripts confusing and it is difficult to track which version of the variable is currently being used by the program.

Using Built-in JavaScript Functions

In addition to custom functions that you create yourself, JavaScript includes the built-in functions listed in Table 3-1.

Function	Description
decodeURI(*string*)	Decodes text strings encoded with encodeURI()
decodeURIComponent(*string*)	Decodes text strings encoded with encodeURIComponent()
encodeURI(*string*)	Encodes a text string so that it becomes a valid URI
encodeURIComponent(*string*)	Encodes a text string so that it becomes a valid URI component
eval(*string*)	Evaluates expressions contained within strings
isFinite(*number*)	Determines whether a number is finite
isNaN(*number*)	Determines whether a value is the special value NaN (Not a Number)
parseFloat(*string*)	Converts string literals to floating-point numbers
parseInt(*string*)	Converts string literals to integers

Table 3-1   Built-in JavaScript functions

NOTE
In this chapter, you also study the `window.alert()`, `window.prompt()`, and `window.confirm()` methods. However, these methods are not built-in JavaScript functions. Rather, they are methods of the `Window` object, which you will study in Chapter 4.

In this book, you will examine several of the built-in JavaScript functions as you need them. For now, you just need to understand that you call built-in JavaScript functions in the same way you call a custom function. For example, the following code calls the `isNaN()` function to determine whether the `socialSecurityNumber` variable is not a number. Because the Social Security number assigned to the `socialSecurityNumber` variable contains dashes, it is not a true number. Therefore, the `isNaN()` function returns a value of true to the `checkVar` variable.

```
var socialSecurityNumber = "123-45-6789";
var checkVar = isNaN(socialSecurityNumber);
document.write(checkVar);
```

One built-in JavaScript function that you will use in this chapter is the `eval()` function, which evaluates expressions contained within strings. You can include a string literal or string variable as the argument for the `eval()` function. If the string literal or string variable you pass to the `eval()` function does not contain an expression that can be evaluated, you will receive an error. The statement `var returnValue = eval("5 + 3");` returns the value 8 and assigns it to the `returnValue` variable. The statement `var returnValue = eval("10");` also evaluates correctly and returns a value of 10, even though the string within the `eval()` function did not contain operators. The `eval()` function has one restriction: you cannot send it a text string that does not contain operators or numbers. If you send the `eval()` function a text string that does not contain operators or numbers, an empty value is returned. For example, the statement `var returnValue = eval("this is a text string");` assigns an empty value to the `returnValue` variable because it does not contain numbers or operators. However, the statement `var returnValue = eval("'this is a text string' + ' and this is another text string'");` evaluates correctly, because the string sent to the `eval()` function contains the concatenation operator.

Another built-in JavaScript function that you will use in this chapter is the `parseInt()` function, which converts string literals to integers. One of the most common uses of the `parseInt()` function is to convert the value obtained from a form field text box from a string to an integer. In some cases, the JavaScript interpreter will not convert a text box value from a string to a number. To ensure that you can use the value from a text box in a mathematical calculation, you use the `parseInt()` function to convert the value to an integer or the `parseFloat()` function to convert the value to a floating-point number. To use the `parseInt()` or `parseFloat()` functions, pass to either function the variable or value that you want to convert to an integer. For example, the following statement assigns the value of a text box named `guests` on a form named `reservations` to a variable named `numGuests`. The `parseInt()` function ensures that the value is converted to an integer.

```
var numGuests = parseInt(document.reservations.guests.value);
```

Understanding Events

One of the primary ways in which JavaScript is executed on a Web page is through events. An **event** is a specific circumstance (such as an action performed by a user, or an action performed by the browser) that is monitored by JavaScript and that your script can respond to in some way. As you will see in this section, you can use JavaScript events to allow users to interact with your Web pages. The most common events are actions that users perform. For example, when a user clicks a form button, a `click` event is generated. You can think of an event as a trigger that fires specific JavaScript code in response to a given situation. User-generated events, however, are not the only kinds of events monitored by JavaScript. Events that are not direct results of user actions, such as the `load` event, are also monitored. The `load` event, which is triggered automatically by a Web browser, occurs when a document finishes loading in a Web browser. Table 3-2 lists some JavaScript events and explains what triggers them.

Event	Triggered when
abort	The loading of an image is interrupted
blur	An element, such as a radio button, becomes inactive
click	The user clicks an element once
change	The value of an element, such as text box, changes
error	An error occurs when a document or image is being loaded
focus	An element, such as a command button, becomes active
load	A document or image loads
mouseout	The mouse moves off an element
mouseover	The mouse moves over an element
reset	A form's fields are reset to its default values
select	A user selects a field in a form
submit	A user submits a form
unload	A document unloads

Table 3-2   JavaScript events

Working with Elements and Events

Events are associated with XHTML elements. The events that are available to an element vary. The `click` event, for example, is available for the `<a>` element and form controls created with the `<input>` element. In comparison, the `<body>` element does not have a `click` event, but does have a `load` event, which occurs when a Web page finishes loading, and an `unload` event, which occurs when a Web page is unloaded.

When an event occurs, your script executes the code that responds to that particular event. Code that executes in response to a specific event is called an **event handler**. You include event handler code as an attribute of the element that initiates the event. For example, you can add to a `<button>` element a `click` attribute that is assigned some sort of JavaScript code, such as code that changes the color of some portion of a Web page. The syntax of an event handler within an element is:

```
<element event_handler ="JavaScript code">
```

Event handler names are the same as the name of the event itself, plus a prefix of "on". For example, the event handler for the click event is onclick, and the event handler for the load event is onload. Like all XHTML code, event handler names are case sensitive and must be written using all lowercase letters in order for a document to be well formed. Table 3-3 lists various XHTML elements and their associated event handlers.

Element	Description	Event
`<a>`	Anchor	onfocus, onblur, onclick, ondblclick, onmousedown, onmouseup, onmouseover, onmousemove, onmouseout, onkeypress, onkeydown, onkeyup
`<img>`	Image	onclick, ondblclick, onmousedown, onmouseup, onmouseover, onmousemove, onmouseout, onkeypress, onkeydown, onkeyup
`<body>`	Document body	onload, onunload, onclick, ondblclick, onmousedown, onmouseup, onmouseover, onmousemove, onmouseout, onkeypress, onkeydown, onkeyup
`<form>`	Form	onsubmit, onreset, onclick, ondblclick, onmousedown, onmouseup, onmouseover, onmousemove, onmouseout, onkeypress, onkeydown, onkeyup
`<input>`	Form control	tabindex, accesskey, onfocus, onblur, onselect, onchange, onclick, ondblclick, onmousedown, onmouseup, onmouseover, onmousemove, onmouseout, onkeypress, onkeydown, onkeyup
`<textarea>`	Text area	onfocus, onblur, onselect, onchange, onclick, ondblclick, onmousedown, onmouseup, onmouseover, onmousemove, onmouseout, onkeypress, onkeydown, onkeyup
`<select>`	Selection	onfocus, onblur, onchange

Table 3-3   XHTML elements and their associated events

The JavaScript code for an event handler is contained within the quotation marks following the name of the JavaScript event handler. The following code uses the `<input>` element to create a push button. The element also includes an onclick event handler that executes the JavaScript window.alert() method, in response to a click event (which occurs when the button is clicked). The **window.alert() method** displays a pop-up dialog box with an OK button. You can pass a single literal string or a variable as an argument to the window.alert() method. The syntax for the alert() method is window.alert(*message*);. The value of the literal string or variable is then displayed in the alert dialog box, as shown in Figure 3-4.

```
<input type="button"
      onclick="window.alert('You clicked a button!')">
```

Figure 3-4
Alert dialog box

Typically, the code executed by the onclick event handler—the window.alert() method—is contained within double quotation marks. In the preceding example, however, the literal string being passed is contained in single quotation marks. This is because the `window.alert()` method itself is already enclosed in double quotation marks.

The `window.alert()` method is the only statement being executed in the preceding event handler. You can, however, include multiple JavaScript statements in an event handler, as long as semicolons separate the statements. For example, to include two statements in the event handler example—a statement that creates a variable and another statement that uses the `window.alert()` method to display the variable—you would type the following:

```
<input type="button"
    onclick="var message='You clicked a button';
    window.alert(message)">
```

Referencing Web Page Elements

You can use JavaScript to reference any element on a Web page by appending the element's name to the name of any elements in which it is nested, starting with the `Document` object. Specific properties of an element can then be appended to the element name. This allows you to retrieve information about an element or change the values assigned to its attributes. For example, form elements such as text boxes have `value` properties that you can use to set or retrieve the value entered into the field. Suppose you have a form with a `name` attribute that is assigned a value of "invoice", containing a text box with a `name` attribute that is assigned a value of "invoice_num". You can change the value of the text box using a statement similar to `document.invoice.invoice_num.value = new value;`. However, the `name` attribute of the `<form>` element is deprecated in XHTML, which means you can only use it with the transitional DTD. You will use this syntax extensively in the next few chapters. In Chapter 5, you will learn how to reference forms using XHTML syntax that conforms to the strict DTD.

Next, you will use JavaScript to create a calculator program using push buttons and `onclick` event handlers. You will use a variable named `inputString` to contain the operands and operators of a calculation. After a calculation is added to the `inputString` variable, the calculation is performed using the `eval()` function. The program will include a single function named `updateString()` that accepts a single value representing a number or operator. The value is then added to the `inputString` variable using the += assignment operator. After the `inputString` variable is updated, it is assigned as the value of a text box in a form.

NOTE
When you refer to a form using the value assigned to its name attribute, you must use the transitional DTD, because the name attribute of the `<form>` element is deprecated in XHTML. In Chapter 5, you will learn how to create and refer to forms that conform to the strict DTD.

To create a calculator program:

1. Create a new document in your text editor.
2. Type the `<!DOCTYPE>` declaration, `<html>` element, header information, and the `<body>` element. Use the transitional DTD and "Calculator" as the content of the `<title>` element.

3. Add the following script section to the document head:

```
<script type="text/javascript">
/* <![CDATA[ */
/* ]]> */
</script>
```

4. Add the following function to the script section. This function is used to update the inputString variable:

```
var inputString = "";
function updateString(value) {
    inputString += value;
    document.Calculator.Input.value = inputString;
}
```

5. Add the following <div> and <form> elements to the document body:

```
<div style="text-align: center">
<form name="Calculator" action="">
</form>
</div>
```

6. Add a text box named "Input" to the form, as follows:

```
<input type="text" name="Input" /><br />
```

7. Add the following <input> elements to the form that create buttons representing the calculator operators. Each element, along with the other elements that you create, sends a value to the updateString() function, using an onclick method:

```
<input type="button" name="plus"    value="  +  "
    onclick="updateString(' + ')" />
<input type="button" name="minus"   value="  -  "
    onclick="updateString(' - ')" />
<input type="button" name="times"   value="  x  "
    onclick="updateString(' * ')" />
<input type="button" name="div"     value="  /  "
    onclick="updateString(' / ')" />
<input type="button" name="mod" value=" mod "
    onclick="updateString(' % ')" /><br />
```

8. Add to the end of the form the following elements for the calculator numbers:

```
<input type="button" name="zero" value="  0  "
    onclick="updateString('0')" />
<input type="button" name="one" value="  1  "
    onclick="updateString('1')" />
<input type="button" name="two" value="  2  "
    onclick="updateString('2')" />
<input type="button" name="three"  value="  3  "
    onclick="updateString('3')" />
```

```
<input type="button" name="four" value="   4    "
    onclick="updateString('4')" /><br />
<input type="button" name="five" value="   5    "
    onclick="updateString('5')" />
<input type="button" name="six" value="   6    "
    onclick="updateString('6')" />
<input type="button" name="seven" value="   7    "
    onclick="updateString('7')" />
<input type="button" name="eight" value="   8    "
    onclick="updateString('8')" />
<input type="button" name="nine" value="   9    "
    onclick="updateString('9')" /><br />
```

9. Finally, add to the end of the form the following elements for the decimal point, clear, and calc (equal) buttons. Notice that the `onclick` event for the calc button performs the calculation by using the `eval()` function with the `inputString` variable. The calculated value is then assigned as the value of the Input text box.

```
<input type="button" name="point"  value="   .   "
    onclick="updateString('.')" />
<input type="button" name="clear"  value=" clear "
    onclick="document.Calculator.Input.value='';
    inputString=''" />
<input type="button" name="calc" value="   =   "
    onclick="document.Calculator.Input.value=eval(inputString);
    inputString=''" />
```

10. Save the document as **Calculator.html** in the **Chapter** folder for Chapter 3, and then validate it with the W3C Markup Validation Service at **validator.w3.org/file-upload.html** and fix any errors that the document contains. Once the document is valid, close it in your text editor.

11. Open the **Calculator.html** document in your Web browser and test the calculation functionality. Figure 3-5 shows how the Calculator.html document looks in a Web browser.

Figure 3-5

Calculator.html in a Web browser

12. Close your Web browser window.

Making Decisions

When you write a computer program, regardless of the programming language, you often need to execute different sets of statements, depending on some predetermined criteria. For example, you might create a program that needs to execute one set of code in the morning, and another set of code at night. Or you might create a program that must execute one set of code when it's running in Windows Explorer, and another when it runs in Firefox. Additionally, you might create a program that depends on user input to determine exactly what code to run. For instance, suppose you create a Web page through which users place online orders. If a user clicks an Add to Shopping Cart button, a set of statements that builds a list of items to be purchased must execute. However, if the user clicks a Checkout button, an entirely different set of statements, which completes the transaction, must execute. The process of determining the order in which statements execute in a program is called **decision making** or **flow control**. The special types of JavaScript statements used for making decisions are called decision-making statements or decision-making structures. The most common type of decision-making statement is the if statement, which you will study first.

if Statements

The if statement is one of the more common ways to control program flow. The **if statement** is used to execute specific programming code if the evaluation of a conditional expression returns a value of true. The syntax for a simple if statement is as follows:

```
if (conditional expression)
     statement;
```

The if statement contains three parts: the keyword if, a conditional expression enclosed within parentheses, and executable statements. Note that the conditional expression *must* be enclosed within parentheses.

If the condition being evaluated returns a value of true, then the statement immediately following the conditional expression executes. After the if statement executes, any subsequent code executes normally. Consider the following code. The if statement uses the equal (==) comparison operator to determine whether the variable exampleVar is equal to 5. (You learned about operators in Chapter 2.) Because the condition returns a value of true, two alert dialog boxes appear. The first alert dialog box is generated by the if statement when the condition returns a value of true, and the second alert dialog box executes after the if statement is completed.

```
var exampleVar = 5;
if (exampleVar == 5)      // CONDITION EVALUATES TO 'TRUE'
     window.alert("<p>The variable is equal to '5'.</p>");
window.alert("<p>Displays after the if statement.</p>");
```

TIP
The statement immediately following the if statement in the preceding code can be written on the same line as the if statement itself. However, using a line break and indentation makes the code easier for the programmer to read.

In contrast, the following code displays only the second alert dialog box. The condition evaluates to false, because exampleVar is assigned the value 4 instead of 5.

```
var exampleVar = 4;
if (exampleVar == 5)      // CONDITION EVALUATES TO 'FALSE'
    window.alert("<p>This dialog box will not appear.</p>");
window.alert("<p>This is the only dialog box that appears.</p>");
```

You can use a command block to construct a decision-making structure containing multiple statements. A **command block** is a set of statements contained within a set of braces, similar to the way function statements are contained within a set of braces. Each command block must have an opening brace ({) and a closing brace (}). If a command block is missing either the opening or closing brace, an error occurs. The following code shows a script that runs a command block if the conditional expression within the if statement evaluates to true.

```
var exampleVar = 5;
if (exampleVar == 5) {      // CONDITION EVALUATES TO 'TRUE'
    document.write("<p>The condition evaluates to true.</p>");
    document.write("<p><code>exampleVar</code> is equal to 5.</p>");
    document.write("<p>Each of these lines will be printed.</p>");
}
document.write(
    "<p>This statement always executes after the if statement.</p>");
```

When an if statement contains a command block, the statements in the command block execute when the if statement condition evaluates to true. After the command block executes, the code that follows executes normally. When the condition evaluates to false, the command block is skipped, and the statements that follow execute. If the conditional expression within the if statement in the preceding code evaluates to false, then only the write() statement following the command block executes.

Next, you will start creating a pilot quiz. The script contains several questions that the Federal Aviation Administration (FAA) includes on a test that it administers to all applicants who apply for a "private pilot" license to fly an airplane. The program will be set up so that users select answer alternatives by means of radio buttons created with the <input> tag.

In this quiz, each question will be scored immediately. The following steps walk you through the process of creating the form with radio buttons, and then through the process of creating a series of if statements to score each question. To save you from a lot of typing, you can use the PilotQuiz.html document from the Chapter folder in the Chapter.03 folder in your data files. (Make a copy of the file and name it PilotQuiz1.html, and then use the copy rather than the original.) If you do not have access to the Data files, then complete the following set of steps to create the PilotQuiz1.html document. Even if you do have the Data files, read through the following steps to understand how the PilotQuiz1.html document is set up.

To create the private pilot quiz program and its form section:

1. Create a new document in your text editor.
2. Type the <!DOCTYPE> declaration, <html> element, header information, and the <body> element. Use the strict DTD and "FAA Private Pilot" as the content of the

<title> element. Include a <link> element that links to the js_styles.css style sheet in your Chapter folder.

3.   Add the following script section to the document head:

```
<script type="text/javascript">
/* <![CDATA[ */
// ADD CODE HERE
/* ]]> */
</script>
```

4.   Add the following elements to the document body:

```
<h1>FAA Private Pilot Quiz</h1>
<form action="">
</form>
```

5.   Add the following lines for the first question to the <form> element. The four radio buttons represent the answers. Because each button within a radio button group requires the same name attribute, these three radio buttons have the same name of "question1". Each radio button is also assigned a value corresponding to its answer letter: *a*, *b*, or *c*. For each radio button group, the onclick event sends the button value to an individual function that scores the answer. Notice that the value for each button is sent to the function as a parameter.

```
<p><strong>1. The term "angle of attack" is defined as the
angle</strong></p>
<p><input type="radio" name="question1" value="a"
onclick="scoreQuestion1('a')" />Between the wing chord line and
the relative wind<br /> <!-- correct answer -->
<input type="radio" name="question1" value="b"
onclick="scoreQuestion1('b')" />Between the airplane's climb
angle and the horizon<br />
<input type="radio" name="question1" value="c"
onclick="scoreQuestion1('c')" />Formed by the longitudinal axis
of the airplane and the chord line of the wing</p>
```

You can build the program quickly by copying the input button code for the first question, pasting it into a new document, and then editing it to create questions two through five. If you use copy and paste to create the input buttons in the following steps, make sure you change the question number for each input button name and the function it calls.

6.   Add the lines for the second question. If you prefer, copy and paste the code you typed earlier, taking care to make the necessary edits.

```
<p><strong>2. What is the purpose of the rudder on an
airplane?</strong></p>
<p><input type="radio" name="question2" value="a"
onclick="scoreQuestion2('a')" />To control roll<br />
<input type="radio" name="question2" value="b"
onclick="scoreQuestion2('b')" />To control overbanking tendency
<br />
```

```
<input type="radio" name="question2" value="c"
onclick="scoreQuestion2('c')" />To control yaw</p><!-- correct
answer -->
```

7. Add the lines for the third question, using copy and paste if you prefer.

```
<p><strong>3. An airplane said to be inherently stable
will?</strong></p>
<p><input type="radio" name="question3" value="a"
onclick="scoreQuestion3('a')" />Be difficult to stall<br />
<input type="radio" name="question3" value="b"
onclick="scoreQuestion3('b')" />Require less effort to control
<br /><!-- correct answer -->
<input type="radio" name="question3" value="c"
onclick="scoreQuestion3('c')" />Not spin</p>
```

8. Add the following lines for the fourth question:

```
<p><strong>4. Which basic flight maneuver increases the load
factor on an airplane as compared to straight-and-level flight?
</strong></p>
<p><input type="radio" name="question4" value="a"
onclick="scoreQuestion4('a')" />Climbs<br />
<input type="radio" name="question4" value="b"
onclick="scoreQuestion4('b')" />Turns<br /><!-- correct
answer -->
<input type="radio" name="question4" value="c"
onclick="scoreQuestion4('c')" />Stalls</p>
```

9. Add the following lines for the fifth question:

```
<p><strong>5. What is one purpose of wing flaps?</strong></p>
<p><input type="radio" name="question5" value="a"
onclick="scoreQuestion5('a')" />To enable the pilot to make
steeper approaches to a landing without increasing the airspeed
<br /><!-- correct answer -->
<input type="radio" name="question5" value="b"
onclick="scoreQuestion5('b')" />To relieve the pilot of
maintaining continuous pressure on the controls<br />
<input type="radio" name="question5" value="c"
onclick="scoreQuestion5('c')" />To decrease wing area to
vary the lift</p>
```

10. Save the document as **PilotQuiz1.html** in the **Chapter** folder for Chapter 3.

Next, you will add the functions to score each of the questions. The functions contain `if` statements that evaluate each answer.

To add JavaScript code to score each of the questions:

1. Replace the line `// ADD CODE HERE` in the script section in the document head with the following function that scores the first question. A response of "Correct

Answer" appears if the user provides the correct answer. A response of "Incorrect Answer" appears if the user provides an incorrect answer.

```
function scoreQuestion1(answer) {
    if (answer == "a")
        window.alert("Correct Answer");
    if (answer == "b")
        window.alert("Incorrect Answer");
    if (answer == "c")
        window.alert("Incorrect Answer");
}
```

2. Add the following scoreQuestion2() function after the scoreQuestion1() function:

```
function scoreQuestion2(answer) {
    if (answer == "a")
        window.alert("Incorrect Answer");
    if (answer == "b")
        window.alert("Incorrect Answer");
    if (answer == "c")
        window.alert("Correct Answer");
}
```

3. Add the following scoreQuestion3() function after the scoreQuestion2() function:

```
function scoreQuestion3(answer) {
    if (answer == "a")
        window.alert("Incorrect Answer");
    if (answer == "b")
        window.alert("Correct Answer");
    if (answer == "c")
        window.alert("Incorrect Answer");
}
```

4. Add the following scoreQuestion4() function after the scoreQuestion3() function:

```
function scoreQuestion4(answer) {
    if (answer == "a")
        window.alert("Incorrect Answer");
    if (answer == "b")
        window.alert("Correct Answer");
    if (answer == "c")
        window.alert("Incorrect Answer");
}
```

5. Add the following scoreQuestion5() function after the scoreQuestion4() function:

```
function scoreQuestion5(answer) {
    if (answer == "a")
        window.alert("Correct Answer");
    if (answer == "b")
        window.alert("Incorrect Answer");
    if (answer == "c")
        window.alert("Incorrect Answer");
}
```

6. Save the **PilotQuiz1.html** document, validate it with the W3C Markup Validation Service at **validator.w3.org/file-upload.html**, and fix any errors that the document contains.

7. Open the **PilotQuiz1.html** document in your Web browser. As you select a response for each question, you will immediately learn whether the answer is correct. Figure 3-6 shows the output that appears if you select the right answer for Question 1.

Figure 3-6

PilotQuiz1.html in a Web browser

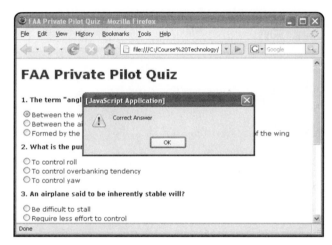

8. Close your Web browser window.

if...else Statements

So far you've learned how to use an `if` statement to execute a statement (or statements) if a condition evaluates to true. In some situations, however, you may want to execute one set of statements when the condition evaluates to true, and another set of statements when the condition evaluates to false. In that case, you need to add an `else` clause to your `if` statement. For instance, suppose you create a script that displays a confirm dialog box that asks users to indicate whether they invest in the stock market by clicking an OK or Cancel radio button. An `if` statement in the script might contain a conditional expression that evaluates the user's input. If the condition evaluates to true (the user clicked the OK button), then the `if` statement would display a Web page on recommended stocks. If the condition evaluates to false (the user clicked the Cancel button), then the statements in an `else` clause would display a Web page on other types of investment opportunities.

The **window.confirm() method** displays a confirm dialog box that contains an OK button and a Cancel button. The syntax for the `window.confirm()` method is `window.confirm(message);`. When a user clicks the OK button in the confirm dialog box, a value of true is returned. When a user clicks the Cancel button, a value of false is returned. For example, the following statement displays the dialog box shown in Figure 3-7:

```
window.confirm("Would you like a cup of coffee?");
```

Figure 3-7
Confirm dialog box

An `if` statement that includes an `else` clause is called an **if...else statement**. You can think of an `else` clause as being a backup plan that is implemented when the condition returns a value of false. The syntax for an `if...else` statement is as follows:

```
if (conditional expression)
     statement;
else
     statement;
```

You can use command blocks to construct an `if...else` statement as follows:

```
if (conditional expression) {
     statements;
}
else {
     statements;
}
```

NOTE
An `if` statement can be constructed without the `else` clause. However, the `else` clause can only be used with an `if` statement.

The following code shows an example of an `if...else` statement:

```
var today = "Tuesday"
if (today == "Monday")
     document.write("<p>Today is Monday</p>");
else
     document.write("<p>Today is not Monday</p>");
```

In the preceding code, the `today` variable is assigned a value of "Tuesday". If the condition (`today == "Monday"`) evaluates to false, control of the program passes to the `else` clause, and the statement `document.write("<p>Today is not Monday</p>");` executes, and the string "Today is not Monday" prints. If the `today` variable had been assigned a value of "Monday", the condition (`today == "Monday"`) would have evaluated to true, and the statement `document.write("<p>Today is Monday</p>");` would have executed. Only one set of statements executes: either the statements following the `if` statement or the statements following the `else` clause. When either set of statements executes, any code following the `if...else` statements executes normally.

The JavaScript code for the PilotQuiz1.html document you created earlier uses multiple `if` statements to evaluate the results of the quiz. Although the multiple `if` statements function properly, they can be simplified using an `if...else` statement. Next, you will simplify the PilotQuiz1.html program by replacing multiple `if` statements with one `if...else` statement.

To add `if...else` statements to PilotQuiz1.html:

1. Return to the **PilotQuiz1.html** document in your text editor and immediately save it as **PilotQuiz2.html**.

2. Because you only need the `if` statement to test for the correct answer, you can group all the incorrect answers in the `else` clause. Modify each of the functions that scores a question so that the multiple `if` statements are replaced with an `if...else` statement. The following code shows how the statements for the `scoreQuestion1()` function should look:

```
if (answer == 'a')
    window.alert("Correct Answer");
else
    window.alert("Incorrect Answer");
```

TIP

Keep in mind that the correct answer for Question 2 is *c*, the correct answer for Question 3 is *b*, the correct answer for Question 4 is *b*, and the correct answer for Question 5 is *a*. You'll need to modify the preceding code accordingly for each question. Copy and paste code and then edit it to save on typing time.

3. Save the **PilotQuiz2.html** document, validate it with the W3C Markup Validation Service at **validator.w3.org/file-upload.html**, and fix any errors that the document contains.

4. Open the **PilotQuiz2.html** document in your Web browser. The program should function the same as when it contained only `if` statements.

5. Close your Web browser window.

Nested `if` and `if...else` Statements

As you have seen, you can use a control structure such as an `if` or `if...else` statement to allow a program to make decisions about what statements to execute. In some cases, however, you may want the statements executed by the control structure to make other decisions. For instance, you may have a program that uses an `if` statement to ask users if they like sports. If users answer yes, you may want to run another `if` statement that asks users whether they like team sports or individual sports. You can include any code you like within the code block for an `if` statement or an `if...else` statement, and that includes other `if` or `if...else` statements.

When one decision-making statement is contained within another decision-making statement, they are referred to as **nested decision-making structures**. An `if` statement contained within an `if` statement or within an `if...else` statement is called a nested `if` statement. Similarly, an `if...else` statement contained within an `if` or `if...else` statement is called a nested `if...else` statement. You use nested `if` and `if...else` statements to perform conditional evaluations that must be executed after the original conditional evaluation. For example, the following code evaluates two conditional expressions before the `write()` statement executes:

```
var salesTotal = window.prompt("What is the sales total?", 0);
if (salesTotal > 50)
        if (salesTotal < 100)
            document.write("<p>The sales total is between 50 and 100.</p>");
```

The `document.write()` statement in the preceding example only executes if the conditional expressions in both `if` statements evaluate to true.

The preceding code uses the **`window.prompt()` method**, which displays a prompt dialog box with a message, a text box, an OK button, and a Cancel button. Any text that is entered into a prompt dialog box by a user can be assigned to a variable. The syntax for the `window.prompt()` method is *variable* = window.prompt(*message*, *default text*);. For example, the following code displays the dialog box shown in Figure 3-8:

```
var yourAge = window.prompt("How old are you?",
    "Enter your age here.");
```

Figure 3-8
Prompt dialog box

The JavaScript code in the PilotQuiz2.html document is somewhat inefficient because it contains multiple functions that perform essentially the same task of scoring the quiz. A more efficient method of scoring the quiz is to include nested decision-making structures within a single function. Next, you will modify the JavaScript code in the PilotQuiz2.html document so that it contains a single function that checks the correct answer for all the questions, using nested `if...else` statements.

To add nested `if...else` statements to the private pilot quiz program:

1. Return to the **PilotQuiz2.html** document in your text editor and immediately save it as **PilotQuiz3.html**.

2. Delete the five functions within the script section, but be sure to leave the JavaScript comments that hide the code from incompatible browsers.

3. Add to the script section the first line for the single function that will check all the answers. The function will receive two arguments: the number argument, which represents the question number, and the answer argument, which will score the answer selected by the user. Code within the body of the function uses the number argument to determine which question to store and the answer argument to determine the answer selected by the user.

    ```
    function scoreQuestions(number, answer) {
    ```

4. Add the following code to score Question 1:

    ```
    if (number == 1) {
        if (answer == "a")
            window.alert("Correct Answer");
        else
            window.alert("Incorrect Answer");
    }
    ```

5. Add the following code to score Question 2:

    ```
    else if (number == 2) {
        if (answer == "c")
            window.alert("Correct Answer");
        else
            window.alert("Incorrect Answer");
    }
    ```

6. Add the following code to score Question 3:

    ```
    else if (number == 3) {
        if (answer == "b")
            window.alert("Correct Answer");
        else
            window.alert("Incorrect Answer");
    }
    ```

7. Add the following code to score Question 4:

    ```
    else if (number == 4) {
        if (answer == "b")
            window.alert("Correct Answer");
        else
            window.alert("Incorrect Answer");
    }
    ```

8. Add the following code to score Question 5:

```
        else if (number == 5) {
            if (answer == "a")
                    window.alert("Correct Answer");
            else
                    window.alert("Incorrect Answer");
    }
```

9. Add a closing brace (}) for the scoreQuestions() function. The completed function should appear in your document as follows:

```
function scoreQuestions(number, answer) {
        if (number == 1) {
                if (answer == "a")
                        window.alert("Correct Answer");
                else
                        window.alert("Incorrect Answer");
        }
        if (number == 2) {
                if (answer == "c")
                        window.alert("Correct Answer");
                else
                        window.alert("Incorrect Answer");
        }
        if (number == 3) {
                if (answer == "b")
                        window.alert("Correct Answer");
                else
                        window.alert("Incorrect Answer");
        }
        if (number == 4) {
                if (answer == "b")
                        window.alert("Correct Answer");
                else
                        window.alert("Incorrect Answer");
        }
        if (number == 5) {
                if (answer == "a")
                        window.alert("Correct Answer");
                else
                        window.alert("Incorrect Answer");
        }
}
```

10. Within each of the <input> elements, change the function called within the onclick event handler to scoreQuestions(*number*, *answer*), changing the number argument to the appropriate question number and the answer argument to the appropriate answer. For example, the event handler for Question 1 should

read: scoreQuestions(1, 'a'). The modified <input> elements in your document should appear as follows:

```
<p><strong>1. The term "angle of attack" is defined as the
angle</strong></p><p><input type="radio" name="question1"
value="a" onclick="scoreQuestions(1, 'a')" />Between the wing
chord line and the relative wind<br /> <!-- correct answer -->
<input type="radio" name="question1" value="b"
onclick="scoreQuestions(1, 'b')" />Between the airplane's climb
angle and the horizon<br />
<input type="radio" name="question1" value="c"
onclick="scoreQuestions(1, 'c')" />Formed by the longitudinal
axis of the airplane and the chord line of the wing</p>
<p><strong>2. What is the purpose of the rudder on an
airplane?</strong></p>
<p><input type="radio" name="question2" value="a"
onclick="scoreQuestions(2, 'a')" />To control roll<br />
<input type="radio" name="question2" value="b"
onclick="scoreQuestions(2, 'b')" />To control overbanking
tendency<br />
<input type="radio" name="question2" value="c"
onclick="scoreQuestions(2, 'c')" />To control yaw</p><!--
correct answer -->
<p><strong>3. An airplane said to be inherently stable
will?</strong></p>
<p><input type="radio" name="question3" value="a"
onclick="scoreQuestions(3, 'a')" />Be difficult to stall<br />
<input type="radio" name="question3" value="b"
onclick="scoreQuestions(3, 'b')" />Require less effort to
control<br /><!-- correct answer -->
<input type="radio" name="question3" value="c"
onclick="scoreQuestions(3, 'c')" />not spin.</p>
<p><strong>4. Which basic flight maneuver increases the load
factor on an airplane as compared to straight-and-level flight?
</strong></p>
<p><input type="radio" name="question4" value="a"
onclick="scoreQuestions(4, 'a')" />Climbs<br />
<input type="radio" name="question4" value="b"
onclick="scoreQuestions(4, 'b')" />Turns<br /><!-- correct
answer -->
<input type="radio" name="question4" value="c"
onclick="scoreQuestions(4, 'c')" />Stalls</p>
<p><strong>5. What is one purpose of wing flaps?</strong></p>
<p><input type="radio" name="question5" value="a"
onclick="scoreQuestions(5, 'a')" />To enable the pilot to make
steeper approaches to a landing without increasing the airspeed
<br /><!-- correct answer -->
```

```
<input type="radio" name="question5" value="b"
onclick="scoreQuestions(5, 'b')" />To relieve the pilot of
maintaining continuous pressure on the controls<br />
<input type="radio" name="question5" value="c"
onclick="scoreQuestions(5, 'c')" />To decrease wing area to
vary the lift</p>
```

11. Save the **PilotQuiz3.html** document, validate it with the W3C Markup Validation Service at **validator.w3.org/file-upload.html**, and fix any errors that the document contains.

12. Open the **PilotQuiz3.html** document in your Web browser. The program should function just as it did with the multiple if statements and the multiple functions.

13. Close your Web browser window.

switch Statements

Another JavaScript statement that is used for controlling program flow is the switch statement. The **switch statement** controls program flow by executing a specific set of statements, depending on the value of an expression. The switch statement compares the value of an expression to a value contained within a special statement called a case label. A **case label** in a switch statement represents a specific value and contains one or more statements that execute if the value of the case label matches the value of the switch statement's expression. For example, your script for an insurance company might include a variable named customerAge. A switch statement can evaluate the variable and compare it to a case label within the switch construct. The switch statement might contain several case labels for different age groups that calculate insurance rates based on a customer's age. If the customerAge variable is equal to 25, the statements that are part of the "25" case label execute and calculate insurance rates for customers who are 25 or older. Although you could accomplish the same task using if or if...else statements, a switch statement makes it easier to organize the different branches of code that can be executed.

A switch statement consists of the following components: the keyword switch, an expression, an opening brace, a case label, executable statements, the keyword break, a default label, and a closing brace. The syntax for the switch statement is as follows:

```
switch (expression) {
    case label:
          statement(s);
          break;
    case label:
          statement(s);
          break;
    ...
    default:
          statement(s);
}
```

A case label consists of the keyword case, followed by a literal value or variable name, followed by a colon. JavaScript compares the value returned from the switch statement expression to the literal value or variable name following the case keyword. If a match is found, the case label statements execute. For example, the case label case 3.17: represents a floating-point integer value of 3.17. If the value of a switch statement expression equals 3.17, then the case 3.17: label statements execute. You can use a variety of data types as case labels within the same switch statement. The following code shows examples of four case labels:

```
case exampleVar:          // variable name
     statement(s)
case "text string":       // string literal
     statement(s)
case 75:                  // integer literal
     statement(s)
case -273.4:              // floating-point literal
     statement(s)
```

NOTE
A single statement or multiple statements can follow a case label. However, unlike if statements, multiple statements for a case label do not need to be enclosed within a command block.

NOTE
Other programming languages, such as Java and C++, require all case labels within a switch statement to be of the same data type.

Another type of label used within switch statements is the default label. The **default label** contains statements that execute when the value returned by the switch statement expression does not match a case label. A default label consists of the keyword default followed by a colon.

When a switch statement executes, the value returned by the expression is compared to each case label in the order in which it is encountered. Once a matching label is found, its statements execute. Unlike the if...else statement, execution of a switch statement does not automatically stop after particular case label statements execute. Instead, the switch statement continues evaluating the rest of the case labels in the list. Once a matching case label is found, evaluation of additional case labels is unnecessary. If you are working with a large switch statement with many case labels, evaluation of additional case labels can potentially slow down your program.

To avoid slow performance, then, you need to give some thought to how and when to end a switch statement. A switch statement ends automatically after the JavaScript interpreter encounters its closing brace (}). You can, however, use a special kind of statement, called a break statement, to end a switch statement once it has performed its required task. A **break statement** is used to exit a control structure. To end a switch statement once it performs its required task, include a break statement within each case label.

TIP

A break statement is used also to exit other types of control statements, such as the while, do...while, and for looping statements. You'll learn about these statements later in this chapter.

The following code shows a switch statement contained within a function. When the function is called, it is passed to an argument named americanCity. The switch statement compares the contents of the americanCity argument to the case labels. If a match is found, the city's state is returned and a break statement ends the switch statement. If a match is not found, the value "United States" is returned from the default label.

```
function city_location(americanCity) {
    switch (americanCity) {
        case "Boston":
            return "Massachusetts";
            break;
        case "Chicago":
            return "Illinois";
            break;
        case "Los Angeles":
            return "California";
            break;
        case "Miami":
            return "Florida";
            break;
        case "New York":
            return "New York";
            break;
        default:
            return "United States";
    }
}
document.write("<p>" + city_location("Boston") + "</p>");
```

Next, you will modify the private pilot quiz program so that the scoreAnswers() function contains a switch statement instead of nested if...else statements. Each case statement in the modified program will check for the question number that is passed from the function number argument. The switch statement makes better programming sense than the nested if...else statements, because it eliminates the need to check the question number multiple times.

To add a switch statement to the private pilot quiz program:

1. Return to the **PilotQuiz3.html** document and immediately save it as **PilotQuiz4.html**.

2. Change the if...else statements within the scoreQuestions() function to the following switch statement.

```
switch (number) {
    case 1:
        if (answer == 'b')
            window.alert("Correct Answer");
        else
            window.alert("Incorrect Answer");
        break;
    case 2:
        if (answer == 'b')
            window.alert("Correct Answer");
        else
            window.alert("Incorrect Answer");
        break;
    case 3:
        if (answer == 'c')
            window.alert("Correct Answer");
        else
            window.alert("Incorrect Answer");
        break;
    case 4:
        if (answer == 'd')
            window.alert("Correct Answer");
        else
            window.alert("Incorrect Answer");
        break;
    case 5:
        if (answer == 'a')
            window.alert("Correct Answer");
        else
            window.alert("Incorrect Answer");
        break;
}
```

3. Save the **PilotQuiz4.html** document, validate it with the W3C Markup Validation Service at **validator.w3.org/file-upload.html**, and fix any errors that the document contains.

4. Open **PilotQuiz4.html** document in your Web browser. The program should function just as it did with the nested if...else statements.

5. Close your Web browser window.

Repeating Code

The statements you have worked with so far execute one after the other in a linear fashion. The if, if...else, and switch statements select only a single branch of code to execute, then continue to the statement that follows. But what if you want to repeat the same statement, function, or code section five times, 10 times, or 100 times? For example, you might want to perform the same calculation until a specific number is found. In that case, you would need to use a **loop statement**, a control structure that repeatedly executes a statement or a series of statements while a specific condition is true or until a specific condition becomes true. In this chapter you'll learn about three types of loop statements: `while` statements, `do...while` statements, and `for` statements.

`while` Statements

One of the simplest types of loop statements is the **`while` statement**, which repeats a statement or series of statements as long as a given conditional expression evaluates to true. The syntax for the `while` statement is as follows:

```
while (conditional expression) {
    statement(s);
}
```

The conditional expression in the `while` statement is enclosed within parentheses following the keyword `while`. As long as the conditional expression evaluates to true, the statement or command block that follows executes repeatedly. Each repetition of a looping statement is called an **iteration**. When the conditional expression evaluates to false, the loop ends and the next statement following the `while` statement executes.

A `while` statement keeps repeating until its conditional expression evaluates to false. To ensure that the `while` statement ends after the desired tasks have been performed, you must include code that tracks the progress of the loop and changes the value produced by the conditional expression. You track the progress of a `while` statement, or any other loop, with a counter. A **counter** is a variable that increments or decrements with each iteration of a loop statement.

TIP

Many programmers often name counter variables `count`, `counter`, or something similar. The letters *i*, *j*, *k*, *l*, *x*, *y*, and *z* are also commonly used as counter names. Using a name such as `count`, or the letter *i* (for increment) or a higher letter, helps you remember (and lets other programmers know) that the variable is being used as a counter.

The following code shows a simple script that includes a `while` statement. The script declares a variable named `count` and assigns it an initial value of 1. The `count` variable is then used in the `while` statement conditional expression (`count <= 5`). As long as the `count` variable is less than or equal to five, the `while` statement loops. Within the body of the `while` statement, the `document.write()` statement prints the value of the `count` variable, then the `count` variable increments by a value of one. The `while` statement loops until the `count` variable increments to a value of 6.

```
var count = 1;
while (count <= 5) {
    document.write(count + "<br />");
    ++count;
```

```
}
document.write("<p>You have printed 5 numbers.</p>");
```

The preceding code uses an increment operator to print the numbers 1 to 5, with each number representing one iteration of the loop. When the counter reaches 6, the message "You have printed 5 numbers." prints, thus demonstrating that the loop has ended. Figure 3-9 shows the output of this simple script.

Figure 3-9

Output of a while statement using an increment operator

You can also control the repetitions in a while loop by decrementing (decreasing the value of) counter variables. Consider the following script:

```
var count = 10;
while (count > 0) {
        document.write(count + "<br />");
        --count;
}
document.write("<p>We have liftoff.</p>");
```

In this example, the initial value of the count variable is 10, and the decrement operator (--) is used to decrease count by one. When the count variable is greater than zero, the statement within the while loop prints the value of the count variable. When the value of count is equal to zero, the while loop ends, and the statement immediately following it prints. Figure 3-10 shows the script output.

Figure 3-10

Output of a while statement using a decrement operator

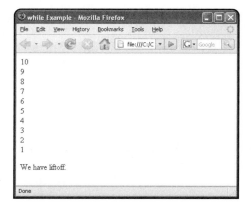

There are many ways to change the value of a counter variable and to use a counter variable to control the repetitions of a while loop. The following example uses the *= assignment operator to multiply the value of the count variable by two. When the count variable reaches a value of 128, the while statement ends. Figure 3-11 shows the script output.

```
var count = 1;
while (count <= 100) {
     document.write(count + "<br />");
     count *= 2;
}
```

Figure 3-11

Output of a while statement using the *= assignment operator

To ensure that the while statement will eventually end, you must include code within the body of the while statement that changes the value of the conditional expression. For example, you may have a while statement that prints odd numbers between 0 and 100. You need to include code within the body of the while statement that ends the loop after the last odd number (99) prints. If you do not include code that changes the value used by the conditional expression, your program will be caught in an infinite loop. In an **infinite loop**, a loop statement never ends because its conditional expression is never false. Consider the following while statement:

```
var count = 1;
while (count <= 10) {
     window.alert("The number is " + count);
}
```

Although the while statement in the preceding example includes a conditional expression that checks the value of a count variable, there is no code within the while statement body that changes the count variable value. The count variable will continue to have a value of 1 through each iteration of the loop. That means an alert dialog box containing the text string "The number is 1" will appear over and over again, no matter how many times the user clicks the OK button.

In most cases, you must force a Web browser that is caught in an infinite loop to close. The method for forcing an application to close varies from one operating system to another. For Windows XP, press Ctrl+Alt+Delete to open the Windows Task Manager, click the Applications tab, click the task containing your browser name, and then click End Task. For Windows 2000, press Ctrl+Alt+Delete, click Task Manager to open the Windows Task Manager, click the Applications tab, click the task containing your browser name, and then click End Task. In Windows

Vista, right-click the taskbar, click Task Manager, click the Applications tab, click the task containing your browser name, and then click End Task.

Next, you will create a new version of the private pilot quiz program that is to be scored by a single `while` statement containing a nested `if` statement. Although this `while` statement is somewhat more complicated than the `if`, `if...else`, and `switch` statements you created previously, it requires many fewer lines of code. You will also include a Score button that grades the entire quiz after a user is finished. (Remember that the earlier version of the program graded the quiz answer by answer.)

To create a version of the private pilot quiz program that is scored by a `while` statement:

1. Return to the **PilotQuiz4.html** document and immediately save it as **PilotQuiz5.html**.

2. Delete the entire `scoreQuestions()` function from the <head> section, and then add the following lines to create two arrays named `answers[]` and `correctAnswers[]`. The `answers[]` array will hold the answers selected each time the quiz runs, and the `correctAnswers[]` array will hold the correct response for each of the questions. The code also assigns the correct responses to each element of the `correctAnswers[]` array.

```
var answers = new Array(5);
var correctAnswers = new Array(5);
correctAnswers[0] = "a";
correctAnswers[1] = "c";
correctAnswers[2] = "b";
correctAnswers[3] = "b";
correctAnswers[4] = "a";
```

3. Add the following function, which assigns the response from each question to the appropriate element in the `answers[]` array. The program sends the actual question number (1–5) to the function using the `onclick` event of each radio button. To assign question responses to the correct element, 1 must be subtracted from the question variable, because the elements in an array start with 0.

```
function recordAnswer(question, answer) {
    answers[question-1] = answer;
}
```

4. Type the following definition for a function that will score the quiz. You will call this function from a new Score button.

```
function scoreQuiz() {
}
```

5. Add to the `scoreQuiz()` function the following statement, which declares a new variable, and assign to it an initial value of 0. The `totalCorrect` variable holds the number of correct answers.

```
var totalCorrect = 0;
```

6. Add the following variable declaration and `while` statement at the end of the `scoreQuiz()` function. In this code, a counter named `count` is declared and initialized to a value of 0, because 0 is the starting index of an array. The conditional expression within the `while` statement checks to see if `count` is less than the length of the array, which is one number higher than the largest element in the `answers[]` array. With each iteration of the loop, the statement in the `while` loop increments the `count` variable by one.

```
var count = 0;
while (count < correctAnswers.length) {
    ++count;
}
```

7. Add the following `if` statement to the beginning of the `while` loop, above the statement that increments the `count` variable. This `if` statement compares each element within the `answers[]` array to each corresponding element within the `correctAnswers[]` array. If the elements match, then the `totalCorrect` variable increments by one.

```
if (answers[count] == correctAnswers[count])
    ++totalCorrect;
```

8. After the `while` loop, add the following code for an alert dialog box that shows how many questions were answered correctly:

```
window.alert("You scored " + totalCorrect
    + " out of 5 answers correctly!");
```

The following code shows how your script section should appear:

```
<script type="text/javascript">
/* <![CDATA[ */
var answers = new Array(5);
var correctAnswers = new Array(5);
correctAnswers[0] = "a";
correctAnswers[1] = "c";
correctAnswers[2] = "b";
correctAnswers[3] = "b";
correctAnswers[4] = "a";
function recordAnswer(question, answer) {
    answers[question-1] = answer;
}
function scoreQuiz() {
    var totalCorrect = 0;
    var count = 0;
    while (count < correctAnswers.length) {
        if (answers[count] == correctAnswers[count])
            ++totalCorrect;
        ++count;
    }
```

```
    window.alert("You scored " + totalCorrect
         + " out of 5 answers correctly!");
}
// STOP HIDING FROM INCOMPATIBLE BROWSERS-->
</script>
```

9. In the onclick event handlers for each radio button, change the name of the called function from scoreQuestions() to **recordAnswer()**, but use the same arguments that you used for the scoreQuestions() function. For example, the onclick event handlers for the Question 1 radio buttons should now read onclick="recordAnswer(1, 'a')".

10. Finally, add the following <input> element immediately above the closing </form> tag. The <input> element creates a command button whose onclick event handler calls the scoreQuiz() function.

```
<p><input type="button" value="Score"
onclick="scoreQuiz();" /></p>
```

11. Save the **PilotQuiz5.html** document, validate it with the W3C Markup Validation Service at **validator.w3.org/file-upload.html**, and fix any errors that the document contains.

12. Open the **PilotQuiz5.html** document in your Web browser. Test the program by answering all five questions and clicking the **Score** button. Figure 3-12 shows how the program appears in a Web browser.

Figure 3-12

PilotQuiz5.html in a Web browser

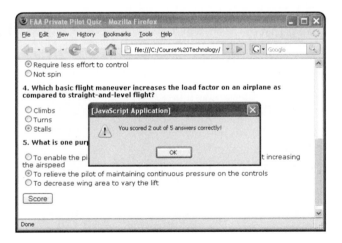

13. Close your Web browser window.

do...while Statements

Another JavaScript looping statement, similar to the while statement, is the do...while statement. The **do...while statement** executes a statement or statements once, then repeats the execution as long as a given conditional expression evaluates to true. The syntax for the do...while statement is as follows:

```
do {
    statement(s);
} while (conditional expression);
```

As you can see in the syntax description, the statements execute before a conditional expression is evaluated. Unlike the simpler while statement, the statements in a do...while statement always execute once, before a conditional expression is evaluated.

The following do...while statement executes once before the conditional expression evaluates the count variable. Therefore, a single line that reads "The count is equal to 2" prints. After the conditional expression (count < 2) executes, the count variable is equal to 3. This causes the conditional expression to return a value of false, and the do...while statement ends.

```
var count = 2;
do {
    document.write("<p>The count is equal to " + count + "</p>");
    ++count;
} while (count < 2);
```

Note that this do...while example includes a counter within the body of the do...while statement. As with the while statement, you need to include code that changes the conditional expression in order to prevent an infinite loop.

In the following example, the while statement never executes, because the count variable does not fall within the range of the conditional expression:

```
var count = 2;
while (count > 2) {
    document.write("<p>The count is equal to " + count + "</p>");
    ++count;
}
```

The following script shows an example of a do...while statement that prints the days of the week, using an array:

```
var daysOfWeek = new Array();
daysOfWeek[0] = "Monday"; daysOfWeek[1] = "Tuesday";
daysOfWeek[2] = "Wednesday"; daysOfWeek[3] = "Thursday";
daysOfWeek[4] = "Friday"; daysOfWeek[5] = "Saturday";
daysOfWeek[6] = "Sunday";
var count = 0;
do {
    document.write(daysOfWeek[count] + "<br />");
    ++count;
} while (count < daysOfWeek.length);
```

In the preceding example, an array is created containing the days of the week. A variable named count is declared and initialized to zero. (Remember, the first subscript or index in an array is zero.) Therefore, in the example, the statement daysOfWeek[0]; refers to Monday. The first iteration of the do...while statement prints "Monday" and then increments the count variable by one. The conditional expression in the while statement then checks to determine when the last element of the array has been printed. As long as the count is less than then length of the array (which is one number higher than the largest element in the daysOfWeek[] array), the loop continues. Figure 3-13 shows the output of the script in a Web browser.

Figure 3-13

Days of Week script in a Web browser

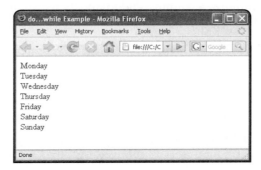

Next, you will replace the while statement in the private pilot quiz program with a do...while statement.

To replace the while statement in the private pilot quiz program with a do...while statement:

1. Return to the **PilotQuiz5.html** document and immediately save it as **PilotQuiz6.html**.

2. Change the while statement within the scoreQuiz() function to the following do...while statement:

```
do {
    if (answers[count] == correctAnswers[count])
        ++totalCorrect;
    ++count;
} while (count < 5);
```

3. Save the **PilotQuiz6.html** document, validate it with the W3C Markup Validation Service at **validator.w3.org/file-upload.html**, and fix any errors that the document contains.

4. Open the **PilotQuiz6.html** document in your Web browser. The program should function just as it did with the nested while statement.

5. Close your Web browser window.

for Statements

So far you have learned how to use the while and the do...while statements to repeat, or loop through, code. You can also use the for statement to loop through code. The **for statement** is used for repeating a statement or series of statements as long as a given conditional expression evaluates to true. The for statement performs essentially the same function as the while statement: if a conditional expression within the `for` statement evaluates to true, then the `for` statement executes and will continue to execute repeatedly until the conditional expression evaluates to false.

One of the primary differences between the `while` statement and the `for` statement is that in addition to a conditional expression, the `for` statement can also include code that initializes a counter and changes its value with each iteration. This is useful because it provides a specific place for you to declare and initialize a counter, and to update its value, which helps prevent infinite loops. The syntax of the `for` statement is as follows:

```
for (counter declaration and initialization; condition;
    update statement) {
    statement(s);
}
```

When the JavaScript interpreter encounters a `for` loop, the following steps occur:

1. The counter variable is declared and initialized. For example, if the initialization expression in a `for` loop is `var count = 1;`, then a variable named `count` is declared and assigned an initial value of 1. The initialization expression is only started once, when the `for` loop is first encountered.

2. The `for` loop condition is evaluated.

3. If the condition evaluation in Step 2 returns a value of true, then the `for` loop statements execute, Step 4 occurs, and the process starts over again with Step 2. If the condition evaluation in Step 2 returns a value of false, then the `for` statement ends and the next statement following the `for` statement executes.

4. The update statement in the `for` statement is executed. For example, the count variable may increment by one.

TIP

You can omit any of the three parts of the `for` statement, but you must include the semicolons that separate each section. If you omit a section, be sure you include code within the body that will end the `for` statement or your program may get caught in an infinite loop.

The following script shows a `for` statement that prints the contents of an array:

```
var brightestStars = new Array();
brightestStars[0] = "Sirius";
brightestStars[1] = "Canopus";
brightestStars[2] = "Arcturus";
brightestStars[3] = "Rigel";
brightestStars[4] = "Vega";
for (var count = 0; count < brightestStars.length; ++count) {
    document.write(brightestStars[count] + "<br />");
}
```

As you can see in this example, the counter is initialized, evaluated, and incremented within the parentheses. You do not need to include a declaration for the count variable before the `for` statement, nor do you need to increment the `count` variable within the body of the `for` statement. Figure 3-14 shows the output.

Figure 3-14

Output of brightest stars script

Using a `for` statement is more efficient because you do not need as many lines of code. Consider the following `while` statement:

```
var count = 1;
while (count < brightestStars.length) {
     document.write(count + "<br />");
     ++count;
}
```

You could achieve the same flow control more efficiently by using a `for` statement as follows:

```
for (var count = 1; count < brightestStars.length; ++count) {
     document.write(count + "<br />");
}
```

There are times, however, when using a `while` statement is preferable to using a `for` statement, especially for looping statements that do need to declare, initialize, or update a counter variable. The following code relies on a Boolean value returned from a confirm dialog box, rather than a counter, for program control.

```
var i = true;
while (i == true)
     i = window.confirm(
          "Do you want to redisplay this dialog box?");
```

You could accomplish the same task using a `for` statement, but in this case, the third part of the `for` statement, which updates the counter, would be unnecessary. This is because the counter is updated by the value returned from the `window.confirm()` method; a value of true would cause the loop to reiterate, while a value of false would cause the loop to exit. Therefore, this code is better written using a `while` statement. If you use a `for` statement instead of a `while` statement in the preceding example, you must not include the update section in the `for` statement. You must also remember to retain the semicolon that separates the conditional section from the update section. If you include the update section, you could create an infinite loop.

CHAPTER 3

The following code shows an example of the Days of Week script you saw earlier. This time, however, the script includes a for statement instead of a do...while statement. Notice that the declaration of the count variable, the conditional expression, and the statement that increments the count variable are now all contained within the for statement. Using a for statement instead of a do...while statement simplifies the script somewhat, because you do not need as many lines of code.

```
var daysOfWeek = new Array();
daysOfWeek[0] = "Monday"; daysOfWeek[1] = "Tuesday";
daysOfWeek[2] = "Wednesday"; daysOfWeek[3] = "Thursday";
daysOfWeek[4] = "Friday"; daysOfWeek[5] = "Saturday";
daysOfWeek[6] = "Sunday";
for (var count = 0; count < daysOfWeek.length; ++count) {
     document.write(daysOfWeek[count] + "<br />");
}
```

Next, you will create a final version of the private pilot quiz program that is scored with a for statement instead of a do...while statement.

To replace the do...while statement in the private pilot quiz program with a for statement:

1. Return to the **PilotQuiz6.html** document and immediately save it as **PilotQuiz7.html**.

2. Delete the declaration for the count variable within the scoreQuiz() function.

3. Change the do...while statement within the scoreQuiz() function to the following for statement:

```
for (var count = 0; count < correctAnswers.length; ++count) {
     if (answers[count] == correctAnswers[count])
          ++totalCorrect;
}
```

4. Save the **PilotQuiz7.html** document, validate it with the W3C Markup Validation Service at **validator.w3.org/file-upload.html**, and fix any errors that the document contains.

5. Open the **PilotQuiz7.html** document in your Web browser. The program should function just as it did with the nested do...while statement.

6. Close your Web browser window and text editor.

Using CONTINUE Statements to Restart Execution

When you studied switch statements, you learned how to use a break statement to exit switch, while, do...while, and for statements. A similar statement, used only with looping statements, is the **continue statement**, which halts a looping statement and restarts the loop with a new iteration. You use the continue statement when you want to stop the loop for the current iteration, but want the loop to continue with a new iteration. For example, suppose a company stores employee salaries in an array and wants to increase the salary by 5% for every employee who earns less than $50,000. The following script contains a `for` loop. This `for` loop contains a `continue` statement that iterates through the values in an array named `salaries[]`. The `continue` statement executes for any values in the `salaries[]` array that are lower than $50,000. The values in the `salaries[]` array that are lower than $50,000 are increased by 5% and the new value is printed.

```
var salaries = new Array(5);
salaries[0] = 42000;
salaries[1] = 52000;
salaries[2] = 44000;
salaries[3] = 46000;
salaries[4] = 65000;
<p>Salary increases:</p>
for (var count = 0; count < salaries.length; ++count) {
    if (salaries[count] >= 50000)
        continue;
    salaries[count] *= 1.05;
    document.write(salaries[count] + "<br />");
}
```

The preceding code skips the two values that are higher than $50,000 and prints the results shown in Figure 3-15.

Figure 3-15

Output of a `for` loop with a `continue` statement

Chapter Summary

▶ In JavaScript programming, you can write your own procedures, called functions, which are similar to the methods associated with an object.

▶ The term "variable scope" refers to where in your program a declared variable can be used. A global variable is one that is declared outside a function and is available to all parts of your program. A local variable is declared inside a function and is only available within the function in which it is declared.

▶ An event is a specific circumstance (such as an action performed by a user, or an action performed by the browser) that is monitored by JavaScript and that your script can respond to in some way.

▶ Code that executes in response to a specific event is called an event handler.

▶ The process of determining the order in which statements execute in a program is called decision making or flow control.

▶ The if statement is used to execute specific programming code if the evaluation of a conditional expression returns a value of true.

▶ A command block is a set of statements contained within a set of braces, similar to the way function statements are contained within a set of braces.

▶ An if statement that includes an else clause is called an if...else statement.

▶ When one decision-making statement is contained within another decision-making statement, they are referred to as nested decision-making structures.

▶ The switch statement controls program flow by executing a specific set of statements, depending on the value of an expression.

▶ A loop statement is a control structure that repeatedly executes a statement or a series of statements, while a specific condition is true or until a specific condition becomes true.

▶ The while statement is used for repeating a statement or series of statements as long as a given conditional expression evaluates to true.

▶ Each repetition of a looping statement is called an iteration.

▶ An infinite loop is a situation in which a loop statement never ends because its conditional expression is never false.

▶ The do...while statement executes a statement or statements once, then repeats the execution as long as a given conditional expression evaluates to true.

▶ The for statement is used for repeating a statement or series of statements as long as a given conditional expression evaluates to true.

▶ The continue statement halts a looping statement and restarts the loop with a new iteration.

Review Questions

1. A function definition must contain arguments. True or false?
2. Explain how to return a value from a function to the calling statement.

3. Which of the following built-in functions can you use to determine whether a value is a number?

    a. `eval()`

    b. `isNaN()`

    c. `parseInt()`

    d. `parseFloat()`

4. You must declare a local variable _____.

    a. with the `local` keyword

    b. before a function

    c. after a function

    d. within the braces of a function definition

5. A variable within a function definition without the `var` keyword is a local variable. True or false?

6. Code that executes in response to a specific event is called a(n) _____.

    a. function

    b. procedure

    c. event handler

    d. method

7. The _____ event occurs when an element becomes active.

    a. `select`

    b. `focus`

    c. `load`

    d. `change`

8. Which of the following statements successfully displays an alert dialog box? (Choose all that apply.)

    a. `alert("Please come again!");`

    b. `document.alert("Please come again!");`

    c. `window.alert("Please come again!");`

    d. `dialog.alert("Please come again!");`

9. Which of the following statements assigns the value of a text box named `comments` on a form named `survey` to a variable named `surveyComments`?

    a. `var surveyComments = document.survey.comments.value`

    b. `var surveyComments = survey.comments.value`

    c. `var surveyComments = document.survey.comments`

    d. `var surveyComments = document.survey.comments.value`

CHAPTER 3

10. Which of the following is the correct syntax for an `if` statement?

    a. ```
       if (singleIncome > 326450),
           window.alert("Your federal income tax rate is 35%.");
       ```
    b. ```
       if (singleIncome > 326450);
           window.alert("Your federal income tax rate is 35%.");
       ```
    c. ```
       if (singleIncome > 326450)
           window.alert("Your federal income tax rate is 35%.");
       ```
    d. ```
       if singleIncome > 326450
           window.alert("Your federal income tax rate is 35%.");
       ```

11. Explain how to construct an `if` statement that executes multiple statements.

12. Which is the correct syntax for an `else` clause?

    a. ```
       else "document.write('Your federal income tax rate is
       28%.')";
       ```
    b. ```
       else; document.write("Your federal income tax rate is
       28%.");
       ```
    c. ```
       else (document.write("Your federal income tax rate is
       28%.");
       ```
    d. ```
       else document.write("Your federal income tax rate is
       28%.");
       ```

13. The `switch` statement controls program flow by executing a specific set of statements, depending on _____.

    a. whether an `if` statement executes from within a function
    b. the version of JavaScript being executed
    c. the value returned by a conditional expression
    d. the result of an `if...else` statement

14. When the value returned by a `switch` statement expression does not match a `case` label, then the statements within the _____ label execute.

    a. `error`
    b. `else`
    c. `exception`
    d. `default`

15. You can exit a `switch` statement using a(n) _____ statement.

    a. `complete`
    b. `end`
    c. `quit`
    d. `break`

16. Each repetition of a looping statement is called a(n) _____.

    a. iteration

    b. cycle

    c. synchronization

    d. recurrence

17. Which of the following is the correct syntax for a `while` statement?

    a.
```
while (i <= population.length) {
    document.write(population[i]);
    ++i;
}
```

    b.
```
while (i <= population.length, ++i) {
    document.write(population[i]);
}
```

    c.
```
while (i <= population.length);
    document.write(population[i]);
    ++i;
```

    d.
```
while (i <= population.length; document.write(i)) {
    ++ population[i];
}
```

18. Which of the following is the correct syntax for a `do...while` statement?

    a.
```
do {
    document.write(counties[i]);
    while (i < counties.length)
}
```

    b.
```
do { while (i < counties.length)
    document.write(counties[i]);
}
```

    c.
```
do {
document.write(counties[i]);
} while (i < counties.length);
```

    d.
```
do while (i < counties.length) {
    document.write(counties[i]);
}
```

19. Which of the following is the correct syntax for a `for` statement?

    a.
```
for (var i = ; i < federalHoliday.length; ++i)
    document.write(federalHoliday[i]);
```

    b.
```
for (var i = 0, i < holiday.length, ++i)
    document.write(federalHoliday[i]);
```

c. ```
for {
    document.write(federalHoliday[i]);
} while (var i = 0; i < holiday.length; ++i)
```

d. ```
for (var i = 0; i < holiday.length);
    document.write(federalHoliday[i]);
    ++i;
```

20. Explain how an infinite loop is caused.

Hands-On Projects

Project 3-1

In this project, you will create a script for Walt's Lawn Service with a function that returns a string value.

1. Create a new document in your text editor.

2. Type the `<!DOCTYPE>` declaration, `<html>` element, document head, and `<body>` element. Use the Strict DTD and "Walt's Lawn Service" as the content of the `<title>` element.

3. Create a script section in the document head that contains the following `favoriteLawnService()` function:

```
<script type="text/javascript">
/* <![CDATA[ */
function favoriteLawnService() {
    var companyName = "Walt's Lawn Service";
}
/* ]]> */
</script>
```

4. Modify the `favoriteLawnService()` function so that it returns the company name to another calling function.

5. Create another script section in the document body.

6. Add statements to the script section in the document body that call the `favoriteLawnService()` function and assign the return value to a variable named `bestLandscaper`.

7. Finally, write code that prints the contents of the `bestLandscaper` variable.

8. Save the document as **WaltsLawnService.html** in the Projects folder for Chapter 3.

9. Use the W3C Markup Validation Service to validate the **WaltsLawnService.html** document and fix any errors that the document contains. Once the document is valid, close it in your text editor and then open it in your Web browser and examine how the elements are rendered.

10. Close your Web browser window.

Project 3-2

In this project, you will create a script that uses a function to print information about financing options for a company named Cahill Cars. The script will include a global variable containing the name of the company, and the function will contain global variables that store financing information.

1. Create a new document in your text editor.

2. Type the `<!DOCTYPE>` declaration, `<html>` element, document head, and `<body>` element. Use the Strict DTD and "Cahill Cars" as the content of the `<title>` element.

3. Create a script section in the document head.

4. Add the following global variable to the script section in the document head:

```
var autoDealer = "Cahill Cars";
```

5. Add to the end of the script section a function named `printFinanceOptions()`. Within the `printFinanceOptions()` function, add the following `document.write()` methods to print the available financing options:

```
document.write("<h2>Financing Options</h2>");
document.write("<ul>");
document.write("<li>24 months: 6.75%</li>");
document.write("<li>48 months: 7.15%</li>");
document.write("<li>72 months: 7.50%</li>");
document.write("</ul>");
```

6. Add a script section to the document body that prints the global variable in an `<h1>` element and that calls the `printFinanceOptions()` function.

7. Save the document as **CahillCars.html** in the Projects folder for Chapter 3.

8. Use the W3C Markup Validation Service to validate the **CahillCars.html** document and fix any errors that the document contains. Once the document is valid, close it in your text editor and then open it in your Web browser and examine how the elements are rendered.

9. Close your Web browser window.

Project 3-3

In this project, you will correct errors in a simple JavaScript program that prints information for the Hotel Tennessee.

1. Create a new document in your text editor.

2. Type the `<!DOCTYPE>` declaration, `<html>` element, document head, and `<body>` element. Use the Strict DTD and "Hotel Tennessee" as the content of the `<title>` element.

3. Create a script section in the document head that contains the following statement:

```
<script type="text/javascript">
/* <![CDATA[ */
document.write(hotelInfo());
/* ]]> */
</script>
```

4. Create a script section in the document body that contains the following `hotelInfo()` function:

```
<script type="text/javascript">
/* <![CDATA[ */
function hotelInfo() {
    return "<p>The Hotel Tennessee in Nashville is within
walking distance of the Country Music Hall of Fame.</p>";
}
/* ]]> */
</script>
```

5. The code you typed in the preceding step should print a single statement that reads "The Hotel Tennessee in Nashville is within walking distance of the Country Music Hall of Fame." However, the code actually contains a design error that generates error messages when you attempt to open the program in a Web browser. Correct the error and make sure the program runs successfully in a browser. (*Hint*: The problem has to do with where the script sections are placed in the document.)

6. Save the document as **HotelTennessee.html** in the Projects folder for Chapter 3.

7. Use the W3C Markup Validation Service to validate the **HotelTennessee.html** document and fix any errors that the document contains. Once the document is valid, close it in your text editor and then open it in your Web browser and examine how the elements are rendered.

8. Close your Web browser window.

Project 3-4

In this project, you will create a document that uses an `if...else` statement and confirm dialog boxes to verify that a passenger meets the eligibility requirements to sit in an airplane's exit row.

1. Create a new document in your text editor.

2. Type the `<!DOCTYPE>` declaration, `<html>` element, document head, and `<body>` element. Use the Strict DTD and "Exit Row Requirements" as the content of the `<title>` element.

3. Create the following script section in the document body:

```
<script type="text/javascript">
/* <![CDATA[ */
/* ]]> */
</script>
```

4. Add the following if...else statements to the script section. These statements use confirm dialog boxes in the conditional expressions to determine whether a passenger meets the eligibility requirements to sit in an airplane's exit row.

```
if (!window.confirm("Are you under 15 years old?"))
        document.write("<p>By federal law, children under age 15
                may not sit in emergency exit rows.</p>");
else if (!window.confirm("Are you capable of lifting 50 or more
        pounds?"))
        document.write("<p>You must be able to life 50 or more
                pounds to sit in an exit row.</p>");
else if (!window.confirm("Are you willing to assist the crew in
        the event of an emergency?"))
        document.write("<p>To sit in an exit row, you must be
                willing to assist the crew in the event of an
                emergency.</p>");
else
        document.write("<p>You meet the criteria for sitting in an
                exit row.</p>");
```

5. Save the document as **ExitRows.html** in the Projects folder for Chapter 3.

6. Use the W3C Markup Validation Service to validate the **ExitRows.html** document and fix any errors that the document contains. Once the document is valid, close it in your text editor and then open it in your Web browser and examine how the elements are rendered.

7. Close your Web browser window.

Project 3-5

In this project, you will write a while statement that prints all even numbers between 1 and 100 to the screen.

1. Create a new document in your text editor.

2. Type the <!DOCTYPE> declaration, <html> element, document head, and <body> element. Use the Strict DTD and "Even Numbers" as the content of the <title> element.

3. Create a script section with a while statement that prints all even numbers between 1 and 100 to the screen.

4. Save the document as **EvenNumbers.html** in the Projects folder for Chapter 3.

5. Use the W3C Markup Validation Service to validate the **EvenNumbers.html** document and fix any errors that the document contains. Once the document is valid, close it in your text editor and then open it in your Web browser and examine how the elements are rendered.

6. Close your Web browser window.

Project 3-6

In this project, you will identify and fix the logic flaws in a `while` statement.

Create a new document in your text editor.

2. Type the `<!DOCTYPE>` declaration, `<html>` element, document head, and `<body>` element. Use the Strict DTD and "While Logic" as the content of the `<title>` element.

3. Create a script section in the document head that includes the following code:

```
<script type="text/javascript">
/* <![CDATA[ */
var count = 0;
var numbers = new Array(100);
while (count > 100) {
    numbers[count] = count;
    ++count;
}
while (count > 100) {
    document.write(numbers[count]);
    ++count;
}
/* ]]> */
</script>
```

4. The code you typed in the preceding step should fill the array with the numbers 1 through 100, and then print them to the screen. However, the code contains several logic flaws that prevent it from running correctly. Identify and fix the logic flaws.

5. Save the document as **WhileLogic.html** in the Projects folder for Chapter 3.

6. Use the W3C Markup Validation Service to validate the **WhileLogic.html** document and fix any errors that the document contains. Once the document is valid, close it in your text editor and then open it in your Web browser and examine how the elements are rendered.

7. Close your Web browser window.

Project 3-7

Standard & Poor's issues a list of bond ratings that determine the investment quality of individual bonds. The bond ratings range from AAA to D with AAA representing the highest quality bonds. In this project, you will create a document with a simple form that displays the investment quality of each particular Standard & Poor's bond rating.

1. Create a new document in your text editor.

2. Type the `<!DOCTYPE>` declaration, `<html>` element, document head, and `<body>` element. Use the Transitional DTD and "Bond Ratings" as the content of the `<title>` element.

3. Create a script section in the document head that includes the following `checkRating()` function and `switch` statement:

```
<script type="text/javascript">
/* <![CDATA[ */
function checkRating(rating) {
    switch (rating) {
            case "AAA":
                    window.alert("Highest Quality");
            case "AA":
                    window.alert("High Quality");
            case "AA":
                    window.alert("Upper Medium");
            case "BBB":
                    window.alert("Medium");
            case "BB":
                    window.alert("Speculative");
            case "B":
                    window.alert("Highly Speculative");
            case "CCC":
                    window.alert("Highly Speculative");
            case "CC":
                    window.alert("Highly Speculative");
            case "D":
                    window.alert("Default");
    }
}
/* ]]> */
</script>
```

4. Add code to the `switch` statement you created in the previous step so that after the statements in a `case` label execute, the `switch` statement ends.

5. Modify the `switch` statement so that a default value of "You did not enter a valid letter grade" is displayed in an alert dialog box if none of the `case` labels match the `grade` variable.

6. Add the following form to the document body that includes an `onclick` event handler which calls the `checkGrade()` function. The value of the single text box is passed to the `checkGrade()` function.

```
<form name="bondRating" action="">
<input type="text" name="rating" />
<input type="button" value="CheckBond Rating"
onclick="checkRating(document.bondRating.rating.value);" />
</form>
```

7. Save the document as **BondRatings.html** in the Projects folder for Chapter 3.

8. Use the W3C Markup Validation Service to validate the **BondRatings.html** document and fix any errors that the document contains. Once the document is valid, close it in your text editor and then open it in your Web browser and examine how the elements are rendered.

9. Close your Web browser window.

Project 3-8

In this project, you will modify a nested if statement so it instead uses a compound conditional expression. You use logical operators such as the || (OR) and && (AND) operators to execute a conditional or looping statement based on multiple criteria.

1. Create a new document in your text editor.

2. Type the <!DOCTYPE> declaration, <html> element, document head, and <body> element. Use the Strict DTD and "Oil Prices" as the content of the <title> element.

3. Create a script section in the document head that includes the following variable declaration and nested if statement:

```
<script type="text/javascript">
/* <![CDATA[ */
var oilPrice = 52.85;
if (oilPrice > 50) {
    if (oilPrice < 60)
            document.write("<p>Oil prices are between $50.00
                and $60.00 a barrel.</p>");
}
/* ]]> */
</script>
```

4. Modify the nested if statement you created in the previous step so it uses a single if statement with a compound conditional expression to determine whether oil prices are between $50.00 and $60.00 a barrel. You will need to use the && (AND) logical operator.

5. Save the document as **OilPrices.html** in the Projects folder for Chapter 3.

6. Use the W3C Markup Validation Service to validate the **OilPrices.html** document and fix any errors that the document contains. Once the document is valid, close it in your text editor and then open it in your Web browser and examine how the elements are rendered.

7. Close your Web browser window.

Case Projects

Save the documents you create for the following projects in the Cases folder for Chapter 3. Be sure to validate the files you create with the W3C Markup Validation Service.

Case Project 3-1

Many companies normally charge a shipping and handling charge for purchases. Create a Web page that allows a user to enter a purchase price into a text box and includes a JavaScript function that calculates shipping and handling. Add functionality to the script that adds a minimum shipping and handling charge of $1.50 for any purchase that is less than or equal to $25.00. For any orders over $25.00, add 10% to the total purchase price for shipping and handling, but do not include the $1.50 minimum shipping and handling charge. The formula for calculating a percentage is *price * percent /* 100. For example, the formula for calculating 10% of a $50.00 purchase price is 50 * 10 / 100, which results in a shipping and handling charge of $5.00. After you determine the total cost of the order (purchase plus shipping and handling), display it in an alert dialog box. Save the document as **CalcShipping.html**.

Case Project 3-2

The American Heart Association recommends that when you exercise, you stay within 50 to 85 percent of your maximum heart rate. This range is called your target heart rate. One common formula for calculating maximum heart rate is to subtract your age from 220. Create a Web page that you can use to calculate your target heart rate. Use a form that contains a text box in which users can enter their age and a command button that uses an `onclick` event handler to call a function named `calcHeartRate()`. Within the `calcHeartRate()`, include a statement that calculates the maximum heart rate and assigns the result to a variable. Use two other statements that calculate the minimum (50%) and maximum (85%) target heart rates. To calculate the minimum target heart rate, you use the formula *maximum_heart_rate * .5* and to calculate the maximum target heart rate, you use the formula *maximum_heart_rate * .85*. After you calculate the minimum and maximum target heart rates, display the result in another text box in the form. For example, for someone 35 years old, the target heart rate text box should display "92 to 157 beats per minute". Save the document as **TargetHeartRate.html**.

Case Project 3-3

Create a Web page that you can use to calculate miles per gallon. Add a form to the Web page that contains four text `<input>` elements: starting mileage, ending mileage, gallons used, and miles per gallon. Assign initial starting values of 0 to each of the `<input>` element's value attribute. Add `onchange` event handlers to the starting mileage, ending mileage, and gallons used text boxes that call a JavaScript function named `calcMPG()`. Create the `calcMPG()` function in a script section in the document head. Within the `calcMPG()` function, declare three variables (`startMiles`, `endMiles`, and `gallons`), and initialize each variable with the value assigned to the `startMiles`, `endMiles`, and `gallons` variables. Create an `if...else` statement that uses the `isNaN()` function within a compound conditional expression to determine whether the `startMiles`, `endMiles`, and `gallons` variables contain numeric values. If the variables do not contain numeric variables, display an alert dialog box informing the user that they must enter numeric values. If the variables do contain numeric values, the `else` clause should perform the miles per gallon calculation and assign the result to the miles per gallon text box in the form. The formula for calculating miles per gallon is (*ending_mileage - starting_mileage*) / *gallons*. The formula includes parentheses to force the order of precedence to calculate the subtraction operation before the division operation. (Recall from Chapter 2 that a division operation has higher precedence than a subtraction operation.) One problem with performing the calculation is that if you attempt to divide by zero, you will receive an error. For this reason, you need to use a nested `if` statement within the `else` clause to verify that the `gallons` variable contains a numeric value greater than zero. If the variable does not contain a value greater than zero, the statements within the `if` statement should not execute. Save the document as **GasMileage.html**.

Case Project 3-4

You can determine whether a year is a leap year by testing if it is divisible by 4. However, years that are also divisible by 100 are not leap years, unless they are also divisible by 400, in which case they are leap years. Write a script that allows a user to enter a year and then determines whether the year entered is a leap year. Include a form with a single text box where the user can enter a year. Display an alert dialog box to the user stating whether the year they entered is a standard year or a leap year. Save the document as **LeapYear.html**.

Case Project 3-5

A prime number is a number than can only be divided by itself or by one. Examples of prime numbers include 1, 3, 5, 13, and 17. Write a script that prints the prime numbers between 1 and 999 in a table that consists of 10 columns. You will need to use several looping and conditional statements to test all division possibilities. Use `document.write()` statements to create the table elements and a counter variable to create the table so it consists of 10 columns. The counter variable should start with an initial value of 0 and be incremented by one each time your code identifies a prime number and prints it in a table cell. Once the counter variable reaches a value of 10 (meaning that 10 cells have been added to the current row), print `</tr><tr>` to start a new row and reset the variable back to 0. Save the document as **PrimeNumbers.html**.

4

Manipulating the Browser Object Model

In this chapter you will:

- Study the browser object model
- Work with the `Window` object
- Study the `History`, `Location`, and `Navigator` objects
- Use JavaScript to refer to windows and frames

There may be situations in which you want to use JavaScript to control the Web browser. For example, you may want to change the Web page being displayed or write information to the Web browser's status bar. Or, you may want to control elements of the Web page itself. To control the Web browser window or the Web page, you use the browser object model. This chapter discusses the components of the browser object model.

Understanding the Browser Object Model

The **browser object model (BOM)** or **client-side object model** is a hierarchy of objects, each of which provides programmatic access to a different aspect of the Web browser window or the Web page. You can use the methods and properties of objects in the browser object model to manipulate the window, frames, and elements displayed in a Web browser. The most basic objects in the browser object model are illustrated in Figure 4-1.

TIP

The browser object model is also called the JavaScript object model or the `Navigator` object model. However, other scripting technologies, such as VBScript, can also control aspects of the Web browser window or Web page. Therefore, the terms "browser object model" or "client-side object model" are more accurate.

Figure 4-1

Browser object model

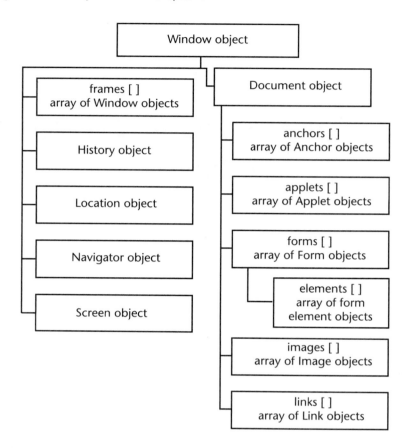

NOTE
The concept of object models is fairly complex. You do not need to understand the details of working with object models in order to work with the browser object model in JavaScript. Instead, you should simply understand that object models define groups of interrelated objects.

You do not have to create any of the objects or arrays explicitly in the browser object model; they are created automatically when a Web browser opens a Web page. The top-level object in the browser object model is the **Window object**, which represents a Web browser window or an individual frame within a window. The Web browser automatically creates the Window object for you. The Window object is called the **global object** because all other objects in the browser object model are contained within it. For example, the Window object contains the Document object, just as a Web browser window contains a Web page document. You use the methods and properties of the Window object to control the Web browser window while you use the methods and properties of the Document object to control the Web page. Figure 4-2 illustrates the concept of the Window object and the Document object.

Figure 4-2

Window object and
Document object

Web browser
window
represented by
the Window
object

Web page
represented by
the Document
object

The Document Object

The Document object is arguably the most important object in the browser object model because
it represents the Web page displayed in a browser. The write() and writeln() methods,
with which you are familiar, refer to the Document object. The statement document.write
("Welcome to my Web page"); adds the text "Welcome to my Web page" to a Web page
when it is rendered by a Web browser. All elements on a Web page are contained within the
Document object, and each element is represented in JavaScript by its own object. Therefore, the
Document object contains all of the elements you create on a Web page. For example, the Form
object, which is used by JavaScript to represent forms created with the <form> element, is contained within the Document object, which is contained within the Window object. The Radio
object, which is used by JavaScript to represent a radio button created with an <input> element,
is contained within the Form object, which is contained within the Document object, which is
contained within the Window object.

NOTE

The Document object branch of the browser object model is represented by its own
object model called the Document Object Model, or DOM. You will learn more
about the DOM in Chapter 10.

In this book, objects in the browser object model are referred to with an initial uppercase letter
(Document object). However, when you use the object name in code, you must always use a
lowercase letter. For example, the following statement refers to the Document object:
document.write ("Welcome to my Web page"); . Note the use of the lowercase "d" in
document.

Referencing JavaScript Objects

Some of the objects in the browser object model represent arrays. In Figure 4-1, those objects that are arrays are followed by brackets, such as `frame[]`, `forms[]`, or `images[]`. The arrays contain objects created from the corresponding elements on a Web page. For example, the `images[]` array contains `Image` objects that represent all the `<img>` elements on a Web page. `Image` objects for each `<img>` element are assigned to the elements of the `images[]` array in the order that they appear on the Web page. The first `Image` object is represented by `images[0]`, the second `Image` object is represented by `images[1]`, and so on.

To refer to a JavaScript object in code, you must refer to all of the objects that contain it, with the object names, separated by periods. Consider an `Image` object, which contains an `src` property that contains the URL assigned to an `<img>` element's `src` attribute. To refer to the `src` property of an `Image` object, you must include the `Document` object. The following `<img>` element includes an `onclick` event handler that uses the `Document` object to display the image's URL in an alert dialog box:

```
<img src="company_logo.gif" height="100" width="200"
    onclick="window.alert('This image is located at the following URL: '
    + document.images[0].src);" alt="Image of a company logo." />
```

Next, you start working on a simple Web site for a real estate company named Pine Knoll Properties. You will find six prewritten Web pages, PineKnollProperties.html, colonial.html, contemporary.html, cottage.html, ranch.html, and townhouse.html, in your Chapter folder for Chapter 4. The PineKnollProperties.html document is the home page; the rest of the pages display photos and information about different property listings. You will modify these Web pages throughout the chapter.

In this exercise, you add an advertisement to the Pine Knoll Properties home page that changes when users click on the image. You will change the image using the `images[]` array.

To add an advertisement to the Pine Knoll Properties home page that changes when users click on the image:

1. Open your text editor, then open the **PineKnollProperties.html** document located in your Chapter folder for Chapter 4.

2. Immediately following the opening `<body>` tag is a table that contains a single row with two cells. The first cell contains two heading elements and the second cell contains a nonbreaking space character entity (` `). Replace the nonbreaking space character entity with the following `<img>` element, `<br>` element, and text. The `<img>` element displays an image named sell1.jpg. When the user clicks the image, an `onclick` event handler changes the image to another image named sell2.jpg.

    ```
    <img src="sell1.jpg" height="60" width="370"
    onclick="document.images[0].src='sell2.jpg';" alt="Advertising
    image for the Pine Knoll Properties." /><br />
    (Click the image to see the answer.)
    ```

3. Save the **PineKnollProperties.html** document and open it in your Web b
    Figure 4-3 shows how the Web page appears. Click on the image to make
    it changes to sell2.jpg.

Figure 4-3

Pine Knoll Properties
Web page with an
advertisement

4. Close your Web browser window.

The code you entered in the preceding exercise refers to the first element (0) in the `images[]`
array, which assumes that the image is the first image on the page. If other images are added
to the Web page before the preceding statement, then referring to the first element in the
`images[]` array would result in the wrong URL being displayed. When referring to the current
object (in this case, the `Image` object for the preceding statement), you can simply use the `this`
keyword instead of including the `Document` object and `images[]` array. The `this` keyword refers
to the current object. The following code shows the same statement, but this time written with
the `this` keyword:

```
<img src="company_logo.gif" height="100" width="200"
     onclick="window.alert('This image is located at the following URL: '
     + this.src);" alt="Image of a company logo." />
```

Next, you modify the `onclick` event handler in the PineKnollProperties.html document so it
uses `this` references instead of referring to the `Document` object and `images[]` array.

To modify the event handlers in the PineKnollProperties.html document so they use `this` references instead of referring to the `Document` object and `images[]` array:

1. Return to the **PineKnollProperties.html** file in your text editor.

2. Modify the `onclick` event handler so it uses a `this` reference instead of referring
    to the `Document` object and `images[]` array:

    ```
    <img src="sell1.jpg" height="60" width="370"
    onclick="this.src='sell2.jpg';" alt="Advertising image for Pine
    Knoll Properties" /><br />
    (Click the image to see the answer.)
    ```

3.   Save the **PineKnollProperties.html** document and open it in your Web browser. Figure 4-4 shows how the Web page appears after clicking the image.

Figure 4-4

Pine Knoll Properties
Web page after adding
this references

4.   Close your Web browser window.

Because the `Window` object is the global object, it is not necessary to include it in your statements. In order for JavaScript to access any other objects in the browser object model, it must first go through the `Window` object. Therefore, if you do not include the `Window` object in statements that access the browser object model, JavaScript automatically assumes that the objects you need to access are contained within the `Window` object. You can list the `Window` object in statements that access the browser object model. For example, the statement `window.alert (window.document.images[0].src);` works just as well as the statement `window.alert (document.images[0].src);`. However, because JavaScript automatically assumes you are referring to the global object, listing the `Window` object is usually unnecessary.

NOTE
It *is* necessary to include the `Window` object when you need to clearly distinguish between the `Window` object and the `Document` object. For example, event-handling code automatically assumes you are referring to the `Document` object instead of the `Window` object. Therefore, in event-handling code, you should include the `Window` object when you are explicitly referring to the Web browser window.

The `WINDOW` Object

The `Window` object includes several properties that contain information about the Web browser window. For instance, the `status` property contains information displayed in a Web browser's status bar. Also contained in the `Window` object are various methods that allow you to manipulate the Web browser window itself. You have already used some methods of the `Window` object, including the `window.alert()`, `window.confirm()`, and `window.prompt()` methods, which all display dialog boxes. Table 4-1 lists the `Window` object properties and Table 4-2 lists the `Window` object methods.

Property	Description
`closed`	Returns a Boolean value that indicates whether a window has been closed
`defaultStatus`	Sets the default text that is written to the status bar
`document`	Returns a reference to the `Document` object
`frames[]`	Returns an array listing the `Frame` objects in a window
`history`	Returns a reference to the `History` object
`location`	Returns a reference to the `Location` object
`name`	Returns the name of the window
`navigator`	Returns a reference to the `Navigator` object
`opener`	Refers to the window that opened the current window
`parent`	Returns the parent frame that contains the current frame
`screen`	Returns a reference to the `Screen` object
`self`	Returns a self-reference to the `Window` object; identical to the `window` property
`status`	Specifies temporary text that is written to the status bar
`top`	Returns the topmost `Window` object that contains the current frame
`window`	Returns a self-reference to the `Window` object; identical to the `self` property

Table 4-1   Window object properties

Note

Some Web browsers, including Internet Explorer, have custom properties and methods for the `Window` object. This book describes only properties and methods that are common to browser objects in all current Web browsers.

Another way of referring to the `Window` object is by using the **self property**, which refers to the current `Window` object. Using the `self` property is identical to using the `window` property to refer to the `Window` object. For example, the following lines are identical:

```
window.alert("text string");
self.alert("text string");
```

Some JavaScript programmers prefer to use the `window` property, while other JavaScript programmers prefer to use the `self` property. The choice is yours. However, when attempting to decipher JavaScript code created by other programmers, be aware that both of these properties refer to the current `Window` object.

Because a Web browser assumes you are referring to the global object, you do not need to refer explicitly to the `Window` object when using one of its properties or methods. For example, the `alert()` method is a method of the `Window` object. Throughout this text, you have used the full

Method	Description
alert()	Displays a simple message dialog box with an OK button
blur()	Removes focus from a window
clearInterval(*variable*)	Cancels an interval that was set with setInterval()
clearTimeout(*variable*)	Cancels a timeout that was set with setTimeout()
close()	Closes a Web browser window
confirm(*message*)	Displays a confirmation dialog box with OK and Cancel buttons
focus()	Makes a Window object the active window
moveBy(*x-pixels, y-pixels*)	Moves the window relative to the current position
moveTo(*x-position, y-position*)	Moves the window to an absolute position
open(*URL, name[, options]*)	Opens a new Web browser window
print()	Prints the document displayed in the window or frame
prompt(*message[, default]*)	Displays a dialog box prompting a user to enter information
resizeBy(*x-pixels, y-pixels*)	Resizes a window by a specified amount
resizeTo(*x-position, y-position*)	Resizes a window to a specified size
scrollBy(*x-pixels, y-pixels*)	Scrolls the window by a specified amount
scrollTo(*x-position, y-position*)	Scrolls the window to a specified position
setInterval(*"code", milliseconds*)	Repeatedly executes a function after a specified number of milliseconds have elapsed
setTimeout(*"code", milliseconds*)	Executes a function once after a specified number of milliseconds have elapsed

Table 4-2   Window object methods

syntax of window.alert(*text*);, although the syntax alert(*text*); (without the Window object) works equally well. However, it's good practice to use the window or self references when referring to a property or method of the Window object in order to clearly identify them as belonging to the Window object. If you do not use the window or self reference, then you or another programmer may confuse a property or method of the Window object with JavaScript variables or functions.

Windows and Events

In Chapter 3, you learned how to use events with your Web pages. Events are particularly important when it comes to working with the browser object model because they allow you to execute the methods and change the properties of objects in the browser object model. In this section, you learn more about mouse events.

The *click* and *dblclick* Events

You have already extensively used the click event with form controls, such as radio buttons, to execute JavaScript code. However, keep in mind that the click event can be used with other types of elements. Earlier in this chapter, you used the click event to change the image displayed on the Pine Knoll Properties Web page. The `click` event is often used for the anchor element. In fact, the primary event associated with the anchor element is the `click` event. When a user clicks a link, the Web browser handles execution of the `onclick` event handler automatically, so you do not need to add an `onclick` event handler to your anchor elements.

There may be times, however, when you want to override an anchor element's automatic `onclick` event handler with your own code. For instance, you may want to warn the user about the content of a Web page that a particular link will open. In order to override the automatic `click` event with your own code, you add to the `<a>` element an `onclick` event handler that executes custom code. When you override an internal event handler with your own code, your code must return a value of true or false, using the return statement. With the `<a>` element, a value of false indicates that you want the Web browser to perform its default event handling operation of opening the URL referenced in the link. A value of true indicates that you do not want the `<a>` element to perform its default event handling operation. For example, the `<a>` element in the following code includes an `onclick` event handler. The `warnUser()` function that is called by the `onclick` event handler returns a value generated by the `window.confirm()` method. Recall that when a user clicks the OK button in a confirm dialog box, a value of true is returned. When a user clicks the Cancel button, a value of false is returned. Notice that there are two return statements in the following code. The return statement in the `warnUser()` function returns a value to the `onclick` event handler. The return statement in the `onclick` event handler returns the same value to the Web browser.

```
...
<script type="text/javascript">
/* <![CDATA[ */
function warnUser() {
      return window.confirm("This link is only for Red Sox fans.
      Are you sure you want to continue?");
}
/* ]]> */
</script>
</head>
<body>
<p><a href="redsox.html" onclick="return
warnUser();">Red Sox Fan Club</a></p>
</body>
</html>
```

The `dblclick` event works the same as the `click` event, except that users need to double-click the mouse instead of single-clicking it. The `dblclick` event is rarely used. They're not generally used with links, because as you know, links are driven by single mouse clicks, and they are rarely used in other situations because, from the user's point of view, single-clicks are much easier than double-clicks.

The *mouseover* and *mouseout* Events

You use the `mouseover` and `mouseout` events to create rollover effects. A **rollover** is an effect that occurs when your mouse moves over an element. The `mouseover` event occurs when the mouse passes over an element and the `mouseout` event occurs when the mouse moves off an element. One common use of the `mouseover` and `mouseout` events is to change the text that appears in a Web browser status bar. For example, by default a link's URL appears in the status bar when the mouse passes over a link. You can use the `mouseover` event to display your own custom message for a link in the status bar. To make your custom message appear in the status bar, you use the JavaScript `status` property, which stores the text that will appear in the status bar. You can then use the `mouseout` event to reset the text displayed in the status bar after the mouse is moved off a link. Most often, any text that is displayed in the status bar is cleared by using the statement `onmouseout="window.status='';"` to set the `status` property to an empty string. Here, the two single quotation marks specify an empty string. You use single quotation marks instead of double quotation marks because the statement is already contained within a pair of double quotation marks. If you prefer, you could use this statement to display another custom message in the status bar.

The following link uses the `onmouseover` event handler to display the text "If you are a Red Sox fan, visit the Red Sox Fan Club!" in the status bar instead of the link's URL, redsox.html. The `onmouseout` event handler displays the text "You must be a Yankees fan." after the mouse moves off the link. Figure 4-5 shows the message that displays in a Web browser window's status bar while the mouse is over the link. Figure 4-6 shows the message that displays after the mouse moves off the link.

```
<p><a href="redsox.html"
onmouseover="window.status='If you are a Red Sox fan, visit the Red Sox
Fan Club!';return true"
onmouseout="window.status='You must be a Yankees fan.';
return true">Red Sox Fan Club</a></p>
```

Figure 4-5

Status bar message displayed with an onmouseover event handler

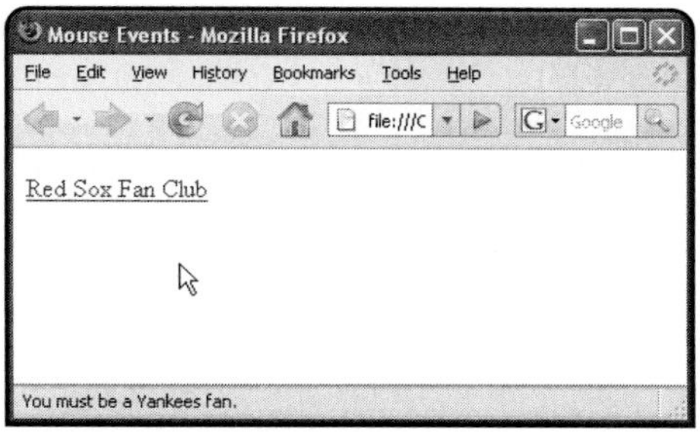

Figure 4-6

Status bar message displayed with an onmouseout event handler

While this section uses the `status` property to introduce the `onmouseover` and `onmouseout` events, it is considered poor Web design technique to hide the target URL of a link. In fact, Firefox includes an option that allows users to prevent scripts from changing status bar text. To allow scripts to change status bar text in Firefox, you must select Options from the Tools menu to display the Options dialog box. In the Options dialog box, select the Content category, and then click the Advanced button to display the Advanced JavaScript Settings dialog box. In the Advanced JavaScript Settings dialog box select the Change status bar text button. Then, click the OK button twice to close the Advanced JavaScript Settings dialog box and the Options dialog box.

The `defaultStatus` property specifies the default text that appears in the status bar whenever the mouse is not positioned over a link. The syntax for the `defaultStatus` property is `window.defaultStatus = "status bar text here";`. For practice, you will now add the `defaultStatus` property to the Pine Knoll Properties Web page so the text "Welcome to Pine Knoll Properties!" displays in the status bar by default. You will also add `onmouseover` event handlers to each of the links that uses the `status` property to modify the status bar text when the mouse pointer passes over the link.

To add `defaultStatus` and `status` properties to the Pine Knoll Properties Web page:

1. Return to the **PineKnollProperties.html** document in your text editor.

2. Add the following script section immediately above the closing `</head>` tag. The script contains a single statement that sets the Web page's default status bar text to "Welcome to Pine Knoll Properties!"

```
<script type="text/javascript">
/* <![CDATA[ */
window.defaultStatus = "Welcome to Pine Knoll Properties!";
/* ]]> */
</script>
```

3. Add `onmouseover` event handlers to each of the links as follows to modify the status bar text when the mouse pointer passes over the link along with `onmouseout` event handlers that resets the status bar to the default text. Notice that the event handlers use the `self` property to refer to the `Window` object.

```
<p><a href="cottage.html"
onmouseover="self.status='View this property.';return true"
onmouseout="self.status=window.defaultStatus;return true">
Cottage: <strong>$149,000</strong></a><br />
<a href="ranch.html"
onmouseover="self.status='View this property.';return true"
onmouseout="self.status=window.defaultStatus;return true">
Ranch: <strong>$189,000</strong></a><br />
<a href="townhouse.html"
onmouseover="self.status='View this property.';return true"
onmouseout="self.status=window.defaultStatus;return true">
Townhouse: <strong>$319,000</strong></a><br />
<a href="colonial.html"
onmouseover="self.status='View this property.';return true"
onmouseout="self.status=window.defaultStatus;return true">
```

```
Colonial: <strong>$389,000</strong></a><br />
<a href="contemporary.html"
onmouseover="self.status='View this property.';return true"
onmouseout="self.status=window.defaultStatus;return true">
Contemporary: <strong>$474,000</strong></a></p>
```

4. Save the **PineKnollProperties.html** document and open it in your Web browser. Figure 4-7 shows how the Web page appears when you hold your mouse pointer over the first property.

Figure 4-7

Pine Knoll Properties Web page after adding `defaultStatus` and `status` properties

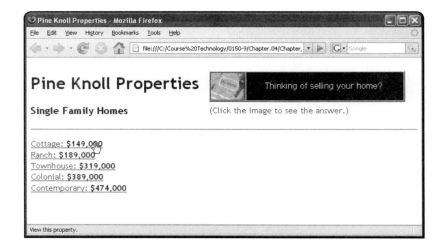

5. Close your Web browser window.

One of the more common uses of rollovers is to replace (or swap) an image on a Web page with another image. Consider the following code, which includes two functions, `price()` and `discount()`. The `price()` function is executed by the `onmouseover` event handler when the mouse passes over the image, while the `discount()` function is executed by the `onmouseout` event handler when the mouse passes off the image. Figure 4-8 shows the Web page before the mouse passes over the image; Figure 4-9 shows the Web page when the mouse is placed on the image. Once the mouse moves off the image, the original image shown in Figure 4-8 displays.

```
<!DOCTYPE html PUBLIC "-//W3C//DTD XHTML 1.0 Strict//EN"
"http://www.w3.org/TR/xhtml1/DTD/xhtml1-strict.dtd">
<html xmlns="http://www.w3.org/1999/xhtml">
<head><title>Mouse Events</title>
<meta http-equiv="content-type" content="text/html;
    charset=iso-8859-1" />
<script type="text/javascript">
/* <![CDATA[ */
function discount() {
document.images[0].src = "discount.jpg";
}
function price() {
```

```
document.images[0].src = "price.jpg";
}
/* ]]> */
</script></head>
<body>
<p><img src="discount.jpg" height="350" width="210"
alt="Image of a sales tag." onmouseover="price();"
onmouseout="discount();" /></p>
</body></html>
```

Figure 4-8

Web page before the
mouse passes over
the image

Figure 4-9

Web page with the
mouse placed over
the image

The mousedown and mouseup Events

The mousedown event occurs when you point to an element and hold the mouse button down; the mouseup event occurs when you release the mouse button. The following code shows the <img> element that displays the "sale tag" images, this time using mousedown and mouseup events:

```
<p><img src="discount.jpg" height="350" width="210"
alt="Image of a sales tag." onmousedown="price();"
onmouseup="discount();" /></p>
```

Next, you modify the <img> element in the PineKnollProperties.html document so the second image in the banner displays when you hold the mouse over it.

To modify the <img> element in the PineKnollProperties.html document so the second image in the banner displays when you hold the mouse over it:

1. Return to the **PineKnollProperties.html** document in your text editor.

2. Replace the onclick event handler in the <img> element with onmousedown and onmouseup event handlers that swap the images. Also, modify the message beneath the <img> element so it instructs users to hold their mouse button down when pointing to the image.

   ```
   <img src="sell1.jpg" height="60" width="370"
   onmousedown="this.src='sell2.jpg';"
   onmouseup="this.src='sell1.jpg';"
   alt="Advertising image for Pine Knoll Properties" /><br />
   Hold your mouse down on the image to see the answer.
   ```

3. Save the **PineKnollProperties.html** document and open it in your Web browser. Press and hold the mouse button over the banner image, then release it. You should see the images change when you press and release the mouse button.

4. Close your Web browser window.

Opening and Closing Windows

Most Web browsers allow you to open new Web browser windows in addition to the Web browser window or windows that may already be open. There are several reasons why you may need to open a new Web browser window. You may want to launch a new Web page in a separate window, allowing users to continue viewing the current page in the current window. Or, you may want to use an additional window to display information such as a picture or an order form.

Whenever a new Web browser window is opened, a new Window object is created to represent the new window. You can have as many Web browser windows open as your system will support, each displaying a different Web page. For example, you can have one Web browser window display Microsoft's Web site, another Web browser window display Firefox's Web site, and so on.

You may be familiar with how to open a link in a new window by using the <a> element's target attribute. For example, the following link opens the National Geographic home page in a new window named ngWindow:

```
<p><a href="http://www.nationalgeographic.com/" target="ngWindow">
   National Geographic home page</a>
```

Whenever the user clicks the preceding link, the Web browser looks for another Web browser window named ngWindow. If the window exists, then the link is opened in it. If the window does not exist, then a new window named ngWindow is created where the link opens.

The links in the Pine Knoll Properties Web page as they exist now open in the current window; they do not open in a new window. Next, you modify the links so they use the <a> element's target attribute to open the URL in a separate window.

To modify the links in the Pine Knoll Properties Web page so they use the <a> element's target attribute to open the URL in a separate window:

1.   Return to the **PineKnollProperties.html** document in your text editor.

2.   Add the following attribute before the closing bracket for each of the five <a> elements:

     target="propertyInfo"

3.   Save the **PineKnollProperties.html** document and open it in your Web browser. Click one of the links to see if the Web page opens in a new browser window. If you click other links on the Pine Knoll Properties Web page, you should notice that each Web page opens in the propertyInfo window (if it is currently open) instead of opening in a separate window. Figure 4-10 shows the propertyInfo window opened to the cottage Web page.

Figure 4-10

Cottage Web page opened in the propertyInfo window

4.   Close your Web browser window.

Opening a Window

The problem with using the target attribute is that it's deprecated in XHTML; you can only use it in the transitional or frameset DTDs. In order to open new windows in the strict DTD, you must use the **open()** **method** of the Window object. The syntax for the open() method is as follows:

```
window.open(url, name, options, replace);
```

Table 4-3 lists the arguments of the `window.open()` method.

Argument	Description
URL	Represents the Web address or filename to be opened
name	Assigns a value to the `name` property of the new `Window` object
options	Represents a string that allows you to customize the new Web browser window's appearance
replace	A Boolean value that determines whether the URL should create a new entry in the Web browser's history list or replace the entry

Table 4-3   Arguments of the `Window` object's `open()` method

You can include all or none of the `window.open()` method arguments. The statement `window.open("http://www.nationalgeographic.com");` opens the National Geographic home page in a new Web browser window, as shown in Figure 4-11. If you exclude the URL argument, then a blank Web page opens. For example, the statement `window.open();` opens the Web browser window displayed in Figure 4-12.

Figure 4-11

Web browser window opened with the URL argument of the `open()` method

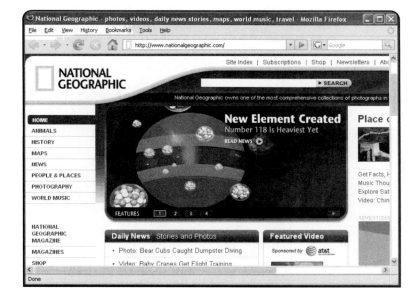

Figure 4-12

Blank Web browser window opened with the `window.open()` statement

When you open a new Web browser window, you can customize its appearance using the `options` argument of the `window.open()` method. Table 4-4 lists some common options that you can use with the `window.open()` method.

Name	Description
height	Sets the window's height
left	Sets the horizontal coordinate of the left of the window, in pixels
location	Includes the URL Location text box
menubar	Includes the menu bar
resizable	Determines if the new window can be resized
scrollbars	Includes scroll bars
status	Includes the status bar
toolbar	Includes the Standard toolbar
top	Sets the vertical coordinate of the top of the window, in pixels
width	Sets the window's width

Table 4-4   Common options of the `Window` object's `open()` method

All the options listed in Table 4-4, with the exception of the `width` and `height` options, are set using values of "yes" or "no", or 1 for yes and 0 for no. To include the status bar, the options string should read "status=yes". You set the `width` and `height` options using integers representing pixels. For example, to create a new window that is 200 pixels high by 300 pixels wide, the string should read "height=200,width=300". When including multiple items in the options string, you must separate the items by commas. If you exclude the options string of the `window.open()` method, then all the standard options are included in the new Web browser window. However, if you include the options string, you must include all the components you want to create for the new window; that is, the new window is created with only the components you explicitly specify.

Figure 4-13 shows the Photo Gallery Web page from the Woodland Park Zoo, located in Seattle, Washington. If you select a link from one of the menus on the page, such as the Cougar link that is highlighted in Figure 4-13, the Photo Gallery Slideshow Web page shown in Figure 4-14 opens.

Note
The menus shown in Figure 4-13 are created using DHTML, which you will study in Chapter 11.

Figure 4-13

Woodland Park Zoo
Photo Gallery Web page

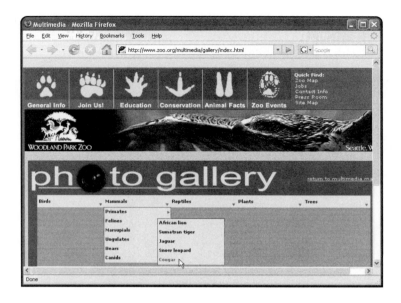

Figure 4-14

Woodland Park Zoo
Photo Gallery Slideshow
Web page displaying a
cougar

Notice that the Photo Gallery Slideshow Web page does not display toolbars, the menu, the URL Location box, or the scrollbars, and is sized to specific dimensions. If you were to attempt to resize the window, you would find that it couldn't be resized. The Photo Gallery Web page uses a JavaScript statement similar to the following to open the Photo Gallery Slideshow Web page:

```
var OpenWin = window.open(page, "CtrlWindow",
 "toolbar=no,menubar=no,location=no,scrollbars=no,resizable=no,
 width=380,height=405");
```

The name argument of the window.open() method is essentially the same as the value assigned to the deprecated target attribute in that it specifies the name of the window where the URL should open. If the name argument is already in use by another Web browser window, then JavaScript changes focus to the existing Web browser window instead of creating a new window.

For instance, the Photo Gallery Web page opens the Photo Gallery Slideshow Web page and assigns it a name of "CtrlWindow". If the `CtrlWindow` Web page already exists when you select another menu item from the Photo Gallery Web page, then the `CtrlWindow` Web page is reused; another window does not open. This is especially important with a Web page such as the Photo Gallery Web page, which allows you to view dozens of different Web pages for each of the animals listed in the menu. Imagine how crowded a user's screen would be if the program kept opening a new Photo Gallery Slideshow Web page window for each selected animal.

Next, you modify the Pine Knoll Properties Web page so the links use the `window.open()` method instead of the `target` attribute to open the URLs in a separate page.

To modify the Pine Knoll Properties Web page so the links use the `window.open()` method instead of the `target` attribute to open the URLs in a separate page:

1. Return to the **PineKnollProperties.html** document in your text editor.

2. Add the following global variable declaration and function to the end of the script section. The function will be called by `onclick` event handlers in each of the links.

```
var propertyWindow;
function showProperty(linkTarget) {
    propertyWindow = window.open(linkTarget, "propertyInfo",
    "toolbar=no,menubar=no,location=no,scrollbars=yes,
    resizable=no,
    width=400,height=350");
}
```

NOTE

Be sure not to add a line break to the options string in the preceding function. The options string is broken in this book due to space limitations.

3. Next, replace the `target` attribute in each `<a>` element with an `onclick` event handler that calls the `showProperty()` function, passing it to the URL of the target Web page. The `onclick` event handler should also return a value of "false" to prevent the PineKnollProperties.html Web page from being replaced with the target Web page that you are opening in a separate window. The modified `<a>` elements should appear as follows:

```
<p><a href="cottage.html"
onmouseover="self.status='View this property.';return true"
onmouseout="self.status=window.defaultStatus;return true"
onclick="showProperty('cottage.html');return false">
Cottage: <strong>$149,000</strong></a><br />
<a href="ranch.html"
onmouseover="self.status='View this property.';return true"
onmouseout="self.status=window.defaultStatus;return true"
```

```
onclick="showProperty('ranch.html');return false">
Ranch: <strong>$189,000</strong></a><br />
<a href="townhouse.html"
onmouseover="self.status='View this property.';return true"
onmouseout="self.status=window.defaultStatus;return true"
onclick="showProperty('townhouse.html');return false">
Townhouse: <strong>$319,000</strong></a><br />
<a href="colonial.html"
onmouseover="self.status='View this property.';return true"
onmouseout="self.status=window.defaultStatus;return true"
onclick="showProperty('colonial.html');return false">
Colonial: <strong>$389,000</strong></a><br />
<a href="contemporary.html"
onmouseover="self.status='View this property.';return true"
onmouseout="self.status=window.defaultStatus;return true"
onclick="showProperty('contemporary.html');return false">
Contemporary: <strong>$474,000</strong></a></p>
```

4.   Save the **PineKnollProperties.html** document and open it in your Web browser. Click one of the links to see if the Web page opens in a new browser window. Figure 4-15 shows how the window appears with the ranch.html Web page displayed.

Figure 4-15
Window opened with the open() method

5.   Close your Web browser window.

A `Window` object's name property can be used only to specify a target window with a link and cannot be used in JavaScript code. If you want to control the new window using JavaScript code located within the Web browser in which it was *created*, then you must assign the new `Window` object created with the `window.open()` method to a variable. The statement that opens the Photo Gallery Slideshow Web page assigns an object representing the new Web browser window to a variable named `OpenWin`. You can use any of the properties and methods of the `Window` object with a variable that represents a `Window` object.

One problem with Web pages such as the Pine Knoll Properties Web page is that windows that open in response to the user clicking a link can get hidden or "lost" behind other windows on the user's screen. For example, suppose the user clicks the cottage link on the Pine Knoll Properties Web page, thereby opening a new window. Then suppose the user returns to the Pine Knoll Properties Web page (without closing the cottage window) and clicks a different link. The window that displays the property is not automatically displayed as the active window on the screen. That is, it does not necessarily appear as the top window; it could instead be hidden behind other windows. The user may continuously click links, thinking that nothing is happening in response to his or her clicks, when in fact the code is actually working fine. The problem might be that the windows are open, but not visible. In order to make a window the active window, you use the **focus()** method of the Window object. You append the focus() method to the variable that represents the window, not to the name argument of the window.open() method. For example, to make the Photo Gallery Slideshow window the active window, you use the following statement:

```
OpenWin.focus();
```

Next, you add a focus() method to the showProperty() function in the Pine Knoll Properties Web page.

To add a focus() method to the showProperty() function in the Pine Knoll Properties Web page:

1. Return to the **PineKnollProperties.html** document in your text editor.
2. Add the following statement to the end of the showProperty() function:

   propertyWindow.focus();

3. Save the **PineKnollProperties.html** document and open it in your Web browser. Click one of the links to open the window that displays the property pages. Leave the Web page open, navigate back to the Pine Knoll Properties Web page, and click a different link. The window that displays the property pages should become the active window and display the URL for the Web page link you clicked.
4. Close your Web browser window.

Closing a Window

The **close()** method, which closes a Web browser window, is the method you will probably use the most with variables representing other Window objects. To close the Web browser window represented by the OpenWin variable, you use the statement OpenWin.close();. To close the current window, you use the statement window.close() or self.close().

NOTE
It is not necessary to include the Window object or self property when using the open() and close() methods of the Window object. However, the Document object also contains methods named open() and close(), which are used for opening and closing Web pages. Therefore, the Window object is usually included with the open() and close() methods, in order to distinguish between the Window object and the Document object.

Next, you add links to each of the property Web pages that call the `close()` method, which will close the window.

To add links to each of the property Web pages that call the `close()` method:

1. Return to your text editor and open the **cottage.html** from the Chapter folder for Chapter 4.

2. Replace the first <p> element with the following table that consists of a single row with two cells. The second cell contains a link that calls the `close()` method, which will close the window.

```
<table width="350">
  <tr>
    <td>Cottage: <strong>$149,000</strong></td>
    <td><a href="" onclick="self.close();">Close Window</a></td>
  </tr>
</table>
```

3. Save and close the **cottage.html** document.

4. Repeat Steps 2 and 3 for the **ranch.html**, **townhouse.html**, **colonial.html**, and **contemporary.html** documents. Be sure to change the text and amount within the first table cell to the appropriate property name.

5. Open the **PineKnollProperties.html** document in your Web browser and click one of the links. Figure 4-16 shows the new link (which closes the window) in the townhouse Web page.

Figure 4-16
Townhouse Web page after adding a link with a `close()` method

6. Click the **Close Window** link to close the window you opened.

7. Close the Web browser window containing the Pine Knoll Properties Web page.

Working with Timeouts and Intervals

As you develop Web pages, you may need to have some JavaScript code execute repeatedly, without user intervention. Alternately, you may want to create animation or allow for some kind of repetitive task that executes automatically. For example, you may want to include an advertising image that changes automatically every few seconds. Or, you may want to use animation to change the ticking hands of an online analog clock (in which case each position of the clock hands would require a separate image).

You use the `Window` object's timeout and interval methods to create code that executes automatically. The **`setTimeout()` method** is used in JavaScript to execute code after a specific amount of time has elapsed. Code executed with the `setTimeout()` method executes only once. The syntax for the `setTimeout()` method is `var variable = setTimeout("code", milliseconds);`. This statement declares that the variable will refer to the `setTimeout()` method. The code argument must be enclosed in double or single quotation marks and can be a single JavaScript statement, a series of JavaScript statements, or a function call. The amount of time the Web browser should wait before executing the code argument of the `setTimeout()` method is expressed in milliseconds.

NOTE

A millisecond is one thousandth of a second; there are 1,000 milliseconds in a second. For example, five seconds is equal to 5,000 milliseconds.

The **`clearTimeout()` method** is used to cancel a `setTimeout()` method before its code executes. The `clearTimeout()` method receives a single argument, which is the variable that represents a `setTimeout()` method call. The variable that represents a `setTimeout()` method call must be declared as a global variable. (Recall from Chapter 2 that a global variable is a variable declared outside of a function and is available to all parts of a JavaScript program.)

The script section in the following code contains a `setTimeout()` method and a `clearTimeout()` method call. The `setTimeout()` method is set to execute after 10,000 milliseconds (10 seconds) have elapsed. If a user clicks the OK button, the `buttonPressed()` function calls the `clearTimeout()` method.

```
...
<script type="text/javascript">
/* <![CDATA[ */
var buttonNotPressed = setTimeout(
     "window.alert('You must press the OK button to continue!')",
10000);
function buttonPressed() {
     clearTimeout(buttonNotPressed);
     window.alert("The setTimeout() method was cancelled!");
}
/* ]]> */
</script>
</head>
<body>
<form action="">
```

```
<input type="button" value=" OK " onclick="buttonPressed();" />
</form>
</body>
</html>
```

Two other JavaScript methods that create code and execute automatically are the
setInterval() method and the clearInterval() method. The **setInterval() method** is
similar to the setTimeout() method, except that it repeatedly executes the same code after
being called only once. The **clearInterval() method** is used to clear a setInterval()
method call in the same fashion that the clearTimeout() method clears a setTimeout()
method call. The setInterval() and clearInterval() methods are most often used for
starting animation code that executes repeatedly. The syntax for the setInterval() method is
the same as the syntax for the setTimeout() method: var *variable* = setInterval
("*code*", *milliseconds*);. As with the clearTimeout() method, the clearInterval()
method receives a single argument, which is the global variable that represents a setInterval()
method call.

By combining the src attribute of the Image object with the setTimeout() or setInterval()
methods, you can create simple animation on a Web page. In this context, "animation" does not
necessarily mean a complex cartoon character, but any situation in which a sequence of images
changes automatically. However, Web animation can also include traditional animation involving cartoons and movement (like the advertising with changing images or the ticking hands of the
clock mentioned above). The following code uses the setInterval() method to automatically
swap two advertising images every couple of seconds. Figure 4-17 shows the two images displayed in a browser.

```
. . .
<script type="text/javascript">
/* <![CDATA[ */
var curBanner="soccer1";
function changeBanner() {
    if (curBanner == "soccer2") {
        document.images[0].src = "soccer1.gif";
        curBanner = "soccer1";
    }
    else {
        document.images[0].src = "soccer2.gif";
        curBanner = "soccer2";
    }
}
/* ]]> */
</script>
</head>
<body onload="var begin=setInterval('changeBanner()',2000);">
<p><img src="soccer1.gif" name="banner" alt="Changing
image for Central Valley Sporting Goods" /></p>
</body>
</html>
```

Figure 4-17
Advertising Images

TIP
You can find a copy of the Jim's Sporting Emporium Web page
(SportingGoods.html) in the Chapter folder for Chapter 4 in your data files.

Next, you modify the Pine Knoll Properties Web page so it uses the setInterval() method to change the image automatically.

To modify the Pine Knoll Properties Web page so it uses the setInterval() method to change the image automatically:

1. Return to the **PineKnollProperties.html** document in your text editor.

2. To the end of the script section, add the following global variables and propertyAd() function. The propertyAd() function will be called by a setInterval() method. As a result, the images will change automatically.

```
var curImage="sell1";
var changeImages;
function propertyAd() {
    if (curImage == "sell2") {
        document.images[0].src = "sell1.jpg";
        curImage = "sell1";
    }
    else {
        document.images[0].src = "sell2.jpg";
        curImage = "sell2";
    }
}
```

3. Modify the opening `<body>` tag so it includes an `onload` event handler that calls the `setInterval()` method and `propertyAd()` function, as follows:

    ```
    <body onload="var changeImages=setInterval('propertyAd()',2000);">
    ```

4. Finally, remove the `onmousedown` and `onmouseup` event handlers from the `<img>` element and delete the explanatory text and `<br>` element from the table cell. The modified table cell should appear as follows:

    ```
    <td><img src="sell1.jpg" height="60" width="370" /><br /></td>
    ```

5. Save the **PineKnollProperties.html** document and then open it in your Web browser. The image should begin alternating automatically.

6. Close your Web browser window.

The HISTORY Object

The **History object** maintains an internal list (known as a history list) of all the documents that have been opened during the current Web browser session. Each Web browser window and frame, regardless of how many windows and frames you have open, contains its own internal `History` object. You cannot view the URLs contained in the history list, but you can write a script that uses the history list to navigate to Web pages that have been opened during a Web browser session.

Two important security features are associated with the `History` object. First, the `History` object will not actually display the URLs contained in the history list. This is important because individual user information in a Web browser, such as the types of Web sites a user likes to visit, is private information. Preventing others from viewing the URLs in a `History` list is an essential security aspect because it keeps people's likes and interests (as evidenced by the types of Web sites a person visits) confidential. This security feature is available in both Firefox and Internet Explorer.

A second important security feature of the `History` object is specific to Internet Explorer and has to do with the domain in which a Web page exists. As mentioned earlier, you can write a script that uses the history list to navigate to Web pages that have been opened during a Web browser session. In Internet Explorer, you can use JavaScript code to navigate through a history list. However, this is only possible if the currently displayed Web page exists within the same domain as the Web page containing the JavaScript code that is attempting to move through the list. For example, a user may open the home page for a company that sells office supplies. Suppose the user then clicks on a link on the office supply company's home page that takes them to another Web page in the company's domain, such as an online ordering page. In this case, the office supply company's home page is added to the user's history list. JavaScript code on the online ordering page can use the `History` object to navigate back to the company's home page. If JavaScript code attempts to access the `History` object of a Web browser that contains a URL located in a different domain, the Web browser ignores the JavaScript code. This security feature helps prevent malicious programmers and unscrupulous Web sites from seizing control of your browser or even your computer. As a general rule, you should only use the `History` object to help visitors navigate through your particular Web site.

The `History` object includes three methods, listed in Table 4-5.

Method	Description
`back()`	Produces the same result as clicking a Web browser's Back button
`forward()`	Produces the same result as clicking a Web browser's Forward button
`go(location)`	Opens a specific document in the history list

Table 4-5   Methods of the `History` object

When you use a method or property of the `History` object, you must include a reference to the `History` object itself. For example, the `back()` and `forward()` methods allow a script to move backward or forward in a Web browser's history. To use the `back()` method, you must use the following: `history.back()`.

The `go()` method is used for navigating to a specific Web page that has been previously visited. The argument of the `go()` method is an integer that indicates how many pages in the history list, forward or backward, you want to navigate. For example, `history.go(-2);` opens the Web page that is two pages back in the history list; the statement `history.go(3);` opens the Web page that is three pages forward in the history list. The statement `history.go(-1);` is equivalent to using the `back()` method, and the statement `history.go(1);` is equivalent to using the `forward()` method.

The `History` object contains a single property, the `length` property, which contains the specific number of documents that have been opened during the current browser session. To use the `length` property, you use the syntax `history.length;`. The `length` property does not contain the URLs of the documents themselves, only an integer representing how many documents have been opened. The following code uses an alert dialog box to display the number of Web pages that have been visited during a Web browser session:

```
window.alert("You have visited " + history.length + " Web pages.");
```

The `History` object is included in this chapter in order to introduce you to all of the major objects in the browser object model. However, you should avoid using the `History` object to navigate to Web pages that have been opened during a Web browser session. Instead, you should use the full URL with the `href` property of the `Location` object, as explained in the next section.

The LOCATION Object

When you want to allow users to open one Web page from within another Web page, you usually create a hypertext link with the `<a>` element. You can also use JavaScript code and the `Location` object to open Web pages. The **Location object** allows you to change to a new Web page from within JavaScript code. One reason you may want to change Web pages with JavaScript code is to redirect your Web site visitors to a different or updated URL. The `Location` object contains several properties and methods for working with the URL of the document currently open in a Web browser window. When you use a method or property of the `Location` object, you must include a reference to the `Location` object itself. For example, to use the `href` property, you must write `location.href` = *URL*;. Table 4-6 lists the `Location` object's properties, and Table 4-7 lists the `Location` object's methods.

Properties	Description
hash	A URL's anchor
host	The host and domain name (or IP address) of a network host
hostname	A combination of the URL's host name and port sections
href	The full URL address
pathname	The URL's path
port	The URL's port
protocol	The URL's protocol
search	A URL's search or query portion

Table 4-6   Properties of the `Location` object

Method	Description
reload(*force*)	Causes the page that currently appears in the Web browser to open again
replace(*URL*)	Replaces the currently loaded URL with a different one

Table 4-7   Methods of the `Location` object

The properties of the `Location` object allow you to modify individual portions of a URL. When you modify any properties of the `Location` object, you generate a new URL, and the Web browser automatically attempts to open that new URL. Instead of modifying individual portions of a URL, it is usually easier to change the `href` property, which represents the entire URL. For example, the statement `location.href` = `"http://www.google.com"`; opens the Google home page.

The `reload()` method of the `Location` object is equivalent to the Reload button in Firefox or the Refresh button in Internet Explorer. It causes the page that currently appears in the Web browser to open again. You can use the `reload()` button without any arguments, as in `location.reload();`, or you can include a Boolean argument of true or false. Including an argument of true forces the current Web page to reload from the server where it is located, even if no changes have been made to it. For example, the statement `location.reload(true);` forces the current page to reload. If you include an argument of false, or do not include any argument at all, then the Web page reloads only if it has changed.

The `replace()` method of the `Location` object is used to replace the currently loaded URL with a different one. This method works somewhat differently from loading a new document by changing the `href` property. The `replace()` method actually overwrites one document with another and replaces the old URL entry in the Web browser's history list. In contrast, the `href` property opens a different document and adds it to the history list.

You use the `Location` object later in this chapter.

The NAVIGATOR Object

The Navigator object is used to obtain information about the current Web browser. It gets its name from Netscape Navigator, but is also supported by Internet Explorer. Some Web browsers, including Internet Explorer, contain unique methods and properties of the Navigator object that cannot be used with other browsers. Table 4-8 lists properties of the Navigator object that are supported by most current Web browsers, including Firefox and Internet Explorer.

Properties	Description
appCodeName	The Web browser code name
appName	The Web browser name
appVersion	The Web browser version
platform	The operating system in use on the client computer
userAgent	The string stored in the HTTP user-agent request header, which contains information about the browser, the platform name, and compatibility

Table 4-8   Properties of the Navigator object

The Navigator object is most commonly used to determine which type of Web browser is running. Due to the incompatibilities between Firefox and Internet Explorer, it is important to be able to distinguish which browser is running in order to execute the correct code for a specific browser. (Cross-browser compatibility issues will be discussed in detail in Chapter 8.) The statement browserType = navigator.appName; returns the name of the Web browser in which the code is running to the browserType variable. You can then use the browserType variable to determine which code to run for the specific browser type. The **with statement** eliminates the need to retype the name of an object when properties of the same object are being referenced in a series. The following with statement prints the five properties of the Navigator object for Internet Explorer 7.0. Figure 4-18 shows the output.

```
with (navigator) {
      document.write("<p>Browser code name: " + appCodeName + "<br />");
      document.write("Web browser name: " + appName + "<br />");
      document.write("Web browser version: " + appVersion + "<br />");
      document.write("Operating platform: " + platform + "<br />");
      document.write("User agent: " + userAgent + "</p>");
}
```

Next, you print the properties of the Navigator object for the Web browser you are using. Because different browsers contain different property names in their Navigator objects, you will use the for...in statement to loop through the properties in your specific type of Web browser.

object
Internet

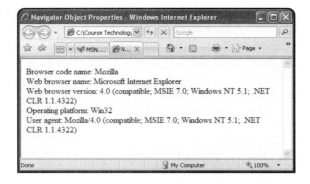

To print the properties of the `Navigator` object for the Web browser you are using:

1. Create a new document in your text editor.

2. Type the `<!DOCTYPE>` declaration, `<html>` element, header information, and the `<body>` element. Use the strict DTD and "Navigator Objects" as the content of the `<title>` element. Include a `<link>` element that links to the js_styles.css style sheet in the Chapter folder for Chapter 4. Your document should appear as follows:

```
<!DOCTYPE html PUBLIC "-//W3C//DTD XHTML 1.0 Strict//EN"
"http://www.w3.org/TR/xhtml1/DTD/xhtml1-strict.dtd">
<html xmlns="http://www.w3.org/1999/xhtml">
<head>
<title>Navigator Objects</title>
<meta http-equiv="content-type" content="text/html;
    charset=iso-8859-1" />
<link rel="stylesheet" href="js_styles.css" type="text/css" />
</head>
<body>
</body>
</html>
```

3. Add the following script section and `for` loop to the document body to print your Web browser's `Navigator` object properties:

```
<script type="text/javascript">
/* <![CDATA[ */
for (prop in navigator) {
    document.write(prop + ": " + navigator[prop] + "<br />");
}
/* ]]> */
</script>
```

4. Save the document as **Navigatorobjects.html** in the Chapter folder for Chapter 4 and validate it with the W3C Markup Validation Service. Once the document is valid, close it in your text editor and open it in your Web browser. Figure 4-19 shows the properties that are available in Firefox.

Figure 4-19
Navigator object
properties in Firefox

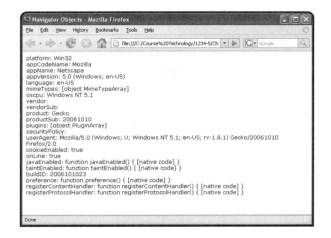

5. Close your Web browser window.

The Screen Object

Computer displays can vary widely, depending on the type and size of the monitor, the type of installed graphics card, and the screen resolution and color depth selected by the user. For example, some notebook computers have small screens with limited resolution while some desktop systems can have large monitors with very high resolution. The wide range of possible display settings makes it challenging to determine the size and positioning of windows generated by JavaScript. The **Screen object** is used to obtain information about the display screen's size, resolution, and color depth. Table 4-9 lists the properties of the Screen object that are supported by most current Web browsers, including Firefox and Internet Explorer.

Properties	Description
availHeight	Returns the height of the display screen, not including operating system features such as the Windows Taskbar
availWidth	Returns the width of the display screen, not including operating system features such as the Windows Taskbar
colorDepth	Returns the display screen's bit depth if a color palette is in use; if a color palette is not in use, returns the value of the pixelDepth property
height	Returns the height of the display screen
pixelDepth	Returns the display screen's color resolution in bits per pixel
width	Returns the width of the display screen

Table 4-9   Properties of the Screen object

The colorDepth and pixelDepth properties are most useful in determining the color resolution that the display supports. For example, if the colorDepth property returns a value of 32, which indicates high color resolution, then you can use JavaScript to display a high color image. However, if the colorDepth property returns a value of 16, which indicates medium color resolution, then you may want to use JavaScript to display a lower color image. The following code illustrates how to use the `colorDepth` property to determine which version of an image to display:

```
if (screen.colorDepth >= 32)
    document.write("<img href='companyLogo_highres.jpg' />");
else if (screen.colorDepth >= 16)
    document.write("<img href='companyLogo_mediumres.jpg' />");
else
    document.write("<img href='companyLogo_lowres.jpg' />");
```

The remaining `Screen` object properties determine the size of the display area. For example, on a computer with a screen resolution of 1024 by 768, the following statements print "Your screen resolution is 1024 by 768.":

```
var screenWidth = screen.width;
var screenHeight = screen.height;
document.write("<p>Your screen resolution is " + screenWidth
    + " by " + screenHeight + ".</p>");
```

One of the more common uses of the `Screen` object properties is to center a Web browser window in the middle of the display area. For windows generated with the `window.open()` method, you can center a window when it first displays by assigning values to the `left` and `top` options of the `options` argument. To center a window horizontally, subtract the width of the window from the screen width, divide the remainder by two, and assign the result to the `left` option. Similarly, to center a window vertically, subtract the height of the window from the screen height, divide the remainder by two, and assign the result to the `top` option. The following code demonstrates how to create a new window and center it in the middle of the display area:

```
var winWidth=300;
var winHeight=200;
var leftPosition = (screen.width-winWidth)/2;
var topPosition = (screen.height-winHeight)/2;
var optionString = "width=" + winWidth + ",height=" + winHeight +
",left=" + leftPosition + ",top=" + topPosition;
OpenWin = window.open("", "CtrlWindow", optionString);
```

Next, you modify the Pine Knoll Properties Web page so the property window is centered in the middle of the display area.

To modify the Pine Knoll Properties Web page so the property window is centered in the middle of the display area:

1. Return to the **PineKnollProperties.html** document in your text editor.
2. Modify the `showProperty()` function as follows so it uses the `Screen` object to calculate the left and top positions of the property window:

```
function showProperty(linkTarget) {
    var propertyWidth=400;
    var propertyHeight=350;
    var winLeft = (screen.width-propertyWidth)/2;
```

```
    var winTop = (screen.height-propertyHeight)/2;
    var winOptions = "toolbar=no,menubar=no,location=no,
        scrollbars=yes,resizable=no";
    winOptions += ",width=" + propertyWidth;
    winOptions += ",height=" + propertyHeight;
    winOptions += ",left=" + winLeft;
    winOptions += ",top=" + winTop;
    propertyWindow = window.open(linkTarget,
        "propertyInfo", winOptions);
      propertyWindow.focus();
}
```

3. Save the **PineKnollProperties.html** document and then validate it with the W3C Markup Validation Service. Once the document is valid, close it in your text editor and open it in your Web browser. Click one of the property links. The property window should open and be centered in the middle of your screen.

4. Close your Web browser window.

Referring to Frames and Windows

In this section, you learn how to refer to frames and windows from within your Web pages.

Using the `target` and `base` Attributes

One popular use of frames is to create a table of contents frame on the left side of a Web browser window with a display frame on the right side of the window. The display frame shows the contents of a URL selected from a link in the table of contents frame. This type of design eliminates the need to open a separate Web browser window when you want to display another document. In other words, it allows you to display a table of contents that users can use to navigate to other documents on a Web site.

Figure 4-20 shows a document that is split into two frames. Each frame displays a different document associated with a different URL. The left frame contains a document that lists the chapters in Jane Austen's *Mansfield Park*, and the right frame contains the author's introduction. When you click a chapter link in the left frame, the selected chapter opens in the right frame, as shown in Figure 4-21.

The following code shows the <frameset> and <frame> elements used to create the Mansfield Park page.

```
<frameset cols="250,*">
    <frame src="toc.html" name="toc" />
    <frame src="intro.html" name="content" />
</frameset>
```

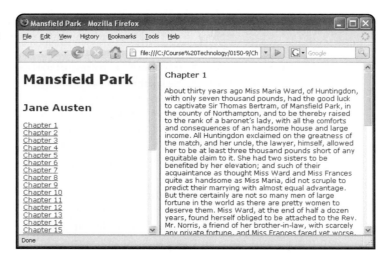

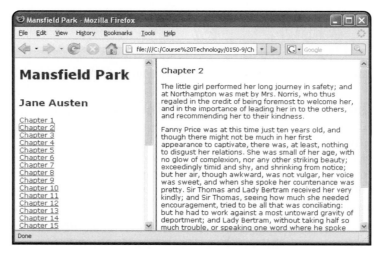

The Mansfield Park Web page creates two column frames. The first column is 250 pixels wide, and the second column takes up the remainder of the window. Two <frame> elements open documents in each individual frame. The document in the left frame contains hyperlinks for each structure name. To cause the document for each hyperlink to open in the right frame, you use the target attribute of the <a> element. You should already be familiar with the **target attribute**; this determines in which frame or Web browser window a document opens, based on the value assigned to an <a> element's target attribute or the value assigned to a <frame> element's name attribute. For example, the name assigned to the right frame in the Mansfield Park Web page is "content." When you click the Chapter 1 hyperlink in the left frame (named toc), the chapter01.html document opens in the content frame. The following is an example of the code that appears in the document displayed in the left frame. Notice that this code uses the target attribute repeatedly.

```
...
<h1>Mansfield Park</h1>
<h2>Jane Austen</h2>
<p><a href="chapter01.html" target="content">Chapter 1</a><br />
<a href="chapter02.html" target="content">Chapter 2</a><br />
<a href="chapter03.html" target="content">Chapter 3</a><br />
<a href="chapter04.html" target="content">Chapter 4</a><br />
...additional chapters
```

Next, you work on a prewritten, frame-based version of the Pine Knoll Properties Web page. You will find the prewritten documents in your Chapter folder for Chapter 4. If you open the main page, PineKnollPropertiesFrames.html, in your Web browser, you will see the Web page shown in Figure 4-22.

Figure 4-22

Frame-based version of the Pine Knoll Properties Web page

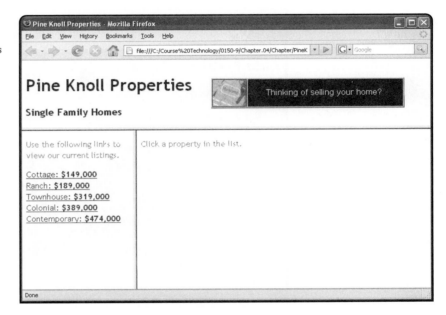

The problem with the Web page is that if you click on one of the links in the left frame (named PropertiesList.html), the target of the link opens in the left frame instead of the right frame. You add `target` attributes to the PropertiesList.html document so the links open in the right frame. The value assigned to the `name` attribute of the right frame is "propertyFrame".

To add `target` attributes to the PropertiesList.html document:

1. Open the **PropertiesList.html** document, located in your Chapter folder for Chapter 4, in your text editor.

2. Modify the <a> elements so they include a `target` attribute assigned a value of "propertyFrame", as follows:

   ```
   <a href="cottage_frame.html" target="propertyFrame">Cottage:
   <strong>$149,000</strong></a><br />
   ```

```
<a href="ranch_frame.html" target="propertyFrame">Ranch:
<strong>$189,000</strong></a><br />
<a href="townhouse_frame.html" target="propertyFrame">Townhouse:
<strong>$319,000</strong></a><br />
<a href="colonial_frame.html" target="propertyFrame">Colonial:
<strong>$389,000</strong></a><br />
<a href="contemporary_frame.html" target="propertyFrame">
Contemporary:<strong>$474,000</strong></a>
```

3. Save the **PropertiesList.html** document, and then open the
    PineKnollPropertiesFrames.html document in your Web browser. Figure 4-23
    shows how the Web page appears after clicking the colonial link.

Figure 4-23

Frames-based version of
the Pine Knoll Properties
Web page after adding
`target` attributes

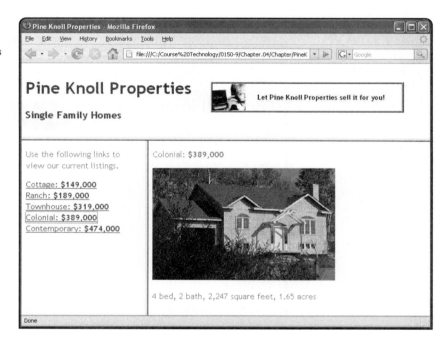

4. Close your Web browser window.

When you are using the same target frame for a long list of hyperlinks, you can also use the
<base> element. You use the `target` attribute with the **<base> element** to specify a default
target for all links in a document, using the assigned name of a window or frame. Although the
<base> element is available in the strict DTD, the `target` attribute is deprecated, so in order to
specify a default target link using the <base> element and the `target` attribute, you must use
the transitional DTD. The <base> element must be placed within the document head, not within
the document body. The following code shows the Mansfield Park Web page written more efficiently using the <base> element.

```
...
<link rel="stylesheet" href="js_styles.css" type="text/css" />
<base target="content" />
</head>
<body>
<h1>Mansfield Park</h1>
<h2>Jane Austen</h2>
<p><a href="chapter01.html">Chapter 1</a><br />
<a href="chapter02.html">Chapter 2</a><br />
<a href="chapter03.html">Chapter 3</a><br />
...additional chapters
```

Next, you modify the PropertiesList.html document so it includes a <base> element instead of multiple target attributes in the <a> elements.

To modify the PropertiesList.html document so it includes a <base> element instead of multiple target attributes in the <a> elements:

1. Return to the **PropertiesList.html** document in your text editor.

2. Add the following <base> element above the closing </head> tag:

   `<base target="propertyFrame" />`

3. Next, delete the `target="propertyFrame"` attributes from each of the <a> elements.

4. Save the **PropertiesList.html** document, and then open the **PineKnollPropertiesFrames.html** document in your Web browser window. The links should function the same as they did before you replaced the `target` attributes with the <base> element.

5. Close your Web browser window.

The `parent` Property

When working with multiple frames and windows, you need to be able to refer to individual frames and windows in JavaScript code. When you create a new window, for instance, you may want to change the content displayed in that window. Or, if you have multiple frames in a window, you may need to change the content displayed in one frame, depending on a link selected in another frame. Recall that the frames[] array contains all the frames in a window. The first frame in a window is referred to as frames[0], the second frame is referred to as frames[1], and so on. If a window contains no frames, then the frames[] array is empty. To refer to a frame within the same frameset, you use the **parent property** of the Window object combined with the frame's index number from the frames[] array. For example, if you have a Web page that creates four frames, the frames can be referred to as parent.frames[0], parent.frames[1], parent.frames[2], and parent.frames[3], respectively.

TIP

For detailed information on how to work with frames, refer to Don Gosselin's *XHTML*, published by Course Technology.

To understand better how to use the `parent` property and `frames[]` array, consider the Web page shown in Figure 4-24.

Figure 4-24

`parent` property and `frames[]` array example

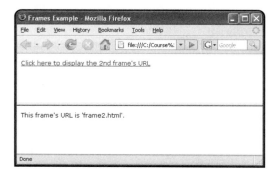

The two frames in Figure 4-24 were created using the following code:

```
<frameset rows="50%, 50%">
    <frame src="frame1.html" name="firstFrame" />
    <frame src="frame2.html" name="secondFrame" />
</frameset>
```

The first frame refers to the second frame's URL by using the following `onclick` event handler in an `<a>` element, as follows:

```
<p><a href=""
onclick="window.alert(parent.frames[1].location.href);return
false">Click here to display the 2nd frame's URL</a></p>
```

As you can see in the preceding code, the statement `parent.frames[1].location.href` returns the URL of the second frame. If the link were returning the first frame's URL, you would use the statement `self.location.href` or `parent.frames[0].location.href`. Note that to display the `href` property of the `Location` object, you must include `location` in the statement, because it is necessary to refer to all of an object's ancestors (with the exception of the `Window` object).

TIP

Remember that each frame contains its own `Window` object, as well as its own `Location`, `History`, and `Navigator` objects.

With nested frames, you can also use the `parent` property along with the name you assigned to a frame with the `<frame>` element. Nested frames are also assigned to the `frames[]` array in the order in which they are encountered. Figure 4-25 shows a variation of the script in Figure 4-24. In Figure 4-25, the column frame on the left is the first frame in the parent frameset. The two frames on the right are nested within the second frame of the parent frameset. For the column frame containing the button to obtain the URL of the last nested frame on the right, you use either `parent.frames[2].location.href` or `parent.thirdFrame.location.href` (assuming the last frame has been assigned a name of `thirdFrame` with the `<frame>` element).

Figure 4-25

Referencing a nested frame

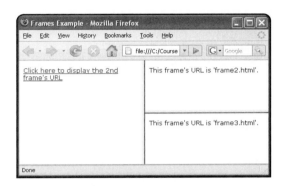

Although the `target` attribute and `<base>` elements work fine for determining in which window or frame to open the target of a link, the `target` attribute is deprecated. Your goal should be to write Web pages that conform to the strict DTD. In order for you to write a Web page that opens the target of a link in a specific frame, and for the Web page to conform to the strict DTD, you can use the `Location` object with the `parent` property and `frames[]` array. For example, to open the target of an `<a>` element in the second frame of the current frame-based Web page, you use an `onclick` event handler with the `<a>` element similar to the following. To prevent the current frame from also displaying the link target, you must return a value of false in the `onclick` event handler.

```
<a href="page.html"
onclick="parent.frames[2].location.href='page.html'" />
```

Next, you modify the PropertiesList.html document so the links open in the right frame using JavaScript.

To modify the PropertiesList.html document so the links open in the right frame using JavaScript:

1. Return to the **PropertiesList.html** document in your text editor.
2. Delete the `<base>` element from the document head.
3. Add `onclick` event handlers to each of the `<a>` elements, as follows:

```
<a href="cottage_frame.html"
onclick="parent.frames[2].location.href='cottage_frame.html';
return false"
>Cottage: <strong>$149,000</strong></a><br />
<a href="ranch_frame.html"
```

```
onclick="parent.frames[2].location.href='ranch_frame.html';
return false"
>Ranch: <strong>$189,000</strong></a><br />
<a href="townhouse_frame.html"
onclick="parent.frames[2].location.href='townhouse_frame.html';
return false"
>Townhouse: <strong>$319,000</strong></a><br />
<a href="colonial_frame.html"
onclick="parent.frames[2].location.href='colonial_frame.html';
return false"
>Colonial: <strong>$389,000</strong></a><br />
<a href="contemporary_frame.html"
onclick="parent.frames[2].location.href='contemporary_frame.html';
return false"
>Contemporary: <strong>$474,000</strong></a>
```

4. Finally, modify the <!DOCTYPE> so the Web page conforms to the strict DTD instead of the transitional DTD.

5. Save the **PropertiesList.html** document and validate it with the W3C Markup Validation Service. Once the document is valid, open the **PineKnollPropertiesFrames.html** document in your Web browser and test the links. The links should function the same as they did before you added the onclick event handlers.

6. Close your Web browser window.

The top Property

In addition to the self property, another property that is used to refer to a window is the top property of the Window object. The **top property** refers to the topmost window on a Web page. When working with frames, the top property refers to the window that constructed the frames. For example, if the code to create a parent frameset is located in a document named FramesExample.html, then the statement top.location.href would return the full URL for the FramesExample.html document, no matter in which frame it was used. When the top property is used on a Web page that does not contain frames, then it refers to the window itself.

Next, you modify the PropertiesList.html document so the links are opened using the top property instead of the parent property.

To modify the PropertiesList.html document so the links are opened using the top property instead of the parent property:

1. Return to the **PropertiesList.html** document in your text editor.

2. Modify the onclick event handlers in the <a> elements so the links are opened using the top property instead of the parent property, as follows:

```
<a href="cottage_frame.html"
onclick="top.frames[2].location.href='cottage_frame.html';
return false">
```

```
Cottage: <strong>$149,000</strong></a><br />
<a href="ranch_frame.html"
onclick="top.frames[2].location.href='ranch_frame.html';
return false">
Ranch: <strong>$189,000</strong></a><br />
<a href="townhouse_frame.html"
onclick="top.frames[2].location.href='townhouse_frame.html';
return false">
Townhouse: <strong>$319,000</strong></a><br />
<a href="colonial_frame.html"
onclick="top.frames[2].location.href='colonial_frame.html';
return false">
Colonial: <strong>$389,000</strong></a><br />
<a href="contemporary_frame.html"
onclick="top.frames[2].location.href='contemporary_frame.html';
return false">
Contemporary: <strong>$474,000</strong></a>
```

3. Save the **PropertiesList.html** document and validate it with the W3C Markup Validation Service. Once the PropertiesList.html document is valid, close it in your text editor, open the **PineKnollPropertiesFrames.html** document in your Web browser, and test the links. The links should function the same as they did before you added the top properties.

4. Close your Web browser window and text editor.

Chapter Summary

▶ The browser object model (BOM) or client-side object model is a hierarchy of objects, each of which provides programmatic access to a different aspect of the Web browser window or the Web page.

▶ The top-level object in the browser object model is the `Window` object, which represents a Web browser window or an individual frame within a window.

▶ To refer to a JavaScript object in code, you must refer to all of the objects that contain it, with the object names separated by periods.

▶ The `Document` object is arguably the most important object in the browser object model because it represents the Web page displayed in a browser.

▶ The `History` object maintains a history list of all the documents that have been opened during the current Web browser session.

▶ The `Location` object allows you to change to a new Web page from within JavaScript code.

▶ The `Navigator` object is used to obtain information about the current Web browser.

▶ The `with` statement eliminates the need to retype the name of an object when properties of the same object are being referenced in a series.

▶ The `Screen` object is used to obtain information about the display screen's size, resolution, and color depth.

▶ The `target` attribute determines in which frame or Web browser window a document opens, based on the value assigned to an `<a>` element's `target` attribute or the value assigned to a `<frame>` element's `name` attribute.

▶ You use the `target` attribute with the `<base>` element to specify a default target for all links in a document, using the assigned name of a window or frame.

▶ To refer to a frame within the same frameset, you use the `parent` property of the `Window` object combined with the frame's index number from the `frames[]` array.

▶ The `top` property refers to the topmost window on a Web page.

Review Questions

1. Which of the following objects is also referred to as the global object?

   a. `Document` object

   b. `Window` object

   c. `Browser` object

   d. `Screen` object

2. Which of the following elements in the browser object model are referenced with arrays? (Choose all that apply.)

   a. images

   b. frames

c. forms

d. paragraphs

3. Which of the following terms does not refer to the browser object model?

a. Firefox object model

b. JavaScript object model

c. client-side object model

d. Navigator object model

4. You must use the `Window` object or `self` property when referencing a property or method of the `Window` object. True or false?

5. Explain how to override an event with an event handler function.

6. Which of the following events are used to create rollover effects? (Choose all that apply.)

a. `onclick`

b. `onload`

c. `onmouseover`

d. `onmouseout`

7. Explain how to open a blank window with the `window.open()` method.

8. You use the options string of the `window.open()` method to specify any elements that you do not want created for the new window. True or false?

9. Which of the following arguments of the options string of the `window.open()` method identifies the horizontal coordinate where the window will be positioned?

a. `left`

b. `leftPosition`

c. `x-axis`

d. `moveTo`

10. Explain why you should include the `Window` object or `self` property when using the `open()` and `close()` methods of the `Window` object.

11. How do you control a new window that you created with JavaScript code?

a. by using the appropriate element in the `windows[]` array of the Windows object

b. by using the `name` argument of the `window.open()` method

c. You cannot control a new window with JavaScript code.

d. by assigning the new `Window` object created with the `window.open()` method to a variable

12. Explain the difference between the `setTimeout()` and `setInterval()` methods. Which method is most often used for starting animation code that executes repeatedly?

13. You can use JavaScript code to navigate through a history list, but only if the currently displayed Web page exists within the same domain as the Web page containing the JavaScript code that is attempting to move through the list. True or false?

14. The full URL of a Web page is located in the _____ property of the `Location` object.

    a. `href`

    b. `hash`

    c. `src`

    d. `url`

15. Which property of the `Navigator` object returns the Web browser name?

    a. `browser`

    b. `browserName`

    c. `appName`

    d. `platform`

16. Explain how to use the `with` statement to reference an object's properties.

17. Which of the following properties of the `Screen` object returns the height of the display screen, not including operating system features such as the Windows Taskbar?

    a. `displayHeight`

    b. `screenHeight`

    c. `availHeight`

    d. `height`

18. Explain how to center a window when it is created with the `window.open()` method.

19. To refer to a frame within the same frameset, you use the _____ property of the `Window` object combined with the frame's index number from the `frames[]` array.

    a. `target`

    b. `parent`

    c. `base`

    d. `frame`

20. Which of the following properties of the `Window` object refers to the topmost window on a Web page?

    a. `main`

    b. `core`

    c. `top`

    d. `principal`

Hands-On Projects

Project 4-1

Most Windows applications include an About dialog box that displays copyright and other information about the program. In this project, you create a script that opens a new window that is similar to an About dialog box.

1. Create a new document in your text editor and type the `<!DOCTYPE>` declaration, `<html>` element, header information, and the `<body>` element. Use the strict DTD and "About Dialog Box Example" as the content of the `<title>` element.

2. Add a form to the document body that includes a single command button that reads "About this JavaScript Program."

3. Add code to the Web page that opens a new browser window when a user clicks the command button. Make the new window 100 pixels high by 300 pixels wide, and centered in the middle of the screen. Do not use any other display options. The new browser window should display a document named About.html (which you will create later in this exercise).

4. Save the document as **AboutExample.html** in the Projects folder for Chapter 4.

5. Use the W3C Markup Validation Service to validate the **AboutExample.html** document and fix any errors that the document contains. Once the document is valid, close it in your text editor.

6. Create a Web page that conforms to the strict DTD that displays a single paragraph with the following text. Be sure to use your name in the paragraph.

   `<p>This program was created by your name. </p>`

7. Add a button to the document body that closes the current window.

8. Save the document as **About.html** in the Projects folder for Chapter 4.

9. Use the W3C Markup Validation Service to validate the **About.html** document and fix any errors that the document contains. Once the document is valid, close it in your text editor.

10. Open **AboutExample.html** in your Web browser and test the script's functionality. The About window should appear centered in the middle of your screen.

11. Close your Web browser window.

Project 4-2

In this exercise, you create a script that repeatedly flashes advertising messages in a text box for a company named "Forestville Foods".

1. Create a new document in your text editor and type the `<!DOCTYPE>` declaration, `<html>` element, header information, and the `<body>` element. Use the transitional DTD and "Forestville Foods" as the content of the `<title>` element.

2. Add a script section to the document head, as follows:

```
<script type="text/javascript">
/* <![CDATA[ */
/* ]]> */
</script>
```

3. Next, add the following heading elements and form to the document body, which will display the quote:

```
<h1>Forestville Foods</h1>
<h2>Party Platters</h2>
<form action="">
<p><input type="text" name="message" size="60"
value="Place your Thanksgiving orders today!" /></p>
</form>
```

4. Add to the script section the following code, which changes the portion of the warning that is displayed in a text box:

```
var curMessage="message1";
var changeMessage;
function adMessage() {
      if (curMessage == "message2") {
            document.advertising.message.value
                  = "Place your Thanksgiving orders today!";
            curMessage = "message1";
      }
      else {
            document.advertising.message.value
              = "All orders must be received by November 20th!";
            curMessage = "message2";
      }
}
```

5. Finally, add the following `onload` event handler to the opening `<body>` tag:

```
<body onload="var changeQuote=setInterval('adMessage()',
2000);">
```

6. Save the document as **ThanksgivingOrders.html** in the Projects folder for Chapter 4.

7. Use the W3C Markup Validation Service to validate the **ThanksgivingOrders.html** document and fix any errors that the document contains. Once the document is valid, close it in your text editor and then open it in your Web browser. The quote should change every few seconds.

8. Close your Web browser window.

Project 4-3

In this exercise, you create a script that changes that status bar text every few seconds.

1. Create a new document in your text editor and type the <!DOCTYPE> declaration, <html> element, header information, and the <body> element. Use the strict DTD and "Holiday Sale" as the content of the <title> element.

2. Add a script section to the document head, as follows:

```
<script type="text/javascript">
/* <![CDATA[ */
/* ]]> */
</script>
```

3. Add the following onload event handler to the opening <body> tag. The onload event handler uses the setInterval() method to continuously call a function named changingStatus() every 2,000 milliseconds.

```
<body onload="begin=setInterval('changingStatus()', 2000);">
```

4. Add the following global variable and function to the script section. The function uses an if...else statement to change the value displayed in the status bar.

```
window.defaultStatus = "Don's Department Store";
function changingStatus() {
        if (window.status == "From now until January 1!")
                window.status = "Prices slashed by 30%!";
        else
                window.status = "From now until January 1!";
}
```

5. Add the following text and elements to the document body:

```
<h1>Don's Department Store</h1>
<h2>Holiday Sale</h2>
```

6. Save the document as **HolidaySale.html** in the Projects folder for Chapter 4.

7. Use the W3C Markup Validation Service to validate the **HolidaySale.html** document and fix any errors that the document contains. Once the document is valid, close it in your text editor and then open it in your Web browser. The status bar text should change every two seconds.

8. Close your Web browser window.

Project 4-4

In this project, you will create a script that redirects users to a different Web page after 10 seconds, or allows them to click a hyperlink.

1. Create a new document in your text editor and type the <!DOCTYPE> declaration, <html> element, header information, and the <body> element. Use the strict DTD and "New Web Address" as the content of the <title> element.

2. Add a script section to the document head, as follows:

```
<script type="text/javascript">
/* <![CDATA[ */
/* ]]> */
</script>
```

3. Add to the script section the following global variable declaration and function to handle the task of redirecting the Web page:

```
var killRedirect;
function newURL() {
        location.href="NewURL.html";
}
```

4. Add the following `onload` event handler to the opening `<body>` tag:

```
<body onload="killRedirect = setTimeout('newURL()', 10000);">
```

5. Now add the following elements and text to the document body:

```
<h2>The URL for the Web page you are trying to reach has
changed!</h2>
<p><strong>You will be automatically redirected in ten
seconds. Click the link if JavaScript is disabled in your
browser.</strong></p>
<p>Be sure to update your bookmark!</p>
<p><a href="UpdatedURL.html">UpdatedURL.html</a></p>
```

6. Save the document as **Redirect.html** in the Projects folder for Chapter 4.

7. Use the W3C Markup Validation Service to validate the **Redirect.html** document and fix any errors that the document contains. Once the document is valid, close it in your text editor.

8. Create a Web page that conforms to the strict DTD that displays a single paragraph with the following text:

```
<p>You have reached the updated Web page.</p>
```

9. Save the document as **UpdatedURL.html** in the Projects folder for Chapter 4.

10. Use the W3C Markup Validation Service to validate the **UpdatedURL.html** document and fix any errors that the document contains. Once the document is valid, close it in your text editor and then open the **Redirect.html** document in your Web browser. In 10 seconds, the UpdatedURL.html document should open automatically.

11. Close your Web browser window.

Project 4-5

In addition to specifying the size and position of a window when it first opens, you can also change the size and position of an open window by using methods of the `Window` object. The `resizeTo()` method resizes a window to a specified size, and the `moveTo()` method moves a window to an absolute position. Using these methods, along with properties of the Screen object, you will create a script that resizes and repositions an open window so it fills the screen.

1. Create a new document in your text editor and type the `<!DOCTYPE>` declaration, `<html>` element, header information, and the `<body>` element. Use the strict DTD and "Maximize Browser Window" as the content of the `<title>` element.

2. Add a form to the document body that includes two command buttons: one that reads "Create New Window" and another that reads "Maximize New Window".

3. Add a script section to the document head, as follows:

```
<script type="text/javascript">
/* <![CDATA[ */
/* ]]> */
</script>
```

4. Add the following function for the Create New Window button. This function opens a document named MaxWindow.html (which you create shortly) in a new browser window, centered in the middle of the screen, when a user clicks the command button.

```
var maxWindow;
function createWindow() {
        var winWidth=300;
        var winHeight=100;
        var winLeft = (screen.width-winWidth)/2;
        var winTop = (screen.height-winHeight)/2;
        var winOptions = ",width=" + winWidth;
        winOptions += ",height=" + winHeight;
        winOptions += ",left=" + winLeft;
        winOptions += ",top=" + winTop;
        maxWindow = window.open("MaxWindow.html", "newWindow",
        winOptions);
        maxWindow.focus();
}
```

5. Add the following function for the Maximize New Window button. The first statement in the function uses the `moveTo()` method of the `Window` object to move the window named maxWindow (which is created by the `createWindow()` function) to position 0, 0, which represents the upper-left corner of the screen. The second statement uses the `resizeTo()` method of the `Window` object and the `availWidth` and `availHeight` properties of the `Screen` object to maximize the window. The final statement changes focus to the maximized window.

```
function maximizeWindow() {
        maxWindow.moveTo(0,0);
        maxWindow.resizeTo(screen.availWidth, screen.availHeight);
        maxWindow.focus();
}
```

6. Save the document as **MaximizeBrowser.html** in the Projects folder for Chapter 4.

7. Use the W3C Markup Validation Service to validate the **MaximizeBrowser.html** document and fix any errors that the document contains. Once the document is valid, close it in your text editor.

8. Create a Web page that conforms to the strict DTD and add the following text and elements to the document body:

```
<p><strong>Resizing and Repositioning Example</strong></p>
<form action="">
<p><input type="button" value="Close Window"
    onclick="window.close();" /></p>
</form>
```

9. Save the document as **MaxWindow.html** in the Projects folder for Chapter 4.

10. Use the W3C Markup Validation Service to validate the **MaxWindow.html** document and fix any errors that the document contains. Once the document is valid, close it in your text editor.

11. Open **MaximizeBrowser.html** in your Web browser and click the **Create New Window** button. The new window should appear centered in the middle of your screen. Return to the **MaximizeBrowser.html** in your Web browser and click the Maximize New Window button. The new window should be resized and repositioned to fill the screen.

12. Close your Web browser window.

Project 4-6

In this project, you will create a Web page for a greeting card company. The page will contain links that display images of greeting cards in a separate window. Your Projects folder for Chapter 4 contains the following greeting card images that you can use for this project: birthday.jpg, halloween.jpg, mothersday.jpg, newyear.jpg, and valentine.jpg.

1. Create a new document in your text editor and type the <!DOCTYPE> declaration, <html> element, header information, and the <body> element. Use the strict DTD and "Gervais Greeting Cards" as the content of the <title> element.

2. Add the following text and elements to the document body. The onclick events in the links call a function named showCard() that handles the process of displaying each greeting card in a separate window. You create the showCard() function next.

```
<h1>Gervais Greeting Cards</h1>
<h2>All Occasions</h2>
<hr />
<p><a href="valentine.jpg" onclick="showCard('valentine.jpg');
return false">
Valentine's Day</a><br />
<a href="mothersday.jpg" onclick="showCard('mothersday.jpg');
return false">
Mother's Day</a><br />
```

```
<a href="halloween.jpg" onclick="showCard('halloween.jpg');
return false">
Halloween</a><br />
<a href="newyear.jpg" onclick="showCard('newyear.jpg');
return false">
New Year</a><br />
<a href="birthday.jpg" onclick="showCard('birthday.jpg');
return false">
Birthday</a></p>
```

3. Add a script section to the document head, as follows:

```
<script type="text/javascript">
/* <![CDATA[ */
/* ]]> */
</script>
```

4. Add the following global variable to the script section. This variable will represent the window that will display the greeting card images.

```
var cardWindow;
```

5. Add the following function to the end of the script section. The function opens a new window, centered in the middle of the screen, that displays the selected greeting card image.

```
function showCard(linkTarget) {
    var propertyWidth=400;
    var propertyHeight=350;
    var winLeft = (screen.width-propertyWidth)/2;
    var winTop = (screen.height-propertyHeight)/2;
    var winOptions = "toolbar=no,menubar=no,location=no,
        scrollbars=yes,resizable=no";
    winOptions += ",width=" + propertyWidth;
    winOptions += ",height=" + propertyHeight;
    winOptions += ",left=" + winLeft;
    winOptions += ",top=" + winTop;
    cardWindow = window.open(linkTarget, "propertyInfo",
    winOptions);
    cardWindow.focus();
}
```

6. Save the document as **GreetingCards.html** in the Projects folder for Chapter 4.

7. Use the W3C Markup Validation Service to validate the **GreetingCards.html** document and fix any errors that the document contains. Once the document is valid, close it in your text editor, open it in your Web browser, and test the functionality.

8. Close your Web browser window.

Case Projects

For the following projects, save the files you create in your Cases folder for Chapter 4. Be sure to validate each Web page with the W3C Markup Validation Service.

Case Project 4-1

Your Cases folder for Chapter 4 contains five advertising images for a concert series, concert1.gif through concert5.gif. Create a script that cycles through the images, displaying each image for five seconds. Save the document as **ConcertAds.html**.

Case Project 4-2

Create a Web page that opens a new window when the user leaves the page. The new window should display the text "Thanks for visiting" and contain a button that closes the window. Also include the text "Be sure to visit our partner Web sites", followed by a list of at least five of your favorite Web sites. Include a <base> element in the document head that opens the partner Web pages in a window named partnerSite. Use the options argument of the Window object's open() method so the window fills the screen when it first opens. Do not make the window resizable and do not display any other options, such as the scroll bars and status bar. Save the main document as **Exit.html** and the document that opens in the new window as **ExitWindow.html**.

Case Project 4-3

Many online real estate companies include multiple photos for the properties they list. Your Cases folder for Chapter 4 contains four additional photos of the townhouse property, townhouse2.jpg through townhouse5.jpg, which show interior views of the townhouse. Copy these images to your Chapter folder for Chapter 4 and modify the townhouse.html document so users can navigate through all five photos. Use two separate functions for the forward and backward navigational functionality. Each function should allow users to cycle forward or backward continuously through the five images. A common use of the onmouseover and onmouseout event handlers is to change the button image displayed for a navigational link on a Web page. For example, holding your mouse over an image of a Home button (that jumps to the Web site's home page) will replace the image with one that is somehow more vivid in order to clearly identify the page that is the target of the link. Your Cases folder for Chapter 4 contains four images, next_blue.gif, next_red.gif, previous_blue.gif, and previous_red.gif, which represent typical forward and backward navigational buttons you will find on a Web site. Copy these images to your Chapter folder for Chapter 4, and use them to represent next and previous links that users can click to move forward or backward through the townhouse images. Holding your mouse over the blue version of each image should display the red version of the image, while moving your mouse off the image should display the blue version. Make any other changes that are necessary to the PineKnollProperties.html or townhouse.html documents.

5

Validating Form Data with JavaScript

In this chapter you will:

- Study form elements and objects
- Use JavaScript to manipulate and validate form elements
- Learn how to submit and reset forms
- Learn how to validate submitted form data

Forms are one of the most common Web page elements used with JavaScript. Typical forms you may encounter on the Web include order forms, surveys, and applications. You can use JavaScript to make sure data was entered properly into the form fields and to perform other types of pre-processing before the data is sent to the server. Without JavaScript, the only action that a Web page can take on form data is to send it to a server for processing.

Overview of Forms

Many Web sites use forms to collect information from users and transmit that information to a server for processing. Typical forms you may encounter on the Web include order forms, surveys, and applications. Figure 5-1 shows part of a form that people can use to apply for an account on MySpace.com.

Another type of form frequently found on Web pages gathers search criteria from a user. After the user enters search criteria, the data is sent to a database on a Web server. The server then queries the database, using the data gathered in the search form, and returns the results to a Web browser. Figure 5-2 shows an example of the advanced search form from Barnes & Noble.com. If you enter "Don Gosselin" in the Author's Name field and click the Search button, the Web server returns results similar to those shown in Figure 5-3.

Forms are usually set up so that the data collected is transmitted to a server-side scripting language program on a Web server. As you learned in Chapter 1, such programs execute on the Web server and not in a browser, as is the case with the JavaScript programs you have created in this book. Some of the more popular server-side scripting languages that are used to process form data include PHP, Common Gateway Interface (CGI), Active Server Pages (ASP), and Java Server Pages (JSP). Because the focus of this book is on client-side JavaScript, you will create a program that submits forms to a document named FormProcessor.html rather than to a Web server. The document FormProcessor.html, located in your Chapter folder for Chapter 5, uses JavaScript code to display the values submitted from a form. The only purpose of the FormProcessor.html document is to display form data and provide a simple simulation of the response you would normally receive from a server-side scripting program.

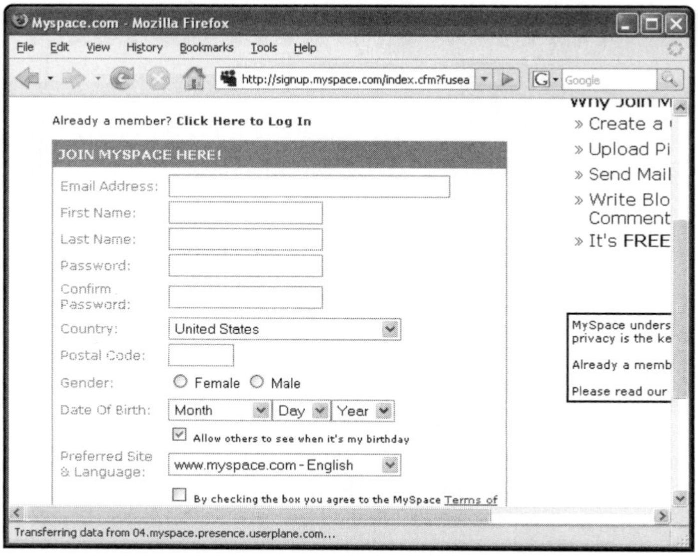

Figure 5-1

MySpace.com sign-up form

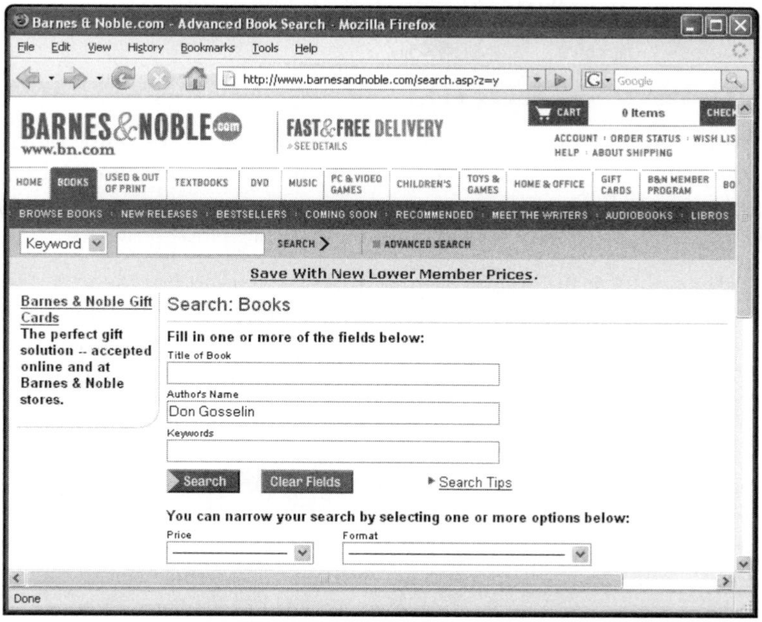

Figure 5-2

Barnes & Noble.com advanced search page

Figure 5-3

Barnes & Noble.com
results page

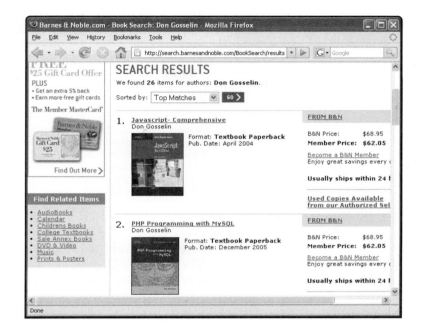

TIP

If a form requires advanced or complex validation or processing, it is a good idea to have a server-side script do the work. Servers are usually much more powerful than a desktop computer or workstation.

Understanding Form Elements and Objects

In this section, you learn about the primary form elements and how to access them with JavaScript.

The `<form>` Element

The `<form>` element designates a form within a Web page and contains all the text and elements that make up a form. You can include as many forms as you like on a Web page, although you cannot nest one form inside another form. Table 5-1 lists the attributes you can use with the `<form>` element.

TIP

To help ensure that your Web pages are well formed, you should always type the opening `<form>` tag and the closing `</form>` tag at the same time, and then go back and fill in the elements and content that you want to appear in the form.

Attribute	Description
accept-charset	Specifies a comma-separated list of possible character sets that the form supports
action	Required attribute that specifies a URL to which form data is submitted If this attribute is excluded, the data is sent to the URL that contains the form Typically you would specify an e-mail address or the URL of a program on a server
enctype	Specifies the MIME type of the data being submitted The default value is application/x-www-form-urlencoded
method	Determines how form data is submitted: the two options for this attribute are "get" and "post"; the default option, "get", appends form data as one long string to the URL specified by the action attribute; the "post" option sends form data as a transmission separate from the URL specified by the action attribute; although "get" is the default, "post" is considered the preferred option, because it allows the server to receive the data separately from the URL

Table 5-1   Attributes of the <form> element

The enctype attribute is important because a server-side scripting program can use its value to determine how to process the form data. The default MIME type of application/x-www-form-urlencoded specifies that form data should be encoded as one long string. The only other MIME types allowed with the enctype attribute are multipart/form-data, which encodes each field as a separate section, and text/plain, which is used to upload a document to a Web server or to submit form data to an e-mail address. With the exception of when you submit form data to an e-mail address, you should normally use the default MIME type of application/x-www-form-urlencoded.

NOTE

MIME is a protocol that was originally developed to allow different document types to be transmitted as attachments to e-mail messages. Now MIME has become a standard method of exchanging files over the Internet. You specify MIME types with two-part codes separated by a forward slash (/). The first part specifies the MIME type, and the second part specifies the MIME subtype.

Instead of submitting form data to a Web server, you can set up a form to send data to an e-mail address. Sending form data to an e-mail address is much simpler than creating and managing a script on a Web server. Instead of relying on a complex script on a Web server to process the data, you rely on the recipient of the e-mail message to process the data. For large organizations that deal with hundreds or thousands of orders a day, e-mailing form data is not an ideal solution. But for smaller companies or Web sites that do not have a high volume of orders, e-mailing form data is an option. To e-mail form data, you replace the Web server script's URL in the <form> element's action attribute with the mailto protocol, as follows: action="mailto:email_address". Separate multiple recipients with commas. You can also use a question mark (?) to append the following options to the e-mail address in a mailto protocol: to, cc, bcc, subject, and body. (Using the to option is the equivalent of separate multiple recipients with commas.) Options appended to the mailto protocol are also separated by commas. For example, the mailto protocol assigned to the following action attribute sends the form data to two recipients, copies a third recipient, and specifies a subject line:

```
action="mailto:reservations@skywardflyers.com,billing@skywardflyers.com?
cc=group_tours@skywardflyers.com, subject=group reservations"
```

When you use the `mailto` protocol, be sure to use the `enctype` of "text/plain", which ensures that the data arrives at the e-mail address in a readable format.

TIP

You can also use the `mailto` protocol with anchor (`<a>`) elements.

Form Controls

There are four primary elements used within the `<form>` element to create form controls: `<input>`, `<button>`, `<select>`, and `<textarea>`. The `<input>` and `<button>` elements are used to create input fields with which users interact. The `<input>` element is the most commonly used form element and allows you to create the following types of form controls:

- Text boxes
- Password boxes
- Radio buttons
- Check boxes
- Push buttons
- File boxes
- Hidden form fields
- Submit buttons
- Image submit buttons
- Reset buttons

The `<select>` element displays choices in a drop-down menu or scrolling list known as a selection list. The `<textarea>` element is used to create a text field in which users can enter multiple lines of information. Any form element into which a user can enter data (such as a text box) or that a user can select or change (such as a radio button) is called a **field**.

The `<input>`, `<textarea>`, and `<select>` elements can include `name` and `value` attributes. The `name` attribute defines a name for an element, and the `value` attribute defines a default value. When you submit a form to a Web server, the form data is submitted in name=value pairs, based on the `name` and `value` attributes of each element. For example, consider the following element, which creates a text `<input>` field:

```
<input type="text" name="company_info" value="Skyward Flyers" />
```

For the preceding element, a name=value pair of "company_info=Skyward Flyers" will be sent to a Web server (unless the user types something else into the field). If you intend to have your script submit forms to a Web server, you must include a `name` attribute for each `<input>`, `<textarea>`, and `<select>` element.

TIP
You are not required to include a `value` attribute or enter a value into a field before the form data is submitted.

NOTE
How form controls are rendered depends on the type of Web browser as well as the operating system. You may notice differences in how form controls appear between Windows and Macintosh operating systems and between different versions of the same operating system. For instance, there is a noticeable difference in how form controls are rendered in Windows 2000 and how they render in Windows XP. The figures in this chapter were generated using Firefox 2.0 running on Windows XP.

Using JavaScript with Forms

JavaScript is often used with forms to validate or process form data before the data is submitted to a server-side script. For example, customers may use an online order form to order merchandise from your Web site. When customers click the form's Submit button, you need to make sure that their information, such as the shipping address and credit card number, is entered correctly. To use JavaScript to access form controls and verify form information, you use the **Form object**, which represents a form on a Web page. The `Form` object is part of the browser object model, which you studied in Chapter 4, and contains properties, methods, and events that you can use to manipulate forms and form controls.

You can use JavaScript to access form controls created with any of the primary form elements, `<input>`, `<button>`, `<select>`, and `<textarea>`. This chapter focuses on how to use JavaScript with the `<input>` and `<select>` elements. However, you can also use many of the JavaScript techniques you learn in this chapter with the `<button>` and `<textarea>` elements.

Referencing Forms and Form Elements

Recall from Chapter 4 that some of the objects in the browser object model are arrays of other objects. For instance, the `Window` object includes a `frames[]` array that contains all the frames in a window. Similarly, the `Document` object includes a `forms[]` array that contains all the forms on a Web page. If a window does not contain any forms, then the `forms[]` array is empty. The first form in a document is referred to as `document.forms[0]`, the second form is referred to as `document.forms[1]`, and so on.

Prior to the development of XHTML, the most common way to refer to a form with JavaScript was to append the value assigned to the `<form>` element's `name` attribute to the `Document` object. For example, if you had a form with a `name` attribute that was assigned a value of "orderForm", you referred to the form in JavaScript as `document.orderForm`. However, the `<form>` element's `name` attribute is deprecated in XHTML. Although you can still use it with the transitional DTD, it is no longer available with the strict DTD. Therefore, if you want your Web pages to be well formed according to the strict DTD, you must avoid using the `name` attribute with your `<form>` elements. Referencing a form by its position in the `forms[]` array is usually not that difficult because most Web pages rarely include more than one form.

Just as the `Document` object has a `forms[]` array, the `Form` object has an `elements[]` array. You can use it to reference each element on a form. The **`elements[]` array** contains objects representing each of the controls in a form. Each element on a form is assigned to the `elements[]` array in the order in which it is encountered by the JavaScript interpreter. To refer to an element on a form, you reference the index number of the form in the `forms[]` array, followed by the appropriate element index number from the `elements[]` array. For example, if you want to refer to the first element in the first form on a Web page, use the statement `document.forms[0].elements[0];`. The third element in the second form is referenced using the statement `document.forms[1].elements[2];`. The following code shows an example of how each element on a form is assigned to the `elements[]` array:

```
<form action="post">
// The following element is assigned to elements[0]
Customer name: <input type="text" name="customer" /><br />
// The following element is assigned to elements[1]
E-mail address: <input type="text" name="email" /><br />
// The following element is assigned to elements[2]
Telephone: <input type="text" name="phone" /><br />
// The following element is assigned to elements[3]
Fax: <input type="text" name="fax" /><br />
</form>
```

Although the `name` attribute is deprecated in XHTML for the `<form>` element, it is still available for form control elements. In fact, if you plan to have your script submit a form to a server-side script, you must include a `name` attribute for each form element. This gives the server-side script a way to identify each piece of form data. Naming an element also gives you an alternative to referencing the element by its position in the `elements[]` array, which can be tedious if you have many fields on a form. For example, if you have an element named `quantity` in the first form on a Web page, you can refer to it using the statement `document.forms[0].quantity;`.

The `Form` Object

Tables 5-2, 5-3, and 5-4 list the properties, events, and methods of the `Form` object.

Property	Description
acceptCharset	Returns a comma-separated list of possible character sets that the form supports
action	Returns the URL to which form data is submitted
elements[]	Returns an array of a form's elements
enctype	Sets or returns a string representing the MIME type of the data being submitted
length	Returns an integer representing the number of elements in the form
method	Sets or returns a string representing one of the two options for submitting form data: "get" or "post"
name	Sets or returns the value assigned to the form's name attribute
target	Sets or returns the target window where responses are displayed after submitting the form

Table 5-2   Form object properties

CHAPTER 5

Event	Description
reset	Executes when a form's reset button is clicked
submit	Executes when a form's submit button is clicked

Table 5-3   Form object events

Method	Description
reset()	Resets a form without the use of a reset button
submit()	Submits a form without the use of a submit button

Table 5-4   Form object methods

Next, you start creating a Web page for a newspaper called *The Gosselin Gazette*. The Web page will contain a subscription form that you will work on throughout this chapter.

To start creating *The Gosselin Gazette* Newspaper Subscription form:

1. Start your text editor and create a new document.

2. Type the `<!DOCTYPE>` declaration, `<html>` element, header information, and the `<body>` element. Use the strict DTD and "Gosselin Gazette Subscription Form" as the content of the `<title>` element. Include a `<link>` element that links to the js_styles.css style sheet in your Chapter folder. Your document should appear as follows:

```
<!DOCTYPE html PUBLIC "-//W3C//DTD XHTML 1.0 Strict//EN"
"http://www.w3.org/TR/xhtml1/DTD/xhtml1-strict.dtd">
<html xmlns="http://www.w3.org/1999/xhtml">
<head>
<title>Gosselin Gazette Subscription Form</title>
<meta http-equiv="content-type" content="text/html;
charset=iso-8859-1" />
<link rel="stylesheet" href="js_styles.css" type="text/css" />
</head>
<body>
</body>
</html>
```

3. Add the following script section to the end of the document head:

```
<script type="text/javascript">
/* <![CDATA[ */
/* ]]> */
</script>
```

4. Add the following heading elements to the document body:

```
<h1>Gosselin Gazette Subscription Form</h1>
<h2>Customer Information</h2>
```

5. Add the following two tags to the end of the document body to create the form section. Throughout the following sections of this chapter, you will add form elements between these tags. Notice that the form's `action` attribute submits the form data to the FormProcessor.html document, and the `method` attribute submits the form data using the "get" option in order to append the form data as one long string to the FormProcessor.html URL. This allows the JavaScript code within the FormProcessor.html document to display the data in the Web browser.

```
<form action="FormProcessor.html" method="get"
enctype="application/x-www-form-urlencoded">
</form>
```

6. Save the document as **Subscription.html** in your Chapter folder for Chapter 5. Do not open the Subscription.html document in a Web browser, because it does not yet contain any form elements.

Working with Input Fields

The empty `<input>` element is used to generate **input fields** that create different types of interface elements, such as text boxes, radio buttons, and so on. The input fields are used to gather information from the user. Table 5-5 lists the attributes of the `<input>` element.

NOTE
Table 5-5 lists only attributes of the `<input>` element that are available in the strict DTD.

The `checked` attribute in Table 5-5, along with several other attributes you will encounter in HTML and XHTML, is a Boolean attribute, which specifies one of two values: true or false. In HTML, you can specify that the check box control is selected, or checked, by default by including the Boolean `checked` attribute within the `<input>` element, as follows:

```
<input type="checked" checked />
```

When a Boolean attribute is not assigned a value, as in the preceding code, it is referred to as having a **minimized form**. However, recall from Chapter 1 that all attribute values must appear within quotation marks. This syntax also means that an attribute must be assigned a value. For this reason, minimized Boolean attributes are illegal in XHTML. You can still use Boolean attributes in XHTML provided you use their full form. You create the **full form** of a Boolean attribute by assigning the name of the attribute itself as the attribute's value. For example, to use the `<input>` element's `checked` Boolean attribute in XHTML, you use the full form of the attribute as follows:

```
<input type="checked" checked="checked" />
```

Attribute	Description
accept	Determines the MIME type of a document that is uploaded with a file box
alt	Provides alternate text for an image submit button
checked	Determines whether or not a radio button or a check box is selected; a Boolean attribute
disabled	Disables a control
maxlength	Accepts an integer value that determines the number of characters that can be entered into a field
name	Designates a name for the element; part of the name=value pair that is used to submit data to a Web server
readonly	Prevents users from changing values in a control
size	Accepts an integer value that determines the width of a text box in characters
src	Specifies the URL of an image
type	Specifies the type of element to be rendered; type is a required attribute; valid values are text, password, radio, check box, reset, button, submit, image, file, and hidden
value	Sets an initial value in a field or a label for buttons; part of the name=value pair that is used to submit data to a Web server

Table 5-5   Attributes of the <input> element

Remember that to specify a value of false for a Boolean attribute, you simply exclude the attribute from the element. If you do not want a check box control to be selected by default, for instance, you simply exclude the checked attribute from the <input> element as follows:

```
<input type="checked" />
```

One of the most important attributes of the <input> element is the type attribute, which determines the type of element to be rendered and is a required attribute. Valid values for the type attribute are text, password, radio, check box, reset, button, submit, image, file, and hidden. Each of these attributes creates a different element. You will study how to use JavaScript with the controls created with the text, password, button, radio, and check box values next. Later in this chapter, you will learn how to use JavaScript with controls created with the reset and submit values.

Input Field Objects

The elements[] array stores objects that represent each type of form control. For the different types of controls that can be created with an <input> element, each control is represented by an object that is similar to the name of the control; a text box is represented by an Input object, a radio button list is represented by a Radio object, a check box is represented by a Checkbox object, and so on. Don't worry about the exact names of each type of input field object because you will never need to refer to them in your scripts. You do need to understand that each of these objects includes various properties and methods. The availability of each property or method depends on the type of form control. For example, the Input object includes a checked property that is only available to check boxes and radio buttons. Tables 5-6 and 5-7 list the properties and methods of the input field object, along with the form controls for which they are available.

Property	Description	Form controls
accept	Sets or returns a comma-separated list of MIME types that can be uploaded	File boxes
accessKey	Sets or returns a keyboard shortcut that users can press to jump to a control, or select and deselect a control	Check boxes, radio buttons, reset buttons, submit buttons, image submit buttons, text boxes, password boxes, file boxes,hidden text boxes
alt	Sets or returns alternate text for an image	Image submit buttons
checked	Sets or returns the checked status of a check box or radio button	Check boxes, radio buttons
defaultChecked	Determines the control that is checked by default in a check box group or radio button group	Check boxes, radio buttons
defaultValue	Sets or returns the default text that appears in a form control	Text boxes, password boxes, file boxes
disabled	Sets or returns a Boolean value that determines whether a control is disabled	Check boxes, radio buttons, reset buttons, submit buttons, image submit buttons, text boxes, password boxes, file boxes, hidden text boxes
form	Returns a reference to the form that contains the control	Check boxes, radio buttons, reset buttons, submit buttons, image submit buttons, text boxes, password boxes, file boxes, hidden text boxes
maxLength	Sets or returns the maximum number of characters that can be entered into a field	Text boxes, password boxes
name	Sets or returns the value assigned to the element's name attribute	Check boxes, radio buttons, reset buttons, submit buttons, image submit buttons, text boxes, password boxes, file boxes, hidden text boxes
readOnly	Sets or returns a Boolean value that determines whether a control is read only	Text boxes, password boxes
size	Sets or returns how many characters wide a field is	Text boxes, password boxes
src	Sets or returns the URL of an image	Image submit buttons
tabIndex	Sets or returns a control's position in the tab order	Check boxes, radio buttons, reset buttons, submit buttons, image submit buttons, text boxes, password boxes, file boxes, hidden text boxes
type	Returns the type of input element: button, check box, file, hidden, image, password, radio, reset, submit, or text	Check boxes, radio buttons, reset buttons, submit buttons, image submit buttons, text boxes, password boxes, file boxes, hidden text boxes
useMap	Sets or returns the name of an image map	Image submit buttons
value	Sets or returns the value of form controls	Check boxes, radio buttons, reset buttons, submit buttons, image submit buttons, text boxes, password boxes, file boxes, hidden text boxes

Table 5-6   Input field object properties and their associated form controls

CHAPTER 5

Method	Description	Form controls
blur()	Removes focus from a form control	Check boxes, radio buttons, reset buttons, submit buttons, text boxes, text areas, password boxes, file boxes
click()	Activates a form control's click event	Check boxes, radio buttons, reset buttons, submit buttons
focus()	Changes focus to a form control	Check boxes, radio buttons, reset buttons, submit buttons, text boxes, password boxes, file boxes
select()	Selects the text in a form control	Text boxes, password boxes, file boxes

Table 5-7   Input field object methods and their associated form controls

You will use several of the input field object properties and methods in this chapter. One property you have already used is the value property. Recall that in Chapter 3 you created a calculator using a form. The Web page included a script with the following function that updated the value in the form's text box:

```
function updateString(value) {
    inputString += value;
    document.Calculator.Input.value = inputString;
}
```

The last statement in the preceding function uses the Document object to set the value property in a control named Input located in a form named Calculator. The following code shows the same function, but this time the last statement in the function uses the forms[] and elements[] arrays to set the value in the text box:

```
function updateString(value) {
    inputString += value;
    document.forms[0].elements[0].value = inputString;
}
```

Text Boxes

An <input> element with a type of "text" (<input type="text" />) creates a simple **text box** that accepts a single line of text. When used with a text box, the value attribute specifies text to be used as the default value at the moment a form first loads. The following code shows an example of some text boxes that include name, value, and size attributes. Figure 5-4 shows the form in a Web browser.

```
<form action="FormProcessor.html" method="get"
enctype="application/x-www-form-urlencoded">
<p>Name<br />
<input type="text" name="name" value="Office of the Mayor"
size="50" /></p>
<p>Address<br />
<input type="text" name="address"
value="City Hall"
```

```
size="50" /></p>
<p>City, State, Zip<br />
<input type="text" name="city" value="New York" size="30" />
<input type="text" name="state" value="NY" size="2"
maxlength="2" />
<input type="text" name="zip"  value="38116" size="10"
maxlength="10" /></p>
</form>
```

Figure 5-4

Form with several text
<input> elements

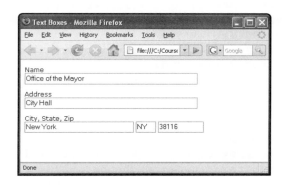

Next, you add text <input> elements to the Subscription form to collect basic customer data.

To add text <input> elements to the Subscription form:

1. Return to the **Subscription.html** document in your text editor.

2. Within the <form> element, add the following table to contain the billing and shipping information text boxes. The table will consist of a single row containing two cells.

    ```
    <table border="0">
    </table>
    ```

3. Within the table, add the following text <input> elements, which will be used to gather a customer's billing information and shipping information. The left cell contains the billing information and the right cell contains the shipping information.

    ```
    <tr>
    <td valign="top"><h3>Billing Information</h3>
    <p>Name<br />
    <input type="text" name="name_billing" size="50" /></p>
    <p>Address<br />
    <input type="text" name="address_billing" size="50" /></p>
    <p>City, State, Zip<br />
    <input type="text" name="city_billing" size="34" />
    <input type="text" name="state_billing" size="2" maxlength="2" />
    <input type="text" name="zip_billing" size="10"
    maxlength="10" /></p>
    ```

```
</td>
<td valign="top">
<h3>Shipping Information</h3>
<p>Name<br />
<input type="text" name="name_shipping" size="50" /></p>
<p>Address<br />
<input type="text" name="address_shipping" size="50" /></p>
<p>City, State, Zip<br />
<input type="text" name="city_shipping" size="34" />
<input type="text" name="state_shipping" size="2"
maxlength="2" />
<input type="text" name="zip_shipping" size="10"
maxlength="5" /></p></td>
</tr>
```

4. After the closing `</table>` tag, add the following elements for the telephone number:

```
<p>Telephone</p>
<p>(<input type="text" name="area" size="3" maxlength="3" />)
<input type="text" name="exchange" size="3" maxlength="3" />
<input type="text" name="phone" size="4" maxlength="4" /></p>
```

5. Save the **Subscription.html** document and then open it in your Web browser. The text `<input>` elements you entered should appear as shown in Figure 5-5.

Figure 5-5

Subscription form after adding text `<input>` elements

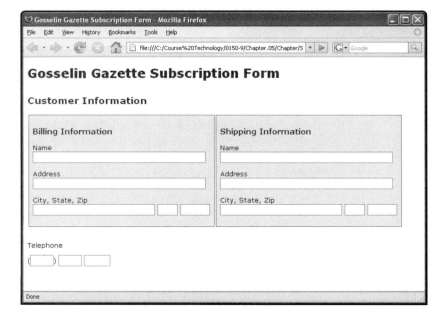

6. Close your Web browser window.

Most form validation with JavaScript takes place when you submit the form. You will learn how to accomplish this kind of validation at the end of this chapter. However, there are some tricks you can use to ensure that users enter the correct information in the first place. For any fields that require numeric values, for instance, you can use JavaScript's built-in `isNaN()` function to determine whether the value entered by the user is a number. Recall from Chapter 3 that the `isNaN()` function determines whether a value is the special value NaN (Not a Number). The `isNaN()` function returns a value of true if the value passed to it is not a number and a value of false if the value passed to it is a number. The following function shows a statement that passes the value of a text box named "subtotal" in the first form on a Web page to the `isNaN()` function:

```
isNaN(document.forms[0].subtotal.value);
```

Next, you will add a function to the Subscription.html document that uses the `isNaN()` function to check whether a value entered into the Zip code or telephone number fields in the subscription form is a number. The function will be called from the `change` event within each field. The `change` event is called when the value in a control changes. If the value entered is not a number, then the function returns a value of false, forcing the user to enter a numeric value into the field.

To add a function to the Subscription.html document that checks whether a value entered into the Zip code or telephone number fields in the subscription form is a number:

1. Return to the **Subscription.html** document in your text editor.

2. Add the following `checkForNumber()` function to the script section in the document head. The function checks whether the argument passed to it is a number. If it is not a number, an alert message is displayed and the function returns a value of false to prevent the `change` event from occurring. Otherwise, the function returns a value of true, allowing the `change` event to occur.

```
function checkForNumber(fieldValue) {
    var numberCheck = isNaN(fieldValue);
    if (numberCheck == true) {
        window.alert("You must enter a numeric value!");
        return false;
    }
}
```

3. Next, add the following `onchange` event handler to the `<input>` elements for the two Zip code fields and the three telephone number fields. Notice that the function is passed a value of `this.value`, which uses the `this` reference to refer to the `value` property of the current form element.

```
onchange="return checkForNumber(this.value);"
```

4. Save the **Subscription.html** document and then open it in your Web browser. Test the validation code by entering some nonnumeric numbers into the area code and telephone number fields.

5. Close your Web browser window.

Password Boxes

An <input> element with a type of "password" (<input type="password" />) creates a **password box** that is used for entering passwords or other types of sensitive data. Each character that a user types in a password box appears as an asterisk or bullet, depending on the operating system and Web browser, in order to hide the password from anyone who may be looking over the user's shoulder. The following code creates a password box with a maximum length of eight characters. Figure 5-6 shows how the password box appears in a Web browser after the user enters some characters.

```
<form action="FormProcessor.html" method="get"
enctype="application/x-www-form-urlencoded">
<p>Please enter a password of 8 characters or less:<br />
<input type="password" name="password" maxlength="8" /></p>
</form>
```

Figure 5-6

Password box in a Web browser

Next, you add a password <input> element to the Subscription.html document that prompts users to enter a password required for managing subscriptions online.

To add a password <input> element to the Subscription.html document:

1. Return to the **Subscription.html** document in your text editor.

2. Above the closing </form> tag, add the following lines for the password <input> element, which prompts users for a password:

   ```
   <p>Enter a password that you can use to manage your subscription
   online:</p>
   <p><input type="password" name="password" size="50" /></p>
   ```

3. Save the **Subscription.html** document and then open it in your Web browser. Test the password field to see if the password you entered appears as asterisks or bullets. Figure 5-7 shows how the form appears in a Web browser after typing a password.

4. Close your Web browser window.

You've probably had experience entering a password on a computer system and then being asked to enter the password again in a confirmation field to verify it. In JavaScript you can check whether a user entered the same password in the password field and in the confirmation field by using an if statement to compare the two values entered into each field. You will now add a password confirmation field to the Subscription.html document.

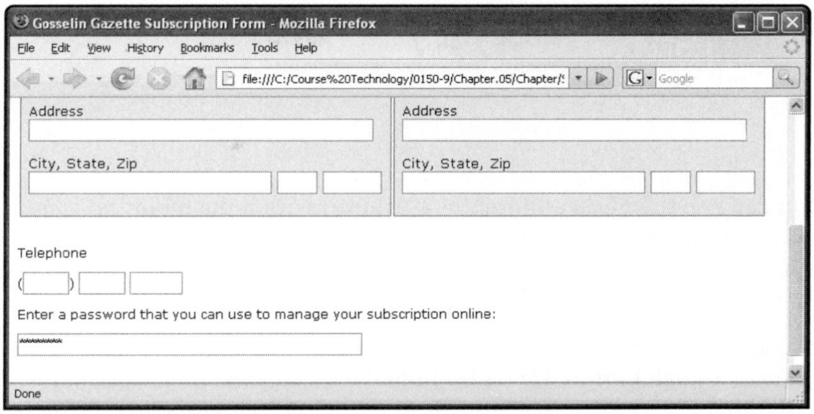

Figure 5-7

Subscription form after
adding a password
`<input>` element

To add a password confirmation field to the Subscription.html document:

1. Return to the **Subscription.html** document in your text editor.

2. Add the following `confirmPassword()` function to the end of the script section. The function compares the values entered into both the password and password confirmation fields. If the values are not the same, then the function uses the `focus()` method to move the cursor back into the password field.

```
function confirmPassword() {
    if (document.forms[0].password_confirm.value
            != document.forms[0].password.value) {
        window.alert("You did not enter the same password!");
    document.forms[0].password.focus();
    }
}
```

3. Above the closing `</form>` tag, add the following lines for a password confirmation field. The `<input>` field includes an `onblur` event handler to call the `confirmPassword()` function.

```
<p>Type the password again to confirm it.</p>
<p><input type="password" name="password_confirm" size="50"
onblur="confirmPassword();" /></p>
```

4. Save the **Subscription.html** document and then open it in your Web browser. Test the password fields to ensure that they properly validate the entered passwords.

5. Close your Web browser window.

Push Buttons

An `<input>` element with a type of "button" (`<input type="button" />`) creates a **push button** that is similar to the OK and Cancel buttons you see in dialog boxes. You have already used push buttons in several projects in this book. Therefore, you may already understand that the primary purpose of push buttons is to execute JavaScript code that performs some type of function, such as a calculation.

NOTE
Push buttons are also called "command buttons."

You can use the `name` and `value` attributes with a push button `<input>` element. The text you assign to a push button's `value` attribute is the text that appears on the button face. The width of a push button created with the `<input type="button">` element is based on the number of characters in its `value` attribute.

You are not required to include the `name` and `value` attributes, because a user cannot change the value of a push button. If you include the `name` and `value` attributes, then the default value set with the `value` attribute is transmitted to a Web server along with the rest of the form data. The following code creates a push button that uses JavaScript code to display a simple dialog box:

```
<p><input type="button" name="push_button" value="Click Here"
onclick="window.alert('You clicked a push button.');" /></p>
```

The code for the `<input>` element creates a button with a value of "Click Here" and a name of `push_button`. As shown in Figure 5-8, if you click the push button, you will see a dialog box containing the text "You clicked a push button."

Figure 5-8
A push button in a Web browser

Radio Buttons

An `<input>` element with a type of "radio" (`<input type="radio" />`) is used to create a group of **radio buttons**, or **option buttons**, from which the user can select only one value. To create a group of radio buttons, all radio buttons in the group must have the same `name` attribute. Each radio button requires a `value` attribute that identifies the unique value associated with that button. Only one selected radio button in a group creates a name=value pair when a form is submitted to a Web server. You can also include the `checked` attribute in a radio `<input>` element to set an initial value for a group of radio buttons. For example, you might have a group of radio buttons that lists the cost of magazine subscriptions. One button lists the cost of a three-month subscription, another button lists the cost of a six-month subscription, and another lists the cost of a yearly subscription. In order to encourage subscribers to purchase the yearly subscription, you could include the `checked` attribute with the yearly subscription radio button. If the `checked` attribute is not included in any of the `<input type="radio">` elements in a radio button group, then none of the buttons in the group are selected when the form loads. The following code creates a group of five radio buttons. Because the married radio button includes the checked attribute, it is selected when the form first loads. Figure 5-9 shows how the radio buttons appear in a Web browser.

```
<form action="FormProcessor.html" method="get"
enctype="application/x-www-form-urlencoded">
<p>What is your current marital status?<br />
<input type="radio" name="marital_status"
value="single" />Single<br />
<input type="radio" name="marital_status"
value="married" checked="checked" />Married<br />
<input type="radio" name="marital_status"
value="divored" />Divorced<br />
<input type="radio" name="marital_status"
value="separated" />Separated<br />
<input type="radio" name="marital_status"
value="widowed" />Widowed</p>
</form>
```

Figure 5-9
Form with radio buttons

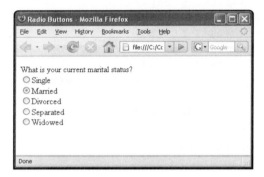

Next, you add radio buttons to the Subscription.html document that allow users to select their desired delivery option. The radio buttons you add are created within a table in order to make it easier to align the radio buttons on the page.

To add radio buttons to the Subscription.html document:

1. Return to the **Subscription.html** document in your text editor.

2. Add the following <h3> element and opening <table> element and the table's header information to the end of the form:

```
<h3>Delivery Rates</h3>
<table border="0">
<colgroup align="left" width="100" />
<colgroup span="4" align="center" width="100" />
<tr><th> </th>
<th>4 weeks</th>
<th>13 weeks</th>
```

```
<th>26 weeks</th>
<th>52 weeks</th></tr>
```

3. Next, add the following table row elements that include payment options for delivery on Monday through Saturday. Notice that each radio button's name attribute is assigned the same name of "delivery" so that the radio buttons are part of the same group.

```
<tr><td><strong>Mon-Sat</strong></td>
<td><input type="radio" name="delivery"
value="12.60" />$12.60</td>
<td><input type="radio" name="delivery"
value="40.95" />$40.95</td>
<td><input type="radio" name="delivery"
value="81.90" />$81.90</td>
<td><input type="radio" name="delivery"
value="156.00" />$156.00</td></tr>
```

4. Next, add the following table row elements that include payment options for delivery every day of the week:

```
<tr><td><strong>Every Day</strong></td>
<td><input type="radio" name="delivery"
value="13.56" />$13.56</td>
<td><input type="radio" name="delivery"
value="44.07" />$44.07</td>
<td><input type="radio" name="delivery"
value="88.14" />$88.14</td>
<td><input type="radio" name="delivery"
value="159.74" />$159.74</td></tr>
```

5. Type the closing **</table>** tag.

6. Save the **Subscription.html** document and then open it in your Web browser. Test the radio buttons to see if you can select only a single button at a time. Figure 5-10 shows how the radio buttons appear in a Web browser.

Figure 5-10

Subscription form after adding radio buttons

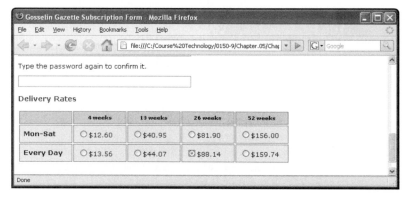

7. Close your Web browser window.

When multiple form elements share the same name, JavaScript creates an array out of the elements using the shared name. Radio buttons, for instance, share the same name so that a single name=value pair can be submitted to a server-side script. For example, assume you have a group of radio buttons named `maritalStatus`. You can use the following statement to access the value of the second radio button in the group:

```
document.forms[0].maritalStatus[1].value;
```

When you have an array that is created from a group of buttons that share the same name, you can use the `checked` property to determine which element in a group is selected. The `checked` property returns a value of true if a check box or radio button is selected, and a value of false if it is not. For example, if you have a group of radio buttons named `maritalStatus`, then you can use a statement similar to the following to determine if the first radio button in the group is selected:

```
document.forms[0].maritalStatus[0].checked;
```

Next, you will add another group of radio buttons to the subscription form. The group contains two buttons, Yes and No, that determine whether the customer wants to be billed continuously on a monthly basis. If the user selects Yes from this option group, then the selected radio button in the payment options group should be deselected, and vice versa. In order to deselect a radio button in a group, you need to loop through the array that represents the group and assign a value of false to the checked button.

To add monthly subscription radio buttons to the Subscription.html document:

1. Return to the **Subscription.html** document in your text editor.

2. Add the following two functions to the end of the script section. The `noDelivery()` function disables the selected radio button in the weekly delivery group, and the `noSunday()` function disables the selected radio button in the Sunday delivery group.

```
function noDelivery() {
    for (var i=0;i<document.forms[0].delivery.length;++i) {
        if (document.forms[0].delivery[i].checked == true)
            document.forms[0].delivery[i].checked = false;
    }
}
function noSunday() {
    for(var i=0;i<document.forms[0].sunday.length;++i) {
        if (document.forms[0].sunday[i].checked == true)
            document.forms[0].sunday[i].checked = false;
    }
}
```

3. Add `onclick` event handlers to the radio buttons in the weekly delivery group that call the `noSunday()` function, as follows:

```
<td><input type="radio" name="delivery"
value="12.60" onclick="noSunday();" />$12.60</td>
<td><input type="radio" name="delivery"
```

```
value="40.95" onclick="noSunday();" />$40.95</td>
<td><input type="radio" name="delivery"
value="81.90" onclick="noSunday();" />$81.90</td>
<td><input type="radio" name="delivery"
value="156.00" onclick="noSunday();" />$156.00</td></tr>
<tr><td><strong>Every Day</strong></td>
<td><input type="radio" name="delivery" value="13.56"
onclick="noSunday();" />$13.56</td>
<td><input type="radio" name="delivery" value="44.07"
onclick="noSunday();" />$44.07</td>
<td><input type="radio" name="delivery" value="88.14"
onclick="noSunday();" />$88.14</td>
<td><input type="radio" name="delivery" value="159.74"
onclick="noSunday();" />$159.74</td>
```

4. Finally, add the following radio buttons for Sunday delivery above the closing </form> tag, but after the closing </table> tag:

```
<p><strong>Sundays only ($3.50 per week)</strong>
<input type="radio" name="sunday" value="weekly"
onclick="noDelivery();" />Bill me weekly
<input type="radio" name="sunday" value="weekly"
onclick="noDelivery();" />Bill me monthly</p>
```

5. Save the **Subscription.html** document, and then open it in your Web browser. Test the radio buttons to ensure that you can only select one button from either group.

6. Close your Web browser window.

Check Boxes

An <input> element with a type of "checkbox" (<input type="checkbox" />) creates a box that can be set to Yes (checked) or No (unchecked). You use **check boxes** when you want users to select whether or not to include a certain item or to allow users to select multiple values from a list of items. Include the checked attribute in a check box <input> element to set the initial value of the check box to Yes. If a check box is selected (checked) when a form is submitted, then the check box name=value pair is included in the form data. If a check box is not selected, a name=value pair is not included in the data submitted from the form.

The following code creates several check boxes. Note that the Fundraising check box is checked when the form first loads because it includes the checked attribute. Figure 5-11 shows how the check boxes appear in a Web browser.

```
<form action="FormProcessor.html" method="get"
enctype="application/x-www-form-urlencoded">
<h3>Which committees would you like to serve on? </h3>
<p><input type="checkbox" name="committees"
value="program_dev" />Program Development<br />
<input type="checkbox" name="committees"
value="fundraising" checked="checked" />Fundraising<br />
<input type="checkbox" name="committees"
```

```
value="pub_relations" />Public Relations <br />
<input type="checkbox" name="committees"
value="education" />Education</p>
</form>
```

Figure 5-11
Form with check boxes

Like radio buttons, you can group check boxes by giving each check box the same name value, although each check box can have a different value. Unlike radio buttons, users can select as many check boxes in a group as they like. When multiple check boxes on a form share the same name, then multiple name=value pairs, each using the same name, are submitted to a Web server. In the preceding example, if the Fundraising and Public Relations check boxes are selected, then two name=value pairs, committees=fundraising and committees=pub_relations are submitted. Note that you are not required to group check boxes with the same name attribute. Although a common group name helps to identify and manage groups of check boxes, it is often easier to keep track of individual values when each check box has a unique name attribute.

Next, you add check boxes to the Subscription.html document to allow users to select any other newspapers to which they are currently subscribed.

To add check boxes to the Subscription.html document:

1. Return to the **Subscription.html** document in your text editor.

2. Above the closing </form> tag, add the following check box elements:

```
<p>Do you subscribe to any other newspapers?</p>
<p><input type="checkbox" name="newspapers"
value="nytimes" />New York Times<br />
<input type="checkbox" name="newspapers"
value="bostonglobe" />Boston Globe<br />
<input type="checkbox" name="newspapers"
value="sfchronicle" />San Francisco Chronicle<br />
<input type="checkbox" name="newspapers"
value="miamiherald" />Miami Herald<br />
<input type="checkbox" name="newspapers"
value="other" />Other</p>
```

3. Save the **Subscription.html** document and then open it in your Web browser. Figure 5-12 shows how the check boxes appear.

CHAPTER 5

Figure 5-12
Subscription form after
adding check boxes

4. Close your Web browser window.

You can use a check box element in Billing Information and Shipping Information at the top of the form in the Subscription.html document. Because it is common to have the same billing and shipping address, you will add a check box element to the subscription form that copies the values of the billing information fields to the shipping information fields.

To add a check box element to the subscription form that copies the values of the billing information fields to the shipping information fields:

1. Return to the **Subscription.html** document in your text editor.

2. Add the following sameShippingInfo() function to the end of the script section. The function uses an if...else statement to copy the values from the billing information fields to the shipping information fields when the check box is selected. When the check box is deselected, empty strings are assigned to the shipping information fields. Notice that the conditional expression in the if statement uses the elements[] array to refer to the check box control. You will not assign a name to the check box control because you do not want its value submitted to the Web server. Therefore, you must refer to it with the elements[] array.

```
function sameShippingInfo() {
    if (document.forms[0].elements[5].checked == true) {
        document.forms[0].name_shipping.value
                = document.forms[0].name_billing.value;
        document.forms[0].address_shipping.value
                = document.forms[0].address_billing.value;
        document.forms[0].city_shipping.value
                = document.forms[0].city_billing.value;
        document.forms[0].state_shipping.value
                = document.forms[0].state_billing.value;
        document.forms[0].zip_shipping.value
                = document.forms[0].zip_billing.value;
    }
    else {
        document.forms[0].name_shipping.value = "";
```

```
document.forms[0].address_shipping.value = "";
document.forms[0].city_shipping.value = "";
document.forms[0].state_shipping.value = "";
document.forms[0].zip_shipping.value = "";
    }
}
```

3.   Now add the following check box element above the closing `</td>` tag for the table cell that contains the billing information fields:

```
<p><input type="checkbox" onclick="sameShippingInfo();" />
Same shipping information</p>
```

4.   Save the **Subscription.html** document and then open it in your Web browser. Enter some fields into the billing information fields and test the check box to see if it copies the values to the shipping information fields.

5.   Close your Web browser window.

Creating Selection Lists

The `<select>` element creates a selection list that presents users with fixed lists of options from which to choose. The options displayed in a selection list are created with `<option>` elements, which you will study next. As with other form elements that create controls, the `<select>` element must appear within a block-level element such as the `<p>` element. The selection list can appear as an actual list of choices or as a drop-down menu. Depending on the number of options in the list, a selection list can also include a scroll bar. Table 5-8 lists the attributes of the `<select>` element.

Attribute	Description
disabled	Disables the selection list
multiple	Specifies whether a user can select more than one option from the list; a Boolean attribute
name	Designates a name for the selection list
size	Determines how many lines of the selection list appear

Table 5-8   Attributes of the `<select>` element

Like other form controls, the `<select>` element includes a name attribute that is submitted to a Web server. However, the value portion of a `<select>` element's name=value pair is the value assigned to an option that is created with the `<option>` element (which you study next). If a `<select>` element includes the Boolean `multiple` attribute, which specifies whether a user can select more than one option from the list, and a visitor selects more than one option in the list, then multiple name=value pairs for the `<select>` element are submitted with the form. Each instance of a `<select>` element's name=value pair includes a value assigned to one of the selected list options created with the `<option>` element.

The size attribute designates how many lines of the selection list appear when the form is rendered in a Web browser. If this attribute is excluded or set to 1, and the <select> element does not include the multiple attribute, then the selection list is a drop-down style menu. For dropdown style menus, the first option element is automatically selected.

Menu Options

You use **<option> elements** to specify the options that appear in a selection list. The content of an <option> element appears as a menu option in a selection list. Table 5-9 lists the attributes of the <option> element.

Attribute	Description
disabled	Disables the option
label	Designates alternate text to display in the selection list for an individual option
selected	Determines if an option is initially selected in the selection list when the form first loads; a Boolean attribute
value	Specifies the value submitted to a Web server

Table 5-9   Attributes of the <option> element

You specify a selection list's menu options using <option> elements placed within a <select> element. Each selection list must contain at least one <option> element. For example, the following code creates two selection lists. Figure 5-13 shows the code in a Web browser. Notice that because the first list's <select> element includes the multiple attribute, you can select multiple options, as shown in the figure. Also notice that the "$2,000 to $2,999" option is the selected value in the second list.

```
<h1>Pine Knoll Appliances</h1>
<h2>Televisions</h2>
<form action="FormProcessor.html" method="get"
enctype="application/x-www-form-urlencoded">
<table border="0">
<tr><td
style="background:white;border:0"><strong>Brand</strong></td><td
style="background:white;border:0"><strong>Price
Range</strong></td></tr>
<tr><td>
<select name="brand" multiple="multiple" size="6">
<option value="hitachi">Hitachi</option>
<option value="magnovox">Magnovox</option>
<option value="panasonic">Panasonic</option>
<option value="samsung">Samsung</option>
<option value="sharp">Sharp</option>
<option value="sony">Sony</option>
</select></td>
<td>
<select name="price" size="6">
```

```
<option value="199">Under $200</option>
<option value="499">$200 to $499</option>
<option value="999">$500 to $999</option>
<option value="1999">$1,000 to $1,999</option>
<option value="2999" selected="selected">$2,000 to $2,999</option>
<option value="3000_plus">Over $3,000</option>
</select></td></tr></table></form>
```

Figure 5-13
Two selection lists

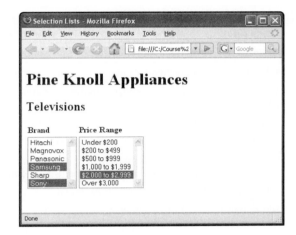

Next, you add a selection list to the Subscription.html document that a subscriber uses to select any magazines to which they are currently subscribed.

To add a selection list to the Subscription.html document:

1. Return to the **Subscription.html** document in your text editor.

2. Add the following selection list to the end of the form:

   ```
   <p>Do you subscribe to any magazines?</p>
   <p><select name="magazine">
   <option value="time">Time</option>
   <option value="newsweek">Newsweek</option>
   <option value="harpers">Harpers</option>
   <option value="bus_week">Business Week</option>
   <option value="entrepreneur">Entrepreneur</option>
   <option value="people">People</option>
   <option value="cosmo">Cosmopolitan</option>
   </select></p>
   ```

3. Save the **Subscription.html** document and then open it in your Web browser. You should see the selection list at the bottom of the page. Because you did not include size and multiple attributes in the `<select>` element, the selection list appears as a drop-down menu.

4. Close your Web browser window.

The `Select` and `Option` Objects

The **`Select` object** represents a selection list in a form. The `Select` object includes an `options[]` array containing an `Option` object for each `<option>` element in the selection list. The **`Option` object** represents an option in a selection list. You use the `Select` and `Option` objects with JavaScript to manipulate the options displayed in a selection. The `Select` object contains the properties listed in Table 5-10 and the methods listed in Table 5-11.

Property	Description
disabled	Sets or returns a Boolean value that determines whether a control is disabled
form	Returns a reference to the form that contains the control
length	Returns the number of elements in the `options[]` array
multiple	Sets or returns a Boolean value that determines whether multiple options can be selected in a selection list
name	Sets or returns the value assigned to the element's name attribute
options[]	Returns an array of the options in a selection list
selectedIndex	Returns a number representing the element number in the `options[]` array of the first option selected in a selection list; returns -1 if No option is selected
size	Sets or returns the number of options to display
tabIndex	Sets or returns a control's position in the tab order
type	Returns the type of selection list; returns "select-one" if the `<select>` element does not include the `multiple` attribute, or it returns "select-multiple" if the `<select>` element does includes the `multiple` attribute

Table 5-10   Properties of the `Select` object

Method	Description
add(*element, before*)	Adds a new option to a selection list
blur()	Removes focus from a form control
focus()	Changes focus to a form control
remove(*index*)	Removes an option from a selection list

Table 5-11   Methods of the `Select` object

You append the properties in Table 5-11 to the name representing the `<select>` element. For example, for the selection list you saw earlier with a `name` attribute of "brand", you use the following statement to assign the number of elements in the selection list to a variable named `numItems`:

```
var numItems = document.forms[0].brand.length;
```

Similarly, the following statement assigns the currently selected option in the selection list to a variable named `curSelection`:

```
var curSelection = document.forms[0].brand.selectedIndex;
```

If the `size` attribute is excluded or set to 1, and the `<select>` element does not include the `multiple` attribute, then the selection list is a drop-down style menu. For drop-down style menus, the first option element is automatically selected. However, for `<select>` elements that assign a value greater than 1 to the `size` attribute or that include the `multiple` attribute, to determine whether an option is selected in a selection list, you need to test whether the `selectedIndex` property contains a value of -1. If it does, then no option is selected. For example, the following code tests whether an option is selected in the `brand` selection list:

```
if (document.forms[0].brand.selectedIndex == -1)
    window.alert("No option is selected.");
else
    window.alert("An option is selected.");
```

The `Option` object contains the properties listed in Table 5-12.

Property	Description
defaultSelected	Returns a Boolean value that determines whether the `<option>` element representing the currently selected item includes the `selected` attribute
disabled	Sets or returns a Boolean value that determines whether a control is disabled
form	Returns a reference to the form that contains the control
index	Returns a number representing the element number within the `options[]` array
label	Sets or returns alternate text to display for the option in the selection list
selected	Sets or returns a Boolean value that determines whether an option is selected
text	Sets or returns the text displayed for the option in the selection list
value	Sets or returns the text that is assigned to the `<option>` element's value attribute; this is the value that is submitted to the server

Table 5-12   Properties of the `Option` object

You append the properties in Table 5-12 to the `options[]` array. For example, the following code tests whether the first element in the `options[]` array for the `brand` selection list is selected:

```
if (document.forms[0].brand.options[0].selected == true)
    window.alert("The first option is selected.");
else
    window.alert("The first option is not selected.");
```

NOTE
The `Select` and `Option` objects do not contain methods.

Adding Options to a Selection List

Although the current ECMAScript recommendations suggest using the add() method of the Select object to add new options to a selection list, this method is not consistently implemented in current Web browsers. For instance, according to the ECMAScript recommendations, you should be able to add a new option to the end of a selection list by passing a value of null as the second parameter of the add() method. While this works in Firefox 2.0, it will not work in Internet Explorer 7.0 unless you eliminate the second parameter altogether from the function call. Similarly, you should be able to pass an integer as the second parameter to indicate before which element the new element should be added. While this works in Internet Explorer 7.0, it does not appear to work in Firefox 2.0. Until this method is consistently available, you should avoid using it to add a new option to a selection list. Instead, to add a new option to a selection list after a Web page renders it, you must create a new option with the Option() constructor. Creating a new option with the Option() constructor is similar to creating an array with the Array() constructor. The syntax for the Option() constructor is as follows:

```
var variable_name = new Option(text, value,
    defaultSelected, selected);
```

Notice that the arguments passed to the Option() constructor match several of the properties of the Option object listed in Table 5-12. The arguments allow you to set the properties of the new option in a single statement. For example, the following statement declares a new option and assigns values to each of the properties of the Option object:

```
var gardeningItem = new Option("mulch", "mulch", false, false);
```

The preceding statement creates a new Option object represented by the gardeningItem variable, and assigns values to the object's properties. You can also assign values to the properties after the new Option object is created. The following code performs the same tasks as the preceding statement:

```
var gardeningItem = new Option();
gardeningItem.text = "mulch";
gardeningItem.value = "mulch";
```

TIP
You do not have to assign values to all of the properties of a new Option object; you only need to assign values to the properties you need.

After you create a new Option object and assign values to its properties, you assign the object to an empty element in an options[] array. For example, to assign the Option object created in the preceding code to the third element in an options[] array in a selection list named gardeningList, you use the following statement:

```
document.forms[0].gardeningList.options[2] = gardeningItem;
```

Next, you add code to the Subscription.html document that allows subscribers to build a selection of the magazines to which they are currently subscribed.

To add code to the Subscription.html document that allows subscribers to build a selection of the magazines to which they are currently subscribed:

1. Return to the **Subscription.html** document in your text editor.

2. Replace the current <select> and <option> elements for the magazine subscriptions with the following elements. The first element is a text box where users can enter the name of a magazine to which they subscribe. Note that the text box does not include a name argument; this prevents the field value from being submitted along with the rest of the form data. The Add Magazine button includes an onclick event handler that calls a function named addMagazine(), which you will add next. In order for the document to be well formed, the <select> element must include at least one <option> element. Therefore, you add a single <option> element that displays "Enter the magazines you subscribe to" in the selection list. In the next section, you will add code to the addMagazine() function that deletes this unnecessary element when the subscriber adds a magazine to the selection list.

```
<p>Magazine <input type="text" size="68" /></p>
<p><input type="button" value="Add Magazine"
onclick="addMagazine();" style="width: 120px" /></p>
<p><select name="magazines" multiple="multiple"
size="10" style="width: 500px">
<option value="none">Enter the magazines you subscribe
to</option>
</select></p>
```

3. Add the following addMagazine() function to the end of the script section. Notice that the code uses the elements[] array to refer to the text box where users enter the names of magazines to which they subscribe; this is necessary because the text box does not include a name argument. (Again, the lack of the name argument prevents the contents of the text box from being submitted with the other form data.) Also notice how the function determines where to add the new item in the options[] array. The number of items in the options[] array is retrieved using the Select object's length property and assigned to a variable named nextItem. The value assigned to the nextItem variable represents the number of elements in the array. As you'll recall, the length of the array is one more than the number of elements in the array (because the array begins with an element of 0). That means you can use the value to identify the next available element.

```
function addMagazine() {
    if (document.forms[0].elements[31].value == "")
        window.alert("You must enter a magazine name.");
    else {
        var magazine = new Option();
        magazine.text = document.forms[0].elements[31].value;
```

```
magazine.value = document.forms[0]
        .elements[31].value;
nextItem = document.forms[0].magazines.length;
document.forms[0].magazines.options[nextItem]
        = magazine;
document.forms[0].elements[31].value = "";
    }
}
```

4. Save the **Subscription.html** document and then open it in your Web browser. Scroll to the end of the Web page and try adding some magazines to the magazine list. One problem you may notice is that the "Enter the magazines you subscribe to" option remains in the selection list after the user adds magazines. You will fix this in the next section.

5. Close your Web browser window.

Removing Options from a Selection List

To remove a single option from a selection list, you pass the option's index number in the options[] array to the remove() method of the Select object. For example, use the following statement to remove the first element in the options[] array of the gardeningList selection list.

```
document.forms[0].gardeningList.remove(0);
```

When you remove an element from the options[] array using a statement similar to the preceding statement, the remaining elements are reordered. In other words, all of the element numbers following the deleted element are decreased by a value of one.

You can remove all the options from an options array by appending the Selection object's length property to the options[] array without the brackets, and then by assigning the length property a value of 0. For example, to remove all the options in the options[] array of the gardeningList selection list, you use the following statement:

```
document.forms[0].gardeningList.options.length = 0;
```

Next, you add code to the Subscription.html document that deletes magazine names from the selection list.

To add code to the Subscription.html document that deletes magazine names from the selection list:

1. Return to the **Subscription.html** document in your text editor.

2. Add the following elements to the end of the <p> element that contains the Add Magazine button. The Delete Magazine button includes an onclick event handler, which calls a function named deleteMagazine(). You will add this function next. To the onclick event handler in the Clear List button, you will assign a statement that deletes all the items in the list.

```
<input type="button" value="Delete Magazine"
onclick="deleteMagazine()" style="width: 120px" />
```

```
<input type="button" value="Clear List"
onclick="document.forms[0].magazines.options.length = 0;"
style="width: 120px" />
```

3. Add the following `deleteMagazine()` function to the end of the script section. The function is very familiar to the `deleteItem()` function you saw in the shopping list form.

```
function deleteMagazine() {
    var selectedItem =
        document.forms[0].magazines.selectedIndex;
    if (selectedItem == -1)
        window.alert(
            "You must select a magazine name in the list.");
    else
        document.forms[0].magazines.remove(selectedItem);
}
```

4. Finally, add the following `if` statement to the beginning of the `else` statement in the `addMagazine()` function. This statement deletes the "Enter the magazines you subscribe to" option that is displayed by default in the selection list.

```
if (document.forms[0].magazines.options[0]
    && document.forms[0].magazines.options[0].value == "none")
        document.forms[0].magazines.options[0] = null;
```

5. Save the **Subscription.html** document and then open it in your Web browser. Scroll to the end of the Web page and try adding some magazines to the magazine list. After you add the first magazine, "Enter the magazines you subscribe to" should be removed from the list. Also, test the Delete Magazine and Clear List buttons.

6. Close your Web browser window.

Changing Options in a Selection List

To change an option in a selection list, you simply assign new values to the option's `value` and `text` properties. For example, use the following statements change the value of the first option in the `gardeningList` selection list from "Pruners" to "Mulch":

```
document.forms[0].gardeningList.options[0].value = "Mulch";
document.forms[0].gardeningList.options[0].text = "Mulch";
```

The following shows a completed example of the shopping list to which you can add new items. An Add Item button in the form calls a function named `addItem()`, which adds new items to the selection list. A new `Option` object named `gardeningList` is created, and its text and value properties are assigned the value of the text box named `newItem`. A function named `deleteItem()`, which is called from the Delete Item button, handles deleting single items from the list. The `onclick` event handler in the Clear List button is assigned a statement that deletes all of the items in the list. A function named `changeItem()` changes the value of a selected item in the list to the value in the New Item text box. Figure 5-14 shows how the form appears in a Web browser.

```
<script type="text/javascript">
/* <![CDATA[ */
function addItem() {
    if (document.forms[0].elements[0].value == "")
        window.alert("You must enter an item.");
    else {
        var gardeningItem = new Option();
        gardeningItem.text = document.forms[0].elements[0].value;
        gardeningItem.value = document.forms[0].elements[0].value;
        nextItem = document.forms[0].gardeningList.length;
        document.forms[0].gardeningList.options[nextItem]
            = gardeningItem;
        document.forms[0].elements[0].value = "";
    }
}
function deleteItem() {
    var selectedItem
        = document.forms[0].gardeningList.selectedIndex;
    if (selectedItem == -1)
        window.alert("You must select an item in the list.");
    else
        document.forms[0].gardeningList.options[selectedItem]
            = null;
}
function changeItem() {
    var selectedItem= document.forms[0].gardeningList.selectedIndex;
    if (selectedItem == -1)
        window.alert("You must select an item in the list.");
    document.forms[0].gardeningList.options[selectedItem].value
        = document.forms[0].elements[0].value;
    document.forms[0].gardeningList.options[selectedItem].text
        = document.forms[0].elements[0].value;
}
/* ]]> */
</script>
</head>
<body>
<h1>Spring Planting</h1>
<h2>Gardening List</h2>
<form action="">
<p>New Item <input type="text" size="68" name="elements[0]" /></p>
<p><input type="button" value="Add Item" onclick="addItem()"
style="width: 120px" />
<input type="button" value="Delete Item" onclick="deleteItem()"
style="width: 120px" />
<input type="button" value="Clear List"
onclick="document.forms[0].gardeningList.options.length = 0;"
```

```
style="width: 120px" />
<input type="button" value="Change Item" onclick="changeItem()"
style="width: 120px" /><br />
<p><select name="gardeningList" size="10" style="width: 500px">
<option value="pruners">Pruners</option>
<option value="seeds">Seeds</option>
</select></p>
</form>
```

Figure 5-14

Shopping list form

Next, you add code to the Subscription.html document that modifies magazine names in the selection list.

To add code to the Subscription.html document that modifies magazine names in the selection list:

1. Return to the **Subscription.html** document in your text editor.

2. Add the following elements to the end of the <p> element that contains the other buttons. The Change Magazine button includes an `onclick` event handler, which calls a function named `changeMagazine()`. You will add this function next.

   ```
   <input type="button" value="Change Magazine"
   onclick="changeMagazine()" style="width: 120px" />
   ```

3. Add the following `changeMagazine()` function to the end of the script section. The function is very familiar to the `changeItem()` function you saw in the shopping list form.

   ```
   function changeMagazine() {
        var selectedItem =
             document.forms[0].magazines.selectedIndex;
   ```

```
if (selectedItem == -1)
      window.alert("You must select a magazine
             name in the list.");
else {
      document.forms[0].magazines.options[selectedItem]
             .value = document.forms[0].elements[31].value;
      document.forms[0]. magazines.options[selectedItem]
             .text = document.forms[0].elements[31].value;
   }
}
```

4. Save the **Subscription.html** document and then open it in your Web browser. Scroll to the end of the Web page and try adding and changing some magazines in the magazine list. Figure 5-15 shows how the document appears.

Figure 5-15

Subscription form with a selection list

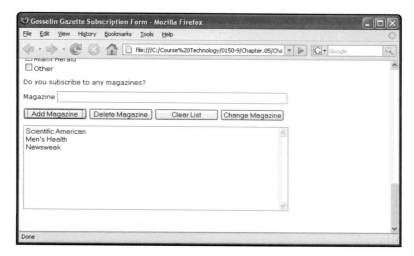

5. Close your Web browser window.

Submitting and Resetting Forms

In this section, you will learn how to submit forms to a server-side script and how to reset form fields to their default values. You will also learn how to use JavaScript to validate submitted data and to confirm whether users really want to reset their form fields.

Submit Buttons

An `<input>` element with a type of "submit" (`<input type="submit" />`) creates a **submit button** that transmits a form's data to a Web server. The `action` attribute of the `<form>` element that creates the form determines to what URL the form is submitted. Although you can include the `name` attribute for a submit button, it is not required because submit buttons do not have values that are submitted to a Web server as part of the form data. The width of a button created with the submit <input> element is based on the number of characters in its value attribute. If you do not include a value attribute, then the default label of the submit button, "Submit Query", is used.

The following statement creates a submit button with a label that reads "Place Order":

```
<p><input type="submit" value="Place Order" /></p>
```

An <input> element with a type of *image* (<input type="image">) creates an **image submit button** that displays a graphical image and transmits a form's data to a Web server. The image <input> element performs exactly the same function as the submit <input> element. You include the src attribute to specify the image to display on the button. You can also include the name and value attributes with the image <input> element, along with the alt attribute to define alternate text for user agents that do not display images.

Next, you will add a submit button to the Subscription.html document.

To add a submit button to the Subscription.html document:

1. Return to the **Subscription.html** document in your text editor.

2. Before the closing </form> tag, add the following elements to create the submit button:

   ```
   <p><input type="image" alt="Graphical image of a subscribe
   button" src="subscribe.gif" /></p>
   ```

3. Save the **Subscription.html** document and then open it in your Web browser. The submit button should appear at the bottom of the page, as shown in Figure 5-16.

Figure 5-16
Subscription form after adding an image submit button

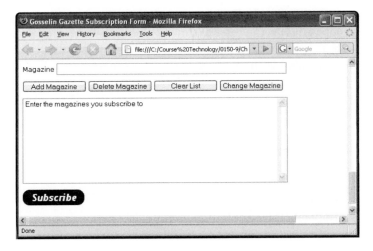

4. Complete the form and then click the **Subscribe** button. The FormProcessor.html document should open and display the data you entered. Figure 5-17 shows how the FormProcessor.html document appears in a Web browser.

Figure 5-17

FormProcessor.html after submitting the Subscription form

5.   Close your Web browser window.

Reset Buttons

An `<input>` element with a type of "reset" (`<input type="reset" />`) creates a **reset button** that clears all form entries and resets each form element to the initial value specified by its `value` attribute. Although you can include the `name` attribute for a reset button, it is not required because reset buttons do not have values that are submitted to a Web server as part of the form data. The text you assign to the reset button's `value` attribute appears as the button label. If you do not include a `value` attribute, then the default label of the reset button, "Reset", appears. The width of a button created with the reset `<input>` element depends on the number of characters in its `value` attribute.

The following statement creates a reset button with a label that reads "Start Over".

```
<p><input type="reset" value="Start Over" /></p>
```

Next, you add a reset button to the Subscription.html document.

To add a reset button to the Subscription.html document:

1.   Return to the **Subscription.html** document in your text editor.

2.   To create the reset button, add the following elements to the end of the form section:

```
<p><input type="reset" /></p>
```

3.   Save the **Subscription.html** document and then open it in your Web browser. Enter some data in the form's fields and test the reset button to see how it works. Figure 5-18 shows how the reset buttons appear in a Web browser.

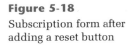

Figure 5-18
Subscription form after
adding a reset button

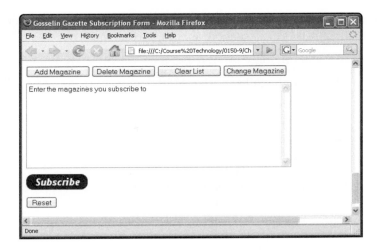

4. Close your Web browser window.

Validating Submitted Data

In Chapter 3, you learned about many of the event handlers that can be used in JavaScript. Two additional event handlers, onsubmit and onreset, are available for use with the <form> element. The **onsubmit event handler** executes when a form is submitted to a server-side script (in other words, when a submit button is selected on a form). The onsubmit event handler is often used to verify or validate a form's data before it is sent to a server. The **onreset event handler** executes when a reset button is selected on a form. You use the onreset event handler to confirm that a user really wants to reset the contents of a form. Both the onsubmit and onreset event handlers are placed before the closing bracket of an opening <form> tag. The following code shows how a form tag with onsubmit and onreset event handlers is written:

```
<form action="FormProcessor.html" method="post"
onsubmit="JavaScript statements;"
onreset="JavaScript statements;">
```

The onsubmit and onreset event handlers must return a value of true or false, depending on whether the form should be submitted (true) or reset (false). For example, the onsubmit and onreset event handlers in the following code return values of true or false, depending on whether the user clicks the OK button or the Cancel button in the Confirm dialog box. If the user clicks the OK button, the Confirm dialog box returns a value of true, and the onsubmit or onreset event executes. If the user clicks the Cancel button, the Confirm dialog box returns a value of false, and the onsubmit or onreset event does not execute.

```
<form action="FormProcessor.html" method="post"
onsubmit="return window.confirm('Are you sure you want
to submit the form?');"
onreset="return window.confirm('Are you sure you want
to reset the form?');">
```

Next, you will add onsubmit and onreset event handlers to the Subscription.html document to confirm that the user really wants to submit or reset the form.

To add onsubmit and onreset event handlers to the Subscription.html document:

1. Return to the **Subscription.html** document in your text editor.

2. Add the following confirmSubmit() and confirmReset() function to the end of the script section:

```
function confirmSubmit() {
    var submitForm = window.confirm("Are you sure you want to
        submit the form?");
    if (submitForm == true)
        return true;
    return false;
}
function confirmReset() {
    var resetForm = window.confirm("Are you sure you want to
        reset the form?");
    if (resetForm == true)
        return true;
    return false;
}
```

3. Before the closing bracket of the opening <form> tag, add the following onsubmit and onreset event handler that calls the confirmSubmit() and confirmReset() functions:

```
onsubmit="return confirmSubmit();"
onreset="return confirmReset();"
```

4. Save the **Subscription.html** document and then open it in your Web browser. Enter some data in the form's fields and click the **Reset** button to see if you receive the warning. Click the **Cancel** button and then click the **Subscribe** button to see if you receive the warning. Click the **OK** button in the Confirm dialog box. The data you entered should appear in the FormProcessor.html document.

5. Close your Web browser window.

Although the onsubmit event handler is useful for confirming that a user really wants to submit a form, its most important purpose is to validate form data. The validation of form data can mean many things ranging from simply ensuring that a field is not empty to performing complex validation of credit card numbers. You have already seen several examples of validation at the form level when you wrote code that checked whether a value entered in the Zip code or telephone number fields in the subscription form was a number. You also wrote code that confirmed that the user entered the same value in the password and password confirmation boxes. In the next section you'll learn how to perform the final step in the validation of these types of fields, ensuring that they are not empty when the form is submitted.

Validating Text and Password Boxes

To verify that text and password boxes are not empty, you can use an `if` statement in the `onsubmit` event handler that checks whether the field's value property contains a value. For example, the following code (which could be called from an `onsubmit` event handler) uses an `if` statement to check whether two text fields (`firstName` and `lastName`) contain text. If they do contain text, a value of true is returned and the form is submitted. If they do not contain text, a value of false is returned and the form is not submitted. Notice that the conditional expression uses the `||` (Or) operator to confirm that both fields have been filled.

```
function submitForm() {
    if (document.forms[0].firstName.value == ""
            || document.forms[0].lastName.value == "") {
            window.alert("You must enter your first and
                    last names!");
            return false;
    }
    else
            return true;
}
```

Next, you add code to the `confirmSubmit()` function in the Subscription form that validates the text and password boxes.

To add code to the `confirmSubmit()` function in the Subscription form that validates the text and password boxes:

1. Return to the **Subscription.html** document in your text editor.

2. Replace the statements within the `confirmSubmit()` function with the following statements, which validate the billing fields. The conditional statement uses multiple `||` (Or) operators to validate all of the billing fields in one expression.

```
if (document.forms[0].name_billing.value == ""
        || document.forms[0].address_billing.value == ""
        || document.forms[0].city_billing.value == ""
        || document.forms[0].state_billing.value == ""
        || document.forms[0].zip_billing.value == "") {
    window.alert("You must enter your billing information.");
    return false;
}
```

3. Add the following statements to the end of the `confirmSubmit()` function to validate the shipping fields:

```
else if (document.forms[0].name_shipping.value == ""
        || document.forms[0].address_shipping.value == ""
        || document.forms[0].city_shipping.value == ""
        || document.forms[0].state_shipping.value == ""
        || document.forms[0].zip_shipping.value == "") {
    window.alert("You must enter your shipping information.");
```

```
        return false;
    }
```

4. Add the following statements to the end of the `confirmSubmit()` function to validate the telephone fields:

```
else if (document.forms[0].area.value == ""
    || document.forms[0].exchange.value == ""
    || document.forms[0].phone.value == "") {
    window.alert("You must enter your telephone number.");
    return false;
}
```

5. Add the following statements to the end of the `confirmSubmit()` function to validate the password fields:

```
else if (document.forms[0].password.value == ""
    || document.forms[0].password_confirm.value == "") {
    window.alert("You must enter a password.");
    return false;
}
```

6. Finally, add the following return statement to the end of the `confirmSubmit()` function:

```
return true;
```

7. Save the **Subscription.html** document and then open it in your Web browser. Enter some data in the form's billing, shipping, telephone, and password fields, but leave some fields blank. Click the **Subscribe** button. Depending on which fields you left blank, you should see an alert message telling you which fields need to be filled in.

8. Click the **OK** button, fill in the fields you left blank, and then click the **Subscribe** button. The data you entered should appear in the FormProcessor.html document.

9. Close your Web browser window.

Validating Radio Buttons

Recall that when multiple form elements share the same name, JavaScript creates an array out of the elements using the shared name. Radio buttons, for instance, share the same name so that a single name=value pair can be submitted to a server-side script. When you have an array that is created from a group of buttons that share the same name, you can use the `checked` property to determine which element in a group is selected. The `checked` property returns a value of true if a check box or radio button is selected, and a value of false if it is not.

When you have an array that is created from a group of buttons that share the same name, you can use the `checked` property to determine which element in a group is selected. The `checked` property returns a value of true if a check box or radio button is selected, and a value of false if it is not. For example, if you have a group of radio buttons named `maritalStatus`, then you can use an `onsubmit` event handler similar to the following to determine if one of the radio buttons in the group is selected:

```
function submitForm() {
    var maritalStatusSelected = false;
    for (var i=0; i<5; ++i) {
        if (document.forms[0].maritalStatus[i].checked == true) {
            maritalStatusSelected = true;
            break;
        }
    }
    if (maritalStatusSelected == false) {
        window.alert("You must select your marital status.");
        return false;
    }
    else
        return true;
}
```

Next, you add code to the `confirmSubmit()` function in the Subscription form that validates the Delivery Rates radio buttons.

To add code to the `confirmSubmit()` function in the Subscription form that validates the Delivery Rates radio buttons:

1. Return to the **Subscription.html** document in your text editor.

2. The Delivery Rates radio buttons are contained within two groups: `delivery` and `sunday`. You need to ensure that a button is selected in one of the groups. First, add the following variable declaration and `for` statement above the `return true;` statement at the end of the `confirmSubmit()` function. The `for` statement checks whether a button is selected in the `delivery` group.

```
var deliverySelected = false;
for (var i=0; i<8; ++i) {
    if (document.forms[0].delivery[i].checked == true) {
        deliverySelected = true;
        break;
    }
}
```

3. Next, add the following `for` statement above the `return true;` statement at the end of the `confirmSubmit()` function to check whether a button is selected in the `sunday` group:

```
for (var j=0; j<2; ++j) {
    if (document.forms[0].sunday[j].checked == true) {
        deliverySelected = true;
        break;
    }
}
```

4. Finally, add the following code above the `return true;` statement at the end of the `confirmSubmit()` function to cancel the form submission if one of the Delivery Rates radio buttons is not selected:

```
if (deliverySelected != true) {
    window.alert("You must select a delivery rate option.");
    return false;
}
```

5. Save the **Subscription.html** document and then open it in your Web browser. Enter some data in the form's billing, shipping, telephone, and password fields, and then click the **Subscribe** button. You should see an alert message instructing you to select a delivery option. Click the **OK** button, select a delivery option, and then click the **Subscribe** button. The data you entered should appear in the FormProcessor.html document.

6. Close your Web browser window.

Validating Check Boxes

You can use the `checked` property to determine whether an individual check box has been selected. If check boxes are part of a group, then you can validate them using the same functionality as the validation code for radio buttons, because JavaScript creates an array out of elements with the same name. The following `onsubmit` event handler determines whether at least one check box in a group of check boxes named `committees` is selected:

```
function submitForm() {
    var committeesSelected = false;
    for (var i=0; i<4; ++i) {
        if (document.forms[0].committees[i].checked == true) {
            committeesSelected = true;
            break;
        }
    }
    if (committeesSelected == false) {
        window.alert("You must select at least one committee.");
        return committeesSelected;
    }
    else
        return committeesSelected;
}
```

Because the newspaper subscription check boxes in the Subscription form are optional, you can skip adding validation code for them.

Validating Selection Lists

Validating selection lists is a little easier than validating radio buttons and check boxes because you only need to test whether the selection list's `selectedIndex` property contains a value of -1. If it does, then no option is selected.

TIP

Remember that if the size attribute is excluded or set to 1, and the <select> element does not include the multiple attribute, then the selection list is a drop-down style menu. For drop-down style menus, the first option element is auto-matically selected.

The following onsubmit event handler determines whether at least one option in a selection list named brand is selected:

```
function submitForm() {
    if (document.forms[0].brand.selectedIndex == -1) {
        window.alert("You must select at least one brand.");
        return false;
    }
    else
        return true;
}
```

The selection list in the subscription form allows subscribers to build a list of magazines to which they subscribe. However, one or more options (depending on whether the <select> element includes the multiple attribute) must be selected in the selection list in order to be submitted to a Web server with the rest of the form data. Because you cannot count on subscribers to select all of the magazines they entered in the selection list before clicking the Subscribe button, you need to add code to the Subscription form that selects all of the magazines when the form is submitted. You will do this by adding a looping statement to the confirmSubmit() event handler function that selects each option in the magazine selection list using the selected property of the Option object.

To add a looping statement to the confirmSubmit() event handler function that selects each option in the magazine selection list:

1. Return to the **Subscription.html** document in your text editor.

2. Locate the return true; statement at the end of the confirmSubmit() function. Above the return true; statement, add the following code to select all of the magazines in the selection list when the form is submitted:

   ```
   for (var k=0; k<document.forms[0].magazines.length; ++k) {
       document.forms[0].magazines.options[k].selected = true;
   }
   ```

3. Save the **Subscription.html** document, then validate it with the W3C Markup Validation Service and fix any errors that the document contains. Once the document is valid, open it in your Web browser. Enter some data in all of the form's fields, and be sure to enter some magazine names. Click the **Subscribe** button. The data you entered, including the magazine names, should appear in the FormProcessor.html document.

4. Close your Web browser window and text editor.

CHAPTER 5

Chapter Summary

▶ Forms collect information from users and transmit that information to a server for processing.

▶ The <form> element designates a form within a Web page and contains all the text and elements that make up a form.

▶ Four primary elements are used within the <form> element to create form controls: <input>, <button>, <select>, and <textarea>.

▶ Any form element into which a user can enter data (such as a text box), or that a user can select or change (such as a radio button), is called a field.

▶ The Form object represents a form on a Web page, while the Input object represents a form control, such as a text box.

▶ The Document object includes a forms[] array that contains all of the forms on a Web page.

▶ The empty <input> element is used to generate input fields that create different types of interface elements, such as text boxes, radio buttons, and so on.

▶ The <select> element creates a selection list that presents users with fixed lists of items from which to choose.

▶ You use <option> elements to specify the options that appear in a selection list.

▶ The Select object represents a selection list in a form.

▶ The Option object represents an option in a selection list.

▶ An <input> element with a type of "submit" (<input type="submit" />) creates a submit button that transmits a form's data to a Web server.

▶ An <input> element with a type of reset (<input type="reset" />) creates a reset button that clears all form entries and resets each form element to the initial value specified by its value attribute.

▶ The onsubmit event handler executes when a form is submitted to a server-side script—that is, when a submit button is selected on a form using a submit <input> element or an image <input> element.

▶ The onreset event handler executes when a reset button is selected on a form.

Review Questions

1. Which of the following MIME types can you use with the <form> element's enctype attribute? (Choose all that apply.)

   a. application/x-www-form-urlunencoded

   b. application/x-www-form-urlencoded

   c. text/plain

   d. multipart/form-data

2. Why would you submit form data to an e-mail address instead of to a Web server? For what types of companies or Web sites is submitting form data to an e-mail address best suited?

3. Documents that reference a form's `name` attribute are well formed according to the strict DTD. True or false?

4. Objects representing each of the controls in a form are stored in the _____ array.

    a. `forms[]`
    b. `controls[]`
    c. `inputs[]`
    d. `elements[]`

5. You can refer to a form control object with which of the following methods? (Choose all that apply.)

    a. with the control's `name` attribute
    b. with the `elements[]` array
    c. with the `controls[]` array
    d. with the `fields[]` array

6. Which of the following elements correctly uses the Boolean `checked` attribute in XHTML?

    a. `<option value="freshman" selected="1" />`
    b. `<option value="sophomore" selected="selected" />`
    c. `<option value="junior" selected />`
    d. `<option value="senior" selected="true" />`

7. Explain how to ensure that users enter a number into a text field.

8. Only one selected radio button in a group creates a name=value pair when a form is submitted to a Web server. True or false?

9. When multiple form elements share the same name, JavaScript creates an array out of the elements using the shared name. True or false?

10. Which property sets and returns a Boolean value indicating whether multiple options can be selected in a selection list?

    a. `sizeable`
    b. `select`
    c. `multiple`
    d. `many`

11. Selections lists must include at least one `<option>` element. True or false?

12. What value does the `selectedIndex` property of the `Select` object return if no option is selected?

a.   -1

b.   0

c.   1

d.   false

13.   How do you use the `Option()` constructor to add a new option after a Web page renders a selection list?

14.   What is the correct syntax for removing the first element from an `options[]` array in a selection list named `customers`?

a.   `document.forms[0].customers.options[0] = null;`

b.   `document.forms[0].customers.options[0] = "";`

c.   `document.forms[0].customers.options[0] = 0;`

d.   `document.forms[0].customers.options[0] = -1;`

15.   Where do you place the `onsubmit` event handler?

a.   in a submit `<input>` element

b.   in the closing `</form>` tag

c.   in the form control that calls the submit event

d.   in the opening `<form>` tag

16.   Explain how to add, remove, and change selection list options.

17.   Explain how to create a reset event handler function.

18.   Explain how to verify that text and password boxes are not empty

19.   Which of the following properties indicates whether a check box or radio button is selected?

a.   `selected`

b.   `checked`

c.   `active`

d.   `isSelected`

20.   Explain how to validate selection lists.

Hands-On Projects

 ### Project 5-1

In addition to using `<input>` elements with type attributes of "submit" or "reset" to create submit and reset buttons, you can also use the `<button>` element to create submit buttons, reset buttons, as well as push buttons, which are similar to the OK and Cancel buttons you see in dialog boxes. The buttons you create with the `<button>` element are virtually identical to the buttons you create with the `<input>` element. The big difference, however, is that you create the <button> element using an opening and closing tag pair, which allows more flexibility in the labels you can create for a button. You can use the standard name and value attributes with the <button> element, along with type attribute, which allows you to specify the button type to be rendered. Valid values for the <button> element's type attribute are submit, reset, and button. However, the value you assign to the value attribute is not used as the button's label (although it will be sent to the Web server as part of the control's name=value pair). Instead, the content placed within the <button> element tag pair determines the button label. You can embed an <img> element within the <button> tag or use text elements to modify the appearance of the text that appears as a button's label.

In this project, you will modify the Subscription form so the reset button is created with the <button> element. You will also use an image to represent the reset button. Your Chapter folder for Chapter 5 contains an image file named reset.gif that you can use for this project.

1. Open in your text editor the **Subscription.html** document, located in your Chapter folder for Chapter 5.

2. Navigate to the end of the document, then delete the following reset <input> element and the paragraph element that contains it:

   ```
   <p><input type="reset" /></p>
   ```

3. Add the following <button> element just before the last closing </p> tag. The element's type attribute is assigned a value of "reset". The element also includes a style attribute that suppresses the button's default border and background color.

   ```
   <button style="border:0; background:white" type="reset"><img
   src="reset.gif" alt="Graphical image of reset button." />
   </button>
   ```

4. Save the **Subscription.html** document.

5. Use the W3C Markup Validation Service to validate the **Subscription.html** document and fix any errors that the document contains. Once the document is valid, close it in your text editor and then open it in your Web browser.

6. Enter some data in the form, and then scroll to the end of the document. You should see the new Reset image button. Click the Reset image button and you should see the prompt asking if you really want to reset the form. Click OK.

7. Close your Web browser window.

Project 5-2

In this project, you will create a script that automatically moves a user's curser to the next field after a specified number of characters have been entered into the current field. The project will use a simple form that allows users to enter their 10-digit telephone number. The form will contain three text boxes for the area code, exchange, and number portions of the telephone number.

1. Create a new document in your text editor.

2. Type the `<!DOCTYPE>` declaration, `<html>` element, header information, and the `<body>` element. Use the strict DTD and "Auto Next Field" as the content of the `<title>` element.

3. Add the following form to the document body. The form contains three text boxes. The first two text boxes, for the area code and exchange, use the `onkeyup` event to call an event handler function named `nextField()`. Two arguments are passed to the `nextField()` function: a `this` reference, which passes the name of the current control, and the name of the destination control. Notice that each of the text boxes includes `maxlength` attributes.

```
<form action="FormProcessor.html" method="get"
enctype="application/x-www-form-urlencoded">
<p><strong>Enter your 10-digit telephone number:</strong>
<input type="text" name="area_code" size="4"
onkeyup="nextField(this, document.forms[0].exchange)"
maxlength="3" />
<input type="text" name="exchange" size="4"
onkeyup="nextField(this, document.forms[0].number)"
maxlength="3" />
<input type="text" name="number" size="5" maxlength="4" /></p>
</form>
```

4. Add the following script section and paragraph elements to the document body:

```
<script type="text/javascript">
/* <![CDATA[ */
/* ]]> */
</script>
```

5. Add to the script section the following `nextField()` function, which is called from the `onkeyup` events in the `<input>` elements. Notice how the conditional expression compares length of the field to the `maxlength` attribute. The current value assigned to the field is retrieved with the `value` property. Then, a property named `length` is appended to the `value` property. The `length` property is a property of the `String` class, and it returns the number of characters in a string. (You will study the `String` class in Chapter 7.) If the length of the field is equal to the value assigned to the `maxlength` attribute, then the `focus()` statement moves the focus to the field identified by the `destField` parameter.

```
function nextField(startField, destField) {
    if (startField.value.length==startField.maxLength)
    destField.focus();
}
```

6. Save the document as **AutoNextField.html** in the Projects folder for Chapter 5.

7. Use the W3C Markup Validation Service to validate the **AutoNextField.html** document and fix any errors that the document contains. Once the document is valid, close it in your text editor and then open it in your Web browser.

8. Enter an area code into the first text box. After you enter the third number in the area code, focus transfers to the second text box. Enter an area code into the second text box. After you enter the third number in the exchange, focus transfers to the third text box.

9. Close your Web browser window.

Project 5-3

When you first open a Web page with a form in a browser, none of the form controls have the focus. In this project, you create a Web page that sets the focus when the Web page first opens. The Web page you create will contain a simple inquiry form that might be sent to a real estate agent.

1. Create a new document in your text editor and type the `<!DOCTYPE>` declaration, `<html>` element, document head, and `<body>` element. Use the strict DTD and "Realtor Inquiry" as the content of the `<title>` element.

2. Add the following heading element and form to the document body. The form contains several text boxes that gather details of the property that a customer is looking for along with a selection list that allows customers to select a specific type of property.

```
<h1>Real Estate Inquiry</h1>
<form action="FormProcessor.html" method="get"
enctype="application/x-www-form-urlencoded">
<p>Name<br />
<input type="text" name="visitor_name" size="50" /></p>
<p>E-mail address<br />
<input type="text" name="e-mail" size="50" /></p>
<p>Phone<br />
<input type="text" name="phone" size="50" /></p>
<p>Area of town<br />
<input type="text" name="area" size="50" /></p>
<p>Property <select name="property_type">
<option value="unselected">Select a Property Type</option>
<option value="condo">Condos</option>
<option value="single">Single Family Homes</option>
<option value="multi">Multifamily Homes</option>
<option value="mobile">Mobile Homes</option>
<option value="mobile">Land</option>
</select>
Sq. feet <input type="text" name="feet" size="5" /> </p>
<p>Bedrooms <input type="text" name="bedrooms" size="5" />
Maximum price <input type="text" name="price" size="12" /></p>
```

```
<p>How should we contact you? <input type="radio"
name="contactHow"value="call_me" /> Call me
<input type="radio" name="contactHow" value="e-mail_me" />
E-mail me</p>
<p><input type="submit" /></p>
</form>
```

3.   Add a script section to the document head, as follows:

```
<script type="text/javascript">
/* <![CDATA[ */
/* ]]> */
</script>
```

4.   Add to the script section the following setFormFocus() function, which uses the focus() method of the Input object to set the focus on the first control in the form, named visitor_name:

```
function setFormFocus() {
    document.forms[0].visitor_name.focus();
}
```

5.   Add to the opening <body> tag the following onload event handler, which calls the setFormFocus() method when the page first loads:

```
onload="setFormFocus();"
```

6.   Save the document as **RealEstateInquiry.html** in the Projects folder for Chapter 5, and then open it in your Web browser. The first control on the form should receive the focus as soon as the form is rendered.

7.   Close your Web browser window.

Project 5-4

In this project, you will add default values to the text boxes you created in the last project. You will also add onfocus event handlers to each text box to remove the default values when the text box receives the focus.

1.   Return to the **RealEstateInquiry.html** document you created in the last project.

2.   Add value attributes to each of the text <input> elements to create default values, as follows:

```
<form action="FormProcessor.html" method="get"
enctype="application/x-www-form-urlencoded">
<p>Name<br />
<input type="text" name="visitor_name" size="50"
value="Enter your name" /></p>
<p>E-mail address<br />
<input type="text" name="e-mail" size="50"
```

```
value="Enter your e-mail address" /></p>
<p>Phone<br />
<input type="text" name="phone" size="50"
value="Enter your phone number" /></p>
<p>Area of town<br />
<input type="text" name="area" size="50"
value="What area of town are you interested in?" /></p>
<p>Property <select name="property_type">
<option value="unselected">Select a Property Type</option>
<option value="condo">Condos</option>
<option value="single">Single Family Homes</option>
<option value="multi">Multifamily Homes</option>
<option value="mobile">Mobile Homes</option>
<option value="mobile">Land</option>
</select>
Sq. feet <input type="text" name="feet" size="5"
value="???" /> </p>
<p>Bedrooms <input type="text" name="bedrooms" size="5"
value="???" />
Maximum price <input type="text" name="price" size="12"
value="$$$" /></p>
<p>How should we contact you? <input type="radio"
name="contactHow" value="call_me" /> Call me
<input type="radio" name="contactHow" value="e-mail_me" />
E-mail me</p>
<p><input type="submit" /></p>
</form>
```

3. Add `onclick` event handlers to each `<input>` element to check whether the value of the control is equal to its default value. If so, then change the value to an empty string (`" "`). For example, the `onclick` event handler for the `visitor_name` `<input>` element is as follows:

```
onclick="if (this.value == 'Enter your name') this.value = '';")
```

4. Add validation code to the RealEstateInquiry.html document that verifies the text boxes are not empty and do not contain the default values when the form is submitted. For the square feet, number of bedrooms, and maximum price fields, include validation code that verifies the user entered a numeric value. Also, add validation code that verifies whether users have selected values from the selection list and the radio button group.

5. Save the **RealEstateInquiry.html** document, validate it the W3C Markup Validation Service, and fix any errors that the document contains. Once the document is valid, close it in your text editor and then open it in your Web browser. Selecting each control should remove the default values.

6. Close your Web browser window.

Case Projects

For the following projects, save the documents you create in your Cases folder for Chapter 5. Be sure to validate each Web page with the W3C Markup Validation Service.

Case Project 5-1

Create a Web page that a Web site can use to ensure that customers read and agree to the terms and conditions of visiting the Web site. Include some legal text explaining the terms and conditions. (You can make this up.) Include a button that reads "Enter Site". Also, include a check box that reads "I accept the terms and conditions". Add code that forces the user to select the check box before clicking the Enter Site button. Save the document as **Terms.html**.

Case Project 5-2

Create a Web page that contains a table with three columns. In the left and right columns, create two selection lists. Fill both selection lists with unique items, such as baby names. In the middle column, add two buttons: one button should contain the characters ">>" and the other button should contain the characters "<<". Write a script that moves the selection list items between the two columns. For example, if the left column contains the name "David", clicking the >> button should move the name to the right column. Save the script as **MoveMenuItems.html**.

Case Project 5-3

Create a registration form, similar to what you may encounter when registering for an online Web site. Include three sections: Personal Information, Security Information, and Preferences. In the Personal Information section, add name, e-mail address, and telephone fields. Include default text in the name and e-mail text boxes, but write some code that removes the default text from each text box when a user clicks it. Write code for the telephone field that prevents users from entering any values except for numbers. In the Security Information section, add password and password confirmation fields. Write code that ensures that the same value was entered into both fields. Also add a security challenge question selection list and a security answer text box that the Web site will use to help identify a user in the event that he or she loses his or her password. The security challenge selection list should contain questions such as "What is your mother's maiden name?", "What is the name of your pet?", and "What is your favorite color?". In the Preferences section, add radio buttons that confirm whether a user wants special offers sent to his or her e-mail address. Also, include check boxes with special interests the user may be interested in, such as entertainment, business, and shopping. Add submit and reset buttons that call `submit()` and `reset()` event handler functions when they are clicked. The `submit()` event handler function should ensure that the user has entered values into each text box, and that the values submitted are not the same as the default text. The `submit()` event handler function should also ensure that the user selects a security challenge question, selects a radio button to confirm whether he or she wants special offers sent to his or her e-mail address, and selects at least one interest check box. Submit the form to the FormProcessor.html script (there is a copy in your Cases folder for Chapter 5). Save the document as **Registration.html**.

6

Using Object-Oriented JavaScript

In this chapter you will:

- Study object-oriented programming
- Learn about the built-in JavaScript objects
- Work with the `Date`, `Number`, and `Math` objects
- Define custom JavaScript objects

In this chapter, you will learn how to use object-oriented programming techniques in your JavaScript programs. Essentially, object-oriented programming allows you to use and create self-contained "objects" that can be reused in your programs. You already have some experience with object-oriented programming, after working with browser objects (including the `Window`, `Document`, and `Form` objects) in Chapters 4 and 5. The browser objects, however, are part of the Web browser itself. The objects you study in this chapter are part of the JavaScript programming language. Additionally, you will learn how to create your own custom JavaScript objects.

Introduction to Object-oriented Programming

The JavaScript programs you have written so far have mostly been self-contained; most code, such as variables, statements, and functions, exists within a script section. For example, you might create a Web page for an online retailer that uses JavaScript to calculate the total for a sales order that includes state sales tax and shipping. However, the retailer might sell different types of products on different Web pages; one page may sell baseball uniforms, another page may sell jellybeans, and so on. If you want to reuse the JavaScript sales total code on multiple Web pages, you must copy all of the statements or recreate them from scratch for each Web page. Object-oriented programming takes a different approach. It allows you to reuse code without having to copy or recreate it.

Reusing Software Objects

Object-oriented programming (OOP) refers to the creation of reusable software objects that can be easily incorporated into multiple programs. The term **object** specifically refers to programming code and data that can be treated as an individual unit or component. (Objects are also called **components**.) The term **data** refers to information contained within variables or other types of storage structures. In Chapter 1, you learned that the functions associated with an object are called methods, and the variables that are associated with an object are called properties or attributes.

Objects can range from simple controls such as a button, to entire programs such as a database application. In fact, some programs consist entirely of other objects. You'll often encounter objects that have been designed to perform a specific task. For example, in a retail sales program, you could refer to all of the code that calculates the sales total as a single object. You could then reuse that object over and over again in the same program just by typing the object name.

Popular object-oriented programming languages include C++, Java, and Visual Basic. Using any of these or other object-oriented languages, programmers can create objects themselves or use objects created by other programmers.

For example, if you are creating an accounting program in Visual Basic, you can use an object named Payroll that was created in C++. The Payroll object may contain one method that calculates the amount of federal and state tax to deduct, another method that calculates the FICA amount to deduct, and so on. Properties of the Payroll object may include an employee's number of tax withholding allowances, federal and state tax percentages, and the cost of insurance premiums. You do not need to know how the Payroll object was created in C++, nor do you need to re-create it in Visual Basic. You only need to know how to access the methods and properties of the Payroll object from the Visual Basic program.

TIP

You have already used object-oriented programming techniques when you included objects of the browser object model (BOM) in your scripts.

One way of understanding object-oriented programming is to compare it to how personal computers (PCs) are assembled. There are many manufacturers of PCs, but few manufacturers build all of the components that go into a particular unit. Instead, computer manufacturers usually include components from other vendors. For example, there are many different brands of monitors, keyboards, mice, and so on. Even though different manufacturers build each of these hardware components, if they are designed for a PC, then they all share common ways of attaching to the main computer. Monitors plug into standard monitor ports, keyboards plug into standard keyboard ports, mice plug into mouse ports, and so. In fact, most of today's hardware components can plug into a Universal Serial Bus (USB) port, which is a standard interface for connecting computer hardware. Just as all hardware components can plug into the same PC, the software components of an object-oriented program can all "plug" into one application.

An object-oriented accounting program is conceptually illustrated in Figure 6-1. In the figure, the accounting program is composed of four separate components that are plugged into the main accounting program: an Accounts Receivable object, an Accounts Payable object, an Expense Reporting object, and the Payroll object. The important thing to understand is that you do not need to rewrite the Accounts Receivable object, Accounts Payable object, Expense Reporting object, or the Payroll object for the accounting program; the accounting program only needs to call their methods and provide the correct data to their properties.

Figure 6-1

Conceptual illustration of
an accounting program

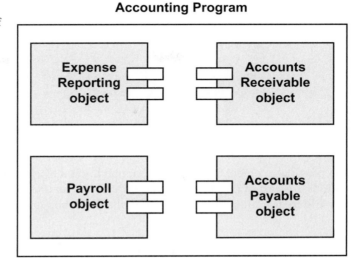

Accounting Program

What Is Encapsulation?

Objects are **encapsulated**, which means that all code and required data are contained within the object itself. In most cases, an encapsulated object consists of a single computer file that contains all code and required data. Encapsulation places code inside what programmers like to call a "black box"; when an object is encapsulated, you cannot see "inside" it—all internal workings are hidden. The code (methods and statements) and data (variables and constants) contained in an encapsulated object are accessed through an interface. An **interface** represents elements required for a source program to communicate with an object. For example, interface elements required to access a `Payroll` object might be a method named `calcNetPay()`, which calculates an employee's net pay, and properties containing the employee's name and pay rate.

When you include encapsulated classes in your programs, users can see only the methods and properties of the object that you allow them to see. Essentially, the principle of **information hiding** states that any methods and properties that other programmers do not need to access or know about should be hidden. By removing the ability to see inside the black box, encapsulation reduces the complexity of the code, allowing programmers who use the code to concentrate on the task of integrating the code into their programs. Encapsulation also prevents other programmers from accidentally introducing a bug into a program, or from possibly even stealing the code and claiming it as their own.

You can compare a programming object and its interface to a handheld calculator. The calculator represents an object, and you represent a program that wants to use the object. You establish an interface with the calculator object by entering numbers (the data required by the object) and then pressing calculation keys (which represent the methods of the object). You do not need to know, nor can you see, the inner workings of the calculator object. As a programmer, you are concerned only with an object's methods and properties. To continue the analogy, you are only concerned with the result you expect the calculator object to return. Figure 6-2 illustrates the idea of the calculator interface.

Figure 6-2
Calculator interface

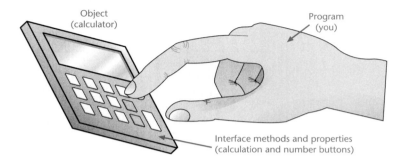

Object
(calculator)

Program
(you)

Interface methods and properties
(calculation and number buttons)

In JavaScript, the Document object is encapsulated, making it a black box. The write() and writeln() methods are part of the interface that JavaScript can use to communicate with the Document object. Figure 6-3 illustrates the concept of a black box using JavaScript and the Document object.

Figure 6-3
Conceptual example of the Document object black box

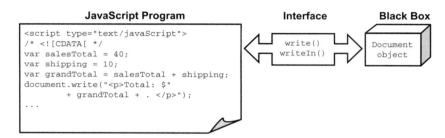

```
<script type="text/javaScript">
/* <![CDATA[ */
var salesTotal = 40;
var shipping = 10;
var grandTotal = salesTotal + shipping;
document.write("<p>Total: $"
        + grandTotal + . </p>");
...
```

JavaScript Program

Interface

write()
writeln()

Black Box

Document
object

Another example of an object and its interface is Microsoft Word. Word itself is actually an object made up of numerous other objects. The program window (or user interface) is one object. The items you see in the interface, such as the menu and toolbars, are used to execute methods. For example, the Bold button on the toolbar executes a bold method. The text of your document is the data you provide to the program. Microsoft Word is a helpful tool that you can use without knowing how the various methods work. You only need to know what each method does. To get full satisfaction out of Microsoft Word, you only need to provide the data (text) and execute the appropriate methods (such as the bold method), when necessary. In the same way, when using objects in your code, you only need to provide the necessary data (such as an employee's gross pay) and execute the appropriate method (such as the calcNetPay() method).

Understanding Classes

In object-oriented programming, the code, methods, attributes, and other information that make up an object are organized into **classes**. Essentially, a class is a template, or blueprint, that serves as the basis for new objects. When you use an object in your program, you actually create an instance of the class of the object. An **instance** is an object that has been created from an existing class. When you create an object from an existing class, you are said to be **instantiating** the object.

Later in this chapter, you will learn how to create, or instantiate, an object from built-in JavaScript classes and from custom classes that you write yourself. However, as a conceptual example, consider an object named BankAccount that contains methods and properties that you might use to record transactions associated with a checking or savings account. The BankAccount object is created from a `BankAccount` class. To use the `BankAccount` class, you create an instance of the class. A particular instance of an object **inherits** its methods and properties from a class—that is, it takes on the characteristics of the class on which it is based. The `BankAccount` object, for instance, would inherit all of the methods and properties of the `BankAccount` class. To give another example, when you create a new word processing document, which is a type of object, it usually inherits the properties of a template on which it is based. The template is a type of class. The document inherits characteristics of the template such as font size, line spacing, and boiler-plate text. In the same manner, programs that include instances of objects inherit the object's functionality.

TIP

Class names in traditional object-oriented programming usually begin with an uppercase letter. This convention is also followed in JavaScript.

Because objects in the browser object model are actually part of the Web browser, you do not need to instantiate them in order to use them in your programs. For example, you do not need to instantiate a `Document` object from the `Document` class in your JavaScript programs because the Web browser automatically instantiates one for you. However, you do need to instantiate objects from the built-in JavaScript classes that you will study next.

Built-in JavaScript Classes

The JavaScript language includes the 11 built-in classes listed in Table 6-1. Each object contains various methods and properties for performing a particular type of task.

Class	Description
Array	Creates new array objects
Boolean	Creates new Boolean objects
Date	Retrieves and manipulates dates and times
Error	Returns run-time error information
Function	Creates new function objects
Global	Stores global variables and contains various built-in JavaScript functions
Math	Contains methods and properties for performing mathematical calculations
Number	Contains methods and properties for manipulating numbers
Object	Represents the base class for all built-in JavaScript classes; contains several of the built-in JavaScript functions
RegExp	Contains methods and properties for finding and replacing characters in text strings
String	Contains methods and properties for manipulating text strings

Table 6-1   Built-in JavaScript classes

NOTE

You will study the `Date`, `Number`, `Math`, and `Object` classes in this chapter. You will study the `Array`, `String`, and `RegExp` classes in Chapter 7 and the `Error` object in Chapter 8.

Instantiating an Object

You can use some of the built-in JavaScript objects directly in your code, while other objects require you to instantiate a new object. The `Math` object is one that you can use directly in your programs without instantiating a new object. The following example shows how to use the `Math` object's `PI` (π) property in a script:

```
<script type="text/javascript">
// The following statement prints 3.141592653589793
document.write("The value of PI is " + Math.PI);
</script>
```

Unlike the `Math` object, an `Array` object requires you to instantiate a new object before you can use it. As you learned in Chapter 2, arrays are represented in JavaScript by the `Array` object, which contains a constructor named `Array()`. You create new arrays in your code using the `new` keyword and the `Array()` constructor. The following statement shows an example of how to instantiate an array named `teamRoster[]`:

```
var teamRoster = new Array();
```

You may be wondering why the preceding statement instantiates the new object using the `var` keyword. As you recall, the `var` keyword is used for declaring variables. The name you use for an instantiated object is really a variable just like an integer or string variable. In fact, programmers use the terms "variable" and "object" interchangeably. The difference is that the data the variable represents happens to be an object instead of a number or string. Recall from Chapter 2 that variables are the values a program stores in computer memory. Recall, too, that the JavaScript language also supports reference data types, which can contain multiple values or complex types of information, as opposed to the single values stored in primitive data types. In other words, in the same manner that you use a variable name to represent a primitive data type, such as an integer, in computer memory, you also use a variable name to represent an object. Because the objects you declare in your JavaScript program are actually a certain type of variable, you can use the `var` keyword to identify them as variables. You are not required to identify them; however, it is good practice always to use the `var` keyword when declaring any variables or objects in your programs.

NOTE

The `Option` object is the only object in the W3C browser object model from which you can instantiate a new object. The Web browser creates all other objects in the browser object model automatically. (You studied the `Option` object in Chapter 5.)

Performing Garbage Collection

If you have worked with other object-oriented programming languages, then you may be familiar with the term **garbage collection**, which refers to cleaning up, or reclaiming, memory that is reserved by a program. When you declare a variable or instantiate a new object, you are actually reserving computer memory for the variable or object. With some programming languages, you must write code that deletes a variable or object after you are through with it in order to free the memory for use by other parts of your program, or by other programs running on your computer. With JavaScript, you do not need to worry about reclaiming memory that is reserved for your variables or objects; JavaScript knows when your program no longer needs a variable or object and automatically cleans up the memory for you.

Using the `Date` Class

You can use dates in your programs to create a calendar, calculate how long it will take to do something, and so on. For instance, a Web page for a dry cleaning business may need to use the current date to calculate when a customer's dry cleaning order will be ready. The **Date class** contains methods and properties for manipulating the date and time. The `Date` class allows you to use the current date and time (or a specific date or time element, such as the current month) in your JavaScript programs. You create a `Date` object with one of the constructors listed in Table 6-2.

Constructor	Description
`Date()`	Creates a `Date` object that contains the current date and time from the local computer
`Date(milliseconds)`	Creates a `Date` object based on the number of milliseconds that have elapsed since midnight, January 1, 1970
`Date(date_string)`	Creates a `Date` object based on a string containing a date value
`Date(year, month[, date, hours, minutes, seconds, milliseconds])`	Creates a `Date` object with the date and time set according to the passed arguments; the year and month arguments are required

Table 6-2   Date class constructors

The following statement demonstrates how to create a `Date` object that contains the current date and time from the local computer:

```
var today = new Date();
```

The dates of the month and year in a `Date` object are stored using numbers that match the actual date and year. However, the days of the week and months of the year are stored in a `Date` object using numeric representations, starting with zero, similar to an array. The numbers 0 through 6 represent the days Sunday through Saturday, and the numbers 0 through 11 represent the months January through December. The following statement demonstrates how to specify a specific date with a `Date` constructor function. In this example, the date assigned to the `mozartsBirthday` variable is January 27, 1756.

```
var mozartsBirthday = new Date(1756, 0, 27);
```

After you create a new `Date` object, you can then manipulate the date and time in the variable, using the methods of the `Date` class. Note that the date and time in a `Date` object are not updated over time like a clock. Instead, a `Date` object contains the static (unchanging) date and time as of the moment the JavaScript code instantiates the object.

Table 6-3 lists commonly used methods of the `Date` class.

Method	Description
getDate()	Returns the date of a `Date` object
getDay()	Returns the day of a `Date` object
getFullYear()	Returns the year of a `Date` object in 4-digit format
getHours()	Returns the hour of a `Date` object
getMilliseconds()	Returns the milliseconds of a `Date` object
getMinutes()	Returns the minutes of a `Date` object
getMonth()	Returns the month of a `Date` object
getSeconds()	Returns the seconds of a `Date` object
getTime()	Returns the time of a `Date` object
setDate(*date*)	Sets the date (1-31) of a `Date` object
setFullYear(*year*[, *month*, *day*])	Sets the 4-digit year of a `Date` object; optionally allows you to set the month and the day
setHours(*hours*[, *minutes*, *seconds*, *milliseconds*])	Sets the hours (0-23) of a `Date` object; optionally allows you to set the minutes (0-59), seconds (0-59), and milliseconds (0-999)
setMilliseconds(*milliseconds*)	Sets the milliseconds (0-999) of a `Date` object
setMinutes(*minutes*[, *seconds*, *milliseconds*])	Sets the minutes (0-59) of a `Date` object; optionally allows you to set seconds (0-59) and milliseconds (0-999)
setMonth(*month*[, *date*])	Sets the month (0-11) of a `Date` object; optionally allows you to set the date (1-31)
setSeconds(*seconds*[, *milliseconds*])	Sets the seconds (0-59) of a `Date` object; optionally allows you to set milliseconds (0-999)
toLocaleString()	Converts a `Date` object to a string, set to the current time zone
toString()	Converts a `Date` object to a string
valueOf()	Converts a `Date` object to a millisecond format

Table 6-3   Commonly used methods of the `Date` class

NOTE
The `Date` class does not contain any properties.

Each portion of a `Date` object, such as the day, month, year, and so on, can be retrieved and modified using the `Date` object methods. For example, if you create a new `Date` object using the statement `var curDate = new Date();`, you can retrieve just the date portion stored in the `curDate` object by using the statement `curDate.getDate();`.

If you want to display the full text for days and months (for example, Wednesday, or January), then you can use a conditional statement to check the value returned by the `getDay()` or `getMonth()` method. For example, the following code uses an `if...else` construct to print the full text for the day of the week returned by the `getDay()` function. Figure 6-4 shows the output when the script is run on a Saturday.

```
<script type="text/javascript">
var today = new Date();
var curDay = today.getDay();
if (curDay == 0)
    document.write("Today is Sunday");
else if (curDay == 1)
    document.write("Today is Monday");
else if (curDay == 2)
    document.write("Today is Tuesday");
else if (curDay == 3)
    document.write("Today is Wednesday");
else if (curDay == 4)
    document.write("Today is Thursday");
else if (curDay == 5)
    document.write("Today is Friday");
else if (curDay == 6)
    document.write("Today is Saturday");
</script>
```

Figure 6-4

Output of a script with a `getDay()` method

If you need to return the full text of the day or month, you should assign the days of the week or the months of the year to an array. You can then combine the `getDay()` or `getMonth()` method with the array name to return the full text of the day or month. For example, the following code includes an array named `months[]` with 12 elements that are assigned the full text names of the months of the year.

```
<script type="text/javascript">
var today = new Date();
```

```
var months = new Array();
months[0] = "January"; months[1] = "February"; months[2] = "March";
months[3] = "April"; months[4] = "May"; months[5] = "June";
months[6] = "July"; months[7] = "August"; months[8] = "September";
months[9] = "October"; months[10] = "November"; months[11] =
"December";
var curMonth = months[today.getMonth()];
document.write("The current month is " + curMonth);
</script>
```

In the preceding code, the full text name of the month is assigned to the curMonth variable using the statement var curMonth = months[today.getMonth()];. The value of the element is retrieved by placing the today object with the getMonth() method appended to it between the brackets of the months[] array name. Figure 6-5 shows the output.

Figure 6-5

Output of a script with a getMonth() method

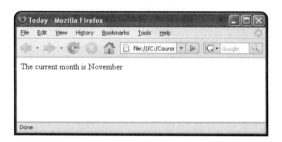

Next, you start creating a Web page for Central Valley Snowboarding that visitors can use to make group reservations. You will use the Date object to generate a monthly calendar that visitors can use to select reservation dates. The script will submit the reservation information to the same FormProcessor.html document that you used in Chapter 5. The FormProcessor.html document, located in your Chapter folder for Chapter 6, uses JavaScript code to display the values submitted from a form. The only purpose of the FormProcessor.html document is to display form data and provide a simple simulation of the response you would normally receive from a server-side scripting program.

To create a group reservations page for Central Valley Snowboarding that uses the Date object to generate a monthly calendar:

1. Start your text editor and create a new document.

2. Type the <!DOCTYPE> declaration, <html> element, header information, and the <body> element. Use the strict DTD and "Central Valley Snowboarding" as the content of the <title> element. Include a <link> element that links to the js_styles.css style sheet in your Chapter folder. Your document should appear as follows:

```
<!DOCTYPE html PUBLIC "-//W3C//DTD XHTML 1.0 Strict//EN"
"http://www.w3.org/TR/xhtml1/DTD/xhtml1-strict.dtd">
<html xmlns="http://www.w3.org/1999/xhtml">
<head>
<title>Central Valley Snowboarding</title>
```

```
<meta http-equiv="content-type" content="text/html;
    charset=iso-8859-1" />
<link rel="stylesheet" href="js_styles.css" type="text/css" />
</head>
<body>
</body>
</html>
```

3. Add the following text and elements to the document body. The form submits the data to the FormProcessor.html document.

```
<h1>Central Valley Snowboarding</h1>
<h2>Group Reservations</h2><hr />
<form action="FormProcessor.html" method="get"
    enctype="application/x-www-form-urlencoded">
</form>
```

4. Add the following elements to the end of the form section:

```
<h3>Snowboarding Date</h3>
<p><input type="text" name="reservationDate" /> </p>
<h3>Group Leader</h3>
<table border="0">
<tr valign="top">
    <td>Last name<br />
    <input type="text" name="leaderLastName" size="50" />
    <br />
        First name<br />
    <input type="text" name="leaderFirstName" size="50" />
    <br />
        Telephone<br />
    <input type="text" name="leaderTelephone" size="50" />
    <br />
        Address<br />
    <input type="text" name="leaderAddress" size="50" /><br />
        City, State, Zip<br />
    <input type="text" name="leaderCity" size="34" />
        <input type="text" name="leaderState" size="2"
        maxlength="2" />
    <input type="text" name="leaderZip" size="5"
    maxlength="5" /></td>
</tr></table>
<p><input type="submit" value="Submit Group Reservation" /></p>
```

5. Add the following script section after the closing </table> tag, but before the <p> tag that precedes the <input> element for the Submit button:

```
<script type="text/javascript">
/* <![CDATA[ */
```

```
/* ]]> */
</script>
```

6. Add the following statements to the script section, which declare a `Date` object at the global level, return the number representing the current month, and declare an array to contain the full text for the months of the year. The last two statements create a variable named `dateToday` and assign it as the value of the Snowboarding Date field in the form.

```
var dateObject = new Date();
var month = dateObject.getMonth();
var monthArray = new
Array("January","February","March","April","May","June",
"July","August","September","October","November","December");
var dateToday = monthArray[month] + " " + dateObject.getDate() + ",
" + dateObject.getFullYear();
document.forms[0].reservationDate.value = dateToday;
```

7. Save the document as **CVSGroups.html** in your Chapter folder for Chapter 6, and then open it in your Web browser. Figure 6-6 shows how the document appears in a Web browser. The current date should appear in the Snowboarding Date field.

Figure 6-6

Central Valley Snowboarding group reservations page

8. Close your Web browser window.

Next, you modify the Central Valley Snowboarding page so it includes functionality that allows users to select a date from a separate date picker window.

To add date picking functionality to the Central Valley Snowboarding page:

1. Return to the **CVSGroups.html** document in your text editor.

2. Add the following anchor element before the closing <p> tag in the paragraph element that contains the Snowboarding Date field. The anchor element contains an onclick event handler that calls a function named displayCalendar(), which you create next.

```
<a href="" onclick="displayCalendar(); return false">Select Date</a>
```

3. Next, start building the following displayCalendar() function. The statements in the function use the window.open() method to create a new window that will display the calendar. Notice that the statements use the calendarWin variable (which represents the new window) with document.write() statements to create the new window. In order for the contents of the window to be well formed, the code includes document.write() statements that create the <!DOCTYPE> declaration, <html> element, and header information. The last statement begins creating the table that will display the calendar. Add the following function to the end of the script section:

```
function displayCalendar() {
    calendarWin = window.open("", "CalWindow",
    "status=no,resizable=yes,width=400,height=320,left=200,
    top=200");
    calendarWin.focus();
    calendarWin.document.write("<!DOCTYPE html PUBLIC '-//W3C//
    DTD XHTML 1.0 Strict//EN' 'http://www.w3.org/TR/xhtml1/
    DTD/xhtml1-strict.dtd'><html xmlns='http://www.w3.org/
    1999/xhtml'>
    <head><title>Central Valley Snowboarding</title><meta
    http-equiv='content-type' content='text/html;
    charset=iso-8859-1' />
    <link rel='stylesheet' href='js_styles.css' type='text/
    css' /></head><body>");
    calendarWin.document.write("<table cellspacing='0'
    border='1' width='100%'>");
}
```

CAUTION
Be sure to type the literal strings in this exercise on the same line. They are broken here due to space limitations.

4. Start building the table by adding the following statements to the end of the displayCalendar() function. Notice that the second statement uses the monthArray[] and the month variables to print the name of the current month and the getFullYear() method of the dataObject variable to print the year.

```
calendarWin.document.write("<colgroup span='7' width='50' />");
calendarWin.document.write(
        "<tr><td colspan='7' align='center'><strong>"
        + monthArray[month] + " " + dateObject.getFullYear()
        + "</strong></td></td></tr>");
calendarWin.document.write("<tr align='center'><td>Sun</td>
<td>Mon</td><td>Tue</td><td>Wed</td><td>Thu</td><td>Fri</td>
<td>Sat</td></tr>");
calendarWin.document.write("<tr align='center'>");
```

5. Add the following statements to the end of the `displayCalendar()` function. The first statement uses the `setDate()` function to set the date of the `Date` object to the first day of the month. The second statement uses the `getDay()` function to determine which day of the week it is. For instance, if the `getDay()` function returns a value of 3, then the first day of the number starts on Wednesday. Any table cells for days in the first week that are part of the previous month are assigned a nonbreaking space character (` `) by the `for` statement.

```
dateObject.setDate(1);
var dayOfWeek = dateObject.getDay();
for (var i=0; i<dayOfWeek; ++i) {
        calendarWin.document.write("<td> </td>");
}
```

6. Add the following statements to the end of the `displayCalendar()` function. The first statement calculates the number of days in the first week that require date values. The second statement declares a variable named `dateCounter` that is used to keep track of the next date to write to the calendar. The `for` statement then finishes creating the first row in the table, which represents the first week of the month. Notice that the `for` statement creates anchor elements for each of the dates. When a user clicks on a date, an onclick event uses the `opener` property of the `self` object to assign the data value to the Snowboarding Date field in the form on the main Central Valley Snowboarding Web page, and then close the calendar window. (Recall that the `opener` property refers to the window that opened the current window.)

```
var daysWithDates = 7 - dayOfWeek;
var dateCounter = 1;
for(var i=0; i<daysWithDates; ++i) {
        var curDate = monthArray[month] + " " + dateCounter + ", "
        + dateObject.getFullYear();
        calendarWin.document.write("<td><a href=''
        onclick='self.opener.document.forms[0]
                .reservationDate.value=\""
        + curDate + "\";self.close()'>" + dateCounter + "</a></td>");
        ++dateCounter;
}
```

7. Next, add the following variable declaration and if...else statement to determine the number of days in the month variable, which represents the Date object. You need the number of days in the current month in order to determine the number of days to display in the calendar. Add the statements to the end of the displayCalendar() function.

```
var numDays = 0;
// January, March, May, July, August, October, December
if (month == 0 || month == 2 || month == 4 || month == 6 ||
month == 7 || month == 9 || month == 11)
     numDays = 31;
// February
else if (month == 1)
     numDays = 28;
// April, June, September, November
else if (month == 3 || month == 5 || month == 8 || month == 10)
     numDays = 30;
```

8. Next, add the following for statement to the end of the displayCalendar() function. The calendar needs to consist of six body rows in order to display all of the dates for each month. You already added the first row in Steps 6 and 7. In the following for statement add the remaining five rows, starting and ending each row with <tr align='center'> and </tr>:

```
for (var rowCounter = 0; rowCounter < 5; ++rowCounter) {
     var weekDayCounter = 0;
     calendarWin.document.write("<tr align='center'>");
     calendarWin.document.write("</tr>");
}
```

9. Add the following code between the two write() statements in the for loop. This code adds the dates for each week. The while statement loops through the seven days in a week. While the dateCounter variable is less than or equal to the numDays variable (which represents the total number of days in the month), a table cell and the value of the dateCounter are created for each day. If the dateCounter variable is greater than the numDays variable, nonbreaking characters are added to each table cell for the remaining days in the week that are not part of the current month.

```
while (weekDayCounter < 7) {
        var curDate = monthArray[month] + " " + dateCounter + ", "
          + dateObject.getFullYear();
        if (dateCounter <= numDays)
               calendarWin.document.write("<td><a href=''
               onclick='self.opener.document.forms[0].
               reservationDate.value=\""
               + curDate + "\";self.close()'>" + dateCounter +
               "</a></td>");
        else
```

```
                          calendarWin.document.write("<td> </td>");
                  ++weekDayCounter;
                  ++dateCounter;
          }
```

10. Finally, add the following statements to the end of the `displayCalendar()` function. The first statement closes the `<table>`, `<body>`, and `<html>` elements. The second statement, which calls the `close()` method of the new window's `Document` object, notifies the Web browser window that you are finished writing to the window and the document should be displayed. (You learn more about the `Document` object's `close()` method in Chapter 10.)

```
calendarWin.document.write("</table></body></html>");
calendarWin.document.close();
```

11. Save the **CVSGroups.html** document, open it in your Web browser, and then click the **Select Date** link to display the calendar window. Figure 6-7 shows how the calendar window appears. Click a date in the calendar window. The date should be added to the Snowboarding Date field on the Group Reservations page and the calendar window should close.

Figure 6-7

Calendar window that appears after clicking the Select Date link

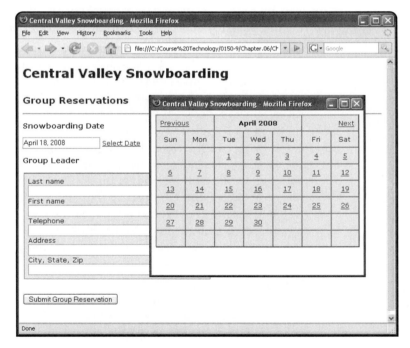

12. Close your Web browser window.

Next, you complete the calendar functionality by modifying the script so it displays different months instead of just the current month.

To add functionality to the calendar script so it displays different months:

1. Return to the **CVSGroups.html** document in your text editor.

2. Modify the first statement in the `displayCalendar()` function definition as follows so it accepts a single parameter named `whichMonth`:

```
function displayCalendar(whichMonth) {
. . .
```

3. Locate the following statement in the `displayCalendar()` function:

```
calendarWin.document.write("<tr><td colspan='7'
align='center'><strong>" + monthArray[month] + " " +
dateObject.getFullYear() + "</strong></td></td></tr>");
```

4. Replace the preceding statement with the following statements. The `if` statement determines whether the value assigned to the `whichMonth` parameter is either -1 or 1. If the value is -1, then the `setMonth()` function sets the date assigned to the date object to one month earlier by subtracting a value of one from the value returned with the `getMonth()` function. If the value is 1, then the `setMonth()` function sets the date assigned to the date object to one month later by adding a value of one to the value returned with the `getMonth()` function. The variable declaration statement then uses another `getMonth()` function to assign the new month to the `month` variable. The `document.write()` statement builds the same header row at the beginning of the calendar that you saw in the last exercise, but this time it also creates Previous and Next links that rerun the `displayCalendar()` function when they are clicked.

```
if (whichMonth == -1)
        dateObject.setMonth(dateObject.getMonth()-1);
else if (whichMonth == 1)
        dateObject.setMonth(dateObject.getMonth()+1);
var month = dateObject.getMonth();
calendarWin.document.write("<tr><td colspan='2'><a href=''
        onclick='self.opener.displayCalendar(-1);return false'>
        Previous</a></td><td colspan='3' align='center'><strong>"
        + monthArray[month] + " " + dateObject.getFullYear()
        + "</strong></td><td colspan='2' align='right'><a href=''
        onclick='self.opener.displayCalendar(1);return false'>
        Next</a></td></tr>");
```

NOTE
Be sure to type the text string that is printed with the `calendarWin.document.write()` statement on a single line.

CHAPTER 6

5. Save the **CVSGroups.html** document, open it in your Web browser, and then click the **Select Date** link to display the calendar window. The calendar window now includes Previous and Next links, as shown in Figure 6-8.

Figure 6-8
Calendar window with Previous and Next links

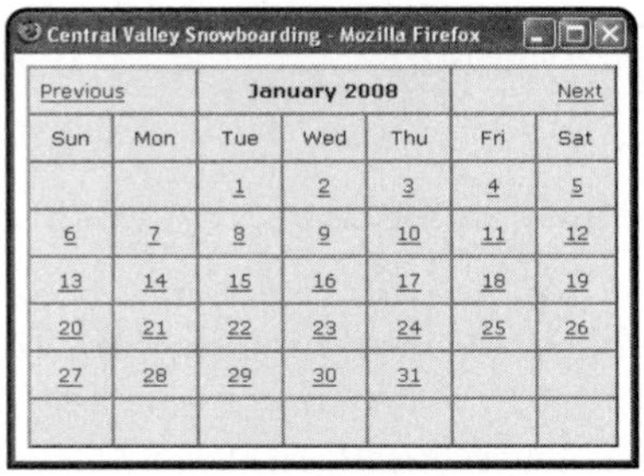

6. Test the **Previous** and **Next** links. The calendar window should update and display the correct dates for the selected month. Click a date in the calendar window to ensure that the date is still added to the Snowboarding Date field on the Group Reservations page and that the calendar window closes.
7. Close your Web browser window.

Manipulating Numbers with the `Number` Class

The `Number class` contains methods for manipulating numbers and properties that contain static values representing some of the numeric limitations in the JavaScript language (such as the largest positive number that can be used in JavaScript). While you can create a `Number` object using a statement similar to `var myNum = new Number();`, you are not required to do so. Instead, you can simply append the name of any `Number` class method or property to the name of an existing variable that contains a numeric value.

Using `Number` Class Methods

Table 6-4 lists the methods of the `Number` class.

Method	Description
`Number()`	Number object constructor
`toExponential(decimals)`	Converts a number to a string in exponential notation using a specified number of decimal places
`toFixed(decimals)`	Converts a number to a string with a specified number of decimal places
`toLocaleString()`	Converts a number to a string that is formatted with local numeric formatting conventions
`toPrecision(decimals)`	Converts a number to a string with a specific number of decimal places, either in exponential notation or in fixed notation
`toString(radix)`	Converts a number to a string using a specified radix
`valueOf()`	Returns the numeric value of a `Number` object

Table 6-4   Number class methods

The primary reason for using any of the "to" methods listed in Table 6-4 is to convert a number to a string value with a specific number of decimal places that will be displayed to a user. If you don't need to display the number for a user, there is no need to use any of the methods. The most useful Number class method is the toFixed() method, which you can use to display a numeric value with a specified number of decimal places. For example, you may have a number in your program that represents a dollar value. However, depending on the result of a calculation or a value entered by a user, the number may contain more than the two decimal places that are acceptable in a currency value. The following code shows a simple example of a numeric variable named salesTotal that is assigned a value of 49.95. If you apply a discount of 10% to the variable, the new number is equal to 44.995. Before displaying the value, the write() statement uses the toFixed() method to convert the value of the salesTotal variable to a string containing two decimal places.

```
var salesTotal = 49.95;
var discount = salesTotal * .1;
salesTotal -= discount; // new value is 44.995
document.write("$" + salesTotal.toFixed(2));
```

Accessing Number Class Properties

Table 6-5 lists the properties of the Number class. Note that there is little reason for you to use these properties. However, they are listed here for the sake of completeness.

Property	Description
MAX_VALUE	The largest positive number that can be used in JavaScript
MIN_VALUE	The smallest positive number that can be used in JavaScript
NaN	The value NaN, which stands for "not-a-number"
NEGATIVE_INFINITY	The value of negative infinity
POSITIVE_INFINITY	The value of positive infinity

Table 6-5   Number class properties

Next, you add code to the Group Reservations page that calculates group discounts.

To add code to the Group Reservations page that calculates group discounts:

1. Return to the **CVSGroups.html** document in your text editor.
2. Add the following text and elements to the end of the form section, but above the Submit button. The text and elements display group discounts and the first <input> element allows users to enter the number of snowboarders in their groups. The onchange event handler in the first <input> element then calls a function named calcGroupDiscount() that will calculate the group discount according to the size of the group. Notice that an argument of this.value is passed to the function.

```
<h3>Group Discounts</h3>
<ul>
<li>Daily Rate: $49</li>
<li>5-10 snowboarders: 10% discount</li>
<li>11-24 snowboarders: 20% discount</li>
<li>25+ snowboarders: 25% discount</li>
</ul>
<p>How many snowboarders are in your group? <input type="text"
size="5" value="0" onchange="calcGroupDiscount(this.value)">
<br />
Your group rate is $<input type="text" name="discount" size="60"
value="0" readonly="readonly" style="border: none" /></p>
```

3. Add the following calcGroupDiscount() function to the end of the script section. The if...else statements in the function calculate the group discount according to the value assigned to the groupSize parameter. The last statement in the function then assigns the discount rate to the discount field in the form.

```
function calcGroupDiscount(groupSize) {
    var dailyRate = 49;
    if (groupSize > 5 && groupSize < 10)
        dailyRate = 49 / 1.1;
    else if (groupSize > 10 && groupSize < 25)
        dailyRate = 49 / 1.2;
    else if (groupSize > 24)
        dailyRate = 49 / 1.25;
    var groupRate = groupSize * dailyRate;
    document.forms[0].discount.value = groupRate;
}
```

4. Save the **CVSGroups.html** document and then open it in your Web browser. Enter a number in the group size field, then press the **Tab** key or click off the field so that the calcGroupDiscount() function is called by the onchange event handler. Notice that the group rate field displays all the digits in the calculated number. For example, Figure 6-9 shows a group rate of $356.3636363636363 after entering a value of 8 in the group size field.

5. Return to the **CVSGroups.html** document in your text editor

6. Modify the last statement in the calcGroupDiscount() function as follows so the groupRate includes the toFixed() method to convert the value of the groupRate variable to two decimal places.

```
document.forms[0].discount.value = groupRate.toFixed(2);
```

7. Save the **CVSGroups.html** document and then reopen it in your Web browser. Enter a number in the group size field, then press the **Tab** key or click off the field

so that the `calcGroupDiscount()` function is called by the `onchange` event handler. The group rate field should display the calculated number with two decimal places.

Figure 6-9

Group Reservations page after adding the Group Discounts section

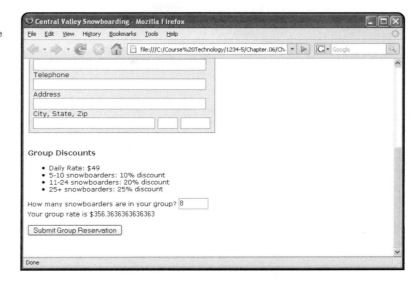

8. Close your Web browser window.

Performing Math Functions with the `Math` Class

The **`Math` class** contains methods and properties for performing mathematical calculations in your programs.

Using `Math` Class Methods

Table 6-6 lists the methods of the `Math` class.

Unlike the `Array`, `Date`, and `Number` classes, the `Math` class does not contain a constructor. This means that you cannot instantiate a `Math` object using a statement such as `var mathCalc = new Math()`. Instead, you use the `Math` object and one of its methods or properties directly in your code. For example, the `sqrt()` method returns the square root of a number. The following code shows how to use the `sqrt()` method to determine the square root of 144:

```
var curNumber = 144;
squareRoot = Math.sqrt(curNumber); // returns '12'
document.write("The square root of " + curNumber
    + " is " + squareRoot); // prints '12'
```

Method	Description
abs(x)	Returns the absolute value of x
acos(x)	Returns the arc cosine of x
asin(x)	Returns the arc sine of x
atan(x)	Returns the arc tangent of x
atan2(x, y)	Returns the angle from the x-axis
ceil(x)	Returns the value of x rounded to the next highest integer
cos(x)	Returns the cosine of x
exp(x)	Returns the exponent of x
floor(x)	Returns the value of x rounded to the next lowest integer
log(x)	Returns the natural logarithm of x
max(x, y)	Returns the larger of two numbers
min(x, y)	Returns the smaller of two numbers
pow(x, y)	Returns the value of x raised to the y power
random()	Returns a random number
round(x)	Returns the value of x rounded to the nearest integer
sin(x)	Returns the sine of x
sqrt(x)	Returns the square root of x
tan(x)	Returns the tangent of x

Table 6-6   Math class methods

Accessing `Math` Class Properties

Table 6-7 lists the properties of the Math class.

Property	Description
E	Euler's constant e, which is the base of a natural logarithm; this value is approximately 2.7182818284590452354
LN10	The natural logarithm of 10, which is approximately 2.302585092994046
LN2	The natural logarithm of 2, which is approximately 0.6931471805599453
LOG10E	The base-10 logarithm of e, the base of the natural logarithms; this value is approximately 0.4342944819032518
LOG2E	The base-2 logarithm of e, the base of the natural logarithms; this value is approximately 1.4426950408889634
PI	A constant representing the ratio of the circumference of a circle to its diameter, which is approximately 3.1415926535897932
SQRT1_2	The square root of 1/2, which is approximately 0.7071067811865476
SQRT2	The square root of 2, which is approximately 1.4142135623730951

Table 6-7   Math class properties

As an example of how to use the properties of the `Math` object, the following code shows how to use the `PI` property to calculate the area of a circle based on its radius. The code also uses the `round()` method to round the value returned to the nearest whole number.

```
var radius = 25;
var area = Math.round(Math.PI * radius * radius);
document.write("A circle with a radius of " + radius
     + " has an area of " + area); // prints 1963
```

Next, you modify the `calcGroupDiscount()` function so it uses the `round()` function of the `Math` object to round the group discount to the nearest integer instead of displaying decimal places. If you entered a large number in the last exercise when you tested the script, you may have noticed that although the group discount displayed only two decimal places, the number was not formatted with commas or whatever the formatting convention is for your locale. For example, if you entered a value of 38, the group rate is displayed as $1489.60. In English, the numeric formatting convention is to include commas to separate thousands. This means that the value $1489.60 should display as $1,489.60. To ensure that numbers are correctly displayed according to local numeric formatting conventions, you must use the `toLocaleString()` function, which you will also add to the `calcGroupDiscount()` function.

To modify the Group Reservations page so it uses the `round()` function of the `Math` object and the `toLocaleString()` function:

1. Return to the **CVSGroups.html** document in your text editor.
2. Add the following statement immediately after the statement in the `calcGroupDiscount()` function that declares and initializes the `groupRate` variable. This statement uses the `round()` function of the `Math` object to round the number to the nearest integer.

    ```
    groupRate = Math.round(groupRate);
    ```

3. Modify the last statement in the `calcGroupDiscount()` function so it calls the `toLocaleString()` function instead of the `toFixed()` function, as follows:

    ```
    document.forms[0].discount.value = groupRate.toLocaleString();
    ```

4. Save the **CVSGroups.html** document and then reopen it in your Web browser. Enter a number larger than 25 in the group size field, then press the **Tab** key or click off the field so that the `calcGroupDiscount()` function is called by the onchange event handler. The value in the group rate field should display with a comma separator and no decimal places. Figure 6-10 shows how the page appears after entering a value of 35 in the group size field.
5. Close your Web browser window.

Figure 6-10
Group Reservations
page after adding
`Math.round()` and
`toLocaleString()`
functions

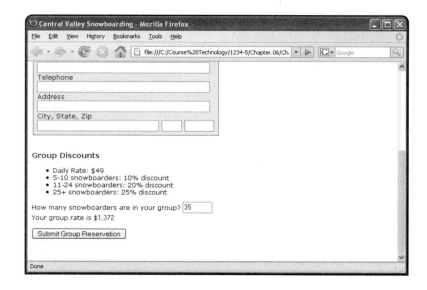

Defining Custom JavaScript Objects

JavaScript is not a true object-oriented programming language. You can base objects in your programs on built-in JavaScript classes such as the `Array` and `Date` objects. However, you cannot create your own classes in JavaScript. For this reason, JavaScript is said to be an object-based programming language instead of an object-oriented programming language.

Although JavaScript is not a true object-oriented programming languages, it does allow you to define your own custom objects. Unlike objects that are based on classes, custom objects in JavaScript are not encapsulated, which means that other programmers who use your custom object can see inside of the black box. Even though custom JavaScript objects cannot be encapsulated, you may find them useful, especially if you need to replicate the same functionality an unknown number of times in a script. For example, you may have a Web site that allows customers to place online orders for concert tickets. For each order, you may want to create a new object that uses properties to store information such as the customer's name, concert name, number of tickets, concert date, and so on. The object may also contain methods that calculate sales tax and sales total. Although you could use standard functions and variables to create the same functionality, the ability to treat each order as a self-contained object would make your job as a programmer a little easier.

NOTE
The most recent implementation of the JavaScript language, ECMAScript Edition 3, includes support for true classes. However, at the time of this writing, no Web browsers support the new JavaScript class functionality.

Declaring Basic Custom Objects

Although JavaScript is not a true object-oriented programming language, you can create basic objects and properties by using the `Object` object. To declare a custom object with the `Object` object, you use the following statement:

```
var objectName = new Object();
```

You can also create a custom object by assigning a pair of empty braces to a variable name, as follows:

```
var objectName = {};
```

After you create a custom object, you can assign properties to the object by appending the property name to the object name with a period. For example, the following code creates a new object named `ConcertTickets` and assigns four properties to it: `customerName`, `concertName`, `ticketQuantity`, and `concertDate`. You can then access the values assigned to each property the same as you would for other types of objects, as demonstrated with the `document.write()` statements. Notice that the `concertDate` property is created as a `Date` object that stores the date and time of the concert. Figure 6-11 shows the output.

```
var ConcertTickets = new Object();
ConcertTickets.customerName = "Don Gosselin";
ConcertTickets.concertName = "Jimmy Buffett";
ConcertTickets.ticketQuantity = 2;
ConcertTickets.concertDate = new Date(2008, 6, 18, 20);
document.write("<h1>Ticket Order</h1>");
document.write("<p>Customer: " + ConcertTickets.customerName);
document.write("<br />Concert: " + ConcertTickets.concertName);
document.write("<br />Quantity: " + ConcertTickets.ticketQuantity);
document.write("<br />Date: " +
ConcertTickets.concertDate.toLocaleString() + "</p>");
```

Figure 6-11

Output of custom object properties

Custom objects created as described in this section are limited to containing only properties. Although you may find it useful to create objects in this manner to organize complex data, in most cases you can use standard variables just as effectively. Objects are most useful when they contain both properties and methods. To create custom objects that contain methods, you must use constructor functions, which are described later in this chapter.

Next, you start adding a Group Members section to the Central Valley Snowboarding page. This section allows you to enter information about each snowboarder in the group, including name, address, and phone number.

To add a Group Members form section to the Central Valley Snowboarding page:

1. Return to the **CSVGroups.html** document in your text editor and type the following text and elements above the `<h3>Group Discounts</h3>` section:

```
<h3>Group Members</h3>
<p><input type="button" value="Add Snowboarder" />
<input type="button" value="Delete Snowboarder" />
<input type="button" value="Update Info" /></p>
<table border="0">
<tr>
<td><select name="contacts" size="13" style="width: 150px">
<option value="contacts">Group Members</option>
</select></td>
<td>Last name<br />
<input type="text" name="lastname" size="50" /><br />
First name<br />
<input type="text" name="firstname" size="50" /><br />
Telephone<br />
<input type="text" name="telephone" size="50" /><br />
Address<br />
<input type="text" name="address" size="50" /><br />
City, State, Zip<br />
<input type="text" name="city" size="34" />
<input type="text" name="state" size="2" maxlength="2" />
<input type="text" name="zip" size="5" maxlength="5" /></td>
</tr>
</table>
```

2. Add the following object declaration to the end of the script section. The object properties will contain other objects that represent each snowboard added to the Group Members list. Using one object to store other objects makes it easier to manage each group member as it is added to and deleted from the program.

```
var contactList = new Object();
```

3. Save the **CVSGroups.html** document and open it in your Web browser. You still need to add functionality to the section before you can enter any snowboarder information. Figure 6-12 shows how the Web page appears after adding the Group Members section.

4. Close your Web browser window.

Figure 6-12

Group Reservations Web page after adding the Group Members section

Defining Constructor Functions

You can define your own custom objects using a **constructor function**, which is a function that is used as the basis for a custom object. (Another term for constructor function is **object definition**.) As with traditional class-based objects, JavaScript objects inherit all the variables and statements of the constructor function on which they are based. Any JavaScript function can serve as a constructor. The following code defines a function named `ConcertTickets()` with four parameters that can serve as a constructor function:

```
function ConcertTickets(customer, concert, tickets, eventDate) {
...
}
```

Use a statement similar to the following to instantiate an instance of a `ConcertTickets` object:

```
var newOrder = new ConcertTickets();
```

Next, you add a constructor function to the Group Reservations page.

To add a constructor function to the Group Reservations page:

1. Return to the **CSVGroups.html** document in your text editor.

2. Type the following constructor function above the `contactList` declaration statement in the script section:

   ```
   function Contact() {
   }
   ```

3. Save the **CVSGroups.html** document.

Adding Properties

To add a property to a constructor function, you must add a statement to the function body that uses the `this` keyword with the following syntax: `this.property_name = value;`. In the case of a custom JavaScript object, the `this` keyword refers to the object that calls the constructor function. For example, the following constructor function includes three properties: `customerName`, `concertName`, and `ticketQuantity`, and `concertDate`.

```
function ConcertTickets(customer, event, quantity, eventDate) {
    this.customerName = customer;    // customer name
    this.concertName = event; // event name
    this.ticketQuantity = quantity; // number of tickets
    this.concertDate = eventDate; // concert date
}
```

The statements in the preceding constructor function use the `this` keyword to assign the values of the four arguments (`name`, `type`, `quantity`, and `date`) to the `customerName`, `concertName`, `ticketQuantity`, and `concertDate` properties of whichever object called the function. The use of the `this` reference is one of the primary differences between standard functions and constructor functions. Standard functions do not include a `this` reference, because they are not used as the basis of objects.

The following code declares a `ticketOrder` object based on the `ConcertTickets()` constructor function, assigns values to its four properties, and then prints the properties. The output is the same as that shown in Figure 6-11.

```
var ticketOrder = new ConcertTickets();
ticketOrder.customerName = "Don Gosselin";
ticketOrder.concertName = "Jimmy Buffett";
ticketOrder.ticketQuantity = 2;
ticketOrder.concertDate = new Date(2008, 6, 18, 20);
document.write("<h1>Ticket Order</h1>");
document.write("<p>Customer: " + ticketOrder.customerName);
document.write("<br />Concert: " + ticketOrder.concertName);
document.write("<br />Quantity: " + ticketOrder.ticketQuantity);
document.write("<br />Date: " +
ticketOrder.concertDate.toLocaleString() + "</p>");
```

You can also assign values to the properties of an object when you first instantiate the object using statements similar to the following:

```
var ticketOrder = new ConcertTickets("Don Gosselin",
    "Jimmy Buffett", 2, new Date(2008, 6, 18, 20));
document.write("<h1>Ticket Order</h1>");
document.write("<p>Customer: " + ticketOrder.customerName);
document.write("<br />Concert: " + ticketOrder.concertName);
document.write("<br />Quantity: " + ticketOrder.ticketQuantity);
document.write("<br />Date: "
    + ticketOrder.concertDate.toLocaleString()
    + "</p>");
```

Next, you will add properties to the `Contact` constructor function.

To add properties to the `Contact` constructor function, along with a function that copies the values from the Contacts form to the properties:

1. Return to the **CVSGroups.html** document in your text editor.

2. Add the following properties to the `Contact` constructor function. Each property is initially assigned an empty string.

```
this.lastName = "";
this.firstName = "";
this.telephone = "";
this.address = "";
this.city = "";
this.state = "";
this.zip = "";
```

3. Save the **CVSGroups.html** document.

Enumerating Custom Object Properties

Some custom objects can contain dozens of properties. For example, a script may create new custom object properties that store sales prices for each item a customer wants to purchase. Suppose you want to discount the individual sales prices by 10% of any items that cost more than $100. Because there is no way to determine in advance which items a customer will purchase, you have no way of knowing which properties have been added to the object for each individual customer. To execute the same statement or command block for all the properties within a custom object, you can use the `for...in statement`, which is a looping statement similar to the `for` statement. The syntax of the `for...in` statement is as follows:

```
for (variable in object) {
     statement(s);
}
```

The variable name in the `for...in` statement constructor holds an individual object property. The object name in the constructor represents the name of an object that has been instantiated in a program. Unlike the other loop statements, the `for...in` statement does not require a counter or any other type of code to control how the loop functions. Instead, the `for...in` statement automatically assigns each property in an object to the variable name, performs the necessary statements on the property, then moves to the next property and starts over. The `for...in` statement ends automatically once it reaches the last property in an object. A typical use of the `for...in` statement is to retrieve the names of properties within an object, as shown in the following code:

```
var ConcertTickets = new Object();
ConcertTickets.customerName = "Don Gosselin";
ConcertTickets.concertName = "Jimmy Buffett";
ConcertTickets.ticketQuantity = 2;
ConcertTickets.concertDate = new Date(2008, 6, 18, 20);
for (prop in ConcertTickets) {
     document.write(prop + "<br />");
}
```

In the preceding code, the variable name `prop` holds the names of each property in the `ConcertTickets` object. The `document.write()` statement then writes the name of each property to the Web browser window, as shown in Figure 6-13.

Figure 6-13

Property names printed with a `for...in` statement

The preceding example demonstrates how to use the `for...in` statement with objects instantiated from the `Object` object. Using the `for...in` statement with objects instantiated from constructor functions is very similar, as follows:

```
function ConcertTickets(customer, concert, tickets, eventDate) {
    this.customerName = customer;      // customer name
    this.concertName = concert; // concert name
    this.ticketQuantity = tickets; // number of tickets
    this.concertDate = eventDate; // concert date
}
var ticketOrder = new ConcertTickets("Don Gosselin",
    "Jimmy Buffett", 2, new Date(2008, 6, 18, 20));
for (prop in ticketOrder) {
    document.write(prop + "<br />");
}
```

One of the benefits of the `for...in` statement is that it **enumerates**, or assigns an index to, each property in an object. This is similar to the way elements in an array are indexed. You can use an enumerated object property to access the values contained within object properties. For example, in the following code, the `document.write()` statement within the body of the `for...in` statement refers to the `prop` variable as an index of the `ticketOrder` object:

```
for (prop in ticketOrder) {
    document.write(ticketOrder[prop] + "<br />");
}
```

Each iteration of the `for...in` statement in the preceding code now prints the contents of each property rather than just the property names. The code passes the `ticketOrder` object to the `document.write()` method, along with the `prop` variable enclosed in brackets (`ticketOrder[prop]`). You would use this same technique to print the contents of an array. Unlike the elements in an array, however, you cannot refer to the enumerated properties of an object outside of a `for...in` loop; doing so generates an error. The statement `document.writeln(ticketOrder[prop]);` causes an error outside of a `for...in` loop.

Next, you start adding a function named `addContact()` that will add snowboarders to the contact list.

To start adding the `addContact()` function:

1. Return to the **CVSGroups.html** document in your text editor.

2. Add the following `addContact()` function definition to the end of the script section:

    ```
    function addContact() {
    }
    ```

3. Add the following variable declaration to the `addContact()` function. This variable will store a number that will represent the new contact.

    ```
    var newContact = 0;
    ```

4. Add the following `for...in` statement to the end of the `addContact()` function. This statement enumerates the properties in the `contactList` object and increments the `newContact` variable for each contact. The value assigned to the `newContact` variable will be used to represent each new contact that is added to the Group Members form.

    ```
    for (contact in contactList) {
        ++newContact;
    }
    ```

5. Save the **CVSGroups.html** document.

Referring to Object Properties as Associative Arrays

JavaScript allows you to refer to object properties using associative array syntax. An **associative array** is an array whose elements are referred to with an alphanumeric key instead of an index number. For example, with associative arrays you can create a company's payroll information that uses each employee's last name instead of an index number to refer to an element in the array. To refer to an element in an associative array, you place an element's key in single or double quotation marks inside the array brackets. For example, the following statements create the elements in an array named `hotelReservation[]` using associative array syntax:

```
var hotelReservation = new Array(4);
hotelReservation["guest"] = "Don Gosselin";
hotelReservation["nights"] = 2;
hotelReservation["price"] = 89.95;
hotelReservation["nonsmoking"] = true;
document.write("<p>Guest: " + hotelReservation["guest"]);
document.write("<br />Nights: " + hotelReservation["nights"]);
document.write("<br />Price: " + hotelReservation["price"]);
document.write("<br />Non-smoking room: "
    + hotelReservation["nonsmoking"] + "</p>");
```

You can also use associative array syntax to refer to the properties of an object. The following example demonstrates how to refer to the `customerName` property of the `ConcertTickets` object using associative array syntax (`ConcertTickets["customerName"]`) instead of standard property syntax (`ConcertTickets.customerName`):

```
var ConcertTickets = new Object();
ConcertTickets.customerName = "Don Gosselin";
document.write("<p>Customer: " + ConcertTickets["customerName"]);
```

One of the benefits of using associative array syntax with object properties is that you can dynamically build property names at runtime. For example, the following statements use associative array syntax to create a property consisting of the word "employee" and an employee ID in an object named `employeeList`:

```
var employeeList = new Object();
var employeeID = 56725;
employeeList["employee" + employeeID] = "Don Gosselin";
```

You can print the contents of the property created with the preceding statements by using any of the following:

```
document.write(employeeList["employee" + employeeID]);
document.write(employeeList.employee56725);
document.write(employeeList["employee56725"]);
```

Next, you complete the `addContact()` function. The function will use associative array syntax to create the properties of each `Contact` object that is stored in properties of the `contactList` object.

To complete the `addContact()` function:

1. Return to the **CVSGroups.html** document in your text editor.

2. Add the following statements to the end of the `addContact()` function. The `if` statement checks to see if the last name and first name fields have been filled in. If not, then an alert dialog box appears instructing users to enter the contact's first and last name. If both fields contain values, then an `else` statement instances a new `Contact` object and assigns it as a property of the `contactList` object. The remaining statements assign values to the `Contact` object property, create a new `Option` object, and assign the contents of the new `Contact` property to the new `Option` object. Notice that the statements use associative array syntax to build the name of the `Contact` objects that are assigned as properties of the `contactList` object.

```
if (document.forms[0].lastname.value == ""
       || document.forms[0].firstname.value == "")
    window.alert("You must enter the contact's first and
    last names.");
else {
    contactList["contact" + newContact] = new Contact();
    contactList["contact" + newContact].lastName
          = document.forms[0].lastname.value;
    contactList["contact" + newContact].firstName
```

```
        = document.forms[0].firstname.value;
contactList["contact" + newContact].telephone
        = document.forms[0].telephone.value;
contactList["contact" + newContact].address
        = document.forms[0].address.value;
contactList["contact" + newContact].city = document.forms
[0].city.value;
contactList["contact" + newContact].state
        = document.forms[0].state.value;
contactList["contact" + newContact].zip = document.forms
[0].zip.value;
var createContact = new Option();
createContact.value = contactList["contact"
        + newContact].lastName + ", " + contactList["contact"
        + newContact].firstName;
createContact.text = contactList["contact" + newContact].
lastName + ", "
        + contactList["contact" + newContact].firstName;
document.forms[0].contacts.options[newContact] =
createContact;
    }
```

3. Add the following event handler to the Add Snowboarder element:

    ```
    <input type="button" value="Add Snowboarder" onclick=
    "addContact()" />
    ```

4. Save the **CVSGroups.html** document and open the document in your Web browser. Test the script by adding some contacts to the contact list.

5. Close your Web browser window.

Deleting Properties

To delete a specific property in a custom object, you use the `delete` operator with the syntax `delete object.property`. For example, the following statement deletes the `concertDate` property of the `ConcertTickets` object:

```
delete ConcertTickets.concertDate;
```

TIP

You can use the `delete` operator to delete properties created with either the `Object` object or with a constructor function.

Next, you add a `deleteContact()` function to the Group Reservations page that deletes selected snowboarders from the Group Members section.

To add a `deleteContact()` function:

1. Return to the **CVSGroups.html** document in your text editor.

2. Add the following `deleteContact()` function definition to the end of the script section:

```
function deleteContact() {
}
```

3. Add the following statements to the `deleteContact()` function. These statements loop through each option in the selection list to determine which option is selected. Once the selected item is located, its index value is assigned to the `selectedContact` variable. The last statement deletes the item from the select list by assigning a value of null to the element in `option[]` array.

```
var contactSelected = false;
var selectedContact = 0;
for (var i=0; i<document.forms[0].contacts.options.length;++i) {
    if (document.forms[0].contacts.options[i].selected == true) {
        contactSelected = true;
        selectedContact = i;
        break;
    }
}
document.forms[0].contacts.options[i] = null;
```

4. Add the following statements to the end of the `deleteContact()` function. The `if...else` statement first checks the value assigned to the `contactSelect` variable. If the `contactSelect` variable contains a value of false, an alert dialog box informs the user that they must select a contact in the list. If the `contactSelect` variable contains a value of true, the `for...in` statement deletes all of the properties in the `contactList` object. Then, the `for` statement rebuilds the properties in the `contactList` object from the options that are displayed in the selection list.

```
if (contactSelected == true) {
    for (prop in contactList) {
        delete contactList[prop]
    }
    for (var i=0; i<document.forms[0].contacts.options
            .length;++i) {
        contactList["contact" + i] = new Contact();
        contactList["contact" + i].lastName
            = document.forms[0].lastname.value;
        contactList["contact" + i].firstName
            = document.forms[0].firstname.value;
        contactList["contact" + i].telephone
            = document.forms[0].telephone.value;
        contactList["contact" + i].address
```

```
                    = document.forms[0].address.value;
        contactList["contact" + i].city = document.forms[0].
          city.value;
        contactList["contact" + i].state = document.forms[0].
          state.value;
        contactList["contact" + i].zip = document.forms[0].
          zip.value;
    }
}
else
        window.alert("You must select a contact in the list.");
```

5.   Add the following event handler to the Delete Snowboarder element:

```
<input type="button" value="Delete Snowboarder"
onclick="deleteContact()" />
```

6.   Save the **CVSGroups.html** document and open the document in your Web browser. Test the script by adding and deleting some contacts to the contact list.

7.   Close your Web browser window.

Creating Methods

You can create a function that will be used as an object method by referring to any object properties it contains with the this reference. For example, the following code defines a method that prints the customerName, concertName, ticketQuantity, and concertDate properties of the ConcertTickets constructor function:

```
function displayConcertTickets() {
    document.write("<p>Customer: " + this.customerName);
    document.write("<br />Concert: " + this.concertName);
    document.write("<br />Quantity: " + this.ticketQuantity);
    document.write("<br />Date: "
        + this.concertDate.toLocaleString() + "</p>");
}
```

After a method is created, it must be added to the constructor function, using the syntax this.*methodName* = functionName;. The *methodName* following the this reference is the name that is being assigned to the function within the object. Remember not to include the parentheses following the function name, as you would when calling a function in JavaScript. The statement this.*methodName* = *functionName*(); is incorrect, because it includes parentheses. To add the displayConcertTickets() function to the ConcertTickets function definition as a method named showOrder(), you include the statement this.showOrder = displayConcertTickets; within the function definition braces.

The following code shows the ConcertTickets() constructor function, the displayConcertTickets() function that creates the showOrder() method, and statements that instantiate two ConcertTickets objects and print the values of their properties. Figure 6-14 shows the output.

```
function ConcertTickets(customer, concert, tickets, eventDate) {
    this.customerName = customer;      // customer name
    this.concertName = concert; // concert name
    this.ticketQuantity = tickets; // number of tickets
    this.concertDate = eventDate; // concert date
    this.showOrder = displayConcertTickets;
}
function displayConcertTickets() {
    document.write("<p>Customer: " + this.customerName);
    document.write("<br />Concert: " + this.concertName);
    document.write("<br />Quantity: " + this.ticketQuantity);
    document.write("<br />Date: "
        + this.concertDate.toLocaleString() + "</p>");
}
var ticketOrder = new ConcertTickets("Don Gosselin",
    "Jimmy Buffett", 2, new Date(2008, 6, 18, 20));
ticketOrder.showOrder();
var ticketOrder = new ConcertTickets("Don Gosselin",
    "John Mayer", 2, new Date(2008, 8, 30, 20));
ticketOrder.showOrder();
```

Figure 6-14

Output of a script with
two instantiated custom
objects

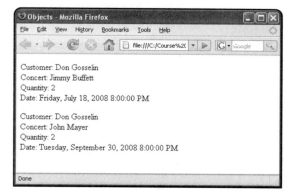

Now you will add methods to the Contact constructor function.

To add methods to the Contact constructor function:

1. Return to the **CVSGroups.html** document in your text editor and add the following function above the contactList declaration in the script section. The function updates the fields in the contacts form with the properties of the selected Contact object. An onclick event handler you will add to the <select> element later in these steps will call the function.

    ```
    function getContactInfo() {
        document.forms[0].lastname.value = this.lastName;
        document.forms[0].firstname.value = this.firstName;
        document.forms[0].telephone.value = this.telephone;
    ```

```
      document.forms[0].address.value = this.address;
      document.forms[0].city.value = this.city;
      document.forms[0].state.value = this.state;
      document.forms[0].zip.value = this.zip;
}
```

2. Next, add the following function after the `getContactInfo()` function. This function updates the selected contacts information within the `Contact` object. You will pass the `curIndex` parameter from an `onclick` event handler for an Update Contact button you will add in the contacts form.

```
function updateSelectedContact(curIndex) {
      this.lastName = document.forms[0].lastname.value;
      this.firstName = document.forms[0].firstname.value;
      this.telephone = document.forms[0].telephone.value;
      this.address = document.forms[0].address.value;
      this.city = document.forms[0].city.value;
      this.state = document.forms[0].state.value;
      this.zip = document.forms[0].zip.value;
      document.forms[0].contacts.options[curIndex].value
            = this.lastName + ", " + this.firstName;
      document.forms[0].contacts.options[curIndex].text
            = this.lastName + ", " + this.firstName;
      window.alert("Contact information updated.");
}
```

3. Add the following two statements to the end of the `Contact` constructor function, which declare the `getContactInfo()` and `updateSelectedContact()` as methods of the `Contact` object:

```
this.getContacts = getContactInfo;
this.updateContact = updateSelectedContact;
```

4. Add an `onclick` event handler to the Update Snowboarder button, as follows. The event handler passes to the `updateContact()` function the `selectedIndex` property of the option that is selected in the selection list.

```
<input type="button" value="Update Info" onclick
="contactList['contact' + document.forms[0].contacts
.selectedIndex].updateContact(
document.forms[0].contacts.selectedIndex);" />
```

5. Finally, add the following event handler to the `<select>` element. The event handler updates the data displayed in the contact information fields after a new option is clicked in the selection list.

```
onclick="contactList['contact'
+ this.selectedIndex].getContacts();"
```

6. Save the **CVSGroups.html** document and then open it in your Web browser. Test the script by adding some contacts to the contact list. Try clicking on a previously entered contact. The contact's information should display in the contact

information fields. Also, try updating a previously entered contact. Figure 6-15 shows how the form appears after adding several contacts.

Figure 6-15

Contacts form after adding several contacts

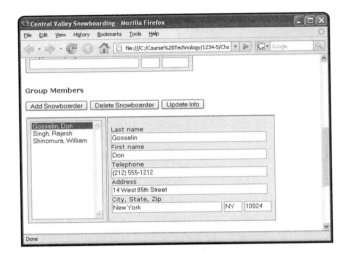

7. Close your Web browser window.

Your final step is to modify the Group Reservations page so the group discount is automatically calculated as individuals are added and deleted from the Group Members list.

To modify the Group Reservations page so it automatically calculates group discounts:

1. Return to the **CVSGroups.html** document in your text editor and add the following statement to the end of the `addContact()` function. This statement calls the `calcGroupDiscount()` function and passes to it the value of the `newContact` variable incremented by one.

    `calcGroupDiscount(newContact+1);`

2. Add the following statement to the end of the `deleteContact()` function. This statement also calls the `calcGroupDiscount()` function, but instead passes to it the `length` property of the `options[]` array, which indicates the number of items in the group members list.

    `calcGroupDiscount(document.forms[0].contacts.options.length);`

3. Finally, delete the following text and elements from the Group Discounts section:

    `How many snowboarders are in your group? <input type="text" size="5" value="0" onchange="calcGroupDiscount(this.value)"> <br />`

4. Save the **CVSGroups.html** document and then validate it with the W3C Markup Validation Service at **validator.w3.org/file-upload.html**. Once the document is valid, close it in your text editor.

5. Open the **CVSGroups.html** document in your Web browser and try adding and deleting some snowboarders. The group discount should update automatically.

Using the `prototype` Property

As explained earlier, objects inherit the properties and methods of the constructor functions from which they are instantiated. When you instantiate a new object named `ticketOrder` based on the `ConcertTickets` constructor function, the new object includes the `customerName`, `eventName`, `numTickets`, and `concertDate` properties along with the `showOrder()` method. After instantiating a new object, you can assign additional properties to the object, using a period. The following code creates a new object based on the `ConcertTickets` constructor function, then assigns to the object a new property named `orderDate`. The statement uses the `Date()` constructor function without any arguments, which assigns the current date to the `orderDate` property.

```
var ticketOrder = new ConcertTickets("Don Gosselin",
     "Jimmy Buffett", 2, new Date(2008, 6, 18, 20));
ticketOrder.orderDate = new Date();
```

When you add a new property to an object that has been instantiated from a constructor function, the new property is only available to that specific object; the property is not available to the constructor function or to any other objects that were instantiated from the same constructor function. However, if you use the `prototype` property with the name of the constructor function, any new properties you create will also be available to the constructor function and any objects instantiated from it. The **prototype property** is a built-in property that specifies the constructor from which an object was instantiated. The following code uses the `prototype` property to add the `orderDate` property to the `ConcertTickets` constructor function. By using a `prototype` property, you ensure that all objects that extend the `ConcertTickets` constructor function also have access to the `orderDate` property.

```
var ticketOrder = new ConcertTickets("Don Gosselin",
     "Jimmy Buffett", 2, new Date(2008, 6, 18, 20));
ticketOrder.prototype.orderDate = new Date();
```

Object definitions can use the `prototype` property to extend other object definitions. That is to say, you can create a new object based on an existing object. The new object inherits the properties and methods of the original object. You can then add additional properties and methods to the new object that will not be available to the existing object. Consider an object definition named `Event` that contains generic properties and methods that might be used for planning an event. You may need to create additional object definitions that extend `Event` and that contain properties and methods specific to certain types of events. To extend one object definition (the derived object definition) from another object definition (the base object definition), append the `prototype` property to the derived object definition, followed by the new keyword and the name of the base object definition using the following syntax: *derived_object*`.prototype = new` *base_object*`();`. The following code shows an example of a `RetirementEvent` object definition that extends the `Event` object definition. The `Event` class definition contains some generic properties, `eventLocation`, `eventDate`, and `eventCost`, that apply to all types of events, along with a `calcEventCost()` method that calculates the cost of an event. The `RetirementEvent` class includes `guestOfHonor` and `company` properties along with a `showEventDetails()` method. Figure 6-16 shows the output.

```
<script type="text/javascript">
/* <![CDATA[ */
function Event(location, date) {
     this.eventLocation = location;
     this.eventDate = date;
     this.eventCost = 0;
     this.calcEventCost = calcCost;
}
function calcCost(guests) {
     this.eventCost = guests * 25; // $25 per head
}
function RetirementEvent(retiree, company) {
     this.guestOfHonor = retiree;
     this.companyName = company;
     this.showEventDetails = eventDetails;
}
function eventDetails() {
     document.write("<h1>Retirement Party</h1>");
     document.write("<p>Guest of honor: " + this.guestOfHonor);
     document.write("<br />Company: " + this.companyName);
     document.write("<br />Event date: " + this.eventDate);
     document.write("<br />Event location: " + this.eventLocation);
     document.write("<br />Event cost: $" +
             this.eventCost.toLocaleString() + "</p>");
}
RetirementEvent.prototype = new Event();
var wertherRetirement = new RetirementEvent("Jacob Werther",
"Forestville Funding");
wertherRetirement.eventLocation = "Forestville, CA";
wertherRetirement.eventDate = "April 20, 2008";
wertherRetirement.calcEventCost(175);
wertherRetirement.showEventDetails();
/* ]]> */
</script>
```

Figure 6-16
Output of a script with
an extended object
definition

NOTE

Some object-oriented programming languages allow objects to inherit from more than one object definition. JavaScript, however, only allows objects to inherit from a single object definition.

Chapter Summary

▶ The term object-oriented programming (or OOP) refers to the creation of reusable software objects that can be easily incorporated into another program.

▶ Reusable software objects are often referred to as components.

▶ In object-oriented programming, an object is programming code and data that can be treated as an individual unit or component. Data refers to information contained within variables or other types of storage structures.

▶ Objects are encapsulated, which means that all code and required data are contained within the object itself.

▶ An interface represents elements required for a source program to communicate with an object.

▶ The principle of information hiding states that any class members that other programmers do not need to access or know about should be hidden.

▶ In object-oriented programming, the code, methods, attributes, and other information that make up an object are organized using classes.

▶ An instance is an object that has been created from an existing class. When you create an object from an existing class, you are said to be instantiating the object.

▶ An object inherits, or takes on, the characteristics of the class on which it is based.

▶ The Date class contains methods and properties for manipulating the date and time.

▶ The Number class contains methods for manipulating numbers and properties that contain static values representing some of the numeric limitations in the JavaScript language (such as the largest positive number that can be used in JavaScript).

▶ The Math class contains methods and properties for performing mathematical calculations in your programs.

▶ You can define your own custom objects using a constructor function (also known as an object definition), which is a function that is used as the basis for a custom object.

▶ The this keyword refers to the current object.

▶ The prototype property is a built-in property that specifies the constructor from which an object was extended.

Review Questions

1. Which of the following terms refer to programming code and data that can be treated as an individual unit or component? (Choose all that apply.)

   a. methods
   b. components
   c. objects
   d. properties

2. Explain the principle of information hiding. What does the term "black box" refer to?

3. A(n) _____ is an object that has been created from an existing class.

    a. constructor
    b. instance
    c. template
    d. structure

4. Explain why programmers use the terms "variable" and "object" interchangeably.

5. JavaScript automatically performs garbage collection. True or false?

6. Which of the following `Date` class constructors creates a `Date` object that contains the current date and time from the local computer?

    a. `Date()`
    b. `Date(milliseconds)`
    c. `Date(date_string)`
    d. `Date(year, month[, date, hours, minutes, seconds, milliseconds])`

7. Explain how to display the full text for days and months in a `Date` object.

8. Which of the following methods of the `Number` class converts a number to a string that is formatted with local numeric formatting conventions?

    a. `toString()`
    b. `toLocaleString()`
    c. `toFixed()`
    d. `valueOf()`

9. What is the primary reason for using most of the `Number` class methods?

10. What is the correct syntax for using the `max()` method of the `Math` class?

    a. `firstNumber = Math.sqrt(secondNumber);`
    b. `var result = firstNumber.sqrt(secondNumber);`
    c. `var result = sqrt.Math(firstNumber, secondNumber);`
    d. `var result = Math.sqrt(firstNumber, secondNumber);`

11. A function that is used as the basis for an object is called an object definition or a(n) _____.

    a. object variable
    b. class
    c. method
    d. constructor function

12. Explain why JavaScript is not a true object-oriented programming language.

13. In the case of a custom JavaScript object, the `this` keyword refers to _____.

    a. the currently executing JavaScript statement

    b. the current object that called the constructor function

    c. the XHTML document

    d. the Web browser window

14. What is the correct syntax for creating an object named `currentSale` from a constructor function named `Transaction` that requires two arguments: `quantity` and `price`?

    a. `currentSale = new Transaction (2, 59.95);`

    b. `currentSale(2, 59.95) = new Transaction;`

    c. `new Transaction(2, 59.95) = currentSale;`

    d. `currentSale() = new Transaction 2, 59.95;`

15. Explain how to assign properties to a custom object created with the `Object` object.

16. The `Object` object can contain both properties and methods. True or false?

17. Which of the following statements is the correct syntax for assigning the value of a parameter named `priceQuote` to a property named `quote` in a constructor function?

    a. `quote = priceQuote;`

    b. `this.quote = priceQuote;`

    c. `this.quote = this.priceQuote;`

    d. `quote = this.priceQuote;`

18. What is the correct syntax for adding a new property named `squareFeet` to a constructor function named `RealEstate`?

    a. `RealEstate.prototype = squareFeet("");`

    b. `prototype.RealEstate.squareFeet = "";`

    c. `squareFeet.RealEstate.prototype = "";`

    d. `RealEstate.prototype.squareFeet = "";`

19. What is the correct syntax for adding an object method named `submitBid()` to a constructor function named `Auction`?

    a. `Auction = new submitBid();`

    b. `myMethod = this.submitBid;`

    c. `this.submitBid = myMethod();`

    d. `this.submitBid = submitBid;`

20. The built-in property that specifies the constructor from which an object was extended is called the _____ property.

   a. `source`

   b. `origination`

   c. `default`

   d. `prototype`

Hands-On Projects

Project 6-1

One problem with the calendar in the Group Reservations Web page that you created in this chapter is that it does not display 29 days for the month of February during leap years. In Chapter 3, you created a simple form that tested for leap years. As you may recall, you can determine whether a year is a leap year by testing if it is divisible by 4. However, years that are also divisible by 100 are not leap years, unless they are also divisible by 400, in which case they are leap years. (1900 was not a leap year; 2000 was.) In this project, you will add code to the Group Reservations Web page that displays 29 days for the month of February during leap years.

1. Copy the **CVSGroups.html** document from your Chapter folder for Chapter 6 to your Projects folder for Chapter 6. Rename the document as **CVSGroupsLeapYear.html**.

2. In the `displayCalendar()` function, locate the following `else...if` statement that determines the number of days for the month of February:

```
else if (month == 1)
    numDays = 28;
```

3. Modify the `else...if` statement so it includes the calculations for determining whether it is a leap year, as follows:

```
else if (month == 1) {
    var thisYear = dateObject.getYear();
    if (thisYear %4 != 0)
        numDays = 28;
    else if  (thisYear % 400 == 0)
        numDays = 29;
    else if (thisYear % 100 == 0)
        numDays = 28;
    else
        numDays = 29;
}
```

4. Save the **CVSGroupsLeapYear.html** document.

5. Use the W3C Markup Validation Service to validate the **CVSGroupsLeapYear.html** document and fix any errors that the document contains. Once the document is valid, close it in your text editor and then open it in your Web browser.

6. Open the **CVSGroupsLeapYear.html** document in your Web browser and click the **Select Date** link to display the calendar window. Click the **Next** or **Previous** link to navigate to the month of February in a leap year, such as 2008. The calendar should display 29 days.

7. Close your Web browser window.

Project 6-2

Another problem with the Group Reservations Web page is that if you submit the form, none of the snowboarders in the Group Members list are submitted unless their names are selected in the selection list. Even if you select the names in the list, only the last and first names are submitted. Further, the values of the group member information fields (last name, first name, telephone, and so on) are submitted; these fields should not be submitted because their values are stored in the Contact objects that contain the information for each snowboarder. In this project, you will add an onsubmit event handler that selects all the options in the Group Members selection list and submits the properties in each Contact object along with each group member name. You will also remove the name attributes from each of the group member information fields to prevent them from being submitted with the form. (Recall that only form fields with name attributes are submitted with a form.) Finally, you will modify the script so it refers to each group member information field by its position in the options[] array instead of by its name attribute.

1. In your text editor, open the **CVSGroupsLeapYear.html** document from your Projects folder for Chapter 6 and immediately save it as **CVSGroupsSubmission.html**.

2. Add to the opening <form> tag an onsubmit attribute that calls an event handler function named submitReservation(). (You create the event handler function in Step 3.)

   ```
   <form action="FormProcessor.html" method="get" enctype=
   "application/x-www-form-urlencoded" onsubmit="return
   submitReservation();">
   ```

3. Type the following submitReservation() function at the end of the script section. The for loop iterates through the items in the group members selection list. For each item, it appends the properties of the associated object to the value property using associative array syntax; this ensures that all information for each snowboarder is submitted with the form. The last statement in the for loop uses the selected property to select the item.

   ```
   function submitReservation() {
       for (var k=0; k<document.forms[0].contacts.length; ++k) {
           document.forms[0].contacts.options[k].value += ", "
           + contactList["contact" + k].telephone + ", "
   ```

```
        + contactList["contact" + k].address + ", "
        + contactList["contact" + k].city + ", "
        + contactList["contact" + k].state + ", "
        + contactList["contact" + k].zip;
      document.forms[0].contacts.options[k].selected = true;
   }
   return true;
}
```

4. Remove the name attributes from the lastname, firstname, telephone, address, city, state, and zip elements in the Group Members fields.

5. Finally, replace each of the references to the name properties in the script section of each of the Group Members fields to the element's associated index in the elements[] array. The indexes for each field in the elements[] array are: lastname=elements[12], firstname=elements[13], telephone=elements[14], address=elements[15], city=elements[16], state=elements[17], and zip=elements[18]. For example, the statements in the getContactInfo() function should be modified as follows:

```
function getContactInfo() {
     document.forms[0].elements[12].value = this.lastName;
     document.forms[0].elements[13].value = this.firstName;
     document.forms[0].elements[14].value = this.telephone;
     document.forms[0].elements[15].value = this.address;
     document.forms[0].elements[16].value = this.city;
     document.forms[0].elements[17].value = this.state;
     document.forms[0].elements[18].value = this.zip;
}
```

NOTE
Be sure to replace the name property references for the Group Members fields everywhere in the script section, not just in the getContactInfo() function.

6. Save the **CVSGroupsSubmission.html** document

7. Use the W3C Markup Validation Service to validate the **CVSGroupsSubmission.html** document and fix any errors that the document contains. Once the document is valid, close it in your text editor and then open it in your Web browser. Add several entries to the Group Members list and submit the form. The FormProcessor.html file should display the values for each of your entries, but it should not display the group member information fields.

8. Close your Web browser window.

Project 6-3

In this project, you will create a script that displays the current date and time and welcomes the user with "Good morning!", "Good afternoon!", or "Good evening!", depending on the time of day.

1. Create a new document in your text editor.

2. Type the `<!DOCTYPE>` declaration, `<html>` element, header information, and the `<body>` element. Use the strict DTD and "Welcome" as the content of the `<title>` element.

3. Add the following text and elements to the document body:

```
<h1>Welcome to my Web Page</h1>
```

4. Add the following script section to the end of the document body:

```
<script type="text/javascript">
/* <![CDATA[ */
/* ]]> */
</script>
```

5. Add the following variable declarations to the script section. The first variable instantiates a `Date` object. The second and third variables will be assigned text strings containing a greeting and the current time. The fourth and fifth variables are assigned the minute and hour values from the `Date` object.

```
var dateObject = new Date();
var greeting = "";
var curTime = "";
var minuteValue = dateObject.getMinutes();
var hourValue = dateObject.getHours();
```

6. Add the following code to the end of the script section. The first `if` statement evaluates the `minuteValue` variable and adds a 0 to the beginning of the value if it is less than 10. This forces the minutes to always display as two decimals. The `if...else` structure evaluates the `hourValue` variable and builds the strings that are assigned to the `greeting` and `curTime` variables.

```
if (minuteValue < 10)
    minuteValue = "0" + minuteValue;
if (hourValue < 12) {
    greeting = "<p>Good morning! "
    curTime = hourValue + ":" + minuteValue + " AM";
}
else if (hourValue == 12) {
    greeting = "<p>Good afternoon! ";
    curTime = hourValue + ":" + minuteValue + " PM";
}
else if (hourValue < 17) {
    greeting = "<p>Good afternoon!"
    curTime = (hourValue-12) + ":" + minuteValue + " PM"
```

```
}
else {
    greeting = "<p>Good evening! "
    curTime = (hourValue-12) + ":" + minuteValue + " PM"
}
```

7. Add the following arrays to the end of the script section. These arrays contain the full text for days and months.

```
var dayArray = new Array("Sunday", "Monday", "Tuesday",
"Wednesday", "Thursday", "Friday", "Saturday");
var monthArray = new Array("January", "February", "March",
"April", "May", "June", "July", "August", "September", "October",
"November", "December");
```

8. Type the following statements at the end of the script section to retrieve the current day and month values from the `dateObject` variable:

```
var day =  dateObject.getDay();
var month = dateObject.getMonth();
```

9. Finally, add the following statement to the end of the script section to display the current date and time and a welcome message:

```
document.write("<p>"+ greeting + "It is " + curTime
    + " on " + dayArray[day] + ", " + monthArray[month]
    + " " + dateObject.getDate() + ", " + dateObject.
    getFullYear() + ".</p>");
```

10. Save the **WelcomeDateTime.html** document in your Projects folder for Chapter 6.

11. Use the W3C Markup Validation Service to validate the **WelcomeDateTime.html** document and fix any errors that the document contains. Once the document is valid, close it in your text editor and then open it in your Web browser. You should see the appropriate welcome message along with the time and date.

12. Close your Web browser window.

Project 6-4

In this project, you will create a tip calculator.

To create a tip calculator:

1. Create a new document in your text editor.

2. Type the `<!DOCTYPE>` declaration, `<html>` element, header information, and the `<body>` element. Use the strict DTD and "Tip Calculator" as the content of the `<title>` element.

3. Add the following heading and form to the document body. The form uses a table to format the display of the fields. The form is fairly straightforward. Several of the fields use an `onchange` event handler to call a `figureTip()` method, which you will add in the next step.

```
<h2>Tip Calculator</h2>
<form action="">
<table border="0">
<tr><td>Bill:</td><td><input type="text" name="bill" value="0"
onchange="figureTip();" /></td></tr>
<tr><td>Tip %:</td><td><input type="text" name="tip_percent"
value="0"
onchange="figureTip();" /> (enter as a whole number)</td></tr>
<tr><td># of People:</td><td><input type="text" name="num_people"
value="1" onchange="figureTip();" /> </td></tr>
<tr><td>Tip amount:</td><td><input type="text" name="tip_amount"
value="0" readonly="readonly" /></td></tr>
<tr><td>Total:</td><td><input type="text" name="total" value="0"
readonly="readonly" /></td></tr>
<tr><td>Total per Person:</td><td><input type="text"
name="total_person" value="0" readonly="readonly" /></td></tr>
</table>
</form>
```

4. Next, add the following script section to the document head. The function uses the
   Document object to retrieve the values entered in the form fields. The calculated
   results use the Math.round() method to round the figures to whole numbers and
   the toFixed() method to format the results to two decimal places.

```
<script type="text/javascript">
/* <![CDATA[ */
function figureTip() {
    var bill = document.forms[0].bill.value;
    var tipPercent = document.forms[0].tip_percent.value;
    var numPeople = document.forms[0].num_people.value;
    var tipAmount = Math.round(bill * ("." + tipPercent));
    var total = Math.round(bill * (1 + "." + tipPercent));
    var totalPerPerson = Math.round(total / numPeople);
    document.forms[0].tip_amount.value = tipAmount.
    toLocaleString();
    document.forms[0].total.value = total.toLocaleString();
    document.forms[0].total_person.value
        = totalPerPerson.toLocaleString();
}
/* ]]> */
</script>
```

5. Save the document as **TipCalculator.html** in the Projects folder for Chapter 6,
   and then validate it with the W3C Markup Validation Service at **validator.w3.org/
   file-upload.html**. Once the TipCalculator.html document is valid, close it in your
   text editor, and then open it in your Web browser. Test the calculator's functionality.

6. Close your Web browser window.

Case Projects

For the following projects, save the files you create in your Cases folder for Chapter 6. Be sure to validate each Web page with the W3C Markup Validation Service.

Case Project 6-1

A popular use of the Date object is to create a digital clock. However, recall that the date and time in a Date object are not updated over time like a clock. Instead, a Date object contains the static date and time as of the moment the JavaScript code instantiates the object. You can simulate a digital clock that appears to "tick" off each second by using a setInterval() method that continuously executes code to retrieve the current time. Use this technique to create a digital clock that displays a 12-hour clock in a form's text box. The clock should display hours, minutes, seconds, and either AM or PM. Format the displayed time so that any minutes or seconds that are less than 10 are preceded by a 0, such as 10:08:07 AM. Save the document as **DigitalClock.html**.

Case Project 6-2

Create a Web page for a digital photo development company. Include a form that allows clerks at the company to enter orders for each customer. The form should allow you to enter one item per order. Include radio buttons for different types of items that can be created with digital images, including hard copy prints, posters, coffee mugs, and t-shirts. Use a Date object to automatically calculate the date an item will be ready, based on the current date. For example, hard copy prints and posters should be ready one day from today, coffee mugs two days from today, t-shirts three days from today, and so on. Submit the form to the FormProcessor.html document (a copy is in your Cases folder for Chapter 6). Save the document as **DigitalPhotos.html**.

Case Project 6-3

Create a Web page that allows a coach to submit a roster for a baseball team. Include fields for the team name and head coach's contact information. Create a Team Members section, similar to the Group Members section on the Group Reservations page, to allow the coach to enter information for each team member, including contact information and the position played. Include functionality that allows the coach to add, delete, and modify player information. Also include a check box that the coach can select if permission has been received from the player's guardian. Write functionality that submits all of the team member information (including the permission field) to the FormProcessor.html document (a copy is in your Cases folder for Chapter 6), and create the form so the team member information fields are not submitted. Save the document as **TeamRoster.html**.

7

Manipulating Data in Strings and Arrays

In this chapter you will:

- Manipulate strings
- Work with regular expressions
- Manipulate arrays
- Convert between strings and arrays

One of the most common uses of JavaScript is for processing form data submitted by users. Because form data is submitted as strings, a good JavaScript programmer must be adept at dealing with strings. Another critical skill for a JavaScript programmer is the ability to manipulate arrays. Earlier in this book, you learned basic skills for working with both strings and arrays. In this chapter, you learn how to use advanced techniques for both strings and arrays. You also learn how to employ regular expressions, which are used for matching and manipulating strings according to specified rules.

Manipulating Strings

As you learned in Chapter 1, a string is text contained within double or single quotation marks. You can use text strings as literal values or assign them to a variable. For example, the first statement in the following code prints a literal text string, whereas the second statement assigns a text string to a variable. The third statement then uses the `document.write()` statement to print the text string assigned to the variable.

```
document.write("2003-04 NBA All-Star Game MVP: ");
var basketballPlayer = "Shaquille O'Neal";
document.write("<p>" + basketballPlayer + "</p>");
```

Whether you use single or double quotation marks, a string must begin and end with the same type of quotation mark. For example, `document.write("<p>This is a text string.</p>");` is valid because the string starts and ends with double quotation marks. Likewise, `document.write('<p>This is a text string.</p>');` is valid because the string begins and ends with single quotation marks. By contrast, the statement `document.write ("<p>This is a text string.</p>');` is invalid because the string starts with a double quotation mark and ends with a single quotation mark. In this case, you would receive an error message because the JavaScript interpreter cannot tell where the literal string begins and ends.

The preceding example demonstrates some of the basic techniques for creating and combining strings. You will often find it necessary to parse the text strings in your scripts. When applied to text strings, the term **parsing** refers to the act of extracting characters or substrings from a larger string. This is essentially the same concept as the parsing (rendering) that occurs in a Web browser when the Web browser extracts the necessary formatting information from a Web page before displaying it on the screen. In the case of a Web page, the document itself is one large text string from which formatting and other information needs to be extracted. However, when working on a programming level, parsing usually refers to the extraction of information from string literals and variables.

To parse the text strings in your scripts, you use the methods and `length` property of the `String` class. All literal strings and string variables in JavaScript are represented by a **String class**, which contains methods for manipulating text strings.

NOTE

This chapter only discusses class methods that are part of ECMAScript.

In this chapter, you create a JavaScript program that validates e-mail information that is entered into a form on a Web page. The form information will be submitted to the FormProcessor.html document that you have used in the past two chapters, while the validation functionality will be achieved with an `onsubmit` event handler. Your Chapter folder for Chapter 7 includes a Web page named EmailForm.html that contains the form you will validate along with the FormProcessor.html document. Figure 7-1 shows how the EmailForm.html document appears in a Web browser.

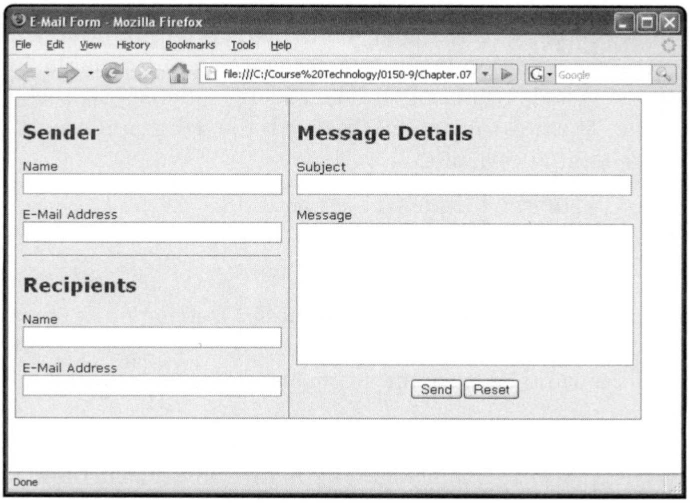

Figure 7-1

EmailForm.html in a Web browser

To add an `onsubmit` event handler to the e-mail form:

1. Open in your text editor the **EmailForm.html** document, located in your Chapter folder for Chapter 7.

2. Add the following script section above the closing `</head>` tag:

```
<script type="text/javascript">
/* <![CDATA[ */
/* ]]> */
</script>
```

3. Add the following `validateSubmission()` function to the script section. You will modify the `validateSubmission()` function throughout this chapter.

```
function validateSubmission() {
}
```

4. Add to the opening `<form>` tag an `onsubmit` event handler that calls the `validateSubmission()` function, as follows:

```
<form action="FormProcessor.html" method="get"
onsubmit="return validateSubmission()">
```

5. Save the **EmailForm.html** document and then open it in your Web browser. Type some information into the form fields and click the **Send** button. The data you entered should appear in the FormProcessor.html page.

6. Close your Web browser window.

Formatting Strings

This section describes how to use special characters and how to change the letter case of strings.

Using Special Characters

You learned in Chapter 2 that when you want to include basic types of special characters, such as quotation marks, within a literal string, you must use an escape sequence. The escape sequence for double quotation marks is `\"` and the escape sequence for single quotation marks is `\'`. For example, the text string assigned to the `basketballPlayer` variable includes escape sequences for both double and single quotation marks. Figure 7-2 shows the output in a Web browser.

```
var basketballPlayer = "Shaquille \"Shaq\" O\'Neal";
MVP = "2003-04 NBA All-Star Game MVP: " + basketballPlayer;
document.write("<p>" + MVP + "</p>");
```

For other types of special characters, you need to use Unicode, which is a standardized set of characters from many of the world's languages. A number represents each character in the Unicode character set. For instance, the Unicode numbers for the uppercase letters A, B, and C, are 65, 66, and 67, respectively. In most cases, you can use XHTML numeric character references or character entities to represent Unicode characters in text strings. For example, the copyright symbol (©) can be represented in HTML by the numeric character reference

Figure 7-2
Output of a text string
created with escape
sequences and the con-
catenation operator

`&#169;` and the character entity is `&copy;`. To assign the text "© 1995 - 2006" to a variable named `copyrightInfo` in JavaScript, you can use either of the following statements:

```
copyrightInfo = "<p>&#169; 1995-2006</p>"; // numeric character ref.
copyrightInfo = "<p>&copy; 1995-2006</p>"; // character entity
```

Instead of using numeric character references or character entities within text strings, as shown in the preceding example, you can use the **`fromCharCode()` method**, which constructs a text string from Unicode character codes that are passed as arguments. The `fromCharCode()` method is called a static method because it is not used as a method of any string objects (which can be literal strings or variables) in your scripts. Instead, you must call `fromCharCode()` as a method of the `String` class with the following syntax `String.fromCharCode(char1, char2, ...)`. The following statement uses the `fromCharCode()` method to print "JavaScript" with Unicode characters:

```
document.write("<p>" + String.fromCharCode(74,97,118,97,83,99,114,
     105,112,116) + "</p>");
```

The numeric characters in the preceding statement would render in a Web browser as "JavaScript:. The following statement uses the `fromCharCode()` method to print "© 1995 - 2006":

```
document.write("<p>" + String.fromCharCode(169) + " 1995 - 2006</p>");
```

NOTE

The character set that is most commonly used today is American Standard Code for Information Interchange, or ASCII, which is a standardized set of numeric representations for English characters. The Unicode character set contains the ASCII character set as a subset. Unicode will eventually replace ASCII entirely because of ASCII's limitation to English characters.

Changing Case

To change the case of letters in a string, you use the `toLowerCase()` and `toUpperCase()` methods of the `String` class. The **`toLowerCase()` method** converts a text string to lowercase, while the **`toUpperCase()` method** converts a text string to uppercase. You append either method to a string or variable that contains the text for which you want to change letter case. For example, the following code uses the `toUpperCase()` method to print the contents of the `agency` variable ("fema") in uppercase letters ("FEMA"):

```
var agency = "fema";
document.write("<p>" + agency.toUpperCase() + "</p>");
```

Note that the `toUpperCase()` method in the preceding statement does not convert the contents of the `agency` variable to uppercase letters; it only prints the text in uppercase letters. If you want to change the contents of a variable to upper- or lowercase letters, you must assign the value returned from the `toLowerCase()` or `toUpperCase()` methods to the variable or to a different variable. The following statements demonstrate how to change the contents of the `agency` variable to uppercase letters:

```
var agency = "fema";
agency = agency.toUpperCase()
document.write("<p>" + agency + "</p>");
```

Because e-mail addresses are case-insensitive, you will modify the e-mail form so it converts the case of the e-mail addresses to lowercase letters.

To modify the e-mail form so it converts the case of the e-mail addresses to lowercase letters:

1. Return to the **EmailForm.html** document in your text editor.

2. Add the following statements to the `validateSubmission()` function. The first statement declares a Boolean variable named `retValue` that will be returned from the `validateSubmission()` function. Recall that the value returned from an `onsubmit` event handler (the `validateSubmission()` function) determines whether the JavaScript interpreter submits the form data. The second statement passes to the `validateEmail()` function the form object that contains the sender e-mail address, not just the value entered into the field. This allows the `validateEmail()` function to modify the form value directly. Notice that the value returned from the `validateEmail()` function is assigned to the `retValue` variable. If the `validateEmail()` function returns a value of false (meaning the e-mail address did not pass validation), the `if` statement returns that value, which cancels the form submission.

   ```
   var retValue = true;
   retValue = validateEmail(document.forms[0].sender_email);
   if (retValue == false)
        return retValue;
   ```

3. Add the following statements to the end of the `validateSubmission()` function. These statements pass the recipient e-mail object to the `validateEmail()` function. If the `validateEmail()` function returns a value of false (meaning the e-mail address did not pass validation), the `if` statement returns that value, which cancels the form submission.

   ```
   retValue = validateEmail(document.forms[0].recipient_email);
   if (retValue == false)
        return retValue;
   ```

4. Add the following `validateEmail()` function to the end of the script section. The function accepts a single argument containing a form object that you want

to make lowercase. The first statement in the function assigns the value of the form object to a variable named `email`, while the second statement converts the contents of the `email` variable to lowercase and then assigns the converted value back to the form object. The third statement returns a value of true.

```
function validateEmail(formObject) {
    var email = formObject.value;
    formObject.value = email.toLowerCase();
    return true;
}
```

5. Save the **EmailForm.html** document and then open it in your Web browser. Enter some uppercase e-mail addresses into the sender and recipient e-mail fields, and then click the **Send** button. The e-mail addresses you entered should appear in the FormProcessor.html page in lowercase letters.

6. Close your Web browser window.

Counting Characters in a String

You will often find it necessary to count characters and words in strings, particularly with strings from form submissions. For example, you might need to count the number of characters in a password to ensure that a user selects a password with a minimum number of characters. Or, you might have a Web page that allows users to submit classified ads that cannot exceed a maximum number of characters. The `String` class contains a single property, the **length property**, which returns the number of characters in a string. To return the total number of characters in a string, you append the `length` property of the `String` class to a literal string, variable, or object containing text. For example, the following code uses the `length` property to count the number of characters in a variable named `country`. The `document.write()` statement prints "The country name contains 18 characters."

```
var country = "Kingdom of Morocco";
document.write("<p>The country name contains " + country.length
    + " characters.</p>");
```

TIP
The `length` property counts escape sequences such as \n as one character.

The e-mail form includes a Subject field in which users can enter the subject of a message. Next, you modify the script so it uses the `length` property to prevent users from entering a subject of more than 40 characters.

To modify the script so it uses the `length` property to prevent users from entering a subject of more than 40 characters:

1. Return to the **EmailForm.html** document in your text editor.

2. Add the following `if...else` statement after the statement in the `validateSubmission()` function that declares the `retValue` variable. Notice that the `length` property is appended to the `value` property of the `subject` object. If the length of the subject field is greater than 40 characters, a message displays to the user that she has exceeded the maximum number of characters and the `if` statement returns a value of false, preventing the form submission. The `else` statement ensures that the `sender_email, recipient_email`, and `subject` fields are filled in.

```
if (document.forms[0].subject.value.length > 40) {
    window.alert("The subject must be 40 characters or less!");
    return false;
}
else if (document.forms[0].sender_email.value == ""
    || document.forms[0].recipient_email.value == ""
    || document.forms[0].subject.value == "") {
    window.alert("You did not fill in one of the
            following required fields: sender e-mail,
            recipient e-mail, or subject.");
    retValue = false;
}
```

3. Add the following statements after the closing brace of the `else` clause to check if the `retValue` variable was set to false:

```
if (retValue == false)
    return retValue;
```

4. Save the **EmailForm.html** document and then open it in your Web browser. For the Subject field, enter more than 40 characters and click the **Send** button. You should see the message informing you that the subject contains more than 40 characters.

5. Close your Web browser window.

Finding and Extracting Characters and Substrings

In some situations, you will need to find and extract characters and substrings from a string. For example, if your script receives an e-mail address, you may need to extract the name portion of the e-mail address or domain name. To search for and extract characters and substrings in JavaScript, you use the methods listed in Table 7-1.

Method	Description
charAt(*index*)	Returns the character at the specified position in a text string; returns an empty string if the specified position is greater than the length of the string
charCodeAt(*index*)	Returns the Unicode character code at the specified position in a text string; returns NaN if the specified position is greater than the length of the string
indexOf(*text*[, *index*])	Performs a case-sensitive search and returns the position number in a string of the first character in the text argument; if the *index* argument is included, then the indexOf() method starts searching at that position within the string; returns -1 if the character or string is not found
lastIndexOf(*text*[, *index*])	Performs a case-sensitive search and returns the position number in a string of the last instance of the first character in the text argument; if the index argument is included, then the lastIndexOf() method starts searching at that position within the string; returns -1 if the character or string is not found
match(*pattern*)	Performs a case-sensitive search and returns an array containing the results that match the *pattern* argument; returns null if the text is not found
search(*pattern*)	Performs a case-sensitive search and returns the position number in a string of the first instance of the first character in the *text* argument; returns -1 if the character or string is not found
slice(*starting index* [, *ending index*])	Extracts text from a string starting with the position number in the string of the *starting index* argument and ending with the position number of the *ending index* argument; allows negative argument values
substring(*starting index* [, *ending index*])	Extracts text from a string starting with the position number in the string of the *starting index* argument and ending with the position number of the *ending index* argument; does not allow negative argument values

Table 7-1   Search and extraction methods of the String class

There are two types of string search methods: methods that return a numeric position in a text string and methods that return a character or substring. To use methods that return the numeric position in a text string, you need to understand that the position of characters in a text string begins with a value of 0, the same as with indexed array elements. For example, the search() method returns the position of the first instance of the first character of a text string that is passed as an argument. If the search string is not found, the search() method returns a value of -1. The following code uses the search() method to determine whether the email variable contains an @ character. Because the position of text strings begins with 0, the document.write() statement returns a value of 9, even though the @ character is the tenth character in the string.

```
var email = "president@whitehouse.gov";
document.write(email.search("@")); // returns 9
```

As another example, the indexOf() method returns the position of the first occurrence of one string in another string. The primary difference between the search() method and the indexOf() method is that you can pass to the indexOf() method a second optional argument that specifies the position in the string where you want to start searching. If the search string is not found, the indexOf() method returns a value of -1. The following code uses the indexOf() method to determine whether the email variable contains an @ character. Because the `indexOf()` method includes a value of 10 as the second optional argument, the `document.write()` statement returns a value of -1 (indicating that the search string was not found) because the method began searching in the string after the position of the @ character.

```
var email = "president@whitehouse.gov";
document.write(email.indexOf("@", 10)); // returns -1
```

To extract characters from a string, you use the `substring()` or `slice()` methods. In both cases, you pass to the method the starting index and ending index of the characters you want to extract. Both methods return a substring containing the specified characters or an empty string if the specified starting index does not exist. For example, the second statement in the following code uses the `search()` method to identify the position of the @ character in the `email` variable. The `substring()` method then returns the name portion of the e-mail address by using a starting index position of 0 (the first character in the string) and the value assigned to the `nameEnd` variable as the ending index position.

```
var email = "president@whitehouse.gov";
var nameEnd = email.search("@");
document.write("<p>The name portion of the e-mail address is '"
      + email.substring(0, nameEnd) + "'.</p>");
```

To extract characters from the middle or end of a string, you need to identify the position of the character in the string where you want to start the extraction. One way to do this is by using the `search()`, `indexOf()`, or `lastIndexOf()` methods. The `lastIndexOf()` method works the same as the `indexOf()` method except that it returns the position of the last occurrence of one string in another string instead of the first. The following code uses the `lastIndexOf()` method to return the position of the period within the e-mail address in the `email` variable. The `substring()` method then uses the index returned from the `lastIndexOf()` method to return the domain identifier of the e-mail address.

```
var email = "president@whitehouse.gov";
var startDomainID = email.lastIndexOf(".");
document.write("<p>The domain identifier of the e-mail address is " +
      email.substring(startDomainID) + ".</p>"
```

The only difference between the `slice()` and `substring()` methods is that the `slice()` method allows you to specify negative argument values for the index arguments. If you specify a negative value for the starting index, the `slice()` method starts at the end of the text string; -1 represents the last character in the string, -2 represents the second to last character, and so on. If you specify a negative value for the ending index, the number of characters that the `slice()` method extracts also starts at the end of the text string. Note that the `slice()` method does not return the character represented by the ending index; it returns the character immediately before the ending index. For example, the first `slice()` method in the following statements uses a starting index of -6, which represents the letter 'S' in the *JavaScript* text string, and an ending index of -3, which represents the letter 'i' in the *JavaScript* text string. Remember that both positions are counted from the end of the text string. In comparison, the second `slice()` method uses a starting index of 2, which represents the letter 'v' in the *JavaScript* text string and an ending index is 5, which represents the letter 'S' in the *JavaScript* text string. Because the index values are positive, they are counted from the beginning of the text string. Figure 7-3 shows how the following statements print in a Web browser.

```
var language = "JavaScript";
document.write("<p>" + language.slice(-6,-3) + "</p>");
document.write("<p>" + language.slice(2,5) + "</p >");
```

Figure 7-3

Examples of the slice() method with negative and positive index values

The following code uses the slice() method to return the domain identifier of the e-mail address in the email variable:

```
var email = "president@whitehouse.gov";
document.write("<p>The domain identifier of the e-mail address is "
    + email.slice(-4) + ".</p>");
```

The following code contains another example of the slice() method. In this version, the code uses search() and lastIndexOf() methods to return the domain name of the e-mail address. Notice that the second statement increments the position returned from the search() method by one. This prevents the @ character from being included in the substring returned from the slice() method.

```
var email = "president@whitehouse.gov";
var domainBegin = email.search("@") + 1;
var domainEnd = email.lastIndexOf(".");
document.write("<p>The domain name portion of the e-mail address is '"
    + email.slice(domainBegin, domainEnd) + "'.</p>");
```

Later in this chapter, you learn how to use regular expressions to validate strings, including e-mail addresses. For now, you use the search() and lastIndexOf() methods simply to check whether the e-mail addresses entered into the form contain ampersands and a period to separate the domain and identifier.

To use the search() and lastIndexOf() methods to check whether the e-mail addresses entered into the form contain ampersands and a period to separate the domain and identifier:

1. Return to the **EmailForm.html** document in your text editor.

2. Add the following bolded statements to the validateEmail() function. The function uses search() and lastIndexOf() methods to determine whether the string passed to it contains an ampersand and a period. If the string does contain both characters, a value of true is returned. If not, a value of false is returned.

```
function validateEmail(formObject) {
    var email = formObject.value;
    if (email.search("@") == -1
            || email.lastIndexOf(".") == -1) {
```

```
window.alert("One or more of the e-mail addresses
        you entered does not appear to be valid.");
return false;
```

}

```
formObject.value = email.toLowerCase();
return true;
```

}

3. Save the **EmailForm.html** document and then open it in your Web browser. Enter e-mail addresses in the sender and recipient e-mail fields that do not include ampersands or periods, and then click the **Send** button. You should see the message informing you that one or more of the e-mail addresses are invalid.

4. Close your Web browser window.

Replacing Characters and Substrings

In addition to finding and extracting characters in a string, you might also need to replace them. The **replace()** method of the String class creates a new string with all instances of a specified pattern replaced with the value of the text argument. The syntax for the replace() method is *string*.replace(*pattern*, *text*). Essentially, the replace() method replaces any patterns it finds in the string with the text.

TIP

The replace() method is case sensitive.

The following example demonstrates how to use the replace() method to replace "president" in the email variable with "vice.president".

```
var email = "president@whitehouse.gov";
var newEmail = email.replace("president", "vice.president");
document.write("<p>" + newEmail + "</p>"); // prints
    'vice.president@whitehouse.gov'
```

NOTE

When you pass a simple text string as the pattern argument of the replace() method, only the first instance of the pattern is replaced with the specified text. To replace all instances of a pattern, you must use a regular expression as the pattern argument and set the property of the RegExp object's global property. Regular expressions and the RegExp object are discussed later in this chapter.

Combining Characters and Substrings

So far, you have used the concatenation operator (+) and the compound assignment operator (+=) to combine text strings. The JavaScript `String` class also includes the **concat() method**, which creates a new string by combining strings that are passed as arguments. The syntax for the `concat()` method is *string*`.concat(`*value1*`, `*value2*`, ...)`. Note that the `concat()` method does not change the original string but returns a new string. The *value* arguments are appended to the string in the order in which they are passed to the `concat()` method. For example, the following statements demonstrate how to use the `concat()` method to build a string that is printed using a `document.write()` statement. Figure 7-4 shows the output in a Web browser.

```
var name = "Theodor Seuss Geisel";
var penName = "Dr. Seuss";
document.write("<p>" + penName.concat(" was the pen name of ", name)
     + ".</p>");
```

Figure 7-4

Output generated with the `concat()` method of the `String` class

In most cases, you do not need to use the `concat()` method. Instead, it is usually easier to use the concatenation operator and the compound assignment operator to combine text strings. The following code shows the same statements from the preceding example, but this time using concatenation operators:

```
var name = "Theodor Seuss Geisel";
var penName = "Dr. Seuss";
document.write("<p>" + penName + " was the pen name of "
     + name + ".</p>");
```

Comparing Strings

In Chapter 2, you studied various operators that you can use with JavaScript, including comparison operators. Although comparison operators are most often used with numbers, they can also be used with strings. The following statements use the comparison operator (==) to compare two variables containing text strings:

```
var florida = "Miami is in Florida.";
var cuba = "Havana is in Cuba.";
if (florida == cuba)
     document.write("<p>Same location.</p>");
else
     document.write("<p>Different locations.</p>");
```

Because the text strings are not the same, the `else` clause prints the text "Different locations." You can also use comparison operators to determine whether one letter is higher in the alphabet than another letter. In the following code, the first `document.write()` statement executes because the letter "B" is higher in the alphabet than the letter "A":

```
var firstLetter = "A";
var secondLetter = "B";
if (secondLetter > firstLetter)
    document.write("<p>The second letter is higher in the alphabet
    than the first letter.</p>");
else
    document.write("<p>The second letter is lower in the alphabet
            than the first letter.</p>");
```

The comparison operators actually compare individual characters according to their Unicode position. Lowercase letters are represented by the values 97 ("a") to 122 ("z"). Uppercase letters are represented by the values 65 ("A") to 90 ("Z"). Because lowercase letters have higher values than uppercase letters, the lowercase letters are evaluated as being "greater" than the uppercase letters. For example, an uppercase letter "A" is represented by Unicode value 65, whereas a lowercase letter "a" is represented by Unicode value 96. For this reason, the statement `"a" > "A"` returns a value of true because the uppercase letter "A" has a lower Unicode value than the lowercase letter "a."

In addition to using standard comparison operators, the `String` class includes a **`localeCompare()` method**, which compares strings according to the particular sort order of a language or country. The syntax for the `localeCompare()` method is *sourceString*.`localeCompare(`*compareString*`)`. If *compareString* is equivalent to *sourceString*, the method returns a value of 0; if *compareString* sorts before *sourceString*, the method returns a value greater than 0, usually 1; if *compareString* sorts after *sourceString*, the method returns a value less than 0, usually -1. For example, consider the following `localeCompare()` method, which compares the strings "Dan" and "Don". Because "Dan" sorts before "Don", the method returns a value of 1.

```
var sourceString = "Don";
var compareString = "Dan";
document.write(sourceString.localeCompare(compareString)); // returns 1
```

In comparison, the following statement, which switches the "Dan" and "Don" arguments, returns a value of -1:

```
var sourceString = "Dan";
var compareString = "Don";
document.write(sourceString.localeCompare(compareString));
// returns -1
```

If both strings values are equal, the `localeCompare()` method returns a value of 0, as in the following example:

```
var sourceString = "Don";
var compareString = "Don";
document.write(sourceString.localeCompare(compareString)); // returns 0
```

Keep in mind that the `localeCompare()` method performs a case-sensitive comparison of two strings. The following statements return a value of 1 because the lowercase "d" in the comparison string sorts before the uppercase "D" in the source string:

```
var sourceString = "Don";
var compareString = "don";
document.write(sourceString.localeCompare(compareString ));
// returns 1
```

To perform a case-insensitive comparison of two strings, you must first use the `toLowerCase()` or `toUpperCase()` methods to convert the strings to the same case. The `localeCompare()` statement in the following code returns a value of 0 because both the source string and comparison string are converted to lowercase before the comparison is performed:

```
var sourceString = "Don";
var compareString = "don";
sourceString = sourceString.toLowerCase();
compareString = compareString.toLowerCase();
document.write(sourceString.localeCompare(compareString ));
// returns 0
```

Next, you add a function to the e-mail form that determines whether a user entered the same e-mail address for the sender and recipient.

To add a function to the e-mail form that determines whether a user entered the same e-mail address for the sender and recipient:

1. Return to the **EmailForm.html** document in your text editor.

2. Add the following statements to the end of the `validateSubmission()` function. The first statement calls a function named `compareAddresses()`, which you create next. Notice that parameters are passed to the `compareAddresses()` function: one for the sender e-mail object and one for the recipient e-mail object. The second statement returns the `retValue` variable from the `validateSubmission()` function.

   ```
   retValue = compareAddresses(document.forms[0].sender_email,
       document.forms[0].recipient_email);
   return retValue;
   ```

3. Add the following `compareAddresses()` function to the end of the script section. The function accepts two parameters for the sender and recipient e-mail objects, which it assigns to two variables: `senderEmail` and `recipientEmail`. Both variables are converted to lowercase with the `toLowerCase()` method and then compared with the `localeCompare()` method. If both e-mail addresses are the same, a message displays to the user and the function returns a value of false.

   ```
   function compareAddresses(senderObject, recipientObject) {
       var senderEmail = senderObject.value;
       var recipientEmail = recipientObject.value;
       senderEmail = senderEmail.toLowerCase();
   ```

```
        recipientEmail = recipientEmail.toLowerCase();
        if (senderEmail.localeCompare(recipientEmail) == 0) {
            window.alert("You entered the same e-mail address for
                    sender and recipient.");
            return false;
        }
        else
            return true;
    }
```

4. Save the **EmailForm.html** document and then open it in your Web browser. Enter the same e-mail address in the sender and recipient e-mail fields and click the **Send** button. You should see the message informing you that you entered the same e-mail address for both the sender and recipient.

5. Close your Web browser window.

Working with Regular Expressions

One of the more complex methods of working with strings involves the use of **regular expressions**, which are patterns that are used for matching and manipulating strings according to specified rules. With scripting languages such as JavaScript, regular expressions are most commonly used for validating submitted form data. For example, you can use a regular expression to ensure that a user enters a date in a specific format, such as *mm/dd/yyyy*, or a telephone number in the format (###) ###-####. Most scripting languages support some form of regular expressions.

NOTE
ECMAScript regular expressions are based on the regular expression functionality of the Perl 5 programming language.

Defining Regular Expressions in JavaScript

Regular expression patterns in JavaScript must begin and end with forward slashes. The following statement defines a regular expression pattern for determining whether a text string contains "https" and assigns it to a variable named `urlProtocol`. Notice that the regular expression pattern is not enclosed in quotations.

```
var urlProtocol = /https/;
```

You can use regular expressions with several of the `String` class methods, including the `search()` and `replace()` methods. The value you pass to either of these methods can be either a text string or a regular expression. The following statements pass the `urlProtocol` regular expression to the `search()` method, which then searches the text contained within the `url` variable for "https". Because the `url` variable contains a protocol of "http" instead of "https", the `search()` method returns a value of -1, indicating that the regular expression pattern was not found.

```
var urlProtocol = /https/;
```

```
var url = "http://www.dongosselin.com";
document.write("<p>" + url.search(urlProtocol) + "</p>"); // returns -1
```

In addition to assigning a regular expression to a variable, you can also pass the pattern directly to a method that accepts regular expressions. The following example demonstrates how to pass the /https/ regular expression directly to the search() method. Again, notice that the regular expression is not enclosed within quotations.

```
var url = "http://www.dongosselin.com";
document.write("<p>" + url.search(/https/) + "</p>"); // returns -1
```

A final approach for creating a regular expression is to use the RegExp() constructor. The RegExp() constructor is part of the **RegExp object**, which contains methods and properties for working with regular expressions in JavaScript. The syntax for creating a regular expression with the RegExp() constructor is as follows:

```
var regExpName = new RegExp("pattern"[, attributes]);
```

Notice that the pattern in the preceding syntax is surrounded by quotation marks instead of forward slashes. The following example demonstrates how to use the RegExp() constructor with the "https" pattern:

```
var urlProtocol = new RegExp("https");
var url = "http://www.dongosselin.com";
document.write("<p>" + url.search(urlProtocol) + "</p>"); // returns -1
```

All three ways of defining regular expressions result in the same functionality, so which one you use makes little difference. Because the value passed to the RegExp() constructor is a text string, the JavaScript interpreter must convert it to a regular expression before it can be used as a regular expression. This added step can make RegExp() constructors slightly slower than assigning a regular expression to a text string or passing one as an argument. For this reason, some programmers prefer not to use RegExp() constructors to define regular expressions. However, you may find them helpful for keeping your scripts organized and easy to read.

Next, you modify the search() method in the validateEmail() function so it searches for the ampersand in the e-mail addresses using a regular expression instead of the "@" text string.

To modify the search() method in the validateEmail() function so it searches for the ampersand in the e-mail addresses using a regular expression instead of the "@" text string:

1.   Return to the **EmailForm.html** document in your text editor.
2.   Locate the if statement in the validateEmail() function and modify the conditional expression so that the value passed to the search() method is passed as a regular expression instead of a string, as shown in the following bolded code:

```
. . .
if (email.search(/@/)
      == -1 || email.lastIndexOf(".") == -1) {
. . .
```

CAUTION
You cannot use regular expressions with the `indexOf()` and `lastIndexOf()` methods.

3. Save the **EmailForm.html** document and then open it in your Web browser. Enter e-mail addresses in the sender and recipient e-mail fields that do not include ampersands, and then click the **Send** button. You should see the message informing you that one or more of the e-mail addresses are invalid.

4. Close your Web browser window.

Using Regular Expression Methods

Although you can use regular expressions with several of the `String` class methods, the `RegExp` object includes two methods, `test()` and `exec()`, which are specifically designed for working with regular expressions. The `exec()` method is a little complex, so you will study the `test()` method in this book. The `test()` method returns a value of true if a string contains text that matches a regular expression or false if it doesn't. The syntax for the `test()` method is as follows:

```
var pattern = test(string);
```

The following code demonstrates how to use the `test()` method to determine whether the `url` variable contains the text "dongosselin". Because the variable does contain the text, the `document.write()` statement prints "true".

```
var urlDomain = new RegExp("dongosselin");
var url = "http://www.dongosselin.com";
document.write("<p>" + urlDomain.test(url) + "</p>"); // returns true
```

The preceding examples simply demonstrate how to use the `test()` method. In fact there is no point in using regular expression methods with such examples because you can more easily determine whether the two strings match by using the `search()` method or one of the other `String` class methods. The real power of regular expressions comes from the patterns you write, as you'll learn in the next section.

Writing Regular Expression Patterns

The hardest part of working with regular expressions is writing the patterns and rules that are used for matching and manipulating strings. As an example of a common, albeit complicated, regular expression, consider the following code:

```
emailPattern = /^[_a-z0-9\\-]+(\.[_a-z0-9\\-]
    +)*@[a-z0-9\\-]+(\.[a-z0-9\\-]+)*(\.[a-z]{2,3})$/;
email = "dongosselin@compuserve.com";
if (emailPattern.test(email))
    document.write("<p>You entered a valid e-mail address.</p.");
else
```

```
document.write("<p>You did not enter a valid e-mail
        address.</p.");
```

The preceding code uses the `test()` method to determine whether the `email` variable contains a valid e-mail address. If the `test()` method returns a value of true, then a `document.write()` statement prints "You entered a valid e-mail address." As you can see, the logic is straightforward: if the e-mail address doesn't match the regular expression, then a `document.write()` statement prints "You did not enter a valid e-mail address." The complex part of the code is the pattern that is defined in the first statement.

NOTE
You can find many types of prewritten regular expressions on the Regular Expression Library Web page at *http://www.regexlib.com/*.

Regular expression patterns consist of literal characters and **metacharacters**, which are special characters that define the pattern matching rules in a regular expression. Table 7-2 lists the metacharacters that you can use with JavaScript regular expressions.

Metacharacter	Description
.	Matches any single character
\	Identifies the next character as a literal value
^	Matches characters at the beginning of a string
$	Matches characters at the end of a string
()	Specifies required characters to include in a pattern match
[]	Specifies alternate characters allowed in a pattern match
[^]	Specifies characters to exclude in a pattern match
-	Identifies a possible range of characters to match
|	Specifies alternate sets of characters to include in a pattern match

Table 7-2   JavaScript regular expression metacharacters

Matching any Character

You use a period (.) to match any single character in a pattern. A period in a regular expression pattern really specifies that the pattern must contain a value where the period is located. For example, the following code specifies that the `zip` variable must contain five characters. Because the variable only contains three characters, the `test()` method returns a value of false.

```
var zipPattern = /...../;
var zip = "015";
document.write(zipPattern.test(zip)); // returns false
```

In comparison, the following `test()` method returns a value of true because the `zip` variable contains five characters:

```
var zipPattern = /...../;
var zip = "01562";
document.write(zipPattern.test(zip)); // returns true
```

Because the period only specifies that a character be must included in the designated location within the pattern, you can also include additional characters within the pattern. The following `test()` method returns a value of true because the `zip` variable contains the required five characters along with the ZIP+4 characters.

```
var zipPattern = /...../;
var zip = "01562-2607";
document.write(zipPattern.test(zip)); // returns true
```

Matching Characters at the Beginning or End of a String

The ^ metacharacter matches characters at the beginning of a string, and the $ metacharacter matches characters at the end of a string. A pattern that matches the beginning or end of a line is called an **anchor**. To specify an anchor at the beginning of a line, the pattern must begin with the ^ metacharacter. The following example specifies that the `url` variable begin with "http". Because the variable does begin with "http", the `test()` method returns true.

```
var urlProtocol = /^http/;
var url = "http://www.dongosselin.com";
document.write(urlProtocol.test(url)); // returns true
```

All literal characters following the ^ metacharacter in a pattern compose the anchor. This means that the following example returns false because the `url` variable does not begin with "https" (only "http" without the 's'), as is specified by the anchor in the pattern:

```
var urlProtocol = /^https/;
var url = "http://www.dongosselin.com";
document.write(urlProtocol.test(url)); // returns false
```

To specify an anchor at the end of a line, the pattern must end with the $ metacharacter. The following demonstrates how to specify that a URL end with "com":

```
var urlIdentifier = /com$/;
var url = "http://www.dongosselin.com";
document.write(urlIdentifier.test(url)); // returns true
```

The preceding code returns true because the URL assigned to the `urlIdentifier` variable ends with "com". However, the following code returns false because the URL assigned to the `urlIdentifier` variable does not end with "gov".

```
var urlIdentifier = /gov$/;
var url = "http://www.dongosselin.com";
document.write(urlIdentifier.test(url)); // returns false
```

Matching Special Characters

To match any metacharacters as literal values in a regular expression, you must precede the character with a backslash. For example, a period (.) metacharacter matches any single character in pattern. If you want to ensure that a string contains an actual period and not any character, you need to escape it with a backslash. The domain identifier in the following code is appended to the domain name with a comma instead of a period. However, the regular expression returns true because the period in the expression is not escaped.

```
var urlIdentifier = /.com$/;
var url = "http://www.dongosselin,com";
document.write(urlIdentifier.test(url)); // returns true
```

To correct the problem, you must escape the period as follows:

```
var urlIdentifier = /\.com$/;
var url = "http://www.dongosselin,com";
document.write(urlIdentifier.test(url)); // returns false
```

Next, you modify the conditional expression in the validateEmail() function so it uses test() methods and determines whether a domain identifier is appended to the domain name with period.

To add test() methods to the validateEmail() function:

1. Return to the **EmailForm.html** document in your text editor.

2. Locate the if statement in the validateEmail() function and modify the conditional expression so it uses the test() method to search for an ampersand in the e-mail address. Also, replace the lastIndexOf() method with a test() that determines whether a domain identifier is appended to the domain name with a period. The modified conditional expression should appear as follows:

   ```
   ...
   if (/@/.test(email) == false
        || /\....$/.test(email) == false) {
   ...
   ```

3. Save the **EmailForm.html** document and then open it in your Web browser. Enter e-mail addresses in the sender and recipient e-mail fields that do not include ampersands or a domain identifier appended to the domain name with a period, and then click the **Send** button. You should see the message informing you that one or more of the e-mail addresses are invalid.

4. Close your Web browser window.

Specifying Quantity

Metacharacters that specify the quantity of a match are called **quantifiers**. Table 7-3 lists the quantifiers that you can use with JavaScript regular expressions.

Quantifier	Description
?	Specifies that the preceding character is optional
+	Specifies that one or more of the preceding characters must match
*	Specifies that zero or more of the preceding characters can match
{n}	Specifies that the preceding character repeat exactly n times
{n,}	Specifies that the preceding character repeat at least n times
{n1, n2}	Specifies that the preceding character repeat at least n1 times but no more than n2 times

Table 7-3   JavaScript regular expression quantifiers

The question mark quantifier specifies that the preceding character in the pattern is optional. The following code demonstrates how to use the question mark quantifier to specify that the protocol assigned to the beginning of the `url` variable can be either http or https:

```
var urlProtocol = /^https?/;
var url = "http://www.dongosselin.com";
document.write(urlProtocol.test(url)); // returns true
```

The addition quantifier (+) specifies that one or more of the preceding characters match, while the asterisk quantifier (*) specifies that zero or more of the preceding characters match. As a simple example, the following code demonstrates how to ensure that a variable containing a string of name=value pairs contains at least one equal sign:

```
var stringPattern = /=+/;
var queryString = "sport=football";
document.write(stringPattern.test(queryString)); // returns true
```

Similarly, for a string that consists of multiple name=value pairs separated by ampersands (&), the following code demonstrates how to check whether the `queryString` variable contains zero or more ampersands:

```
var stringPattern = /=+&*/;
var queryString = "sport=football&sport=baseball";
document.write(stringPattern.test(queryString)); // returns true
```

The { } quantifiers allow you to specify more precisely the number of times that a character must repeat. The following code shows a simple example of how to use the { } quantifiers to ensure that a Zip code consists of at least 5 characters:

```
var zipPattern = /.{5}/;
var zip = "01562";
document.write(zipPattern.test(zip)); // returns true
```

NOTE
You can validate a Zip code much more efficiently with character classes, which are covered later in this chapter.

CHAPTER 7

Specifying Subexpressions

As you learned earlier, regular expression patterns can include literal values; any strings you validate against a regular expression must contain exact matches for the literal values contained in the pattern. You can also use parentheses metacharacters ( ) to specify the required characters to include in a pattern match. Characters contained in a set of parentheses within a regular expression are referred to as a **subexpression** or **subpattern**. Subexpressions allow you to determine the format and quantities of the enclosed characters as a group. As an example, consider the following pattern, which defines a regular expression for a telephone number:

```
/^(1-)?(\(.{3}\) )?(.{3})(\-.{4})$/
```

TIP
Notice that the preceding pattern includes the ^ and $ metacharacters to anchor both the beginning and end of the pattern. This ensures that a string exactly matches the pattern in a regular expression.

The first and second groups in the preceding pattern include the ? quantifier. This allows a string to optionally include a 1 and the area code. If the string does include these groups, they must be in the exact format of 1-*nnn* (where *nnn* represents the area code), including the space following the area code. Similarly, the telephone number itself includes two groups that require the number to be in the format of "555-1212". Because the 1 and area code are optional, each of the test() methods in the following code returns a value of true:

```
var phonePattern = /^(1 )?(\(.{3}\) )?(.{3})(\-.{4})$/;
document.write("<p>" + phonePattern.test("555-1234") + "</p>");
// returns true
document.write("<p>" + phonePattern.test("(707) 555-1234") + "</p>");
// returns true
document.write("<p>" + phonePattern.test("1 (707) 555-1234") + "</p>");
// returns true
```

Defining Character Classes

You use **character classes** in regular expressions to treat multiple characters as a single item. You create a character class by enclosing the characters that make up the class with bracket [ ] metacharacters. Any characters included in a character class represent alternate characters that are allowed in a pattern match. As an example of a simple character class, consider the word "analyze", which the British spell as "analyse". Both of the following statements return true because the character class allows either spelling of the word:

```
var wordPattern = /analy[sz]e/;
document.write("<p>" + wordPattern.test("analyse") + "</p>");
// returns true
document.write("<p>" + wordPattern.test("analyze") + "</p>");
// returns true
```

In comparison, the following regular expression returns false because "analyce" is not an accepted spelling of the word:

```
document.write("<p>" + wordPattern.test("analyce") + "</p>");
// returns false
```

You use a hyphen metacharacter (-) to specify a range of values in a character class. You can include alphabetical or numerical ranges. You specify all lowercase letters as "[a-z]" and all uppercase letters as "[A-Z]". The following statements demonstrate how to ensure that only the values A, B, C, D, or F are assigned to the letterGrade variable. The character class in the regular expression specifies a range of A-D or the character 'F' as valid values in the variable. Because the variable is assigned a value of "B", the test() method returns true.

```
var gradeRange = /[A-DF]/;
var letterGrade = "B";
document.write("<p>" + gradeRange.test(letterGrade) + "</p>");
// returns true
```

In comparison, the following test() method returns false because "E" is not a valid value in the character class:

```
var gradeRange = /[A-DF]/;
var letterGrade = "E";
document.write("<p>" + gradeRange.test(letterGrade) + "</p>");
// returns false
```

To specify optional characters to exclude in a pattern match, include the ^ metacharacter immediately before the characters in a character class. The following examples demonstrate how to exclude the letters "E" and G-Z from an acceptable pattern in the letterGrade variable. The first test() method returns a value of true because the letter "A" is not excluded from the pattern match, while the second test() method returns a value of false because the letter "E" is excluded from the pattern match.

```
var gradeRange = /[^EG-Z]/;
var letterGrade = "A";
document.write("<p>" + gradeRange.test(letterGrade)
    + "</p>"); // returns true
letterGrade = "E";
document.write("<p>" + gradeRange.test(letterGrade)
    + "</p>"); // returns false
```

The following statements demonstrate how to include or exclude numeric characters from a pattern match. The first statement returns true because it allows any numeric character, while the second statement returns false because it excludes any numeric character.

```
document.write("<p>" + /[0-9]/.test("5") + "</p>"); // returns true
document.write("<p>" + /[^0-9]/.test("5") + "</p>"); // returns false
```

Note that you can combine ranges in a character class. The first of the following statements demonstrates how to include all alphanumeric characters, and the second demonstrates how to exclude all lowercase and uppercase letters:

```
document.write("<p>" + /[0-9a-zA-Z]/.test("7")
    + "</p>"); // returns true
document.write("<p>" + /[^a-zA-Z]/.test("Q")
    + "</p>"); // returns false
```

The following statement demonstrates how to use character classes to create a phone number regular expression pattern:

```
var phonePattern = /^(1 )?(\([0-9]{3}\) )?([1-9]{3})(\-[1-9]{4})$/;
document.write("<p>" + phonePattern.test("1 (707) 555-1234") + "</p>");
var phonePattern = /^(1 )?(\([0-9]{3}\) )?([1-9]{3})(\-[1-9]{4})$/;
document.write("<p>" + phonePattern.test("1 (707) 555-1234") + "</p>");
```

As a more complex example of a character class, examine the following e-mail validation regular expression you saw earlier in the chapter. At this point, you should recognize how the regular expression pattern is constructed. The anchor at the beginning of the pattern specifies that the first part of the e-mail address must include one or more of the characters A-Z (upper- or lower-case), 0-9, or an underscore (_), or hyphen (-). The second portion of the pattern specifies that the e-mail address can optionally include a dot separator, as in "don.gosselin". The pattern also requires the @ character. Following the literal @ character, the regular expression uses patterns that are similar to the patterns in the name portion of the e-mail address to specify the required structure of the domain name. The last portion of the pattern specifies that the domain identifier must consist of at least two, but not more than three alphabetic characters.

```
var emailPattern = /^[_a-z0-9\-]+(\.[_a-z0-9\-]
    +)*@[a-z0-9\-]+(\.[a-z0-9\-]+)*(\.[a-z]{2,3})$/;
```

JavaScript regular expressions include special escape characters that you can use in character classes to represent different types of data. For example, the "\w" expression can be used instead of the "0-9a-zA-Z" pattern to allow any alphanumeric characters in a character class. Table 7-4 lists the JavaScript character class expressions.

Expression	Description
\w	Alphanumeric characters
\D	Alphabetic characters
\d	Numeric characters
\S	All printable characters
\s	Whitespace characters
\W	Any character that is not an alphanumeric character
\b	Backspace character

Table 7-4   JavaScript character class escape characters

The following statements demonstrate how to include and exclude numeric characters from a pattern match using the \d escape character:

```
document.write("<p>" + /[\d]/.test("5") + "</p>"); // returns true
document.write("<p>" + /[\d]/.test("A") + "</p>"); // returns false
```

TIP
Be sure to include the brackets that make up each escape character within the character class brackets.

As a more complex example, the following statement demonstrates how to compose the e-mail validation regular expression with class expressions:

```
var emailPattern = /^[_\w\-]+(\.[_\w\-]+)*@[\w\-]
    +(\.[\w\-]+)*(\.[\D]{2,3})$/;
```

Next, you modify the `validateEmail()` function so it uses an e-mail regular expression to validate e-mail addresses.

To validate the e-mail addresses in the e-mail form with a regular expression:

1. Return to the **EmailForm.html** document in your text editor.

2. Add the following e-mail regular expression variable above the `if` statement in the `validateEmail()` function:

   ```
   var emailCheck = /^[_\w\-]+(\.[_\w\-]+)*@[\w\-]
       +(\.[\w\-]+)*(\.[\D]{2,3})$/;
   ```

3. Modify the conditional expression in the `if` statement so it validates e-mail addresses with the `test()` method and the `emailCheck` regular expression, as follows:

   ```
   . . .
   if (emailCheck.test(email) == false) {
   . . .
   ```

4. Save the **EmailForm.html** document and then open it in your Web browser. Enter some invalid e-mail addresses in the sender and recipient e-mail fields and click the **Send** button. You should see the message informing you that one or more of the e-mail addresses are invalid.

5. Close your Web browser window.

Matching Multiple Pattern Choices

To allow a string to contain an alternate set of substrings, you separate the strings in a regular expression pattern with the | metacharacter. This is essentially the same as using the Or operator (||) to perform multiple evaluations in a conditional expression. For example, to allow a string to contain either "vegetarian" or "vegan", you include the pattern "vegetarian | vegan".

The following code demonstrates how to check whether a domain identifier at the end of a string contains a required value of either .com, .org, or .net. The first `document.write()` statement returns a value of false because the URL contains a domain identifier of .gov, while the second `document.write()` statement returns a value of true because the domain identifier contains a valid value of .com.

```
emailPattern = /\.(com|org|net)$/;
email = "dongosselin@compuserve.gov";
document.write("<p>" + emailPattern.test("http://www.dongosselin.gov")
    + "</p>"); // returns false
document.write("<p>" + emailPattern.test("http://www.dongosselin.com")
    + "</p>"); // returns true
```

Setting Regular Expression Properties

The RegExp object includes several properties that you can use to configure how JavaScript executes regular expressions. Table 7-5 lists the properties of the RegExp object. Note that several of the properties can be set with flags, which represent specific values that can be assigned to the property.

Property	Flag	Description
global	g	Determines whether to search for all possible matches within a string
ignoreCase	i	Determines whether to ignore letter case when executing a regular expression
lastIndex	--	Stores the index of the first character from the last match
multiline	m	Determines whether to search across multiple lines of text
source	--	Contains the regular expression pattern

Table 7-5   Properties of the RegExp object

The values of the lastIndex and source properties are automatically set by the JavaScript interpreter, although you can set the values of the global, ignoreCase, and multiline properties from within your scripts. You have two options for setting the values of these properties. First, you can assign a value of true or false to the property by creating a regular expression with the RegExp() constructor. For example, the first statement in the following code declares a RegExp object named opecCountry that searches for the pattern "saudi arabia". The second statement then assigns a value of true to the ignoreCase property of the opecCountry variable so the case of the regular expression is ignored when it executes.

```
var opecCountry = new RegExp("saudi arabia");
opecCountry.ignoreCase = true;
```

The second option for setting the values of the global, ignoreCase, and multiline properties is to use the flags that are listed in Table 7-5 when you assign a regular expression to a variable without using the RegExp() constructor. To use one of the property flags, you place it after the closing slash at the end of the regular expression. For example, the first statement in the following code declares the regular expression that searches for the pattern "saudi arabia", and sets the ignoreCase attribute to true by appending the *i* flag after the closing forward slash. The test() method then returns a value of true, even though the letter case of "Saudi Arabia" in the OPEC variable does not match the letter case of "saudi arabia" in the opecCountry regular expression variable.

```
var opecCountry = /saudi arabia/i;
var OPEC = "Algeria, Angola, Indonesia, Iran, Iraq, Kuwait,
```

```
        Libya, Nigeria, Qatar, Saudi Arabia,
        United Arab Emirates, Venezuela";
document.write("<p>" + opecCountry.test(OPEC) + "</p>");
// returns true
```

Recall that you can use regular expressions with several methods of the `String` class, including the `search()` and `replace()` methods. By default, the `replace()` method only replaces the first occurrence of a specified pattern in the target string. To replace all instances of a specified pattern with the `replace()` method, you set the value of the `RegExp` object's `global` property to true, either with the `RegExp()` constructor or by including the *g* flag in the regular expression pattern that is assigned to a variable. The following example demonstrates how to use the *g* flag to replace all instances of colon symbols in the `infoString` variable with equal signs:

```
var infoString = "firstName:Don,lastName:Gosselin,occupation:writer";
infoString = infoString.replace(/:/g, "=");
```

Manipulating Arrays

To manipulate arrays in your scripts, you use the methods and `length` property of the **Array class**. You already know how to use the `new` keyword and the `Array()` constructor to create an array in your programs. When you create an array in your programs using the `Array()` constructor, you are really instantiating an object from the `Array` class. The methods of the `Array` class are discussed throughout this section.

In the following steps, you modify the recipient section of the e-mail form in order to allow users to enter multiple recipients. You will use a selection list that users can use to add and delete recipient information dynamically. Later in this section, you will use methods of the `Array` class to modify the contents of the selection list.

To add a selection list to the recipient section to the e-mail form:

1. Return to the **EmailForm.html** document in your Web browser.

2. Add the following text and elements immediately after the paragraph tag that contains the `recipient_email` element. These elements create three command buttons: Add, Remove, and Update. Each of the buttons contains `onclick` event handlers that call functions, which you will work on for the rest of this chapter.

```
<p><input type="button" value="Add"
onclick="addRecipient()" /> <input type="button"
value="Remove" onclick="deleteRecipient()" /> 
<input type="button" value="Update"
onclick="updateSelectedRecipient()" /></p>
<select name="recipients" size="4" style="width: 265px"
onclick="getRecipientInfo()">
<option value="recipients">Recipients</option>
</select>
```

3. Add the following `addRecipient()` function to the end of the script section. This function executes when a user clicks the Add button. The `if` statement first

determines whether the user entered a recipient name and e-mail address. The `else` clause then uses the `validateEmail()` function to validate the e-mail address. If the e-mail address is valid, the remainder of the statements in the `else` clause remove the default "recipients" entry from the selection list, and then add the recipient's name and e-mail address to the selection list. (You learned how to dynamically add new elements to a selection list in Chapter 5.)

```
function addRecipient() {
    if (document.forms[0].recipient_name.value == ""
            || document.forms[0].recipient_email.value == "")
        window.alert("You must enter the recipient's name
                and e-mail address.");
    else {
            retValue = validateEmail(
            document.forms[0].recipient_email);
            if (retValue == false)
            return retValue;
            if (document.forms[0].recipients.options[0]
                    && document.forms[0].recipients
                    .options[0].value == "recipients")
                document.forms[0].recipients.options[0] = null;
            var nextRecipient = document.forms[0]
                    .recipients .options.length;
            var createRecipient = new Option(document
                    .forms[0].recipient_name.value
                    + ", " + document.forms[0]
                    .recipient_email.value);
            document.forms[0].recipients
                    .options[nextRecipient] = createRecipient;
    }
}
```

4. Add the following `deleteRecipient()` function to the end of the script section. This simple function includes two statements that delete a selected recipient from the selection list.

```
function deleteRecipient() {
    var selectedIndex = document.forms[0]
            .recipients.selectedIndex;
    var recipientInfo= document.forms[0].recipients.options
            [selectedIndex] = null;
}
```

5. It is possible that someone may want to send a message to him or herself, so delete the entire `compareAddresses()` function from the script section.

6. Delete the following statement from the `validateSubmission()` function that called the `compareAddresses()` function:

```
retValue = compareAddresses(document.forms[0].sender_email,
    document.forms[0].recipient_email);
```

7. Delete the following statements from the `validateSubmission()` function that validated the recipient e-mail; this functionality is now being handled by the `addRecipients()` function.

```
retValue = validateEmail(document.forms[0].recipient_email);
if (retValue == false)
    return retValue;
```

8. Save the **EmailForm.html** document and then open it in your Web browser. Test the selection list functionality by adding and deleting some e-mail addresses. Figure 7-5 shows the form in a Web browser.

Figure 7-5

EmailForm.html after adding multiple recipient functionality

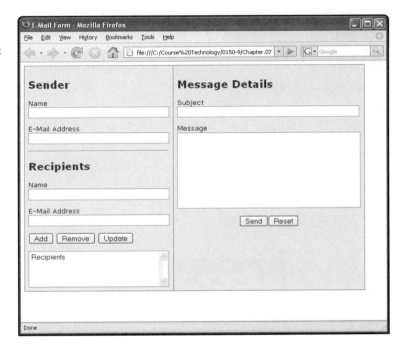

9. Close your Web browser window.

Finding and Extracting Elements and Values

This section discusses methods for finding and extracting elements and values in an array. The primary method for finding a value in an array is to use a looping statement to iterate through the array until you find a particular value. For example, the `for` statement in the following code loops through the `hospitalDepts[]` array to see if it contains "Neurology." If it does, a message prints and the `break` statement ends the `for` loop.

```
var hospitalDepts = new Array("Anesthesia",
    "Molecular Biology", "Neurology", "Pediatrics");
```

```
for (var i=0; i<hospitalDepts.length; ++i) {
        if (hospitalDepts[i] == "Neurology") {
                document.write("<p>The hospital has a
                        Neurology department.</p>");
                break;
        }
}
```

To extract elements and values from an array, you use the `slice()` method to return (copy) a portion of an array and assign it to another array. The syntax for the `slice()` method is `array_name.slice(start, end);`. The `array_name` argument indicates the name of the array from which you want to extract elements. The `start` argument indicates the start position within the array to begin extracting elements. The `end` argument is an integer value that indicates the number of elements to return from the array, starting with the element indicated by the `start` argument.

The following example demonstrates how to use the `slice()` method to return the first five elements in the `topGolfers[]` array. The elements are assigned to a new element named `topFiveGolfers[]`. Figure 7-6 shows the output.

```
var topGolfers = new Array("Tiger Woods", "Vijay Singh",
     "Ernie Els", "Phil Mickelson", "Retief Goosen",
     "Padraig Harrington", "David Toms", "Sergio Garcia",
     "Adam Scott", "Stewart Cink");
var topFiveGolfers = topGolfers.slice(0, 5);
document.write("<p>The top five golfers in the world are:</p><p>");
for (var i=0; i<topFiveGolfers.length; ++i) {
     document.write(topFiveGolfers[i] + "<br />");
}
```

Figure 7-6

Output of an array returned with the `slice()` method

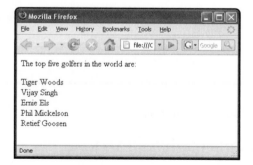

Manipulating Elements

As you use arrays in your scripts, you will undoubtedly need to add and remove elements. For example, suppose you have a shopping cart program that uses an array to store the names of products that a customer plans to purchase. As the customer selects additional products to purchase, or changes her mind about an item, you will need to manipulate the elements in the array of products.

Adding and Removing Elements from the Beginning of an Array

To add or remove elements from the beginning of an array, you need to use the `shift()` and `unshift()` methods. The `shift()` method removes and returns the first element from the beginning of an array, whereas the `unshift()` method adds one or more elements to the beginning of an array. You append the `shift()` method to the name of the array whose first element you want to remove. You append the `unshift()` method to the name of an array and pass to the method a comma-separated list of values for each element you want to add. For example, the following code declares and initializes an array containing the names of the world's top-ranked golfers in 2005. The `shift()` method removes the first golfer, Ernie Els, from the top of the array and the `unshift()` method adds the two highest-ranked players, Tiger Woods and Vijay Singh, to the top of the array. Figure 7-7 shows the output.

```
var topGolfers = new Array(
     "Ernie Els",
     "Phil Mickelson",
     "Retief Goosen",
     "Padraig Harrington",
     "David Toms",
     "Sergio Garcia",
     "Adam Scott",
     "Stewart Cink");
topGolfers.shift();
topGolfers.unshift("Tiger Woods", "Vijay Singh");
for (var i=0; i<topGolfers.length; ++i) {
     document.write(topGolfers[i] + "<br />");
}
```

Figure 7-7

Output of an array modified with the `shift()` and `unshift()` methods

Adding and Removing Elements from the End of an Array

The easiest way to add additional elements to the end of an array is to use array's `length` property to determine the next available index. For example, the first statement in the following code uses the `Array()` constructor to create the initial `hospitalDepts[]` array. The second statement then adds a new value, "Pediatrics," as the fourth element of the array by using the array's `length` property as the element index.

```
var hospitalDepts = new Array(
     "Anesthesia",
     "Molecular Biology",
     "Neurology");
hospitalDepts[hospitalDepts.length] = "Pediatrics";
```

You can also add and remove elements from the end of an array by using the pop() and push() methods. The pop() method removes the last element from the end of an array, whereas the push() method adds one or more elements to the end of an array. You append the pop() method to the name of the array whose last element you want to remove. You append the push() method to the name of an array and pass to the method a comma-separated list of values for each element you want to add. In the following example, the pop() method removes the last department, "Pediatrics," from the end of the array and the push() method adds the two additional departments, "Psychiatry" and "Pulmonary Diseases," to the end of the array.

```
hospitalDepts = array(
     "Anesthesia",
     "Molecular Biology",
     "Neurology",
"Pediatrics");
hospitalDepts.pop();
hospitalDepts.push("Psychiatry", "Pulmonary Diseases");
```

Adding and Removing Elements Within an Array

So far, you have learned to add and remove elements from the beginning and end of an array. To add or remove elements anywhere else in an array, you need to use the splice() method. After adding or removing array elements, the splice() method also renumbers the indexes in the array. The syntax for the splice() method is *array_name*.splice(*start*, *characters_to_delete*, *value1*, *value2*, ...);. The *array_name* argument indicates the name of the array you want to modify. The *start* argument indicates the element within the array at which point elements should be added or removed. The *characters_to_delete* argument is an integer value that indicates the number of elements to remove from the array, starting with the element indicated by the *start* argument. The *value* arguments represent the values you want to add as new elements to an array.

To add an element within an array, include a value of 0 as the second argument to the splice() method. The splice() method in the following code adds a new element with a value of "Ophthalmology" between the "Neurology" and "Pediatrics" elements and renumbers the elements:

```
var hospitalDepts = new Array(
     "Anesthesia",
     "Molecular Biology",
     "Neurology",
     "Pediatrics");
hospitalDepts.splice(3, 0, "Ophthalmology");
```

To add more than one element within an array, pass additional values to the `splice()` method. The following example shows how to add two new elements, "Ophthalmology" and "Otolaryngology", between the "Neurology" and "Pediatrics" elements:

```
var hospitalDepts = new Array(
    "Anesthesia",
    "Molecular Biology",
    "Neurology",
    "Pediatrics");
hospitalDepts.splice(3, 0, "Ophthalmology", "Otolaryngology");
```

You can also delete array elements by omitting the third argument from the `splice()` method. After you delete array elements with the `splice()` method, the remaining indexes are renumbered, just as when you add new elements. For example, to delete the second and third elements in the `hospitalDepts[]` array, you use the following statement:

```
var hospitalDepts = new Array(
    "Anesthesia",
    "Molecular Biology",
    "Neurology",
    "Pediatrics");
hospitalDepts.splice(1, 2);
```

CAUTION

If you do not include the second argument (*characters_to_delete*), the *splice()* method deletes all the elements from the first argument (*start*) to the end of the array.

If the `hospitalDepts[]` array contains four elements with the values "Anesthesia," "Molecular Biology," "Neurology," and "Pediatrics" (in that order), then executing the preceding statement removes the elements containing "Molecular Biology" and "Neurology" from the array.

Methods of the `Array` class are not available to a form's `options[]` array. In order to use the methods of the `Array` class with an `options[]` array, you must first create a new array and copy the elements from the `options[]` array to the new array. Once you are through using the methods of the `Array` class on the new array, you must copy its elements back to the `options[]` array. The procedures you added in the last exercise are sufficient for adding and deleting options to and from a selection list. For practice, in the next section you modify the recipient functions in the e-mail form so they use methods of the `Array` class to add and delete recipients.

To use methods of the `Array` class in the e-mail form:

1. Return to the **EmailForm.html** document in your text editor.

2. Delete the following statements from the `addRecipient()` function:

    var nextRecipient = document.forms[0].recipients
    .options.length;

```
var createRecipient = new Option(document.forms[0]
    .recipient_name.value + ", "
    + document.forms[0].recipient_email.value);
document.forms[0].recipients.options[nextRecipient]
    = createRecipient;
```

3. Add the following statements to the end of the else clause in the addRecipient()
    function. The first statement declares a new array, and the first for loop assigns
    the values of the options[] array to the new array. The push() statement then
    adds the new recipient to the end of the new array. The final for loop then
    recreates the options[] array from the new array.

```
var recipientsArray = new Array();
for (var i=0; i<document.forms[0].recipients.options.length;
    ++i) {
    recipientsArray.push(document.forms[0].recipients
        .options[i].value);
}
recipientsArray.push(document.forms[0].recipient_name.value
    + ", " + document.forms[0].recipient_email.value);
for (var j=0; j<recipientsArray.length; ++j) {
    var createRecipient = new Option(recipientsArray[j]);
    document.forms[0].recipients.options[j] = createRecipient;
}
```

4. Delete the following two statements from the deleteRecipient() function:

```
var selectedIndex = document.forms[0]
    .recipients.selectedIndex;
document.forms[0].recipients.options[selectedIndex] = null;
```

5. Add the following statements to the deleteRecipient() function. The first
    statement declares a new array, and the for loop assigns the values of the
    options[] array to the new array.

```
var recipientsArray = new Array();
for (var i=0; i<document.forms[0].recipients.options.length;
    ++i) {
    recipientsArray.push(document.forms[0].recipients
        .options[i].value);
}
```

6. Add the following statements to the end of the deleteRecipient() function.
    The if statement uses the shift() method to remove the first element if the
    selected index in the options list is 0. The else...if clause uses the pop()
    method to remove the last element if the selected index is equal to the length of
    the options[] array minus one. If the selected index is not equal to 0 or to the
    length of the options array minus one, the else clause uses the splice() method
    to remove the element.

```
if (document.forms[0].recipients.selectedIndex == 0)
    recipientsArray.shift();
else if (document.forms[0].recipients.selectedIndex
    == document.forms[0].recipients.options.length-1)
    recipientsArray.pop();
else
    recipientsArray.splice(document.forms[0]
        .recipients.selectedIndex, 1);
```

7. Add the following statements to the end of the deleteRecipient() function to recreate the options array. Notice that the first statement removes all the options from the options array by assigning a value of 0 to the length property.

```
document.forms[0].recipients.options.length = 0;
for (var j=0; j<recipientsArray.length; ++j) {
    var createRecipient = new Option(recipientsArray[j]);
    document.forms[0].recipients.options[j] = createRecipient;
}
```

8. Save the **EmailForm.html** document and then open it in your Web browser. Test the selection list functionality by adding and deleting some e-mail addresses.

9. Close your Web browser window.

Manipulating Arrays

In the preceding section, you studied techniques for working with the individual elements in an array. In this section, you study techniques for manipulating entire arrays. More specifically, this section discusses how to sort and compare arrays. First, you learn how to sort arrays.

Sorting Arrays

To sort elements of an array alphabetically, you use the sort() method. You append the sort() method to the name of the array you want to sort using the following syntax: *array_name*.sort();. For example, the following code shows how to use the sort() method to sort the elements of an array named scientificFishNames[]. Notice the order in which the values are assigned to the array elements. Figure 7-8 shows the order of the elements after executing the sort() method.

```
<script type="text/javascript">
scientificFishNames = new Array();
scientificFishNames[0] = "Quadratus taiwanae";
scientificFishNames[1] = "Macquaria australasica";
scientificFishNames[2] = "Jordania zonope";
scientificFishNames[3] = "Abudefduf sparoides";
scientificFishNames[4] = "Dactylopterus volitans";
scientificFishNames[5] = "Wattsia mossambica";
scientificFishNames[6] = "Bagrus urostigma";
scientificFishNames.sort();
for(var i=0;i<scientificFishNames.length;++i) {
```

```
        document.write(scientificFishNames[i] + "<br />");
}
</script>
```

Figure 7-8
Output of a sorted array

The reverse() method simply transposes, or reverses, the order of the elements in an array; it does not perform a reverse sort (Z to A instead of A to Z). If you want to perform a reverse sort on an array, then you first need to execute the sort() method to sort the array alphabetically, and then call the reverse() method to transpose the array elements. The following code shows how to perform a reverse sort on the scientificFishNames[] array. Figure 7-9 shows the output of the code in a Web browser.

```
<script type="text/javascript">
scientificFishNames = new Array();
scientificFishNames[0] = "Quadratus taiwanae";
scientificFishNames[1] = "Macquaria australasica";
scientificFishNames[2] = "Jordania zonope";
scientificFishNames[3] = "Abudefduf sparoides";
scientificFishNames[4] = "Dactylopterus volitans";
scientificFishNames[5] = "Wattsia mossambica";
scientificFishNames[6] = "Bagrus urostigma";
scientificFishNames.sort();
scientificFishNames.reverse();
for(var i=0;i<scientificFishNames.length;++i) {
    document.write(scientificFishNames[i] + "<br />");
}
</script>
```

Figure 7-9
Output of a reverse-sorted array

Combining Arrays

If you want to combine arrays, you use the concat() method. The syntax for the concat() method is *array1*.contact(*array2, array3, ...*);. The *array2* array is appended to the *array1* array, the *array3* array is appended to the *array2* array, and so on. For example, consider the following code, which declares and initializes Provinces[] and Territories[] arrays. The Territories[] array is appended to the Provinces[] array with the concat() method and the result is then assigned to a new array named Canada[]. Figure 7-10 shows the output.

```
var Provinces = new Array("Newfoundland and Labrador",
    "Prince Edward Island", "Nova Scotia", "New Brunswick",
    "Quebec", "Ontario", "Manitoba", "Saskatchewan", "Alberta",
    "British Columbia");
var Territories = new Array("Nunavut", "Northwest Territories",
    "Yukon Territory");
var Canada = new Array();
Canada = Provinces.concat(Territories);
for(var i=0;i<Canada.length;++i) {
    document.write(Canada[i] + "<br />");
}
```

Figure 7-10

Output of two arrays combined with the concat() method

Converting Between Strings and Arrays

Depending on the type of data stored in a string, you may often find it easier to manipulate the data by converting it into an array. You use the **split() method** of the String class to split a string into an indexed array. The split() method splits each character in a string into an array element, using the syntax *array = string*.split(*separator[, limit]*);. The *separator* argument specifies the character or characters where the string will be separated into array elements, and the *limit* argument determines the maximum length of the array. If the string does not contain the specified separators, the entire string is assigned to the first element of the array.

To split the individual characters in a string into an array, pass an empty string (" ") as the *separator* argument.

The following code demonstrates how to convert a variable named OPEC into an array named opecArray. A comma and a space separate the country names in the opecNations variable. After the split() method converts the string to an array, a for loop prints the contents of each array element. Figure 7-11 shows the output.

```
var OPEC = "Algeria, Angola, Indonesia, Iran, Iraq, Kuwait, Libya,
     Nigeria, Qatar, Saudi Arabia, United Arab Emirates,
     Venezuela";
var opecArray = OPEC.split(", ");
for (var i=0; i<opecArray.length; ++i) {
     document.write(opecArray[i] + "<br />");
}
```

Figure 7-11

Output of an array that was converted from a string

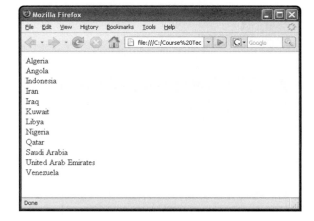

The opposite of the split() method is the Array class's **join() method**, which combines array elements into a string, separated by a comma or specified characters. The syntax for the join() method is *array*.join(["*separator*"]);. The *separator* argument specifies the character or characters that will separate the contents of each array element in the returned string. If you do not include the *separator* argument, the join() method automatically separates elements with a comma. To prevent the elements from being separated by any characters in the new string, pass an empty string ("") as the *separator* argument. The following code demonstrates how to use the join() method to create a string from an array containing the names of the OPEC nations. Because the join() method does not include a *separator* argument, the OPEC nations are automatically separated by commas, as shown in Figure 7-12.

```
var OPEC = new Array("Algeria", "Angola", "Indonesia", "Iran",
     "Iraq", "Kuwait", "Libya", "Nigeria", "Qatar",
     "Saudi Arabia", "United Arab Emirates", "Venezuela");
var opecString = OPEC.join();
document.write("<p>" + opecString + "</p>");
```

Figure 7-12

Output of a string that was converted from an array

In comparison, because the `join()` method in the following example includes a *separator* argument of ";", the OPEC nations are separated by semicolons, as shown in Figure 7-13.

```
var OPEC = new Array("Algeria", "Angola", "Indonesia", "Iran", "Iraq",
    "Kuwait", "Libya", "Nigeria", "Qatar", "Saudi Arabia",
    "United Arab Emirates", "Venezuela");
var opecString = OPEC.join(";");
document.write("<p>" + opecString + "</p>");
```

Figure 7-13

Output of a string that was converted from an array with a custom separator

In addition to the `join()` and `toString()` methods, you can also use the `toString()` and `toLocaleString()` method to convert an array to a string. The `toString()` method automatically separates converted array elements with commas. The `toLocaleString()` method formats the returned string according to the conventions of a particular language or country and also automatically separates each converted array element with that locale's separator character. The syntax for the `toString()` method is *array*.`toString();` and the syntax for the `toLocaleString()` method is *array*.`toLocaleString();`.

Next, you add code to the e-mail form that allows you to update recipient information and to submit the recipient's list as a single string. The code will use `split()` and `join()` methods.

To add code containing `split()` and `join()` methods to the e-mail form:

1. Return to the **EmailForm.html** document in your text editor.

2. Add the following `getRecipientInfo()` function to the end of the script section. When you select a recipient in the selection list, this function copies the name and e-mail address to the recipient form fields. Notice that the last three statements use the `split()` method to copy the name and e-mail address into elements of an array named `infoArray`.

```
function getRecipientInfo() {
    var selectedIndex = document.forms[0]
        .recipients.selectedIndex;
    var recipientInfo = document.forms[0].recipients.options[
        selectedIndex].value;
    var infoArray = recipientInfo.split(", ");
    document.forms[0].recipient_name.value = infoArray[0];
    document.forms[0].recipient_email.value = infoArray[1];
}
```

3. Add the following `updateSelectedRecipient()` function to the end of the script section. This function updates the recipient information in the selection list and is called when the user clicks the Update button.

```
function updateSelectedRecipient() {
    var selectedIndex = document.forms[0]
        .recipients.selectedIndex;
    document.forms[0].recipients.options[selectedIndex].value
        = document.forms[0].recipient_name.value + ", "
        + document.forms[0].recipient_email.value;
    document.forms[0].recipients.options[selectedIndex].text
        = document.forms[0].recipient_name.value + ", "
        + document.forms[0].recipient_email.value;
}
```

4. Add the following statements to the end of the `validateSubmission()` function, but above the `return` statement. The first statement declares a new array and the `for` loop assigns the values of the `options[]` array to the new array. The last statement then uses the `join()` method to convert the array values to a string, which is then assigned to a hidden form field named `recipientsList`.

```
var recipientsArray = new Array();
for (var i=0; i<document.forms[0].recipients.options.length;
    ++i) {
    recipientsArray.push(document.forms[0].recipients
        .options[i].value);
}
document.forms[0].recipientsList.value
    = recipientsArray.join(";");
```

5. Save the **EmailForm.html** document and validate it with the W3C Markup Validation Service. Once the document is valid, close it in your text editor and then open it in your Web browser. Enter values in each of the fields and test the update functionality by adding and modifying some recipient e-mail addresses. Click the **Submit** button and you should see the recipient list assigned to the `recipientsList` field.

6. Close your Web browser window and text editor.

Chapter Summary

▶ When applied to text strings, the term parsing refers to the act of extracting characters or substrings from a larger string.

▶ All literal strings and string variables in JavaScript are represented by the String class, which contains methods for manipulating text strings.

▶ The fromCharCode() method of the String class constructs a text string from Unicode character codes that are passed as arguments.

▶ To change the case of letters in a string, you use the toLowerCase() and toUpperCase() methods of the String class.

▶ The String class contains a single property, the length property, which returns the number of characters in a string.

▶ There are two types of string search methods: methods that return a numeric position in a text string and methods that return a character or substring.

▶ The replace() method of the String class creates a new string with all instances of a specified pattern replaced with the value of the text argument.

▶ The concat() method of the JavaScript String class creates a new string by combining strings that are passed as arguments.

▶ The localeCompare() method of the String class compares strings according to the particular sort order of a language or country.

▶ Regular expressions are patterns that are used for matching and manipulating strings according to specified rules.

▶ The RegExp object contains methods and properties for working with regular expressions in JavaScript.

▶ Regular expression patterns consist of literal characters and metacharacters, which are special characters that define the pattern matching rules in a regular expression.

▶ A pattern that matches the beginning or end of a line is called an anchor.

▶ Metacharacters that specify the quantity of a match are called quantifiers.

▶ Characters contained in a set of parentheses within a regular expression are referred to as a subexpression or subpattern.

▶ You use character classes in regular expressions to treat multiple characters as a single item.

▶ To allow a string to contain an alternate set of substrings, you separate the strings in a regular expression pattern with the | metacharacter.

▶ You use the methods and length property of the Array class to manipulate arrays in your scripts.

▶ To extract elements and values from an array, you use the slice() method of the Array class to return (copy) a portion of an array and assign it to another array.

▶ You use the shift() and unshift() methods of the Array class to add or remove elements from the beginning of an array.

▶ You use the pop() and push() methods of the Array class to add and remove elements from the end of an array.

▶ The `splice()` method of the `Array` class adds or removes elements within an array.

▶ The `sort()` method of the `Array` class alphabetically sorts the elements of an array.

▶ The `reverse()` method of the `Array` class transposes, or reverses, the order of the elements in an array.

▶ The `concat()` method of the `Array` class combines arrays.

▶ The `split()` method of the `String` class splits a string into an indexed array.

▶ The `join()` method of the `Array` class combines array elements into a string, separated by a comma or specified characters.

Review Questions

1. When applied to text strings, the term _____ refers to the act of extracting characters or substrings from a larger string.

    a. stripping
    b. compiling
    c. rendering
    d. parsing

2. The `toUpperCase()` and `toLowerCase()` methods do not convert the contents of the string to which they are appended. True or false?

3. Which of the following properties returns the number of characters in a string?

    a. `size`
    b. `length`
    c. `chars`
    d. `width`

4. Which of the following functions return a value of -1 if the character or string is not found? (Choose all that apply.)

    a. `indexOf()`
    b. `lastIndexOf()`
    c. `search()`
    d. `substring()`

5. What is the difference between the `search()` and `indexOf()` methods?

6. Explain why you would specify negative argument values for the `splice()` method.

7. Which of the following is the correct syntax for using the `replace()` method to replace commas with semicolons in a variable named `userQuery`?

    a. `userQuery.replace(",", ";")`
    b. `replace.userQuery(",", ";")`

```
c.  userQuery = replace(",", ";")
d.  userQuery(",").replace(";")
```

8. Which of the following can you use to combine text strings? (Choose all that apply.)

    a. `concat()` method

    b. `join()` method

    c. concatenation operator (`+`)

    d. compound assignment operator (`+=`)

9. Because lowercase letters have higher values than uppercase letters, lowercase letters are evaluated as being "greater" than uppercase letters. True or false?

10. Which of the following provide correct syntax for creating a regular expression variable named `ftpProtocol` that contains the text ftp://? (Choose all that apply.)

```
a.  var ftpProtocol = new RegExp("ftp://");
b.  var ftpProtocol = new RegExp(ftp://);
c.  var ftpProtocol = "ftp://";
d.  var ftpProtocol = /ftp:\/\//;
```

11. Which of the following regular expression metacharacters matches characters at the beginning of a string?

    a. `^`

    b. `$`

    c. `()`

    d. `[]`

12. Which of the following regular expression quantifiers specifies that zero or more of the preceding characters can match?

    a. `?`

    b. `+`

    c. `*`

    d. `{n}`

13. Explain why you would use subexpressions.

14. Which of the following correctly specify that case should be ignored when executing the regular expression that is assigned to the `newsStation` variable? (Choose all that apply.)

```
a.  var newsStation = new RegExp("CNN");
    newsStation.ignoreCase = true;
b.  var newsStation = new RegExp("CNN", ignoreCase);
c.  var newsStation = /CNN/i;
d.  var newsStation = /CNN/ & i;
```

15. Which of the following functions removes the first element from the beginning of an array?

    a. `shift()`

    b. `unshift()`

    c. `push()`

    d. `pop()`

16. Explain how to use the `splice()` function to add and remove elements to and from an array.

17. Explain how to use the `slice()` function to return a portion of an array and assign it to another array.

18. Explain how to perform a reverse sort of an array's elements.

19. Which of the following is the correct syntax for splitting a string variable that contains stock prices separated by semicolons into an array named `stockPriceArray[]`?

    a. `stockPrices.split(";") = new Array(stockPricesArray);`

    b. `split(stockPrices, stockArray, ";");`

    c. `var stockPriceArray.split(";",stockPrices);`

    d. `var stockPriceArray = stockPrices.split(";");`

20. By default, the `join()` method combines array elements into a string separated by forward slashes. True or false?

Hands-On Projects

Project 7-1

In this project, you create a document that uses `String` class methods and the `length` property.

1. Create a new document in your text editor.

2. Type the `<!DOCTYPE>` declaration, `<html>` element, document head, and document body. Use the strict DTD and "String Class Examples" as the content of the `<title>` element.

3. Add the following script section to the document head:

```
<script type="text/javascript">
/* <![CDATA[ */
/* ]]> */
</script>
```

4. Add the following statements containing examples of string operators to the script section. Use your own name and place of birth where indicated.

```
var name;
firstName = "your first name";
lastName = "your last name";
var placeOfBirth;
name = firstName + " ";
name += lastName;
placeOfBirth = "city where you were born";
placeOfBirth += ", state where you were born";
```

5. Add the following statements (which use `String` class methods and the `length` property) to the end of the script section:

```
nameArray = name.split(" ");
document.write("<p>My first name is: " + nameArray[0]
    + "<br />");
document.write("My last name is: " + nameArray[1]
    + "<br />");
document.write("There are " + firstName.length
    + " characters in my first name" + "<br />");
document.write("I was born in " + placeOfBirth + "<br />");
document.write("My initials are: " + firstName.charAt(0) +
    lastName.charAt(0) + "</p>");
```

6. Save the document as **StringExamples.html** in your Projects folder for Chapter 7, and then validate the document with the W3C Markup Validation Service. Once the document is valid, close it in your text editor and then open it in your Web browser to see how it renders.

7. Close your Web browser window.

Project 7-2

You have probably seen Web pages with text that appears to scroll across the status bar or within a text box. Text scrollers are created using the `String` object. Although you may find them useful on your Web pages, use them sparingly, because some visitors find them annoying. In this project you will create scrolling text in the status bar.

1. Create a new document in your text editor.

2. Type the `<!DOCTYPE>` declaration, `<html>` element, header information, and the `<body>` element. Use the strict DTD and "Scrolling Text" as the content of the `<title>` element.

3. Add the following script section to the document head:

```
<script type="text/javascript">
/* <![CDATA[ */
/* ]]> */
</script>
```

4. Add the following statements to the script section. The first statement assigns a value to the status property of the `Window` object. The `scrollStatusBar()` function

then uses the substring() method of the String object to modify the order of the characters in the text string.

```
window.status = "Elvis has left the building ... ";
function scrollStatusBar() {
    var message = window.status;
    window.status = message.substring(1)
        + message.substring(0, 1);
}
```

5. Finally, add an onload event handler to the opening <body> tag that uses a setInterval() method to continuously call the scrollStatusBar() function every second:

```
<body onload="setInterval('scrollStatusBar()', 100)">
```

6. Save the document as **ScrollingText.html** in your Projects folder for Chapter 7, and validate it with the W3C Markup Validation Service. Once the ScrollingText.html document is valid, open it in your Web browser. The text should scroll across the status bar.

7. Close your Web browser window.

 ## Project 7-3

In this project, you create a To Do list using arrays. This project is not practical for use on a live Web page because it does not store the information you enter into a database; the data you enter will disappear after you refresh or leave the Web page. However, creating the To Do list is useful for learning how to work with arrays in JavaScript.

1. Create a new document in your text editor.

2. Type the <!DOCTYPE> declaration, <html> element, header information, and the <body> element. Use the strict DTD and "To Do List" as the content of the <title> element.

3. Add the following script section to the document head:

```
<script type="text/javascript">
/* <![CDATA[ */
/* ]]> */
</script>
```

4. Add the following heading level element and form to the document body. The Add Task and Delete Selected Task buttons include onclick event handlers that call functions, which you will add in the next step.

```
<h1>To Do List</h1>
<form action="">
<p>New Task <input type="text" size="68" name="newtask" />
</p><p><input type="button" value="Add Task" onclick="addTask()"
```

```
style="width: 150px" />
<input type="button" value="Delete Selected Task"
onclick="deleteTask()" style="width: 150px" /><br />
<input type="button" value="Ascending Sort"
 onclick="ascendingSort()" style="width: 150px" /></p>
<p><select name="tasks" size="10" style="width: 500px">
<option value="tasks">Tasks</option></select></p>
</form>
```

5. Add to the script section the following addTask() function, which adds a new task to the selection list. The if statement first checks to ensure that the user has entered a value into the New Task field. If the field does not contain a value, then a window.alert() dialog box appears and informs the user that they must enter a value in the field. If the field does contain a value, then an else statement executes. The else statement first checks to see if the default option of "Tasks" is present as the first element in the options[] array. If so, it is deleted. Then, the addTask() function uses the Option object to add a new task.

```
function addTask() {
    if (document.forms[0].newtask.value == "")
        window.alert("You must enter a value in the
            New Task field.");
    else {
        if (document.forms[0].tasks.options[0].value
            == "tasks")
            document.forms[0].tasks.options[0] = null;
        var newTask = new Option();
        newTask.value = document.forms[0].newtask.value;
        newTask.text = document.forms[0].newtask.value;
        var numTasks = document.forms[0].tasks
            .options.length;
        document.forms[0].tasks.options[numTasks]
            = newTask;
        document.forms[0].newtask.value = "";
    }
}
```

6. Add the following deleteTask() function, which deletes a task from the selection list. The function uses a while statement to loop through each option in the selection list to determine which option is selected. Once the selected option is located, it is deleted from the options[] array.

```
function deleteTask() {
    var selectedTask = 0;
    var taskSelected = false;
    while (selectedTask < document.forms[0].tasks.length) {
```

```
        if (document.forms[0].tasks
            .options[selectedTask].selected == true) {
            taskSelected = true;
            break;
         }
        ++selectedTask;
    }
    if (taskSelected == true)
        document.forms[0].tasks.options[selectedTask]
            = null;
    else
        window.alert(
            "You must select a task in the list.");
}
```

7. To the end of the script section, add the following function, which sorts the tasks in the task list in ascending order. One problem with a form's options[] array is that you cannot use any of the array methods that are available to other types of arrays. Therefore, the following function creates a new array named newTasks[] and copies to it the values from each of the elements in the options[] array. The sort() method is then executed on the new array. Finally, the values from each of the elements in the newTasks[] array are copied back into the options[] array.

```
function ascendingSort() {
    var newTasks = new Array();
    for (var i =0; i < document.forms[0].tasks.length;
        ++i) {
        newTasks[i] = document.forms[0].tasks
            .options[i].value;
    }
    newTasks.sort();
    for (var j =0; j < document.forms[0].tasks.length;
        ++j) {
        document.forms[0].tasks.options[j].value
            = newTasks[j];
        document.forms[0].tasks.options[j].text
            = newTasks[j];
    }
}
```

8. Save the document as **ToDoList.html** in your Projects folder for Chapter 7, and validate it with the W3C Markup Validation Service. Once the ToDoList.html document is valid, open it in your Web browser and test the functionality.

9. Close your Web browser window.

Project 7-4

In this project, you add code to the To Do Web page that performs a reverse sort of the To Do list items.

1. Return to the **ToDoList.html** document in your text editor.

2. Add the following function to the end of the script section to perform a reverse sort on the To Do list:

```
function descendingSort() {
    var newTasks = new Array();
    for (var i =0; i < document.forms[0].tasks.length;
        ++i) {
        newTasks[i] = document.forms[0].tasks
            .options[i].value;
    }
    newTasks.sort();
    newTasks.reverse();
    for (var j =0; j < document.forms[0].tasks.length;
        ++j) {
        document.forms[0].tasks.options[j].value
            = newTasks[j];
        document.forms[0].tasks.options[j].text
            = newTasks[j];
    }
}
```

3. Modify the form so it includes a Descending Sort button, which calls the descendingSort() function, as follows:

```
...
<input type="button" value="Ascending Sort"
onclick="ascendingSort()" style="width: 150px" />
<input type="button" value="Descending Sort"
onclick="descendingSort()" style="width: 150px" />
</p>
<p><select name="tasks" size="10" style="width: 500px">
...
```

4. Save the **ToDoList.html** document and then validate the document with the W3C Markup Validation Service. Once the document is valid, close it in your text editor and then open it in your Web browser and test the code.

5. Close your Web browser window.

Case Projects

Save the documents you create for the following projects in the Cases directory for Chapter 7.

Case Project 7-1

Create a script that presents a word guessing game. Allow users to guess the word one letter at a time by entering a character in a form. Start by assigning a secret word to a variable. After each guess, print the word using asterisks for each remaining letter, but fill in the letters that the user guessed correctly. Store the user's guess in a form field. For example, if the word you want users to guess is "suspicious" and the user has successfully guessed the letters "s" and "i," then store s*s*i*i**s in the form field. You need to use multiple arrays along with the split() and join() methods to create the game's functionality. Clear the guessed character from the form each time it is submitted, and add functionality that displays an alert dialog box if the user fails to enter a character. Save the document as **GuessingGame.html**.

Case Project 7-2

A palindrome is a word or phrase that is identical forward or backward, such as the word "racecar." A standard palindrome is similar to a perfect palindrome except that spaces and punctuation are ignored. For example, "Madam, I'm Adam" is a standard palindrome because the characters are identical forward or backward, provided you remove the spaces and punctuation marks. Write a script that checks whether a word or phrase entered by a user is a palindrome. Use a form where the user can enter the word or phrase, and include one button that checks if the word or phrase is a perfect palindrome and another button that checks if the word or phrase is a standard palindrome. Both buttons should display an alert dialog box that states whether the word or phrase is a perfect or standard palindrome. For both types of palindromes, you need to use the reverse() method of the Array class. For the standard palindrome, use a regular expression to determine whether each character is an alphanumeric character; if not, then you need to remove the non-alphanumeric character (or space) before you can determine if the word or phrase is a standard palindrome. Save the document as **Palindromes.html**.

Case Project 7-3

Although the `String` object includes the `toUpperCase()` and `toLowerCase()` methods for converting strings to upper- or lowercase letters, it does not include a method for converting text to title case capitalization (Text That Appears Like This). Create a script that takes text that a user enters into a form field and converts it to title case capitalization. To accomplish this, use the `split()` method to split the words in the string into an indexed array. Then, create a `for` loop that uses another `split()` method that splits each word in the elements of the indexed array into another indexed array of characters. Within the `for` loop, use the `toUpperCase()` method to convert the first element in the second array (which represents the first character in the word to uppercase) to uppercase, and then use the `join()` method to rebuild the array of words in the text string. Execute a final `join()` method to convert the array of words back into a single text string. Call the JavaScript code that converts the text to title case by clicking a command button. Save the script as **TitleCase.html**.

Case Project 7-4

Create a Web page that contains a text box in which users can enter a date. Also include a button that executes the `test()` method to validate the date against a regular expression. Write a regular expression pattern that allows users to enter a one or two digit month, one or two digit date, and two or four digit year. Also, allow users to separate the month, day, and year by using either dashes or forward slashes. Users should be able to enter any of the following date formats: 1-25-07, 1-25-2007, or 01/25/2007. Save the script as **DateValidation.html**.

8

Debugging and Error Handling

In this chapter you will:

- Study debugging concepts
- Learn how to trace error messages
- Learn how to use comments to locate bugs
- Trace errors with debugging tools
- Study exception and error handling
- Study additional debugging techniques

The more JavaScript programs you write, the more likely you are to write programs that generate error messages. At times it may seem like your programs never function quite the way you want. Regardless of experience, knowledge, and ability, all programmers incorporate errors in their programs at one time or another. Thus, all programmers must devote part of their programming education to mastering the art of debugging. As you learned at the start of this book, debugging is the process of tracing and resolving errors in a program. Debugging is an essential skill for any programmer, regardless of the programming language.

In this chapter, you will learn techniques and tools that you can use to trace and resolve errors in JavaScript programs. You will not create any new programs. Instead, you will learn how to use JavaScript debugging techniques to locate errors in an existing program named Moving Estimator. The Moving Estimator program is designed to be used by a shipping company to calculate the costs of moving a household from one location to another, based on distance, weight, and several other factors. The program is fairly simple and uses functions to calculate the various types of moving costs, along with a function named `calcTotalEstimate()` that totals the estimate. Before you proceed with this chapter, try out the completed version of the program named MovingEstimatorNoBugs.html in the Chapter folder for Chapter 8. It includes six text boxes. Each time a user enters a value into one of the text boxes, an `onchange` event handler calls a function that calculates the item's cost. Each function then calls a function named `calcTotalEstimate()`, which calculates the total cost and places it in the Moving Estimate text box. Figure 8-1 shows an example of the program running in a Web browser after some moving costs have been entered.

Figure 8-1

Moving Estimator program

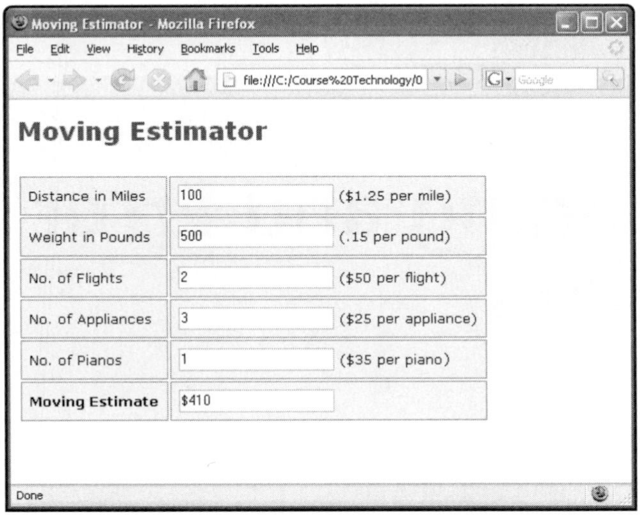

Note that you will not be working with the MovingEstimatorNoBugs.html document in this chapter. Rather, you will work with a version of the document that contains bugs, MovingEstimatorWithBugs.html. You need to use the "buggy" version in order to learn the debugging techniques presented in this chapter. If you get stuck, however, you can use the no-bugs version as a reference.

Understanding Debugging

Three types of errors can occur in a program: syntax errors, run-time errors, and logic errors. **Syntax errors** occur when the interpreter fails to recognize code. In JavaScript, statements that are not recognized by a browser's scripting engine generate syntax errors. (Recall from Chapter 1 that a scripting engine is just one kind of interpreter, with the term "interpreter" referring generally to any program that executes scripting language code.) Syntax errors can be caused by incorrect usage of JavaScript code or references to objects, methods, and variables that do not exist. For example, if a programmer attempts to use a method that does not exist or omits a method's closing parenthesis, the scripting engine generates a syntax error. Many syntax errors are generated by incorrectly spelled or mistyped words. For example, the statement `writln("Hello World");` causes a syntax error because the `writeln()` method is misspelled as *writln()*. Similarly, the statement `Document.writeln("Hello World");` causes a syntax error because the `Document` object is incorrectly typed with an uppercase *D*. (Remember that most JavaScript objects, such as the `Document` object, should be all lowercase letters.)

NOTE

Syntax errors in compiled languages, such as C++, are also called compile-time errors, because they are usually discovered when a program is compiled. Because JavaScript is an interpreted language, syntax errors are not discovered until a program executes.

The second type of error, a **run-time error**, occurs when the JavaScript interpreter encounters a problem while a program is executing. Run-time errors differ from syntax errors in that they do not necessarily represent JavaScript language errors. Instead, run-time errors occur when the interpreter encounters code that it cannot execute. For example, consider the statement `customFunction();`, which calls a custom JavaScript function named `customFunction()`. This statement does not generate a syntax error, because it is legal (and usually necessary) to create and then call custom functions in a JavaScript program. However, if your program includes the call statement but does not include code that creates the function in the first place, your program generates a run-time error. The error occurs when the interpreter attempts to call the function and is unable to find it.

The following shows another example of a run-time error. In this example, a `writeln()` method attempts to print the contents of a variable named `messageVar`. Because the `messageVar` variable is not declared (you can assume it has not been declared in another script section elsewhere in the document), a run-time error occurs.

```
document.writeln(messageVar);
```

Another point to remember is that a run-time error can be caused by a syntax error, because a syntax error does not occur until the interpreter attempts to execute the code. For example, you may have a function that contains a statement with a syntax error. However, the syntax error will not be caught until the function executes at run time. When the function does execute, it generates a run-time error because of the syntax error within the function.

The third type of error, a **logic error**, is a flaw in a program's design that prevents the program from running as anticipated. In this context, the term "logic" refers to the execution of program statements and procedures in the correct order to produce the desired results. You're already accustomed to performing ordinary, nonprogramming tasks according to a certain logic. For example, when you do the laundry, you normally wash, dry, iron, then fold your clothes. If you decided to iron, fold, dry, and then wash the clothes, you would end up with a pile of wet laundry rather than the clean and pressed garments you desired. The problem, in that case, would be a type of logic error—you performed the steps in the wrong order.

One example of a logic error in a computer program is multiplying two values when you mean to divide them, as in the following code:

```
var divisionResult = 10 * 2;
document.write("Ten divided by two is equal to "
     + divisionResult);
```

Another example of a logic error is the creation of an infinite loop, in which a loop statement never ends because its conditional expression is never updated or is never false. The following code creates a `for` statement that results in the logic error of an infinite loop. The cause of the infinite loop is that the third argument in the `for` statement's parentheses never changes the value of the count variable.

```
for (var count = 10; count >= 0; count) {
     window.alert("We have liftoff in " + count);
}
```

Because the `count` variable is never updated in the preceding example, it continues to have a value of 10 through each iteration of the loop, resulting in the repeated display of an alert dialog box containing the text "We have liftoff in 10". To correct this logic error, you add a decrement operator to the third argument in the `for` statement's constructor, as follows:

```
for (var count = 10; count >= 0; --count) {
    window.alert("We have liftoff in " + count);
}
```

Error Messages

The first line of defense in locating bugs in JavaScript programs are the error messages you receive when the JavaScript interpreter encounters a syntax or run-time error. Two important pieces of information displayed in error message dialog boxes are the line number in the document where the error occurred and a description of the error. Note that the line number in an error message is counted from the start of the document, not just from the start of a script section. All error messages generated by a Web browser are run-time errors. However, keep in mind that run-time errors can be caused by syntax errors. Logic errors do not generate error messages because they do not prevent the script from running (as syntax errors do) or from executing properly (as run-time errors do). Instead, they prevent the program from running the way you anticipated. Computers are not smart enough (yet) to identify a flaw in a program's logic. For example, if you create an infinite loop with a `for` statement, the interpreter has no way of telling whether you really wanted to continually execute the `for` statement's code. Later in this chapter, you will learn how to trace the flow of your program's execution in order to locate logic errors.

Consider the following function, which causes a syntax error because it is missing the closing brace (}). Figure 8-2 shows the error message in Firefox Error Console. Figure 8-3 shows the error message in Internet Explorer.

```
function missingClosingBrace() {
    var message = "This function is missing a closing brace.";
    window.alert(message);
```

Figure 8-2
Firefox error message

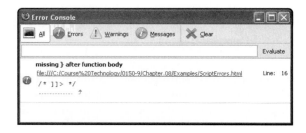

To view errors in Firefox Web browsers, you need to select Error Console from the Tools menu in Firefox 2.0 or later, or JavaScript Console in Firefox versions earlier than 2.0. If you are using a version of Internet Explorer higher than 4.0, you need to turn on error notification. To verify that error notification is turned on in Internet Explorer, click Tools on the menu bar, click Internet Options, click the Advanced tab, in the Browsing category click the Display a notification about every script error check box to select it (if necessary), and then click OK. Other Web browsers may also require you to turn on error notification.

Figure 8-3

Internet Explorer error message

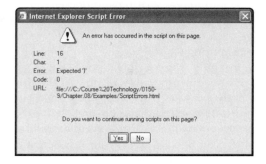

Regardless of which browser you use, you can rely on error messages only to find the general location of an error in a program and not as the exact indicator of an error. You cannot always assume that the line specified by an error message is the actual problem in your program. For example, the var result = amount * percentage; statement in the following code causes a run-time error because the interpreter cannot locate the amount and percentage variables included in the statement. The amount and percentage variables are declared within the variableDeclarations() function, making them local variables which are only available inside the function. Because the amount and percentage variables are not global variables, they are not visible to the calculatePercentage() function, which causes a run-time error. The var result = amount * percentage; statement generates the run-time error because it attempts to access variables that are local to another function. However, the real problem is that the percentage and amount variables are not declared at a global level.

```
function variableDeclarations() {
     var percentage = .25;
     var amount = 1600;
}
function calculatePercentage() {
     var result = amount * percentage;
     document.write("<p>Twenty-five percent of " + amount + " is ");
     document.write(result + "</p>");
}
```

When debugging JavaScript, it is important that you understand how a browser interprets a Web page and JavaScript code. A common complaint among professional programmers is that Web browsers do not strictly enforce JavaScript syntax. For example, browsers can interpret JavaScript statements that do not end in a semicolon. In contrast, in high-level languages such as C++ and Java, you *must* end a statement with a semicolon or you receive an error.

You can compare the way Web browsers render XHTML and interpret JavaScript to the way human beings comprehend language. Someone can speak to you using bad grammar or with a strong regional or foreign accent. Yet, provided the other person is speaking to you in the same root language, you can usually understand what he or she is saying. The same applies to a Web browser and JavaScript: even if you write sloppy JavaScript code, the Web browser can often (but not always) figure out what the code is supposed to do. This means that a Web browser can run JavaScript code and render XHTML, even though your program contains bugs.

This lack of common bug enforcement makes writing and debugging programs more difficult. What can you do to mitigate bugs in your JavaScript programs? First, always use good syntax, such as ending statements with semicolons and declaring variables with `var` keywords. The more disciplined you are in your programming technique, the fewer bugs you will find in your programs. Second, be sure to thoroughly test your JavaScript programs with every browser type and version on which you anticipate your program will run. At the time of this writing, Internet Explorer has the majority share of the browser market (approximately 62%), although at one time Internet Explorer controlled almost 95% of the market. Given Microsoft's dominance over the past decade, some JavaScript programmers ignore Firefox and other browsers altogether. Because browser loyalties continually shift, you need to write your JavaScript code so it is compatible with as many Web browsers as possible. One rule of thumb is that if a browser is used by more than one percent of the market, then you need to write and debug your JavaScript programs for that browser.

TIP

You can find a great deal of information on the popularity of the various browsers by searching for "browser statistics" in a search engine.

Next, you will use error messages to help locate bugs in the Moving Estimator program. The error messages shown in this exercise are generated with Firefox 2.0 and Internet Explorer 7. If you use a different Web browser, the error messages you see will differ.

To use error messages to help locate bugs in the Moving Estimator program:

1. Open in your Web browser the **MovingEstimatorWithBugs.html** document located in your Chapter folder for Chapter 8. If you are using Firefox, select **Error Console** from the **Tools** menu to display the Error Console, as shown in Figure 8-4. If you are using Internet Explorer, you will receive a dialog box with either an OK button or Yes and No buttons, depending on your configuration. The dialog box with Yes and No buttons will ask you if you want to continue running scripts on the Web page or if you want to debug the script (again, depending on your configuration). Figure 8-5 shows an example of the dialog box that asks if you want to continue running scripts. Click the **No** or **OK** button to close the dialog box.

Figure 8-4

First run-time error message in Firefox Error Console

Figure 8-5

First run-time error message in Internet Explorer

2. Leave the MovingEstimatorWithBugs.html document open in your Web browser, but also open the document in your text editor. As shown in Figures 8-4 and 8-5, the error is located on line 14. Locate line 14 and notice that the statement that declares the `appliancesCost` variable is missing the letter *v* in the `var` keyword.

3. Add the missing *v* so the statement reads as follows:

```
var appliancesCost = 0;
```

4. Save the **MovingEstimatorWithBugs.html** document in your text editor, then return to your Web browser and reload the Web page. If you are using Firefox, the Error Console should display the error message shown in Figure 8-6. If you are using Internet Explorer, the dialog box shown in Figure 8-7 should display; click the **No** or **OK** button to close the dialog box.

Figure 8-6

Second run-time error message in Firefox Error Console

Figure 8-7

Second run-time error message in Internet Explorer

5. Return to the **MovingEstimatorWithBugs.html** document in your text editor and locate line 21, which contains this statement: `laborCost = pounds * .15;`. In this instance, the Web browser expected to find an opening ({) character before

the `laborCost = pounds * .15;` statement in the `calcLaborCosts()` function. Add the missing ({) character so the function looks like the following:

```
function calcLaborCost(pounds) {
    laborCost = pounds * .15;
    calcTotalEstimate();
}
```

6. Save the **MovingEstimatorWithBugs.html** document in your text editor, then return to your Web browser and reload the Web page. Another run-time error displays, this time on line 26. If you are using Internet Explorer, click the **No** or **OK** button to close the dialog box.

7. Return to the **MovingEstimatorWithBugs.html** document in your text editor and locate line 26. The problem is that the statement is missing an assignment operator. Add an assignment operator to the statement so it appears as follows:

```
flightsCost = flights * 50;
```

8. Save the **MovingEstimatorWithBugs.html** document in your text editor, then return to your Web browser and reload the Web page. Another run-time error occurs, this time on line 35. If you are using Internet Explorer, click the **No** or **OK** button to close the dialog box.

9. Return to the **MovingEstimatorWithBugs.html** document in your text editor and locate line 35, which is a statement in the `calcPianosCost()` function that calls the `calcTotalEstimate()` function. Notice that the function is missing its closing parenthesis. Add the missing parenthesis so the statement appears as follows:

```
calcTotalEstimate();
```

10. Save the **MovingEstimatorWithBugs.html** document in your text editor, then return to your Web browser and reload the Web page a final time. You should receive no more error messages. However, do not try and use the program yet because it still contains plenty of bugs. Leave the document open in your Web browser.

Tracing Errors with the `window.alert()` Method

If you are unable to locate a bug in your program by using error messages, or if you suspect a logic error (which does not generate error messages), then you must trace your code. Tracing is the examination of individual statements in an executing program. The `window.alert()` method provides one of the most useful ways to trace JavaScript code. You place a `window.alert()` method at different points in your program and use it to display the contents of a variable, an array, or the value returned from a function. Using this technique, you can monitor values as they change during program execution.

For example, examine the following function, which calculates weekly net pay, rounded to the nearest integer. The program is syntactically correct and does not generate an error message.

However, the function is not returning the correct result, which should be 485. Instead, the function is returning a value of 5169107.

```
function calculatePay() {
    var payRate = 15; numHours = 40;
    var grossPay = payRate * numHours;
    var federalTaxes = grossPay * .06794;
    var stateTaxes = grossPay * .0476;
    var socialSecurity = grossPay * .062;
    var medicare = grossPay * .0145;
    var netPay = grossPay - federalTaxes;
    netPay *= stateTaxes;
    netPay *= socialSecurity;
    netPay *= medicare;
    return Math.round(netPay);
}
```

To trace the problem, you can place a window.alert() method at the point in the program where you think the error may be located. For example, the first thing you may want to check in the calculatePay() function is whether the grossPay variable is being calculated correctly. To check whether the program calculates grossPay correctly, place a window.alert() method in the function following the calculation of the grossPay variable as follows:

```
function calculatePay() {
    var payRate = 15; numHours = 40;
    var grossPay = payRate * numHours;
window.alert(grossPay);
    var federalTaxes = grossPay * .06794;
    var stateTaxes = grossPay * .0476;
    var socialSecurity = grossPay * .062;
    var medicare = grossPay * .0145;
    var netPay = grossPay - federalTaxes;
    netPay *= stateTaxes;
    netPay *= socialSecurity;
    netPay *= medicare;
    return Math.round(netPay);
}
```

NOTE

It is helpful to place any window.alert() methods you use to trace program execution at a different level of indentation to distinguish them clearly from the actual program.

Because the grossPay variable contained the correct value (600), you would move the window.alert() method to check the value of the netPay variable. You then continue with this technique until you discover the error. If you did, you would discover that the calculatePay()

function does not perform properly because the lines that add the stateTaxes, socialSecurity, and medicare variables to the netPay variable are incorrect; they use the multiplication assignment operator (*=) instead of the subtraction assignment operator (-=).

TIP

Instead of using the window.alert() method, you can write information to the status bar, using the status property of the Window object.

An alternative to using a single window.alert() method is to place multiple window.alert() methods throughout your code to check values as the code executes. For example, you could trace the calculatePay() function by using multiple window.alert() methods, as follows:

```
function calculatePay() {
     var payRate = 15; numHours = 40;
     var grossPay = payRate * numHours;
window.alert(grossPay);
     var federalTaxes = grossPay * .06794;
     var stateTaxes = grossPay * .0476;
     var socialSecurity = grossPay * .062;
     var medicare = grossPay * .0145;
     var netPay = grossPay - federalTaxes;
window.alert(netPay);
     netPay *= stateTaxes;
window.alert(netPay);
     netPay *= socialSecurity;
window.alert(netPay);
     netPay *= medicare;
window.alert(netPay);
     return Math.round(netPay);
}
```

One drawback to using multiple window.alert() methods to trace values is that you must close each dialog box for your code to continue executing. However, using multiple window.alert() methods is sometimes more efficient than moving a single window.alert() method. The key to using multiple window.alert() methods to trace program values is using them selectively at key points throughout a program. For example, suppose you were debugging a large accounting program with multiple functions. You could place a window.alert() method at key positions within the program, such as wherever a function returns a value or a variable is assigned new data. In this way, you could get the general sense of what portion of the program contains the bug. Once you discover the approximate location of the bug, for instance in a particular function, you can then concentrate your debugging efforts on that one function.

Next, you will use alert dialog boxes to locate a bug in the Moving Estimator program.

To use alert dialog boxes to locate a bug in the Moving Estimator program:

1. Return to the **MovingEstimatorWithBugs.html** document in your Web browser.

2. Click the **No. of Appliances** text box, type **3**, and press the **Tab** key. Each of the text boxes in the form uses an onchange event handler to call a function, which updates the value of the associated item. Each item's function then calls the calcTotalEstimate() function, which should update the Moving Estimate text box. The onchange event handler for the No. of Appliances text box calls the calcAppliancesCost() function. The value in the Moving Estimate text box should have changed to $75. Instead, it changes to $0.

CAUTION
Do not enter values into any of the other text boxes—the program still contains many bugs.

3. To trace the problem, return to the **MovingEstimatorWithBugs.html** document in your text editor and locate the calcAppliancesCost() function. Add two window.alert() functions to the calcAppliancesCost() function, as follows. The first window.alert() function checks to see if the value from the text box that is passed to the function's appliances parameter is correct. The second window.alert() function checks to see if the calculation that totals the cost of moving the appliances assigns the correct value to the appliancesCost variable.

```
function calcAppliancesCost(appliances) {
window.alert(appliances);
      appliancesCost - appliances * 25;
window.alert(appliancesCost);
      calcTotalEstimate();
}
```

4. Save the **MovingEstimatorWithBugs.html** document in your text editor, then return to your Web browser and reload the Web page.

5. Click the **No. of Appliances** text box, type **3**, and press the **Tab** key. The first alert dialog box appears and correctly displays 3, which is the number you typed into the text box.

6. Click the **OK** button. The second alert dialog box appears and displays a value of 0 instead of the correct cost for moving three appliances ($75). This tells you that there is something wrong with the statement preceding the second alert dialog box.

7. Click the **OK** button. Return to your text editor and examine the statement above the second window.alert() statement. Note that instead of an assignment operator, the statement includes a subtraction operator.

8. Replace the subtraction operator with an assignment operator as follows:

```
appliancesCost = appliances * 25;
```

9. Remove the two `window.alert()` statements from the `calcAppliancesCost()` function.

10. Save the **MovingEstimatorWithBugs.html** document in your text editor, then return to your Web browser and reload the Web page.

11. Click the **No. of Appliances** text box, type **2**, and press the **Tab** key. The value in the Moving Estimate text box should correctly change to $50. Leave the document open in your Web browser.

Tracing Errors with the `write()` and `writeln()` Methods

There may be situations in which you want to trace a bug in your program by analyzing a list of values rather than by trying to interpret the values displayed in alert dialog boxes on a case-by-case basis. You can create such a list by opening a new browser window and using the `write()` and `writeln()` methods to print values to this separate window. The following code shows an example of the `calculatePay()` function printing values to a separate window. Multiple `write()` methods that print values to the new window are included throughout the function. Figure 8-8 shows the contents of the new window after executing the `calculatePay()` function.

```
function calculatePay() {
valueWindow = window.open("", "", "height=150,width=350");
    var payRate = 15; numHours = 40;
    var grossPay = payRate * numHours;
    valueWindow.document.open();
valueWindow.document.write("grossPay is " + grossPay + "<br />");
    var federalTaxes = grossPay * .06794;
    var stateTaxes = grossPay * .0476;
    var socialSecurity = grossPay * .062;
    var medicare = grossPay * .0145;
    var netPay = grossPay - federalTaxes;
valueWindow.document.write("netPay minus Federal taxes is "
    + netPay + "<br />");
    netPay *= stateTaxes;
valueWindow.document.write("netPay minus State taxes is "
    + netPay + "<br />");
    netPay *= socialSecurity;
valueWindow.document.write("netPay minus Social Security is "
    + netPay + "<br />");
    netPay *= medicare;
valueWindow.document.write("netPay minus Medicare is "
    + netPay + "<br />");
valueWindow.document.close();
    return Math.round(netPay);
}
calculatePay();
```

Figure 8-8

Contents of new window
after executing the
`calculatePay()`
function

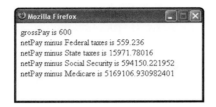

Using the contents of the window in Figure 8-8, you can evaluate each variable in the `calculatePay()` function as values change throughout the function execution. Quickly viewing a list of variable values in a separate window is a simple, yet effective technique for testing many types of code.

TIP

When using `write()` and `writeln()` methods to trace bugs, it is helpful to use a **driver program**, which is a simplified, temporary program that is used for testing functions and other code. A driver program is simply a JavaScript program that contains only the code you are testing. Driver programs do not have to be elaborate; they can be as simple as a single function you are testing. This technique allows you to isolate and test an individual function without having to worry about Web page elements, event handlers, global variables, and other code that form your program's functionality as a whole.

Next, you will use `write()` statements and another browser window to help locate bugs in the Moving Estimator program's `calcTotalEstimate()` function. The `calcTotalEstimate()` function should calculate the total of the `mileageCost`, `laborCost`, `flightsCost`, `appliancesCost`, and `pianosCost` variables. However, you need to be sure that the calculations are being performed properly before you can confidently include the function in the Moving Estimator program. The `calcTotalEstimate()` function is a very simple function, but it serves the purpose of demonstrating how to use a driver program to debug a function.

To use `write()` statements and another browser window to help locate bugs in the Moving Estimator program's `calcTotalEstimate()` function:

1. Return to the **MovingEstimatorWithBugs.html** document in your text editor, highlight the `calcTotalEstimate()` function, and then copy it to the Clipboard by clicking **Copy** on the **Edit** menu (or by pressing Ctrl+C).

2. Create a new document in your text editor and add a script section to the document as follows. Because you are only using this document for testing purposes, you do not need to include a `<!DOCTYPE>` declaration, `<html>` element, or header and body sections.

```
<script type="text/javascript">
/* <![CDATA[ */
/* ]]> */
</script>
```

CHAPTER 8

3. Paste the `calcTotalEstimate()` function, which you copied from the Moving Estimator program, into the script section by clicking **Paste** on the **Edit** menu (or by pressing Ctrl+V).

4. Following the `calcTotalEstimate()` function's closing brace, add a single statement that calls the `calcTotalEstimate()` function, as follows:

```
calcTotalEstimate();
```

5. The `total` variable should be assigned the combined values of the five other variables. Therefore, if each of the other variables contains a value of 100, the `total` variable should be assigned a total value of 500. To test how the calculations perform under these conditions, add the declarations and assignments for each variable, as follows. In the actual version of the program, the variables are global variables that receive their values from text boxes in a form. Each of the text boxes calls an associated function using an `onchange` event handler, which assigns the value entered into a text box to the associated global function.

```
function calcTotalEstimate() {
var mileageCost = 100;
var laborCost = 100;
var flightsCost = 100;
var appliancesCost = 100;
var pianosCost = 100;
    var total = mileageCost;
    total += laborCost;
    total = flightsCost;
    total = appliancesCost;
    total += pianosCost;
    document.forms[0].total.value = "$" + total.toLocaleString();
}
```

6. Next, add `write()` statements to the `calcTotalEstimate()` function that print the value of the total variable each time it is assigned a new value. Also, add a line comment to the last statement because this simple driver program does not include the form that displays the final total.

```
function calcTotalEstimate() {
...
    var total = mileageCost;
document.write("total variable after adding mileageCost: "
    + total + "<br />");
    total += laborCost;
document.write("total variable after adding laborCost: "
    + total + "<br />");
    total = flightsCost;
document.write("total variable after adding flightsCost: "
    + total + "<br />");
    total = appliancesCost;
document.write("total variable after adding appliancesCost: "
```

```
        + total + "<br />");
    total += pianosCost;
document.write("total variable after adding pianosCost: "
    + total + "<br />");
//    document.forms[0].total.value = "$" + total.toLocaleString();
}
```

7. Save the document as **MovingEstimatorFunctionTest.html** in your Chapter folder for Chapter 8, and then close it in your text editor.

8. Open **MovingEstimatorFunctionTest.html** in your Web browser. Your Web browser should resemble Figure 8-9. You can see from the output statements that the calcTotalEstimate() function did not assign a final value of 500 to the total variable. Instead, it assigned a value of 200 to the total variable. Looking back over the individual statements that printed the value of the total variable each time it was assigned a new value, you can see that the flightsCost and appliancesCost values were not added to the value of the total variable, but instead replaced its value. As you probably already noticed, the two statements that assign these values to the total variable used the assignment operator (=) instead of the compound addition assignment operator (+=). Although this is a very simple example, it demonstrates how output statements can help you analyze a variable's changing values.

Figure 8-9

Output of the MovingEstimatorFunctionTest.html document

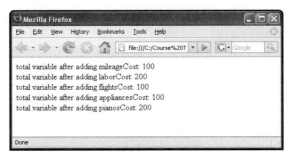

9. Close the browser window displaying the **MovingEstimatorFunctionTest.html** document.

10. Return to the **MovingEstimatorWithBugs.html** document in your text editor and modify the calcTotalEstimate() function so that the statements that assign the flightsCost and appliancesCost values to the total variable use the compound addition assignment operator (+=) instead of the assignment operator (=), as follows:

```
function calcTotalEstimate() {
    var total = mileageCost;
    total += laborCost;
    total += flightsCost;
    total += appliancesCost;
    total += pianosCost;
```

```
        document.forms[0].total.value = "$" + total.toLocaleString();
    }
```

11. Save the **MovingEstimatorWithBugs.html** document, but do not try to use the program yet because it still contains some bugs.

Using Comments to Locate Bugs

Another method of locating bugs in a JavaScript program is to transform lines that you think may be causing problems into comments. In other words, you can "comment out" problematic lines. This technique helps you isolate the statement that is causing the error. In some cases you may choose to comment out individual lines that could be causing the error, or you may choose to comment out all lines except the lines that you know work. When you first receive an error message, start by commenting out only the statement specified by the line number in the error message. Save the document, and then open it again in your Web browser to see if you receive another error. If you receive additional error messages, comment out those statements as well. Once you eliminate the error messages, examine the commented out statements for the cause of the bug.

TIP
The cause of an error in a particular statement is often the result of an error in a preceding line of code.

The last five statements in the following code are commented out because they generate error messages stating that `yearlyIntrest` is not defined. The problem with the code is that the `yearlyInterest` variable is incorrectly spelled as `yearlyIntrest` in several of the statements. Commenting out the lines isolates the problem statements.

```
var amount = 100000;
var percentage = .08;
document.write("<p>The interest rate for a loan in the amount of "
    + amount + " is " + percentage + "<br />");
var yearlyInterest = amount * percentage;
// document.writeln("The amount of interest for one year is "
    + yearlyIntrest + "<br />");
// var monthlyInterest = yearlyIntrest / 12;
// document.writeln("The amount of interest for one month is "
    + monthlyInterest + "<br />");
// var dailyInterest = yearlyIntrest / 365;
// document.writeln("The amount of interest for one day is "
    + dailyInterest + "</p>");
```

Although the error in the preceding code may seem somewhat simple, it is typical of the types of errors you will encounter. Often you will see the error right away and not need to comment out code or use any other tracing technique. However, when you have been staring at the same code for long periods of time, simple spelling errors, like `yearlyIntrest`, are not always easy to spot. Commenting out the lines you know are giving you trouble is a good technique for isolating and correcting even the simplest types of bugs.

Combining Debugging Techniques

You can combine debugging techniques to aid in your search for errors. For example, the following code uses comments combined with an alert dialog box to trace errors in the `calculatePay()` function. Suppose that the `var grossPay = payRate * numHours;` statement is the last statement in the function that operates correctly. Therefore, all of the lines following that statement are commented out. You would then use an alert dialog box to check the value of each statement, removing comments from each statement in a sequential order, and checking and correcting syntax as you go.

```
function calculatePay() {
     var payRate = 15; numHours = 40;
     var grossPay = payRate * numHours;
window.alert(grossPay);
//    var federalTaxes = grossPay * .06794;
//    var stateTaxes = grossPay * .0476;
//    var socialSecurity = grossPay * .062;
//    var medicare = grossPay * .0145;
//    var netPay = grossPay - federalTaxes;
//    netPay *= stateTaxes;
//    netPay *= socialSecurity;
//    netPay *= medicare;
//    return Math.round(netPay);
}
```

Next, you will use comments to locate bugs in the Moving Estimator program.

To use comments to locate bugs in the Moving Estimator program:

1. Return to the **MovingEstimatorWithBugs.html** document in your Web browser, reload or refresh the Web page, and then enter the following data:

   Distance in Miles: **400**
   Weight in Pounds: **900**
   No. of Flights: **2**

2. Note the total value displayed in the Moving Estimate box. Instead of a correct value of 735, you see an incorrect value of 3,135. In order to locate the code that is causing this problem, you need to add comments to the `calcTotalEstimate()` function.

3. Return to the **MovingEstimatorWithBugs.html** document in your text editor and add comments to all of the statements in the `calcTotalEstimate()` function, except the first statement, which assigns the `mileageCost` variable to the `total` variable, and the last statement, which assigns the value of the `total` variable to its associated text box in the form. Your function should appear as follows:

```
function calcTotalEstimate() {
    var total = mileageCost;
//  total += laborCost;
//  total += flightsCost;
//  total += appliancesCost;
//  total += pianosCost;
    document.forms[0].total.value = "$" + total.toLocaleString();
}
```

4. Save the **MovingEstimatorWithBugs.html** document in your text editor, then return to your Web browser and reload or refresh the Web page.

5. Enter **400** as the Distance in Miles value and press the **Tab** key. The correct value of 500 is assigned to the Moving Estimate box. Therefore, the mileageCost variable is not the problem.

6. Return to the **MovingEstimatorWithBugs.html** document in your text editor and remove the comment from the total += laborCost; statement. Save the **MovingEstimatorWithBugs.html** document in your text editor, then return to your Web browser and reload or refresh the Web page.

7. Enter **400** as the Distance in Miles value, press the **Tab** key, enter **900** as the Weight in Pounds value, and press the **Tab** key. At 15 cents a pound, the total cost of 900 pounds is $135. Adding 135 to the Distance in Miles amount of 500 results in a total of 635. Therefore, the program is functioning correctly so far.

8. Return to the **MovingEstimatorWithBugs.html** document in your text editor and remove the comment from the total += flightsCost; statement. Save the **MovingEstimatorWithBugs.html** document in your text editor, then return to your Web browser and reload or refresh the Web page.

9. Enter **400** as the Distance in Miles value, press the **Tab** key, enter **900** as the Weight in Pounds value, press the **Tab** key, enter **2** as the No. of Flights value and then press the **Tab** key. At $50 per flight, a value of 2 should only increase the moving estimate by 100, for a total of 735. However, the Moving Estimate box incorrectly displays 3135. The program functioned correctly until it tried to call the calcFlightsCost() function.

10. Scroll to the calcFlightsCost() function in your text editor and note that the function includes an unnecessary statement, flights = 50;, which causes the calculation error. Do not think this is a trivial example. As you develop your own applications, you will often find yourself adding and deleting statements that can introduce simple, hard-to-detect bugs in your programs.

11. Delete the flights = 50; statement from the calcFlightsCost() function.

12. Remove the remainder of the comments from the statements in the calcTotalEstimate() function, save the **MovingEstimatorWithBugs.html** document, and then refresh your Web browser. Enter the data listed in Step 1. The correct value of 735 should appear in the Moving Estimate box. Do not enter any numbers for the other calculations because the program still contains some errors.

Tracing Errors with Debugging Tools

Many high-level programming languages such as Visual C++ have debugging capabilities built directly into their development environments. These built-in debugging capabilities provide sophisticated commands for tracking errors. The JavaScript programming language does not have a development environment other than your text editor. The only true debugging tools you have in JavaScript are the error messages generated by a browser. To provide JavaScript with debugging capabilities, both Mozilla and Microsoft developed debugging tools that can be used with their browsers to debug JavaScript code. Mozilla's debugging tool is called **JavaScript Debugger** and can be used to debug JavaScript code in Mozilla-based Web browsers, including Firefox. JavaScript Debugger is available to Firefox as an extension. (The term "extension" refers to additional functionality that can be added to a program.) To install JavaScript Debugger in Firefox, select Add-ons from the Tools menu, and then click Get Extensions in the Add-ons dialog box. In the Firefox Add-ons Web page that opens, search for "JavaScript Debugger" and follow the instructions for installing it.

Microsoft's debugging tool, called **Script Debugger**, can be used with Internet Explorer to debug JavaScript code. You can also use it to debug VBScript, Java applets, JavaBeans, and ActiveX components in addition to JavaScript programs. You can download Script Debugger from the Microsoft Developer Network at *msdn.microsoft.com/downloads/*. Note that Script Debugger refers to JavaScript as JScript. This text, however, always uses the original name of the language, JavaScript.

Up to this point, you have learned how to interpret error messages and correct the statements that cause the errors. As helpful as they are, error messages are useful only in resolving syntax and run-time errors. You have also learned some techniques that assist in locating logic errors. Examining your code manually is usually the first step to take when you have a logic error, or you may use an alert dialog box to track values. These techniques work fine with smaller programs. However, when you are creating a large program that includes multiple objects, methods, and functions, logic errors can be very difficult to spot. For instance, you may have a function that instantiates objects from several different constructor functions. Each instantiated object may then call methods or use properties from its parent object or from other ancestor objects. Attempting to trace the logic and flow of such a program using simple tools such as the alert dialog box can be difficult. Mozilla JavaScript Debugger and Microsoft Script Debugger provide several tools that can help you trace each line of code, creating a much more efficient method of finding and resolving logic errors.

NOTE
This chapter discusses the basic aspects of how to use JavaScript Debugger and Script Debugger to debug your JavaScript programs.

Understanding the JavaScript Debugger and Script Debugger Windows

This section describes the main windows for both JavaScript Debugger and Script Debugger.

Using JavaScript Debugger

To debug JavaScript with JavaScript Debugger, you open the document you want to debug in Firefox and then select JavaScript Debugger from the Tools menu. This opens the JavaScript Debugger window. All of the scripts that are currently loaded in the browser window or that are used by JavaScript Debugger itself are listed in the Loaded Scripts view portion of the JavaScript Debugger window. In Loaded Scripts view, icons represent different types of files, including a "J" icon for .js (JavaScript) files, an "H" icon for HTML files, and a square icon for a JavaScript function. To open a particular file, double-click it in Loaded Scripts view. The file opens in Source Code view, which is a read-only file viewer that you can use to help debug your scripts. Figure 8-10 displays the JavaScript Debugger window with the nsMicrosoftsummaryService.js file (a JavaScript file that Firefox uses) opened in Source Code view.

Figure 8-10

Document opened in JavaScript Debugger

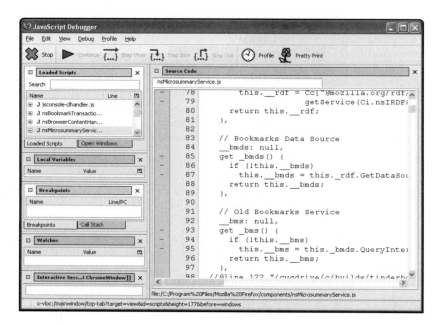

TIP

Use the Show/Hide submenu on the View menu to toggle the display of the various views in JavaScript Debugger.

NOTE

JavaScript Debugger also includes some more advanced features, such as Interactive Session view, which allow you to debug your scripts from a command line instead of from JavaScript Debugger's graphical user interface (GUI).

TIP

In addition to Loaded Scripts view, you can also use Open Windows view to open files in JavaScript Debugger. Open Windows view organizes each open file by the Web browser window where it is opened. However, note that you have limited debugging functionality with the files that are open in Open Windows view. For example, in Open Windows view you cannot set hard breakpoints, which you study next.

Using Script Debugger

To debug JavaScript with Script Debugger, you open the document you want to debug in Internet Explorer and use the Script Debugger submenu on the View menu. The Script Debugger submenu contains two commands: Open and Break at Next Statement. The Open command opens the current document in the Script Debugger window. Once you open a document in Script Debugger, icons appear in the left margin to indicate various elements. For example, a yellow arrow points to the statement that executes next. The types of code elements in a JavaScript program are distinguished by syntax color coding. This color coding makes it easier to understand the structure and code in a JavaScript program. For example, the default syntax coloring for JavaScript keywords is blue. Figure 8-11 shows an example of a document opened in Script Debugger. Although you can't see colors in the figure, the arrow and the highlighted statement are yellow.

Figure 8-11

Document opened in
Script Debugger

```
Microsoft Script Debugger  · [Read only: file:///C:/Course%20Technology/0150-9/Ch...
File  Edit  View  Debug  Window  Help
File          Edit                    Debug
        <input type="text" name="leaderZip" size="5" maxlength="5" /></td>
    </tr>
    </table>
    <script type="text/javascript">
    /* <![CDATA[ */
    var dateObject = new Date();
    var month = dateObject.getMonth();
    var monthArray = new Array("January","February","March","April","May","
    var dateToday = monthArray[month] + " " + dateObject.getDate() + ", " +
    document.forms[0].reservationDate.value = dateToday;
    function displayCalendar(whichMonth) {
        calendarWin = window.open("", "CalWindow", "status=no,resizable=yes,
        calendarWin.focus();
        calendarWin.document.write("<!DOCTYPE html PUBLIC '-//W3C//DTD XHTMl
        calendarWin.document.write("<table cellspacing='0' border='1' width=
        calendarWin.document.write("<colgroup span='7' width='50' />");

        if (whichMonth == -1)
            dateObject.setMonth(dateObject.getMonth()-1);
        else if (whichMonth == 1)
            dateObject.setMonth(dateObject.getMonth()+1);
        var month = dateObject.getMonth();
        calendarWin.document.write("<tr><td colspan='2'><a href='' onclick='
Ready                                        Ln 41
```

NOTE

The next section explains how to use the Break at Next Statement command.

The following steps walk you through the process of opening the Moving Estimator program in JavaScript Debugger. The subsequent set of steps walks you through the process of opening the Moving Estimator program in Script Debugger instead. The steps you follow at this point depend on which browser you prefer. Before you start either set of steps, make sure you have downloaded and installed JavaScript Debugger or Script Debugger as described at the beginning of this section.

To open the Moving Estimator program in JavaScript Debugger:

1. Return to the **MovingEstimatorWithBugs.html** document in Firefox.

2. Select **JavaScript Debugger** from the **Tools** menu. The JavaScript Debugger window opens.

3. Locate **MovingEstimatorWithBugs.html** in Loaded Scripts view and double-click it. The MovingEstimatorWithBugs.html document opens in Source Code view, as shown in Figure 8-12. Leave the JavaScript Debugger window open.

Figure 8-12

MovingEstimatorWith-Bugs.html open in JavaScript Debugger

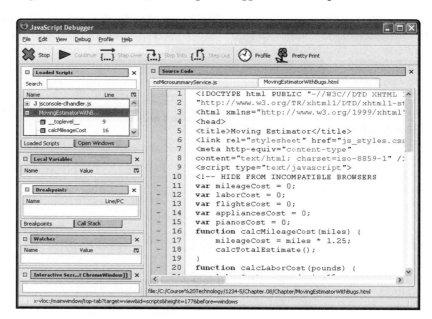

To open the Moving Estimator program in Script Debugger:

1. Return to the **MovingEstimatorWithBugs.html** document in Internet Explorer.

2. Select **Open** from the **Script Debugger** submenu on the **View** menu. The Script Debugger window opens, as shown in Figure 8-13. Leave the Script Debugger window open.

Figure 8-13
MovingEstimatorWith-Bugs.html open in Script Debugger

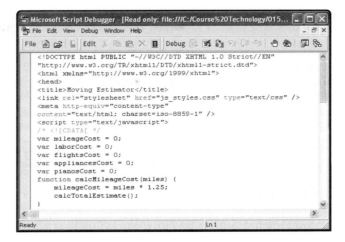

Setting Breakpoints

Both JavaScript Debugger and Script Debugger include commands that you can use to control program execution after your scripts enter break mode. The term **break mode** refers to the temporary suspension of program execution so that you can monitor values and trace program execution. Entering break mode requires inserting breakpoints into your code. A **breakpoint** is a statement in the code at which program execution enters break mode. Once a program is paused at a breakpoint, you can use the commands on the JavaScript Debugger or Script Debugger Debug menus to trace program execution. When a program enters break mode, program execution is not stopped—it is only suspended. This section describes how to set breakpoints in JavaScript Debugger and Script Debugger.

TIP

This text instructs you to use the JavaScript Debugger and Script Debugger menus to execute commands. However, many of the commands are also available as icons on the JavaScript Debugger and Script Debugger toolbars.

Entering Break Mode in JavaScript Debugger

JavaScript Debugger allows you to enter two types of breakpoints: hard breakpoints and future breakpoints. **Hard breakpoints** can be set for executable statements within a local function and notify JavaScript Debugger to enter break mode before the statement executes. **Future breakpoints** can be set for any type of statement and notify JavaScript Debugger to enter break mode as soon as possible before the statement executes. In most cases, you only need to use future breakpoints for statements that exist outside of any local functions, such as variable declaration statements or function calls. As soon as JavaScript Debugger can enter break mode for a future breakpoint, it changes the future breakpoint to a hard breakpoint. The steps for working with breakpoints in JavaScript Debugger are as follows:

1. Open the document you want to debug in Firefox and select JavaScript Debugger from the Tools menu.

2. To set a breakpoint in the script, right-click the line in Source Code view where you want to set the breakpoint and select Set Breakpoint or Set Future Breakpoint from the shortcut menu. For hard breakpoints, a "B" icon appears in the left column next to the line in Source Code view. For future breakpoints, an "F" icon appears in the left column next to the line in Source Code view. The breakpoints you set also appear in Breakpoints view.

3. To execute the script and stop at the first set breakpoint, return to the Web browser window where the script is running and click the Reload icon or press Ctrl+R. The script begins to execute and then focus changes to the JavaScript Debugger, paused at the first set breakpoint.

Once a program is paused at a breakpoint, you can use the commands on the Debug menu to trace program execution. When a program enters break mode, program execution is not stopped—it is only suspended. To resume program execution after entering break mode, select Continue from the Debug menu. The **Continue command** executes the rest of the program normally or until another breakpoint is encountered. Multiple breakpoints provide a convenient way to pause program execution at key positions in your code at which you think there may be a bug. You can also end a debugging session without executing the rest of the program by selecting the **Stop command** from the Debug menu.

Next, you will practice using breakpoints with the Moving Estimator program in Firefox.

To practice using breakpoints with the Moving Estimator program in Firefox:

1. Return to the **MovingEstimatorWithBugs.html** document in the JavaScript Debugger window.

2. Right-click the first statement in the script section, `var mileageCost = 0;`, and select **Set Future Breakpoint** from the shortcut menu. An "F" icon appears in the left margin of Source Code view next to the line containing the breakpoint.

3. In the `calcMileageCost()` function, right-click the `mileageCost = miles * 1.25;` statement and select **Set Breakpoint** from the shortcut menu. A "B" icon appears in the left margin of Source Code view next to the line containing the breakpoint. Figure 8-14 shows the JavaScript Debugger window with the two breakpoints.

4. Switch back to the Web browser window and click the **Reload** icon or press **Ctrl+R**. The script begins to execute and then focus changes to the JavaScript Debugger, paused at the future breakpoint. Notice that the "F" icon has changed to a "B" icon.

5. Select **Continue** from the **Debug** menu. The remainder of the initialization statements execute.

6. Switch back to the Web browser window, type **900** in the **Distance in Miles** text box, and press the **Tab** key. Focus switches to the JavaScript Debugger window, paused at the breakpoint in the `calcMileageCost()` function.

7. Select **Continue** from the **Debug** menu. The code finishes executing.

Figure 8-14

Breakpoints in JavaScript Debugger

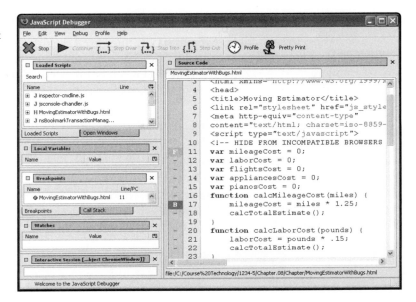

Entering Break Mode in Script Debugger

The Break at Next Statement command instructs Script Debugger to enter break mode as soon as it encounters JavaScript code. The steps for opening a document in the Script Debugger window and entering break mode at the first statement are as follows:

1. Open the document in Internet Explorer, and then select Break at Next Statement from the Script Debugger submenu on the View menu. This command tells Internet Explorer that you want to debug the current document.

2. In Internet Explorer, click the **Refresh** button or perform some event (such as clicking a form button) that executes JavaScript code. The document opens in the Script Debugger window at the first executed JavaScript statement.

TIP

Alternately, you can open the document in the Script Debugger window and select Break at Next Statement from the Script Debugger Debug menu. Then, switch back to Internet Explorer and click the Refresh button or perform some event that executes JavaScript code.

To resume program execution after entering break mode, select Run from the Debug menu. The **Run command** executes the rest of the program normally or until another breakpoint is encountered. Multiple breakpoints provide a convenient way to pause program execution at key positions in your code at which you think there may be a bug. You can also end a debugging session without executing the rest of the program by selecting the **Stop Debugging command** from the Debug menu.

Next, you will practice using breakpoints with the Moving Estimator program in Internet Explorer.

CHAPTER 8

To practice using breakpoints with the Moving Estimator program in Internet Explorer:

1. Return to the **MovingEstimatorWithBugs.html** document in Internet Explorer, select **Break at Next Statement** from the **Script Debugger** submenu on the **View** menu, and then click the **Refresh** button or press **F5**. The script begins to execute and then focus changes to the Script Debugger, paused at the first statement, `var mileageCost = 0;`.

2. Select the **Stop Debugging** command from the **Debug** menu to end the debugging session without executing the rest of the program.

3. Return to the **MovingEstimatorWithBugs.html** document in Script Debugger.

4. Move your cursor to the first statement in the `calcMileageCost()` function, `mileageCost = miles * 1.25;`, and select **Toggle Breakpoint** from the **Debug** menu. A red circle appears in the left margin of the Script Debugger window next to the line containing the breakpoint, as shown in Figure 8-15.

Figure 8-15
Breakpoint in Script
Debugger

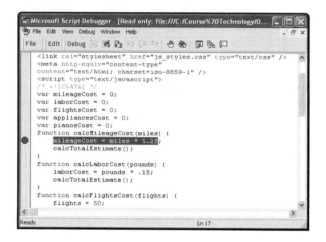

5. Switch back to the Web browser window, type **900** in the **Distance in Miles** text box, and press the **Tab** key. Focus switches to the Script Debugger window, paused at the breakpoint in the `calcMileageCost()` function.

6. Select **Run** from the **Debug** menu. The code finishes executing.

Stepping Through Your Scripts

The Step Into, Step Over, and Step Out commands on the Debug menus in both JavaScript Debugger and Script Debugger allow you to continue program execution after you enter break mode. The **Step Into command** executes an individual line of code and then pauses until you instruct the debugger to continue. This feature gives you an opportunity to evaluate program flow and structure as code is being executed.

As you use the Step Into command to move through code, the debugger stops at each line within every function of the JavaScript program. However, when stepping through a program to trace a logical error, it is convenient to be able to skip functions that you know are functioning correctly.

The **Step Over command** allows you to skip function calls. The program still executes the function that you step over, but it appears in each debugger as if a single statement executes.

The **Step Out command** executes all remaining code in the current function. If the current function was called from another function, all remaining code in the current function executes and the debugger stops at the next statement in the calling function.

Next, you will practice tracing program execution using the Step commands.

To practice tracing program execution using the Step commands in either JavaScript Debugger or Script Debugger:

1. Return to the **MovingEstimatorWithBugs.html** document in your Web browser window and type **900** in the **Distance in Miles** text box, and press the **Tab** key. Focus switches to the JavaScript Debugger (for Firefox) window or Script Debugger (for Internet Explorer) window, paused at the breakpoint in the `calcMileageCost()` function.

2. Select **Step Into** from the **Debug** menu to execute the `mileageCost = miles * 1.25;`. Control transfers to the `calcTotalEstimate()` statement.

3. Select **Step Into** from the **Debug** menu again to execute the `calcTotalEstimate()` statement. Control transfers to the `calcTotalEstimate()` function.

4. Because you already know the `calcTotalEstimate()` function works correctly, select **Step Out** from the **Debug** menu to finish executing the remainder of the `calcMileageCost()` function.

5. Select **Continue** or **Run** from the **Debug** menu to complete debugging and program execution.

Clearing Breakpoints

This section explains how to clear breakpoints in JavaScript Debugger and Script Debugger.

Clearing Breakpoints in JavaScript Debugger

To clear a breakpoint in JavaScript Debugger, right-click a line in Source Code view that contains the breakpoint and select Clear Breakpoint or Clear Future Breakpoint from the shortcut menu. To remove all breakpoints from a document in JavaScript Debugger, right-click anywhere in Breakpoints view and select Clear All Breakpoints or Clear All Future Breakpoints from the shortcut menu. Note that when you clear a hard breakpoint, it automatically changes to a future breakpoint. This means that after you clear a hard breakpoint, you must then clear the resulting future breakpoint.

To remove breakpoints from the Moving Estimator program in JavaScript Debugger:

1. Return to the **MovingEstimatorWithBugs.html** document in JavaScript Debugger.

2. Right-click anywhere in **Breakpoints** view and select **Clear All Breakpoints** from the shortcut menu.

3. Right-click anywhere in **Breakpoints** view and select **Clear All Future Breakpoints** from the shortcut menu.

Clearing Breakpoints in Script Debugger

To clear a breakpoint in Script Debugger, place your cursor anywhere in a line that contains the breakpoint and select Toggle Breakpoint from the Debug menu. To remove all breakpoints from a document in Script Debugger, select Clear All Breakpoints from the Debug menu.

To remove breakpoints from the Moving Estimator program in Script Debugger:

1. Return to the **MovingEstimatorWithBugs.html** document in Script Debugger.
2. Select **Clear All Breakpoints** from the Debug menu.

Tracing Variables and Expressions

As you trace program execution using Step commands and breakpoints, you may also need to trace how variables and expressions change during the course of program execution. For example, suppose you have a statement that reads `resultNum = firstNum / secondNum;`. You know this line is causing a divide-by-zero error, but you do not know exactly when `secondNum` is being changed to a zero value. To pinpoint the cause of the logic problem, you need a way to trace program execution and locate the exact location at which `secondNum` is being changed to a zero value.

Tracing Variables and Expressions in JavaScript Debugger

JavaScript Debugger includes two views that you can use to trace variables and expressions during the course of program execution: Local Variables and Watches. **Locals Variables view** displays all local variables within the currently executing function, regardless of whether they have been initialized. Local Variables view helps you see how different values in the currently executing function affect program execution. You use Local Variables view when you need to be able to see all of a function's variables, regardless of whether they have been assigned a value. You can change the value of a variable in Local Variables view by right-clicking the variable and selecting Change Value from the shortcut menu. **Watches view** monitors both variables and expressions in break mode. To open Watches view, select Watches from the Show/Hide submenu on the View menu. To display the value of a variable or expression, you right-click Watches view and select Add Watch Expression from the shortcut menu. Enter the variable or expression you want to watch and click OK. The variable or expression you enter displays in Watches view, along with its value. Figure 8-16 shows Watches view as it monitors the value of the `mileageCost` and `total` variables in the `calcTotalEstimate()` function. The other JavaScript Debugger views have been hidden to make it easier for you to locate Watches view.

TIP
To remove a watch expression, right-click the expression in Watches view and select Remove Watch.

Figure 8-16
Variables in Watches
view

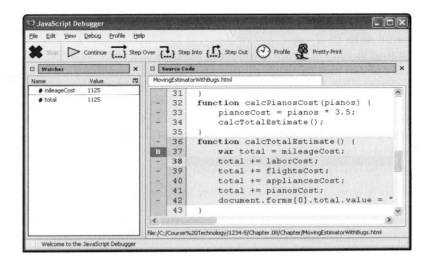

Tracing Variables and Expressions in Script Debugger

In Script Debugger, you can use the **Command window** to monitor variables and expressions in break mode. You can also change variables and expressions in break mode from within the Command window. To open the Command window, click View on the menu bar and then click Command Window.

To display the value of a variable or expression in the Command window, you enter the variable or expression and press Enter. The value prints directly beneath the variable or expression in the Command window. To change the value of a variable, type the variable name in the Command window followed by an equal sign and the new value, and then press Enter. The new value prints beneath the statement you entered. Figure 8-17 shows the Command window as it monitors the value of the `mileageCost` and `total` variables in the `calcTotalEstimate()` function.

Figure 8-17
Variables in the
Command window

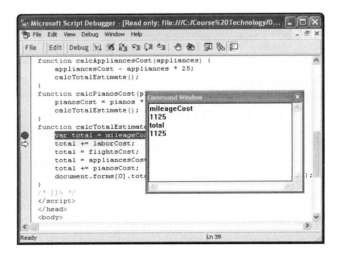

TIP

The Command window also allows you to change the value of object properties during a debugging session. For example, if you want to change the car_color property of the myCar object to blue during a debugging session, type myCar.car_color = "blue" in the Command window and press Enter.

Next, you use Watches view or the Command window to find a bug in the Moving Estimator program.

To use Watches view or the Command window to find a bug in the Moving Estimator program:

1. Return to the **MovingEstimatorWithBugs.html** document in your Web browser.

2. Enter the following data for each of the moving cost calculations:

   ```
   Distance in Miles: 1000
   Weight in Pounds: 500
   No. of Flights: 2
   No. of Appliances: 3
   No. of Pianos: 2
   ```

3. After you enter the preceding numbers, the Moving Estimate text box displays a value of $1,507, which isn't right. (The value should be $1,570.) Because you have already corrected the Distance in Miles, Weight in Pounds, and No. of Flights calculations earlier in this chapter, you will start by examining the No. of Appliances calculation. You will examine the two values required by the appliances calculation: the appliances variable, which receives its value from the associated form text box, and the appliancesCost variable, which receives the result of the calculation. First, return to the **MovingEstimatorWithBugs.html** document in the JavaScript Debugger or Script Debugger window and insert a breakpoint on the **appliancesCost = appliances * 25;** statement.

4. Return to the **MovingEstimatorWithBugs.html** document in the Web browser window and enter the values from Step 2 into the Distance in Miles, Weight in Pounds, and No. of Flights text boxes. Click the **No. of Appliances** text box, type **3** for the number of appliances, then press the **Tab** key. The program enters break mode on the appliancesCost = appliances * 25; statement. Select the **Step Into** command to execute the function's calculation statement.

5. If you are using JavaScript Debugger, right-click anywhere in Watches view, select **Add Watch Expression** from the shortcut menu, and type **appliancesCost** in the prompt dialog box and press **Enter**. If you are using Script Debugger, select **Command Window** from the **View** menu, type **appliancesCost**, and press **Enter**. The correct value, 75, appears in both Watches view in JavaScript Debugger and the Command window in Script Debugger. Therefore, the problem does not appear to be related to the appliances cost calculation.

6. Select **Continue** or **Run** from the **Debug** menu.

7. Remove the breakpoint from the **appliancesCost = appliances * 25;** statement in the calcAppliancesCost() function.

8. Next, you will examine the two values required by the piano calculation: the `pianos` variable and the `pianosCost` variable. Insert a breakpoint on the **`pianosCost = pianos * 3.5;`** statement in the `calcPianosCost()` function.

9. Return to the **MovingEstimatorWithBugs.html** document in the Web browser window and re-enter the values from Step 2.

10. Press the **Tab** key after you type **2** for the number of pianos. The program enters break mode on the `pianosCost = pianos * 3.5;` statement. Select the **Step Into** command to execute the function's calculation statement.

11. If you are using JavaScript Debugger, right-click anywhere in Watches view, select **Add Watch Expression** from the shortcut menu, type **pianosCost** in the prompt dialog box and press **Enter**. If you are using Script Debugger, select **Command Window** from the **View** window, type **pianosCost**, and press **Enter**. Because the cost to move a single piano is $35, the `pianosCost` variable should be updated to 70 after you execute the `pianosCost = pianos * 3.5;` statement. The correct value of 75 should appear in Watches view or the Command window. Instead, a value of 7 appears. If you are observant, you have probably already noticed that the calculation is multiplying the `pianos` variable by 3.5 instead of 35.

12. Select **Continue** or **Run** from the **Debug** menu. Return to the **MovingEstimatorWithBugs.html** document in your text editor and modify the incorrect statement in the `calcPianosCost()` function so the `pianos` variable is multiplied by 35 instead of 3.5, as follows:

```
pianosCost = pianos * 35;
```

13. Remove the breakpoint from the `pianosCost = pianos * 35;` statement in the `calcAppliancesCost()` function.

14. Save the **MovingEstimatorWithBugs.html** document in your text editor, then return to your Web browser and reload the Web page. Enter the values from Step 2. The program should now function correctly, calculating a moving estimate of $1,570.

Examining the Call Stack

When you are working with a JavaScript program that contains multiple functions, the computer must remember the order in which functions are executed. For example, if you have an `accountsPayable()` function that calls an `accountsReceivable()` function, the computer must remember to return to the `accountsPayable()` function after the `accountsReceivable()` function finishes executing. Similarly, if the `accountsReceivable()` function calls a `depositFunds()` function after it has been called by the `accountsPayable()` function, then the computer must remember to return to the `accountsReceivable()` function after the `depositFunds()` function finishes executing, then return to the `accountsPayable()` function after the `accountsReceivable()` function finishes executing. The term **call stack** refers to the order in which procedures, such as functions, methods, or event handlers, execute in a program. Each time a program calls a procedure, the procedure is added to the top of the call stack, and then removed after it finishes executing.

The ability to view the contents of a call stack is very useful when tracing logic errors in large programs with multiple functions. For example, suppose you have a variable that is passed as an argument among several functions. Suppose also that the variable is being assigned the wrong value. Viewing the call stack, along with using tracing commands, makes it easier to locate the specific function causing the problem. JavaScript Debugger and Script Debugger include Call Stack features that provide the ability to view the contents of a call stack when debugging a program. To display Call Stack view in JavaScript Debugger, select Show/Hide on the View menu, and then click Call Stack. To display the Call Stack window in Script Debugger, select Call Stack from the View menu.

Handling Exceptions and Errors

Although standard error messages that are generated by programming languages such as JavaScript are very helpful to programmers, they tend to scare users, who might think that they somehow caused the error. Errors can and will occur, but you should never let your users think that they did something wrong. Your goal should be to write code that anticipates any problems that may occur and includes graceful methods of dealing with those problems. Writing code that anticipates and handles potential problems is often called **bulletproofing**. One bulletproofing technique you have already used has to do with validating submitted form data. For example, in Chapter 7, you created the following function to validate an e-mail addresses. This example contains a nested if statement that uses a regular expression to test whether the passed formObject variable contains a valid e-mail address.

```
function validateEmail(formObject) {
    var email = formObject.value;
    var emailCheck = /^[_\w-]+(\.[_\w-]+)*@[\w-]+(\
        .[\w-]+)*(\.[\D]{2,3})$/;
    if (emailCheck.test(email) == false) {
        window.alert("One or more of the e-mail addresses
            you entered does not appear to be valid.");
        return false;
    }
    formObject.value = email.toLowerCase();
    return true;
}
```

Another method of bulletproofing your code is to use **exception handling**, which allows programs to handle errors as they occur in the execution of a program. The term **exception** refers to some type of error that occurs in a program. Many advanced programming languages, including ECMAScript Edition 3, include exception-handling capabilities. You use exception handling to test any type of input or functionality that is external to a program. For most programming languages, exception handling is most useful when connecting to a database or when trying to access some other type of external program. Because JavaScript cannot connect to databases and is mostly limited to working within the confines of a user's Web browser, the main reason for using exception handling is to evaluate user input. Although you could technically use exception handling for all of your JavaScript programs, your code should be tested thoroughly enough that it anticipates any potential problems that may occur. However, one area that you cannot control is whether users enter the correct type of data.

Throwing Exceptions

You execute code that may contain an exception in a **try statement**. The syntax for a `try` statement is as follows:

```
try {
    statements;
}
```

You use a **throw statement** to indicate that an error occurred within a `try` block. Using a `throw` statement to indicate that an error occurred is called "throwing an error". The error that you "throw" with a `throw` statement can be any type of expression. The following example demonstrates how to use a `try` statement with a regular expression to test whether the passed `formObject` variable contains a valid e-mail address:

```
try {
    var email = formObject.value;
    var emailCheck = /^[_\w-]+(\.[_\w-]+)*@[\w-]+(\
        .[\w-]+)*(\.[\D]{2,3})$/;
    if (emailCheck.test(email) == false)
        throw "One or more of the e-mail addresses
            you entered does not appear to be valid.";
}
```

Catching Exceptions

After you throw an error, you use a **catch statement** to handle, or "catch" the error. The syntax for a `catch` statement is as follows:

```
catch(error) {
    statements;
}
```

The `catch` statement accepts a single argument that you can use to refer to the thrown exception. The following `catch` statement demonstrates how to catch the exception that is thrown by the `try` statement that evaluates the e-mail address. Notice that the `window.alert()` statement displays the passed `emailError` variable as its value. The `catch` statement also returns a value of false to the calling statement, which indicates that the form's `onsubmit` event handler should not execute.

```
catch(emailError) {
    window.alert(emailError)
    return false;
}
```

Executing Final Exception Handling Tasks

JavaScript's exception handling functionality also includes a **`finally` statement** that executes regardless of whether its associated `try` block throws an exception. You normally use a `finally` statement to perform some type of cleanup or any necessary tasks after code is evaluated with a `try` statement. The syntax for a `finally` statement is as follows:

```
finally {
    statements;
}
```

NOTE

Whenever a `try` statement throws an exception, the JavaScript interpreter executes the nearest `catch` statement. If a `catch` statement is not located within the construct that throws an exception, the JavaScript interpreter looks at the next higher level of code for a `catch` statement. For example, if an `if` statement contains a `throw` statement, but it does not contain a `catch` statement, the JavaScript interpreter looks in a function that contains the `if` statement. Then, if the function does not contain a `catch` statement, the JavaScript interpreter looks for a `catch` statement at the global level. If a construct that contains `try` and `finally` statements but no `catch` statement, the `finally` statement executes before the JavaScript constructor begins searching at a higher level for a `catch` statement.

The following example contains the entire `validateEmail()` function from Chapter 7, with `try`, `throw`, `catch`, and `finally` statements that evaluate the e-mail address:

```
function validateEmail(formObject) {
    try {
        var email = formObject.value;
        var emailCheck = /^[_\w-]+(\.[_\w-]+)*@[\w-]+(\
            .[\w-]+)*(\.[\D]{2,3})$/;
        if (emailCheck.test(email) == false)
            throw "One or more of the e-mail addresses
                you entered does not appear to be valid.";
    }
    catch(emailError) {
        window.alert(emailError)
        return false;
    }
    finally {
        formObject.value = email.toLowerCase();
    }
    return true;
}
```

Next, you will modify the Moving Estimator program so it uses exception handling to prevent users from entering any values except numbers in the form's text boxes. Before you can add this functionality, you need to understand how to find out more information about events that occur in JavaScript. An `Event` object represents every event in JavaScript. When you call an event handler function, you can pass an argument named `event`, which is an object that contains information about the event that occurred. For example, the `Event` object contains a `type` property that specifies the type of event that occurred. The button created with the following statement generates an alert dialog box that uses the `type` property of the `Event` object to display the type of event that occurred. Clicking the button displays "You executed a click event." in the alert dialog box.

```
<input type="button" onclick="window.alert('You executed a ' +
event.type + ' event.')" value="Click Me" />
```

NOTE

You must refer to the `Event` object in your JavaScript statements with lowercase letters.

To prevent users from entering any values except for numbers, you can use the `onkeypress` event with the `Event` object to determine which values were entered. The `Event` object generated by the `onkeypress` event contains the Unicode character that represents the pressed key. Unfortunately, Internet Explorer and Netscape-based browsers (including Firefox) store the Unicode characters in different properties; Internet Explorer stores the Unicode character in the `keyCode` property while Netscape-based browsers store the Unicode character in the `charCode` property. You can handle this by using the `Navigator` object to determine which browser type is running, and then use this information to access the Unicode character from the correct property. Next, you can use the `fromCharCode()` method of the `String` class to convert the Unicode character to its equivalent print character. Finally, you will use a regular expression within the exception handling structure to determine the type of character the user pressed. If the user did not press a numeric character, the `onkeypress` event is canceled and a message is displayed to the user.

To add exception handling to the Moving Estimator program:

1. Return to the **MovingEstimatorWithBugs.html** document in your Web browser.
2. Add the following function, named `validateInput()`, to the end of the script section. The function accepts a single parameter representing the generated event.

   ```
   function validateInput(keyPressEvent) {
   }
   ```

3. Add to the `validateInput()` function the following `if...else` structure, which determines whether the Web browser is Internet Explorer or a Netscape-based browser. If the browser is Internet Explorer, the value of the Event object's `keyCode` property is assigned to the `enteredKey` variable. For Netscape-based browsers, the value of the `charCode` property is assigned to the `enteredKey` variable.

```
if (navigator.appName == "Microsoft Internet Explorer")
    var enteredKey = keyPressEvent.keyCode;
else if (navigator.appName == "Netscape")
    var enteredKey = keyPressEvent.charCode;
```

4. Next, add the following two statements to the end of the validateInput()
    function. The first statement uses the fromCharCode() method of the String
    class to convert the Unicode character in the enteredKey variable to its
    equivalent print character. The result is assigned to a variable named
    enteredChar. The second statement declares a variable named retValue that is
    assigned a value of true. The value assigned to the retValue variable will be
    returned from the function in the finally statement, which you will add next.

```
var enteredChar = String.fromCharCode(enteredKey);
var retValue = true;
```

5. Add the following exception handling code to the end of the validateInput()
    function. The try statement uses the \d character class expression to determine
    whether the value assigned to the enteredChar variable is not a numeric value
    and the \W character class expression to determine if the character is not a
    nonalphanumeric character, such as a Tab character. (You studied character class
    expressions in Chapter 7.) If the value is not a number or a non-alphanumeric
    character, then an exception is thrown to the catch statement, which displays the
    error in an alert dialog box and assigns a value of false to the retValue variable.
    The finally statement returns the retValue variable, which tells the calling
    statement whether the entered character is a numeric value.

```
try {
    if (!/\d/.test(enteredChar) &&  !/\W/.test(enteredChar))
        throw "You did not enter a numeric value.";
}
catch(inputError) {
    window.alert(inputError);
    retValue = false;
}
finally {
    return retValue;
}
```

6. Finally, add the following onkeypress event handler to each of the <input>
    elements in the form. The event handler calls the validateInput() function and
    passes to it the Event object. If an entered character is a numeric value, then the
    validateInput() function returns a value of true and the character is allowed
    in the text box. If the entered character is not a numeric value, then the
    validateInput() function returns a value of false, which prevents the character
    from being allowed in the text box.

```
onkeypress="return validateInput(event)"
```

7. Save the **MovingEstimatorWithBugs.html** document, validate it with the W3C Markup Validation Service, and fix any errors that the document contains. Once the document is valid, close it in your text editor and open it in your Web browser. Test the form fields to ensure that you can only enter numeric values.

8. Close your Web browser window and text editor.

Implementing Custom Error Handling

The primary purpose of exception handling is to test specific types of code. As you learned earlier in this chapter, the main reason for using exception handling with JavaScript is to evaluate user input. Instead of just using exception handling with specific types of code, you can also write your own custom code for handling any types of errors that occur on a Web page. Regardless of the programming language, many programmers often prefer to write their own error handling code. Not only does this allow programmers to write user-friendly messages, but it also gives them greater control over any errors that occur in their programs. You will also find custom error handling useful in debugging your scripts, particularly with browsers, such as Firefox, that display error messages in a separate window. This section explains how you can add custom error handling code to your JavaScript programs.

CAUTION

In the early days of JavaScript, most Web browsers displayed alert dialog boxes for each and every error that occurred on a Web page. These alert dialog boxes grew extremely annoying to users, especially when they visited Web pages containing poorly written JavaScript programs. To help make the Web surfing experience more enjoyable, most modern Web browsers suppress error messages or display them in a separate Window that must be specifically opened by the user. Be warned that this section explains how to override a Web browser's default error handling functionality. In most cases, you should just thoroughly test and debug your scripts, and then let a Web browser's default error handling functionality deal with whatever errors you missed. However, there may be cases when you will find it necessary to write your own error handling functionality, particularly with interactive Web pages that require user input.

Catching Errors with the `onerror` Event

JavaScript includes an `onerror` event that executes whenever an error occurs on a Web page. Unlike other types of events, you do not call the `onerror` event handler with an XHTML tag. Instead, you must call the `onerror` event handler as a property of the Window object. You assign to the `onerror` event handler the name of a function that you want to handle JavaScript errors. For example, the following statement assigns a function named `processErrors()` to handle any JavaScript errors that occur on a page. Notice that you do not include parentheses following the function name.

```
window.onerror=processErrors;
```

TIP
To ensure that all of the JavaScript code on your Web page can find the error handling function, add the function to the beginning of a script section in the document head, immediately followed by a `window.onerror` statement that assigns the function as the event handler function.

To prevent a Web browser from executing its own error handling functionality, you return a value of true from the `onerror` event handler function, as demonstrated in the following example of the `processErrors()` function:

```
function processErrors() {
    return true;
}
```

NOTE
The `onerror` event handler does not fix errors in your JavaScript programs; its only purpose is to prevent them from being reported by a Web browser and to give you an opportunity to handle them with custom code. Also note that some versions of Internet Explorer ignore the `onerror` event handler if the Disable Script Debugging option is selected on the Advanced tab of the Internet Options dialog box. You display the Internet Options dialog box in Internet Explorer by selecting Internet Options from the Tools menu.

Writing Custom Error Handling Functions

When you specify a custom error handling function by assigning it to the `onerror` event handler, the JavaScript interpreter automatically passes three arguments in the following order to the function for any JavaScript errors that occur: error message, URL, and line number. You can use the values in your custom error handling function by adding parameters to the function definition. You can then use the parameters in your function to point out to a user the location of any JavaScript errors that may occur. For example, the following code shows a modified version of the `processErrors()` function containing parameters which are assigned the three arguments that are passed by the JavaScript interpreter:

```
function processErrors(errMessage, errURL, errLineNum) {
    window.alert("The file " + errLineNum
        + " generated the following error: " + errMessage
        + " on line " + errLineNum);
    return true;
}
window.onerror=processErrors;
```

If you include the preceding code on your Web page, an alert dialog box will be displayed for any JavaScript errors the page contains. The following code displays the alert dialog box shown in Figure 8-18 because the `document.write()` statement is misspelled as `document.wrte()`:

```
<!DOCTYPE html PUBLIC "-//W3C//DTD XHTML 1.0 Strict//EN"
"http://www.w3.org/TR/xhtml1/DTD/xhtml1-strict.dtd">
<html xmlns="http://www.w3.org/1999/xhtml">
<head>
<title>onerror Event Handler</title>
<meta http-equiv="content-type"
content="text/html; charset=iso-8859-1" />
<script type="text/javascript">
/* <![CDATA[ */
function processErrors(errMessage, errURL, errLineNum) {
    window.alert("Error: " + errMessage + "\n"
            + "File: " + errURL + "\n"
            + "Line: " + errLineNum);
    return true;
}
window.onerror=processErrors;
/* ]]> */
</script>
</head>
<body>
<script type="text/javascript">
/* <![CDATA[ */
document.wrte("My name is Don.");
/* ]]> */
</script>
</body>
</html>
```

Figure 8-18

Alert dialog box displayed by a custom error handler function

Additional Debugging Techniques

The rest of this section discusses additional methods and techniques for locating and correcting errors in your JavaScript programs, including checking XHTML elements, analyzing logic, testing statements with JavaScript URLs, and reloading a Web page.

Checking XHTML Elements

There will be occasions when you cannot locate the source of a bug, no matter how long you search. In such cases, the flaw may not lie in your JavaScript code at all, but in your XHTML elements. If you cannot locate a bug using any of the methods described in this chapter, then perform a line-by-line analysis of your XHTML code, making sure that all tags have opening and closing brackets. Also, be sure that all necessary opening and closing tags, such as the

`<script>...</script>` tag pair, are included. Better yet, use the W3C Markup Validation Service to validate your Web page; this is usually much easier than performing a line-by-line analysis.

The following code contains a flawed XHTML element that can cause problems with JavaScript. Examine the code and look for the error, which can be difficult to spot.

```
<!DOCTYPE html PUBLIC "-//W3C//DTD XHTML 1.0 Strict//EN"
"http://www.w3.org/TR/xhtml1/DTD/xhtml1-strict.dtd">
<html xmlns="http://www.w3.org/1999/xhtml">
<head>
<title>Error Example</title>
<meta http-equiv="content-type"
content="text/html; charset=iso-8859-1" />
<script type="text/javascript"
    document.write("<p>Hello World</p>");
</script>
</head>
<body>
<h2>Error Example</h2>
</body>
</html>
```

The problem with the preceding code is that the opening `<script>` element is missing a closing bracket. Without the closing bracket, the browser sees only the script section that you want to include in the head section of the document. Because the contents of the head section are not rendered, you never receive an error message, nor do you see the output from the `document.write()` method. In your debugging efforts, you may think the JavaScript code is not functioning properly when actually it does not function at all. It's worth mentioning again that the W3C Markup Validation Service would have caught this immediately, so validate your Web pages frequently.

Analyzing Logic

At times, errors in JavaScript code stem from logic problems that are difficult to spot using tracing techniques. When you suspect that your code contains logic errors, you must analyze each statement on a case-by-case basis. For example, the following code contains a logic flaw that prevents it from functioning correctly:

```
var displayAlert = false, conditionTrue;
if (displayAlert == true)
    conditionTrue = "condition is true";
    window.alert(conditionTrue);
```

If you were to execute the preceding code, you would always see the alert dialog box, although it should not appear, because the `displayAlert` variable is set to false. However, if you examine the `if` statement more closely, you would see that the `if` statement ends after the declaration of the `conditionTrue` variable. The `window.alert()` method following the variable declaration is not part of the `if` structure, because the `if` statement does not include a set of braces to enclose the lines it executes when the conditional evaluation returns true. The `window.alert()` method also displays the value "undefined". This is because the `conditionTrue` variable was not assigned a value when it was declared in the first statement, and because the statement that assigns a value to the `conditionTrue` variable is bypassed when the `if` statement conditional expression evaluates to false. For the code to execute properly, the `if` statement must include braces as follows:

```
var displayAlert = false, conditionTrue;
if (displayAlert == true) {
    conditionTrue = "condition is true";
    window.alert(conditionTrue);
}
```

The following `for` statement shows another example of an easily overlooked logic error:

```
var count = 0;
for (count = 1; count < 6; ++count);
    document.write(count + "<br />");
```

The preceding code should print the numbers 1 through 5 to the screen. However, the line `for (var count = 1; count < 6; ++count);` contains an ending semicolon, which marks the end of the `for` loop. The loop executes five times and changes the value of `count` to 6, but does nothing else, because there are no statements before its ending semicolon. The line `document.write(count + "<br />");` is a separate statement that executes only once, printing the number 6 to the screen. The code is syntactically correct, but does not function as you anticipated. As you can see from these examples, it is easy to overlook very minor logic errors in your code.

Testing Statements with JavaScript URLs

If you find that the error in your code is the result of a single statement, you can test the statement using a JavaScript URL without rerunning the entire program. A **JavaScript URL** is used for testing and executing JavaScript statements without an XHTML document or JavaScript source file. The syntax for a JavaScript URL is `javascript:statement(s)`. You enter a JavaScript URL into your Web browser's address box, just like a normal URL. When your browser sees the URL's `javascript:` protocol, it executes the JavaScript statements that follow. For example, to display an alert dialog box without executing a script, enter `javascript:window.alert("Hello World")` into your browser Address or Location box. You can include multiple statements in a JavaScript URL if a semicolon separates them. To declare a variable and display its value using an alert dialog box, you use the following statement syntax:

```
javascript:var stringVar="Hello World";window.alert(stringVar)
```

JavaScript URLs are particularly useful if you are trying to construct the correct syntax for a mathematical expression. The following code calculates the total amount due on a mortgage of $100,000. The calculation adds eight percent interest and a $35 late fee. However, the calculation does not function correctly because of an order of precedence problem.

```
mortgageBalance = 100000;
interest = .08;
```

```
lateFees = 35;
document.write(mortgageBalance + lateFees * 1 + interest);
```

Although you can modify the structure of the formula directly within a JavaScript program, you can also use a JavaScript URL to test the calculation. The following statement displays the result of the formula in an alert dialog box, using a JavaScript URL. Parentheses that correct the order of precedence problem have been added to the formula.

```
javascript:mortgageBalance=100000;
interest=.08; lateFees=35;
window.alert((mortgageBalance + lateFees) * (1 + interest));
```

TIP
The preceding code example is broken onto multiple lines due to space limitations in this text. To check code using a JavaScript URL, you must enter the JavaScript code all on one line before pressing Enter.

Reloading a Web Page

When you edit the JavaScript code in a document, it is usually sufficient to save the document and click the Reload or Refresh button in your browser to test your changes. However, it is important to understand that with complex scripts, a Web browser cannot always completely clear its memory of the remnants of an old bug, even though you have fixed the code. Therefore, it is sometimes necessary to close and then reopen the document in your browser. You can also force the reload of a Web page by holding your Shift key and clicking the browser's Reload or Refresh button. At times, however, even reopening the file does not completely clear the browser memory of the old JavaScript code. Instead, you must close the browser window completely and start a new session. You may also find it necessary to delete the frequently visited Web pages that your browser temporarily stores either in your computer's memory or on the hard drive. To delete temporary files in Firefox, select Options from the Tools menu, click the Privacy tab in the Options dialog box, and then click Clear Now. To delete temporary files in Internet Explorer, select Internet Options from the Tools menu, click the General tab, and then click Delete in the Browsing history section. Do not forget to perform these tasks if you are certain that you have fixed an error in your code, but are unable to get your program to perform properly.

Using a `for...in` Statement to Check Object Properties

Sometimes program errors are caused by using the wrong object properties or by assigning the wrong value to an object property. As you learned in Chapter 5, the `for...in` statement is a looping statement that executes the same statement or command block for all of the properties within an object. You can use a `for...in` loop to determine if values are being assigned to the correct properties in an object. This technique is useful when you have an object with many properties, and you cannot trace the cause of incorrect values being assigned to properties. Consider the following constructor function, which creates a `CandyOrder` object:

```
function CandyOrder(customer, candy, boxes) {
    this.customerName = customer;    // customer name
```

```
    this.candyType = candy; // chocolate, caramel, and so on
    this.numBoxes = boxes; // number of boxes ordered
}
```

When you instantiate a new `CandyOrder` object using the statement `var valentinesDay = new CandyOrder("Don", 2, "chocolate");`, you discover that the type of candy is being assigned to the `numBoxes` property, and the number of boxes is being assigned to the `candyType` property. To help trace the problem, you can use the following `for...in` statement to loop through the properties in the `CandyOrder` object and display their values in an alert dialog box:

```
var valentinesDay = new CandyOrder("Don", 2, "chocolate");
var propertiesList = "";
for (prop in valentinesDay) {
    propertiesList += prop + "=" + valentinesDay[prop] + "\n";
}
window.alert(propertiesList);
```

The preceding code creates the dialog box displayed in Figure 8-19.

Figure 8-19

Alert dialog box created
with a `for...in`
statement

From the values listed in the alert box, you can see that the `candyType` and `numBoxes` properties are assigned the wrong values because the argument list in the statement that instantiates the `valentinesDay` object is incorrect. Instead of `var valentinesDay = new CandyOrder ("Don", 2, "chocolate");`, the statement should be `var valentinesDay = new CandyOrder("Don", "chocolate", 2);`. Although this example of using the `for...in` statement to track down property values is fairly simple, it gives you an idea of how to use this technique to locate bugs in the assignment of object properties.

Identifying JavaScript Language and Browser Bugs

If you have tried everything you can think of to fix a bug in your program, consider the possibility that you may be encountering a bug in the JavaScript language or in a specific Web browser. As an example of a bug that exists in Firefox, consider the following statement, which uses the `Window` object's `status` property to write the text "Student Healthcare Services" to the Web browser's status bar:

```
window.status("Student Healthcare Services");
```

Because the `Window` object is the global object, it is technically not necessary to include it in your statements. However, if you exclude the `Window` object, as shown in the following example, Firefox ignores the statement and doesn't generate an error message while Internet Explorer correctly interprets the statement and writes the text to the status bar:

```
status("Student Healthcare Services");
```

Even though Firefox ignores the preceding statement because it does not reference the `Window` object, it does correctly interpret the following statement, which assigns a value to the `defaultStatus` property, even though it also does not reference the `Window` object:

```
defaultStatus("Student Healthcare Services");
```

Unfortunately, there is no comprehensive or official list of JavaScript language bugs. If you suspect that you have encountered a JavaScript language bug or a browser bug, your best bet is to visit the browser vendor's support site. Mozilla's support site is *http://www.mozilla.com/en-US/support/* and Microsoft's support site is *http://msdn.microsoft.com*. Note, however, that the manufacturer of a software program is not always the first to know about a bug in its product. Innovative users often discover bugs first, and then report them to the program creator. These users also usually love to share their bug discoveries with other users. Take advantage of the many JavaScript programmers who are often more than happy to help you solve a problem or track down a bug. You can find help on many different Web sites by searching for "JavaScript" in any search engine.

Chapter Summary

▶ Three types of errors can occur in a program: syntax errors, run-time errors, and logic errors. Syntax errors occur when the interpreter fails to recognize code. Run-time errors occur when the JavaScript interpreter encounters a problem while a program is executing. Logic errors are flaws in a program's design that prevent the program from running as you anticipate.

▶ The first line of defense in locating bugs in JavaScript programs are the error messages you receive when the JavaScript interpreter encounters a syntax or run-time error.

▶ Tracing is the examination of individual statements in an executing program. You can use the `window.alert()`, `document.write()`, and `document.writeln()` methods to trace JavaScript code.

▶ When using `write()` and `writeln()` methods to trace bugs, it is helpful to use a driver program, which is a simplified, temporary program that is used for testing functions and other code.

▶ Another method of locating bugs in a JavaScript program is to transform lines that you think may be causing problems into comments.

▶ Mozilla's debugging tool is called JavaScript Debugger and can be used to debug JavaScript code in Mozilla-based Web browsers including Firefox. Microsoft's debugging tool, called Script Debugger, can be used with Internet Explorer to debug JavaScript code.

▶ The term break mode refers to the temporary suspension of program execution so that you can monitor values and trace program execution.

▶ A breakpoint is a statement in the code at which program execution enters break mode.

▶ The Step Into, Step Over, and Step Out commands on the Debug menus in both JavaScript Debugger and Script Debugger Debug menu allow you to continue program execution after you enter break mode.

▶ JavaScript Debugger includes two views that you can use to trace variables and expressions during the course of program execution: Local Variables and Watches. In Script Debugger, you can use the Command window to monitor variables and expressions in break mode.

▶ The term call stack refers to the order in which procedures, such as functions, methods, or event handlers, execute in a program.

▶ Writing code that anticipates and handles potential problems is often called bulletproofing.

▶ Exception handling allows programs to handle errors as they occur in the execution of a program. The term exception refers to some type of error that occurs in a program.

▶ You execute code that may contain an exception in a `try` statement. You use a `throw` statement to indicate that an error occurred within a `try` block. After you throw an error, you use a `catch` statement to handle, or "catch" the error. A `finally` statement that is included with a `try` statement executes regardless of whether its associated `try` block throws an exception.

▶ JavaScript includes an `onerror` event that executes whenever an error occurs on a Web page. You can combine the `onerror` event with your own custom code for handling any types of errors that occur on a Web page. When you specify a custom error handling function by assigning it to the `onerror` event handler, the JavaScript interpreter automatically passes three arguments in the following order to the function for any JavaScript errors that occur: error message, URL, and line number.

▶ Additional methods and techniques for locating and correcting errors in your JavaScript programs include checking your XHTML elements, analyzing your logic, testing statements with JavaScript URLs, reloading a Web page, using a `for...in` statement to check object properties, and identifying JavaScript language and browser bugs.

Review Questions

1. _____ errors are problems in the design of a program that prevent it from running as you anticipate.

   a. Syntax
   b. Logic
   c. Run-time
   d. Application

2. If the JavaScript interpreter encounters a problem while a program is executing, that problem is called a(n) _____ error.

   a. run-time
   b. logic
   c. application
   d. syntax

3. Which of the following statements causes a syntax error?

   a. `myDate = New Date();`
   b. `document.writeln("Available points: " + availPoints)`
   c. `return salesTotal;`
   d. `window.prompt("Do you really want to submit the form?");`

4. Which of the following functions causes a run-time error?

   a.
   ```
   function calcProfit() {
           var grossProfit = 50000;
           var netProfit = 40000;
           var margin = grossProfit - netProfit;
           var marginPercent = margin / grossProfit;
   }
   ```
   b.
   ```
   function calcProfit() {
           var grossProfit = 60000;
           var netProfit = 50000;
           var margin = grossProfit - netProfit;
           var marginPercent = margin / grossProfit;
   }
   ```
   c.
   ```
   function calcProfit() {
           var grossProfit = 50000;
   ```

```
        var netProfit = 50000;
        var margin = grossProfit - netProfit;
        var marginPercent = margin / grossProfit;
    }
```

d.
```
    function calcProfit() {
        var grossProfit = 20000;
        var netProfit = 30000;
        var margin = grossProfit - netProfit;
        var marginPercent = margin / grossProfit;
    }
```

5. Which of the following `if` statements is logically incorrect?

   a. `if (/\.(com|org|net)$/.test(urlVariable))`
      `    document.write("Invalid URL.");`

   b. `if (/\.(com|org|net)$/.test(urlVariable)) document.write(`
      `    "Invalid URL.");`

   c. `if (/\.(com|org|net)$/.test(urlVariable));`
      `    document.write("Invalid URL.");`

   d. `if (/\.(com|org|net)$/.test(urlVariable)) {`
      `    document.write("Invalid URL.");`
      `}`

6. JavaScript error messages identify the exact location in a document where the error occurred. True or false?

7. Explain the various techniques and tools that you can use to trace the individual statements in an executing program.

8. The following simple form should call a function named `checkEmail()` when the user clicks the Submit button. What is wrong with the function that prevents the function from executing? (Note that there are two possible solutions to this question.)

```
<form action="FormProcessor.html" method="get"
    onsubmit="return checkEmail()">
<p>E-Mail Address<br />
<p><input type="button" value="Submit" /></p>
</form>
```

9. Explain how to use a driver program.

10. Which of the following modes temporarily suspends, or pauses, program execution so that you can monitor values and trace program execution?

    a. Step

    b. Break

    c. Continue

    d. Suspend

11. In most cases, you only need to use future breakpoints in JavaScript Debugger for statements that exist outside of any local functions, such as variable declaration statements or function calls. True or false?

12. Explain how to open a JavaScript document in JavaScript Debugger and Script Debugger, and how to enter break mode.

13. Which of the following commands do you use in Script Debugger to execute the rest of the program normally or until another breakpoint is encountered?

    a. Continue

    b. Run

    c. End

    d. Stop

14. Which command executes all the statements in the next function in both JavaScript Debugger and Script Debugger?

    a. Step

    b. Step Into

    c. Step Out

    d. Step Over

15. What is the purpose of the call stack? How can you use it to debug your JavaScript programs?

16. When and why should you use exception handling with your JavaScript programs?

17. After you throw an error, you use a(n) _____ statement to handle the error.

    a. `exception`

    b. `try`

    c. `catch`

    d. `finally`

18. Which of the following statements assigns a function named `handleProblems()` to handle any JavaScript errors that occur on a page?

    a. `handleProblems(throw);`

    b. `window.onerror=(handleProblems);`

    c. `window.onerror=handleProblems;`

    d. `window.onerror=handleProblems();`

19. Which of the following arguments does the JavaScript interpreter automatically pass to the `onerror` event handler for any JavaScript errors that occur? (Choose all that apply.)

    a. Error number

    b. Error message

    c. Line number

    d. URL

20. Explain how to use at least three additional debugging methods and techniques for locating and correcting errors in your JavaScript programs.

Hands-On Projects

Project 8-1

In this project, you create and fix a script that prints text strings.

1. Create a new document in your text editor.

2. Type the `<!DOCTYPE>` declaration, `<html>` element, header information, and the `<body>` element. Use the strict DTD and "Babe Ruth" as the content of the `<title>` element.

3. Add the following script section to the document body:

```
<script type="text/javascript">
/* <![CDATA[ */
/* ]]> */
</script>
```

4. Add the following statements to the script section:

```
document.write("<p>Babe Ruth was also known as the "Bambino"
      and the "Sultan of Swat".</p>");
```

5. Save the document as **BabeRuth.html** in your Projects folder for Chapter 8, and then open it in your Web browser. You should receive an error message about a missing parenthesis. The problem with the code is that the string in the `document.write()` statement contains nested double quotations. To fix the problem, you need to escape the double quotations with a backslash character.

6. Return to the BabeRuth.html document in your text editor and add escape characters to the string in the `document.write()` statement, as follows:

```
document.write("<p>Babe Ruth was also known as the \"Bambino\"
      and the \"Sultan of Swat\".</p>");
```

7. Save the **BabeRuth.html** document, and then validate the document with the W3C Markup Validation Service. Once the document is valid, close it in your text editor and reload it in your Web browser window. The text should display correctly without any error messages.

8. Close your Web browser window.

Project 8-2

In this project, you will create and fix a script that contains the formula for converting Celsius temperatures to Fahrenheit.

1. Create a new document in your text editor.

2. Type the `<!DOCTYPE>` declaration, `<html>` element, header information, and the `<body>` element. Use the strict DTD and "Convert to Fahrenheit" as the content of the `<title>` element.

3. Add the following script section to the document body:

```
<script type="text/javascript">
/* <![CDATA[ */
/* ]]> */
</script>
```

4. Add to the script section the following declaration for a variable named `cTemp` that represents a Celsius temperature. The variable is assigned a value of 20 degrees.

```
var cTemp = 20;
```

5. Add the following two statements to the end of the script section. The first statement declares a variable named `fTemp` that will store the converted temperature. The right operand includes the formula for converting from Celsius to Fahrenheit. The last statement prints the value assigned to the `fTemp` variable.

```
var cTemp = 20;
var fTemp = 9 / 5 * (cTemp + 32);
document.write("<p>" + cTemp + " degrees Celsius is equal to "
        + fTemp.toFixed(0) + " degrees Fahrenheit.</p>");
```

6. Save the document as **ConvertToFahrenheit.html** in the Projects folder for Chapter 8, and then open it in your Web browser. 20 degrees Celsius is equivalent to 68 degrees Fahrenheit. However, the formula incorrectly calculates that 20 degrees Celsius is equivalent to a value of 94 Fahrenheit. You will need to modify the formula so that it uses the correct order of precedence to convert the temperature.

7. Close your Web browser window and return to the **ConvertToFahrenheit.html** document in your text editor.

8. Modify the order of precedent in the Celsius-to-Fahrenheit formula by adding parentheses as follows:

```
var fTemp = ((9 / 5) * cTemp) + 32;
```

9. Save the document as **ConvertToFahrenheit.html** document, and then validate the document with the W3C Markup Validation Service. Once the document is valid, close it in your text editor, and then open it in your Web browser. The temperature should calculate correctly as 68 degrees Fahrenheit.

10. Close your Web browser window.

Project 8-3

In this project, you will create and fix a document with a simple form that displays the value of a letter grade.

1. Create a new document in your text editor.

2. Type the `<!DOCTYPE>` declaration, `<html>` element, document head, and `<body>` element. Use the Transitional DTD and "Letter Grades" as the content of the `<title>` element.

3. Create a script section in the document head that includes the following `checkGrade()` function and `switch` statement:

```
<script type="text/javascript">
/* <![CDATA[ */
function checkGrade() {
    switch (grade)
            case "A":
                window.alert("Your grade is excellent.";
                break;
            case "B":
                window.alert("Your grade is good.";
                break;
            case "C":
                window.alert("Your grade is fair.";
                break;
            case "D":
                window.alert("You are barely passing.";
                break;
            case "F":
                window.alert("You failed.";
                break;
            default:
                window.alert("Invalid letter!";
    }
/* ]]> */
</script>
```

4. Add the following form to the document body that includes an `onclick` event handler which calls the `checkGrade()` function. The value of the single text box is passed to the `checkGrade()` function.

```
<form action="" enctype="application/x-www-form-urlencoded">
<p><input type="text" name="grade" /><input type="button" value="Check
Grade" onclick="checkGrade(this.value);" /></p>
</form>
```

5. Save the document as **LetterGrades.html** in the Projects folder for Chapter 8, and then open it in your Web browser. You should receive an error message about a missing brace. The problem is that the statements within the `switch` statement are

not contained within braces. Modify the `switch` statement so it includes braces, as follows:

```
switch (grade) {
    case "A":
        window.alert("Your grade is excellent.";
    break;
    case "B":
        window.alert("Your grade is good.";
        break;
    case "C":
        window.alert("Your grade is fair.";
        break;
    case "D":
        window.alert("You are barely passing.";
        break;
    case "F":
        window.alert("You failed.";
        break;
    default:
        window.alert("Invalid letter!";
}
```

6. Save the **LetterGrades.html** document and reload it in your Web browser window. You should receive another error message about a missing closing parenthesis. Each of the `window.alert()` statements in the `switch` statement is missing a closing parenthesis. Add the closing parenthesis to each of the `window.alert()` statements, between the closing quotation and the semicolon.

7. Save the **LetterGrades.html** document and reload it in your Web browser window. You should not receive any more error messages when you reload the page. However, if you enter a grade into the text box and click the Check Grade button, you will see an additional error about "grade" not being defined. This error is caused by the fact that the `checkGrade()` function definition does not include the `grade` parameter, which is used in the `switch` statement to evaluate the letter grade. Add the `grade` parameter to the `checkGrade()` function definition, as follows:

```
function checkGrade(grade) {
    ...
```

8. Save the **LetterGrades.html** document and reload it in your Web browser window. Try entering a valid grade into the text box and clicking the Check Grade button. No matter what value you enter, you will always see the message "Invalid letter!" in the alert box. The cause of this error is the button element, which calls the `checkGrade()` function, and incorrectly passes a value to the function of `this.value`. The value of the grade text box, not the value of the button, must be passed to the `checkGrade()` function. Modify the argument that is passed to the `checkGrade()` function, as follows:

```
onclick="checkGrade(document.forms[0].grade.value);"
```

9. Save the **LetterGrades.html** document, and then validate the document with the W3C Markup Validation Service. Once the document is valid, close it in your text editor and reload it in your Web browser window. The script should now function correctly.

10. Close your Web browser window.

 ## Project 8-4

In this project, you will create a password validation script that uses exception handling and a regular expression to ensure that the password entered by a user is between 6 and 15 characters long, and contains at least one uppercase letter, one lowercase letter, and one numeric digit.

1. Create a new document in your text editor.

2. Type the `<!DOCTYPE>` declaration, `<html>` element, document head, and `<body>` element. Use the Transitional DTD and "Validate Password" as the content of the `<title>` element.

3. Create a script section in the document head that includes the following `validatePassword()` function. The `try` block uses an `if` statement with a regular expression to determine whether an entered password matches the regular expression. The regular expression requires that the password be between 6 and 15 characters long, and contain at least one uppercase letter, one lowercase letter, and one numeric digit. If the password does not match the regular expression, an exception is thrown. The `try` block also uses another `if` statement that determines whether the values in a password field and a password confirmation field match. If not, an exception is also thrown. The `finally` block removes the values that the user entered into the password and password confirmation fields. If the `catch` block does not return a value of false, meaning that no exception was thrown, the final statements in the function print the text "You entered a valid password."

```
function validatePassword(password) {
    try {
        if (document.forms[0].password.value
            != document.forms[0].password_confirm.value)
            throw "You did not enter the same password.";
        else if (!/^(?=.*\d)(?=.*[a-z])(?=.*
            [A-Z]).{6,15}$/.test(password))
            throw "You did not enter a valid password.";
    }
    catch(inputError) {
        window.alert(inputError);
        return false;
    }
    finally {
        document.forms[0].password.value = "";
        document.forms[0].password_confirm.value = "";
```

```
      }
      document.open();
      document.write("<strong>You entered a valid password.
            </strong>");
      document.close();
    }
```

4. Add the following form to the document body. The form contains a password field, a password confirmation field, and a command button that calls the `validatePassword()` function.

```
<form action="" enctype="application/x-www-form-urlencoded">
<p>Password<br />
<input type="password" name="password" /></p>
<p>Confirm Password<br />
<input type="password" name="password_confirm" /></p>
<p><input type="button" value="Validate Password"
onclick="validatePassword(document.forms[0].password.value);" /></p>
</form>
```

5. Save the document as **ValidatePassword.html** in your Projects folder for Chapter 8, and then validate the document with the W3C Markup Validation Service. Once the document is valid, close it in your text editor and then open it in your Web browser and test the code.

6. Close your Web browser window.

Case Projects

After you fix the bugs in the following projects, be sure to validate each document with the W3C Markup Validation Service.

Case Project 8-1

The Cases folder for Chapter 8 on your Data Disk contains copies of some of the programs you created earlier in this text. However, all of the programs contain errors. Use any of the debugging skills you have learned in this section to correct the errors. You may review earlier tutorials to see how the program should function—but do *not* copy or review the correct syntax. Use these exercises as an opportunity to test and improve your debugging skills. The tutorial number in which you created each program is appended to the name of the document. After you fix each document, rename the file by replacing the _Chapter0x portion of the filename with "_Fixed" and save the document. The documents you must correct are:

- ► BondRatings_Chapter03.html
- ► TargetHeartRate_Chapter03.html
- ► Redirect_Chapter04.html
- ► ThanksgivingOrders_Chapter04.html

▶ AutoNextField_Chapter05.html
▶ DigitalClock_Chapter06.html
▶ TipCalculator_Chapter06.html
▶ GuessingGame_Chapter07.html
▶ ToDoList_Chapter07.html

Case Project 8-2

Many Web sites today use "challenge questions" that you can use to reset a forgotten password. Common challenge questions ask you to provide your mother's maiden name, the name of your favorite pet, or the city where you were born. Create a Web page that contains a form with several challenge questions. For challenge questions that require alphabetic answers, such as mother's maiden name, use an `onkeypress` event to call an event handler function. Within the function, use exception handling with a regular expression to prevent users from entering numeric values in fields that require text answers. If a user enters a numeric value in a field that requires a text answer, display an alert dialog box with the text "You can only enter letters into this field" and return a value of false to prevent the character from being entered. Also include challenge question fields that require numeric answers, such as Social Security number and number of siblings. Use the `onkeypress` event with another event handler function to prevent users from entering text values in the fields that require numeric answers. The second function should also use exception handling with a regular expression to prevent users from entering text values in fields that require numeric answers. If a user enters a text value in a field that requires a numeric answer, display an alert dialog box with the text "You can only enter numbers into this field" and return a value of false to prevent the character from being entered. Remember that you need to use different code to retrieve the Unicode character for Internet Explorer and Mozilla-based Web browsers. Save the document as ChallengeQuestions.html in your Cases folder for Chapter 8.

Case Project 8-3

One of the most important aspects of creating a good program is the design and analysis phase of the project. Conducting a good design and analysis phase is critical to minimizing bugs in your program. Search the Internet or your local library for information on this topic. Explain the best way to handle the design and analysis phase of a software project.

Case Project 8-4

Equally important as minimizing bugs during software development is the testing phase. Search the Internet or your local library for information on software testing. Then design a plan for thoroughly testing your JavaScript programs before deploying them on the Web.

9

Managing State Information and Security

In this chapter you will:

- Learn about state information
- Save state information with hidden form fields, query strings, and cookies
- Learn about security issues

The Web was not originally designed to store information about a user's visit to a Web site. However, the ability to store user information, including preferences, passwords, and other data, is now considered essential because it allows you to improve the usability of a Web page. The three most common tools for maintaining state information are hidden form fields, query strings, and cookies, which you study in this chapter. Given the sensitive nature of user information, it's also essential that you have a good understanding of the JavaScript security issues described in this chapter.

Understanding State Information

Hypertext Transfer Protocol (HTTP) manages the hypertext links used to navigate the Web and ensures that Web browsers correctly process and display the various types of information contained in Web pages. Information about individual visits to a Web site is called **state information**. HTTP was originally designed to be **stateless**, which means that Web browsers stored no persistent data about a visit to a Web site. The original stateless design of the Web allowed early Web servers to quickly process requests for Web pages, since they did not need to remember any unique requirements for different clients. Similarly, Web browsers did not need to know any special information to load a particular Web page from a server. Although this stateless design was efficient, it was also limiting; because a Web server could not remember individual user information, the Web browser was forced to treat every visit to a Web page as an entirely new session. This was true regardless of whether the browser had just opened a different Web page on the same server. This design hampered interactivity and limited the amount of personal attention a Web site could provide. Today, there are many reasons for maintaining state information. Among other things, maintaining state information allows a server to:

- Customize individual Web pages based on user preferences.
- Temporarily store information for a user as a browser navigates within a multipart form.

- Allow a user to create bookmarks for returning to specific locations within a Web site.
- Provide shopping carts that store order information.
- Store user IDs and passwords.
- Use counters to keep track of how many times a user has visited a site.

To learn how to maintain state information, you will work on a frame-based Color Printer Product Registration Web page. The Color Printer Product Registration Web page consists of two Web pages: the first page contains a form for recording customer information, and the second page contains a form for recording product information. The documents are already created for you; you can find them in your Chapter folder for Chapter 9. Figure 9-1 shows the Customer Information form and Figure 9-2 shows the Product Information form of the Color Printer Product Registration page.

Figure 9-1

Customer Information form of the Color Printer Product Registration Web page

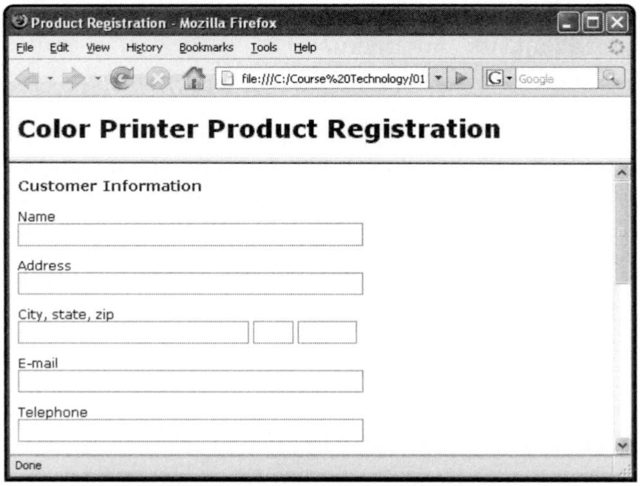

Figure 9-2

Product Information form of the Color Printer Product Registration Web page

The forms are designed so that data entered by the user on both forms can be submitted to a Web server simultaneously. This makes sense because the data collected by both forms are really parts of the same data set; the forms are broken into two Web pages only to make it easier for the user to enter the necessary information. The problem with the Web pages is that if a user moves from the Customer Information page to the Product Information page, the data entered on the Customer Information page is lost. In this chapter you will learn how to save the values entered into the two Web pages by using hidden form fields, query strings, and cookies.

Saving State Information with Hidden Form Fields

A special type of form element, called a **hidden form field**, is not displayed by the Web browser and therefore allows you to hide information from users. You create hidden form fields with the `<input>` element. Hidden form fields temporarily store data that needs to be sent to a server along with the rest of a form, but that a user does not need to see. Examples of data stored in hidden fields include the result of a calculation or some other type of information that a program on the Web server might need. You create hidden form fields using the same syntax used for other fields created with the `<input>` element: `<input type="hidden">`. The only attributes that you can include with a hidden form field are the `name` and `value` attributes.

The following code contains a version of the calculator script you created in Chapter 3. The script has been modified to store and recall numbers using a hidden form field.

```
...
<script type="text/javascript">
/* <![CDATA[ */
var inputString = "";
function updateString(value) {
inputString += value;
document.forms[0].Input.value = inputString;
}
/* ]]> */
</script>
</head><body>
<div style="text-align: center">
<form action="">
<p><input type="text" name="Input" /><br />
<input type="button" name="plus"    value="  +  "
onclick="updateString(' + ')" />
<input type="button" name="minus"   value="  -  "
onclick="updateString(' - ')" />
<input type="button" name="times"   value="  x  "
onclick="updateString(' * ')" />
<input type="button" name="div"     value="  /  "
onclick="updateString(' / ')" />
<input type="button" name="mod" value=" mod "
onclick="updateString(' % ')" /><br />
```

```
<input type="button" name="zero"    value="  0   "
onclick="updateString('0')" />
<input type="button" name="one"     value="  1   "
onclick="updateString('1')" />
<input type="button" name="two"     value="  2   "
onclick="updateString('2')" />
<input type="button" name="three"   value="  3   "
onclick="updateString('3')" />
<input type="button" name="four"    value="  4   "
onclick="updateString('4')" /><br />
<input type="button" name="five"    value="  5   "
onclick="updateString('5')" />
<input type="button" name="six"     value="  6   "
onclick="updateString('6')" />
<input type="button" name="seven"   value="  7   "
onclick="updateString('7')" />
<input type="button" name="eight"   value="  8   "
onclick="updateString('8')" />
<input type="button" name="nine"    value="  9   "
onclick="updateString('9')" /><br />
<input type="button" name="point"   value="  .   "
onclick="updateString('.')" />
<input type="button" name="clear"  value=" clear "
onclick="document.Calculator.Input.value='';
inputString=''" />
<input type="button" name="calc"    value="  =   "
onclick="document.Calculator.Input.value=eval(inputString);
inputString=''" /><br />
<input type="button" name="mem" value=" M +"
onclick="document.forms[0].storedValue.value
= parseInt(document.forms[0].storedValue.value)
+ parseInt(document.forms[0].Input.value)" />
<input type="button" name="recall" value=" MRC " onclick=
"updateString(document.forms[0].storedValue.value)" />
<input type="button" name="memClear" value=" MC "
onclick="document.forms[0].storedValue.value=0" />
<input type="hidden" name="storedValue" value="0" /></p>
</form></div></body></html>
```

The four new elements used to add storage functionality to the script are as follows:

```
<input type="button" name="mem" value=" M +"
onclick="document.forms[0].storedValue.value
= parseInt(document.forms[0].storedValue.value)
+ parseInt(document.forms[0].Input.value)" />
<input type="button" name="recall" value=" MRC " onclick=
"updateString(document.forms[0].storedValue.value)" />
<input type="button" name="memClear" value=" MC "
```

```
onclick="document.forms[0].storedValue.value=0" />
<input type="hidden" name="storedValue" value="0" />
```

The first new button, named mem, adds the value of the Input text box to the value stored in the hidden form field named storedValue. Notice that the mem button's onclick event handler uses two calls to the parseInt() function. Form text fields only store data in the form of text strings. For this reason, you must use the built-in parseInt() function to convert the contents of a text field to an integer. After this conversion, the contents of the text field can be used in a JavaScript calculation. If you do not use the parseInt() function in the mem button's onclick event handler, when you attempt to assign another number to the hidden storedValue field, the new number is concatenated with the contents of the storedValue field, just as when you combine two text fields. The second new button, named recall, retrieves the information stored in the hidden storedValue field and passes it to the updateString() function. The third new button, named memClear, clears the contents of the hidden storedValue field. Figure 9-3 shows how the script appears in a Web browser.

Figure 9-3

Calculator script in a Web browser

TIP
You can also use a global JavaScript variable to add storage functionality to the calculator script.

Next, you add hidden form fields to the Color Printer Product Registration program. These fields will store customer information when the user moves from the Customer Information form to the Product Information form. The Web pages containing the forms are displayed in the bottom frame of a frame-based Web page. The Product Information form is displayed when a user clicks the Next button at the bottom of the Customer Information form. The problem is that once you click the Next button, the values stored in the Customer Information form are lost. To fix this problem, you will add hidden form fields to the top frame (which currently only contains a heading element that reads "Color Printer Product Registration"). When you click the Next button, the values in the Customer Information form fields will be copied into the hidden form fields in the top frame. You will also add a submit button to the Product Information form that will not, in fact, submit the Product Information form to a Web server. Instead, the Submit button will copy the values of the Product Information form's fields into the hidden form fields in the top frame. Then, the form within the top frame will be submitted to the FormProcessor.html document using the Form object's `submit()` method. (The FormProcessor.html document you use in this chapter is the same document you used in Chapter 5 to display the results of submitted forms.) First, you will add the hidden form fields to the top frame.

NOTE
You will not add validation code to the Color Printer Product Registration forms; this way you can focus on the techniques presented in this chapter.

To add the hidden form fields to the top frame of the Color Printer Product Registration frameset:

1. Start your text editor and open the **TopFrame.html** document from the Chapter folder for Chapter 9.

2. Add the following form and hidden form fields above the closing `</body>` tag. The form contains hidden form fields that will store values from both the Customer Information form and the Product Information form. Notice that the form will be submitted to the FormProcessor.html document.

```
<form action="FormProcessor.html" method="get"
enctype="application/x-www-form-urlencoded">
<p><input type="hidden" name="name" />
<input type="hidden" name="address" />
<input type="hidden" name="city" />
<input type="hidden" name="state" />
<input type="hidden" name="zip" />
<input type="hidden" name="email" />
<input type="hidden" name="telephone" />
<input type="hidden" name="platform" />
<input type="hidden" name="quality" value="false" />
<input type="hidden" name="speed" value="false" />
<input type="hidden" name="functions" value="false" />
<input type="hidden" name="price" value="false" />
<input type="hidden" name="design" value="false" />
<input type="hidden" name="comments" />
<input type="hidden" name="location" />
<input type="hidden" name="serial" />
<input type="hidden" name="date" />
<input type="hidden" name="where" /></p>
</form>
```

3. Save the **TopFrame.html** document.

Next, you add code to the Customer Information document that copies its form field values to the hidden form fields in the top frame of the Color Printer Product Registration frameset.

To copy the Customer Information document's form fields to hidden form fields in the top frame of the Color Printer Product Registration frameset:

1. Open the **CustomerInfo.html** document in your Chapter folder for Chapter 9 in your text editor.

2. The form in the CustomerInfo.html document includes a Next button with an `onclick` event handler that calls a function named `nextForm()`. The `nextForm()` function contains a single statement that opens the Product Information document, named ProductInfo.html, using the `href` property of the `Location` object. Add the following statements above the single statement in the `nextForm()` function. The statements use the `parent` property to copy the values of the Customer Information form to the corresponding hidden form fields in the top frame.

```
parent.topframe.document.forms[0].name.value =
    document.forms[0].name.value;
parent.topframe.document.forms[0].address.value =
    document.forms[0].address.value;
parent.topframe.document.forms[0].city.value =
    document.forms[0].city.value;
parent.topframe.document.forms[0].state.value =
    document.forms[0].state.value;
parent.topframe.document.forms[0].zip.value =
    document.forms[0].zip.value;
parent.topframe.document.forms[0].email.value =
    document.forms[0].email.value;
parent.topframe.document.forms[0].telephone.value =
    document.forms[0].telephone.value;
for (var i=0; i<document.forms[0].platform.length; ++i) {
    if (document.forms[0].platform[i].checked == true)
        parent.topframe.document.forms[0].platform.value
            = document.forms[0].platform[i].value;
}
if (document.forms[0].quality.checked == true)
    parent.topframe.document.forms[0].quality.value = true;
if (document.forms[0].speed.checked == true)
    parent.topframe.document.forms[0].speed.value = true;
if (document.forms[0].functions.checked == true)
    parent.topframe.document.forms[0].functions.value = true;
if (document.forms[0].price.checked == true)
    parent.topframe.document.forms[0].price.value = true;
if (document.forms[0].design.checked == true)
    parent.topframe.document.forms[0].design.value = true;
parent.topframe.document.forms[0].location.value =
document.forms[0].location.value;
parent.topframe.document.forms[0].comments.value =
document.forms[0].comments.value;
```

3. Save the **CustomerInfo.html** document.

Next, you add code to the Product Information document that copies its form field values to the hidden form fields in the top frame of the Color Printer Product Registration frameset before submitting the form to the FormProcessor.html document.

To add code to the Product Information document that copies its form field values to the hidden form fields in the top frame of the Color Printer Product Registration frameset:

1. Open the **ProductInfo.html** document in your Chapter folder for Chapter 9.

2. Add a submit button to the end of the form, before the `<input>` element for the reset button, as follows:

```
<p><input type="submit" value="Register Product" />
<input type="reset" /></p>
```

3. Add to the opening `<form>` tag the following `onsubmit` event handler, which calls a function named `submitForm()`:

```
onsubmit="return submitForm()"
```

4. Now add the following `submitForm()` function to the end of the script section in the document head. The statements at the beginning of the function copy the values in the Product Information form to the corresponding hidden form fields in the top frame. The second-to-last statement uses the `Form` object's `submit()` function to submit the form in the top frame to the FormProcessor.html document. (The `action` attribute in the `<form>` element in the top frame is assigned "FormProcessor.html", which submits the top frame's form to the FormProcessor.html document.) Notice that the last statement returns a value of false, which prevents the form in the ProductInfo.html document from submitting its data.

```
function submitForm() {
    parent.topframe.document.forms[0].serial.value =
        document.forms[0].serial.value;
    parent.topframe.document.forms[0].date.value =
        document.forms[0].date.value;
    if (document.forms[0].where[0].checked == true)
        parent.topframe.document.forms[0].where.value
            = document.forms[0].where[0].value;
    if (document.forms[0].where[1].checked == true)
        parent.topframe.document.forms[0].where.value
            = document.forms[0].where[1].value;
    if (document.forms[0].where[2].checked == true)
        parent.topframe.document.forms[0].where.value
            = document.forms[0].where[2].value;
    if (document.forms[0].where[3].checked == true)
        parent.topframe.document.forms[0].where.value
            = document.forms[0].where[3].value;
    parent.topframe.document.forms[0].submit();
    return false;
}
```

5. Save the **ProductInfo.html** document and then open the **ProductRegistration.html** document in a Web browser. Enter some data into the Customer Information form fields and click the **Next** button. Then, enter some data into the Product Information form fields and click the **Register Product** button. The FormProcessor.html document should open and display the data you entered.

6. Close your Web browser window.

Saving State Information with Query Strings

One way to preserve information following a user's visit to a Web page is to append a query string to the end of a URL. A **query string** is a set of name=value pairs appended to a target URL. It consists of a single text string containing one or more pieces of information. You can use a query string to pass information, such as search criteria, from one Web page to another.

Passing Data with a Query String

To pass data from one Web page to another using a query string, add a question mark (?) immediately after a URL, followed by the query string (in name=value pairs) for the information you want to preserve. In this manner, you are passing information to another Web page, similar to the way you can pass arguments to a function or method. You separate individual name=value pairs within the query string using ampersands (&). The following code provides an example of an <a> element that contains a query string consisting of three name=value pairs:

```
<a href="http://www.URL.com/TargetPage.html?firstName=Don
&lastName=Gosselin&occupation=writer">Link Text</a>
```

The passed query string is then assigned to the search property of the target Web page Location object. The search property of the Location object contains a URL's query or search parameters. For the preceding example, after the TargetPage.html document opens, the query string "?firstName=Don&lastName=Gosselin&occupation=writer" is available as the value of the search property of the Location object.

NOTE

The search property of the Location object gets its name from the fact that many Internet search engines use the query string it contains to store search criteria.

Next, you modify the Color Printer Product Registration page so the registration information is passed as query strings instead of being stored in hidden form fields. First, you will modify the TopFrame.html document.

To modify the TopFrame.html document so the registration information is passed as query strings instead of being stored in hidden form fields:

1. Return to the **TopFrame.html** document in your text editor.

2. Delete the form containing the hidden form fields. You do not need the form because the data will be saved in a query string.

3. Save the **TopFrame.html** document and validate it with the W3C Markup Validation Service. Once the document is valid, close it in your text editor.

Next, you modify the CustomerInfo.html document.

To modify the CustomerInfo.html document so the registration information is passed as query strings instead of being stored in hidden form fields:

1. Return to the **CustomerInfo.html** document in your text editor.

2. Replace all of the statements in the nextForm() function with the following code, which builds the query string using each form element name and value in a variable named savedData. The name of each form element is entered as a literal string and concatenated with the value property of each element, using the + and += assignment operators. All the name=value pairs are concatenated into a single string that is assigned to the savedData variable. Notice that each name=value pair is separated by an ampersand. The last statement appends a question mark along with the savedData query string to the ProductInfo.html URL that is assigned to the href property of the Location object.

```
var savedData;
savedData = "name=" + document.forms[0].name.value;
savedData += "&address=" + document.forms[0].address.value;
savedData += "&city=" + document.forms[0].city.value;
savedData += "&state=" + document.forms[0].state.value;
savedData += "&zip=" + document.forms[0].zip.value;
savedData += "&email=" + document.forms[0].email.value;
savedData += "&telephone=" + document.forms[0].telephone.value;
for (var i=0; i<document.forms[0].platform.length; ++i) {
        if (document.forms[0].platform[i].checked == true)
                savedData += "&platform="
                        + document.forms[0].platform[i].value;
}
if (document.forms[0].quality.checked == true)
    savedData += "&quality=true";
if (document.forms[0].speed.checked == true)
    savedData += "&speed=true";
if (document.forms[0].functions.checked == true)
    savedData += "&functions=true";
if (document.forms[0].price.checked == true)
    savedData += "&price=true";
if (document.forms[0].design.checked == true)
    savedData += "&design=true";
savedData += "&location=" + document.forms[0].location.value;
```

```
savedData += "&comments=" + document.forms[0].comments.value;
location.href="ProductInfo.html" + "?" + savedData;
```

3. Save the **CustomerInfo.html** document.

Finally, you will modify the ProductInfo.html document.

To modify the ProductInfo.html document so the registration information is passed as query strings instead of being stored in hidden form fields:

1. Return to the **ProductInfo.html** document in your text editor.

2. Delete all of the statements in the submitForm() function. Then, add the following code, which creates a new savedData variable.

```
var savedData = location.search;
savedData += "&serial=" + document.forms[0].serial.value;
savedData += "&date=" + document.forms[0].date.value;
if (document.forms[0].where[0].checked == true)
    savedData += "&where=retail";
else if (document.forms[0].where[1].checked == true)
    savedData += "&where=catalog_mail";
else if (document.forms[0].where[2].checked == true)
    savedData += "&where=internet";
else if (document.forms[0].where[3].checked == true)
    savedData += "&where=other";
```

3. You cannot use a form's submit event to send a query string to a URL on the Web server because the form's own data is appended to the URL, and not to the query string you want to submit. In other words, if you submit the Product Information form, only the fields on the Product Information form (serial number, purchase date, and place of purchase) are appended to the FormProcessor.html document. Therefore, you need to replace the Submit button that calls the submitForm() event with an <input> button. This way, the query string you append to the URL is submitted to the FormProcessor.html document instead of the form data. Delete the onsubmit event handler in the opening <form> tag. Then, replace the Submit button with the following <input> button:

```
<input type="button" value="Register Product"
onclick="submitForm();" />
```

4. Finally, add the following statement to the end of the submitForm() function. The statement uses the top property to replace the main frameset document with a document named Register.html, which you will create shortly. The query string is appended to the URL.

```
top.location.href = "Register.html" + savedData;
```

5. Save the **ProductInfo.html** document.

Before you test the code, you need to create the Register.html document. You'll do that next, when you learn to manipulate strings.

Parsing Data from a Query String

For a Web page to use the information in a query string, your JavaScript program must first parse the string, using a combination of several methods and the length property of the String object. (This is also true when you want to use data contained in a cookie. You'll learn about cookies later in this chapter.) The first parsing task is to remove the question mark at the start of the query string, using the substring() method combined with the length property. As you recall from Chapter 7, the substring() method takes two arguments: a starting index number and an ending index number. The first character in a string has an index number of 0, similar to the first element in an array. Because you want to exclude the first character of the string (the question mark), which has an index of 0, you use a starting index of 1. For the ending index number, you use the length property, which tells the substring() method to include the rest, or length, of the string. The following code assigns the search property of the Location object to a variable named queryData and uses the substring() method and length property to remove the starting question mark:

```
// Assigns the query string to the queryData variable
var queryData = location.search;
// Removes the opening question mark from the string
queryData = queryData.substring(1, queryData.length);
```

The next step is to convert the individual pieces of information in the queryData variable into array elements using the split() method. You pass to the split() method the character that separates each individual piece of information in a string. In this case, you will pass the ampersand character, because that is the character that separates the name=value pairs in the query string. However, keep in mind that you can split a string at any character. The code to convert the information in the queryData variable into an array named queryArray[] is as follows:

```
// splits queryData into an array
var queryArray = queryData.split("&");
```

The following code shows a completed version of the parsing script that uses a for loop to print the values in queryArray[]:

```
// Assigns the query string to the queryData variable
var queryData = location.search;
// Removes the opening question mark from the string
queryData = queryData.substring(1, queryData.length);
// splits queryData into an array
var queryArray = queryData.split("&");
for (var i=0; i<queryArray.length; ++i) {
    document.write(queryArray[i] + "<br />");
}
```

Figure 9-4 shows the output in a Web browser when the location.search property in the preceding code contains the following string value:

```
?firstName=Don&lastName=Gosselin&occupation=writer
```

Figure 9-4

Parsing script in a Web browser

In the past few chapters, you used the FormProcessor.html document to display the results of submitted forms. The FormProcessor.html document has only two purposes: to display form data and to provide a simple simulation of the response you would normally receive from a program on a Web server created with a server-side scripting language. The FormProcessor.html document contains JavaScript that uses parsing techniques to read the query string containing form data that is attached to a URL. The query string is attached to the URL when the form is submitted.

Next, you write your own parsing script that extracts and displays the data in the query string. This script is similar to a server-side scripting program you might write to extract data from a query string. The difference is that, instead of being stored in a database or used in some sort of operation, the data is instead displayed on a Web page.

To create a parsing script:

1. Create a new document in your text editor.

2. Type the `<!DOCTYPE>` declaration, `<html>` element, document head, and document body. Use the strict DTD and "Register" as the content of the `<title>` element.

3. Add the following statements to the document body:

    ```
    <h2>Your product registration has been received.</h2>
    <p><strong>You entered the following data:</strong></p>
    ```

4. Add the following script section to the end of the document body:

    ```
    <script type="text/javaScript">
    /* <![CDATA[ */
    /* ]]> */
    </script>
    ```

5. Add the following statement to the script section. This statement assigns the query string in the `Location` object's `search` property to a variable named `formData`.

    ```
    var formData = location.search;
    ```

6. Add the following statement to the end of the script section, which uses the `substring()` method combined with the `length` property to remove the question mark at the start of the query string:

    ```
    formData = formData.substring(1, formData.length);
    ```

7. Now add the following statement. This statement contains a `split()` method, which separates the name=value pairs in the query string into the elements of an array named `formArray[]`.

```
var formArray = formData.split("&");
```

8. Finally, add the following `for` loop, which prints the name=value pairs in the elements of `formArray[]`.

```
for (var i=0; i < formArray.length; ++i) {
    document.write(formArray[i] + "<br />");
}
```

9. Save the document as **Register.html** in your Chapter folder for Chapter 9.

10. Open **ProductRegistration.html** in your Web browser. Enter some data into the Customer Information form fields and click the **Next** button. Then enter some data into the Product Information form fields and click the **Register Product** button. The Register.html document should open and display the data you entered, as shown in Figure 9-5.

Figure 9-5

Data submitted to Register.html

NOTE

The %20 characters in the fields in Figure 9-5 are encoded characters. You will learn about encoded characters in the next section.

11. Close your Web browser window.

Saving State Information with Cookies

Query strings do not permanently maintain state information. The information contained in a query string is available only during the current session of a Web page. Once a Web page that reads a query string closes, the query string is lost. Hidden form fields maintain state information between Web pages, but the data they contain are also lost once the Web page that reads the hidden fields closes. You can save the contents of a query string or hidden form fields by submitting the form data using a server-side scripting language, but that method requires a separate server-based application. To make it possible to store state information beyond the current Web page session, Netscape created cookies. **Cookies** are small pieces of information about a user that are stored by a Web server in text files on the user's computer. The W3C DOM defines cookie specifications.

Each time the Web client visits a Web server, saved cookies for the requested Web page are sent from the client to the server. The server then uses the cookies to customize the Web page for the client. Cookies were originally created for use with CGI scripts, but are now commonly used by JavaScript and other scripting languages.

You have probably seen cookies in action if you have ever visited a Web site where you entered a username in a prompt dialog box or in a text field, and then found that you were greeted by that username the next time you visited the Web site. This could occur with each subsequent visit to the same Web site, whether during the same browser session or during a different browser session days or weeks later. The Web page remembers this information by storing it locally on your computer in a cookie. Another example of a cookie is a counter that counts the number of times an individual user has visited a Web site.

Cookies can be temporary or persistent. **Temporary cookies** remain available only for the current browser session. **Persistent cookies** remain available beyond the current browser session and are stored in a text file on a client computer. In this section, you will create both persistent and temporary cookies.

There are a number of limitations on the use of cookies that are enforced by Web browsers. Each individual server or domain can store only a maximum of 20 cookies on a user's computer. In addition, the total cookies per browser cannot exceed 300, and the largest cookie size is 4 kilobytes. If these limits are exceeded, a Web browser may start discarding older cookies.

Creating Cookies

You use the `cookie` property of the `Document` object to create cookies in name=value pairs, the same way you used name=value pairs with a query string. The syntax for the `cookie` property is as follows:

```
document.cookie = name + value;
```

The cookie property is created with a required `name` attribute and four optional attributes: `expires`, `path`, `domain`, and `secure`.

The *name* Attribute

The only required parameter of the `cookie` property is the `name` attribute, which specifies the cookie's name=value pair. Cookies created with only the `name` attribute are temporary cookies, because they are available for only the current browser session. The following code creates a cookie with a name=value pair of "firstName=Don":

```
document.cookie = "firstName=" + "Don";
```

The `cookie` property of the `Document` object can be confusing. For other JavaScript properties, assigning a new value to a property *replaces* the old value. In contrast, assigning a new value to the `cookie` property builds a list of cookies, rather than replaces the last value. The following example builds a list of cookies:

```
document.cookie = "firstName=" + "Don";
document.cookie = "lastName=" + "Gosselin";
document.cookie = "occupation=" + "writer";
```

A Web browser automatically separates each name=value pair in the `cookie` property with a semicolon and a space. Therefore, the value assigned to the `cookie` property for the preceding cookies contains the following value:

```
firstName=Don; lastName=Gosselin; occupation=writer
```

By default, cookies themselves cannot include semicolons or other special characters, such as commas or spaces. Cookies cannot include special characters because they are transmitted between Web browsers and Web servers using HTTP, which does not allow certain nonalphanumeric characters to be transmitted in their native format. However, you can use special characters in your cookies if you use **encoding**, which involves converting special characters in a text string to their corresponding hexadecimal ASCII value, preceded by a percent sign. For example, 20 is the hexadecimal ASCII equivalent of a space character, and 25 is the hexadecimal ASCII equivalent of a percent sign (%). In URL encoded format, each space character is represented by %20, and each percent sign is represented by %25. After encoding, the contents of the string "tip=A standard tip is 15%" would read as follows:

```
tip=A%20standard%20tip%20is%2015%25
```

The built-in **encodeURIComponent() function** is used in JavaScript for encoding the individual parts of a URI. More specifically, the `encodeURIComponent()` function converts special characters in the individual parts of a URI to their corresponding hexadecimal ASCII value, preceded by a percent sign. The syntax for the `encodeURIComponent()` function is `encodeURIComponent(text);`. The `encodeURIComponent()` function does not encode standard alphanumeric characters such as A, B, C, or 1, 2, 3, or any of the following special characters: - _ . ! ~ * ' ( ). It also does not encode the following characters which have special meaning in a URI: ; / ? : @ & = + $,. For example, the / character is not encoded because it is used for designating a path on a file system. When you read a cookie or other text string encoded with the `encodeURIComponent()` function, you must first decode it with the **decodeURIComponent() function**. The syntax for the `decodeURIComponent()` function is `decodeURIComponent(text);`. The following code encodes several cookies with the `encodeURIComponent()` function and assigns them to the `cookie` property of the `Document` object:

```
document.cookie = "firstName=" + encodeURIComponent("Don");
document.cookie = "lastName=" + encodeURIComponent("Gosselin");
document.cookie = "occupation=" + encodeURIComponent("writer");
```

TIP

JavaScript also includes the `encodeURI()` and `decodeURI()` functions, which can be used to encode and decode entire URIs. Be sure to distinguish these functions from the `encodeURIComponent()` and `decodeURIComponent()` functions, which encode and decode the individual parts of a URI.

If you transmit a URI containing spaces from recent Web browsers (including Firefox and Internet Explorer), the Web browser automatically encodes the spaces for you before transmitting the cookie. However, special characters such as the percent sign are not automatically encoded. This can cause problems with older browsers and Web servers that do not recognize certain special characters unless they are encoded. Additionally, older Web browsers do not automatically encode spaces in URIs. For these reasons, you should manually encode and decode cookies using the `encodeURIComponent()` and `decodeURIComponent()` functions if you anticipate that your scripts will run in older Web browsers.

NOTE

Older versions of JavaScript use the deprecated `escape()` and `unescape()` methods for encoding and decoding text strings.

Next, you modify the Customer Information form so its fields are saved in temporary cookies instead of in query strings.

To modify the Customer Information form so its fields are saved in temporary cookies instead of in query strings:

1. Return to the **CustomerInfo.html** document in your text editor.

2. Delete the first statement in the `nextForm()` function that declares the `savedData` variable.

3. Next, in each of the lines that builds the `savedData` variable, replace the `savedData +=` portion with **document.cookie =**. Also, remove the ampersands (&) from the name portion of each name=value pair and encode each of the values that are assigned as cookies using the `encodeURIComponent()` method. Finally, delete the portions of the `location.href` statement that append the query string, so that it reads **location.href = "ProductInfo.html";**. The modified `nextForm()` function should appear as follows:

```
document.cookie = "name=" + encodeURIComponent(
    document.forms[0].name.value);
document.cookie = "address=" + encodeURIComponent(
    document.forms[0].address.value);
document.cookie = "city=" + encodeURIComponent(
    document.forms[0].city.value);
document.cookie = "state=" + encodeURIComponent(
```

```
        document.forms[0].state.value);
document.cookie = "zip=" + encodeURIComponent(
        document.forms[0].zip.value);
document.cookie = "email=" + encodeURIComponent(
        document.forms[0].email.value);
document.cookie = "telephone=" + encodeURIComponent(
        document.forms[0].telephone.value);
for (var i=0; i<document.forms[0].platform.length; ++i) {
        if (document.forms[0].platform[i].checked == true)
                document.cookie = "platform=" +
encodeURIComponent(document.forms[0].platform[i].value);
}
if (document.forms[0].quality.checked == true)
        document.cookie = "quality=" + encodeURIComponent("true");
if (document.forms[0].speed.checked == true)
        document.cookie = "speed=" + encodeURIComponent("true");
if (document.forms[0].functions.checked == true)
        document.cookie = "functions=" + encodeURIComponent("true");
if (document.forms[0].price.checked == true)
        document.cookie = "price=" + encodeURIComponent("true");
if (document.forms[0].design.checked == true)
        document.cookie = "design=" + encodeURIComponent("true");
document.cookie = "location=" + encodeURIComponent(
        document.forms[0].location.value);
document.cookie = "comments=" +
encodeURIComponent(document.forms[0].comments.value);
location.href="ProductInfo.html";
```

4. Save the **CustomerInfo.html** document. Before you can open the Color Printer Product Registration document, you need to learn how to read cookies.

Before you learn how to read cookies, you will learn about other cookie parameters.

The *expires Attribute*

For a cookie to persist beyond the current browser session, you must use the expires attribute of the cookie property. The **expires attribute** of the cookie property determines how long a cookie can remain on a client system before it is deleted. Cookies created without an expires attribute are available for only the current browser session. The syntax for assigning the expires attribute to the cookie property, along with an associated name=value pair, is expires=*date*. The name=value pair and the expires=*date* pair are separated by a semicolon. The *date* portion of the expires attribute must be a text string in Coordinated Universal Time (usually abbreviated as UTC) format as follows:

```
Weekday Mon DD HH:MM:SS Time Zone YYYY
```

The following is an example of Coordinated Universal Time:

```
Mon Dec 27 14:15:18 PST 2008
```

NOTE
Coordinated Universal Time is also known as Greenwich Mean Time (GMT), Zulu time, and world time.

Be sure not to encode the `expires` attribute using the `encodeURIComponent()` method. JavaScript does not recognize a UTC date when it is in URI-encoded format. If you use the `encodeURIComponent()` method with the `expires` attribute, JavaScript is not able to set the cookie expiration date.

You can manually type a string in UTC format, or you can create the string with the `Date` object, which automatically creates the string in UTC format. (You first learned about the `Date` object in Chapter 6.) To use a `Date` object with the `expires` attribute, you specify the amount of time you want a cookie to be valid by using a combination of the "set" and "get" methods of the `Date` object. The following statement declares a `Date` object named `cookieDate`, and then changes the date portion of the new object using the `setDate()` and `getDate()` methods. Notice that you can nest `Date` object methods inside other `Date` object methods. In the example, the `setDate()` method sets the date portion of `cookieDate` by using the `getDate()` method to retrieve the date, and adding seven to increase the date by one week. You might use a cookie that expires after one week (or less) to store data that needs to be maintained for a limited amount of time. For example, a travel agency may store data in a cookie that temporarily holds a travel reservation that expires after a week.

```
cookieDate.setDate(myDate.getDate() + 7);
```

After you create a `Date` object and specify the date you want the cookie to expire, you must use the `toUTCString()` method to convert the `Date` object to a string, formatting it in Coordinated Universal Time. The following code creates a new cookie and assigns an expiration date one year from now. Before the `expires` attribute is assigned to the `cookie` property, the `Date` object uses the `toUTCString()` method to convert the date to a string in Coordinated Universal Time.

```
var expiresDate = new Date();
expiresDate.setFullYear(expiresDate.getFullYear() + 1);
document.cookie = "firstName=" + encodeURIComponent("Don") + "; expires="
    + expiresDate.toUTCString();
```

When developing a JavaScript program, you may accidentally create, but not delete, persistent cookies that your program does not need. Unused persistent cookies can sometimes interfere with the execution of a JavaScript cookie program. For this reason, it's a good idea to delete your browser cookies periodically, especially while developing a JavaScript program that uses cookies. To delete cookies in Firefox, select Options from the Tools menu, select the Privacy tab in the Options dialog box, and then click the Clear Now button. Select the Cookies check box and click Clear Private Data Now. To delete cookies in Internet Explorer, select Internet Options from the Tools menu, click the General tab of the Internet Options dialog box, and then click the Delete button. In the Delete Browsing History dialog box, select Delete cookies and select Yes when prompted.

CHAPTER 9

Next, you will add to the ProductInfo.html document a persistent cookie named `registered` that is assigned a value of true when the user clicks the Submit button. The cookie will be used to determine whether a user has already submitted the product registration information if he or she opens the ProductRegistration.html document again.

To add a persistent cookie to the ProductInfo.html document:

1. Return to the **ProductInfo.html** in your text editor.

2. Add the following statements to the end of the `submitForm()` function, but above the statement that assigns the Register.html document and the query string to the `href` property of the `Location` object. These statements create a cookie named `registered`. The cookie `registered` is assigned a value of true and is set to expire in one year.

   ```
   var expiresDate = new Date();
   expiresDate.setFullYear(expiresDate.getFullYear() + 1);
   document.cookie = "registered=" + encodeURIComponent(true)
   + ";expires=" + expiresDate.toUTCString();
   ```

3. Save **ProductInfo.html** document. Although the document saves the cookie, you need to learn how to read cookies with JavaScript before you can write code that determines whether the user has already submitted product registration information. You will learn how to read cookies later in this section.

The path Attribute

The **path attribute** determines the availability of a cookie to other Web pages on a server. The `path` attribute is assigned to the `cookie` property, along with an associated name=value pair, using the syntax `path=path name`. By default, a cookie is available to all Web pages in the same directory. However, if you specify a path, then a cookie is available to all Web pages in the specified path as well as to all Web pages in all subdirectories in the specified path. For example, the following statement makes the cookie named `firstName` available to all Web pages located in the /marketing directory or any of its subdirectories:

```
document.cookie = "firstName=" + encodeURIComponent("Don"
    + ";path=/marketing");
```

To make a cookie available to all directories on a server, use a slash to indicate the root directory, as in the following example:

```
document.cookie = "firstName=" + encodeURIComponent("Don"
    + ";path=/");
```

When you are developing JavaScript programs that create cookies, your programs may not function correctly if the directory containing your Web page contains other programs that create cookies. Cookies from other programs that are stored in the same directory along with unused cookies you created during development can cause your JavaScript cookie program to run erratically. Therefore, it is a good idea to always place JavaScript cookie programs in their own directory and use the `path` attribute to specify any subdirectories your program requires.

The domain Attribute

Using the path attribute allows cookies to be shared across a server. Some Web sites, however, are very large and use a number of servers. The **domain attribute** is used for sharing cookies across multiple servers in the same domain. Note that you cannot share cookies outside of a domain. The domain attribute is assigned to the cookie property, along with an associated name=value pair, using the syntax domain=*domain name*. For example, if the Web server programming.gosselin.com needs to share cookies with the Web server writing.gosselin.com, the domain attribute for cookies set by programming.gosselin.com should be set to .gosselin.com. That way, cookies created by programming.gosselin.com are available to writing.gosselin.com and to all other servers in the domain gosselin.com.

The following code shows how to make a cookie at programming.gosselin.com available to all servers in the gosselin.com domain:

```
document.cookie = "firstName=" + encodeURIComponent("Don"
    + ";domain=.gosselin.com";
```

The secure Attribute

Internet connections are not always considered safe for transmitting sensitive information. It is possible for unscrupulous people to steal personal information, such as credit card numbers, passwords, Social Security numbers, and other types of private information online. To protect private data transferred across the Internet, Netscape developed Secure Sockets Layer, or SSL, to encrypt data and transfer it across a secure connection. The URLs for Web sites that support SSL usually start with the HTTPS protocol instead of HTTP. The **secure attribute** indicates that a cookie can only be transmitted across a secure Internet connection using HTTPS or another security protocol. Generally when working with client-side JavaScript, the secure attribute should be omitted. However, if you wish to use this attribute, you assign it to the cookie property with a Boolean value of true or false, along with an associated name=value pair, using the syntax secure=*boolean value*. For example, to activate the secure attribute for a cookie, you use a statement similar to the following:

```
document.cookie = "firstName=" + encodeURIComponent("Don"
    + ";secure=true";
```

Reading Cookies

So far, you have stored both temporary and persistent cookies. Next, you need to learn how to retrieve stored cookie values. The cookies for a particular Web page are available in the cookie property of the Document object. Cookies consist of one continuous string that must be parsed before the data they contain can be used. To parse a cookie, you must:

1. Decode it using the decodeURIComponent() function.
2. Use the methods of the String object to extract individual name=value pairs.

To give you an idea of what is involved in extracting data from cookies, the following code creates three encoded cookies, then reads them from the cookie property and decodes them. The split() method is then used to copy each name=value pair into the elements of an array named cookieArray[].

```
document.cookie = "city=" + encodeURIComponent("Boston");
document.cookie = "team=" + encodeURIComponent("Red Sox");
document.cookie = "sport=" + encodeURIComponent("baseball");
var cookieString = decodeURIComponent(document.cookie);
var cookieArray = cookieString.split("; ");
```

Notice that the split() method in the preceding code splits the cookies using two characters: a semicolon and a space. Recall that when you assign a name=value pair to the cookie property of the Document object, JavaScript automatically separates cookies with a semicolon and space. If you do not include the space in the split() method, then the name portion of each name=value pair in the new array has an extra space before it. Once you split the cookies into separate array elements, you still need to determine which cookie holds the value you need. The following for loop cycles through each element in the array and uses an if statement and several string methods to check if the name portion of each name=value pair is equal to *team*. The conditional expression in the if statement uses the substring() method to return the name portion of the name=value pair in the variable named yourTeam. The first argument in the substring() method specifies the starting point of the substring as the first character (0). The second argument in the substring() method is the indexOf() method appended to the yourTeam variable, which returns the index number of the equal sign. If the substring is equal to *team*, then the for loop ends using a break statement, and the text *Your team* is written to the browser along with the value portion of the name=value pair. The statements that return the value portion of the name=value pair also use the substring() method along with the indexOf() method. However, this time the first argument starts the substring at the index number of the equal sign plus one, which is the character following the equal sign. The second argument in the substring() method specifies the ending point of the substring to be the length of the data variable.

```
var yourTeam;
for (var count = 0; count < 3; ++count) {
    yourTeam = cookieArray[count];
    if (yourTeam.substring(0,yourTeam.indexOf("="))
        == "team") {
        document.writeln("Your team is the "
        + yourTeam.substring(yourTeam.indexOf("=") + 1,
            yourTeam.length));
        break;
    }
}
```

The preceding code is a little difficult to understand at first. If you are having trouble understanding how to manipulate strings, try experimenting with different string methods and see what you come up with. Using string methods to parse a cookie is the only way to extract individual pieces of information from a long cookie string, so it is important that you understand how they work.

Next, you will modify the code in the ProductInfo.html document so it does not refer to the query string that was originally passed from the CustomerInfo.html document.

To modify the code in the ProductInfo.html document so it does not refer to the query string that was originally passed from the CustomerInfo.html document:

1. Return to the **ProductInfo.html** document in your text editor.

2. Delete the following first statement in the `submitForm()` function. You no longer need this statement because the CustomerInfo.html document now stores persistent data in cookies instead of with a query string.

    ```
    var savedData = location.search;
    ```

3. Replace the statement that saves the serial number to the `savedData` variable with the following statement. This version of the statement now includes a `var` keyword and appends the name=value pair for the serial number to a question mark, which is necessary because the serial number will now be the first name=value pair in the query string.

    ```
    var savedData = "?serial=" + document.forms[0].serial.value;
    ```

4. Save **ProductInfo.html** and validate it with the W3C Markup Validation Service. Once the document is valid, close it in your text editor.

Next, you need to add code to the Register.html document that reads and prints the contents of the cookies from the CustomerInfo.html document.

To add code to the Register.html document that reads and prints the contents of the cookie:

1. Return to the **Register.html** document in your text editor.

2. Add the following statements to the beginning of the script section. The first statement decodes the cookie with the `decodeURIComponent()` method and assigns the decoded value to a variable named `cookieData`. The second statement uses the `split()` method to create an array named `cookieArray[]` that contains the name=value pairs in the `cookieData` variable. The `for` statement then prints each of the values in the array.

    ```
    var cookieData = decodeURIComponent(document.cookie);
    var cookieArray = cookieData.split("; ");
    for (var i=0; i < cookieArray.length; ++i) {
        document.write(cookieArray[i] + "<br />");
    }
    ```

3. Save the **Register.html** document and validate it with the W3C Markup Validation Service. Once the document is valid, close it in your text editor. Open the **ProductRegistration.html** document in your Web browser. Enter some data into the Customer Information form fields and click the **Next** button. Then, enter some data into the Product Information form fields and click the **Register Product** button. The Register.html document should open and display the data for both the customer information form and the product information form.

4. Close your Web browser window.

Next, you modify the CustomerInfo.html document so it reads the persistent registered cookie to determine whether the user has already submitted the product registration. If so, a confirmation dialog box prompts the user to select whether he or she wants to reregister the product. If the user selects Cancel, some text is written to the Web browser window thanking the user for registering the color printer.

To modify the CustomerInfo.html document so it reads the persistent registered cookie:

1. Return to the **CustomerInfo.html** document in your text editor.

2. Add the following checkRegistration() function to the script section. This function will be called by the document onload event handler in the opening <body> tag. First, the cookie is decoded with the decodeURIComponent() method and assigned to a variable named registrationCheck. Next, the function uses the split() method to split the cookie into an array named regValue[].The if statement then checks the value in the second element of the regValue[] array. If the element contains a value of true, a confirm dialog box prompts the user to choose whether he or she wants to register another printer. If the user selects the OK button in the confirm dialog box, the function ends and the user is returned to the CustomerInfo.html document. However, if the user selects the Cancel button, then "Thank you for registering your color printer!" is printed to the document window.

```
function checkRegistration() {
    if (document.cookie) {
        var registrationCheck
            = decodeURIComponent(document.cookie);
        var regValue = registrationCheck.split("=");
        if (regValue[1] == "true") {
            var registerAgain = window.confirm(
                "You have already registered
                your color printer! Do you want to
                register another printer?");
            if (registerAgain == false) {
                document.open();
                document.write("<p>Thank you for
                    registering your color
                    printer!</p>");
                document.close();
            }
        }
    }
}
```

3. Add the following onload event handler to the opening <body> element, which calls the checkRegistration() function:

```
<body onload="checkRegistration()">
```

4. Save the **CustomerInfo.html** document and validate it with the W3C Markup Validation Service. Once the document is valid, close it in your text editor. Open the **ProductRegistration.html** document in your Web browser. If you submitted data to the Register.html document in the last exercise, you should see the confirm dialog box. Select **Cancel**; the text "Thank you for registering your color printer!" should print to the browser window.

5. Close your Web browser window.

Understanding Security Issues

This section discusses security issues that relate to Web browsers and JavaScript.

Secure Coding with JavaScript

Viruses, worms, data theft by hackers, and other types of security threats are now a fact of life when it comes to Web-based applications. If you put an application into a production environment without considering security issues, you are asking for trouble. To combat security violations, you need to consider both Web server security issues and secure coding issues. Web server security involves technologies such as firewalls, which combine software and hardware to prevent access to private networks connected to the Internet. One very important technology is the Secure Sockets Layer (SSL) protocol, which encrypts data and transfers it across a secure connection. These types of security technologies work well in the realm of the Internet. However, JavaScript programs are downloaded and execute locally within the Web browser of a client computer, and are not governed by security technologies such as firewalls and Secure Sockets Layer.

TIP
Although Web server security issues are critical, they are properly covered in books on Apache, Internet Information Services, and other types of Web servers. Be sure to research security issues for your Web server and operating system before activating a production Web site.

To provide even stronger software security, many technology companies, including Microsoft and Oracle, now require their developers and other technical staff to adhere to secure coding practices and principles. **Secure coding**, or **defensive coding**, refers to the writing of code in such a way that minimizes any intentional or accidental security issues. Secure coding has become a major goal for many information technology companies, primarily due to the exorbitant cost of fixing security flaws in commercial software. According to one study, it is 100 times more expensive to fix security flaws in released software than it is to apply secure coding techniques during the development phase. The National Institute of Standards & Technology estimates that $60 billion a year is spent identifying and correcting software errors. In addition, politicians have recently shown a great deal of interest in regulating software security. Tom Ridge, former Secretary of the U.S. Department of Homeland Security, recently said, "A few lines of code can wreak more havoc than a bomb." Intense government scrutiny gives information technology companies strong incentive to voluntarily improve the security of software products before state and federal governments pass legislation that requires security certification of commercial software.

Basically, all code is insecure unless proven otherwise. Unfortunately, there is no magic formula for writing secure code, although there are various techniques that you can use to minimize security threats in your programs. Your first line of defense in securing your JavaScript programs is to validate all user input. You have studied various techniques in this book for validating user input, including how to validate data with regular expressions and how to use exceptions to handle errors as they occur in your scripts. Be sure to use these techniques in your scripts, especially scripts that run on commercial Web sites. The remainder of this section discusses security issues that relate to Web browsers and JavaScript.

JavaScript Security Concerns

The Web was originally designed to be read-only, which is to say its primary purpose was to locate and display documents that existed on other areas of the Web. With the development of programming languages such as JavaScript, Web pages can now contain programs in addition to static content. This ability to execute programs within a Web page raises several security concerns. The security areas of most concern to JavaScript programmers are:

- Protection of a Web page and JavaScript program against malicious tampering
- Privacy of individual client information
- Protection of the local file system of the client or Web site from theft or tampering

Another security concern is the privacy of individual client information in the Web browser window. Your e-mail address, bookmarks, and history list are valuable pieces of information that many direct marketers would love to get their hands on in order to bombard you with advertising geared toward your likes and dislikes. Without security restrictions, a JavaScript program could read this information from your Web browser. One of the most important JavaScript security features is its *lack* of certain types of functionality. For example, many programming languages include objects and methods that make it possible for a program to read, write, and delete files. To prevent mischievous scripts from stealing information or causing damage by changing or deleting files, JavaScript does not allow any file manipulation whatsoever. Similarly, JavaScript does not include any sort of mechanism for creating a network connection. This limitation prevents JavaScript programs from infiltrating a private network or intranet from which information may be stolen or damaged. Another helpful limitation is the fact that JavaScript cannot run system commands or execute programs on a client. The ability to read and write cookies is the only type of access to a client that JavaScript has. Web browsers, however, strictly govern cookies and do not allow access to cookies from outside the domain that created them.

The Same Origin Policy

Another JavaScript security feature has to do with the same origin policy, which restricts how JavaScript code in one window or frame accesses a Web page in another window or frame on a client computer. For windows and frames to view and modify the elements and properties of documents displayed in other windows and frames, they must have the same protocol (such as HTTP) and exist on the same Web server. For example, documents from the following two domains cannot access each others' elements and properties because they use different protocols.

The first domain's protocol is HTTP and the second domain's protocol is HTTPS, which, as mentioned earlier, is used on secure networks (that is, networks that run SSL).

```
http://www.gosselin.com
https://www.gosselin.com
```

The same origin policy applies not only to the domain name, but also to the server on which a document is located. Therefore, documents from the following two domains cannot access each others' elements and properties, since they are located on different servers, even though they exist in the same domain of gosselin.com:

```
http://www.programming.gosselin.com
http://www.writing.gosselin.com
```

The same origin policy prevents malicious scripts from modifying the content of other windows and frames and prevents the theft of private browser information and information displayed on secure Web pages. How necessary is the same origin policy? Consider the src attribute of the Document object, which determines the URL displayed in a window or frame. If a client has multiple windows or frames open on its system and the same origin policy did not exist, then a Web page in one window or frame could change the Web pages displayed in other windows or frames. There are plenty of unscrupulous or simply malicious advertisers who would try to force you to view only their Web pages. The security of private networks and intranets would also be at risk without the same origin policy. Consider a user who has one Web browser open to a page on the Internet and another Web browser open to a secure page from his or her private network or intranet. Without the same origin policy, the Internet Web page would have access to the information displayed on the private Web page.

The same origin policy also protects the integrity of the design of your Web page. For example, without the same origin policy, a frame in one window or frame could modify the elements and properties of JavaScript objects and XHTML code in other windows and frames. To give you an idea of how the same origin policy prevents this type of scenario from occurring, you will now create a frame set in which one frame uses JavaScript code to try to change the status bar text of another frame, using the status property of the Document object.

To test the same origin policy:

1. Create a new document in your text editor.

2. Type the following code to create a frameset document. The code causes the Yahoo! Web page to appear in the second frame.

```
<!DOCTYPE html PUBLIC "-//W3C//DTD XHTML 1.0 Frameset//EN"
"http://www.w3.org/TR/xhtml1/DTD/xhtml1-frameset.dtd">
<html xmlns="http://www.w3.org/1999/xhtml">
<head>
<title>Same Origin Policy</title>
<meta http-equiv="content-type" content="text/html;
charset=iso-8859-1" />
</head>
<frameset cols="20%, *">
<frame src="WrongOrigin.html" name="wrongFrame" />
```

```
<frame src="http://www.yahoo.com" name="yahooFrame" />
</frameset>
</html>
```

3. Save the document as **MainFrame.html** in your Chapter folder for Chapter 9, and then validate it with the W3C Markup Validation Service. Once the MainFrame.html document is valid, close it in your text editor.

4. Create another document in your text editor. Type the `<!DOCTYPE>` declaration, `<html>` element, document head, and document body. Use the strict DTD and "Same Origin Policy" as the content of the `<title>` element.

5. Add the following simple form, which contains a single button called Change Status. The button uses an `onclick` event that tries to change the status bar text of the frame containing the Yahoo! Web page.

```
<form action="">
<p><input type="button" value="Change Status"
onclick="parent.yahooFrame.document.status='Visit Don\'s Bait and
Tackle Shop!'" /></p>
</form>
```

6. Save the document as **WrongOrigin.html** in your Chapter folder for Chapter 9, and then validate it with the W3C Markup Validation Service. Once the WrongOrigin.html document is valid, close it in your text editor.

7. Open the MainFrame.html document in your Web browser and click the **Change Status** button. If you are using Firefox and the Error Console is open, you should receive an error message similar to the one shown in Figure 9-6.

Figure 9-6

Error message demonstrating the same origin policy

8. Close your Web browser window.

In some circumstances you will want two documents from related Web sites on different servers to be able to access each other's elements and properties. Consider a situation in which a document in the `programming.gosselin.com` domain needs to access content, such as form data, from a document in the `writing.gosselin.com` domain. To allow documents from different origins in the same domain to access each other's elements and properties, you use the `domain` property of the `Document` object. The **domain property** of the `Document` object changes the origin of a document to its root domain name using the statement `document.domain = "domain";`. Adding the statement `document.domain = "gosselin.com";` to documents from both `programming.gosselin.com` and `writing.gosselin.com` allows the documents to access each other's elements and properties, even though they are located on different servers.

Chapter Summary

▶ Information about individual visits to a Web site is called state information.

▶ HTTP was originally designed to be stateless, which means that Web browsers stored no persistent data about a visit to a Web site.

▶ A special type of form element, called a hidden form field, is not displayed by the Web browser. You can hide information from users in a hidden form field.

▶ The three most common tools for maintaining state information are hidden form fields, query strings, and cookies.

▶ A query string is a set of name=value pairs appended to a target URL. A query string consists of a single text string containing one or more pieces of information.

▶ Cookies are small pieces of information about a user that are stored by a Web server in text files on the user's computer.

▶ Cookies can be temporary or persistent. Temporary cookies remain available only for the current browser session. Persistent cookies remain available beyond the current browser session and are stored in a text file on a client computer.

▶ The `cookie` property is created with a required name attribute and four optional attributes: `expires`, `path`, `domain`, and `secure`.

▶ You can use special characters in your cookies if you use encoding, which involves converting special characters in a text string to their corresponding hexadecimal ASCII value, preceded by a percent sign.

▶ The built-in `encodeURIComponent()` function encodes the individual parts of a URI.

▶ When you read a cookie or other text string encoded with the `encodeURIComponent()` function, you must first decode it with the `decodeURIComponent()` function.

▶ Cookies consist of one continuous string that must be parsed before the data they contain can be used.

▶ The term "secure coding," or "defensive coding," refers to the writing of code in such a way that minimizes any intentional or accidental security issues.

▶ The same origin policy restricts how JavaScript code in one window or frame accesses a Web page in another window or frame on a client computer.

▶ The `domain` property of the `Document` object changes the origin of a document to its root domain name using the statement `document.domain = "domain";`.

Review Questions

1. HTTP was originally designed to allow Web browsers to store persistent data about a visit to a Web site. True or false?

2. Which of the following attributes can you use with an `<input type="hidden">` element? (Choose all that apply.)

    a. `name`

    b. `type`

    c. value

    d. visible

3. The data stored in a hidden form field is not sent to a server along with the rest of the form. True or false?

4. Explain how you can use hidden form fields to store data when navigating between Web pages.

5. What character is used for appending a query string to a URL?

    a. %

    b. *

    c. $

    d. ?

6. From where can you access a query string that is passed to a Web page? (Choose all that apply.)

    a. at the end of the query string

    b. the search property of the Window object

    c. the search property of the Document object

    d. the search property of the Location object

7. What characters separate entries in a query string? (Choose all that apply.)

    a. @

    b. ^

    c. &

    d. ~

8. What is the first task in parsing data from a query string?

    a. Encode the string with the encodeURIComponent() function.

    b. Use the toString() method to convert the query string to a JavaScript text string.

    c. Remove the question mark from the beginning of the string.

    d. Use the split() method to convert the individual pieces of information in the query string into array elements.

9. Temporary cookies remain available as long as the client computer is connected to the Internet. True or false?

10. What is the correct syntax for creating a transient cookie?

    a. cookie = name + value;

    b. cookie = name + "=" + value;

```
c.  cookie.transient = name + "=" + value;
d.  document.cookie = "?" + name + "=" + value;
```

11. What is the only required attribute of the `cookie` property?

    a. `domain`

    b. `expires`

    c. `path`

    d. `name`

12. What character do you use to separate attributes in a cookie value?

    a. `=`

    b. `&`

    c. `:`

    d. `;`

13. Explain why you should use encoding with cookie values. What methods and procedures do you use to encode and decode cookie values?

14. In URL encoded format, what character is represented by %20?

    a. a space character

    b. an ampersand (&)

    c. an uppercase letter 'A'

    d. a dollar sign ($)

15. You should always encode the value assigned to the `expires` attribute. True or false?

16. The availability of a cookie to other Web pages on a server is determined by the _____ attribute.

    a. `system`

    b. `path`

    c. `directory`

    d. `server`

17. Which attribute is used for sharing cookies outside of a domain?

    a. `share`

    b. `secure`

    c. `domain`

    d. You cannot share cookies outside of a domain.

18. Explain some of the steps you can take to write secure JavaScript code.

19. Which of the following statements best describes the same origin policy?

    a. The same origin policy determines if and how a user allows cookies to be set on his or her computer.

    b. The same origin policy restricts how JavaScript code in one window or frame accesses a Web page in another window or frame on a client computer

    c. The same origin policy allows Web sites to access e-mail addresses, bookmarks, history lists, and other types of client information that are stored in a user's Web browser.

    d. The same origin policy is a security protocol that verifies whether JavaScript code is running secure or unsecure mode as determined by the Web site's domain protocol.

20. To allow documents from different origins in the same domain to access each other's elements and properties, you use the _____.

    a. `path` attribute of the `cookie` property

    b. `domain` attribute of the `cookie` property

    c. `domain` property of the `Document` object

    d. `origin` property of the `Window` object

Hands-On Projects

 ## Project 9-1

In this project, you will create a cookies program that stores the date and time of your last visit.

1. Create a new document in your text editor.

2. Type the `<!DOCTYPE>` declaration, `<html>` element, header information, and the `<body>` element. Use the strict DTD and "Last Visit" as the content of the `<title>` element.

3. Add the following script section to the document body:

```
<script type="text/javascript">
/* <![CDATA[ */
/* ]]> */
</script>
```

4. First, add the following `if` statement to the script section, which checks to see if a cookie exists for the current Web page. If it does, then statements within the `if` statement will extract and display the date and time of the last visit.

```
if (document.cookie) {
    var cookieString = decodeURIComponent(document.cookie);
```

```
    var cookieArray = cookieString.split("; ");
    var lastVisit =
        cookieArray[0].substring(cookieArray[0].indexOf("=")
        + 1, cookieArray[0].length);
    document.write("<p>Your last visit was " + lastVisit
    + "</p>");
}
else
    document.write("<p>This is your first visit.</p>");
```

5. Next, to the end of the script section, add the following statements, which use a `Date` object to assign the date and time of the current visit to the document's cookie:

```
var now = new Date();
var day = now.getDay();
var date = now.getDate();
var year = now.getFullYear();
var month = now.getMonth();
var hours = now.getHours();
var minutes = now.getMinutes();
var seconds = now.getSeconds();
var days = new Array();
days[0] = "Sunday"; days[1] = "Monday"; days[2] = "Tuesday";
days[3] = "Wednesday"; days[4] = "Thursday"; days[5] = "Friday";
days[6]="Saturday";
var thisVisit = days[day] + " " + month + "/" + date + "/"
    + year + " at "+ hours + ":" + minutes + ":" + seconds;
document.cookie = encodeURIComponent(thisVisit);
```

6. Save the document as **LastVisit.html** in your Projects folder for Chapter 9, and then validate the document with the W3C Markup Validation Service. Once the document is valid, close it in your text editor.

7. Open the LastVisit.html document in your Web browser. The first time you open the document, you should see the text "This is your first visit." Refresh your Web browser and you should see the date and time of your last visit.

8. Close your Web browser window.

Project 9-2

In the next few projects, you will create a Web site that simulates online banking for a company named Forestville Funding. Each customer's user information will be stored in cookies. When a user visits the Web page again, he or she will be prompted to enter the stored user name and password. If the user does not enter the correct information within three tries, the script will prompt him or her to reregister. Note that for security reasons, browser cookies should never be the primary repository for a user's login name and password. The purpose of this exercise is to demonstrate how you can use cookies to remember user data, including login information.

NOTE

The Forestville Funding site will not include validation functionality in order to allow you to focus on the cookie techniques.

In this project, you will create the registration page for the Forestville Funding online banking site.

1. Create a new document in your text editor.

2. Type the `<!DOCTYPE>` declaration, `<html>` element, document head, and document body. Use the strict DTD and "Forestville Funding Online Banking" as the content of the `<title>` element.

3. Add the following text and elements to the document body. The form gathers each customer's first name, last name, account number, user ID, and password. Clicking the Register button will call a function named `registerForm()` that stores the form values in cookies. You will create the `registerForm()` function next.

```
<h1>Forestville Funding</h1><hr />
<h2>Online Banking Registration</h2>
<form action="" method="get" enctype="application/x-www-form-
urlencoded">
<p><strong>First Name</strong><br />
<input type="text" name="firstname" /></p>
<p><strong>Last Name</strong><br />
<input type="text" name="lastname" /></p>
<p><strong>Account Number</strong><br />
<input type="text" name="acctnum" /></p>
<p><strong>User ID</strong><br />
<input type="text" name="username" /></p>
<p><strong>Password</strong><br />
<input type="password" name="userpassword" /></p>
<p><input type="button" value="Register"
onclick="registerForm();" /></p>
</form>
```

4. Add the following script section to the document head:

```
<script type="text/javascript">
/* <![CDATA[ */
/* ]]> */
</script>
```

5. Start creating the `registerForm()` function in the script section, as follows:

```
function registerForm() {
}
```

6. Add the following statements to the `registerForm()` function. These statements declare and initialize variables with the contents of the form fields.

```
var firstName = document.forms[0].firstname.value;
var lastName = document.forms[0].lastname.value;
var acctnum = document.forms[0].acctnum.value;
var userName = document.forms[0].username.value;
var userPassword = document.forms[0].userpassword.value;
```

7. Add the following statements to the end of the registerForm() function. These statements declare a new Date object and set the year to one year from the current date. You will use the Date object to make the user information cookies persistent.

```
var myDate = new Date();
myDate.setFullYear(myDate.getFullYear() + 1);
```

8. Next, add the following statements to the end of the registerForm() function. These statements create persistent cookies out of the variables containing the values from the form fields.

```
document.cookie = "firstname=" + encodeURIComponent(firstName)
    + "; expires=" + myDate.toUTCString();
document.cookie = "lastname=" + encodeURIComponent(lastName)
    + "; expires=" + myDate.toUTCString();
document.cookie = "acctnum=" + encodeURIComponent(acctnum)
    + "; expires=" + myDate.toUTCString();
document.cookie = "name=" + encodeURIComponent(userName)
    + "; expires=" + myDate.toUTCString();
document.cookie = "password=" + encodeURIComponent(userPassword)
    + "; expires=" + myDate.toUTCString();
```

9. Finally, add the following statements to the end of the function. The first statement displays an alert dialog box after the cookies are successfully created. The last statement opens the Forestville Funding online banking login page, which you will create in the next project.

```
window.alert("Thank you for registering!");
location.href = "ForestvilleFundingLogin.html";
```

10. Save the document as **ForestvilleFundingRegistration.html** in a folder named ForestvilleFunding in your Projects folder for Chapter 9, and then validate the document with the W3C Markup Validation Service. Once the document is valid, close it in your text editor.

Project 9-3

In this project, you create the login page for the Forestville Funding online banking Web site.

1. Create a new document in your text editor.

2. Type the <!DOCTYPE> declaration, <html> element, document head, and document body. Use the strict DTD and "Forestville Funding Online Banking" as the content of the <title> element.

3. Add the following text and elements to the document body. The form allows customers to enter their user IDs and passwords. Clicking the Log In button will call a function named `checkUser()` that determines whether the user entered a valid ID and password. You will create the `checkUser()` function next.

```
<h1>Forestville Funding</h1><hr />
<h2>Online Banking</h2>
<form action="" method="get" enctype="application/x-www-form-
urlencoded">
<p><strong>User ID</strong><br />
<input type="text" name="username" /></p>
<p><strong>Password</strong><br />
<input type="password" name="userpassword" /></p>
<p><input type="button" value="Log In" onclick="checkUser();" /></p>
</form>
<p><a href="ForestvilleFundingRegistration.html">Register</a></p>
<hr />
<p>Forestville Funding. Member FDIC. Equal Housing Lender.<br />
&copy; 2008 Forestville Funding. All rights reserved.</p>
```

4. Add the following script section to the document head:

```
<script type="text/javascript">
/* <![CDATA[ */
/* ]]> */
</script>
```

5. Start creating the checkUser() function in the script section, as follows:

```
function checkUser() {
}
```

6. Add the following statements to the `checkUser()` function. The `if` statement checks whether the the `cookie` property exists. If it doesn't, then the ForestvilleFundingRegistration.html document opens. The `attempts` variable will track the number of times the user has attempted to log in.

```
if (document.cookie.length == 0)
    location.href = "ForestvilleFundingRegistration.html";
var attempts = 0;
```

7. Add the following statements to the end of the `checkUser()` function. These statements declare and initialize variables with the contents of the form fields. The first statement decodes the contents of the document cookie and assigns its value to a variable named `savedData`. The second statement declares two variables, `storedName` and `storedPassword`, which will store the user ID and password from the cookies. The third and fourth statements assign the user ID and password values that the user entered into the form to variables named `userName` and `userPassword`. The final statement uses the `split()` method to create a variable named `dataArray[]` that contains the contents of the cookie, split into array elements.

```
var savedData = decodeURIComponent(document.cookie);
var storedName, storedPassword;
var userName = document.forms[0].username.value;
var userPassword = document.forms[0].userpassword.value;
var dataArray = savedData.split("; ");
```

8. Add to the end of the checkUser() function the following for statement, which retrieves and assigns the user name and password values from dataArray[] to the storedName and storedPassword variables.

```
for (var i = 0; i < dataArray.length; ++i) {
    if (dataArray[i].substring(0,dataArray[i].indexOf("="))
        == "name") {
        storedName = dataArray[i].substring(
            dataArray[i].indexOf("=")
                + 1,dataArray[i].length);
    }
    if (dataArray[i].substring(0,dataArray[i].indexOf("="))
        == "password") {
        storedPassword = dataArray[i].substring(
            dataArray[i].indexOf("=")
                + 1,dataArray[i].length);
    }
}
```

9. Finally, add the following statements to the end of the checkUser() function. The first statement increments the attempts variable by a value of one. The if statement determines whether the user ID and password entered by the user match the values stored in the cookies. If so, a new transient "login=successful" cookie is created and the ForestvilleFunding.html page opens. (You will create the ForestvilleFunding.html page in the next project.) The else statement displays an alert dialog box informing the user that his or her login attempt was unsuccessful. If the user has made three attempts to log in (as determined by the attempts variable), the ForestvilleFundingRegistration.html page opens.

```
++attempts;
if (userName == storedName && userPassword == storedPassword) {
    document.cookie = "login=" + encodeURIComponent("successful");
    location.href = "ForestvilleFunding.html";
}
else {
    window.alert("Incorrect login or password. Please try again.");
    if (attempts == 3)
        location.href = "ForestvilleFundingRegistration.html";
}
```

10. Save the document as **ForestvilleFundingLogin.html** in a folder named ForestvilleFunding in your Projects folder for Chapter 9, and then validate the document with the W3C Markup Validation Service. Once the document is valid, close it in your text editor.

Project 9-4

In this project, you create the main Forestville Funding online banking page that users see after they log in successfully.

1. Create a new document in your text editor.

2. Type the `<!DOCTYPE>` declaration, `<html>` element, document head, and document body. Use the strict DTD and "Forestville Funding Online Banking" as the content of the `<title>` element.

3. Add the following text and elements to the document body:

    ```
    <h1>Forestville Funding</h1><hr />
    <h2>Online Banking</h2>
    <hr />
    <p>Forestville Funding. Member FDIC. Equal Housing Lender.<br />
    &copy; 2008 Forestville Funding. All rights reserved.</p>
    ```

4. Add the following script section to the document head:

    ```
    <script type="text/javascript">
    /* <![CDATA[ */
    /* ]]> */
    </script>
    ```

5. Add the following statements to the end of the script section. The first statement assigns the cookie value to the `savedData` variable. The `if` statement uses the `search()` method of the `String` object to determine whether the cookie value that is assigned to the `savedData` variable contains the value "login=successful". If it does not, then the user has not logged in during the current browser session and the ForestvilleFundingLogin.html document is opened. If the "login=successful" cookie is found, then the `split()` method creates a variable named `dataArray[]` that contains the contents of the cookie, split into array elements. The final statement declares `firstName`, `lastName`, and `acctNum` variables that will be assigned to the values stored in the cookies.

    ```
    var savedData = decodeURIComponent(document.cookie);
    if (savedData.search("login=successful") == -1)
        location.href = "ForestvilleFundingLogin.html";
    var dataArray = savedData.split("; ");
    var firstName, lastName, acctNum;
    ```

6. Add to the end of the script section the following `for` statement, which retrieves and assigns the user's first name, last name, and account number from `dataArray[]` to the `firstName`, `lastName`, and `acctNum` variables:

    ```
    for (var i = 0; i < dataArray.length; ++i) {
        if (dataArray[i].substring(0,dataArray[i].indexOf("="))
            == "firstname") {
            firstName = dataArray[i].substring(
                dataArray[i].indexOf("=")
                    + 1,dataArray[i].length);
    ```

```
        }
        if (dataArray[i].substring(0,dataArray[i].indexOf("="))
                == "lastname") {
            lastName = dataArray[i].substring(
                    dataArray[i].indexOf("=")
                        + 1,dataArray[i].length);
        }
        if (dataArray[i].substring(0,dataArray[i].indexOf("="))
                == "acctnum") {
            acctNum = dataArray[i].substring(
                    dataArray[i].indexOf("=")
                        + 1,dataArray[i].length);
        }
    }
```

7. Finally, add the following script section to the document body, immediately after the `<h2>` element. The script section prints the values assigned to the `firstName`, `lastName`, and `acctNum` variables:

```
<script type="text/javascript">
/* <![CDATA[ */
document.write("<p>You are currently logged in as "
    + firstName + " " + lastName + ".<br />");
document.write("Your account number is " + acctNum + ".</p>");
/* ]]> */
</script>
```

8. Save the document as **ForestvilleFunding.html** in a folder named ForestvilleFunding in your Projects folder for Chapter 9, and then validate the document with the W3C Markup Validation Service. Once the document is valid, close it in your text editor and open it in your Web browser. Because you have not yet logged in, the ForestvilleFunding.html document should open the ForestvilleFundingLogin.html document. The ForestvilleFundingLogin.html document should in turn open the ForestvilleFundingRegistration.html document because you have not yet entered any registration information.

9. Enter information into the fields on the registration page and click **Register**. An alert dialog box should appear, thanking you for registering. Clicking the alert dialog box's **OK** button displays the login page.

10. Enter the user ID and password for the account that you just created into the fields on the login page and click **Log In**. The main Forestville Funding online banking page should appear and display the name and account number you entered.

11. Close your Web browser window.

Project 9-5

Many Web sites require cookies to be enabled in order to support certain types of Web page functionality, especially when it comes to logging into a Web site. For example, if you attempt to log in to American Express at *https://www.americanexpress.com* and cookies are disabled in your browser, the login attempt will fail because the American Express Web site requires cookies to be enabled on client browsers to store security information and other types of data. Cookies are also required for the Forestville Funding online banking page. In this project you will add functionality to the Forestville Funding login page that uses the cookieEnabled property of the Navigator object to determine whether cookies are enabled in the Web browser. You will also add functionality that "remembers" login names and passwords so users won't need to log in every time they visit the Forestville Funding Web site. Note that with commercial applications, a user's login name and password are stored in cookies and are then retrieved by a Web server. Because you already stored the login name and password in cookies, you will just create another cookie named remember that is assigned a value of true.

1. Create a new document in your text editor.

2. Type the <!DOCTYPE> declaration, <html> element, document head, and document body. Use the strict DTD and "Forestville Funding Online Banking" as the content of the <title> element.

3. Add the following text and elements to the document body:

```
<h1>Forestville Funding</h1><hr />
<h2>Online Banking</h2>
<p>This Web site requires that your browser accept cookies.</p>
<hr />
<p>Forestville Funding. Member FDIC. Equal Housing Lender.<br />
&copy; 2008 Forestville Funding. All rights reserved.</p>
```

4. Save the document as **ForestvilleFundingNoCookies.html** in a folder named ForestvilleFunding in your Projects folder for Chapter 9, and then validate the document with the W3C Markup Validation Service. Once the document is valid, close it in your text editor.

5. Open in your text editor the **ForestvilleFundingLogin.html** document from the ForestvilleFunding folder in your Projects folder for Chapter 9. Add to the script section the following statements, which check whether the cookieEnabled property of the Navigator object contains a value of false. If so, then the ForestvilleFundingNoCookies.html is opened. Also, modify the if statement that checks whether the document.cookie property exists into an else...if statement.

```
if (!navigator.cookieEnabled)
    location.href = "ForestvilleFundingNoCookies.html";
else if (!document.cookie)
    location.href = "ForestvilleFundingRegistration.html";
```

6. Add the following text and elements immediately above the paragraph in the document body that contains the Log In button:

```
<p><input type="checkbox" name="remember_me" /> Remember my login
information</p>
```

7. Modify the if statement at the end of the `checkUser()` function so it includes the following bolded `if` statement, which creates a "remember=true" cookie if the remember_me check box is selected:

```
if (userName == storedName && userPassword == storedPassword) {
    document.cookie = "login=" + encodeURIComponent("successful");
    if (document.forms[0].elements[2].checked) {
        var myDate = new Date();
        myDate.setFullYear(myDate.getFullYear() + 1);
        document.cookie = "remember=" + encodeURIComponent
        ("true")
            + "; expires=" + myDate.toUTCString();
    }
    location.href = "ForestvilleFunding.html";
}
```

8. Save the **ForestvilleFundingLogin.html** document and validate it with the W3C Markup Validation Service. Once the document is valid, close it in your text editor.

9. Open in your text editor the **ForestvilleFunding.html** document from the ForestvilleFunding folder in your Projects folder for Chapter 9 and modify the statement that checks for the "login=successful" cookie so it also checks for the "remember=true" cookie, as shown with the following bolded code. If both `search()` methods return a value of -1 for both cookies, then the ForestvilleFundingLogin.html document opens because the user: 1) is not logged in for the current session, and 2) has not selected the remember_me button on the ForestvilleFundingLogin.html page.

```
if (savedData.search("login=successful") == -1
    && savedData.search("remember=true") == -1)
        location.href = "ForestvilleFundingLogin.html";
```

10. Save the **ForestvilleFunding.html** document and validate it with the W3C Markup Validation Service. Once the document is valid, close it in your text editor.

11. Open your Web browser and disable cookies. To disable cookies in Firefox, select **Options** from the **Tools** menu and click the **Privacy** tab. On the Privacy tab, deselect the **Accept cookies from sites** box and click **OK**. To disable cookies in Internet Explorer, select **Internet Options** from the **Tools** menu and click the **Privacy** tab. On the **Privacy** tab, select the **Advanced** button to display the Advanced Privacy Settings dialog box. In the Advanced Privacy Settings dialog box, select the **Override automatic cookie handling** box and then select the **Block** radio buttons in the **First-party Cookies** and **Third-party Cookies** sections. Click **OK** to close the Advanced Privacy Settings dialog box and click **OK** again to close the Internet Options dialog box. Close your Web browser after you have disabled cookies.

12. Open the **ForestvilleFunding.html** document in your Web browser. Because you have disabled cookies, the ForestvilleFundingNoCookies.html document should open. Follow the same procedures listed in Step 11 to reenable cookies, and then close your Web browser.

13. Open the **ForestvilleFunding.html** document again in your Web browser. Because you are starting a new brower session, the transient "login=successful" cookie has ceased to exist, so the ForestvilleFundingLogin.html document should open. Enter your user ID and password, click the **Remember my login information** box, and then click **Log In**. Your account information should display on the ForestvilleFunding.html page.

14. Close your Web browser and the reopen the **ForestvilleFunding.html** document again in your Web browser. Because you selected the Remember my login information box, your account information should display immediately on the ForestvilleFunding.html page; you will not be redirected to the ForestvilleFundingLogin.html page.

15. Close your Web browser window.

Project 9-6

In this project, you will correct errors in a cookie program.

1. Create a new document in your text editor.

2. Type the `<!DOCTYPE>` declaration, `<html>` element, header information, and the `<body>` element. Use the strict DTD and "Cookie Errors" as the content of the `<title>` element.

3. Add the following script section to the document body:

```
<script type="text/javascript">
/* <![CDATA[ */
var visitData = decodeURIComponent(document.cookie);
if (visitData.length = 0)
    document.write("<p>You have visited before.</p>");
else
    document.write("<p>This is your first visit.</p>");
var expiresDate = new Date();
expiresdate.setFullYear(expiresDate.getFullYear() - 1);
document.cookie = encodeURIComponent("expires="
    + expiresDate.toUTCString());
/* ]]> */
</script>
```

4. Save the document as **CookieErrors.html** in a folder named CookieErrors in your Projects folder for Chapter 9, and validate it with the W3C Markup Validation Service. Once the CookieErrors.html document is valid, open it in your Web browser. The first time you open the document, you should see the text "This is your first visit". If you close and then reopen your Web browser (rather than refreshing your Web browser window), you will continue to receive the message "This is your first visit". Fix the errors in the document. (*Hint*: There is more than one error in the program.)

5. Close your Web browser window.

Case Projects

For the following projects, save the documents you create in your Cases folder for Chapter 9. Be sure to validate the documents you create with the W3C Markup Validation Service. Also, be sure to create each document in its own folder in order to avoid conflicts with cookies that are set by other Web pages.

Case Project 9-1

Create a document that stores and reads cookies that track the number of times a user has visited your Web site and the date of his or her last visit. The first time the user visits, display a message welcoming him or her to your Web site and remind them to bookmark the page. Whenever a user visits the site, display the cookies using `document.write()` statements, increment the counter cookie by one, and then reset the counter cookie expiration date to one year from the current date. Save the document as **Counter.html**.

Case Project 9-2

Create a document with a "nag" counter that reminds users to register. Save the counter in a cookie and display a message reminding users to register every third time they visit your site. Create a form in the body of the document that includes text boxes for a user's name and e-mail address along with a Register button. Once a user fills in the text boxes and clicks the Register button, delete the nag counter cookie and replace it with cookies containing the user's name and e-mail address. After registering, display the name and e-mail address cookies in an alert message whenever the user revisits the site. Save the document as **NagCounter.html**.

Case Project 9-3

Create a document with a form that registers users for a marketing seminar. When a user submits the registration form, store cookies containing the user's information such as name, company, and so on. If a user attempts to register a second time with the same name, display a confirm dialog box asking if he or she wants to register again. Save the document as **MarketingSeminar.html**.

Case Project 9-4

Create a document with a form for reserving a rental car. As a user creates a reservation, store cookies containing the user's reservation information, including name and address, telephone, pickup and return dates, and car type. Also, create buttons that redisplay a user's reservation information with an alert message. Set the cookies so that they expire one day after a visit. Save the document as **CarRentals.html**.

10

Introduction to the Document Object Model (DOM)

In this chapter you will:

- Learn about dynamic Web pages
- Study the Document Object Model (DOM)
- Learn how to open and close the `Document` object
- Learn how to access document elements
- Work with the `Image` object

Today, more and more businesses want their Web sites to include formatting and images that can be updated without the user having to reload a Web page from the server. They also want innovative ways to use animation and interactive Web pages to attract and retain visitors and to make their Web sites effective and easy to navigate. You cannot create these kinds of effects with standard Extensible Hypertext Markup Language (XHTML); instead, you need to use Dynamic HTML (DHTML). One of the most important aspects of DHTML is the Document Object Model (DOM). In this chapter, you will learn about the DOM and how it fits in with DHTML.

Creating Dynamic Web Pages

As you have probably realized by now, Web pages are much more useful when they are dynamic. In Internet terminology, the word **dynamic** means several things. Primarily, it refers to Web pages that respond to user requests through buttons or other kinds of controls. Among other things, a dynamic Web page can allow a user to change the document background color, submit a form and process a query, and participate in an online game or quiz. The term "dynamic" also refers to various kinds of effects, such as animation, that appear automatically in a Web browser.

You can simulate limited dynamism and interactivity with simple hypertext links. Consider the Web page shown in Figure 10-1, which displays a photo of a pig weathervane that is sold by a company named Weathervane Warehouse. This single Web page has links to six other Web pages that are identical to the one shown in Figure 10-1, except that each displays a different weathervane picture.

Figure 10-1
Pig weathervane

The following code shows the document body for the Web page that displays the flying pig weathervane:

```
<body>
<h1>Weathervane Warehouse</h1>
<h2>Copper Weathervanes</h2>
<p>Click the name of a weathervane to view its photo.</p>
<table border="1" width="100%">
<colgroup span="1" width="40%" />
<tr><td><a href="Weathervanes_rooster.html">Barn
Rooster</a></td>
<td align="center" rowspan="7" style="background:white">
<img src="flying_pig.jpg"
width="198" height="180" alt="Photo of a flying pig
weathervane." /></td></tr>
<tr><td><a href="Weathervanes_eagle.html">Eagle</a>
</td></tr>
<tr><td><a href="Weathervanes_duck.html">Landing
Duck</a></td></tr>
<tr><td><a href="Weathervanes_pig.html">Flying
Pig</a></td></tr>
<tr><td><a href="Weathervanes_whale.html">Whale</a>
</td></tr>
<tr><td><a href="Weathervanes_ship.html">Clipper
Ship</a></td></tr>
<tr><td><a href="Weathervanes_salmon.html">Salmon</a>
</td></tr>
</table>
</body>
```

TIP
You can find files for the Weathervane Warehouse Web site in the Chapter folder for Chapter 10 on your Data Disk.

Hyperlinks such as those found in the weathervane document do not change the currently displayed document, but load new ones from the server instead, so they cannot produce true dynamic effects. When a user clicks a link on the weathervane page, it appears as if only the graphic changes. In reality, the entire page is replaced. This means the Web browser has to find the correct Web page on the server, transfer that file to your computer, and then render the new document. Although you might not notice the time it takes for these steps to occur in this simple example, the transfer and rendering time for a large, complex Web page could be significant. If the Weathervane Warehouse Web page were dynamic, only the image displayed by the `<img>` element would change, and the work would be performed locally by a Web browser rather than by a server. Changing only the image would be much more effective and efficient.

To make Web pages truly dynamic, you need more than just XHTML. **Dynamic HTML (DHTML)** refers to a combination of technologies that make Web pages dynamic. The term DHTML is actually a combination of JavaScript, XHTML, CSS, and the Document Object Model. You should already be familiar with JavaScript, XHTML, and CSS. In order to be successful with JavaScript, you also need to learn about the Document Object Model.

TIP
Remember that "DHTML" does not refer to a single technology, but to several combined technologies.

Understanding the HTML Document Object Model

At the core of DHTML is the **Document Object Model**, or **DOM**, which represents the HTML or XML of a Web page that is displayed in a browser. The Document Object Model that represents HTML content is referred to as the HTML DOM, and the Document Object Model that represents XML content is referred to as the XML DOM. Throughout this book, you have created Web pages that conform to XHTML. Because XHTML documents are just another type of XML document, you can manipulate them with both the HTML DOM and the XML DOM. But which is preferable? The W3C formally recommends using the XML DOM instead of the HTML DOM. Nonetheless, it's easier to use the HTML DOM with basic types of DHTML techniques, such as those discussed in this and the next chapter. Keep in mind, however, that you must use the XML DOM when using some advanced JavaScript techniques, such as AJAX, which is discussed in Chapter 12.

Each element on a Web page is represented in the HTML DOM by its own object. The fact that each element is an object makes it possible for a JavaScript program to access individual elements on a Web page and change them individually, without having to reload the page from the server. Although the individual technologies that make up DHTML have been accepted standards for some time, the implementation of DHTML has evolved slowly. One of the main delays in implementation has to do with the DOM. Earlier versions of Internet Explorer and Navigator included DOMs that were almost completely incompatible with each other. This meant that you needed to write different JavaScript code sections for different browsers. At the time of this writing, Mozilla-based Web browsers including Firefox, Internet Explorer 5.0 and higher, and Netscape 6 and higher are all compatible with a standardized version of the DOM, Level 3, that is recommended by the World Wide Web Consortium (W3C).

When it comes to Web page authoring, the most important part of the HTML DOM is the Document object. Through the Document object you can access other objects that represent elements on a Web page. Throughout this book, you have used the HTML DOM to access and manipulate form elements. Similarly, you can use JavaScript to manipulate the images on a Web page through the Image object. The value you assign to an <img> element's name attribute becomes the name of an associated Image object. In order to access an Image object named companyLogo, you must append the image name to the Document object as follows: document.companyLogo. (You will learn how to work with the Image object in the next section.)

TIP

For a complete listing of objects in the HTML DOM, see the W3Schools' HTML DOM reference at *http://w3schools.com/htmldom/dom_reference.asp*.

Next, you spend a little time studying more of the Document object's properties and methods.

HTML DOM Document Object Methods

The Document object contains several methods used for dynamically generating Web pages and manipulating elements. Table 10-1 lists the methods of the Document object that are specified in the WC3 DOM.

Method	Description
close()	Closes a new document that was created with the open() method
getElementById(*ID*)	Returns the element represented by *ID*
getElementsByName(*name*)	Returns a collection of elements represented by *name*
getElementsByTagName(*tag name*)	Returns a collection of elements represented by *tag name*
open()	Opens a new document in a window or frame
write(*text*)	Writes new text to a document
writeln(*text*)	Writes new text to a document, followed by a line break

Table 10-1   HTML DOM Document object methods

HTML DOM `Document` Object Properties

The HTML DOM `Document` object contains various properties used for manipulating Web page objects. Table 10-2 lists the properties of the `Document` object that are specified in the WC3 DOM.

Property	Description
`anchors[]`	Returns an array of the document's anchor elements
`body`	Returns the document's `<body>` or `<frameset>` element
`cookie`	Returns the current document's cookie string, which contains small pieces of information about a user that are stored by a Web server in text files on the user's computer
`domain`	Returns the domain name of the server where the current document is located
`forms[]`	Returns an array of the document's forms
`images[]`	Returns an array of the document's images
`links[]`	Returns an array of a document's links
`referrer`	Returns the Uniform Resource Locator (URL) of the document that provided a link to the current document
`title`	Returns or sets the title of the document as specified by the `<title>` element in the document `<head>` section
`URL`	Returns the URL of the current document

Table 10-2   HTML DOM's `Document` object properties

The only property you can dynamically change after a Web page is rendered is the `title` property, which allows you to change the title of the document that is specified by the `<title>` element in the document `<head>` section. For example, the following statement can be used to change the text displayed in the title bar after the Web page is rendered:

```
document.title = "Doug's Laundry and Dry Cleaning Home Page";
```

Opening and Closing the `Document` Object

Although the `Document` object's `write()` and `writeln()` methods are part of the DOM, they cannot be used to change content after a Web page has been rendered. You can write code that executes the `write()` and `writeln()` methods in the current document after it is rendered, but they replace the content that is currently displayed in the Web browser window.

You can, however, use the **`open()` method** to create a new document in a window or frame, and then use the `write()` and `writeln()` methods to add content to the new document. The **`close()` method** notifies the Web browser that you are finished writing to the window or frame and that the document should be displayed. Although later versions of Internet Explorer and Netscape do not require you to use the `open()` and `close()` methods with the `write()` and `writeln()` methods, some older browsers do not display any content in the window until you execute the `close()` method. In addition, some browsers, including Firefox, do not stop the spinning icon in the upper-right browser corner that indicates a document is loading until the `close()` method executes. Because Firefox is the second most widely used browser, you should always use the `open()` and `close()` methods when dynamically creating document content.

You should always use the `open()` and `close()` methods when you want to use the `write()` and `writeln()` methods to update the text displayed in an existing window or frame. Specifically, if you do not use the `close()` method to notify the Web browser that you are finished writing to the window or frame, then any new calls to the `write()` and `writeln()` methods are appended to the existing text that is currently displayed in the window or frame. For example, consider the links in the following code. Each link uses a `write()` method to print a property of the `Navigator` object in another frame of a frame-based document. When you click a link, the contents in the right frame should be replaced. However, each time you click a link, the `Navigator` object property value is appended to the frame; the entire contents of the frame are not replaced. Figure 10-2 shows how the target frame appears after clicking the `appCodeName`, `appName`, and `appVersion` links.

```
<p>
<a href=""
onclick="top.frames[2].document.write(navigator.appCodeName);
return false;">appCodeName</a><br />
<a href=""
onclick="top.frames[2].document.write(navigator.appName);
return false;">appName</a><br />
<a href=""
onclick="top.frames[2].document.write(navigator.appVersion);
return false;">appVersion</a><br />
<a href=""
onclick="top.frames[2].document.write(navigator.platform);
return false;">platform</a><br />
<a href=""
onclick="top.frames[2].document.write(navigator.userAgent);
return false;">userAgent</a><br />
</p>
```

Figure 10-2

Output of `document.write()` statements without using the `open()` and `close()` methods

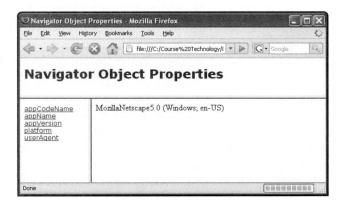

CAUTION
The values assigned to each `onclick` event handler in the preceding code must be typed on the same line because they are part of a literal string; they are broken here due to space limitations.

In order for the links to work correctly, you must add `open()` and `close()` methods to each event handler, as follows:

```
<p>
<a href=""
onclick="top.frames[2].document.open();top.frames[2]
.document.write(navigator.appCodeName);top.frames[2]
.document.close();return false;">appCodeName</a><br />
<a href=""
onclick="top.frames[2].document.open();top.frames[2]
.document.write(navigator.appName);top.frames[2]
.document.close();return false;">appName</a><br />
<a href=""
onclick="top.frames[2].document.open();top.frames[2]
.document.write(navigator.appVersion);top.frames[2]
.document.close();return false;">appVersion</a><br />
<a href=""
onclick="top.frames[2].document.open();top.frames[2]
.document.write(navigator.platform);top.frames[2]
.document.close();return false;">platform</a><br />
<a href=""
onclick="top.frames[2].document.open();top.frames[2]
.document.write(navigator.userAgent);top.frames[2]
.document.close();return false;">userAgent</a><br />
</p>
```

CAUTION
The values assigned to each `onclick` event handler in the preceding code must be typed on the same line because they are part of a literal string; they are broken here due to space limitations.

TIP
You can find copies of the Navigator Object Properties frameset in the Chapter folder for Chapter 10 on your Data Disk.

Next, you start working on a Web site for a flight-training school called Al's Aviation. You will find three prewritten Web pages, Aviation.html, Pilot.html, and Inst.html, in your Chapter folder for Chapter 10. The Aviation.html file is the home page, the Pilot.html file contains information on private pilot training, and the Inst.html file contains information on flight instrument training. You will modify these Web pages throughout the chapter.

The Al's Aviation Web pages do not contain <h1> elements. You will write code that uses the title property of each Al's Aviation Web page as its <h1> element.

To write code that uses the title property of each Al's Aviation Web page as its <h1> element:

1. Start your text editor, open the home page for Al's Aviation, **Aviation.html**, from your Chapter folder for Chapter 10, and immediately save it as **AviationHome.html**.

2. Locate the <h2> element that reads "Welcome to Flight School!" and add the following script section above it. The script section contains statements that add the value of the Document object's title property to the Web page as an <h1> element.

```
<script type="text/javascript">
/* <![CDATA[ */
document.open();
document.write("<h1>" + document.title + "</h1>");
document.close();
/* ]]> */
</script>
```

3. Save the **AviationHome.html** file, but leave the document open in your text editor.

4. Open the **Pilot.html** file and immediately save it as **PrivatePilot.html**. Add the script section shown in Step 2 above its <h2> element.

5. Save the **PrivatePilot.html** file, but leave the document open in your text editor.

6. Open the **Inst.html** file and immediately save it as **Instrument.html**. Add the same script section above its <h2> element.

7. Save the **Instrument.html** file, but leave the document open in your text editor.

8. Open the **AviationHome.html** file in your Web browser. Figure 10-3 shows how it appears. The first heading on the page, Al's Aviation, is created using the value assigned to the Web page's Document object's title property.

9. Close your Web browser window.

Figure 10-3

AviationHome.html

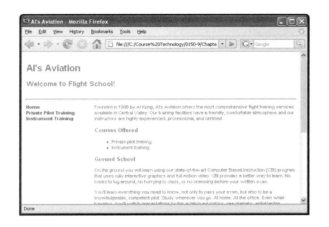

Using the IMAGE Object

There's not enough space in this chapter to investigate all objects in the HTML DOM, but one object you should be familiar with is the Image object. An **Image object** represents an image created using the <img> element. You need to use an Image object if you want to dynamically change an image that is displayed on a Web page. As you learned in Chapter 4, the images[] array contains Image objects that represent all the <img> elements on a Web page. Image objects for each <img> element are assigned to the elements of the images[] array in the order that they appear on the Web page. The first Image object is represented by images[0], the second Image object is represented by images[1], and so on.

The Image object contains various properties that you can use to manipulate your objects. Table 10-3 lists the properties of the Image object.

Property	Description
align	Returns or sets the alignment of an image in relation to the surrounding text; you can assign one of the following values to this property: left, right, top, middle, or bottom
alt	Returns or sets the image's alternate text
border	Returns or sets the border width, in pixels
height	Returns or sets the image height, in pixels
hspace	Returns or sets the amount of horizontal space, in pixels, to the left and right of the image
isMap	Returns a Boolean value that indicates whether the image is a server-side image map
longDesc	Returns or sets an image's long description
name	Returns or sets the image name
src	Returns or sets the URL of the displayed image
useMap	Returns or sets the image to be used as a client-side image map
vspace	Returns or sets the amount of vertical space, in pixels, above and below the image
width	Returns or sets the image width, in pixels

Table 10-3   Image object properties

You have already used one of the most important parts of the Image object, the **src property**, which allows JavaScript to dynamically change an image. Changing the value assigned to the src property also changes the src attribute associated with an <img> element, which dynamically changes an image displayed on a Web page. For instance, you can change the displayed image for an image named companyLogo using a statement such as document.companyLogo.src = "new_image.jpg";.

Next, you will add an image to the Al's Aviation home page that asks visitors if they have ever dreamed of flying. Clicking the image displays another image that advertises a free "discovery flight" from Al's Aviation. Your Chapter folder for Chapter 10 contains two images, dream.gif and discovery.gif, that you can use for the exercise.

To add an image to the Al's Aviation home page:

1. Return to the **AviationHome.html** file in your text editor.

2. In the first table in the file, locate the <td> element that contains a nonbreaking space ( ). Replace the nonbreaking space characters with the following <img> element. Notice that the onclick event handler uses the this reference to refer to the image's src property. Recall that the this reference simply refers to the current element.

    ```
    <img src="dream.gif" height="60" width="468" alt="Banner
    advertising image" onclick="this.src='discovery.gif';" />
    ```

3. Save the **AviationHome.html** file and open it in your Web browser. When the file first opens, it displays the image shown in Figure 10-4.

Figure 10-4

Default image displayed on the Al's Aviation home page

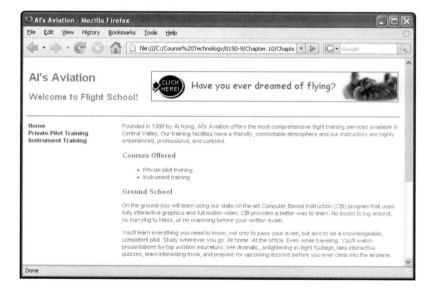

4. Click the image. The current image is replaced with the image shown in Figure 10-5.

5. Close your Web browser window.

Figure 10-5

Al's Aviation home page after clicking the banner image

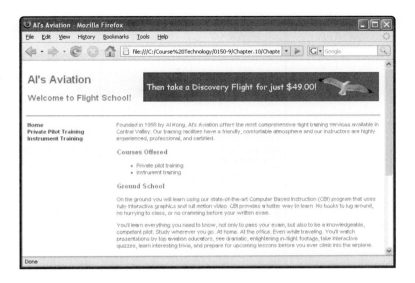

Animation with the `Image` Object

As you learned in Chapter 4, you can create simple animation on a Web page by combining the `src` attribute of the `Image` object with the `setTimeout()` or `setInterval()` methods. In Chapter 4, you saw the following code, which uses the `setInterval()` method to automatically swap two advertising images every couple of seconds. Figure 10-6 shows the two images displayed in a browser.

```
...
<script type="text/javascript">
/* <![CDATA[ */
var curBanner="soccer1";
function changeBanner() {
     if (curBanner == "soccer2") {
          document.images[0].src = "soccer1.gif";
          curBanner = "soccer1";
     }
     else {
          document.images[0].src = "soccer2.gif";
          curBanner = "soccer2";
     }
}
/* ]]> */
</script>
</head>
<body onload="var begin=setInterval('changeBanner()',2000);">
<p><img src="soccer1.gif" name="banner" alt="Changing
image for Central Valley Sporting Goods" /></p>
</body>
</html>
```

Figure 10-6
Advertising images

TIP

The Central Valley Sporting Goods Web page is provided as a file named
SportingGoods.html in the Chapter folder for Chapter 10 on your Data Disk.

While the advertising images can be loosely termed "animation," true animation involving movement requires a different image, or frame, for each movement that a character or object makes. While swapping two images is simple enough, you need to understand a little more about how to work with the Image object when you want your animation to include multiple images.

NOTE

This book does not teach the artistic skills necessary for creating frames in an animation sequence. Instead, the goal is to show how to use JavaScript and the Image object to perform simple animation by swapping frames displayed by an <img> element.

CAUTION

Do not confuse animation frames and frames created with the <frameset> and <frame> elements.

As an example of a more complex animation sequence, Figure 10-7 shows 16 frames, with each frame showing a unicycle in a slightly different position.

Figure 10-7
Unicycle animation
frames

You create an animated sequence with JavaScript by using the `setInterval()` or `setTimeout()` methods to cycle through the frames in an animation series. Each iteration of a `setInterval()` or `setTimeout()` method changes the frame displayed by an `<img>` element. The speed of the animation depends on how many milliseconds are passed as an argument to the `setInterval()` or `setTimeout()` methods.

The following code animates the frames in Figure 10-7. The code assigns the frames to a `unicycle[]` array. Once the Turn button is clicked, a `setInterval()` method calls the `turn()` function, which executes an `if...else` statement that changes the displayed frame based on the `curUnicycle` variable. Once the `curUnicycle` variable reaches 15 (the highest element in an array with sixteen elements), it resets to zero (the first element in the array), and the animation sequence starts over from the beginning. The name of each image for the frames corresponds to an element number in the `unicycle[]` array. The Stop button uses the `clearInterval()` method to stop the `startInterval()` method. Figure 10-8 shows an example of the script in a Web browser.

```
<!DOCTYPE html PUBLIC "-//W3C//DTD XHTML 1.0 Strict//EN"
"http://www.w3.org/TR/xhtml1/DTD/xhtml1-strict.dtd">
<html xmlns="http://www.w3.org/1999/xhtml">
<head>
<title>Unicycle</title>
<meta http-equiv="content-type"
    content="text/html;charset=iso-8859-1" />
<script type="text/javascript">
/* <![CDATA[ */
var turnUnicycle;
var unicycle = new Array(16);
var curUnicycle = 0;
unicycle[0] = "unicycle0.gif"; unicycle[1] = "unicycle1.gif";
unicycle[2] = "unicycle2.gif"; unicycle[3] = "unicycle3.gif";
unicycle[4] = "unicycle4.gif"; unicycle[5] = "unicycle5.gif";
unicycle[6] = "unicycle6.gif"; unicycle[7] = "unicycle7.gif";
unicycle[8] = "unicycle8.gif"; unicycle[9] = "unicycle9.gif";
unicycle[10] = "unicycle10.gif"; unicycle[11] = "unicycle11.gif";
unicycle[12] = "unicycle12.gif"; unicycle[13] = "unicycle13.gif";
unicycle[14] = "unicycle14.gif"; unicycle[15] = "unicycle15.gif";
```

```
function turn() {
    if (curUnicycle == 15)
        curUnicycle = 0;
    else
        ++curUnicycle;
    document.images[0].src = unicycle[curUnicycle];
}
function startTurning() {
    if (turnUnicycle != null)
        clearInterval(turnUnicycle);
    turnUnicycle = setInterval("turn()", 100);
}
/* ]]> */
</script>
</head>
<body>
<p><img src="unicycle1.gif" height="75" width="75" /></p>
<form action="">
<p><input type="button" value=" Turn "
onclick="startTurning();" />
<input type="button" value=" Stop "
onclick="clearInterval(turnUnicycle);" /></p>
</form>
</body>
</html>
```

Figure 10-8

Unicycle animation in a
Web browser

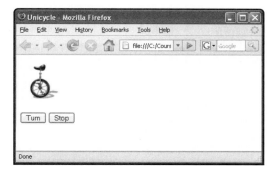

TIP

You can find a copy of the preceding Unicycle animation page, named
Unicycle.html, along with the required image files in the Chapter folder for
Chapter 10 on your Data Disk.

Notice that the preceding code includes a function, startTurning(), which is called from
the Turn button in the document body. The if statement determines whether the animation is

already running by checking to see if the `turnUnicycle` variable is equal to null. This technique enables you to quickly check whether an object exists or if a variable has been initialized. If the `setInterval()` method has been called and assigned to the `turnUnicycle` variable, then the conditional expression returns a value of true, which causes the `if` statement to execute the `clearInterval()` method to cancel the animation. If you do not include the `if` statement, then the user could click the Turn button several times, which would cause multiple instances of the `setInterval()` method to occur. Multiple instances of the same `setInterval()` method causes your computer to execute as many animation sequences as there are instances of the `setInterval()` method, which could make the animation appear to run faster than desired or function erratically.

Next, you will modify the Private Pilot Training page so it includes an animated image of an airplane. Your Chapter folder for Chapter 10 contains 16 images, airplane0.gif through airplane15.gif, that you can use for this exercise.

To modify the Private Pilot Training page so it includes an animated image of an airplane:

1. Return to the **PrivatePilot.html** file in your text editor.

2. Add the following script section to the document head, just above the closing `</head>` tag:

    ```
    <script type="text/javascript">
    /* <![CDATA[ */
    /* ]]> */
    </script>
    ```

3. Add to the script section the following variable definitions and function, which change the displayed image. The code is very similar to the unicycle animation code you saw in this section.

    ```
    var plane = new Array(16);
    var curPlane = 0;
    plane[0] = "airplane0.gif";
    plane[1] = "airplane1.gif";
    plane[2] = "airplane2.gif";
    plane[3] = "airplane3.gif";
    plane[4] = "airplane4.gif";
    plane[5] = "airplane5.gif";
    plane[6] = "airplane6.gif";
    plane[7] = "airplane7.gif";
    plane[8] = "airplane8.gif";
    plane[9] = "airplane9.gif";
    plane[10] = "airplane10.gif";
    plane[11] = "airplane11.gif";
    plane[12] = "airplane11.gif";
    plane[13] = "airplane11.gif";
    plane[14] = "airplane11.gif";
    plane[15] = "airplane11.gif";
    function fly() {
    ```

```
if (curPlane == 15)
      curPlane = 0;
else
      ++curPlane;
document.images[0].src = plane[curPlane];
}
```

4. Add an `onload` event handler to the opening `<body>` element as follows that uses the `setInterval()` method to start the animation:

```
<body onload="setInterval('fly()', 200);">
```

5. In the first table in the file, locate the `<td>` element that contains a nonbreaking space (` `). Replace the nonbreaking space characters with the following `<img>` element:

```
<img src="airplane0.gif" height="100" width="200"
alt="Image of an airplane." />
```

6. Save the **PrivatePilot.html** file and then open it in your Web browser. An image of an airplane appears to fly on your screen, as shown in Figure 10-9.

Figure 10-9

PrivatePilot.html after adding an animated image of an airplane

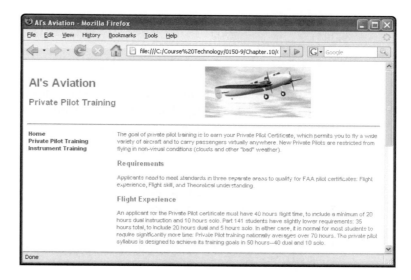

7. Close your Web browser window.

Image Caching

In the airplane program, you may have noticed that the loading of each image appears to be jerky, erratic, or slow, and that the URL for each image flickers in the status bar each time the image changes. This happens because JavaScript does not save a copy of the image in memory that can be used whenever necessary. Instead, each time a different image is loaded by an `<img>` element, JavaScript must open or reopen the image from its source. You probably accessed the airplane image files directly from the Data Disk on your local computer, and if you have a particularly fast computer, you may not have noticed a loading problem. If you did notice erratic loading of the images, then you can imagine how erratic and slow the animation would appear if you had to download the images from the Web server each time they are loaded. A technique for eliminating multiple downloads of the same file is called **image caching**. Image caching temporarily stores image files in memory on a local computer. This technique allows JavaScript to store and retrieve an image from memory rather than download the image each time it is needed.

Images are cached using the `Image()` constructor of the `Image` object. The `Image()` constructor creates a new `Image` object. There are three steps for caching an image in JavaScript:

1. Create a new object using the `Image()` constructor.
2. Assign a graphic file to the `src` property of the new `Image` object.
3. Assign the `src` property of the new `Image` object to the `src` property of an `<img>` element.

In the following code, the `src` attribute of the `<img>` element named `myImage` is initially set to an empty string "". In the script section, a new `Image` object named `newImage` is created. The `newImage` object is used to save and access the memory cache containing the image file. A file named graphic.jpg is assigned to the `src` property of the `newImage` object. The `src` property of the `newImage` object is then assigned to the `src` property of the `<img>` element.

```
<body>
<img src="" height="100" width="100" alt="Description" />
<script type="text/javascript">
/* <![CDATA[ */
var newImage = new Image()
newImage.src = "graphic.jpg"
document.images[0].src = newImage.src
/* ]]> */
</script>
</body>
```

Be sure to understand that in the preceding code, the graphic.jpg file is not assigned directly to the `src` property of the `<img>` element. Instead, the `newImage` object is assigned to the `src` property of the `<img>` element. If you assigned the graphic.jpg file directly to the `src` property of the `<img>` element using the statement `document.myImage.src = "graphic.jpg";`, then the file would reload from its source each time it was needed. The `newImage` object opens the file once and saves it to a memory cache.

The following code shows a version of the unicycle animation code modified to use image caching. The lines that add each image file to the `unicycle[]` array have been replaced by a `for` loop, which assigns a new object to each element of the `unicycle[]` array until the `loadImages` variable is greater than the length of the array. In the `while` loop, each object in the `unicycle[]` array is assigned an image file using the `src` property. In the `turn()` function, the `unicycle[curUnicycle]` operator in the statement `document.images[0].src = unicycle[curUnicycle];` now includes the `src` property so that the statement reads `document.images[0].src = unicycle[curUnicycle].src;`.

```
<!DOCTYPE html PUBLIC "-//W3C//DTD XHTML 1.0 Strict//EN"
"http://www.w3.org/TR/xhtml1/DTD/xhtml1-strict.dtd">
<html xmlns="http://www.w3.org/1999/xhtml">
<head>
<title>Unicycle</title>
<meta http-equiv="content-type"
     content="text/html;charset=iso-8859-1" />
<script type="text/javascript">
/* <![CDATA[ */
var turnUnicycle;
var unicycle = new Array(16);
var curUnicycle = 0;
for (var imagesLoaded=0; imagesLoaded < 16; ++imagesLoaded) {
     unicycle[imagesLoaded] = new Image();
     unicycle[imagesLoaded].src = "unicycle"
          + imagesLoaded + ".gif";
}
function turn() {
     if (curUnicycle == 15)
          curUnicycle = 0;
     else
          ++curUnicycle;
     document.images[0].src = unicycle[curUnicycle].src;
}
function startTurning() {
     if (turnUnicycle != null)
          clearInterval(turnUnicycle);
     turnUnicycle = setInterval("turn()", 100);
}
/* ]]> */
</script>
</head>
<body>
<p><img src="unicycle0.gif" height="75" width="75" /></p>
<form action="">
<p><input type="button" value=" Turn "
onclick="startTurning();" />
<input type="button" value=" Stop "
onclick="clearInterval(turnUnicycle);" /></p>
</form>
</body>
</html>
```

TIP

You can find a copy of the preceding Unicycle Web page, named UnicycleCache1.html, along with the required image files in the Chapter folder for Chapter 10 on your Data Disk.

Next, you will modify the airplane animation in the PrivatePilot.html document to include image caching.

To modify the airplane animation in the PrivatePilot.html document to include image caching:

1. Return to the **PrivatePilot.html** file in your text editor.

2. Replace the 16 statements that assign each airplane frame to the `plane[]` array with the following `for` loop. The `loadImages` variable keeps track of the number of cached images and the `while` loop creates a new `Image` object within each element of the `plane[]` array. Each object in the `plane[]` array is then assigned an image file using the `src` property.

    ```
    for (var imagesLoaded=0; imagesLoaded < 16; ++imagesLoaded) {
        plane[imagesLoaded] = new Image();
        plane[imagesLoaded].src = "airplane" + imagesLoaded
            + ".gif";
    }
    ```

3. Add the `src` property to the `document.images[0].src = plane[curPlane];` statement in the `fly()` function so it reads as follows:

    ```
    document.images[0].src = plane[curPlane].src;
    ```

4. Save the **PrivatePilot.html** document and open it in your Web browser. If you previously experienced erratic animation, the new animation should appear much smoother.

5. Close your Web browser window.

Even when you use image caching, the images must all be loaded into an `Image` object before the animation functions correctly. Often, you will want animation to start as soon as a page finishes loading, as is the case with the airplane animation. However, even though a page has finished loading, all the images may not have finished downloading and may not be stored in image caches. If you run the airplane animation across an Internet connection, the `onload` event handler of the `<body>` element may execute the animation sequence before all the frames are transferred and assigned to `Image` objects (depending on Internet connection speed). The animation will still function, but will be erratic until all the images have been successfully stored in `Image` objects. To be certain that all images are downloaded into a cache before commencing an animation sequence, you use the `onload` event handler of the `Image` object.

The following code shows another modified version of the unicycle script. This time, the program does not include a Turn or Stop button. Instead, the `for` loop now contains an `if` statement that checks whether the `imagesLoaded` variable is equal to 15, which indicates that all the images have been downloaded. Once the `imagesLoaded` variable equals 15, the `turn()` function executes using the same setInterval() statement that was originally located in the onclick event for the Turn button. Notice that the code no longer includes the startTurning() function, nor does it include an onload event handler in the <body> element. Once all the images are cached in the unicycle[] array, the turn() function executes automatically.

```
<!DOCTYPE html PUBLIC "-//W3C//DTD XHTML 1.0 Strict//EN"
"http://www.w3.org/TR/xhtml1/DTD/xhtml1-strict.dtd">
<html xmlns="http://www.w3.org/1999/xhtml">
<head>
<title>Unicycle</title>
<meta http-equiv="content-type"
     content="text/html;charset=iso-8859-1" />
<script type="text/javascript">
/* <![CDATA[ */
var turnUnicycle;
var unicycle = new Array(16);
var curUnicycle = 0;
for (var imagesLoaded=0; imagesLoaded < 16; ++imagesLoaded) {
    unicycle[imagesLoaded] = new Image();
    unicycle[imagesLoaded].src = "unicycle"
          + imagesLoaded + ".gif";
    if (imagesLoaded == 15)
          turnUnicycle = setInterval("turn()", 100);
}
function turn() {
    if (curUnicycle == 15)
          curUnicycle = 0;
    else
          ++curUnicycle;
    document.images[0].src = unicycle[curUnicycle].src;
}
/* ]]> */
</script>
</head>
<body>
<p><img src="unicycle0.gif" height="75" width="75" /></p>
</body>
</html>
```

TIP
You can find a copy of the preceding Unicycle Web page, named UnicycleCache2.html, along with the required image files in the Chapter folder for Chapter 10 on your Data Disk.

Next, you add an image `onload` event handler to the airplane animation that executes the animation after all the images have loaded.

To add an image `onload` event handler to the airplane animation that executes the animation after all the images have loaded:

1. Return to the **PrivatePilot.html** file in your text editor.

2. Add the following `if` statement to the end of the `for` loop. After all the images are loaded, the `if` statement uses the `setInterval()` method to call the `loadImages()` function.

```
if (imagesLoaded == 15)
    setInterval("fly()", 200);
```

3. Delete the `onload` event handler from the opening `<body>` tag. You no longer need it because the animation is started by the image `onload` event handler.

4. Save the **PrivatePilot.html** file and open it in your Web browser. The animation should begin as soon as all the images load.

5. Close your Web browser window.

Accessing Document Elements

Up to this point in the book, you have accessed HTML elements as properties of the `Document` object. For example, the statement `document.forms[0].email.value` returns the value in a text box named `email` from the first form in a document. Although this method works well, it has its limitations because you can only access anchor, form, image, and link elements. But what if you want to access a paragraph (`<p>`) or table (`<table>`) element? To access any element in a document with JavaScript—and modify it dynamically—you must use one of the following methods of the `Document` object: `getElementById()`, `getElementsByName()`, or `getElementsByTagName()`. The use of these methods is required for many types of DHTML and AJAX techniques, so you will use them for the remainder of this book.

Accessing Elements by Name

The `getElementsByName()` method returns an array of elements with a `name` attribute that matches a specified value. You append the `getElementsByName()` method to the `Document` object and pass to it a single argument representing the `name` attribute of the elements you want to retrieve. For example, consider the following form, which creates four check boxes. The name attribute of each check box is assigned a value of `committees`.

```
<form action="FormProcessor.html" method="get"
enctype="application/x-www-form-urlencoded"
onsubmit="return submitForm()">
<h3>Which committees would you like to serve on? </h3>
<p><input type="checkbox" name="committees"
value="program_dev" />Program Development<br />
<input type="checkbox" name="committees"
```

```
value="fundraising" />Fundraising<br />
<input type="checkbox" name="committees"
value="pub_relations" />Public Relations <br />
<input type="checkbox" name="committees"
value="education" />Education</p>
<p><input type="submit" /></p>
</form>
```

In Chapter 5, you saw the following event handler function, which executes when the form is submitted. This function uses the forms[] array to access the array of elements that represent the check boxes with the name attribute of committees to determine whether at least one check box in the group is selected.

```
function submitForm() {
    var committeesSelected = false;
    for (var i=0; i< document.forms[0].committees.length; ++i) {
        if (document.forms[0].committees[i].checked == true) {
            committeesSelected = true;
            break;
        }
    }
    if (committeesSelected == false) {
        window.alert("You must select at least one committee.");
        return committeesSelected;
    }
    else
        return committeesSelected;
}
```

Now, consider the following modified version of the event handler function. In this version, the function uses the getElementsByName() method to return an array of elements that represent the check boxes with the name attribute of committees.

```
function submitForm() {
    var committeesSelected = false;
    var selectedCommittees = document.getElementsByName("committees");
    for (var i=0; i<selectedCommittees.length; ++i) {
        if (selectedCommittees[i].checked == true) {
            committeesSelected = true;
            break;
        }
    }
    if (committeesSelected == false) {
        window.alert("You must select at least one committee.");
        return committeesSelected;
    }
    else
        return committeesSelected;
```

}

Keep in mind that the getElementsByName() method always returns an array, even if there is only one element in the document with a matching name attribute. This means that even if the document only contains a single element with the specified name, you must refer to it in your JavaScript code by using the first index (0) of the returned array. For example, suppose you have a form with a text box whose name attribute is assigned a value of "email", and it is the only element in the document with that value assigned to its name attribute. The following statement demonstrates how to create an array consisting of a single element with a value of "email" assigned to its name attribute, and then display its value in an alert dialog box:

```
var email = document.getElementsByName("email");
window.alert(email[0].value);
```

With methods like the getElementsByName() method that always return an array, you can also append the index number of the element you want to access to the statement containing the method, as follows:

```
window.alert(document.getElementsByName("email")[0].value);
```

Next, you will modify the PrivatePilot.html document so it uses the getElementsByName() method to refer to the element containing the airplane image.

To modify the PrivatePilot.html document so it uses the getElementsByName() method to refer to the element containing the airplane image:

1. Return to the **PrivatePilot.html** file in your text editor.

2. Locate the following statement in the fly() function:

   ```
   document.images[0].src = plane[curPlane].src;
   ```

3. Modify the statement you located in the previous step so it uses the getElementsByName() method to refer to the element containing the airplane image:

   ```
   document.getElementsByName("airplaneImage")[0].src
       = plane[curPlane].src;
   ```

4. Add the following bolded name attribute, assigned a value of "airplaneImage", to the element containing the airplane image:

   ```
   <td align="center"><img src="airplane0.gif" name="airplaneImage"
   height="100" width="200" alt="Image of an airplane." /></td>
   ```

5. Save the **PrivatePilot.html** file and open it in your Web browser. The animation should begin as soon as all the images load.

6. Close your Web browser window.

Accessing Elements by Tag Name

The getElementsByTagName() method is similar to the getElementsByName() method, except that instead of returning an array of elements with a name attribute that matches a specified value, it returns an array of elements that match a specified tag name. You append the getElementsByTagName() method to the Document object and pass to it a single argument representing the name of the elements you want to retrieve. As an example, the following statement returns an array of all the paragraph (<p>) tags in a document:

```
var docParagraphs = document.getElementsByTagName("p");
```

CAUTION

Be sure not to include the tag name's brackets (such as "<p>") in the argument you pass to the getElementsByTagName() method.

Consider the following modified version of the form containing the committee check boxes. This version contains radio buttons that allow users to select "Yes" if they want to serve on a committee or "No" if they don't. Clicking one of the radio buttons calls a function named enableCommittees() and passes to it a Boolean value of either true (to disable the committee check boxes) or false (to enable them).

```
<form action="FormProcessor.html" method="get"
enctype="application/x-www-form-urlencoded"
onsubmit="return submitForm()">
<p>Would you like to serve on a committee?</p>
<p><input type="radio" name="committeeInvolvement" checked="checked"
onclick="enableCommittees(false)" /> Yes
<input type="radio" name="committeeInvolvement"
onclick="enableCommittees(true)" /> No</p>
<p>Which committees would you like to serve on? </p>
<p><input type="checkbox" name="committees"
value="program_dev" />Program Development<br />
<input type="checkbox" name="committees"
value="fundraising" />Fundraising<br />
<input type="checkbox" name="committees"
value="pub_relations" />Public Relations <br />
<input type="checkbox" name="committees"
value="education" />Education</p>
</form>
```

The following enableCommittees() function demonstrates how to use the getElementsBy-TagName() function. The function's first statement uses the getElementsByTagName() method to return an array of all the <input> elements in the document, which is then assigned to a variable named committeeBoxes[]. Then, the for loop iterates through each of the elements in the committeeBoxes[] array and checks the value of each Input object's type property. If the type property is equal to "checkbox", then the element is enabled or disabled by assigning the value of the boolValue variable to the disabled property of the Input object.

```
function enableCommittees(boolValue) {
    var committeeBoxes = document.getElementsByTagName("input");
```

```
    for (var i=0; i<committeeBoxes.length; ++i) {
        if (committeeBoxes[i].type == "checkbox")
            committeeBoxes[i].disabled = boolValue;
        }
}
```

The `getElementsByTagName()` method works the same as the `getElementsByName()` method in that it always returns an array, even if there is only one element in the document that matches the specified tag name. For example, with a document that contains a single form that is submitted with the POST method, the following `document.write()` statement refers to the first element in the array returned from a `getElementsByTagName()` method that is passed a value of "form". The statement prints, "The form will be submitted with the post method."

```
document.write("<p>The form will be submitted with the "
    + document.getElementsByTagName("form")[0].method
    + " method.</p>");
```

Next, you will modify the PrivatePilot.html document so it uses the `getElementsByTagName()` method instead of the `getElementsByName()` method to refer to the element containing the airplane image.

To modify the PrivatePilot.html document so it uses the `getElementsByTagName()` method instead of the `getElementsByName()` method to refer to the element containing the airplane image:

1. Return to the **PrivatePilot.html** file in your text editor.

2. Modify the last statement in the `fly()` function so it uses the `getElementsByTagName()` method and the `<img>` tag name to refer to the element containing the airplane image, as follows:

   ```
   document.getElementsByTagName("img")[0].src
       = plane[curPlane].src;
   ```

3. Save the **PrivatePilot.html** file and open it in your Web browser. The animation should begin as soon as all the images load.

4. Close your Web browser window.

Accessing Elements by ID

The `getElementsByName()` and `getElementsByTagName()` methods are extremely useful if you need to work with collections of elements that have the same `name` attribute or are of the same type. However, if you are only interested in accessing a single element, you should use the **getElementById() method**, which returns the first element in a document with a matching `id` attribute. You append the `getElementById()` method to the Document object and pass to it a single argument representing the ID of the element you want to retrieve. For example, consider again a document that contains a single form that is submitted with the POST method and that is also assigned a value of `customerInfo` to its ID attribute. The following `document.write()` statement uses the `getElementById()` method to access the form and its method attribute:

```
document.write("<p>The form will be submitted with the "
    + document.getElementById("customerInfo").method
    + " method.</p>");
```

As another example, the following statement uses the getElementById() method to retrieve the value entered into a text box that is assigned an id attribute of email:

```
window.alert("You entered the following e-mail address: "
    + document.getElementById("email").value);
```

Be sure to notice that the getElementById() method does not refer to an array because it only returns a single element instead of an array, as do the getElementsByName() and getElementsByTagName() methods. If your document contains multiple elements with the same id attribute, then the getElementById() method only returns the first matching element.

CAUTION

A common mistake when using the getElementById() method is to capitalize the last 'd', as in getElementByID(), which causes an error because JavaScript is case sensitive.

Next, you will modify the PrivatePilot.html document so it uses the getElementById() method instead of the getElementsByTagName() method to refer to the element containing the airplane image.

To modify the PrivatePilot.html document so it uses the getElementById() method instead of the getElementsByTagName() method to refer to the element containing the airplane image:

1. Return to the **PrivatePilot.html** file in your text editor.

2. Modify the name="airplaneImage" attribute in the <img> element to **id="airplaneImage"**.

3. Modify the last statement in the fly() function so it uses the getElementById() method and the airplaneImage ID to refer to the element containing the airplane image, as follows:

    ```
    document.getElementById("airplaneImage").src
        = plane[curPlane].src;
    ```

4. Save the **PrivatePilot.html** file and open it in your Web browser. The animation should begin as soon as all the images load.

5. Close your Web browser window.

Modifying Elements with the `innerHTML` Property

Another element that is used for accessing elements is the **innerHTML property**, which sets and retrieves the content of a specified element. The innerHTML property was originally introduced by Microsoft into Internet Explorer browsers, but has been adopted by most current Web browsers. The W3C has not officially approved the innerHTML property as part of the DOM, but probably will at some point due to the method's growing popularity and versatility. In comparison to the `document.write()` and `document.writeln()` methods, which cannot be used to change content after a Web page has been rendered, the `innerHTML` property allows you to retrieve and modify the contents of almost any element without having to reload the entire Web page. In fact, many JavaScript programmers view the `innerHTML` property as a replacement for the `document.write()` and `document.writeln()` methods.

NOTE

Although the `innerHTML` property is popular with many JavaScript programmers, it also has its detractors. To learn about the arguments against using the `innerHTML` property, along with some alternative solutions, search the Web for "alternatives to innerHTML". The alternative solutions to the `innerHTML` property primarily use some fairly complex techniques involving the XML DOM. Yet, it's important to point out that one of the greatest benefits of JavaScript is its simplicity and ease-of-use, and using the XML DOM to manipulate Web pages is anything but simple. In this author's opinion, any techniques that continue to make JavaScript easier to understand and use, such as the `innerHTML` property, should be embraced, as opposed to more complex solutions.

To use the `innerHTML` property, you append it to an object representing the element whose value you want to retrieve or modify. As an example, the following paragraph element contains an anchor element that displays the text "How's this for a deal?". An `onmouseover` event uses the `innerHTML` property and a `this` reference to change the contents of the anchor element to "Order now and receive 20% off!". Then, an `onmouseout` event uses the `innerHTML` property and a `this` reference to change the contents of the anchor element back to "How\'s this for a deal?".

```
<p><a href="sales.html" id="salesLink"
onmouseover="this.innerHTML='Order now and receive 20% off!'"
onmouseout="this.innerHTML='How\'s this for a deal?'">How's this for a
deal?</a></p>
```

You can also append the `innerHTML` property to an element that is returned from the `getElementById()`, `getElementsByName()`, or `getElementsByTagName()` methods. The following example shows the same code that uses the `innerHTML` property to change the link text, but this version uses the `getElementById()` method instead of a `this` reference:

```
<p><a href="sales.html" id="salesLink"
onmouseover="document.getElementById('salesLink').innerHTML='Order now
and receive 20% off!'"
onmouseout="document.getElementById('salesLink').innerHTML='How\'s this
for a deal?'">How's this for a deal?</a></p>
```

Next, you will modify the Al's Aviation pages so they use the `innerHTML` property to set the value assigned to the `<h1>` element.

To modify the Al's Aviation pages so they use the innerHTML property to set the value assigned to the <h1> element:

1. Return to the **PrivatePilot.html** file in your text editor.

2. Replace the document.open(), document.write(), and document.close() statements in the second script section with the following statements, which use the getElementById() method, getElementsByTagName() method, and innerHTML property to set the value assigned to the <h1> element:

```
document.write("<h1 id='mainHeading'></h1>");
document.getElementById("mainHeading").innerHTML
    = document.getElementsByTagName("title")[0].innerHTML;
```

3. Save the **PrivatePilot.html** file and validate it with the W3C Markup Validation Service. Once the file is valid, close it in your text editor.

4. Return to the **AviationHome.html** file in your text editor and modify the script section with the same changes you made in Step 2.

5. Save the **AviationHome.html** file and validate it with the W3C Markup Validation Service. Once the file is valid, close it in your text editor.

6. Return to the **Instrument.html** file in your text editor and modify the script section with the same changes you made in Step 2.

7. Save the **Instrument.html** file and validate it with the W3C Markup Validation Service. Once the file is valid, close it in your text editor.

8. Open the **AviationHome.html** file in your Web browser. The first heading on the page, Al's Aviation, uses the innerHTML property to access the value assigned to the Web page's document object's title property. Test the links for the Private Pilot Training and Instrument Training Web pages. The headings should appear the same as the home page.

9. Close your Web browser and text editor.

Chapter Summary

▶ Dynamic HTML (DHTML) refers to a combination of technologies that make Web pages dynamic.

▶ DHTML is a combination of JavaScript, XHTML, CSS, and the Document Object Model.

▶ At the core of DHTML is the Document Object Model, or DOM, which represents the Web page displayed in a window.

▶ The Document Object Model that represents HTML content is referred to as the HTML DOM, and the Document Object Model that represents XML content is referred to as the XML DOM.

▶ Through the Document object, you can access other objects that represent elements on a Web page.

▶ The open() method creates a new document in a window or frame.

▶ The close() method notifies the Web browser that you are finished writing to the window or frame and that the document should be displayed.

▶ You should always use the open() and close() methods when you want to use the document.write() and document.writeln() methods to update the text displayed in an existing window or frame.

▶ An Image object represents an image created using the <img> element.

▶ One of the most important properties of the Image object is the src property, which allows JavaScript to change an image dynamically.

▶ By combining the src attribute of the Image object with the setTimeout() or setInterval() methods, you can create simple animation on a Web page.

▶ A technique for eliminating multiple downloads of the same file is called image caching, which temporarily stores image files in memory. This technique allows JavaScript to store and retrieve an image from memory rather than downloading the image each time it is needed.

▶ You use the onload event handler of the Image object to be certain that all images are downloaded into a cache before commencing an animation sequence.

▶ The getElementsByName() method returns an array of elements with a name attribute that matches a specified value.

▶ The getElementsByTagName() method returns an array of elements that matches a specified tag name.

▶ The getElementById() method returns the first element in a document with a matching id attribute.

▶ The innerHTML property sets and retrieves the content of a specified element.

Review Questions

1. Explain what the word "dynamic" means in Internet terminology.

2. Explain how to simulate limited dynamism and interactivity with simple hypertext links.

3. DHTML refers to a combination of which of the following technologies? (Choose all that apply.)

   a. JavaScript
   b. XHTML
   c. CSS
   d. DOM

4. Which of the following Document Object Models can you use to manipulate an XHTML document? (Choose all that apply.)

   a. HTML DOM
   b. XHTML DOM
   c. JSCRIPT DOM
   d. XML DOM

5. Current Mozilla-based Web browsers including Firefox, Internet Explorer 5.0 and higher, and Netscape 6 and higher are not compatible with a standardized version of the DOM; in other words, you must write different JavaScript code sections for each type of browser. True or false?

6. The only element on a Web page that is represented in the DOM by its own object is the `Document` object. True or false?

7. Which of the following `Document` object methods should you always use when you want to use the `write()` and `writeln()` methods to update the text displayed in an existing window or frame? (Choose all that apply.)

   a. `close()`
   b. `open()`
   c. `getElementById()`
   d. `getElementsByName()`

8. Which of the following `Document` object properties can be dynamically changed after a Web page is rendered?

   a. `referrer`
   b. `title`
   c. `URL`
   d. `domain`

9. Which of the following Document object properties returns an array? (Choose all that apply.)

   a. anchors

   b. cookie

   c. images

   d. forms

10. Which of the following can be used to refer to an image with JavaScript code? (Choose all that apply.)

    a. name attribute

    b. id attribute

    c. value attribute

    d. images[]

11. Which property of the Image object allows JavaScript to change an image dynamically?

    a. URL

    b. value

    c. href

    d. src

12. Why should you use image caching and what are the procedures for adding image caching to your Web pages?

13. To be certain that all images are downloaded into a cache before commencing an animation sequence, you use the _____ of the Image object.

    a. images[] array

    b. animation property

    c. loadImages() method

    d. onload event handler

14. Why do you need to use the getElementById(), getElementsByName(), or getElementsByTagName() method?

15. What value must you pass to the getElementsByName() method?

    a. the id attribute of the element you want to retrieve

    b. the tag name of the elements you want to retrieve

    c. the index of the element in the elements[] array

    d. the name attribute of the elements you want to retrieve

16. The getElementsByName() method only returns an array if it locates multiple elements that match the passed argument; a single variable is returned if only one array element is returned. True or false?

17. Which of the following is the correct syntax for executing the `getElementsByTagName()` method and returning all of a document's `<p>` tags?

    a. `document.getElementsByTagName("<p>")`

    b. `document.getElementsByTagName("p")`

    c. `document.getElementsByTagName(<p>)`

    d. `document.getElementsByTagName() = "<p>"`

18. The `getElementById()` method always returns an array even if only one element is returned. True or false?

19. Which of the following can be used to access the `innerHTML` property?

    a. the `this` reference

    b. the `getElementById()` method

    c. the `getElementsByName()` method

    d. the `getElementsByTagName()` method

20. The W3C has not officially approved the `innerHTML` property as part of the DOM. True or false?

Hands-On Projects

Project 10-1

The DOM `Anchor` object represents a link on a Web page that is created with an `<a>` element. Attributes of the `<a>` element, such as the `href` attribute, are also available as properties of the `Anchor` object. This project demonstrates how to use the `href` property of the `Anchor` object, along with the `innerHTML` property, to dynamically change the URL and text of an anchor element. The project is an investment recommendation page that provides a link to a recommended investment on Yahoo! Finance according to a particular sector, such as consumer goods or healthcare.

1. Create a new document in your text editor.

2. Type the `<!DOCTYPE>` declaration, `<html>` element, header information, and the `<body>` element. Use the strict DTD and "Investment Picks" as the content of the `<title>` element.

3. Add the following heading to the document body:

    `<h1>Investment Picks</h1>`

4. Add the following elements and text to the end of the document body. The form contains buttons for stock recommendations in the nine major sectors (according to Yahoo! Finance). Each radio button contains an `onclick` event that calls an event handler named `updateInvestmentLink()`, which you will add next. Two

arguments are passed to the `updateInvestmentLink()` function: the name of the investment (which will be used as link text) and a URL (which will be used as the link's URL).

```
<form action="" enctype="application/x-www-form-urlencoded">
<p><input type="radio" name="industry"
onclick="updateInvestmentLink('Gold',
'http://finance.yahoo.com/q?s=^YHOh714')" /> Basic Materials
<br />
<input type="radio" name="industry" onclick="updateInvestmentLink
('Koor Industries Ltd.', 'http://finance.yahoo.com/q/pr?s=kor')" />
Conglomerates<br />
<input type="radio" name="industry"
onclick="updateInvestmentLink('Tyson Foods Inc.',
'http://finance.yahoo.com/q/pr?s=tsn')" /> Consumer Goods
<br />
<input type="radio" name="industry"
onclick="updateInvestmentLink('Countrywide Financial Corp.',
'http://finance.yahoo.com/q/pr?s=cfc')" /> Financial<br />
<input type="radio" name="industry"
onclick="updateInvestmentLink('Genentech Inc.',
'http://finance.yahoo.com/q/pr?s=dna')" /> Healthcare<br />
<input type="radio" name="industry"
onclick="updateInvestmentLink('Thermoenergy Corp.',
'http://finance.yahoo.com/q/pr?s=tmen.ob')" /> Industrial Goods
<br />
<input type="radio" name="industry"
onclick="updateInvestmentLink('Sinclair Broadcast Group Inc.',
'http://finance.yahoo.com/q/pr?s=sbgi')" /> Services<br />
<input type="radio" name="industry"
onclick="updateInvestmentLink('Verizon Communications Inc.',
'http://finance.yahoo.com/q/pr?s=vz')" /> Technology<br />
<input type="radio" name="industry"
onclick="updateInvestmentLink('Northwest Natural Gas Co.',
'http://finance.yahoo.com/q/pr?s=nwn')" /> Utilities</p>
</form>
<p><a href="http://finance.yahoo.com/"
id="recommendedInvestment">Yahoo! Finance</a></p>
```

5. Add the following script section to the document head:

```
<script type="text/javascript">
/* <![CDATA[ */
/* ]]> */
</script>
```

6. Add the following `updateInvestmentLink()` function to the script section. The first statement uses the `innerHTML` property and the `urlText` parameter (which is passed as the first argument from the radio buttons) to change the text of the anchor

element. The second statement uses the `href` property of the `Anchor` object and the `urlValue` parameter (which is passed as the second argument from the radio buttons) to change the value of the `href` attribute.

```
function updateInvestmentLink(urlText, urlValue) {
     document.getElementById('recommendedInvestment').innerHTML
          = urlText + " (Yahoo! Finance)";
     document.getElementById('recommendedInvestment').href
          = urlValue;
}
```

7. Save the document as **InvestmentPicks.html** in your Projects folder for Chapter 10, and then validate the document with the W3C Markup Validation Service. Once the document is valid, close it in your text editor.

8. Open the **InvestmentPicks.html** document in your Web browser and test the radio buttons. Clicking each radio button should change the text and URL of the link at the bottom of the page. Be sure to test the link to ensure that it opens the correct URL.

9. Close your Web browser window.

Project 10-2

In Chapter 9 you used the `Event` object to check which values a user entered into a text box. Like the `Image` object, the `Event` object is also part of the HTML DOM. Another event type that you haven't studied yet is the `oncontextmenu` event, which is triggered whenever a user attempts to display the context menu (or "shortcut" menu) by clicking his or her right mouse button. Like the `innerHTML` property, the `oncontextmenu` event was originally introduced by Microsoft into Internet Explorer browsers, but has been adopted by most current Web browsers. The `oncontextmenu` event has also not been officially approved by the W3C, but because it is supported by most current Web browsers, you can safely use it in your JavaScript programs.

Users often copy images or document content from Web pages by right-clicking them to display the context menu, from which you can select the Save Picture As or Copy Image command. One trick that some JavaScript programmers employ to prevent users from copying images or other types of content (that may be protected by copyrights) from a Web page is to use the `oncontextmenu` event to prevent users from displaying the context menu. In this project, you will add an image, instrument.jpg, to the Instrument.html page along with code that prevents users from right-clicking the image and saving it. You will also add code that prevents users from copying any content on the page. You can find the instrument.jpg file in your Projects folder for Chapter 10.

NOTE

Using the `oncontextmenu` event to prevent users from displaying the context menu does not completely protect your content. There are various ways that users can circumvent this functionality, including viewing the Web page source code, taking a screen capture of the content, or disabling JavaScript altogether. Therefore, you can really only rely on this method to notify users that the content they are attempting to copy is copyrighted.

TIP

For more information on the `Event` object, see the DOM event Web page in the W3C's DHTML tutorial at *http://ww.w3schools.com/dhtml/dhtml_object_event.asp*.

1. Copy the **Instrument.html** document from your Chapter folder for Chapter 10 to your Projects folder for Chapter 10.

2. Open in a text editor the **Instrument.html** document from your Projects folder for Chapter 10.

3. Locate in the first table the `<td>` element that contains the non-breaking space (` `), and replace the non-breaking space with the following image element that displays the instrument.jpg file.

```
<img src="instrument.jpg" width="175" height="113"
alt="Image of an airplane's instrument panel." />
```

4. Add the following `oncontextmenu` event handler to the image element you added in the last step. When the user right-clicks the image, an alert dialog box informs them that Al's Aviation owns the copyrights to the image. Then, a value of false is returned, which prevents the context menu from displaying.

```
oncontextmenu="window.alert('This image is copyrighted by Al\'s
Aviation.'); return false"
```

5. Save the **Instrument.html** document and open it in your Web browser. Right-clicking the image should display the alert dialog box and prevent the context menu from opening. However, you should be able to use the context menu to copy the text on the page.

6. Now you will add code that prevents users from using the context menu to copy any content on the Instrument.html page. First, add the following script section to the document head:

```
<script type="text/javascript">
/* <![CDATA[ */
/* ]]> */
</script>
```

7. Add the following statement to the script section in the document head. This statement assigns a function named noContextMenu() as the event handler that will handle any oncontextmenu events. Notice that you do not include parentheses following the function name.

```
document.oncontextmenu=noContextMenu;
```

8. Now add the following noContextMenu() function to the end of the script section in the document head. The function displays an alert dialog box informing users that Al's Aviation owns the copyrights to the content. Then, a value of false is returned, which prevents the context menu from displaying.

```
function noContextMenu() {
    window.alert("This content is copyrighted by Al's Aviation.");
    return false;
}
```

9. Save the **Instrument.html** document and reload it in your Web browser. Right-clicking any portion of the Web page should display the alert dialog box and prevent the context menu from opening.

10. Close your Web browser window.

Project 10-3

In this project, you will create a Web page with an animation of a man using a jackhammer. Your Projects folder for Chapter 10 contains 11 images that are required for this program: jackhammer0.gif through jackhammer10.gif.

1. Create a new document in your text editor.

2. Type the <!DOCTYPE> declaration, <html> element, header information, and the <body> element. Use the strict DTD and "Jackhammer" as the content of the <title> element.

3. Add the following script section to the document head:

```
<script type="text/javascript">
/* <![CDATA[ */
/* ]]> */
</script>
```

4. Add the following text and elements to the document body. The text and elements include an <img> element to display the image, and a form with buttons that controls the animation.

```
<h1>Jackhammer Man</h1>
<p><img src="jackhammer1.gif" height="113" width="100" alt=
"Image of a man with a jackhammer." /></p>
<form action="" enctype="text/plain"><p><input type="button"
value="Start Bouncing"
```

```
onclick="startBouncing();" /> <input type="button" value="Stop
Bouncing" onclick="clearInterval(begin);" /></p>
</form>
```

5. Add the following variable declarations to the script section:

```
var jackhammers = new Array(11);
var curJackhammer = 0;
var direction;
var begin;
jackhammers[0] = "jackhammer0.gif";
jackhammers[1] = "jackhammer1.gif";
jackhammers[2] = "jackhammer2.gif";
jackhammers[3] = "jackhammer3.gif";
jackhammers[4] = "jackhammer4.gif";
jackhammers[5] = "jackhammer5.gif";
jackhammers[6] = "jackhammer6.gif";
jackhammers[7] = "jackhammer7.gif";
jackhammers[8] = "jackhammer8.gif";
jackhammers[9] = "jackhammer9.gif";
jackhammers[10] = "jackhammer10.gif";
```

6. Now add the following functions to the script section, which control the animation:

```
function bounce() {
        if (curJackhammer == 10)
                curJackhammer = 0;
        else
                ++curJackhammer;
        document.getElementsByTagName("img")[0].src
           = jackhammers[curJackhammer].src;
        if (curJackhammer == 0)
                direction = "up";
        else if (curJackhammer == 10)
                direction = "down";
        document.getElementsByTagName("img")[0].src
           = jackhammers[curJackhammer];
}
function startBouncing() {
        if (begin)
                clearInterval(begin);
        begin = setInterval("bounce()",90);
}
```

7. Save the document as **Jackhammer.html** in your Projects folder for Chapter 10 and validate it with the W3C Markup Validation Service. Once the document is valid, open it in your Web browser and test the animation buttons.

8. Close your Web browser window.

Project 10-4

In this project, you will add image caching to the jackhammer animation.

1. Return to the Jackhammer.html document in your text editor and immediately save it as **JackhammerCache.html**.

2. First, delete the following statements from the script section, which assign the image file names to the `jackhammers[]` array:

```
jackhammers[0] = "jackhammer0.gif";
jackhammers[1] = "jackhammer1.gif";
jackhammers[2] = "jackhammer2.gif";
jackhammers[3] = "jackhammer3.gif";
jackhammers[4] = "jackhammer4.gif";
jackhammers[5] = "jackhammer5.gif";
jackhammers[6] = "jackhammer6.gif";
jackhammers[7] = "jackhammer7.gif";
jackhammers[8] = "jackhammer8.gif";
jackhammers[9] = "jackhammer9.gif";
jackhammers[10] = "jackhammer10.gif";
```

3. Now add the following variable declaration and `for` statement to handle the image caching. Add the code above the `bounce()` function.

```
var imagesLoaded = 0;
for (var i = 0; i < 11; ++i) {
        jackhammers[i] = new Image();
        jackhammers[i].src = "jackhammer" + i + ".gif";
        if (i == 10)
                begin = setInterval("bounce()", 90);
}
```

4. Replace the last statement in the `bounce()` function with the following statement, which assigns the cached image to the `<img>` element:

```
document.getElementsByTagName("img")[0].src
    = jackhammers[curJackhammer].src;
```

5. Delete the `startBouncing()` function at the end of the script section. You no longer need the function because the animation starts automatically after the images finish loading.

6. Delete the form in the document body. You no longer need the animation buttons either because the animation starts automatically after the images finish loading.

7. Save the **JackhammerCache.html** document and validate it with the W3C Markup Validation Service. Once the document is valid, close it in your text editor and open it in your Web browser. The animation should begin as soon as the images finish loading.

8. Close your Web browser window.

Project 10-5

The DOM also includes `Table`, `TableRow`, and `TableCell` objects that you can use to dynamically manipulate tables on a Web page. Each of these objects includes various methods and properties for manipulating tables. For example, the `Table` object contains `insertRow()` and `deleteRow()` methods that allow you to add and delete rows in a table while the `TableRow` object contains `insertCell()` and `deleteCell()` methods that allow you to add and delete cells in a table. To refer to a table, you use the `getElementById()` method to access the table through its `id` attribute. The `Table` object also contains a `row[]` array that stores all the rows in the selected table. Similarly, the `TableRow` object contans a `cells[]` array that stores all the cells in the selected row. To access an array containing all of the cells in the first row of a table with an `id` attribute of `myTable`, you use a statement similar to `document.getElementById ("myTable").rows[selectedItem].cells`. Next, you will create a Web page for Central Valley Chocolates that allows users to add and remove chocolate orders from a "shopping cart" table.

TIP

For more information on the `Table`, `TableRow`, and `TableCell` objects, see the W3School's HTML DOM Reference at *http://w3schools.com/htmldom/dom_reference.asp*.

1. Create a new document in your text editor.
2. Type the `<!DOCTYPE>` declaration, `<html>` element, header information, and the `<body>` element. Use the strict DTD and "Central Valley Chocolates" as the content of the `<title>` element.
3. Add the following text and heading elements to the document body:

```
<h1>Central Valley Chocolates</h1>
<h2>Gourmet Chocolates</h2>
```

4. Now add the following table to the end of the document body. Each row in the table contains three cells: the first cell describes the type of chocolate, the second cell lists the price, and the third cell contains an Add button that will call a function named `addItem()`, which you will add next. The argument passed to the `addItem()` function uses the `getElementById()` method to access the current row through its `id` attribute. The `rowIndex` property is a property of the `TableRow` object and returns the current row's index number in the `Table` object's `rows[]` array.

```
<table border="1" id="chocolateTable">
<tr id="ch1">
<td>Chocolate Truffles</td><td>$34.99</td><td><input type=
"button" value="Add" onclick="addItem(document.getElementById
('ch1').rowIndex)" /></td></tr>
<tr id="ch2">
```

```
<td>Pecan Caramel Duets</td><td>$14.99</td><td><input type=
"button" value="Add" onclick="addItem(document.getElementById
('ch2').rowIndex)" /></td></tr>
<tr id="ch3">
<td>Chocolate Covered Cherries</td><td>$28.99</td><td><input
type="button" value="Add" onclick="addItem(document.
getElementById('ch3').rowIndex)" /></td></tr>
<tr id="ch4">
<td>White Chocolate Ganaches</td><td>$22.99</td><td><input
type="button" value="Add" onclick="addItem(document.
getElementById('ch4').rowIndex)" /></td></tr>
<tr id="ch5">
<td>Chocolate Mints</td><td>$17.99</td><td><input type="button"
value="Add" onclick="addItem(document.getElementById('ch5').
rowIndex)" /></td></tr>
<tr id="ch6">
<td>Chocolate Caramels</td><td>$14.99</td><td><input type=
"button" value="Add" onclick="addItem(document.getElementById
('ch6').rowIndex)" /></td></tr>
<tr id="ch7">
<td>Chocolate Toffee Bark</td><td>$9.99</td><td><input type=
"button" value="Add" onclick="addItem(document.getElementById
('ch7').rowIndex)" /></td></tr>
</table>
```

5. Add the following text and elements to the end of the document body. The table will store the shopping cart items selected by the user and the paragraph element will display the sales total.

```
<h2>Your Shopping Cart</h2>
<table id="shoppingCart" border="1">
<tr><td>Your shopping cart is empty</td></tr>
</table>
<p id="total"> </p>
```

6. Add the following script section to the document head:

```
<script type="text/javascript">
/* <![CDATA[ */
/* ]]> */
</script>
```

7. Add the following global variables and function definition to the script section. The emptyCart variable will determine whether the shopping cart is empty and the salesTotal variable will store the current sales total. The curOrderRow variable will be used to create unique IDs for each row in the shopping cart table. The function is passed a single parameter representing the current row's index number in the Table object's rows[] array.

```
var emptyCart = true;
var salesTotal = 0;
var curOrderRow = 1;
```

```
function addItem(selectedItem) {
}
```

8. Add the following `if` statement to the `addItem()` function. This code determines whether the shopping cart is empty; if so, then it uses the `deleteRow()` method of the `Table` object to delete the single row in the table that displays the text "Your shopping cart is empty".

```
if (emptyCart == true) {
    document.getElementById('shoppingCart').deleteRow(0);
    emptyCart = false;
}
```

9. Add to the end of the `addItem()` function the following statements, which assign the description and price to the `selectedItem` and `itemPrice` variables. Notice that the statements use the `cells[]` array of the `TableRows` object to access the cell values through the `innerHTML` property.

```
var curItem = document.getElementById("chocolateTable")
        .rows[selectedItem].cells;
var selectedItem = curItem[0].innerHTML;
var itemPrice = curItem[1].innerHTML;
```

10. Add to the end of the `addItem()` function the following statements, which use the `insertRow()` and `insertCell()` methods, and the `innerHTML` property to create a new row and cell in the shopping cart table. The last statement uses the `innerHTML` property to create a button element that calls a function named `removeItem()`. The function is passed a single argument, the `rowIndex` property of the `TableRow` object.

```
var lastItem = document.getElementById(
        "shoppingCart").rows.length;
var cartTable = document.getElementById("shoppingCart");
var newRow = cartTable.insertRow(lastItem);
var itemCell = newRow.insertCell(0);
itemCell.innerHTML = selectedItem;
var priceCell = newRow.insertCell(1);
priceCell.innerHTML = itemPrice;
var actionCell = newRow.insertCell(2);
actionCell.innerHTML = "<input type='button' value='Remove' "
    + "onclick=\"removeItem(" + newRow.rowIndex + ")\"' />";
```

11. Add the following statements to the end of the `addItem()` function. These statements update the sales total and assign the new value to the paragraph element with the `id` attribute of `total`.

```
salesTotal += parseFloat(itemPrice.substring(1));
document.getElementById('total').innerHTML
    = "<strong>Sales total</strong>: $" + salesTotal.toFixed(2);
```

12. Finally, add the following `removeItem()` function to the end of the script section. This function removes items from the shopping cart table when the user clicks the item's Remove button.

```
function removeItem(rowNum) {
        if (document.getElementById(
                "shoppingCart").rows.length >1) {
                document.getElementById(
                        "shoppingCart").deleteRow(rowNum);
                var curItem = document.getElementById(
                        'chocolateTable').rows[rowNum].cells;
            var itemPrice = curItem[1].innerHTML;
            salesTotal = salesTotal - parseFloat(
                    itemPrice.substring(1));
            document.getElementById('total').innerHTML = "$"
                    + salesTotal.toFixed(2);
        }
        else {
                document.getElementById(
                        "shoppingCart").rows[0].innerHTML
                        = "<td>Your shopping cart is empty</td>";
                salesTotal = 0;
                document.getElementById('total').innerHTML = "$"
                        + salesTotal.toFixed(2);
                emptyCart = true;
        }
}
```

13. Save the document as **ChocolateOrder.html** in your Projects folder for Chapter 10 and validate it with the W3C Markup Validation Service. Once the document is valid, open it in your Web browser and test the program's functionality.

14. Close your Web browser window.

Case Projects

For the following projects, save the documents you create in your Cases folder for Chapter 10. Be sure to validate the files you create with the W3C Markup Validation Service.

Case Project 10-1

Create a document with two vertical frames. Create a series of links in the left frame. Each button should represent the name of a country. Use Wikipedia (*http://www.wikipedia.com*) or another source to look up statistical information on different countries, such as the name of the capital, languages spoken, population, and so on. Use the open(), close(), and write() methods to write the information to the right frame when a user clicks a country link and create separate functions for each country. Save the frameset document as **CountryStats.html** and the document containing the list of country links as **CountryInfo.html**.

Case Project 10-2

Create a Web page that generates addition tables and multiplication tables for the values zero through ten. The document should include buttons that open a new window that displays each table. Generate each table using `document.write()` methods. Both tables should reuse the same window. Save the document as **MathTables.html**.

Case Project 10-3

You have probably seen many sites that use thumbnail images to display smaller versions of an image file. If visitors want to see the image in a larger size, they can click the thumbnail version of the image. The link will then open a larger-sized version of the image or another Web page that displays the larger image along with more information. The important thing to understand is that the thumbnail version of the image is not the original image reduced using the height and width attributes of the `<img>` element. Rather, the thumbnail images are entirely separate images that have been resized using image-editing software. Real estate agents commonly use thumbnails on their Web sites to display pictures of homes and other types of property. Create a Web page for a real estate company that allows visitors to toggle between small and large versions of a property photo. Your Cases folder for Chapter 10 includes two photos, cottage_small.jpg and cottage_large.jpg, that you can use for this exercise. Start by displaying the small version of the image on the Web page and include a link that reads "View larger image". Clicking the link should replace the image file on the Web page with the larger version and change the link text to read "View smaller version". Then, clicking the "View smaller version" link should change back to the smaller version. Use the `getElementById()` method to access the image element on the Web page and be sure to remember to change the height and width of the image each time you replace it. Save the document as **PineKnollProperties.html**.

Case Project 10-4

Create a Web page that allows you to dynamically build a table containing a team roster for a bowling league. Use the same techniques that you learned in Hands-on Project 10-5 for dynamically manipulating tables on a Web page, including the `Table`, `TableRow`, and `TableCell` objects. The Web page should include two forms: one form in which users can enter the names of team members and click an Add Bowler button, and another form which contains the dynamic table and which lists the names of the bowling team members in individual rows. Each row should also contain a Remove Bowler button that removes a bowler's name from the list. The second form should be submitted to the FormProcessor.html document (a copy is in your Cases folder for Chapter 10). In order to submit bowler names that are added dynamically to the table, you will need to dynamically add <input> elements for each bowler. Use two functions: addBowler(), which adds bowler names to the list, and removeBowler(), which removes bowler names from the list. Also, include the text "Your team roster is empty" if no bowlers have been entered or if all bowler names have been removed. Save the document as **BowlingTeam.html**.

Case Project 10-5

Your Cases folder for Chapter 10 contains an animated GIF file of a running puppy, along with six individual images (puppy0.gif through puppy5.gif) that are used in the animation. Create a JavaScript program that animates the six images the same as the animated GIF file. Use image caching to start the animation as soon as the images finish loading, and be sure to use either the getElementById(), getElementsByName(), or getElementsByTagName() method to dynamically update the image element. Save the document as **RunningPuppy.html**.

Case Project 10-6

Your Cases folder for Chapter 10 contains an animated GIF file of a pushpin that is bouncing back and forth, along with 9 individual images (pin0.gif through pin08.gif) that are used in the animation. Create a JavaScript program that animates the 9 images the same as the animated GIF file. You will need to write code that displays pin0.gif through pin08.gif, and then from pin08.gif to pin0.gif. Use image caching to start the animation as soon as the images finish loading, and be sure to use either the getElementById(), getElementsByName(), or getElementsByTagName() method to dynamically update the image element. Save the document as **BouncingPushPin.html**.

11

Creating Dynamic HTML (DHTML)

In this chapter you will:

- Use JavaScript to modify CSS styles
- Work with CSS positioning
- Create DHTML menus
- Learn how to check for browser compatibility

In the last chapter, you learned about the DOM and how it fits in with Dynamic HTML (DHTML). In this chapter, you will become acquainted with some basic DHTML techniques. As you work through this chapter, keep in mind that DHTML is a large subject that could take up an entire book. Also, there is a steep learning curve with DHTML, mainly because it requires a strong knowledge of XHTML, Cascading Style Sheets (CSS), and JavaScript. Therefore, this chapter only touches upon the most basic aspects of DHTML. Specifically, you will learn how to use JavaScript to dynamically modify CSS styles and dynamically position elements. You will also learn how to create DHTML menus and check for browser compatibility.

NOTE
You need a solid understanding of CSS in order to be successful in this chapter.

Manipulating CSS with JavaScript

Although the primary purpose of CSS is to format the display of a Web page, you can use JavaScript to modify CSS styles to make the document dynamic after a Web browser renders the document. As mentioned earlier, prior to the release of the W3C standardized version of the DOM, no DHTML standard worked with both Internet Explorer and Netscape Navigator. This incompatibility was particularly evident to programmers who needed to use JavaScript to manipulate CSS styles. Earlier versions of Internet Explorer and Navigator supported incompatible Document object properties and methods. Because JavaScript uses Document object properties and methods to access CSS styles, if you wanted to use JavaScript code to manipulate CSS in older browsers, you had three options:

- Write code that functioned only in Navigator.
- Write code that functioned only in Internet Explorer.
- Write both sets of code and design the script so that the correct set would execute depending on which browser rendered the page.

If you anticipate that your DHTML code will run in older browsers, you need to learn the DHTML techniques for each type of browser. This chapter only focuses on DHTML techniques that are compatible with the W3C standardized version of the DOM.

Modifying Styles with the `this` Reference

The easiest way to refer to a CSS style in JavaScript is to use the `this` reference and the `style` property in an event handler within the element itself. You use the **style property** to modify an element's CSS properties with JavaScript. In order to refer to a style with the `this` reference, you use a period to append the `style` property to it, followed by another period and a CSS property. For example, the following statement includes an `onclick` event handler that changes the text color of the current paragraph element to red:

```
<p onclick="this.style.color='red';">Red paragraph.</p>
```

CSS properties without hyphens are referred to in JavaScript with all lowercase letters. However, when you refer to a CSS property containing a hyphen in JavaScript code, you remove the hyphen, convert the first word to lowercase, and convert the first letter of subsequent words to uppercase. For example, the `text-decoration` property is referred to as `textDecoration`, `font-family` is referred to as `fontFamily`, `font-size` is referred to as `fontSize`, and so on. To use the `onclick` event handler to modify the font size of the current element, you use the statement `onclick="this.style.fontSize = '2em';"`.

The following code shows an example of how to use `onmouseover` and `onmouseout` event handlers to give users the option of changing the text to make it easier to read. Specifically, it allows users to change the text color and weight of a line simply by passing the mouse pointer over it. Moving the mouse pointer away from the line returns it to its original text color and weight. Figure 11-1 shows the document in a Web browser when the mouse pointer passes over the third line.

```
<!DOCTYPE html PUBLIC "-//W3C//DTD XHTML 1.0 Strict//EN"
"http://www.w3.org/TR/xhtml1/DTD/xhtml1-strict.dtd">
<html xmlns="http://www.w3.org/1999/xhtml">
<head>
<title>Major U.S. Coal Mines</title>
<meta http-equiv="content-type" content="text/html;
charset=iso-8859-1" />
<link rel="stylesheet" href="js_styles.css" type="text/css" />
</head>
```

```
<body>
<h1>Major U.S. Coal Mines</h1>
<p><strong>Place your mouse over any line to change its color and
weight.</strong></p><hr />
<p onmouseover="this.style.color = 'blue';this.style.fontWeight = 'bold'"
onmouseout="this.style.color = 'black';this.style.fontWeight = 'normal'">
North Antelope Rochelle Complex/Powder River Coal Company</p>
<p onmouseover="this.style.color = 'blue';this.style.fontWeight = 'bold'"
onmouseout="this.style.color = 'black';this.style.fontWeight = 'normal'">
Black Thunder/Thunder Basin Coal Company LLC</p>
<p onmouseover="this.style.color = 'blue';this.style.fontWeight = 'bold'"
onmouseout="this.style.color = 'black';this.style.fontWeight = 'normal'">
Cordero Mine/Cordero Mining Co.</p>
<p onmouseover="this.style.color = 'blue';this.style.fontWeight = 'bold'"
onmouseout="this.style.color = 'black';this.style.fontWeight = 'normal'">
Jacobs Ranch Mine/Jacobs Ranch Coal Company</p>
<p onmouseover="this.style.color = 'blue';this.style.fontWeight = 'bold'"
onmouseout="this.style.color = 'black';this.style.fontWeight = 'normal'">
Antelope Coal Mine/Antelope Coal Company</p>
</body>
</html>
```

Figure 11-1

Web page with onmouseover and onmouseout event handlers that change text display

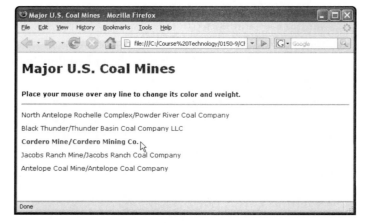

In this chapter, you work on the same Al's Aviation Web pages that you worked with in Chapter 10. The aviation.css style sheet (which each of the Web pages uses) assigns a value of "none" to the text-decoration property for <a> elements so that they are not underlined by default. However, it is more effective to underline the <a> elements when a user places his or her mouse pointer over them, in order to clearly identify the <a> elements as links. Next, you add statements to the onmouseover and onmouseout events that underline the links when the mouse pointer passes over them and then removes the underline when the mouse pointer is removed.

To modify the link underlining in the Al's Aviation Web pages:

1. Copy the **AviationHome.html**, **PrivatePilot.html**, and **Instrument.html** files from your Chapter folder for Chapter 10 to your Chapter folder for Chapter 11.

2. Start your text editor and open the home page for Al's Aviation, **AviationHome.html**.

3. Add onmouseover and onmouseout event handlers for the three <a> elements as follows. In each case, the event handler should display an underline beneath the link only when the mouse pointer passes over the link.

```
<td valign="top"><a href="AviationHome.html"
onmouseover="this.style.textDecoration='underline';"
onmouseout="this.style.textDecoration='none';">Home</a>
<br />
<a href="PrivatePilot.html"
onmouseover="this.style.textDecoration='underline';"
onmouseout="this.style.textDecoration='none';">
Private Pilot Training</a><br/>
<a href="Instrument.html"
onmouseover="this.style.textDecoration='underline';"
onmouseout="this.style.textDecoration='none';">Instrument
Training</a></td>
```

4. Save the **AviationHome.html** document.

5. Open the **PrivatePilot.html** document and add the same text-decoration property to the style declaration for the <a> element and the same statements to the onmouseover and onmouseout event handlers for each <a> element.

6. Save the **PrivatePilot.html** document.

7. Open the **Instrument.html** document and add the same text-decoration property to the style declaration for the <a> element and the same statements to the onmouseover and onmouseout event handlers for each <a> element.

8. Save the **Instrument.html** document.

9. Open the **AviationHome.html** document in your Web browser and test the onmouseover and onmouseout event handlers in the links. Figure 11-2 shows how the Instrument Training link appears when the mouse pointer passes over it.

10. Close your Web browser window.

Figure 11-2

Instrument Training link when the mouse pointer passes over it

You can also pass the `this` reference as an argument to a function. The `onclick` event handler in the following paragraph element calls a function named `changeColor()` and passes it to the `this` reference. When the `this` reference is passed to the function, it becomes the `curElement` variable, which is defined within the function definition's parentheses. The single statement within the function then uses the `curElement` variable to change the element to red.

```
function changeColor(curElement) {
     curElement.style.color = "red";
}
<p onclick="changeColor(this)">
Red paragraph.</p>
```

The following code shows a modified version of the coal mines Web page. This time, however, `this` references are passed to functions that change the display of each line.

```
<!DOCTYPE html PUBLIC "-//W3C//DTD XHTML 1.0 Strict//EN"
"http://www.w3.org/TR/xhtml1/DTD/xhtml1-strict.dtd">
<html xmlns="http://www.w3.org/1999/xhtml">
<head>
<title>Major U.S. Coal Mines</title>
<meta http-equiv="content-type" content="text/html;
charset=iso-8859-1" />
<link rel="stylesheet" href="js_styles.css" type="text/css" />
<script type="text/javascript">
/* <![CDATA[ */
function changeDisplay(curLine) {
     curLine.style.color = "blue";
     curLine.style.fontWeight = "bold";
}
```

CHAPTER 11

```
function restoreDisplay(curLine) {
    curLine.style.color = "black";
    curLine.style.fontWeight = "normal";
}
/* ]]> */
</script>
</head>
<body>
<h1>Major U.S. Coal Mines</h1>
<p><strong>Place your mouse over any line to change its color and
weight.</strong></p><hr />
<p onmouseover="changeDisplay(this)"
onmouseout="restoreDisplay(this)">North Antelope Rochelle Complex/Powder
River Coal Company</p>
<p onmouseover="changeDisplay(this)"
onmouseout="restoreDisplay(this)">Black Thunder/Thunder Basin Coal Company
LLC</p>
<p onmouseover="changeDisplay(this)"
onmouseout="restoreDisplay(this)">Cordero Mine/Cordero Mining Co.</p>
<p onmouseover="changeDisplay(this)"
onmouseout="restoreDisplay(this)">Jacobs Ranch Mine/Jacobs Ranch Coal
Company</p>
<p onmouseover="changeDisplay(this)"
onmouseout="restoreDisplay(this)">Antelope Coal Mine/Antelope Coal
Company</p>
</body>
</html>
```

Next, you will modify the Al's Aviation Web pages so the underlines for the anchor elements are turned on and off using functions.

To modify the code that underlines links in the Al's Aviation Web pages:

1. Return to the **AviationHome.html** document in your text editor.

2. Add the following script section to the document head. The functions use this references to turn the underlining for the links on and off.

```
<script type="text/javascript">
/* <![CDATA[ */
function underlineOn(curLink) {
    curLink.style.textDecoration="underline";
}
function underlineOff(curLink) {
    curLink.style.textDecoration="none";
}
/* ]]> */
</script>
```

3. Next, modify the `onmouseover` and `onmouseout` event handlers in each anchor element so they call the `underlineOn()` and `underlineOff()` functions, passing to each function a `this` reference. Your modified anchor elements should appear as follows:

```
<td valign="top"><a href="AviationHome.html"
onmouseover="underlineOn(this);"
onmouseout="underlineOff(this);">Home</a><br />
<a href="PrivatePilot.html"
onmouseover="underlineOn(this);"
onmouseout="underlineOff(this);">Private Pilot Training</a><br />
<a href="Instrument.html" onmouseover="underlineOn(this);"
onmouseout="underlineOff(this);">Instrument Training</a>
</td>
```

4. Save the **AviationHome.html** document.

5. Return to the **PrivatePilot.html** document in your text editor. Add to the end of the script section the same functions that you added to the AviationHome.html document. Also, modify the `onmouseover` and `onmouseout` event handlers in each `<a>` element so they call the new functions.

6. Save the **PrivatePilot.html** document.

7. Return to the **Instrument.html** document in your text editor. Add a script section to the document head that contains the same functions that you added to the AviationHome.html document. Also, modify the `onmouseover` and `onmouseout` event handlers in each `<a>` element so they call the new functions.

8. Save the **Instrument.html** document.

9. Open the **AviationHome.html** document in your Web browser and test the `onmouseover` and `onmouseout` event handlers in the links. The Web pages should work and appear the same as they did before you added the functions.

10. Close your Web browser window.

Modifying Styles with Methods of the Document Object

In order to modify CSS properties without using the `this` reference, you must first gain access to the styles by using the `getElementById()`, `getElementsByName()`, or `getElementsByTagName()` methods of the `Document` object. The statements in the following function show how to use the `getElementById()` method to access the element with an ID attribute of `ff1` and modify its `color` and `font-size` properties:

```
function changeStyle(curID) {
    var curElement = document.getElementById(curID);
    curElement.style.color = "red";
    curElement.style.fontSize = "18pt";
}
<h1 id="ff1" onclick="changeStyle('ff1')">
Forestville Foods</h1>
```

The following code shows an example of the coal mines page you saw earlier. This time, however, the styles for each line are accessed using getElementById() methods.

```
<!DOCTYPE html PUBLIC "-//W3C//DTD XHTML 1.0 Strict//EN"
"http://www.w3.org/TR/xhtml1/DTD/xhtml1-strict.dtd">
<html xmlns="http://www.w3.org/1999/xhtml">
<head>
<title>Major U.S. Coal Mines</title>
<meta http-equiv="content-type" content="text/html;
charset=iso-8859-1" />
<link rel="stylesheet" href="js_styles.css" type="text/css" />
<script type="text/javascript">
/* <![CDATA[ */
function changeDisplay(curLine) {
    var changeElement = document.getElementById(curLine);
    changeElement.style.color = "blue";
    changeElement.style.fontWeight = "bold";
}
function restoreDisplay(curLine) {
    var changeElement = document.getElementById(curLine);
    changeElement.style.color = "black";
    changeElement.style.fontWeight = "normal";
}
/* ]]> */
</script>
</head>
<body>
<h1>Major U.S. Coal Mines</h1>
<p><strong>Place your mouse over any line to change its color and
weight.</strong></p><hr />
<p id="p1" onmouseover="changeDisplay('p1')"
onmouseout="restoreDisplay('p1')">North Antelope Rochelle Complex/Powder
River Coal Company</p>
<p id="p2" onmouseover="changeDisplay('p2')"
onmouseout="restoreDisplay('p2')">Black Thunder/Thunder Basin Coal Company
LLC</p>
<p id="p3" onmouseover="changeDisplay('p3')"
onmouseout="restoreDisplay('p3')">Cordero Mine/Cordero Mining Co.</p>
<p id="p4" onmouseover="changeDisplay('p4')"
onmouseout="restoreDisplay('p4')">Jacobs Ranch Mine/Jacobs Ranch Coal
Company</p>
<p id="p5" onmouseover="changeDisplay('p5')"
onmouseout="restoreDisplay('p5')">Antelope Coal Mine/Antelope Coal
Company</p>
</body>
</html>
```

Next, you modify the functions in Al's Aviation Web pages so they modify the style of the anchor elements using the `getElementById()` method instead of the `this` reference.

To modify the functions in the Al's Aviation Web pages so they use the `getElementById()` method instead of the `this` reference:

1. Return to the **AviationHome.html** document in your text editor.

2. Modify the `underlineOn()` and `underlineOff()` functions so they use the `getElementById()` function, as follows:

```
function underlineOn(curLink) {
       var selectedLink = document.getElementById(curLink);
       selectedLink.style.textDecoration="underline";
}
function underlineOff(curLink) {
       var selectedLink = document.getElementById(curLink);
       selectedLink.style.textDecoration="none";
}
```

3. Modify the links so they include `id` attributes. Also, modify the event handlers in the anchor elements so they pass each anchor's `id` to the functions instead of the `this` reference. Your modified anchor elements should appear as follows:

```
<td valign="top"><a href="AviationHome.html" id="home"
onmouseover="underlineOn('home');"
onmouseout="underlineOff('home');">Home</a><br />
<a href="PrivatePilot.html" id="pilot"
onmouseover="underlineOn('pilot');"
onmouseout="underlineOff('pilot');">Private Pilot
Training</a><br />
<a href="Instrument.html" id="inst"
onmouseover="underlineOn('inst');"
onmouseout="underlineOff('inst');">Instrument Training</a>
</td>
```

4. Save the **AviationHome.html** document, but leave it open in your text editor.

5. Return to the **PrivatePilot.html** document in your text editor. Modify the functions and event handlers, the same as you did for the AviationHome.html document.

6. Save the **PrivatePilot.html** document, but leave it open in your text editor.

7. Return to the **Instrument.html** document in your text editor. Modify the functions and event handlers, just as you did for the AviationHome.html and PrivatePilot.html documents.

8. Save the **Instrument.html** document, but leave it open in your text editor.

9. Open the **AviationHome.html** document in your Web browser and test the `onmouseover` and `onmouseout` event handlers in the links. The Web pages should work and appear the same as they did before you added the functions.

10. Close your Web browser window.

Understanding CSS Positioning

Although you have used the `<img>` element to create simple animations with JavaScript, you can only use it to create stationary animations. That is, an animation created with the `<img>` element does not travel across the screen. Actually, there is no way to reposition an image on a Web page unless you use **CSS positioning**, which is used to position or lay out elements on a Web page. Table 11-1 lists common CSS positioning properties.

Property	Description
clip	Determines the region of an element that is displayed
display	Specifies whether to display an element
height, width	Determines an image's height and width
top, left	Determines the position of an element's upper-left corner in relation to the upper-left corner of the document window
overflow	Determines how to handle an image that is bigger than its assigned space
position	Specifies the type of CSS positioning
bottom, right	Determines the position of an element's lower-right corner in relation to the upper-left corner of the document window
visibility	Specifies whether an element is visible
z-index	Determines the order in which dynamically positioned elements are layered

Table 11-1   CSS positioning properties

NOTE
CSS positioning is a lengthy topic; this chapter only touches on the very basics.

The most critical CSS positioning property is the `position` property, which determines the type of positioning applied to an element. Table 11-2 lists the values that can be assigned to the `position` property.

Positioning Type	Description
absolute	Positions an element in a specific location on a Web page
fixed	Positions an element in relation to the browser window
relative	Positions an element in relation to other elements on a Web page
static	Positions an element according to the normal flow of other elements and text on a Web page; elements that include a `positioning` property cannot be moved with CSS positioning

Table 11-2   CSS positioning values

A value of "static" essentially means that you cannot use CSS positioning with an element. In order to use CSS positioning, you must use one of the other three values.

Dynamic Positioning

The easiest way to dynamically position an element with CSS is to use the `left` and `top` properties. The `left` property specifies an element's horizontal distance from the upper-left corner of the window, while the `top` property specifies an element's vertical distance from the upper-left corner of the window. Both property values are assigned in pixels. For example, the following code dynamically positions four images of a bird on a Web page. Figure 11-3 shows how the images appear in a Web browser.

```
<body>
<p><img src="goose1.jpg" style="position: absolute; left: 40px;
top: 200px" alt="Image of a bird" height="180"
width="182" /></p>
<p><img src="goose2.jpg" style="position: absolute; left: 80px;
top: 50px" alt="Image of a bird" height="120"
width="118" /></p>
<p><img src="goose3.jpg" style="position: absolute; left: 200px;
top: 100px" alt="Image of a bird" height="150"
width="155" /></p>
<p><img src="goose4.jpg" style="position: absolute; left: 300px;
top: 20px" alt="Image of a bird" height="88"
width="91" /></p>
</body>
```

Figure 11-3
Dynamically positioned images

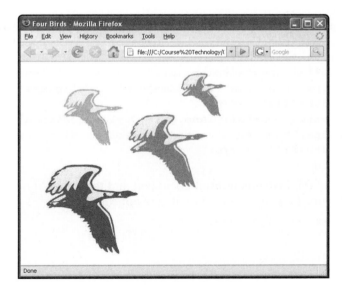

TIP

You can find a copy of the FourBirds.html document and the images it displays in your Chapter folder for Chapter 11.

Next, you dynamically position an image in the Instruments page of the Al's Aviation site. Your Chapter folder for Chapter 11 contains an animated GIF image named airplane.gif that you can use for this exercise.

TIP

An animated GIF is a single file containing a series of individual images that creates simple animation.

To dynamically position an image in the Instruments page of the Al's Aviation site:

1. Return to the **Instrument.html** document in your text editor.

2. In the first table in the document, locate the `<td>` element that contains a nonbreaking space (` `). Replace the nonbreaking space character with the following CSS-positioned `<img>` elements. The CSS properties position the same image in different locations on the screen.

    ```
    <td>
    <p><img src="airplane.gif" style="position: absolute; left:
    225px; top: 40px" alt="Image of an airplane" height="63"
    width="114" /></p>
    <p><img src="airplane.gif" style="position: absolute; left:
    345px; top: 5px" alt="Image of an airplane" height="63"
    width="114" /></p>
    <p><img src="airplane.gif" style="position: absolute; left:
    485px; top: 40px" alt="Image of an airplane" height="63"
    width="114" /></p>
    </td>
    ```

3. Save the **Instrument.html** document and then open it in your Web browser. Figure 11-4 shows how the images appear.

4. Close your Web browser window.

Figure 11-4

Images positioned with CSS in Instrument.html

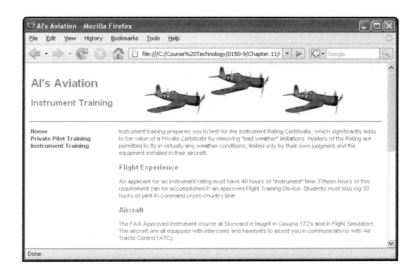

Traveling Animation

The animations you have seen so far have been simple stationary animations that are created by swapping the image files assigned to an `<img>` element's `src` attribute. With DHTML, you can use dynamic positioning to create animations that "travel" across the screen. The following code demonstrates how to create traveling animation with an animated GIF image of a butterfly. The butterfly travels from the lower-left side of the screen, over the paragraph, to the upper-right corner. The global `topPosition` and `leftPosition` variables define the initial starting position of the image. An `onload` event handler in the opening `<body>` tag uses the `setInterval()` function to execute the `flyButterfly()` function, which handles the animation. The first statement in the function gets the element ID of the butterfly image, while the second and third statements assign values to the element's `left` and `top` properties. Be default, the `style` attribute in the image element uses the `visibility` style to hide the image, so the fourth statement in the `flyButterfly()` function displays the image. The remaining statements modify the values assigned to the `topPosition` and `leftPosition` variables, which the function uses to dynamically position the butterfly image. Figure 11-5 shows how the Web page appears in a browser.

```
<!DOCTYPE html PUBLIC "-//W3C//DTD XHTML 1.0 Strict//EN"
"http://www.w3.org/TR/xhtml1/DTD/xhtml1-strict.dtd">
<html xmlns="http://www.w3.org/1999/xhtml">
<head>
<title>Butterfly</title>
<meta http-equiv="content-type" content="text/html;
charset=iso-8859-1" />
<link rel="stylesheet" href="js_styles.css" type="text/css" />
<script type="text/javascript">
/* <![CDATA[ */
var topPosition = 150;
var leftPosition = 0;
function flyButterfly() {
```

```
    var butterfly = document.getElementById("butterfly");
    butterfly.style.left = leftPosition + "px";
    butterfly.style.top = topPosition + "px";
    butterfly.style.visibility = "visible";
    topPosition -= 3;
    leftPosition += 10;
    if (topPosition <= 0) {
        topPosition = 150;
        leftPosition = 0;
    }
}
/* ]]> */
</script>
</head>
<body onload="setInterval('flyButterfly()', 100);">
<p><img src="butterfly.gif" id="butterfly" style="position:
absolute; left: 0px; top: 0px; visibility:hidden" alt="Image of a
butterfly" height="120" width="150" /></p>
<h1>Butterfly</h1>
<p>According to Wikipedia:</p>
<blockquote><p>A butterfly is an insect of the order Lepidoptera, it
belongs to either the Hesperioidea (the skippers) or Papilionoidea (all
other butterflies) superfamilies. Some authors have also suggested the
inclusion of the superfamily Hedyloidea, the American butterfly moths.
They are notable for their unusual life cycle with a larval caterpillar
stage, an inactive pupal stage and a spectacular metamorphosis into a
familiar and colourful winged adult form. The diverse patterns formed by
their brightly coloured wings and their erratic-yet-graceful flight have
made butterfly watching a popular hobby.</p></blockquote>
</body>
</html>
```

Figure 11-5
Butterfly animation
Web page

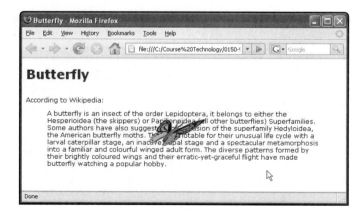

TIP

You can find a copy of the butterfly animation document, named Butterfly.html, in your Chapter folder for Chapter 11.

Next, you will animate the airplane image you added to the Instruments page of the Al's Aviation site so it appears to "fly" across the screen.

To animate the airplane image you added to the Instruments page of the Al's Aviation site so it appears to "fly" across the screen:

1. Return to the **Instrument.html** document in your text editor and add the following global variables to the script section. The `leftPosition` variable sets the initial left position at 250 pixels and the `topPosition` variable sets the initial top position at 0 pixels. The third variable, `verticalDirection`, determines whether the plane is ascending or descending in its flight path.

```
var leftPosition = 250;
var topPosition = 40;
var verticalDirection = "up";
```

2. Add the following `flightCoordinates()` function, which handles the dynamic positioning of the airplane image. The first statement in the function gets the image element's ID, while the second and third statements assign values to the element's `left` and `top` properties. The `if...else` statements then change the values assigned to the global variables in order to set the position of the plane when the `flightCoordinates()` function is called next. The vertical position of the plane cycles between 0 and 40 pixels, while the horizontal position of the plane cycles between 250 pixels (the starting point) and 800 pixels (the right side of the screen). The `verticalDirection` variable determines whether to increase or decrease the value of the `topPosition` variable. The `flightCoordinates()` function is called using a `setInterval()` method from the `onload` event handler of the `<body>` element.

```
function flightCoordinates() {
    var flight = document.getElementById("airplane");
    flight.style.left = leftPosition + "px";
    flight.style.top = topPosition + "px";
    if (verticalDirection == "up")
        --topPosition;
    else if (verticalDirection == "down")
        ++topPosition;
    if (topPosition == 0)
        verticalDirection = "down";
    else if (topPosition == 40)
        verticalDirection = "up";
    ++leftPosition;
```

```
if (leftPosition == 800) {
    leftPosition = 250;
    topPosition = 40;
    verticalDirection = "up"
}
```

3. Replace the three `<img>` elements you added in the last exercise with the following single `<img>` element. Be sure the element includes an `id` attribute that is assigned a value of "airplane".

    ```
    <p><img src="airplane.gif" id="airplane" style="position:
    absolute; left: 250px; top: 40px" alt="Image of an
    airplane" height="63" width="114" /></p>
    ```

4. Finally, add an `onload` event handler to the opening `<body>` tag that calls the `setInterval()` function, as follows:

    ```
    <body onload="setInterval('flightCoordinates()', 25);">
    ```

5. Save the **Instrument.html** document and open it in your Web browser. The airplane image should appear to fly across the upper-right portion of the screen.

6. Close your Web browser window.

Creating DHTML Menus

One of the more popular uses of DHTML is to create menus. The three types of menus discussed in this chapter are expandable menus, navigation menus, and sliding menus. DHTML menus are most often used for organizing navigational links to other Web pages, although they are also useful for displaying and hiding information. As you work through this section, keep in mind that these techniques are only for browsers that are compatible with the W3C DOM. Older browsers that do not support the W3C DOM require different DHTML techniques to achieve the menu effects that are described here.

Expandable Menus

The **display property** specifies whether to display an element on a Web page. You can use the `display` property to simulate expandable and collapsible menus on a Web page. You typically use the `display` property with a **block-level element**, which gives a Web page its structure. Most Web browsers render block-level elements so they appear on their own line. Block-level elements can contain other block-level elements or inline elements. The `<p>` element and heading elements (`<h1>`, `<h2>`, and so on) are examples of common block-level elements with which you have worked. **Inline**, or **text-level, elements** describe the text that appears on a Web page. Unlike block-level elements, inline elements do not appear on their own lines, but appear within the line of the block-level element that contains them. Examples of inline elements include the `<b>` (bold) and `<br />` (line break) elements. One block-level element you may be familiar with is the **`<div>` element**, which formats a group of block-level and inline elements with styles. By placing elements and text within a `<div>` element, you can use the `display` property to simulate expandable and collapsible menus.

If you assign a block-level element's `display` property a value of "none", then the associated element is not displayed. In fact, the Web page does not even allocate space for the element on the page. However, if you use JavaScript to assign a value of "block" to a block-level element's `display` property, the Web page is reformatted to allocate sufficient space for the element and its contents, which are then displayed.

The following code shows a Web page that displays rosters for some American League Baseball teams in 2006. The style section defines a class selector named `collapsed` for the `<div>` element. You should already be familiar with the concept, but, to refresh your memory, a class selector defines different groups of styles for the same element. You create a class selector within a `<style>` element by appending a name for the class to a selector with a period. You then assign the class name to the class attribute of elements in the document that you want to format with the class's style definitions. The `collapsed` class selector includes the `display` property, which turns off the display of each `<div>` element when the Web page is first rendered. Anchor elements within the document body then use onmouseover and onmouseout event handlers to show and hide the `<div>` elements. Figure 11-6 shows the document in a Web browser when the mouse pointer passes over the San Diego Padres link.

```
<!DOCTYPE html PUBLIC "-//W3C//DTD XHTML 1.0 Strict//EN"
"http://www.w3.org/TR/xhtml1/DTD/xhtml1-strict.dtd">
<html xmlns="http://www.w3.org/1999/xhtml">
<head>
<title>2006 American League Baseball Team Rosters</title>
<meta http-equiv="content-type" content="text/html;
charset=iso-8859-1" />
<link rel="stylesheet" href="js_styles.css" type="text/css" />
<style type="text/css">
div.collapsed { display: none }
</style>
</head>
<body>
<h1>American League Baseball</h1>
<h2>Team Rosters for 2006</h2>
<p><a href=""
onmouseover="document.getElementById('padres').style.display='block';"
onmouseout="document.getElementById('padres').style.display='none';">
San Diego Padres</a></p>
<div id="padres" class="collapsed">
<p>Jake Peavy, Jay Witasick, Scott Linebrink, Luther Hackman, Brian
Lawrence, Joe Roa, Mike Matthews, Jaret Wright, Kevin Jarvis, Adam Eaton,
Rod Beck, Ben Howard, Rene Miniel, Kevin Walker, Trevor Hoffman, Mike
Bynum, Brandon Villafuerte, Gary Bennett, Miguel Ojeda, Humberto Quintero,
Khalil Greene, Sean Burroughs, Ramon Vazquez, Dave Hansen, Keith Lockhart,
Mark Loretta, Todd Sears, Brian Giles, Brian Buchanon, Mark Kotsay,
Phil Nevin, Gary Matthews Jr., Xavier Nady</p>
</div>
...
</body>
</html>
```

Figure 11-6
Web page with expand-
able menus

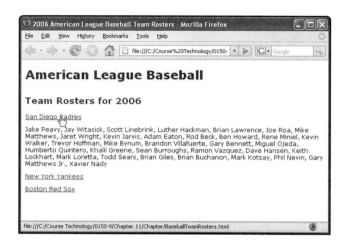

You can find a copy of the BaseballTeamRosters.html file in your Chapter folder for Chapter 11.

Next, you modify the right frame of the Instrument Training Web page so the content beneath each heading is contained within expandable menus.

To add expandable menus to the Instrument Training Web page:

1. Return to the **Instrument.html** document in your text editor.

2. Add the following style section above the closing `</head>` tag. The style section contains a single class selector that hides the content of any `<div>` elements to which it is applied when the Web page first opens.

```
<style type="text/css">
div.collapseInfo { display: none }
</style>
```

3. Place the elements and text beneath the Flight Experience heading within a `<div>` element, as follows. The `<div>` element has an `id` attribute of "experience" and is assigned the `collapseInfo` class selector.

```
<div id="experience" class="collapseInfo">
<p>An applicant for an Instrument rating must have 40 hours
of &quot;instrument&quot; time. Fifteen hours of this requirement
can be accomplished in an approved Flight
Training Device. Students must also log 50 hours of
pilot-in-command cross-country time.</p>
</div>
```

4. Modify the Flight Experience heading so the text is contained within an anchor element. Also, add an `id` attribute and `onclick`, `onmouseover`, and `onmouseout` event handlers to the anchor element. The `onclick` event handler calls a function named `showInfo()`, which displays and hides the information in the `<div>` element. You add the `showInfo()` function next. The `onmouseover` and `onmouseout` event handlers call the `underlineOff()` and

underlineOn() functions, which display and hide the underline beneath the anchor element.

```
<h3><a href="" id="fe"
onmouseover="underlineOn('fe');"
onmouseout="underlineOff('fe');"
onclick="return showInfo('experience');">
Flight Experience</a></h3>
```

5. Add the following showInfo() function to the end of the script section in the document head. The showInfo() function displays and hides the content of the <div> element.

```
function showInfo(heading) {
        var curHeading
        = document.getElementById(heading);
        if (curHeading.style.display == "block")
              curHeading.style.display = "none";
        else
              curHeading.style.display = "block";
      return false;
}
```

6. Add similar elements and event handlers to the remaining headings and information on the page.

7. Save the **Instrument.html** document and then validate it with the W3C Markup Validation Service. Once the document is valid, close it in your text editor, and then open it in your Web browser. Click each of the headings to see if they expand and collapse. Figure 11-7 shows how the Web page appears after clicking the Syllabus heading.

Figure 11-7

Instrument Training
Web page after adding
expandable menus

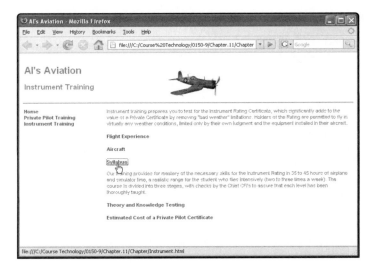

8. Close your Web browser window.

Navigation Menus

You are probably already familiar with drop-down, or pull-down menus, similar to the ones you may find in a Windows application, such as a File menu or an Edit menu. Menus can greatly improve the design of your Web page and are very useful in helping visitors navigate through your Web site. In Chapter 4, you saw some Web pages from the Woodland Park Zoo. The Photo Gallery Web page, shown in Figure 11-8, contains a drop-down menu that assists users in locating the Web page for a particular animal.

Figure 11-8

Navigation menu for the
Woodland Park Zoo
Photo Gallery Web page

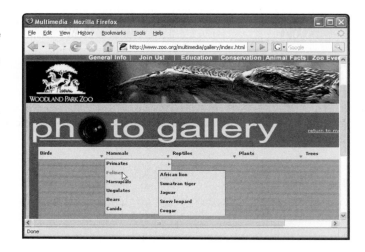

Although there are several ways to create a navigation menu, the easiest way is to use a table to contain your menu items. First, you create a "master" table that will contain nested tables for each individual menu. The following code shows the beginnings of a table that will create a navigation menu for a hardware store. The style section defines various styles to format the table to look something like a menu bar. Figure 11-9 shows the document in a Web browser.

```
<!DOCTYPE html PUBLIC "-//W3C//DTD XHTML 1.0 Strict//EN"
"http://www.w3.org/TR/xhtml1/DTD/xhtml1-strict.dtd">
<html xmlns="http://www.w3.org/1999/xhtml">
<head>
<title>Forestville Hardware Supply</title>
<meta http-equiv="content-type" content="text/html;
charset=iso-8859-1" />
<style type="text/css">
body {
  font-family: Verdana, Arial, Helvetica, sans-serif;
  font-size: 12px;
}
h1 { color: #039 }
table { background-color: aqua; border-style: solid; border-width:
thin; border-color: black }
a.noDecor { text-decoration: none; color: black }
</style>
```

```
</head>
<body>
<table width="75%">
 <tr align="left">
  <td>
   <a href="" class="noDecor">Electrical</a><br />
  </td>
  <td>
   <a href="" class="noDecor">Plumbing</a><br />
  </td>
  <td>
   <a href="" class="noDecor">Heating and Cooling</a><br />
  </td>
 </tr>
</table>
<h1>Forestville Hardware Supply</h1>
<p>Use the menu to help find what you are looking for.</p>
</body>
</html>
```

Figure 11-9
Document with a top
navigation menu

For each navigation menu, you nest another table within the same cell as the menu heading. The following code shows a table nested within the cell for the Electrical menu:

```
...
<table width="75%">
<tr align="left">
<td>
<a href="" class="noDecor">Electrical</a><br />
<table id="electrical" width="25%">
<tr><td><a href="breakers.html">Breakers</a></td></tr>
<tr><td><a href="fuses.html">Fuses</a></td></tr>
<tr><td><a href="tools.html">Tools</a></td></tr>
<tr><td><a href="wire.html">Wire</a></td></tr>
</table>
</td>
...
```

To show and hide each menu, you use the **visibility property**, which determines whether an element is visible. The visibility property differs from the display property in that it allocates space for an element on a Web page. Recall that a Web browser does not allocate space for an element with a value of "none" assigned to its display property. If you assign a value of "hidden" to an element's visibility property, space is allocated for the element, but it is not displayed. You display a hidden element by assigning a value of "visible" to the visibility property. The following code shows another version of the table elements for the Electrical menu. This time, the table cell that contains the menu includes onmouseover and onmouseout event handlers that use the visibility property to show and hide the menu. The <td> element also includes a class selector named noShow. The noShow class selector hides the nested table when the Web page is first rendered. The noShow class selector also assigns the "absolute" value to the position property, which prevents the table from expanding to allocate room for the hidden menus. Figure 11-10 shows the Web page in a browser with the mouse pointer over the Heating and Cooling menu.

```
<style type="text/css">
...
table.noShow {visibility:hidden; position:absolute }
</style>
...
<table width="75%">
 <tr align="left">
  <td onmouseover="document.getElementById('electrical')
     .style.visibility='visible';"
  onmouseout="document.getElementById('electrical')
     .style.visibility='hidden';">
   <a href="" class="noDecor">Electrical</a><br />
     <table class="noShow" id="electrical" width="25%">
     <tr><td><a href="breakers.html">
     Breakers</a></td></tr>
     <tr><td><a href="fuses.html">Fuses</a></td></tr>
     <tr><td><a href="tools.html">Tools</a></td></tr>
     <tr><td><a href="wire.html">Wire</a></td></tr>
     </table>
  </td>
```

Figure 11-10

Heating and Cooling menu in the top navigation menu

TIP
You can find a copy of the HardwareMenuTop.html document in your Chapter folder for Chapter 11.

Next, you will add a navigation menu to the AviationHome.html document.

To add a navigation menu to the AviationHome.html document:

1. Return to the **AviationHome.html** document in your text editor.

2. Add the following style section and class selector declaration above the closing `</head>` tag. The `hideMenu` class selector is applied to the nested table that contains the menu items.

```
<style type="text/css">
table.hideMenu { visibility:hidden; position:relative;
border-style: solid; border-width:
thin; border-color: #C10000 }
</style>
```

3. Replace the three `<a>` elements that provide links to each of the Al's Aviation Web pages with the following code. Be sure not to delete the `<td>...</td>` tag pair that contains the `<a>` elements. The code contains the master table for a menu named "Navigation" that will contain a nested menu commands table. In this exercise, you create a single menu that will contain the three links for each of the Al's Aviation Web pages.

```
<table width="90%">
<tr align="left">
<td onmouseover="document.getElementById('navigation')
.style.visibility='visible';"
onmouseout="document.getElementById('navigation')
.style.visibility='hidden';">
<a href="">Navigation</a><br />
</td>
</tr>
</table>
```

4. Above the closing `</td>` tag that you added in the last step, add the following nested table that contains the links to the Al's Aviation Web pages:

```
<table class="hideMenu" id="navigation" width="100%">
<tr><td><a href="AviationHome.html" id="home"
onmouseover="underlineOn('home');"
onmouseout="underlineOff('home');">Home</a></td></tr>
<tr><td><a href="PrivatePilot.html" id="pilot"
onmouseover="underlineOn('pilot');"
onmouseout="underlineOff('pilot');">Private Pilot
```

```
Training</a></td></tr>
<tr><td><a href="Instrument.html" id="inst"
onmouseover="underlineOn('inst');"
onmouseout="underlineOff('inst');">Instrument
Training</a></td></tr>
</table>
```

5. Save the **AviationHome.html** document and then validate it with the W3C Markup Validation Service. Once the document is valid, close it in your text editor, and then open it in your Web browser. Figure 11-11 shows how the document appears with the navigation menu open and the mouse held over the Private Pilot Training link.

Figure 11-11

Al's Aviation home page with a navigation menu

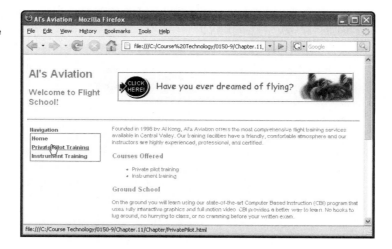

6. Close your Web browser window.

The following code shows a modified version of the hardware store menus. This time, the table is formatted so the menus appear on the left side of the screen. The code also uses the display property instead of the visibility property in order to allow the nested tables to expand and contract beneath each menu heading. Notice that the position property in the noShow class selector is assigned a value of "relative" instead of "absolute". This forces the master table to expand and contract to display the nested tables. Figure 11-12 shows the Web page in a browser with the Plumbing menu expanded.

```
...
<style type="text/css">
body {
   font-family: Verdana, Arial, Helvetica, sans-serif;
   font-size: 12px;
}
h1 { color: #039 }
table { background-color: aqua; border-style: solid; border-width: thin;
border-color: black }
```

```
a.noDecor { text-decoration: none; color: black }
table.noShow {display: none; border-style: none; position: relative }
</style>
</head>
<body>
<h1>Forestville Hardware Supply</h1>
<p>Use the menu to help find what you are looking for.</p>
<table width="50%">
 <tr align="left">
  <td onmouseover=
   "document.getElementById('electrical').style.display='block';"
   onmouseout=
   "document.getElementById('electrical').style.display='none';">
   <a href="" class="noDecor">Electrical</a><br/>
   <table class="noShow" id="electrical" width="100%">
    <tr><td><a href="breakers.html">Breakers</a></td></tr>
    <tr><td><a href="fuses.html">Fuses</a></td></tr>
    <tr><td><a href="tools.html">Tools</a></td></tr>
    <tr><td><a href="wire.html">Wire</a></td></tr>
        </table>
       </td>
     </tr>
     <tr align="left">
      <td onmouseover=
        "document.getElementById('plumbing').style.display='block';"
        onmouseout=
         "document.getElementById('plumbing').style.display='none';">
         <a href="" class="noDecor">Plumbing</a><br />
         <table class="noShow" id="plumbing" width="100%">
           <tr><td><a href="hoseclamps.html">Hose Clamps</a></td></tr>
           <tr><td><a href="pipe.html">Pipe and Fittings</a></td></tr>
          <tr><td><a href="solders.html">Solders and Flux</a></td></tr>
           <tr><td><a href="tools.html">Tools</a></td></tr>
         </table>
        </td>
      </tr>
      <tr align="left"><td onmouseover=
        "document.getElementById('hc').style.display='block';"
        onmouseout=
         "document.getElementById('hc').style.display='none';">
        <a href="" class="noDecor">Heating and Cooling</a><br/>
        <table class="noShow" id="hc" width="100%">
          <tr><td><a href="ac.html">Air Conditioners</a></td></tr>
         <tr><td><a href="dehumidifier.html">Dehumidifiers</a></td></tr>
          <tr><td><a href="heaters.html">Heaters</a></td></tr>
           <tr><td><a href="insulation.html">Insulation</a></td></tr>
           <tr><td><a href="thermostats.html">Thermostats</a></td></tr>
```

```
      <tr><td><a href="ventilation.html">Ventilation</a></td></tr>
        <tr><td><a href="waterheaters.html">Water Heaters</a></td></tr>
       </table>
      </td>
    </tr>
   </table>
</body>
</html>
```

Figure 11-12
Left navigation menu

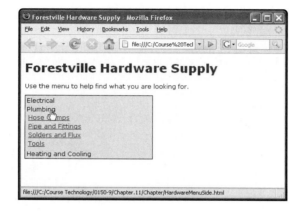

TIP
You can find a copy of the HardwareMenuSide.html document in your Chapter folder for Chapter 11.

Sliding Menus

As their name implies, **sliding menus** are menus that appear to slide open and closed. Although the `visibility` and `display` properties are quite effective in showing and hiding menus, they simply display their associated elements without any sort of effect. In order to simulate a sliding effect, you must use the `left` and `top` properties (depending on whether you are creating a horizontal or vertical menu) along with simple animation techniques.

With a horizontal navigation menu, you must create each individual menu within its own table. The following code shows an example of the tables for the Electrical and Plumbing menus:

```
<h1>Forestville Hardware Supply</h1>
<p>Use the menu to help find what you are looking for.</p>
<table width="160px" class="navMenu" id="electrical"
onmouseover="showMenu('electrical')"
onmouseout="hideMenu('electrical')">
<tr><td><a href="breakers.html">Breakers</a></td>
<td rowspan="4" align="right" valign="middle">
```

```
<img src="electrical.gif" height="65" width="19"
alt="Vertical text that reads 'Electrical'" /></td></tr>
<tr><td><a href="fuses.html">Fuses</a></td></tr>
<tr><td><a href="tools.html">Tools</a></td></tr>
<tr><td><a href="wire.html">Wire</a></td></tr>
</table>
<table width="160px" class="navMenu" id="plumbing"
onmouseover="showMenu('plumbing')"
onmouseout="hideMenu('plumbing')">
<tr><td><a href="hoseclamps.html">Hose Clamps</a></td>
<td rowspan="4" align="right" valign="middle">
<img src="plumbing.gif" height="65" width="19"
alt="Vertical text that reads 'Plumbing'" /></td></tr>
<tr><td><a href="pipe.html">Pipe and Fittings</a></td></tr>
<tr><td><a href="solders.html">Solders and
Flux</a></td></tr>
<tr><td><a href="tools.html">Tools</a></td></tr>
</table>
```

NOTE

You cannot create vertical text (yet) in a Web browser, so this example uses two image files, electrical.gif and plumbing.gif, which contain images of vertical text. The table uses the rowspan attribute so that both images span the other rows in the table.

In order to "hide" the contents of a horizontal navigation menu, you must assign a negative value to the table's left property. The preceding tables use the navMenu class selector, which sets the initial value of the left property to -130px. You must also set the table's position property to "relative". The navMenu class selector style definition appears as follows:

```
table.navMenu { left:-130px; position:relative}
```

The onmouseover event handlers in each <table> element call a function named showMenu(), which uses a setInterval() method to call a function named show(), which makes each menu visible. The show() function continuously changes the left property of the <table> element until it is equal to -12, which aligns the left side of the table with the edge of the browser window. The onmouseout event handlers in each <table> element call a function named hideMenu(). This function uses a setInterval() method to call a function named hide(), which hides each menu. The code in the hide() function is very similar to the code in the show() function. The following code contains the script that gives the sliding menus their functionality. Figure 11-13 shows the Web page in a browser with the Plumbing menu opened.

```
<script type="text/javascript">
/* <![CDATA[ */
var curPosition=-130;
var curMenu;
```

```
var slider;
function showMenu(selectedMenu) {
     clearInterval(slider);
     curMenu = document.getElementById(selectedMenu);
     slider = setInterval("show()", 10);
}
function show() {
     if (curPosition < -12) {
          curPosition = curPosition + 2;
          curMenu.style.left = curPosition + "px";
     }
}
function hideMenu(selectedMenu) {
     clearInterval(slider);
     curMenu = document.getElementById(selectedMenu);
     slider = setInterval("hide()", 10);
}
function hide() {
     if (curPosition > -130) {
          curPosition = curPosition - 2;
          curMenu.style.left = curPosition + "px";
     }
}
/* ]]> */
</script>
```

Figure 11-13
Sliding menus

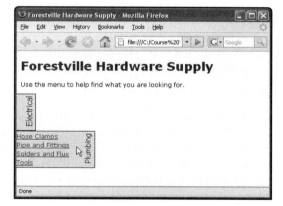

TIP
You can find a copy of the HardwareMenuSliding.html document and the
electrical.gif and plumbing.gif image files in your Chapter folder for Chapter 11.

Next, you add a horizontal sliding menu to the PrivatePilot.html document.

To add a horizontal sliding menu to the PrivatePilot.html document:

1. Return to the **PrivatePilot.html** document in your text editor.

2. Add the following style section and class selector declaration above the closing `</head>` tag. The navMenu class selector will be applied to the table that contains the menu. When the Web page first loads, the class selector sets the table's left margin to -175.

```
<style type="text/css">
table.navMenu { left:-140px; position:relative}
</style>
```

3. Replace the three <a> elements that provide links to each of the Al's Aviation Web pages with the following table, which contains the menu commands. Be sure not to delete the `<td>...</td>` tag pair that contains the <a> elements. This example creates a single sliding menu that will contain the three links for each of the Al's Aviation Web pages. Your Chapter folder for Chapter 11 contains the navigator.gif image file that is included in the table.

```
<table width="180px" class="navMenu" id="electrical"
onmouseover="showMenu('electrical')"
onmouseout="hideMenu('electrical')">
<tr><td><a href="AviationHome.html" id="home"
onmouseover="underlineOn('home');"
onmouseout="underlineOff('home');">Home</a></td>
<td rowspan="4" align="right" valign="middle">
<img src="navigation.gif" height="102" width="36"
alt="Vertical text that reads 'Navigation'" /></td></tr>
<tr><td><a href="PrivatePilot.html" id="pilot"
onmouseover="underlineOn('pilot');"
onmouseout="underlineOff('pilot');">Private Pilot
Training</a></td></tr>
<tr><td><a href="Instrument.html" id="inst"
onmouseover="underlineOn('inst');"
onmouseout="underlineOff('inst');">Instrument
Training</a></td></tr>
</table>
```

4. Add a new script section immediately above the table you just added:

```
<script type="text/javascript">
/* <![CDATA[ */
/* ]]> */
</script>
```

5. Add to the new script section the following script, which gives the sliding menu its functionality:

```
var curPosition=-140;
var curMenu;
var slider;
function showMenu(selectedMenu) {
    clearInterval(slider);
    curMenu = document.getElementById(selectedMenu);
    slider = setInterval("show()", 10);
}
function show() {
    if (curPosition < -6) {
        curPosition = curPosition + 2;
        curMenu.style.left = curPosition + "px";
    }
}
function hideMenu(selectedMenu) {
    clearInterval(slider);
    curMenu = document.getElementById(selectedMenu);
    slider = setInterval("hide()", 10);
}
function hide() {
    if (curPosition > -140) {
        curPosition = curPosition - 2;
        curMenu.style.left = curPosition + "px";
    }
}
```

6. Save the **PrivatePilot.html** document and then validate it with the W3C Markup
    Validation Service. Once the document is valid, close it in your text editor, and
    then open it in your Web browser. Figure 11-14 shows how the Web page appears
    with the Navigation menu open.

Figure 11-14

Al's Aviation home page
with a sliding menu

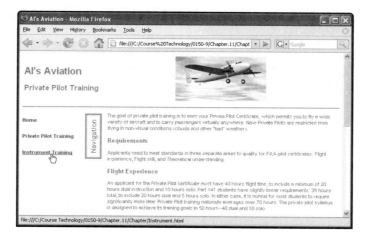

7. Close your Web browser window and text editor.

Checking Browser Compatibility

This chapter primarily discusses DOM techniques that are compatible with the W3C's standardized version of DHTML. However, although books on JavaScript often include sections on how to write different DHTML code for each type of browser, at the time of this writing, well over 90% of Internet users access the Web with a W3C-compliant browser. For this reason, instead of writing different code sections for older browsers that are rarely used, you should write code that checks whether the browser is compliant with the W3C DOM. If the browser is not compliant with the W3C DOM, your script should open an alternate Web page that does not include DHTML or display a message advising the user to upgrade his or her browser.

A JavaScript program that checks which type of browser is running is commonly called a **browser sniffer**. Although there are several ways to write a browser sniffer, including using properties of the Navigator object, the easiest way to test whether a Web browser is compatible with the W3C DOM is to check whether the browser includes the getElementById() method. You can check whether a browser includes the getElementById() method using a statement similar to if (document.getElementById). If the method is available in the browser, then a value of true is returned, meaning that the browser is compatible with the W3C DOM.

The browser sniffer script in the following code opens a DHTML version of the butterfly animation script only if the browser is compatible with the W3C DOM. If the browser is not compatible with the W3C DOM, then a non-DHTML version of the Web page opens.

```
...
<script type="text/javascript">
/* <![CDATA[ */
function checkBrowser() {
    if (document.getElementById)
        document.location.href = "ButterflyDHTML.html";
    else
        document.location.href = "ButterflyNoDHTML.html";
}
/* ]]> */
</script>
</head>
<body onload="checkBrowser();">
</body>
</html>
```

Chapter Summary

▶ The easiest way to refer to a CSS style in JavaScript is to use the `this` reference and the style property in an event handler within the element itself.

▶ You use the `style` property to modify an element's CSS properties with JavaScript.

▶ CSS positioning is used to position or lay out elements on a Web page.

▶ The most critical CSS positioning property is the `position` property, which determines the type of positioning applied to an element.

▶ The easiest way to dynamically position an element with CSS is to use the `left` and `top` properties.

▶ With DHTML, you can use dynamic positioning to create animations that "travel" across the screen by modifying the global `topPosition` and `leftPosition` variables that define an image's position.

▶ DHTML menus are most often used for organizing navigational links to other Web pages, although they are also useful for displaying and hiding information.

▶ The `display` property specifies whether to display an element on a Web page. You can use the `display` property to simulate expandable and collapsible menus on a Web page. You typically use the `display` property with a block-level element, which gives a Web page its structure.

▶ Inline, or text-level, elements describe the text that appears on a Web page.

▶ One block-level element you may be familiar with is the `<div>` element, which formats a group of block-level and inline elements with styles. By placing elements and text within a `<div>` element, you can use the `display` property to simulate expandable and collapsible menus.

▶ A class selector defines different groups of styles for the same element.

▶ To show and hide each menu, you use the `visibility` property, which determines whether an element is visible.

▶ Sliding menus are menus that appear to slide open and closed.

▶ In order to simulate a sliding effect, you must use the `left` and `top` properties (depending on whether you are creating a horizontal or vertical menu) along with simple animation techniques.

▶ A JavaScript program that checks which type of browser is running is commonly called a browser sniffer.

Review Questions

1. Prior to the release of the W3C standardized version of the DOM, no DHTML standard worked with both Internet Explorer and Netscape Navigator. If you want to use JavaScript code to manipulate CSS in older browsers, what options do you have?

2. What is the correct syntax for using the `style` property with an `onmouseover` event handler to display an underline beneath a link?

   a. `onmouseover.this="style.textDecoration=underline"`

   b. `onmouseover(this.style.textDecoration="underline")`

   c. `onmouseover="this.style: textDecoration; underline"`

   d. `onmouseover="this.style.textDecoration='underline'"`

3. If you pass the `this` reference to a function as an argument parameter named `linkTarget`, which of the following statements change the element's text color to blue? (Choose all that apply.)

   a. `linkTarget.style.color = "blue";`

   b. `linkTarget.style.textColor = "blue";`

   c. `this.style.color = "blue";`

   d. `this.style = "textColor: blue";`

4. Which of the following statements changes the value of the `font-family` style to Arial for an element with an `id` value of `salesTotal`?

   a. `document.getElementById("salesTotal")`
       `        .style.font-family = "Arial";`

   b. `document.getElementById("salesTotal")`
       `        .style.FontFamily = "Arial";`

   c. `document.getElementById("salesTotal")`
       `        .style(font-family) = "Arial";`

   d. `document.getElementById("salesTotal")`
       `        .style.fontFamily = "Arial";`

5. How do you use DHTML to show and hide an underline beneath an `<a>` element when a user places his or her mouse pointer over a link?

6. Which of the following CSS properties can you use to dynamically position an element? (Choose all that apply.)

   a. `right`

   b. `left`

   c. `bottom`

   d. `top`

7. Which of the following values (which can be applied to the `position` property) prevents you from using CSS positioning with an element?

   a. relative

   b. absolute

   c. fixed

   d. static

8. Explain the difference between the `display` and `visible` properties.

9. What value do you assign to the `display` property to prevent an element from displaying?

   a. false
   b. hidden
   c. hide
   d. none

10. What value do you assign to the `visible` property to prevent an element from being visible?

    a. hidden
    b. none
    c. false
    d. hide

11. Which of the following `style` attributes prevents an element from being moved with CSS positioning?

    a. `style="position: absolute; left: 100px; top: 120px"`
    b. `style="position: relative; left: 100px; top: 120px"`
    c. `style="position: static; left: 100px; top: 120px"`
    d. `style="position: fixed; left: 100px; top: 120px"`

12. The `bottom` and `right` properties determine the position of an element's lower-right corner in relation to the _____.

    a. lower-right corner of the document window
    b. upper-left corner of the document window
    c. lower-right corner of the visible screen area
    d. upper-left corner of the browser window

13. What value do you assign to the `visible` property to prevent an element from being visible?

    a. hide
    b. none
    c. hidden
    d. false

14. Explain how to create traveling animation with DHTML.

15. What determines an element's starting position when creating traveling animation with DHTML?

    a. The values assigned to the global `topPosition` and `leftPosition` variables
    b. The values assigned to the `left` and `top` style properties in the opening `<body>` tag

    c. The values assigned to an element's `left` and `top` style properties

    d. You cannot determine an element's initial starting position when creating traveling animation with DHTML; the element's position is randomly generated for each animation sequence.

16. You can use the _____ property to simulate expandable and collapsible menus on a Web page.

    a. `display`

    b. `slide`

    c. `static`

    d. `z-order`

17. To allocate sufficient space for a sliding menu, you must assign a value of _____ of the block-level element that contains the text and elements of the sliding menu.

    a. "hide" to the display property

    b. "reserve" to the slide property

    c. "block" to the `display` property

    d. zero (0) to the z-order property

18. If you assign a value of "hidden" to an element's `visibility` property, space is allocated for the element, but it is not displayed. True or false?

19. Explain how to use tables to create a navigation menu.

20. To determine whether a Web browser is compatible with the W3C DOM, you check if the browser includes the _____.

    a. `display` property

    b. `position` property

    c. `setInterval()` or `setTimeout()` methods

    d. `getElementById()` method

Hands-On Projects

Project 11-1

In this chapter, you learned how to use CSS positioning to set and return the position of elements on a Web page. However, you can only use CSS positioning to set and return the position of elements that include properties such as the `position`, `left`, and `top` properties. To find the position of an element that does not include CSS positioning properties, you can use the `offsetLeft` and `offsetTop` properties. Similarly, you can use the `offsetWidth` and `offsetHeight` properties to return the size of an element on a Web page. The `offsetLeft`, `offsetTop`, `offsetWidth`, and `offsetHeight` properties are available to most current Web browsers. In this project, you will create a document that uses the `offsetTop` and `offsetWidth` properties to display context-sensitive help for the fields on a form. The project will also use the CSS `cursor` property to dynamically change the cursor to a help cursor when the mouse pointer passes over a form element that contains context-sensitive help.

1. Create a new document in your text editor.

2. Type the `<!DOCTYPE>` declaration, `<html>` element, document head, and `<body>` element. Use the strict DTD and "Form Help" as the content of the `<title>` element.

3. Add the following elements and text to the document body. The form contains four text boxes for a user name, password, password confirmation, and challenge question. Each text box contains an `onmouseover` event that changes the cursor to a help cursor and an `onclick` event that passes the element's `id` attribute to a function named `showHelp()`, which you will create shortly. The `<div>` element will be used to display the context-sensitive help information for each field. Note that the `<div>` element is initially hidden by assigning a value of "hidden" to the `visibility` property.

```
<h1>Form Help</h1>
<form action="" method="get"
enctype="application/x-www-form-urlencoded">
<p><strong>User name</strong><br />
<input type="text" id="username" size="50"
onmouseover="this.style.cursor='help'"
onclick="showHelp(this.id)" /></p>
<p><strong>Password</strong><br />
<input type="password" id="password" size="50"
onmouseover="this.style.cursor='help'"
onclick="showHelp(this.id)" /></p>
<p><strong>Confirm password</strong><br />
<input type="password" id="password_confirm" size="50"
onmouseover="this.style.cursor='help'"
onclick="showHelp(this.id)" /></p>
<p><strong>What is your mother's maiden name?</strong><br />
<input type="password" id="challenge" size="50"
onmouseover="this.style.cursor='help'"
onclick="showHelp(this.id)" /></p>
</form>
<div id="box" style="position: absolute; visibility: hidden;
width: 250px; background-color:#FFFFC0; font:Comic Sans MS;
color: #A00000;border:1px dashed #D00000"></div>
```

4. Add the following script section to the document head:

```
<script type="text/javascript">
/* <![CDATA[ */
/* ]]> */
</script>
```

5. Create the following showHelp() function in the script section. The first two statements use the getElementById() methods to retrieve the form element represented by the elementId parameter and the <div> element that is assigned an id attribute value of "box".

```
function showHelp(elementId) {
        var curElement = document.getElementById(elementId);
        var helpElement = document.getElementById("box");
}
```

6. Add the following switch statement to the end of the showHelp() function. The statement evaluates the elementId parameter and then uses the innerHTML property to assign the appropriate help text to the <div> element. Be sure to enter each text string on a single line.

```
switch (elementId) {
        case "username":
                helpElement.innerHTML = "Enter a unique user name that is
                        between 5 and 12 characters.";
                break;
        case "password":
                helpElement.innerHTML = "Enter a password between 6 and 10
                        characters that contains both upper and lowercase letters
                        and at least one numeric character. ";
                break;
        case "password_confirm":
                helpElement.innerHTML = "Confirm your selected password. ";
                break;
        case "challenge":
                helpElement.innerHTML = "Enter your mother's maiden name.
                        This value will be used to confirm your identity in
                        the event that you forget your password. ";
        break;
}
```

7. Finally, add the following statements to the end of the showHelp() function. The first statement adds an anchor element to the innerHTML of the <div> element that users can click to hide the context-sensitive help box. The second statement displays the <div> element by assigning a value of "visible" to the visibility property. The third statement obtains the width of the current form field using the offsetWidth property, adds 20 pixels to better position the help box, and then assigns the result to the left property of the <div> element. The fourth statement obtains the top position of the current form field using the offsetTop property and assigns the result to the top property of the <div> element.

```
helpElement.innerHTML += "<a href=''
        onclick=\"document.getElementById('box')
        .style.visibility='hidden';return false;\">Close</a>";
document.getElementById("box").style.visibility = "visible";
```

```
document.getElementById("box").style.left
        = curElement.offsetWidth + 20 + "px";
document.getElementById("box").style.top = curElement.offsetTop + "px";
```

8. Save the document as **FormHelp.html** in your Projects folder for Chapter 11 and validate it with the W3C Markup Validation Service. Once the document is valid, open it in your Web browser and test the context-sensitive help functionality.

9. Close your Web browser window.

 ### Project 11-2

In this project, you will create a document with a link that appears to shake when you move your cursor over it.

1. Create a new document in your text editor.

2. Type the `<!DOCTYPE>` declaration, `<html>` element, document head, and `<body>` element. Use the strict DTD and "Shaking Link" as the content of the `<title>` element.

3. Add a script section to the document head:

```
<script type="text/javascript">
/* <![CDATA[ */
/* ]]> */
</script>
```

4. Add the following link to the document body. The link includes an `onmouseover` event handler that uses the `setInterval()` method to call a function named `shakeLink()`, which you will add next. The `onmouseout` event handler clears the `setInterval()` method.

```
<p><a id="earthquake" style="position: relative"
href="http://www.earthquake.com"
onmouseover="shakeVar=setInterval('shakeLink()', 10);"
onmouseout="clearTimeout(shakeVar);">Global Earthquake
Response Center</a></p>
```

5. Add the following code to the script section. The `shakeLink()` function, which is called by the `onmouseover` event handler in the link, gives the script its functionality.

```
var shakeVar;
var direction = "left";
function shakeLink() {
    if (direction == "left") {
        document.getElementById("earthquake")
                .style.left="3px";
        direction = "right";
    }
    else {
```

```
        document.getElementById("earthquake")
                .style.left="0px";
        direction = "left";
    }
}
```

6. Save the document as **ShakingLink.html** in your Projects folder for Chapter 11 and validate it with the W3C Markup Validation Service. Once the document is valid, open it in your Web browser. Place your mouse pointer over the link and verify that the link starts to shake. Move your mouse pointer off the link and verify that it stops shaking.

7. Close your Web browser window.

Project 11-3

In your Web travels, you have probably encountered "mouse trails"—that is, some sort of image or stylistic element that follows the cursor as it moves around a Web page. You create mouse trails by using DHTML along with the onmousemove event and the screenX and screenY properties of the Event object of the HTML DOM. The screenX property returns the horizontal coordinate of the cursor when an event occurs and the screenY property returns the vertical coordinate of the cursor when an event occurs. In this project you will create a Web page that contains a definition and image of a comet. When the mouse is moved over a <div> element containing the page's text and elements, a mouse trail will display that resembles a comet's tail. Your Projects folder for Chapter 11 contains an image named comet.jpg that you can use for this exercise.

1. Create a new document in your text editor.

2. Type the <!DOCTYPE> declaration, <html> element, header information, and the <body> element. Use the strict DTD and "Mouse Trail" as the content of the <title> element.

3. Add the following style section to the document head:

```
<style type="text/css">
h1 { font-family:arial; color:navy; }
p, td { font-family:arial; font-size:12px; color:black; }
</style>
```

4. Create the following <div> element in the document body. The element's onmousemove event calls an event handler named moveMouse(). The event handler function is passed an argument named event, which is an object that contains information about the event that occurred. You will use the event argument to access the screenX and screenY properties.

```
<div onmousemove="moveMouse(event)">
</div>
```

5. Add the following text and elements as the content of the `<div>` element. The content contains a heading element along with a description of the comet from Wikipedia along with an image of a comet.

```
<h1>Comet</h1>
<p><a href="http://en.wikipedia.org/wiki/Comet">Wikipedia</a>
defines a comet as follows:</p>
<table border="1" cellpadding="5">
<colgroup span="1" width="275" />
<colgroup span="1" width="200" />
<tr><td valign="top">A comet is a small body in the solar system
that orbits the Sun and (at least occasionally) exhibits a coma
(or atmosphere) and/or a tail - both primarily from the effects
of solar radiation upon the comet's nucleus, which itself is a
minor body composed of rock, dust, and ice. Comets' orbits are
constantly changing: their origins are in the outer solar system,
and they have a propensity to be highly affected (or perturbed)
by relatively close approaches to the major planets. Some are
moved into sun grazing orbits that destroy the comets when they
near the Sun, while others are thrown out of the solar system
forever.</td>
<td><img src="comet.jpg" alt="Image of a comet" height="200"
width="250" /></td>
</tr></table>
```

6. Add the following script section and global variables to the document head. The `trailInterval` variable determines the length of the "trail" that follows the mouse. The `xPosition` and `yPosition` variables will store the horizontal and vertical mouse coordinates. The `animationStarted` variable determines whether the animation that controls the mouse trail has been started. Note that the `xPosition` and `yPosition` variables are assigned an initial value of - 10. Each portion of the trail will be created with an empty `<div>` element that is assigned a background color of blue. In this manner, each portion of the trail will appear as a blue square. This allows you to create a mouse trail without any image files. The initial values of -10 that are assigned to the `xPosition` and `yPosition` variables hide the blue squares that are initially displayed when the Web page first loads.

```
<script type="text/javascript">
/* <![CDATA[ */
var trailInterval = 12;
var xPosition = -10;
var yPosition = -10;
var animationStarted = false;
/* ]]> */
</script>
```

7. Add the following `for` loop to the end of the script section. The `for` loop contains a single `document.write()` statement that creates the number of `<div>` elements

that will make up the mouse trail according to the value assigned to the `trailInterval` variable. Each `<div>` element is assigned a unique `id` value of "trail" + i. Because the `trailInterval` variable is assigned a value of 12, the `for` loop creates 12 `<div>` elements with `id` values of "trail0" through "trail11". You will use each `id` value to control the display of the mouse trail. Each `<div>` element's `position` property is assigned a value of "absolute" so it can be dynamically positioned and the `background-color` property is assigned a value of "blue". The `top` and `left` properties are assigned the values of the `xPosition` and `yPosition` variables, respectively. (Recall that the initial value assigned to these variables is -10 to hide the `<div>` elements when the Web page first loads.) Notice the values that are assigned to the `width`, `height`, and `font-size` properties. Each of these properties is assigned a value of i (the `for` loop counter variable) divided by 2. This creates 12 `<div>` elements, starting with a very small element consisting of a width, height, and font size of .5 and ending with a final element consisting of a width, height, and font size of 12. These elements will appear as series of gradually diminishing blue squares that will make up the mouse trail.

```
for (i = 1; i <= trailInterval; i++) {
    document.write("<div id='trail" + i
    + "' style='position:absolute;background-color:blue;top:"
    + yPosition + "px;left:" + xPosition + "px;width:"
    + i/2 + "px;height:" + i/2
    + "px; font-size:" + i/2 + "px'></div>");
}
```

8. Add the following `mouseMove()` function to the end of the script section. The function assigns the horizontal and vertical mouse coordinates to the `xPosition` and `yPosition` variables using the `screenX` and `screenY` properties of the `Event` object. Because Firefox and Internet Explorer use different mappings for the vertical mouse coordinates, the `if...else` statement uses the `appName` property of the `Navigator` object to determine the name of the browser and assign the appropriate value to the `yPosition` variable. The last `if` statement checks the value of the `animationStarted` variable to determine whether the animation that controls the mouse trail has started. If the variable contains a value of false, it is assigned a value of true and the `animate()` function is called. The `animate()` function will contain the code that causes the `<div>` elements to "follow" the cursor to create the mouse trail. You will create the `animate()` function in Step 9.

```
function moveMouse(e) {
    xPosition = e.screenX + 10;
    if (navigator.appName == "Microsoft Internet Explorer") {
        yPosition = e.screenY - 122;
    }
    else if (navigator.appName == "Netscape") {
        yPosition = e.screenY - 65;
    }
    if (!animationStarted) {
```

CHAPTER 11

```
                    animationStarted = true;
                    animate();
              }
      }
```

9. To the end of the script section, add the following `animate()` function. The function declares two local variables, `div1` and `div2`. The `for` loop iterates through `<div>` element and changes its value to the value of the previous `<div>` element. This causes each `<div>` element to replace the previous `<div>`, which creates the mouse trail. The last statement in the function uses the `setTimeout()` method to execute the function every 40 milliseconds.

```
function animate(){
      var div1, div2;
      for (i = 1; i <= trailInterval; i++){
              div1 = document.getElementById("trail"+i);
              if (i < trailInterval-1){
                      div2 = document.getElementById("trail"+(i+1));
                      div1.style.top = div2.style.top;
                      div1.style.left = div2.style.left;
              }
              else {
                      div1.style.top = yPosition + "px";
                      div1.style.left = xPosition + "px";
              }
      }
      setTimeout("animate()",40);
}
```

10. Save the document as **MouseTrail.html** in your Projects folder for Chapter 11, and then validate the document with the W3C Markup Validation Service. Once the document is valid, close it in your text editor.

11. Open the **MouseTrail.html** document in your Web browser and move your mouse over the text and elements to test the mouse trail.

12. Close your Web browser window.

 ## Project 11-4

In this project, you will create a Web page with a ball that bounces randomly within the document area of the Web browser. To create the calculation that causes the ball to bounce randomly, you need to determine the width and height of the document portion of the browser window. With the exception of Internet Explorer, the `Window` object for most current Web browsers include `innerWidth` and `innerHeight` properties. These properties return the width and height, respectively, of the document displayed in a Web browser. To return the width and height of the document displayed in Internet Explorer, you must use the `scrollLeft` and `scrollTop` properties of the `document.documentElement` object. To set the horizontal and vertical positions of an element within the document for most current Web browsers except for Internet Explorer, you use the screenX and screenY properties of the Window object. To set the horizontal and vertical positions of an element within a document in Internet Explorer, you use the scrollLeft and scrollTop properties of the document.documentElement object. Your Projects folder for Chapter 11 contains an image named ball.gif that you can use for this exercise.

1. Create a new document in your text editor.

2. Type the <!DOCTYPE> declaration, <html> element, document head, and <body> element. Use the strict DTD and "Bounce" as the content of the <title> element.

3. Add to the document body the following <div> element, which will dynamically position the ball.gif image:

```
<div id="ballElement" style="position:absolute;left:0px;top:0px">
<img id="ballImage" src="ball.gif" alt="Image of a ball"
height="48" width="48" /></div>
```

4. Add the following script section to the document head:

```
<script type="text/javascript">
/* <![CDATA[ */
/* ]]> */
</script>
```

5. Add to the script section the following global variables, which will store information about the speed, document, position, and direction of the bouncing ball:

```
var bounceSpeed = 5;
var widthMax = 0;
var heightMax = 0;
var xPosition = 0;
var yPosition = 0;
var xDirection = "right";
var yDirection = "down";
```

6. Add to the end of the script section the following setBall() function, which contains an if...else statement to determine the width of the document portion of the window according to the browser type. The last statement uses the setTimeout() method to call a function named bounceBall(), which performs the task of dynamically moving the ball image. You will create the bounceBall() function next.

```
function setBall() {
    if (navigator.appName == "Microsoft Internet Explorer") {
        widthMax = document.documentElement.clientWidth;
        heightMax = document.documentElement.clientHeight;
    }
    else {
        widthMax = window.innerWidth-14;
```

```
            heightMax = window.innerHeight;
        }
        setTimeout('bounceBall()',400);
    }
```

7. Create the following `bounceBall()` function at the end of the script section:

```
function bounceBall() {
}
```

8. Add the following statements to the `bounceBall()` function. These statements calculate the path and direction of the bouncing ball.

```
if (xDirection == "right" && xPosition > (widthMax
        - document.getElementById("ballImage").width - bounceSpeed))
    xDirection = "left";
else if (xDirection == "left" && xPosition < (0 + bounceSpeed))
    xDirection = "right";
if (yDirection == "down" && yPosition > (heightMax
        - document.getElementById("ballImage").height - bounceSpeed))
    yDirection = "up";
else if (yDirection == "up" && yPosition < (0 + bounceSpeed))
    yDirection = "down";
if (xDirection == "right")
    xPosition = xPosition + bounceSpeed;
else if (xDirection == "left")
    xPosition = xPosition - bounceSpeed;
else
    xPosition = xPosition;
if (yDirection == "down")
    yPosition = yPosition + bounceSpeed;
else if (yDirection == "up")
    yPosition = yPosition - bounceSpeed;
else
    yPosition = yPosition;
```

9. Add the following statements to the end of the `bounceBall()` function. These statements use the values that were assigned to the `xPosition` and `yPosition` variables in the preceding `if...else` statements to dynamically position the ball. The last statement uses a `setTimeout()` method to call the function again in 30 milliseconds.

```
if (navigator.appName == "Microsoft Internet Explorer") {
    document.getElementById("ballElement").style.left = xPosition
            + document.documentElement.scrollLeft + "px";
    document.getElementById("ballElement").style.top = yPosition
            + document.documentElement.scrollTop + "px";
}
else {
    document.getElementById("ballElement").style.left = xPosition
```

```
                              + window.screenX + "px";
        document.getElementById("ballElement").style.top = yPosition
                              + window.screenY + "px";
    }
    setTimeout('bounceBall()',30);
```

10. Add the following statement to the end of the script section. If the window is resized, this statement restarts the animation by calling the `setBall()` method, which retrieves the new dimensions of the document and restarts the `bounceBall()` function.

    ```
    window.onresize = setBall;
    ```

11. Finally, add the following `onload` event to the opening `<body>` tag to call the `setBall()` function when the document first loads:

    ```
    <body onload="setBall()">
    ```

12. Save the document as **Bounce.html** in your Projects folder for Chapter 11, and then validate the document with the W3C Markup Validation Service. Once the document is valid, close it in your text editor.

13. Open the **Bounce.html** document in your Web browser. The ball should start bouncing as soon as the page finishes loading. Try resizing the window to see if the animation adjusts to the new document size.

14. Close your Web browser window.

 ## Project 11-5

The `clip` CSS position property determines the region of an element that is displayed. To determine the portions of an element to be displayed, you assign to the `clip` property a value of "rect(*top right bottom left*)". The *top*, *right*, *bottom*, and *left* parameters specify values, in pixels, of the amount of space to clip around the element. Be sure not to separate the parameters in the `rect()` value with commas, as you would with the arguments you pass to a method or function. For example, to clip 10 pixels from all sides of an element, you assign a value of "rect(10px 10px 10px 10px)" to the `clip` property. In this project, you will use the `clip` property to create a screen transition effect of a shrinking box that covers an entire Web page when it first loads, but then shrinks and disappears.

1. Create a new document in your text editor.

2. Type the `<!DOCTYPE>` declaration, `<html>` element, document head, and `<body>` element. Use the strict DTD and "Boxed In" as the content of the `<title>` element.

3. Add to the document body the following `<div>` element, which will be used to create the shrinking box:

    ```
    <div id="i1" style="position:absolute;background-color:blue">
    </div>
    ```

4. Add the following script section to the document head:

```
<script type="text/javascript">
/* <![CDATA[ */
/* ]]> */
</script>
```

5. Add to the script section the following global variables, which will store information about the shrinking box:

```
var clipSpeed=5
var clipRight = 0;
var clipLeft = 0;
var clipTop = 0;
var boxSize;
var stopShrinking;
var clipBottom = 0;
var clipBox=document.getElementById("i1").style;
```

6. Add to the end of the script section the following startShrinking() function, which contains an if...else statement to determine the width of the document portion of the window according to the browser type. The last statement uses the setTimeout() method to call a function named shrinkBox(), which performs the task of dynamically shrinking the box. You will create the shrinkBox() function next.

```
function startShrinking() {
    if (navigator.appName == "Microsoft Internet Explorer") {
        boxSize   = document.documentElement.clientWidth
                  / document.documentElement.clientHeight;
        clipRight=document.documentElement.clientWidth;
        clipBox.width = clipRight + "px";
        clipBottom=document.documentElement.clientHeight;
        clipBox.height=clipBottom + "px";
    }
    else {
        boxToShrink = window.innerWidth/window.innerHeight;
        clipRight=window.innerWidth;
        clipBox.width = clipRight + "px";
        clipBottom=window.innerHeight;
        clipBox.height=clipBottom + "px";
    }
    stopShrinking=setInterval("shrinkBox()",100);
}
```

7. Add the following shrinkBox() function to the end of the script section. The statements in this function dynamically shrink the box until it disappears.

```
function shrinkBox(){
    if (navigator.appName == "Microsoft Internet Explorer")
        minBoxSize=document.documentElement.clientWidth/2;
    else
```

```
            minBoxSize=window.innerWidth/2
    if (clipLeft > minBoxSize){
            clearInterval(stopShrinking);
            clipBox.display="none";
    }
    clipBox.clip="rect(" + clipTop + "px " + clipRight + "px "
            + clipBottom + "px " + clipLeft + "px)"
    clipLeft += boxSize * clipSpeed;
    clipTop += clipSpeed;
    clipRight -= boxSize*clipSpeed;
    clipBottom -= clipSpeed;
}
```

8. Add an onload event to the opening <body> tag that calls the startShrinking() function, as follows:

    ```
    <body onload="startShrinking()">
    ```

9. Save the document as **BoxedIn.html** in your Projects folder for Chapter 11, and then validate the document with the W3C Markup Validation Service. Once the document is valid, close it in your text editor.

10. Open the **BoxedIn.html** document in your Web browser. As soon as the page finishes loading, the document portion of the window should be filled with a blue rectangle that gradually shrinks until it disappears.

11. Close your Web browser window.

Case Projects

For the following projects, save the documents you create in your Cases folder for Chapter 11. Be sure to validate the documents you create with the W3C Markup Validation Service.

Case Project 11-1

Your Cases folder for Chapter 11 contains six images of leaves: leaf1.gif through leaf6.gif. Use each image as many times as you like to create a Web page with falling leaves. Use image caching to ensure that all the images are loaded before the animation begins. Include code that randomly selects which leaf image to display. The formula for randomly selecting a leaf is Math.floor(Math.random() * *numImages*). Because there are six leaf images, the *numImages* argument should be 6. Also, use the Math.random() method to randomly select how fast each leaf falls and the position where it will begin falling. You will need to determine the height and width of the document area by using the document.documentElement.clientHeight and document.documentElement.clientWidth properties in Internet Explorer or the window.innerWidth and window.innerHeight for all other browsers. Save the document as **Autumn.html**.

Case Project 11-2

Your Cases folder for Chapter 11 contains an image file of a mosquito named bug.gif. Use the same coding techniques that you saw in Hands-on Project 11-4, which created a bouncing ball Web page, to dynamically animate the image so the mosquito appears to fly randomly around the page and bounce off the boundaries of the document portion of the window. However, instead of animating a single image, create at least five animated images that move along different paths in the window. To ensure that each image moves along a different path, you only need to set a unique vertical position for each image's starting point. Use a separate <div> element for each image. All images should begin traveling from before the left portion of the document, so the starting horizontal value for each <div> element must be negative. Make sure that some of the images begin traveling in an upward direction and that some of the images begin traveling in a downward direction. You will need to store information about the speed, document, position, and direction of each image in arrays. Use a separate setInterval() or setTimeout() method to begin animating each image. Save the document as **Buzz.html**.

Case Project 11-3

In Hands-on Project 11-5, you used the clip property to create a screen transition effect of a shrinking box that covers an entire Web page when it first loads, but then shrinks and disappears. Use the same technique to create a box that covers an entire Web page, but that gradually opens from right-to-left like a curtain. Remember that you will need to determine the height and width of the document area by using the document.documentElement.clientHeight and document.documentElement.clientWidth properties in Internet Explorer or the window.innerWidth and window.innerHeight for all other browsers. Save the document as **Curtain.html**.

Case Project 11-4

Create a Web page that contains a drop-down menu with menu items for five types of sports, such as football or baseball. Each menu should display at least three links to Web sites that contain information about each particular sport. For example, the Football menu may contain links to NFL.com (http://www.nfl.com), ESPN's NFL page (http://sports.espn.go.com/nfl/index), and Yahoo! Sports NFL page (http://sports.yahoo.com/nfl;_ylt=AsRakGSbKIS7qaEoSsk90ls5nYcB). Save the document as **SportingNews.html**.

Case Project 11-5

You have probably seen the "warp" or "starfield" animation effect that simulates flying through space. With the warp animation, stars usually begin as small points of light in the middle of the computer screen, and then gradually grow large and eventually fly off the screen. Use the DHTML techniques that you learned in this chapter to simulate this type of warp animation. This is an advanced exercise that requires a strong understanding of JavaScript's mathematical functions in order to properly calculate the trajectory or each star and gradually increase its size as it approaches the edge of the screen. If you do not have a strong math background, then do your best to create a simple warp animation with a few stars that begin in the middle of the screen and eventually fly off the edge of the screen. Save the document as **Warp.html**.

12

Updating Web Pages with AJAX

In this chapter you will:

- Study AJAX concepts
- Learn about HTTP
- Use AJAX to request and receive server data

The most recent version of the JavaScript language is ECMAScript Edition 3, which was first released in December of 1999. The next major edition of the JavaScript language will be ECMAScript Edition 4, although at the time of this writing, the developers of the language have not made a great deal of progress on the new version and it is not known when it will be complete. While there have been numerous browser enhancements since Edition 3 was released in 1999, the core JavaScript language has remained essentially unchanged for eight years. This is unusual with software development technologies, because the Web developers who use these technologies are constantly looking for new and better tools for writing their programs. Unwilling simply to await the arrival of Edition 4, JavaScript programmers have managed to accommodate their own demand for increased JavaScript functionality by combining JavaScript with other technologies.

One such technology is DHTML, which makes Web pages dynamic by combining JavaScript, XHTML, CSS, and the Document Object Model. DHTML does a great job of making Web pages more dynamic and will continue to be a vital Web page development technique. The fact that DHTML runs entirely within a user's Web browser used to be considered an advantage, because it made external resources, such as server data, unnecessary. However, as the Internet matured and broadband access became commonplace, Web developers began demanding a way to make their Web pages interact more dynamically with a Web server. For example, consider a Web browser's request for a Web page. In response, the Web server returns the requested page. If the user wants to refresh the Web page, the Web server returns the entire page again—not just the changed portions of the page. For Web page data that must always be up-to-date, such as stock prices, continuously reloading the entire page is too slow, even at broadband speeds. As you will learn in this chapter, the solution is to use AJAX.

Introduction to AJAX

Asynchronous JavaScript and XML (AJAX) refers to a combination of technologies that allow Web pages displayed on a client computer to quickly interact and exchange data with a Web server without reloading the entire Web page. Although its name implies a combination of JavaScript and XML, AJAX primarily relies on JavaScript and HTTP requests to exchange data between a client computer and a Web server. AJAX gets its name from the fact that XML is often the format used for exchanging data between a client computer and a Web server (although it can also exchange data using standard text strings). The other technologies that comprise AJAX include XHTML, CSS, and the Document Object Model (DOM). However, these technologies primarily handle the display and presentation of data within the Web browser (the same as with DHTML) while HTTP and XML are responsible for data exchange. JavaScript ties everything together.

The term AJAX was first used in an article written in 2005 by Jesse James Garrett entitled *Ajax: A New Approach to Web Applications* (http://adaptivepath.com/publications/essays/archives/000385.php). The article discussed how Garrett's company, Adaptive Path, was using a combination of technologies, which they referred to collectively as AJAX, to add richness and responsiveness to Web pages. Since then, AJAX has become hugely popular among JavaScript developers.

It's important to note that Garrett and Adaptive Path did not invent anything new. Rather, they improved Web page interactivity by combining JavaScript, XML, XHTML, CSS, and the DOM with the key component of AJAX, the XMLHttpRequest object, which is available in modern Web browsers. The **XMLHttpRequest object** uses HTTP to exchange data between a client computer and a Web server. Unlike standard HTTP requests, which usually replace the entire page in a Web browser, the XMLHttpRequest object can be used to request and receive data without reloading a Web page. By combining the XMLHttpRequest object with DHTML techniques, you can update and modify individual portions of your Web page with data received from a Web server. The XMLHttpRequest object has been available in most modern Web browsers since around 2001. However, Garrett's article was the first to clearly document the techniques for combining the XMLHttpRequest object with other techniques in order to exchange data between a client computer and a Web server.

Another factor contributing to AJAX's popularity was the release in 2005 of the Google Suggest Web site (*http://www.google.com/webhp?complete=1*), which was one of the first commercial Web sites to implement an AJAX application. Google Suggest is similar to the standard Google Web page, except that, as you type, Google Suggest lists additional search suggestions based on the text you type. For example, if you type "software" in the Google Suggest text box, the search suggestions shown in Figure 12-1 appear. The important thing to understand about Google Suggest is that as you type each letter, JavaScript code uses the XMLHttpRequest object to send the string in the text box to the Google server, which attempts to match the typed characters with matching suggestions. The Google server then returns the suggestions to the client computer (without reloading the Web page), and JavaScript code populates the suggestion list with the response text.

Figure 12-1

Google Suggest Web site

TIP

The AJAX functionality in Google Suggest is now available in several other Google services, including the Google Finance page at *http://finance.google.com/finance*.

NOTE

You can also use frames (created with `<frame>` elements) and inline frames (created with `<iframe>` elements) to change portions of a Web page. However, frames are deprecated and although inline frames are not formally deprecated, they are not included with the XHTML Strict DTD, so you should avoid using them.

Figures 12-2 and 12-3 conceptually illustrate the difference between a standard HTTP request and an HTTP request with the XMLHttpRequest object. In Figure 12-2, the client makes a standard HTTP request for the *http://www.google.com* Web page, which is returned from the server and displayed in the client's Web browser. Figure 12-3 illustrates the request process with the Google Suggest page when a user types the text "las vegas hotels discount" into the text box. Instead of requesting an entire Web page, the XMLHttpRequest object only requests recommended search terms for the "las vegas hotels discount" string. The server returns three recommended search terms to the client, which in turn uses JavaScript to display the terms in the suggestion list.

Figure 12-2
Standard HTTP request

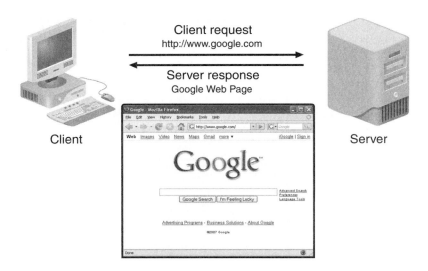

Figure 12-3
HTTP request with the
XMLHttpRequest object

In this chapter, you will create an AJAX application that retrieves the top stories from a selected news agency using RSS feeds. **RSS** (for **RDF Site Summary**, **Rich Site Summary**, or **Really Simple Syndication**) is an XML format that allows Web sites to publish content that can be read by other Web sites. Typical types of data that are published with RSS feeds include news listings, blogs, and digital content such as podcasts. For example, much of the content on MSNBC's Web site at *http://www.msnbc.msn.com* is delivered through RSS feeds. You'll start by creating the main Web page.

To create the main Web page for the top stories application:

1. Start your text editor and create a new document.

2. Type the `<!DOCTYPE>` declaration, `<html>` element, header information, and the `<body>` element. Use the strict DTD and "Top Stories" as the content of the `<title>` element. Your document should appear as follows:

```
<!DOCTYPE html PUBLIC "-//W3C//DTD XHTML 1.0 Strict//EN"
"http://www.w3.org/TR/xhtml1/DTD/xhtml1-strict.dtd">
<html xmlns="http://www.w3.org/1999/xhtml">
<head>
<title>Top Stories</title>
```

```
<meta http-equiv="content-type" content="text/html;
    charset=iso-8859-1" />
</head>
<body>
</body>
</html>
```

3. Add the following style section immediately above the closing </head> tag:

```
<style type="text/css">
h1 {
font-family:arial;
color:navy;
}
p, td {
font-family:arial;
font-size:11px;
color:black;
}
</style>
```

4. Add the following text and elements to the document body. The form will contain radio buttons that represent a list of news agencies from which you can choose to display the selected agency's top stories. The form will be submitted to a PHP script named TopStories that you will create later in the chapter.

```
<h1>Top Stories</h1>
<form method="GET" action="TopStories.php">
</form>
```

5. Add the following table to the form. The table creates the radio buttons that represent the news agencies.

```
<table border="1">
<tr><td valign="top">
<input type="radio" name="agency"
value="http://my.abcnews.go.com/rsspublic/fp_rss20.xml"
checked="checked" /> ABC News<br />
<input type="radio" name="agency"
value="http://newsrss.bbc.co.uk/rss/newsonline_uk_edition/
front_page/rss.xml" /> BBC<br />
<input type="radio" name="agency"
value="http://www.cbsnews.com/feeds/rss/main.rss" /> CBS News<br />
<input type="radio" name="agency"
value="http://rss.cnn.com/rss/cnn_topstories.rss" /> CNN<br />
<input type="radio" name="agency"
```

```
value="http://rss.msnbc.msn.com/id/3032091/device/rss/rss.xml" />
MSNBC<br />
<input type="radio" name="agency"
value="http://rss.news.yahoo.com/rss/topstories" /> Yahoo! News
</td><td id="newsCell" valign="top"></td></tr>
</table>
```

6. Finally, add the following submit button to the end of the form:

```
<p><input type="submit" value="Get Headlines" /></p>
```

7. Save the document as **TopStories.html** in your Chapter folder for Chapter 12, and then open it in your Web browser. Figure 12-4 shows how the document appears in a Web browser. Do not click the submit button yet because you still need to create the PHP script.

Figure 12-4
Top stories Web page

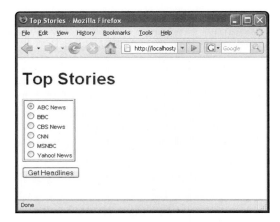

8. Close your Web browser window.

Understanding AJAX's Limitations

Recall from Chapter 9 that the same origin policy restricts how JavaScript code in one window or frame accesses a Web page in another window or frame on a client computer. For windows and frames to view and modify the elements and properties of documents displayed in other windows and frames, they must have the same protocol (such as HTTP) and exist on the same Web server. Because JavaScript is the basis of AJAX programming, you cannot use the XMLHttpRequest object to directly access content on another domain's server; the data you request with the XMLHttpRequest object must be located on the Web server where your JavaScript program is running. In other words, you cannot directly bypass your own Web server and grab data off of someone else's Web server. However, the same origin policy only applies to JavaScript and not to any other programs running on your Web server. This means that you can use a server-side script as a proxy to access data from another domain. The term **proxy** refers to someone or something that acts or performs a request for another thing or person. The server-side proxy script can then return the data to the client computer as it is requested with the XMLHttpRequest object.

Accessing Content on a Separate Domain

The purpose of the same origin policy is to prevent malicious scripts from modifying the content of other windows and frames and prevent the theft of private browser information and information displayed on secure Web pages. However, the ability for one Web server to access Web pages and data on another Web server is the foundation of the World Wide Web. Although you should never attempt to pass off the content from another Web site as your own, there are legitimate reasons why you would use a server-side script to access data from another domain, particularly when it comes to accessing Web services and RSS feeds. A **Web service**, or **XML Web service**, is a software component that resides on a Web server. Web services do not contain any sort of graphical user interface or even a command line interface. Instead, they simply provide services and data in the form of methods and properties; it is up to the client accessing a Web service to provide an implementation for a program that calls a Web service.

As an example of a Web service, consider a Web page that displays the prices of commodities that you want to track, such as crude oil, natural gas, gold, or silver. The Web page may periodically call methods of a Web service that return the most recent trading price for each type of commodity. The developer of a server-side script only needs to know which method of the Web service to call for each type of commodity (such as a `getSilverPrice()` method that returns the current price of silver). The Web service itself does not care what you do with the data once you receive it; it is up to you to display it on a Web page, store it in a database, or use it in some other way in your application. In the case of AJAX, you might pass the data to a JavaScript program running on a client.

This chapter includes an AJAX example that displays streaming stock quote information from Yahoo! Finance. When you enter a stock quote into Yahoo! Finance, the returned results include a link that allows you to download a CSV (comma-separated values) file containing the basic stock quote information, such as opening price and average volume. Because the returned CSV file is a simple text file with each entry separated by commas, you can use a script to parse the file and use the values in your Web pages. You will study the stock quote Web page throughout this chapter. For now, you need to understand that the Web page relies on a server-side PHP script to retrieve and parse stock information from Yahoo! Finance. The PHP script executes when it is passed a stock ticker with the `XMLHttpRequest` object. After the PHP script retrieves the information for the specified stock, it returns the data to the JavaScript code that called it. When you first open the stock quote Web page, it defaults to the quote data for the Nasdaq Composite Index (^IXIC), as shown in Figure 12-5.

Figure 12-5

Stock quote page displaying the default Nasdaq Composite Index quote data

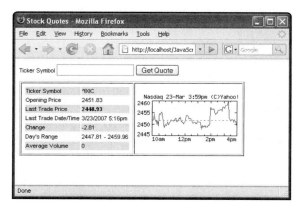

Entering a new ticker symbol and clicking the Get Quote button automatically retrieves the quote data for the specified stock from the Yahoo! Finance page. Figure 12-6 displays the updated stock quotes page after entering the ticker symbol for Oracle Corporation, ORCL.

Figure 12-6

Stock quote page displaying quote data for Oracle Corporation

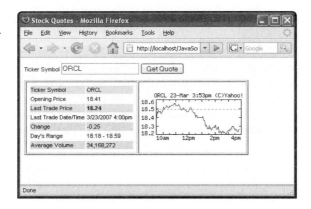

The stock quote page relies on the following PHP script to retrieve data from the Yahoo! Finance page. The script is fairly simple and creates a CSV file from the Yahoo! Finance page that displays the quote data. Then, the script builds an XML tree from the CSV file and returns the result to the client with an echo statement, which is similar to JavaScript's document.write() statement. The purpose of this book is JavaScript programming, not PHP programming, so you will not analyze the following code any further. However, PHP shares a lot of similarities with JavaScript, so you can probably figure out most of the statements in the following code on your own.

```php
<?php
header("Content-Type: text/xml");
$QuoteXML = "<?xml version='1.0' encoding='iso-8859-1' standalone='yes' ?>\n";
$TickerSymbol = $_GET["checkQuote"];
$Quote = fopen("http://quote.yahoo.com/d/quotes.csv?
    s=$TickerSymbol&f=sl1d1t1c1ohgv&e=.csv", "r");
$QuoteString = fread($Quote, 2000);
fclose($Quote);
$QuoteString = str_replace("\"", "", $QuoteString);
$QuoteArray = explode(",", $QuoteString);
$QuoteXML .= "<quote>\n";
$QuoteXML .= "<ticker>{$QuoteArray[0]}</ticker>\n";
$QuoteXML .= "<lastTrade>{$QuoteArray[1]}</lastTrade>\n";
$QuoteXML .= "<lastTradeDate>{$QuoteArray[2]}</lastTradeDate>\n";
$QuoteXML .= "<lastTradeTime>{$QuoteArray[3]}</lastTradeTime>\n";
$QuoteXML .= "<change>{$QuoteArray[4]}</change>\n";
$QuoteXML .= "<open>{$QuoteArray[5]}</open>\n";
$QuoteXML .= "<rangeHigh>{$QuoteArray[6]}</rangeHigh>\n";
$QuoteXML .= "<rangeLow>{$QuoteArray[7]}</rangeLow>\n";
$QuoteXML .= "<volume>{$QuoteArray[8]}</volume>\n";
$QuoteXML .= "<chart>http://ichart.yahoo.com/t?s=$TickerSymbol</chart>\n";
```

```
$QuoteXML .= "</quote>";
header("Content-Length: " . strlen($QuoteXML));
header("Cache-Control: no-cache");
echo $QuoteXML;
?>
```

One lesson you should take away from the preceding code is that PHP, like JavaScript, is not rocket science. Given the JavaScript skills you have learned in this book, and with a little additional study, you can easily learn PHP or any other server-side language. For now, keep in mind that any PHP scripts you see in this chapter are server-side scripting programs; they serve as a counterpoint to JavaScript programs, which are client-side scripting programs. In fact, client-side and server-side scripting languages share much of the same syntax and functionality, although server-side scripting languages can usually do quite a bit more than JavaScript. The exercises in this chapter require you to write some simple PHP scripts. For information on the basics of PHP, refer to Appendix B, "Creating Basic PHP Scripts."

TIP

To learn more about PHP programming, refer to *PHP Programming with MySQL*, by Don Gosselin (the author of this book), published by Course Technology.

Running AJAX from a Web Server

Throughout this book, you have opened Web pages directly from your local computer or network into your Web browser. However, in this chapter, you will open files from a Web server. Opening a local file in a Web browser requires the use of the file:/// protocol. Because AJAX relies on the XMLHttpRequest object to retrieve data, you must open your AJAX files from a Web server with the HTTP protocol (http://) instead. You can turn a computer into a Web server by installing Web server software on it. The most popular Web server software used on the Internet is Apache HTTP Server (typically referred to as Apache), which is used by more than half of today's Web sites. The second most popular Web server is Microsoft Internet Information Services (IIS) for Windows operating systems, which is used on about one-third of today's Web sites. Additionally, several of the examples and projects in this chapter use PHP scripts to retrieve data from other Web servers. If you do not have access to a Web server that can run PHP, follow the instructions in Appendix A, "Building a Web Development Environment", to install and configure either Apache or IIS and the PHP software on your local computer.

In the following steps, you will open the stock quotes Web page from your Web server. After opening the Web page, you will test it.

To open and test the stock quotes Web page:

1. Follow the instructions in Appendix A, "Building a Web Development Environment" to install and configure a Web server and PHP. Be sure to follow the instructions for creating an Alias directive for Apache or a virtual directory in IIS that points to the location of your data files.

2. Open your Web browser and enter the following URL to load the stock quotes Web page:

    ```
    http://localhost/JavaScript_Projects/Chapter.12/Chapter/
    StockQuotes.html
    ```

CAUTION

Remember that you cannot open an AJAX file from your local file system; you must open your AJAX files from a Web server with the HTTP protocol (http://).

3. By default, the stock quotes Web page displays quote data for the Nasdaq Composite Index (^IXIC). Enter another stock symbol, such as MSFT (for Microsoft) or CSCO (for Cisco), and click **Get Quote**. The Web page should automatically update the stock data for the symbol you entered. Figure 12-7 shows how the Web page appears after entering the stock symbol for Microsoft.

Figure 12-7

Stock quotes Web page displaying Microsoft stock data

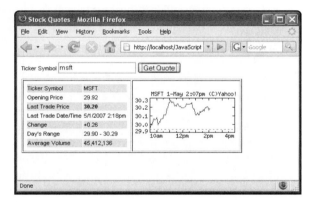

4. Close your Web browser window.

Overview of Creating an AJAX Script

After you have installed and configured your Web server, you perform the following steps to create an AJAX script:

- Instantiate an `XMLHttpRequest` object for the Web browser where the script will run.
- Use the `XMLHttpRequest` object to send a request to the server.
- Read and process the data returned from the server.

Before you can write an AJAX script, you need to know a little more about HTTP to understand how AJAX exchanges data client computers and Web servers.

Working with HTTP

When discussing HTTP, it's helpful to start by reviewing basic terminology. As you know, when a user attempts to access a Web page, either by entering its URL in a browser's Address box or by clicking a link, the user's Web browser asks a Web server for the Web page. The process of asking for a Web page from a Web server is known as a **request**. The Web server's reply (which might consist of the requested Web page or a message about that Web page) is known as the **response**. Every Web page is identified by a unique address called the Uniform Resource Locator, or **URL**. A Web page's URL is similar to a telephone number in that each URL is unique, and refers to a specific Web page. A URL consists of two basic parts: a protocol (usually HTTP), and either the domain name for a Web server or a Web server's Internet Protocol address. Hypertext Transfer Protocol (HTTP) is a set of rules that defines how requests are made by an HTTP client to an HTTP server, and how responses are returned from an HTTP server to an HTTP client. The term **HTTP client** refers to the application, usually a Web browser, which makes the request. The term **HTTP server** is another name for a Web server and refers to a computer that receives HTTP requests and returns responses to HTTP clients. A colon, two forward slashes, and a host follow the protocol portion of a URL. The term **host** refers to a computer system that is being accessed by a remote computer. In a URL, a specific filename, or a combination of directories and a filename, can follow the domain name or IP address. If the URL does not specify a filename, the requesting Web server looks for a default Web page located in the root or specified directory. Default Web pages usually have names similar to index.html or default.html. For instance, if you want help using Google's Web site and you enter *http://www.google.com/support/* in your browser's Address box, the Web server automatically opens a file named index.html.

TIP

An Internet Protocol, or IP address, is another way to uniquely identify computers or devices connected to the Internet. An IP address consists of a series of four groups of numbers separated by periods. Each Internet domain name is associated with a unique IP address.

Although HTTP is probably the most widely used protocol on the Internet, it is not the only one. HTTP is a component of Transmission Control Protocol/Internet Protocol (TCP/IP), a large collection of communication protocols used on the Internet. Other common protocols include Hypertext Transfer Protocol Secure (HTTPS), which provides secure Internet connections that are used in Web-based financial transactions and other types of communication that require security and privacy, and File Transfer Protocol (FTP), which is used for transferring files across the Internet.

The W3C and Internet Engineering Task Force jointly develop HTTP. The Internet Engineering Task Force (IETF) is a volunteer organization devoted to the development and promotion of Internet Standards, most notably TCP/IP. Recall that the W3C does not actually release a version of a particular technology. Instead, it issues a formal recommendation for a technology, which essentially means that the technology is (or will be) a recognized industry standard. The most recent version of HTTP that is commonly used today is 1.1, which is defined by RFC 2616 and recommendations. You can find the HTTP recommendations on the W3C Web site at *http://www.w3.org/Protocols/*.

Understanding HTTP Messages

Most people who use the Web don't realize that there is more going on behind the scenes when it comes to requesting a Web page and receiving a response from a Web server. HTTP client requests and server responses are both known as **HTTP messages**. When you submit a request for a Web page, the HTTP client opens a connection to the server and submits a request message. The Web server then returns a response message that is appropriate to the type of request. Both request and response messages are in the following format:

```
Start line containing the request method for requests or status line for
responses
Header lines (zero or more)
Blank line
Message body (optional)
```

The specific contents of each line depend on whether it is a request or a response message. The first line either identifies the method (such as GET or POST) for requests or the status returned from a response. Following the first line, each message can include zero or more lines containing **headers**, which define information about the request or response message and about the contents of the message body. The RFC2616 recommendation defines 46 HTTP 1.1 headers, categorized by generic headers that can be used in request or response messages and headers that are specific to a request, a response, or the message body. The format for using a header is *header: value*.

For example, the following lines define two generic headers that can be used in either request or response messages: Connection and Date. The Connection header specifies that the HTTP connection should close after the Web client receives a response from the Web server. The Date header identifies the date and time in Greenwich Mean Time format when a message was originated.

```
Connection: close
Date: Fri, 27 June 2008 18:32:07 GMT
```

One generic header that requires special mention for AJAX applications is the Cache-Control header, which specifies how a Web browser should cache any server content it receives. Most Web browsers try to reduce the amount of data that needs to be retrieved from a server by caching retrieved data on a local computer. **Caching** refers to the temporary storage of data for faster access. If caching is enabled in a Web browser, the Web browser will attempt to locate any necessary data in its cache before making a request from a Web server. For example, assume that caching is turned on when you open the stock quotes Web page. If you enter the same stock symbol more than once and click the Get Quotes button, the browser will retrieve the stock data stored in its cache and not the most recent data from the server. While this technique improves Web browser performance, it goes against the reason for using AJAX, which is to update portions of a Web page dynamically with the most recent data from a server. For this reason, you should always include in your AJAX programs the Cache-Control header, with an assigned value of "no-cache", as follows:

```
Cache-Control: no-cache
```

TIP
See RFC 2616 for complete listings and descriptions of the available HTTP 1.1 headers.

NOTE
The HTTP headers are case-insensitive.

A blank line always follows the last header line. Optionally, a message body can follow the blank line in the messages. In most cases, the message body contains form data for POST requests or some type of document (such as a Web page or XML page) or other type of content (such as an image file) that is returned with a server response. However, message bodies are not required for either request or response messages. For example, with a GET request, no message body is necessary because any form data that is part of the request is appended to the URL. Response messages are also not required to include a message body. This may seem a little strange because if a server doesn't return a Web page, then what is returned? What's the point in sending a request to a Web server if it doesn't return anything? Although GET and POST requests are by far the two most common types of HTTP requests, there are five other methods that can be used with an HTTP request: HEAD, DELETE, OPTIONS, PUT, and TRACE. The DELETE, OPTIONS, PUT, and TRACE methods are rarely used. However, the HEAD method is commonly used for returning information about a document, but not the document itself. For example, you may use the HEAD method to determine the last modification date of a Web page before requesting it from the Web server.

Later in this chapter, you will learn more about how to manage the response messages that are returned from a server. But first, you will learn about what's involved when sending a request message.

Sending HTTP Requests

Without a scripting language such as JavaScript, most Web browsers are usually limited to using the GET and POST methods with an HTTP request. The GET method is used for standard Web page requests, but can have a query string or form data appended to the URL. For example, if you enter the address for the United States Postal Service Web site (*http://www.usps.com*) in your Web browser, the browser creates a request message that begins with the following start line:

```
GET / HTTP/1.1
```

The preceding line identifies the method as GET and 1.1 as the HTTP version. Notice the forward slash after GET, which identifies the root directory on the Web server as the location of the requested file. Because no HTML document was specified in the URL, the request looks in the Web server's root directory for a default Web page such as index.htm. However, if the URL contains a specific directory or file name, it is included in the start line. For example, a URL request that contains a directory and file name, such as *http://www.usps.com/business/welcome.htm*, generates the following start line in a request message:

```
GET /business/welcome.htm HTTP/1.1
```

When requesting a URL, most Web browsers include the headers listed in Table 12-1 in generated request messages.

Header	Description
Host	Identifies the host portion of a requested URL
Accept-Encoding	Defines the encoding formats that the HTTP client accepts
Accept	Defines the MIME types that the HTTP client accepts
Accept-Language	Lists the languages that the HTTP client accepts in a response
Accept-Charset	Defines the character sets that the HTTP client accepts
User-Agent	Identifies the user agent, such as a Web browser, that submitted the request
Referer	Identifies the referring URL from which the request was made

Table 12-1   Common request headers

The following shows an example request header. When you search for "pottery barn" on Google and click the Pottery Barn link (*www.potterybarn.com/*) that is returned in the search results, the following request message is generated in Firefox:

```
GET / HTTP/1.1
Host: www.potterybarn.com
User-Agent: Mozilla/5.0 (Windows; U; Windows NT 5.1; en-US; rv:1.8.1.3)
Gecko/20070309 Firefox/2.0.0.3
Accept: text/xml,application/xml,application/xhtml+xml,text/html;q=0.9,
text/plain;q=0.8,image/png,*/*;q=0.5
Accept-Language: en-us,en;q=0.5
Accept-Encoding: gzip,deflate
Accept-Charset: ISO-8859-1,utf-8;q=0.7,*;q=0.7
Keep-Alive: 300
Connection: keep-alive
Referer: http://www.google.com/search?hl=en&q=pottery+barn&btnG=Google+Search
blank line
```

A POST request is similar to a GET request except that any submitted data is included in the message body immediately following the blank line after the last header. Requests made with the POST method also usually include some of the headers listed in Table 12-2 to provide more information about the message body.

Header	Description
Content-Encoding	Defines the encoding format of the message body
Content-Language	Identifies the language of the message body
Content-Length	Identifies the size of the message body
Content-Location	Specifies the location of the message body contents
Content-Type	Identifies the MIME type of the message body
Expires	Defines the expiration date of the message body contents
Last-Modified	Identifies the last modification date of the message body contents

Table 12-2   Common message body headers

NOTE
The message body headers listed in Table 12-2 are used for response messages as well as request messages.

The following code is an example of a POST request message that is generated when submitting a catalog request to Pottery Barn. The message body is a URL-encoded string containing information about the customer who requested the catalog.

```
POST /cust/catalogrequest.cfm HTTP/1.1
Host: secure.potterybarn.com
User-Agent: Mozilla/5.0 (Windows; U; Windows NT 5.1; en-US; rv:1.8.1.3)
Gecko/20070309 Firefox/2.0.0.3
Accept: text/xml,application/xml,application/xhtml+xml,text/html;q=0.9,
text/plain;q=0.8,image/png,*/*;q=0.5
Accept-Language: en-us,en;q=0.5
Accept-Encoding: gzip,deflate
Accept-Charset: ISO-8859-1,utf-8;q=0.7,*;q=0.7
Keep-Alive: 300
Connection: keep-alive
Referer: https://secure.potterybarn.com/cust/catalogrequest.cfm
Content-Type: application/x-www-form-urlencoded
Content-Length: 193
blank line
subid=CRQ_2014_1175186446&rqpb=1&rqod=1&step=info&n0=Don+Gosselin
&a0=100+Main+Street &b0=&c0=Spencer&s0=MA&z0=01562&e0=email%40dongosselin.com
&v0=email%40dongosselin.com&submit.x=24&submit.y=9
```

Next, you will learn about the HTTP responses that the user's browser receives from a Web server.

CHAPTER 12

Receiving HTTP Responses

HTTP response messages take the same format as request messages, except for the contents of the start line and the headers. Instead of containing a request method, the start line, or status line, returns the protocol and version of the HTTP server (such as HTTP/1.1) along with a status code and descriptive text. The status codes returned from an HTTP server consist of three digits. The codes that begin with 1 (101, 102, etc.) are purely information, indicating, for instance, that a request was received. The codes that begin with 2 indicate a successful request. The following list summarizes the types of messages provided by the three digit codes that begin with 1-5. Table 12-3 lists the most common response codes.

- 1*xx* (informational)—Request received
- 2*xx*: (success)—Request successful
- 3*xx*: (redirection)—Request cannot be completed without further action
- 4*xx*: (client error)—Request cannot be fulfilled due to a client error
- 5*xx*: (server error)— Request cannot be fulfilled due to a server error

Code	Text	Description
200	OK	The request was successful.
301	Moved Permanently	The requested URL has been permanently moved.
302	Moved Temporarily	The requested URL has been temporarily moved.
404	Not Found	The requested URL was not found.
500	Internal Server Error	The request could not be completed due to an internal server error.

Table 12-3   Common response codes

For successful requests with HTTP 1.1, the start line in the response message consists of the following status line:

```
HTTP/1.1 200 OK
```

Zero or more response headers follow the status line. Table 12-4 lists the most common response codes.

Header	Description
Vary	Determines whether the server can respond to subsequent requests with the same response
Server	Returns information about the server software that processed the request
Location	Redirects clients to a different URI

Table 12-4   Common response headers

NOTE

Because responses return documents (such as an XHTML document) or other types of files (such as image files), response messages usually include one or more of the message body headers listed in Table 12-4.

The response returned from a server can be much more involved than the original request that generated it. The initial request from an HTTP client for a Web page often results in the server issuing multiple other requests for resources that are required by the requested URL, such as style sheets, images, and so on. As a simplified example, the following statements represent the basic response that is returned for a request for the United States Postal Service Web site, although keep in mind that additional requests may be issued for resources that are required by the URL:

```
HTTP/1.x 200 OK
Server: Netscape-Enterprise/6.0
Date: Fri, 30 Mar 2007 03:18:56 GMT
Content-Type: text/html
Cache-Control: no-cache, must-revalidate, private
Content-Encoding: gzip
Content-Length: 6722
blank line
<!DOCTYPE HTML PUBLIC "-//W3C//DTD HTML 4.01 Transitional//EN">
<html><head><!-- <!DOCTYPE HTML PUBLIC "-//W3C//DTD HTML 4.01
Transitional//EN"
"http://www.w3.org/TR/html4/loose.dtd"> -->
<title>USPS - The United States Postal Service (U.S. Postal
Service)</title>
...
```

Next, you will create a PHP script that returns the RSS feeds for the selected news agency in the top stories program. The response returned from the PHP script will include the Content-Type, Content-Length, and Cache-Control headers.

To create a PHP script that returns the RSS feeds for a selected news agency:

1. Create a new document in your text editor.

2. Add the following PHP script section to the document:

    ```
    <?php
    ?>
    ```

3. Add the following statement to the script section. This statement retrieves the value of the agency field that was passed in the GET request from the TopStories.html page and assigns it to a variable named $NewsSource.

    ```
    $NewsSource=$_GET["agency"];
    ```

4. Add to the end of the script section the following header() functions. PHP uses the header() function to define a header that will be returned with a response. The first statement creates the Content-Type header and assigns it a value of "text/xml". The second statement creates the Content-Type header and assigns it the length of the RSS feed by using the file_get_contents() method to retrieve the file and the strlen() function to obtain the file length. The second statement creates the Cache-Control header and assigns it a value of "no-cache".

```
header("Content-Type: text/xml");
header("Content-Length: " . strlen(file_get_contents($NewsSource)));
header("Cache-Control: no-cache");
```

5. Add to the end of the script section the following statement, which uses the `readfile()` function to return the contents of the RSS feed as a response:

```
readfile($NewsSource);
```

6. Save the document as **TopStories.php** in your Chapter folder for Chapter 12, and then close it in your text editor.

7. Open your Web browser and enter the following URL to load the top stories Web page:

```
http://localhost/JavaScript_Projects/Chapter.12/Chapter/
TopStories.html
```

8. Select a news agency on the top stories Web page and click **Get Headlines**. Most current Web browsers have built-in readers that can automatically read and display RSS feeds. Figure 12-8 displays the RSS feed that appears for ABC News.

Figure 12-8
RSS feed for ABC News

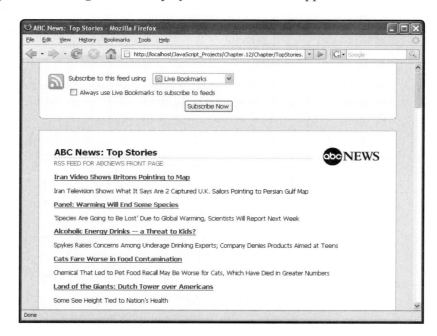

9. Close your Web browser window.

Now that you understand the basics of HTTP requests and responses, you can begin learning about how to use these operations with JavaScript to exchange data between a client computer and a Web server.

Requesting Server Data

The XMLHttpRequest object is the key to turning your JavaScript script into AJAX programs because it allows you to use JavaScript and HTTP to exchange data between a Web browser and a Web server. More specifically, you use the methods and properties of an instantiated XMLHttpRequest object with JavaScript to build and send request messages and to receive and process response messages. The XMLHttpRequest object contains the methods listed in Table 12-5 and the properties listed in Table 12-6.

Method	Description
abort()	Cancels the current HTTP request
getAllResponseHeaders()	Returns a text string containing all of a response's headers that were returned with a response in *header: value*, separated by line breaks
getResponseHeader (*header_name*)	Returns a text string containing the value assigned to the specified header
open(method,URL[,*async, user, password*])	Specifies the method and URL for an HTTP request; assigning a value of true to the *async* argument performs the request asynchrounously while a value of false performs the request synchronously; the default is true
send([*content*])	Submits an HTTP request using the information assigned with the open() method; the optional content argument contains the message body
setRequestHeader (*header_name, value*)	Creates an HTTP header using the *header_name* and *value* arguments

Table 12-5   XMLHttpRequest object methods

Property	Description
onreadystatechange	Specifies the name of the event handler function that executes whenever the value that is assigned to the readyState property changes
readyState	Contains one of the following values, which represent the state of the HTTP request: 0 (uninitialized), 1 (open), 2 (sent), 3 (receiving), or 4 (loaded)
responseText	Contains the HTTP response as a text string
responseXML	Contains the HTTP response as an XML document
status	Contains the HTTP status code (such as 200 for "OK" or 404 for "Not Found) that was returned with the response
statusText	Contains the HTTP status text (such as "OK" or "Not Found) that was returned with the response

Table 12-6   XMLHttpRequest object properties

Before you can use any of the methods and properties listed in Tables 12-5 and 12-6, you must first learn how to instantiate an XMLHttpRequest object.

Instantiating an `XMLHttpRequest` Object

The first step for using AJAX to exchange data between an HTTP client and a Web server is to instantiate an `XMLHttpRequest` object. For Mozilla-based browsers, such as Firefox, and for Internet Explorer 7, you instantiate an `XMLHttpRequest` object with the `XMLHttpRequest` constructor, as follows:

```
var httpRequest = new XMLHttpRequest();
```

Unfortunately, although the `XMLHttpRequest` object is available in most modern Web browsers, it is not standardized by the W3C or any other standards organization. Thankfully, Internet Explorer 7 now uses the same syntax for instantiating an `XMLHttpRequest` object that Mozilla-based browsers use. However, for older versions of Internet Explorer, to instantiate an `XMLHttpRequest` object in Internet Explorer, you must instantiate the `XMLHttpRequest` object as an ActiveX object. **ActiveX** is a technology that allows programming objects to be easily reused with any programming language that supports Microsoft's Component Object Model. The **Component Object Model (COM)** is an architecture for cross-platform development of client/server applications. For Internet Explorer 6, you use the following syntax to instantiate an `XMLHttpRequest` object by passing a value of "Msxml2.XMLHTTP" to the ActiveX object constructor:

```
var httpReq = new ActiveXObject("Msxml2.XMLHTTP");
```

To make things even more confusing, Internet Explorer 5.5 requires the following slightly different syntax to instantiate an `XMLHttpRequest` object by passing a value of "Microsoft.XMLHTTP" instead of "Msxml2.XMLHTTP" to the ActiveX object constructor:

```
var httpReq = new ActiveXObject("Microsoft.XMLHTTP");
```

As of February 2007, Internet Explorer 6 is used by almost 40% of the browser market, and Internet Explorer 5.5 is used by 2.5% of the browser market. Because these versions of Internet Explorer are still in use, you should include the appropriate syntax to instantiate an `XMLHttpRequest` object for each browser. Essentially, your code should test for and instantiate an `XMLHttpRequest` object according to the following rules:

1. For Mozilla-based browsers or Internet Explorer 7, use the `XMLHttpRequest` constructor.
2. For Internet Explorer 6, pass a value of "Msxml2.XMLHTTP" to the ActiveX object constructor.
3. For Internet Explorer 5.5, pass a value of "Microsoft.XMLHTTP" to the ActiveX object constructor.
4. For all other browsers, inform the user that his or her browser does not support AJAX.

Most JavaScript programmers use a series of nested `try...catch` statements to instantiate an `XMLHttpRequest` object according to the Web browser that is running the script. For example, the following code declares a variable named `httpRequest` and then attempts to use the `XMLHttpRequest` constructor in the `try` statement to declare an `XMLHttpRequest` object. If the Web browser running the code does not contain an `XMLHttpRequest` constructor, then it is neither a Mozilla-based browser nor Internet Explorer 7. If this is the case, then the `try` statement throws an exception to the `catch` statement. Notice that the `catch` statement contains a nested `try...catch` statement. The nested `try` statement attempts to declare an `XMLHttpRequest` object by passing a value of "Msxml2.XMLHTTP" to the ActiveX object constructor. If the Web browser running the code does not support a value of "Msxml2.XMLHTTP" with the ActiveX object constructor, then it is not Internet Explorer. If this is the case, then the `try` statement throws an exception to the nested `catch` statement. Finally, if the nested `try` statement cannot instantiate an `XMLHttpRequest` object with the ActiveX object constructor, the nested `catch` statement prints "Your browser does not support AJAX!".

```
var httpRequest;
// instantiate an object for Mozilla-based browsers and Internet Explorer 7
try {
       httpRequest = new XMLHttpRequest();
}
// instantiate an ActiveX object for Internet Explorer 6
catch (requestError) {
       try {
              httpRequest = new ActiveXObject("Msxml2.XMLHTTP");
       }
       catch (requestError) {
              document.write("<p>Your browser does not support AJAX!</p>");
              return false;
       }
}
```

If you only need to support Internet Explorer 6 and higher, then the preceding code is sufficient. However, to support Internet Explorer 5.5, you must include another `try...catch` statement within the nested `catch` statement that attempts to pass a value of "Microsoft.XMLHTTP" (the value that is required for Internet Explorer 5.5) to the ActiveX object constructor. The following code demonstrates how to use two nested `try...catch` statements within a main `try...catch` statement to instantiate an `XMLHttpRequest` object for the appropriate Web browser. If none of the three `try` statements is able to instantiate an `XMLHttpRequest` object, then the final `catch` statement prints "Your browser does not support AJAX!".

```
var httpRequest;
// instantiate an object for Mozilla-based browsers and Internet Explorer 7
try {
       httpRequest = new XMLHttpRequest();
}
catch (requestError) {
       // instantiate an ActiveX object for Internet Explorer 6
       try {
              httpRequest = new ActiveXObject("Msxml2.XMLHTTP");
       }
       catch (requestError) {
              // instantiate an ActiveX object for Internet Explorer 5.5
              try {
                     httpRequest = new ActiveXObject("Microsoft.XMLHTTP");
              }
```

```
        catch (requestError) {
                document.write(
                        "<p>Your browser does not support AJAX!</p>");
                return false;
        }
    }
}
```

Opening and closing HTTP connections takes up a lot of computer memory and processing time. To improve performance between client requests and server responses, HTTP/1.1 automatically keeps the client-server connection open unless it is specifically closed by assigning a value of "close" to the `Connection` header, or until it is closed by the client or server. This means that you can make your AJAX programs faster by reusing an instantiated `XMLHttpRequest` object instead of recreating it each time you send a server request. The following code demonstrates how to create a global variable named `httpRequest` that is assigned an instantiated `XMLHttpRequest` object in a function named `getRequestObject()`. The `getRequestObject()` function is only called once when the Web page first loads. After the `getRequestObject()` function creates the appropriate `XMLHttpRequest` object, the last statement in the function returns the `httpRequest` variable to a calling statement. Notice the `if` statement that follows the `getRequestObject()` function. If the `httpRequest` variable is equal to false, then it has not been instantiated with the `XMLHttpRequest` object and the `getRequestObject()` function is called. However, if the `httpRequest` variable is *not* equal to false (meaning that the Web page has already been loaded), then the `getRequestObject()` function is bypassed because the `XMLHttpRequest` object already exists.

```
var httpRequest = false;
function getRequestObject() {
        try {
                httpRequest = new XMLHttpRequest();
        }
        catch (requestError) {
                try {
                        httpRequest = new ActiveXObject("Msxml2.XMLHTTP");
                }
                catch (requestError) {
                        try {
                                httpRequest = new ActiveXObject("Microsoft.XMLHTTP");
                        }
                        catch (requestError) {
                                window.alert("Your browser does not support AJAX!");
                                return false;
                        }
                }
        }
        return httpRequest;
}
if (!httpRequest)
        httpRequest = getRequestObject();
```

Next, you will add code to the top stories Web page that instantiates an XMLHttpRequest object.

To add code to the top stories Web page that instantiates an XMLHttpRequest object:

1. Return to the **TopStories.html** document in your text editor.

2. Add the following script section above the closing </head> tag:

```
<script type="text/javascript">
/* <![CDATA[ */
/* ]]> */
</script>
```

3. Add to the script section the following global declaration for the httpRequest variable and the getRequestObject() function:

```
var httpRequest = false;
function getRequestObject() {
        try {
                httpRequest = new XMLHttpRequest();
        }
        catch (requestError) {
                try {
                        httpRequest = new ActiveXObject("Msxml2
                        .XMLHTTP");
                }
                catch (requestError) {
                        try {
                                httpRequest = new ActiveXObject
                                ("Microsoft.XMLHTTP");
                        }
                        catch (requestError) {
                                window.alert("Your browser does not
                                support AJAX!");
                                return false;
                        }
                }
        }
        return httpRequest;
}
```

4. Save the **TopStories.html** document.

Opening and Sending a Request

After you instantiate an XMLHttpRequest object, you use the open() method with the instantiated XMLHttpRequest object to specify the request method (such as GET or POST) and URL. The following statement is the open() method used by the stock quotes Web page. The statement specifies the GET method and a URL named StockCheck.php, which is the PHP script that retrieves the stock information from Yahoo! Finance. The requested stock is appended to the URL as a query string in the format `checkQuote=tickerSymbol`. The value assigned to the `tickerSymbol` variable is passed with Get Quote button's `onclick` event to a function containing the `XMLHttpRequest` code.

```
httpRequest.open("get","StockCheck.php?" + "checkQuote="
    + tickerSymbol);
```

The `open()` method also accepts three optional arguments. The first two optional arguments—a user name and password—are only necessary if the Web server requires authentication. The third optional argument, the *async* argument, can be assigned a value of true or false to determine whether the request will be handled synchronously or asynchronously. Assigning a value of true to the *async* argument performs the request asynchrounously while a value of false performs the request synchronously. If you omit the *async* argument, it defaults to a value of true, which performs the request asynchronously. The following statement demonstrates how to specify that the request will be handled synchronously and how to pass a user name ("dongosselin") and password ("rosebud") to the `open()` method:

```
httpRequest.open("get","StockCheck.php?" + "checkQuote="
    + tickerSymbol, false, "dongosselin", "rosebud");
```

In the last section, you learned how to reuse an instantiated `XMLHttpRequest` object instead of recreating it each time you send a server request. When you reuse an existing `XMLHttpRequest` object, it is possible that the object may already have been in the process of sending a request to the server. To improve performance, you should call the `abort()` method of the `XMLHttpRequest` object to cancel any existing HTTP requests before beginning a new one. Append the `abort()` method to an instantiated `XMLHttpRequest` object and call the method before calling the `open()` method, as follows:

```
httpRequest.abort();
httpRequest.open("get","StockCheck.php?" + "checkQuote="
    + tickerSymbol, false, "dongosselin", "rosebud");
```

After you have defined the basic request criteria with the `open()` method, you use the `send()` method with the instantiated `XMLHttpRequest` object to submit the request to the server. The `send()` method accepts a single argument containing the message body. If GET is specified with the `open()` method, you must pass a value of null to the `send()` method, as follows:

```
httpRequest.send(null);
```

Recall that when a Web browser submits an HTTP request, it usually includes various response and message body headers. When running basic GET requests with the `XMLHttpRequest` object, you do not usually need to specify any additional HTTP headers. For example, the following statements are all you need to open and send a request with the stock quotes Web page:

```
httpRequest.abort();
httpRequest.open("get","StockCheck.php?" + "checkQuote="
    + tickerSymbol);
httpRequest.send(null);
```

Requests with the POST method are a little more involved. With form data, a Web browser automatically handles the task of creating name=value pairs from form element name attributes and field values. When submitting form data as the message body with the `XMLHttpRequest` object, you must manually build the name=value pairs that will be submitted to the server. The first statement in the following code creates a variable named `requestBody` that is assigned the value "checkQuote=" and the URI-encoded value assigned to the `tickerSymbol` variable. The last statement then passes the `requestBody` variable as an argument to the `send()` method.

```
var requestBody = "checkQuote=" + encodeURIComponent(tickerSymbol);
httpRequest.send(requestBody);
```

With `POST` requests, you must at least submit the `Content-Type` header before executing the `send()` method to identify the MIME type of the message body. You should also submit the `Content-Length` header to specify the size of the message body and the `Connection` header to specify that the connection with the server be closed after the response is received. You use the `setRequestHeader()` method to specify HTTP headers and values to submit with the HTTP request. You pass two arguments to the `setRequestHeader()` method: the name of the header and its value. For example, the following code uses the `setRequestHeader()` method to define the `Content-Type`, `Content-Length`, and `Connection` headers before submitting the request for the stock quotes Web page:

```
httpRequest.abort();
httpRequest.open("POST","StockCheck.php");
var requestBody = "checkQuote=" + encodeURIComponent(tickerSymbol);
httpRequest.setRequestHeader("Content-Type",
     "application/x-www-form-urlencoded");
httpRequest.setRequestHeader("Content-Length", requestBody.length);
httpRequest.setRequestHeader("Connection", "close");
httpRequest.send(requestBody);
```

Next, you will add a function that instantiates, opens, and submits an `XMLHttpRequest` object.

To add a function that instantiates, opens, and submits an `XMLHttpRequest` object:

1. Return to the **TopStories.html** document in your text editor.
2. Add the following `newsUpdate()` function to the end of the script section. The `if` statement at the beginning of the function calls the `getRequestObject()` function to instantiate the `httpRequest` object if it does not already exist. The `for` loop then iterates through the radio buttons on the form to determine which one is checked, and then copies the checked item's URL (which is stored in the `value` attribute) to a variable named `agency`. The last three statements then abort an existing process (if one is running), and open and send the new request. Notice that the value of the `agency` variable is appended to the URL in the `open()` function as a query string.

```
function newsUpdate() {
    if (!httpRequest)
        httpRequest = getRequestObject();
    for (var i=0; i<6; ++i) {
        if (document.forms[0].agency[i].checked == true) {
            var agency = document.forms[0].agency[i].value;
```

```
                              break;
                    }
            }
            httpRequest.abort();
            httpRequest.open("get","TopStories.php?" + "agency=" + agency);
            httpRequest.send(null);
      }
```

3. Save the **TopStories.html** document.

Receiving Server Data

After you submit a request with the XMLHttpRequest object, the message body in the server response is assigned to the XMLHttpRequest object's responseXML or responseText properties. The responseXML property contains the HTTP response as an XML document, while the responseText property contains the HTTP response as a text string. Note that the message body is only assigned to the responseXML property if the server response includes the Content-Type header, assigned a MIME type value of "text/xml". You can process the contents of the responseXML property using XML DOM node manipulating techniques. In the XML DOM, each XML element is referred to as a **node**. The XML DOM contains numerous properties and methods for manipulating the nodes in an XML document. In this chapter, you will work with the childNodes[] array and the nodeValue property. The childNodes[] array returns an array of child nodes for a particular element while the nodeValue property sets and returns the value of a node. For example, the following statements demonstrate how to manipulate the value assigned to the responseXML property for the stock quotes Web page. The first statement assigns the value of the returned responseXML property to a variable named stockValues. The remaining statements then use the innerHTML() method, childNodes[] array, and nodeValue property to assign the values of the XML document stored in the stockValues variable to the appropriate element.

```
var stockValues = httpRequest.responseXML;
document.getElementById("ticker").innerHTML =
stockValues.getElementsByTagName("ticker")[0].childNodes[0].nodeValue;
document.getElementById("openingPrice").innerHTML
     = stockValues.getElementsByTagName("open")[0].childNodes[0].nodeValue;
document.getElementById("lastTrade").innerHTML = "<strong>"
     + stockValues.getElementsByTagName("lastTrade")[0]
     .childNodes[0].nodeValue + "</strong>";
document.getElementById("lastTradeDT").innerHTML
     = stockValues.getElementsByTagName("lastTradeDate")[0]
     .childNodes[0].nodeValue + " " + stockValues.getElementsByTagName(
     "lastTradeTime")[0].childNodes[0].nodeValue;
document.getElementById("change").innerHTML
     = stockValues.getElementsByTagName("change")[0].childNodes[0].nodeValue;
document.getElementById("range").innerHTML
     = stockValues.getElementsByTagName("rangeLow")[0].childNodes[0]
```

```
        .nodeValue + " - " + stockValues.getElementsByTagName(
        "rangeHigh")[0].childNodes[0].nodeValue;
var volume = parseInt(stockValues.getElementsByTagName(
        "volume")[0].childNodes[0].nodeValue);
document.getElementById("volume").innerHTML = volume.toLocaleString();
document.getElementById("chart").innerHTML = "<img src="
        + stockValues.getElementsByTagName("chart")[0].childNodes[0].nodeValue
        + " alt='Stock line chart from Yahoo.com.' />";
```

TIP

For a complete listing of node types, properties, and methods of the XML DOM, refer to the W3 School's XML DOM reference at http://w3schools.com/dom/dom_nodetype.asp.

To use the `responseText` property, consider the following simplified version of the PHP script you saw earlier, which retrieves data from the Yahoo! Finance page:

```php
<?php
header("Content-Type: text/html");
$TickerSymbol = $_GET["checkQuote"];
$Quote = fopen("http://quote.yahoo.com/d/quotes.csv?
        s=$TickerSymbol&f=sl1d1t1c1ohgv&e=.csv", "r");
$QuoteString = fread($Quote, 2000);
fclose($Quote);
echo $QuoteString;
?>
```

The second statement in the preceding code assigns a value of "text/html" to the `Content-Type` header, and instead of building an XML tree, the code simply returns a text string similar to the following text that is returned for the Nasdaq Composite Index (^IXIC):

```
"^IXIC",2421.64,"3/30/2007","5:16pm",+3.76,2419.91,2432.20,2403.01,0
```

NOTE

Don't worry about understanding the PHP script—the only thing you need to know about the script is that this version returns a text string instead of an XML document.

The following statements demonstrate how to use the returned response string with JavaScript. The first statement uses the `split()` method of the `String` object to split the string at each of the commas into an array named `responseArray`. The remaining statements then use the `innerHTML()` method to assign the values in `responseArray` to the appropriate elements.

```
var responseArray = httpRequest.responseText.split(",");
document.getElementById('ticker').innerHTML
      = responseArray[0].slice(1, responseArray[0].length-1);
document.getElementById('openingPrice').innerHTML
      = responseArray[5];
document.getElementById('lastTradeDT').innerHTML
      = responseArray[2].slice(1, responseArray[2].length-1) + " "
      + responseArray[3].slice(1, responseArray[3].length-1);
document.getElementById('lastTrade').innerHTML = "<strong>"
      +  responseArray[1] + "</strong>";
document.getElementById('change').innerHTML = responseArray[4];
document.getElementById('range').innerHTML = responseArray[7]
      + " - " + responseArray[6];
var volume = parseInt(responseArray[8]);
document.getElementById('volume').innerHTML = volume.toLocaleString();
document.getElementById('chart').innerHTML
      = "<img src=http://ichart.yahoo.com/t?s=" + tickerSymbol
      + " alt='Stock line chart from Yahoo.com.' />";
```

The specific procedures for accessing the values of the responseText and responseXML properties with JavaScript depend on whether you submitted a synchronous or asynchronous request.

Receiving Synchronous Responses

The value of the open() method's third argument determines whether the HTTP request is performed synchronously or asynchronously. A **synchronous request** stops the processing of the JavaScript code until a response is returned from the server. To create a synchronous request, you should check the value of the XMLHttpRequest object's status property, which contains the HTTP status code (such as 200 for "OK" or 404 for "Not Found) that was returned with the response, to ensure that the response was received successfully.

The following statements demonstrate how to use the returned status code and response string. The first statement passes a value of false as the third argument of the open() method to create a synchronous request. The second statement submits the request. The if statement then determines whether the value assigned to the status property is 200. If so, the response was successful and the statements within the if statement execute. Note that the statements within the if statement are the same statements you saw previously for manipulating the value assigned to the responseXML property for the stock quotes Web page. If any other status code is returned, the else statement prints a message with the status code and text.

```
httpRequest.abort();
httpRequest.open("get","StockCheck.php?" + "checkQuote="
      + tickerSymbol, false);
if (httpRequest.status == 200) {
      httpRequest.send(null);
      var stockValues = httpRequest.responseXML;
      document.getElementById("ticker").innerHTML = stockValues
```

```
        .getElementsByTagName("ticker")[0].childNodes[0].nodeValue;
    ...
}
    else {
        document.write("<p>HTTP response error " + httpRequest.status
            + ": " + httpRequest.statusText + "</p>");
    }
```

Next, you will modify the top stories Web page so it sends and receives synchronous requests and responses using RSS feeds. RSS documents are in a standardized XML format contained within a root element named <channel>. The <channel> root element contains four required elements: <title>, <link>, <description>, and <item>. Multiple <item> elements can be included, each of which contains an article or other type of content that is being published as part of the feed. Each <item> element also requires nested <title>, <link>, and <description> elements. There are numerous other optional elements that can be included in an RSS feed. One optional element, the <pubDate> element, which contains an article's publication date, is often used within the <item> elements in the RSS feeds from news agencies. The following is an example of a portion of an RSS feed from ABC News:

```
<?xml version="1.0" encoding="ISO-8859-1" ?>
<rss version="2.0">
<channel>
    <title>ABC News: Top Stories</title>
    <link>http://abcnews.go.com/<</link>
    <description>RSS FEED FOR ABC NEWS FRONT PAGE</description>
    <item>
        <title>Cats Fare Worse in Food Contamination</title>
        <link>http://abcnews.go.com/Business/wireStory?id=2998246&CMP=
        OTC-RSSFeeds0312</link>
        <pubDate>Sat, 31 Mar 2007 20:45:36 -0400</pubDate>
        <description>Chemical That Led to Pet Food Recall May Be Worse
        for Cats, Which Have Died in Greater Numbers</description>
    </item>
    <item>
        <title>Land of the Giants: Dutch Tower over Americans</title>
        <link>http://abcnews.go.com/WNT/Health/story?id=2998245&page=
        1&CMP=OTC-RSSFeeds0312</link>
        <pubDate>Sat, 31 Mar 2007 20:39:01 -0400</pubDate>
        <description>Some See Height Tied to Nation's Health</description>
    </item>
    ...
</channel>
</rss>
```

To retrieve all of the <item> elements, you can use a statement similar to the following:

```
var newsItems=news.getElementsByTagName("item");
```

You can then use the `newsItems` variable with the `getElementsByTagName()` method, the `childNodes[0]` property, and the `lastChild` property to retrieve the values for each news item's title, publication date, link, and description. For example, the following statement assigns the value of the second `<item>` element's `<title>` element ("Land of the Giants: Dutch Tower over Americans") to a variable named `curHeadline`.

```
var curHeadline = newsItems[1].getElementsByTagName(
    "title")[0].childNodes[0].nodeValue;
```

To modify the top stories Web page so it sends and receives synchronous requests and responses:

1. Return to the **TopStories.html** document in your text editor and add a value of false as the third argument of the `open()` method in the `newsUpdate()` function as follows so it sends the request synchronously:

   ```
   httpRequest.open("get","TopStories.php?" + "agency=" + agency, false);
   ```

2. Add the following statements to the end of the `newsUpdate()` function to handle the server response. The first statement assigns the value of the `responseXML` property to a variable named `news`. The news stories will be displayed in a cell with an `id` attribute of `newsCell`. Each time you select a different news agency, the second statement deletes the cell's existing content by assigning an empty string to the `innerHTML` property of the cell.

   ```
   var news = httpRequest.responseXML;
   document.getElementById("newsCell").innerHTML = "";
   ```

3. Add to the end of the `newsUpdate()` function the following statement, which returns a collection of all `<item>` elements in the response and assigns it to a variable named `newsItems`:

   ```
   var newsItems=news.getElementsByTagName("item");
   ```

4. Start creating the following `for` statement at the end of the `newsUpdate()` function. The `for` statement is contained within an `if` statement that first determines whether the RSS feed contains any items. The `for` statement will use the response in the `news` variable to build the cell containing each news item's title, publication date, link, and description.

   ```
   if (newsItems.length > 0) {
       for (var i=0; i<newsItems.length; ++i) {
       }
   }
   else
       document.getElementById("newsCell").innerHTML
           = "RSS feed does not contain any items.";
   ```

5. Add the following statements to the `for` loop. These statements use the `getElementsByTagName()` method, the `childNodes[0]` property, and the `lastChild` property to retrieve the values for each news item's title, publication date, link, and description.

```
var curHeadline = newsItems[i].getElementsByTagName(
    "title")[0].childNodes[0].nodeValue;
var curLink = newsItems[i].getElementsByTagName(
    "link")[0].childNodes[0].nodeValue;
var curPubDate = newsItems[i].getElementsByTagName(
    "pubDate")[0].childNodes[0].nodeValue;
var curDesc = newsItems[i].getElementsByTagName(
    "description")[0].childNodes[0].nodeValue;
```

6. Add the following statements to the end of the `for` loop to build the cell containing the stories:

```
var curStory = "<a href='" + curLink + "'>" + curHeadline
    + "</a><br />";
curStory += "<span style='color: gray'>" + curPubDate
    + "</span><br />";
curStory += curDesc + "<br />";
document.getElementById("newsCell").innerHTML += curStory;
```

7. Add the following `onload` event handler to the opening `<body>` tag. This event handler calls the `newsUpdate()` function when the Web page first loads.

```
onload="newsUpdate()"
```

8. Add the following `onclick` event handler to each of the radio buttons. This event handler calls the `newsUpdate()` function whenever a radio button is selected.

```
onclick="newsUpdate()"
```

9. Delete the following paragraph and input element:

```
<p><input type="submit" value="Get Headlines" /></p>
```

10. Add the following elements immediately after the opening `<table>` tag to handle the display of the table columns:

```
<colgroup span="1" width="125" />
<colgroup span="1" width="350" />
```

11. Save the **TopStories.html** document, and then open it in your Web browser by entering the following URL. After the Web page loads, the top stories for ABC News should display in the right column of the table, as shown in Figure 12-9.

```
http://localhost/JavaScript_Projects/Chapter.12/Chapter/
TopStories.html
```

Figure 12-9

Top stories Web page displaying default ABC News stories

12. Select a different news agency. The stories for the selected agency should display, as shown in Figure 12-10 for MSNBC. Clicking a link will display the full news article in a separate window.

Figure 12-10

Top stories Web page displaying default MSNBC stories

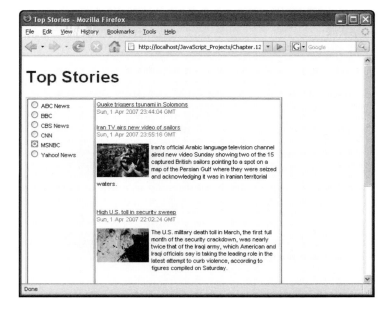

13. Close your Web browser window.

Although synchronous responses are easier to handle, they have a major drawback in that a script will not continue processing until the response is received. This means that if the server doesn't respond for some reason (perhaps because it is running slowly due to high traffic or maintenance requirements), your Web page will appear to be dead in the water. Users can stop the script by clicking the browser's Stop button. However, a synchronous request with the `send()` method does not contain any sort of mechanism for specifying the length of time that is allowed for receiving a response. To ensure that your script continues running in the event of a server problem, you should use asynchronous requests with the `send()` method.

Receiving Asynchronous Responses

In comparison to a synchronous request, an **asynchronous request** allows JavaScript to continue processing while it waits for a server response. To create an asynchronous request, you pass a value of true as the third argument of the `open()` method or omit the argument altogether. To receive a response for an asynchronous request, you must use the `XMLHttpRequest` object's `readyState` property and `onreadystatechange` event. The `readyState` property contains one of the following values, which represent the state of the HTTP request: 0 (uninitialized), 1 (open), 2 (sent), 3 (receiving), or 4 (loaded). The `onreadystatechange` event is triggered whenever the value assigned to the `readyState` property changes. You assign to the `onreadystatechange` event the name of a function that will execute whenever the `readyState` property changes. For example, the `open()` method in the following code defines an asynchronous request because it includes a value of true as the method's third argument. (Recall that you can also simply omit the third argument to define an asynchronous request.) The third statement assigns a function named `fillStockInfo()` as the event handler function for the `onreadystatechange` event.

```
httpRequest.abort();
httpRequest.open("get","StockCheck.php?" + "checkQuote="
      + tickerSymbol);
httpRequest.send(null);
httpRequest.onreadystatechange=fillStockInfo;
```

The value assigned to the `readyState` property is updated automatically according to the current statement of the HTTP request. However, you cannot process the response until the `readyState` property is assigned a value of 4, meaning the response is finished loading. For this reason, you include an `if` statement in the `fillStockInfo()` function that checks the value assigned to the `readyState` property. As shown in the following example, once the `readyState` property is assigned a value of 4 and the `status` property is assigned a value of 200, the statements in the body of the `if` statement process the response:

```
function fillStockInfo() {
      if (httpRequest.readyState==4 && httpRequest.status == 200) {
            var stockValues = httpRequest.responseXML;
            document.getElementById("ticker").innerHTML = stockValues
                .getElementsByTagName("ticker")[0].childNodes[0].nodeValue;
            ...
      }
}
```

CHAPTER 12

To modify the top stories Web page so it sends and receives asynchronous requests and responses:

1. Return to the **TopStories.html** document in your text editor and change the value of the third argument of the `open()` method in the `newsUpdate()` function from false to true as follows so it sends the request asynchronously:

    ```
    httpRequest.open("get","TopStories.php?" + "agency=" + agency, true);
    ```

2. Add the following `fillNewsInfo()` function definition to the end of the script section. The statements in the body of the `if` statement (which you will add next) will process the response once the `readyState` property is assigned a value of 4 and the `status` property is assigned a value of 200.

    ```
    function fillNewsInfo() {
        if (httpRequest.readyState==4 && httpRequest.status == 200) {
        }
    }
    ```

3. Move the following statements from the end of the `newsUpdate()` function to the `if` statement in the `fillNewsInfo()` function:

    ```
    var news = httpRequest.responseXML;
    document.getElementById("newsCell").innerHTML = ""
    var newsItems=news.getElementsByTagName("item");
    if (newsItems.length > 0) {
        for (var i=0; i<newsItems.length; ++i) {
            var curHeadline = newsItems[i].getElementsByTagName(
                "title")[0].childNodes[0].nodeValue;
            var curLink = newsItems[i].getElementsByTagName(
                "link")[0].childNodes[0].nodeValue;
            var curPubDate = newsItems[i].getElementsByTagName(
                "pubDate")[0].childNodes[0].nodeValue;
            var curDesc = newsItems[i].getElementsByTagName(
                "description")[0].childNodes[0].nodeValue;
            var curStory = "<a href='" + curLink + "'>"
                + curHeadline + "</a><br />";
            curStory += "<span style='color: gray'>" + curPubDate
                + "</span><br />";
            curStory += curDesc + "<br />";
            document.getElementById("newsCell").innerHTML
                += curStory;
        }
    }
    else
            document.getElementById("newsCell").innerHTML
                = "RSS feed does not contain any items.";
    ```

4. Add the following statement to the end of the `newsUpdate()` function. This statement assigns the `fillNewsInfo()` function as the event handler function for the `onreadystatechange` event.

    `httpRequest.onreadystatechange=fillNewsInfo;`

5. Save the **TopStories.html** document, and then open it in your Web browser by entering the following URL. The Web page should function the same as it did before you changed it to perform asynchronous requests.

    `http://localhost/JavaScript_Projects/Chapter.12/Chapter/`
    `TopStories.html`

6. Close your Web browser window.

Refreshing Server Data Automatically

To automatically refresh data that is obtained from an HTTP server, you use JavaScript's `setTimeout()` or `setInterval()` methods to send a request to the server, and read and process the data returned from the server. As an example, the following code contains a completed version of the JavaScript section that gives the stock quotes Web page its functionality. A global variable named `tickerSymbol` is declared at the beginning of the script section and assigned a default value of ^IXIC, which is the ticker symbol for the Nasdaq Composite Index. The `getStockQuote()` function, which calls the `getRequestObject()` function and also opens and submits the HTTP request, is initially called from an `onload` event in the `<body>` tag and is subsequently called each time a user clicks the Get Quote button. The last statement in the `getStockQuote()` function uses a `setTimeout()` method to call the `getStockQuote()` function every 10,000 milliseconds (or every 10 seconds). The `setTimeout()` method reinitializes each time the `getStockQuote()` function executes.

```
<script type="text/javascript">
/* <![CDATA[ */
var httpRequest = false;
var tickerSymbol = "^IXIC";
function getRequestObject() {
      try {
            httpRequest = new XMLHttpRequest();
      }
      catch (requestError) {
            try {
                  httpRequest = new ActiveXObject("Msxml2.XMLHTTP");
            }
            catch (requestError) {
                  try {
                        httpRequest = new ActiveXObject("Microsoft.XMLHTTP");
                  }
                  catch (requestError) {
                        window.alert("Your browser does not support AJAX!");
                        return false;
                  }
            }
```

```
                }
        }
        return httpRequest;
}
function getStockQuote(newTicker) {
        if (!httpRequest)
                httpRequest = getRequestObject();
        if (newTicker)
                tickerSymbol = newTicker;
        httpRequest.abort();
        httpRequest.open("get","StockCheck.php?" + "checkQuote="
                + tickerSymbol, true);
        httpRequest.send(null);
        httpRequest.onreadystatechange=fillStockInfo;
        var updateQuote = setTimeout('getStockQuote()', 10000);
}
function fillStockInfo() {
        if (httpRequest.readyState==4 && httpRequest.status == 200) {
                var stockValues = httpRequest.responseXML;
                document.getElementById("ticker").innerHTML
                        = stockValues.getElementsByTagName(
                        "ticker")[0].childNodes[0].nodeValue;
                document.getElementById("openingPrice").innerHTML
                        = stockValues.getElementsByTagName(
                        "open")[0].childNodes[0].nodeValue;
                document.getElementById("lastTrade").innerHTML
                        = "<strong>" + stockValues.getElementsByTagName(
                        "lastTrade")[0].childNodes[0].nodeValue + "</strong>";
                document.getElementById("lastTradeDT").innerHTML
                        = stockValues.getElementsByTagName(
                        "lastTradeDate")[0].childNodes[0].nodeValue + " "
                        + stockValues.getElementsByTagName(
                        "lastTradeTime")[0].childNodes[0].nodeValue;
                document.getElementById("change").innerHTML
                        = stockValues.getElementsByTagName(
                        "change")[0].childNodes[0].nodeValue;
                document.getElementById("range").innerHTML
                        = stockValues.getElementsByTagName(
                        "rangeLow")[0].childNodes[0].nodeValue + " - "
                        + stockValues.getElementsByTagName(
                        "rangeHigh")[0].childNodes[0].nodeValue;
                var volume = parseInt(stockValues.getElementsByTagName(
                        "volume")[0].childNodes[0].nodeValue);
                document.getElementById("volume").innerHTML
                        = volume.toLocaleString();
                document.getElementById("chart").innerHTML = "<img src="
                        + stockValues.getElementsByTagName("chart")[0]
```

```
                     .childNodes[0].nodeValue
                     + " alt='Stock line chart from Yahoo.com.' />";
        }
}
/* ]]> */
</script>
```

Next, you add a `setTimeout()` statement to the top stories Web page that refreshes the currently displayed news stories every five minutes.

To add a `setTimeout()` statement to the top stories Web page that refreshes the currently displayed news stories every five minutes:

1. Return to the **TopStories.html** document in your text editor and add the following statement to the end of the `newsUpdate()` function:

   `var recentNews = setTimeout('newsUpdate()', 5000);`

2. Save the **TopStories.html** file, close it in your text editor, and then validate it with the W3C Markup Validation Service. Once the file is valid, open it in your Web browser by entering the following URL. If you wait five minutes, the most recent stories should refresh for the selected news agency.

   `http://localhost/JavaScript_Projects/Chapter.12/Chapter/`
   `TopStories.html`

3. Close your Web browser window.

Conclusion

Your goal in the study of JavaScript programming, or any technology subject for that matter, should not be memorizing facts and syntax. Instead, your goal should be to comprehend and understand how things work. If you forget everything else you learned in this book, remember this: The best programmers in the world do not necessarily know all the answers. Rather, they know where to *find* the answers. Build yourself a library of reference books that you can use to find the answers you need. Best of luck in your career!

Chapter Summary

▶ "Asynchronous JavaScript And XML" or "AJAX" refers to a combination of technologies that allow a Web page displayed on a client computer to quickly interact and exchange data with a Web server without reloading the entire Web page.

▶ The XMLHttpRequest object uses HTTP to exchange data between a client computer and a Web server.

▶ RSS (for RDF Site Summary or Rich Site Summary) is an XML format that allows Web sites to publish content that can be read by other Web sites.

▶ You cannot use the XMLHttpRequest object to directly access content on another domain's server; the data you request with the XMLHttpRequest object must be located on the Web server where your JavaScript program is running.

▶ Because AJAX relies on the XMLHttpRequest object to retrieve data, you must open AJAX files from a Web server with the HTTP protocol (http://).

▶ Hypertext Transfer Protocol (HTTP) is a set of rules that defines how requests are made by an HTTP client to an HTTP server, and how responses are returned from an HTTP server to an HTTP client. An HTTP client refers to the application, usually a Web browser, which makes the request. An HTTP server is another name for a Web server and refers to a computer that receives HTTP requests and returns responses to HTTP clients.

▶ HTTP client requests and server responses are both known as HTTP messages.

▶ You use the methods and properties of an instantiated XMLHttpRequest object with JavaScript to build and send request messages and to receive and process response messages.

▶ The first step for using AJAX to exchange data between an HTTP client and a Web server is to instantiate an XMLHttpRequest object.

▶ After you instantiate an XMLHttpRequest object, you use the open() method with the instantiated XMLHttpRequest object to specify the request method (such as GET or POST) method and URL.

▶ To improve performance, you should call the abort() method of the XMLHttpRequest object to cancel any existing HTTP requests before beginning a new one.

▶ After you have defined the basic request criteria with the open() method, you use the send() method with the instantiated XMLHttpRequest object to submit the request to the server.

▶ After you submit a request with the XMLHttpRequest object, the message body in the server response is assigned to the XMLHttpRequest object's responseXML or responseText properties.

▶ A synchronous request stops the processing of the JavaScript code until a response is returned from the server; an asynchronous request allows JavaScript to continue processing while it waits for a server response.

▶ To automatically refresh data that is obtained from an HTTP server, you use JavaScript's setTimeout() or setInterval() methods to automatically execute—after a specific amount of time has elapsed—the statements that instantiate an XMLHttpRequest object, send a request to the server, and read and process the data returned from the server.

Review Questions

1. Explain the difference between AJAX and DHTML.

2. You can use the XMLHttpRequest object to directly access content on another domain's server. True or false?

3. The term _____ refers to someone or something that acts or performs a request for another person.

   a. intermediary

   b. firewall

   c. deputy

   d. proxy

4. Explain how JavaScript's same origin policy affects AJAX applications. How can you get around the restrictions imposed by the same origin policy?

5. Which of the following protocols cannot be used to open and run an AJAX Web page? (Choose all that apply.)

   a. file:\\\

   b. ftp:\\

   c. http:\\

   d. https:\\

6. Which of the following steps is not required for creating an AJAX application?

   a. Instantiate an XMLHttpRequest object for the Web browser where the script will run.

   b. Use the XMLHttpRequest object's open() method to fine the request information.

   c. Use the XMLHttpRequest object to send a request to the server.

   d. Close the XMLHttpRequest object after parsing the response data.

7. A(n) _____ is another name for a Web server.

   a. PHP server

   b. client-side scripting engine

   c. server-side scripting engine

   d. XMLHttpRequest server

8. What is the most recent version of HTTP?

   a. 1.0

   b. 1.1

   c. 1.5

   d. 2.0

9. HTTP requests and responses must define at least one header. True or false?

10. Why you should always include the `Cache-Control` header in your AJAX programs? What value should you assign to it?

11. An HTTP message that does not contain a message body must end with what?

    a. a non-breaking space character ( )

    b. a closing `</http>` tag

    c. an EOF statement

    d. a blank line

12. Which of the following HTTP request methods returns information about a document, but not the document itself?

    a. HEAD

    b. OPTIONS

    c. PUT

    d. TRACE

13. Which of the following start lines is returned for a GET request with HTTP 1.1 to http://movies.go.com/reviews?

    a. `GET HTTP/1.1 movies.go.com/reviews`

    b. `GET / HTTP/1.1`

    c. `GET movies.go.com/reviews HTTP/1.1`

    d. `GET /reviews HTTP/1.1`

14. Which of the following response codes is returned with a successful HTTP request?

    a. 100

    b. 200

    c. 404

    d. 500

15. Explain how to write code that instantiates the correct `XMLHttpRequest` object for current Web browsers (such as Firefox and Internet Explorer 7), Internet Explorer 6, and Internet Explorer 5.5.

16. What value do you pass as an argument to the `XMLHttpRequest` object's `send()` method if the request does not include a message body?

    a. null

    b. 0

    c. 1

    d. The `send()` method does not require an argument if the request does not include a message body.

17. What is the difference between synchronous and asynchronous HTTP requests? Which is the preferred method and why?

18. Which of the following headers should be included with HTTP requests that contain message bodies?

    a. `Connection`

    b. `Content-Type`

    c. `Content-Length`

    d. `Last-Modified`

19. An HTTP response has been received from a Web server when the `readystate` property contains which of the following values?

    a. 1

    b. 2

    c. 3

    d. 4

20. Explain how to automatically refresh data that is obtained from an HTTP server.

Hands-On Projects

Project 12-1

In this project, you will create an AJAX program that looks up city and state names based on a ZIP code entered by a user. Your Projects folder for Chapter 12 contains an XML file named zips.xml that you can use for this exercise. Note that the zips.xml file only contains information for the states of Florida and Georgia. This is because the XML file containing information for all U.S. ZIP codes would be approximately five megabytes in size, which is too large to successfully manipulate with JavaScript. Note that the purpose of this exercise is to demonstrate how to use AJAX to look up information on a server. In reality, a better solution for retrieving individual records from such a large collection of data is to use a server-side script to retrieve it from a relational database.

1. Create a new document in your text editor.

2. Type the `<!DOCTYPE>` declaration, `<html>` element, header information, and the `<body>` element. Use the strict DTD and "City and State Lookup" as the content of the `<title>` element.

3. Add the following style section to the document head:

```
<style type="text/css">
h1 {
font-family:arial;
color:navy;
}
p, td {
font-family:arial;
```

```
font-size:11px;
color:black;
}
</style>
```

4. Add the following text and elements to the document body. The form contains three text boxes for ZIP code, city, and state. When a user enters a value into the ZIP code box and leaves the field, the onblur event calls the updateCityState() function, which you will create shortly.

```
<h1>City and State Lookup</h1>
<form action="">
<p>ZIP code <input type="text" size="5" name="zip" id="zip"
onblur="updateCityState()" /></p>
<p>City <input type="text" name="city" />
State <input type="text" size="2" name="state" /></p>
</form>
```

5. Add the following script section to the document head:

```
<script type="text/javascript">
/* <![CDATA[ */
/* ]]> */
</script>
```

6. Add to the script section the following global httpRequest variable definition and getRequestObject() function, which instantiates the XMLHttpRequest object:

```
var httpRequest = false;
function getRequestObject() {
        try {
                httpRequest = new XMLHttpRequest();
        }
        catch (requestError) {
                try {
                        httpRequest = new ActiveXObject
                        ("Msxml2.XMLHTTP");
                }
                catch (requestError) {
                        try {
                                httpRequest = new ActiveXObject
                                ("Microsoft.XMLHTTP");
                        }
                        catch (requestError) {
                                window.alert("Your browser does not
                                support AJAX!");
                                return false;
                        }
                }
        }
```

```
        }
        return httpRequest;
    }
```

7. Add to the end of the script section the following updateCityState() function, which handles the tasks of instantiating, opening, and sending the HTTP request. The onreadystatechange event is assigned getZipInfo() as the event handler function. You will create the getZipInfo() function next.

```
function updateCityState() {
    if (!httpRequest)
            httpRequest = getRequestObject();
    httpRequest.abort();
    httpRequest.open("get","zips.xml");
    httpRequest.send(null);
    httpRequest.onreadystatechange=getZipInfo;
}
```

8. Add to the end of the script section the following getZipInfo() function, which retrieves the city and state from the XML file and adds them to the form fields in the document body after the response is received from the server.

```
function getZipInfo() {
  if (httpRequest.readyState==4 && httpRequest.status == 200) {
    var zips = httpRequest.responseXML;
    var locations = zips.getElementsByTagName("Row");
    var notFound = true;
    for (var i=0; i<locations.length; ++i) {
      if (document.forms[0].zip.value == zips.getElementsByTagName(
          "ZIP_Code")[i].childNodes[0].nodeValue) {
          document.forms[0].city.value = zips.getElementsByTagName(
            "City")[i].childNodes[0].nodeValue;
          document.forms[0].state.value = zips.getElementsByTagName(
            "State_Abbreviation")[i].childNodes[0].nodeValue;
          notFound = false;
          break;
      }
    }
    if (notFound) {
      window.alert("Invalid ZIP code!");
      document.forms[0].city.value = "";
      document.forms[0].state.value = "";
    }
  }
}
```

9. Save the document as **CityStateLookup.html** in your Projects folder for Chapter 12, and then validate the document with the W3C Markup Validation Service. Once the document is valid, close it in your text editor.

10. Open the **CityStateLookup.html** document in your Web browser by entering the following URL: *http://localhost/JavaScript_Projects/Chapter.12/Projects/CityStateLookup.html*. Enter a ZIP code for a city in Florida or Georgia, such as 34136 for Bonita Springs, Florida. The city and state names should automatically be added to the form fields.

11. Close your Web browser window.

Project 12-2

Yahoo! Weather includes an RSS feed that allows you to retrieve a locale's current weather conditions according to its ZIP code. In this project, you will create an AJAX program that allows users to enter a ZIP code to retrieve current weather conditions.

1. Create a new document in your text editor.

2. Type the `<!DOCTYPE>` declaration, `<html>` element, header information, and the `<body>` element. Use the strict DTD and "Weather Report" as the content of the `<title>` element.

3. Add the following style section to the document head:

```
<style type="text/css">
h1 {
font-family:arial;
color:navy;
}
p, td {
font-family:arial;
font-size:11px;
color:black;
}
</style>
```

4. Add the following text and elements to the document body. The form contains a text box and button that includes an `onclick` event, which calls a function named `weatherUpdate()` when clicked. The text box contains a default value of 94558, which is the ZIP code for Napa, California.

```
<h1>Weather Report</h1>
<form method="get">
<p>ZIP code <input type="text" name="zip" value="94558" /> <input
type="button" value="Check Weather" onclick="weatherUpdate()" /></p>
</form>
<p id="weatherPara"></p>
```

5. Add the following script section to the document head:

```
<script type="text/javascript">
/* <![CDATA[ */
/* ]]> */
</script>
```

6. Add to the script section the following global `httpRequest` variable definition and `getRequestObject()` function, which instantiates the `XMLHttpRequest` object:

```
var httpRequest = false;
function getRequestObject() {
        try {
                httpRequest = new XMLHttpRequest();
        }
        catch (requestError) {
                try {
                        httpRequest = new ActiveXObject("Msxml2.XMLHTTP");
                }
                catch (requestError) {
                        try {
                                httpRequest = new ActiveXObject
                                ("Microsoft.XMLHTTP");
                        }
                        catch (requestError) {
                                window.alert("Your browser does not
                                support AJAX!");
                                return false;
                        }
                }
        }
        return httpRequest;
}
```

7. Add to the end of the script section the following `weatherUpdate()` function, which handles the tasks of instantiating, opening, and sending the HTTP request. The `onreadystatechange` event is assigned `fillWeatherInfo()` as the event handler function. You will create the `fillWeatherInfo()` function next.

```
function weatherUpdate() {
        if (!httpRequest)
                httpRequest = getRequestObject();
        var zip = document.forms[0].zip.value;
        httpRequest.abort();
        httpRequest.open("get","WeatherReport.php?zip=" + zip, true);
        httpRequest.send(null);
        httpRequest.onreadystatechange=fillWeatherInfo;
}
```

8. Add to the end of the script section the following `fillWeatherUpdate()` function, which adds the weather information to the empty paragraph element in the document body after the response is received from the server.

```
function fillWeatherInfo() {
  if (httpRequest.readyState==4 && httpRequest.status == 200) {
```

```
var weather = httpRequest.responseXML;
var weatherItems=weather.getElementsByTagName("item");
if (weatherItems.length > 0) {
  for (var i=0; i<weatherItems.length; ++i) {
    var curHeadline = weatherItems[i].getElementsByTagName(
      "title")[0].childNodes[0].nodeValue;
    var curLink = weatherItems[i].getElementsByTagName(
      "link")[0].childNodes[0].nodeValue;
    var curPubDate = weatherItems[i].getElementsByTagName(
      "pubDate")[0].childNodes[0].nodeValue;
    var curDesc = weatherItems[i].getElementsByTagName(
      "description")[0].childNodes[0].nodeValue;
    var weatherSpot = document.getElementById('weatherPara');
    var curStory = "<a href='" + curLink + "'>" + curHeadline
      + "</a><br />";
    curStory += "<span style='color: gray'>" + curPubDate
      + "</span><br />";
    curStory += curDesc + "<br />";
    weatherSpot.innerHTML= curStory;
  }
}
else
  window.alert("Invalid ZIP code.");
  }
}
```

9. Add an onload event to the opening <body> tag so it runs the weatherUpdate () function as soon as the Web page finishes loading, as follows:

```
<body onload="weatherUpdate()">
```

10. Save the document as **WeatherReport.html** in your Projects folder for Chapter 12, and then validate the document with the W3C Markup Validation Service. Once the document is valid, close it in your text editor.

11. Create a new document in your text editor and add the following PHP code, which opens the RSS feed and returns the XML document to the WeatherReport.html document:

```php
<?php
$Zip = $_GET["zip"];
$WeatherURL = "http://weather.yahooapis.com/forecastrss?p=" . $Zip;
header("Content-Type: text/xml");
header("Content-Length: " . strlen(file_get_contents($WeatherURL)));
header("Cache-Control: no-cache");
readfile($WeatherURL);
?>
```

12. Save the document as **WeatherReport.php** in your Projects folder for Chapter 12, close it in your text editor, and then open the **WeatherReport.html** document in your Web browser by entering the following URL: http://localhost/ JavaScript_Projects/Chapter.12/Projects/WeatherReport.html. When the Web page first opens, it displays the weather for Napa, California.

13. Enter a different ZIP code in the text box and click the **Check Weather** button. The page should update with the weather conditions for the ZIP code you entered.

14. Close your Web browser window.

 ## Project 12-3

ESPN.com publishes separate RSS feeds for various sports, such as football, baseball, and golf. In this project, you will create an AJAX program that allows users to view current news for a selected sport.

1. Create a new document in your text editor.

2. Type the `<!DOCTYPE>` declaration, `<html>` element, header information, and the `<body>` element. Use the strict DTD and "Sporting News" as the content of the `<title>` element.

3. Add the following style section to the document head:

```
<style type="text/css">
h1 {
font-family:arial;
color:navy;
}
p, td {
font-family:arial;
font-size:11px;
color:black;
}
</style>
```

4. Add the following text and elements to the document body. This content is very similar to the text and elements you added to the document body for the top stories Web page. Instead of containing information for different news agencies, the radio buttons represent different sports, and their values are the URL for the associated ESPN.com RSS feed. The last cell at the end of the table will contain the sports stories.

```
<h1>Sporting News</h1>
<form method="get" action="TopStories.php">
<table border="1">
<colgroup span="1" width="125" />
<colgroup span="1" width="350" />
```

```
<tr><td valign="top">
<input type="radio" name="sport"
value="http://sports.espn.go.com/espn/rss/nfl/news"
checked="checked" onclick="sportsUpdate()" /> NFL<br />
<input type="radio" name="sport"
value="http://sports.espn.go.com/espn/rss/nba/news"
onclick="sportsUpdate()" /> NBA<br />
<input type="radio" name="sport"
value="http://sports.espn.go.com/espn/rss/mlb/news"
onclick="sportsUpdate()" /> MLB<br />
<input type="radio" name="sport"
value="http://sports.espn.go.com/espn/rss/rpm/news"
onclick="sportsUpdate()" /> NASCAR<br />
<input type="radio" name="sport"
value="http://sports.espn.go.com/espn/rss/nhl/news"
onclick="sportsUpdate()" /> NHL<br />
<input type="radio" name="sport"
value="http://sports.espn.go.com/espn/rss/boxing/news"
onclick="sportsUpdate()" /> Boxing
</td>
<td id="newsCell" valign="top"></td></tr>
</table>
</form>
```

5. Add the following script section to the document head:

```
<script type="text/javascript">
/* <![CDATA[ */
/* ]]> */
</script>
```

6. Add to the script section the following global `httpRequest` variable definition and `getRequestObject()` function, which instantiates the `XMLHttpRequest` object:

```
var httpRequest = false;
function getRequestObject() {
        try {
                httpRequest = new XMLHttpRequest();
        }
        catch (requestError) {
                try {
                    httpRequest = new ActiveXObject("Msxml2.XMLHTTP");
                }
                catch (requestError) {
                        try {
                                httpRequest = new ActiveXObject
                                ("Microsoft.XMLHTTP");
                        }
```

```
                catch (requestError) {
                    window.alert("Your browser does not
                    support AJAX!");
                    return false;
                }
            }
        }
    return httpRequest;
}
```

7. Add to the end of the script section the following `sportsUpdate()` function, which handles the tasks of instantiating, opening, and sending the HTTP request. The `onreadystatechange` event is assigned `getSportsNews()` as the event handler function. You will create the `getSportsNews()` function next.

```
function sportsUpdate() {
    if (!httpRequest)
        httpRequest = getRequestObject();
    for (var i=0; i<6; ++i) {
        if (document.forms[0].sport[i].checked == true) {
            var sport = document.forms[0].sport[i].value;
            break;
        }
    }
    httpRequest.abort();
    httpRequest.open("get","SportingNews.php?" + "sport=" +
    sport, true);
    httpRequest.send(null);
    httpRequest.onreadystatechange=getSportsNews;
    var recentNews = setTimeout('sportsUpdate()', 5000);
}
```

8. Add to the end of the script section the following `getSportsNews()` function, which adds the sports information to the nested table in the document body after the response is received from the server.

```
function getSportsNews() {
  if(httpRequest.readyState==4 && httpRequest.status == 200) {
    var news = httpRequest.responseXML;
    document.getElementById("newsCell").innerHTML = "";
    var newsItems=news.getElementsByTagName("item");
    if (newsItems.length > 0) {
      for (var i=0; i<newsItems.length; ++i) {
        var curHeadline = newsItems[i].getElementsByTagName(
          "title")[0].childNodes[0].nodeValue;
        var curLink = newsItems[i].getElementsByTagName(
          "link")[0].childNodes[0].nodeValue;
        var curPubDate = newsItems[i].getElementsByTagName(
          "pubDate")[0].childNodes[0].nodeValue;
```

```
        var curDesc = newsItems[i].getElementsByTagName(
            "description")[0].childNodes[0].nodeValue;
        var curStory = "<a href='" + curLink + "'>"
            + curHeadline + "</a><br />";
        curStory += "<span style='color: gray'>" + curPubDate
            + "</span><br />";
        curStory += curDesc + "<br />";
      document.getElementById("newsCell").innerHTML += curStory;
      }
    }
    else
      document.getElementById("newsCell").innerHTML
        = "RSS feed does not contain any items.";
  }
}
```

9. Add an `onload` event to the opening `<body>` tag so it runs the `sportsUpdate()` function as soon as the Web page finishes loading, as follows:

    ```
    <body onload="sportsUpdate()">
    ```

10. Save the document as **SportingNews.html** in your Projects folder for Chapter 12, and then validate the document with the W3C Markup Validation Service. Once the document is valid, close it in your text editor.

11. Create a new document in your text editor and add the following PHP code, which opens the RSS feed and returns the XML document to the SportingNews.html document:

    ```php
    <?php
    $SportsLeague=$_GET["sport"];
    header("Content-Type: text/xml");
    header("Content-Length: " . strlen(
            file_get_contents($SportsLeague)));
    header("Cache-Control: no-cache");
    readfile($SportsLeague);
    ?>
    ```

12. Save the document as **SportingNews.php** in your Projects folder for Chapter 12, close it in your text editor, and then open the **SportingNews.html** document in your Web browser by entering the following URL: http://localhost/JavaScript_Projects/ Chapter.12/Projects/ SportingNews.html. When the Web page first opens, it displays news for the NFL.

13. Select a radio button for a different sport. The page should update with the news for the sport you selected.

14. Close your Web browser window.

Project 12-4

In this project, you will modify the stock quotes Web page that was used as the chapter example so it also lists RSS news information for a selected stock.

1. Open the **StockQuotes.html** document from your Projects folder for Chapter 12.

2. First, add the following text and elements immediately above the closing `</table>` tag at the end of the document. This content creates a cell that will display the news information for the selected stock.

```
<tr><td id="stockNews" colspan="2"> </td></tr>
```

3. Next, add the following `getStockNews()` function to the end of the script section. This function uses the existing `httpRequest` object to request the stock news. The `open()` statement opens a PHP file named StockNews.php and passes the stock symbol to it. The `onreadystatechange` event is assigned `fillStockNews()` as the event handler function. You will create the `fillStockNews()` function next.

```
function getStockNews() {
      httpRequest.open("get","StockNews.php?stockFeed="
          + tickerSymbol, true);
      httpRequest.send(null);
      httpRequest.onreadystatechange=fillStockNews;
}
```

4. Add the following function call to the end of the `if` statement in the `fillStockInfo()` function; the stock's news information will be retrieved after the stock quote information:

```
getStockNews();
```

5. Add to the end of the script section the following `fillStockNews()` function, which adds the title, link, and publication date for each stock news item to the last table cell in the document body after the response is received from the server.

```
function fillStockNews() {
  if (httpRequest.readyState==4 && httpRequest.status == 200) {
     var news = httpRequest.responseXML;
       document.getElementById("stockNews").innerHTML = ""'
      var newsItems=news.getElementsByTagName("item");
     if (newsItems.length > 0) {
      for (var i=0; i<newsItems.length; ++i) {
                var curHeadline = newsItems[i].getElementsByTagName(
                    "title")[0].childNodes[0].nodeValue;
                var curLink = newsItems[i].getElementsByTagName(
                    "link")[0].childNodes[0].nodeValue;
                var curPubDate = newsItems[i].getElementsByTagName(
                    "pubDate")[0].childNodes[0].nodeValue;
                var curDesc = newsItems[i].getElementsByTagName(
                     "description")[0].childNodes[0].nodeValue;
                var curStory = "<a href='" + curLink + "'>" + curHeadline
```

```
                            + "</a><br />";
              curStory += "<span style='color: gray'>" + curPubDate
                            + "</span><br />";
              curStory += curDesc + "<br />";
              document.getElementById("stockNews").innerHTML
                            += curStory;
        }
    }
    else
        document.getElementById("stockNews").innerHTML
            = "RSS feed does not contain any items.";
    }
}
```

6. Save the **StockQuotes.html** document and validate it with the W3C Markup Validation Service. Once the document is valid, close it in your text editor.

7. Create a new document in your text editor and add the following PHP code, which opens the Yahoo! Finance RSS feed for the stock and returns the XML document to the StockQuotes.html document. The value assigned to the $NewsSource variable is the URL for the Yahoo! Finance news RSS feed, http://finance.yahoo.com/rss/ headline, combined with a name=value pair consisting of s=*ticker*. (The 's' portion of the name=value pair is required by the Yahoo! Finance RSS news feed.)

```php
<?php
$NewsSource = "http://finance.yahoo.com/rss/headline?s="
    . $_GET["stockFeed"];
header("Content-Type: text/xml");
header("Content-Length: " . strlen(file_get_contents
($NewsSource)));
header("Cache-Control: no-cache");
readfile($NewsSource);
?>
```

8. Save the document as **StockNews.php** in your Projects folder for Chapter 12, close it in your text editor, and then open the **StockQuotes.html** document in your Web browser by entering the following URL: http://localhost/JavaScript_Projects/ Chapter.12/Projects/StockQuotes.html. When the Web page first opens, it should display quote information and news for the Nasdaq Composite Index (^IXIC). Enter another stock symbol (such as ORCL for Oracle) and click **Get Quote**. The stock quote and news should change to display Oracle information.

9. Close your Web browser window.

Case Projects

For the following projects, save the documents you create in your Cases folder for Chapter 12. Be sure to validate the HTML documents you create with the W3C Markup Validation Service.

Case Project 12-1

Movies.com publishes RSS feeds on current movies including what's in theaters, upcoming movies, reviews, and so on. The available RSS feeds are listed on the following URL: *http://movies.go.com/rss*. Create an AJAX application that is similar to the top stories application you created in this chapter. Allow users to display news information using the available RSS feeds on Movies.com. Save the HTML document as MovieNews.html and the PHP document as MovieNews.php.

Case Project 12-2

Online travel sites such as Orbitz.com publish RSS feeds with travel deals. Create an AJAX application that retrieves RSS feeds for travel deals from at least three online travel sites. Design the application using the same techniques that you used to create the top stories application in this chapter. Save the HTML document as TravelDeals.html and the PHP document as TravelDeals.php.

Case Project 12-3

The traffic.com Web site (*http://www.traffic.com*), which contains free, real-time traffic information, publishes RSS feeds for traffic conditions in numerous American cities. The RSS traffic feeds page on traffic.com (*http://www.traffic.com/rss.html*) lists the RSS feeds for the available cities. Create an AJAX program containing a Web page with a text box into which users can enter the name of a city to retrieve its traffic results. The URLs for each of the RSS feeds are in the format *http://cityrss.traffic.com/feeds/rss_*city. For example, the RSS traffic feed for Boston is *http://cityrss.traffic.com/feeds/rss_boston*. You will need to build the string that is passed to the server by appending the city name to the URL. Use the toLowerCase() method of the String object to ensure that the city name is lowercase. When the page first opens, it should default to the traffic information for Albany. Include functionality that displays the message "Invalid city" or "There are no reported traffic incidents" if the user enters an invalid city name or if the selected feed does not contain any traffic incidents. Save the Web page as TrafficReport.html and the PHP page as TrafficReport.php.

Case Project 12-4

In Chapter 7, you created a Web page that displayed scrolling text in the status bar. Use a similar technique to add scrolling headlines to the top stories Web page. First, copy the TopStories.html and TopStories.php documents from your Chapter folder for Chapter 12 to your Cases folder for Chapter 12. Add a text box above the table that displays the list of news organizations and stories. Add functionality to the fillNewsInfo() function that assigns the values from each <title> element in the RSS feed to a global array. Then, add a function that scrolls the headlines in the text box. The scrolling text should start with the first headline displayed in the headlines list and change to each subsequent headline. Once the last headline is displayed, start over with the first headline.

Appendix A

Building a Web Development Environment

Understanding how to install and configure the software required for creating and delivering PHP scripts is considered a critical skill for Web developers. Even if you have an Internet service provider (ISP) hosting your Web site, you will still need to develop your PHP scripts on your local computer before uploading them to your ISP. In this appendix, you build a Web development environment consisting of a Web server and PHP. After you have finished installing and testing your Web development environment, you study the basics of how to create PHP scripts.

Even if you already have access to the necessary software for creating and delivering PHP scripts, or if you install the software in some other manner, be certain to follow the instructions in the Configuring Apache or Configuring Internet Information Services sections later in this appendix (depending on which Web server you install). These sections contain procedures you need to perform to configure your Web server to work with Chapter 12's data files.

Building a Web Development Environment

Before you can write PHP scripts, you need the following:

- A Web browser
- A Web server
- The PHP software

You should already have a Web browser installed on your computer. Be sure to use a recent Web browser such as Firefox 2 or Internet Explorer 7. You can use almost any version of the UNIX/ Linux operating system to develop PHP scripts, including Red Hat Linux and Mac OS X. To develop PHP scripts with the Windows operating systems, the version of Windows you can use depends primarily on the Web server software you decide to install. Although you can install the Apache Web server on Windows platforms as far back as Windows 95, the Apache Foundation does not recommend installing Apache on Windows 95, Windows 98, or Windows Me. Internet Information Services (IIS) is only available on Windows 2000 and newer versions.

NOTE

The instructions in this appendix assume that you are familiar with basic commands for your operating system.

If you have an account with an ISP, you may already have access to a PHP installation on your ISP's Web server. Check with your ISP for more information. Even if you do have an account with an ISP, you should install the necessary software on your local computer so that you can develop your Web pages and scripts before transferring them to your ISP.

CAUTION

Keep in mind that the Web development environment you install in this section should only be used for development and testing purposes, and not for hosting a live Web site. Until you understand the security and maintenance issues involved with hosting a Web site, your best bet is to go through an ISP.

NOTE

A number of companies offer free and commercial installation kits that automatically install and configure a Web server and PHP. You can find an extensive list of these installation kits at *http://www.hotscripts.com/PHP/Software_and_Servers/ Installation_Kits/*. However, the PHP Group (the open source organization that develops PHP) does not endorse any installation kits and recommends that you perform a manual installation for best results.

Understanding Binary and Source Code Installations

You can install open source software from binary format or from source code. **Binary format** (or **binaries**) are compiled files, such as executable installation programs. **Source code** is the original programming code in which an application was written. Before you can use source code, it must be **compiled**, or processed and assembled into an executable format. On Windows platforms, your best bet is to install the open source applications discussed in this section using binaries that are available on each application's Web site. Although you can also compile Windows versions of each program, you must use Microsoft Visual Studio, which is a line of development tools for Windows platforms.

The difference between interpreting and compiling is that, while interpreted programs (such as JavaScript and PHP) are processed and assembled into an executable format each time they execute, compiled programs only need to be recompiled when their code changes.

For UNIX and Linux operating systems, you can also install Apache and PHP from either binary or source code format, although the open source organizations that develop these applications do not usually make binary versions available on their Web sites. However, Apache and PHP come preinstalled on many UNIX and Linux-based operating systems. If they are not preinstalled on your system, then you can probably find binaries in the form of "packages" that can be installed with special programs. For example, various Linux platforms allow you to use an application called the Red Hat Package Manager (RPM) to install binary packages (or "RPMs"). You can probably find binary package versions of Apache and PHP with your UNIX/Linux installation files or on your platform vendor's Web site or another third-party Web site. For example, you can download a binary package of PHP for Mac OS X at *http://www.entropy.ch/software/macosx/php/*.

NOTE

Because so many UNIX/Linux operating systems are available, specific instructions cannot be listed here for determining whether an application is installed and for locating and installing binary packages on each platform. You should be able to find detailed instructions on your platform vendor's Web site.

TIP

Source code for many UNIX/Linux programs is written in the C programming language. To compile C code on UNIX/Linux systems, you must use the make utility with an ANSI C compiler. Even if you already have an ANSI C compiler installed on your system, it is recommended that you install the most recent version of the GNU C compiler, which is freely available at *http://gcc.gnu.org/*.

Although a binary format can be easier to install, it may not contain the most recent version of an open source application, and you may not be able to customize your installation and configuration. To be successful with this book, you do not necessarily need the latest and greatest version of each application, nor do you need to perform advanced installations and configurations. Yet, the ability to install and compile programs from source code is a skill you must possess in order to be a successful Web developer, especially if you work with UNIX/Linux systems for which binary installations do exist. For this reason, the instructions in this appendix describe how to install each open source application from open source format. The instructions use generic steps that are similar for most UNIX-based systems, including Linux platforms and Mac OS X. For detailed instructions on installing each open source application with specific platforms, see the installation documentation on each application's Web site.

Getting Help

You have probably grown to expect a certain level of help and support from vendors of commercial software. For instance, Microsoft provides a great deal of help and support for IIS. The first line of support is the online help that is installed with IIS. Figure A-1 shows the Web page that should appear in your browser for IIS 5.1.

If you cannot find the answers you need with the online help that is installed with IIS, you can obtain more information as well as professional technical support on Microsoft's Web site at *http://www.microsoft.com*.

Figure A-1
Help page for IIS

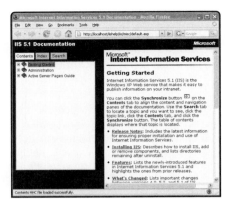

However, of the three applications discussed in this section, IIS is the only commercial offering; Apache and PHP are all open source software. One of the downsides to using open-source software is the lack of official support from a commercial software company such as Microsoft to help you through difficulties. Instead, you must rely on online documentation that is maintained by volunteers. You can access the official online documentation for Apache and PHP at the following URLs:

- **Apache documentation**: *http://httpd.apache.org/docs/*
- **PHP documentation**: *http://www.php.net/docs.php*

If you cannot find your answers in the online documentation, then you can also post a message to various mailing lists that are available for each application. In most cases, other users who monitor the lists will be delighted to help you figure out a problem. You can find mailing lists and other support resources for each product at the following URLs:

- **Apache support resources**: *http://httpd.apache.org/lists.html*
- **PHP support resources**: *http://www.php.net/support.php*

NOTE
Course Technology and the author of this book are more than happy to help with any problems you may have with this book. However, when it comes to installing or running any of the applications discussed in this book, they cannot help you find the answers to your problems as quickly as the open source community can.

Installing and Configuring a Web Server

As you learned earlier, Apache is the most popular Web server software used on the Internet. Apache is developed as open source software by the Apache Software Foundation (*http://apache.org/*) and runs on most platforms, including Windows and Linux.

Microsoft's commercial IIS for Windows operating systems is the second most popular Web server and is used on about a third of today's Web sites. IIS is available as a component of the following Windows platforms:

- Windows 2000 (Professional, Server, and Advanced Server)
- Windows XP Professional
- Windows Server 2003 family for both client and server applications
- Windows Vista

NOTE
IIS can only be installed on Windows platforms.

When you install Apache on UNIX and Linux operating systems, you must start and stop the application manually. When you install Apache or IIS on Windows, each Web server is installed as a service. The term **service** is used in Windows operating systems to refer to a program that performs a specific function to support other programs. Services are usually launched automatically when Windows first starts, so you do not normally need to start Apache or IIS yourself. Yet, there will be times when you will need to restart your Web server, especially after you modify your configuration settings. For this reason, instructions for starting and stopping Apache and IIS are listed in the following sections.

PHP scripts are supported by almost every Web server out there. You can use whatever Web server you like with this book, provided it supports PHP. But because Apache and IIS are two of the most popular Web server applications, the installation and configuration instructions in this book focus on Apache and IIS. If you decide to use a Web server other than Apache or IIS, refer to the documentation that came with the Web server for installation and configuration instructions.

NOTE
Other Microsoft Web servers that support PHP are available for older versions of Windows, including Peer Web Services on Windows NT Workstation 4.0 and Personal Web Server for Windows 95/98/ME. However, because these Web servers have been discontinued by Microsoft, this book only includes instructions for IIS.

Installing and Running Apache on UNIX and Linux

This section explains how to install and configure Apache from source code on UNIX and Linux systems. For more detailed installation instructions, refer to the Apache documentation at *http://httpd.apache.org/docs/install.html*.

CAUTION
Before installing Apache on UNIX and Linux systems, you may need to log in as the root user to ensure that you have the necessary permissions to perform administration tasks.

To install Apache from source code on UNIX and Linux systems:

1. Start your Web browser, and enter the Web address for the Apache HTTP Server download page: **http://httpd.apache.org/download.cgi**. Download the compressed UNIX source file containing the Apache version that the Apache Foundation recommends as the best available. At the time of this writing, the best available version is Apache 2.2.4 and the compressed UNIX source file is named httpd-2.2.4.tar.gz. Save the file to a temporary location such as your usr/src directory or another directory of your choice.

2. Run the following `gunzip` command in the directory where you downloaded the compressed file. This command decompresses the httpd-2.2.4.tar.gz file into a tar file named httpd-2.2.4.tar within the same directory.

    `gunzip httpd-2.2.4.tar.gz`

3. Run the following `tar` command, which extracts the files in the httpd-2.2.4.tar to a directory named httpd-2.2.4 within the current directory:

    `tar xvf httpd-2.2.4.tar`

4. Change to the httpd-2.2.4 directory:

    `cd httpd-2.2.4`

5. The httpd-2.2.4 directory contains a `configure` command that prepares your system for installation of Apache. You can specify several parameters when you run the `configure` command. One parameter that you should be aware of is the `--prefix` parameter, which specifies the location to install Apache. By default, Apache is installed in the /usr/local/apache2 directory. Run the `configure` command using default options, including the default installation location, then run the following command:

    `./configure`

    If you want to install Apache in a location other than the default, run the `configure` command as follows:

    `./configure --prefix=installation directory`

TIP
For a complete listing of parameters and syntax for the `configure` command, type `./configure --help`.

6. After the configuration script finishes, compile the Apache source code by running the **make** command in the httpd-2.2.4 directory.

7. Finally, perform the installation by running the **make install** command in the httpd-2.2.4 directory.

You start, stop, and restart Apache using the `apachectl` control script, located in the bin directory beneath the directory where you installed Apache. The following examples assume that Apache is installed in the /usr/local/apache2 directory.

To start Apache, use the `start` option with the `apachectl` control script, as follows:

```
/usr/local/apache2/bin/apachectl start
```

To stop Apache, use the `stop` option of the `apachectl` control script, as follows:

```
/usr/local/apache2/bin/apachectl stop
```

To restart Apache, use the `restart` option of the `apachectl` control script, as follows:

```
/usr/local/apache2/bin/apachectl restart
```

Installing and Running Apache on Windows

This section explains how to install and configure Apache from binary format on Windows operating systems. For more detailed installation instructions, refer to the Apache documentation at *http://httpd.apache.org/docs/*.

To install Apache from binary format on Windows operating systems:

1. Start your Web browser, and enter the Web address for the Apache HTTP Server download page: **http://httpd.apache.org/download.cgi**. Download the Win32 Binary (MSI Installer) file containing the Apache version that the Apache Foundation recommends as the best available. At the time of this writing, the best available version is Apache 2.2.4 and the Win32 Binary (MSI Installer) file is named apache_2.2.4-win32-x86-no_ssl.msi. Save the file to a temporary folder on your computer.

2. Open **Windows Explorer** or **My Computer** and navigate to the folder where you downloaded the apache_2.2.4-win32-x86-no_ssl.msi installation file. Double-click the file to start the installation program. The Welcome screen of the installation wizard appears.

3. In the Welcome screen, click the **Next** button to proceed with installation. The License Agreement screen appears.

4. On the License Agreement screen, click the button that accepts the terms of the license agreement, and then click the **Next** button. The Read This First screen appears.

5. Read through the contents of the Read This First screen, and then click the **Next** button. The Server Information screen appears.

6. The Server Information screen asks you for information about your Web server, including the network domain, the server name, and the administrator's e-mail address. If you have registered a domain name and already configured your computer as a Web server, enter this information. However, you are probably only using the current computer to perform the exercises in this book. If that is the case, accept the default values that were entered for your system. In the section of the screen that asks for whom to install Apache, accept the default value of **for All**

Users, on Port 80, as a Service — Recommended. Click the **Next** button to continue. The Setup Type screen appears.

7. The Setup Type screen allows you to select whether to perform a typical or custom installation. Accept the default value of **Typical**, and click the **Next** button. The Destination Folder screen appears.

8. The Destination Folder screen allows you to change the folder where Apache will be installed. Change the destination folder if you need to, although in most cases you should accept the default value. Click the **Next** button to continue. The Ready to Install the Program screen appears.

9. The Ready to Install the Program screen is the final screen that appears before Apache is installed. If you want to change any of the installation options you selected, click the **Back** button. Otherwise, click the **Install** button. When the installation is complete, the Installation Wizard Complete screen appears.

10. Click the **Finish** button to close the Installation Wizard Complete screen.

The preceding steps install Apache as a service, so you do not normally need to start Apache yourself. To control Apache manually, click your Start menu and point to All Programs; you should see an Apache HTTP Server 2.2.4 folder, which in turn contains a Control Apache Server folder. The Control Apache Server folder contains Stop, Start, and Restart commands that you can use if you need to control the service manually. The Control Apache Server folder also contains a Monitor Apache Servers command, which places an icon in the notification area to the right of the Windows taskbar. You can also use the Monitor Apache Services icon to stop, start, and restart Apache. The Monitor Apache Services command should start automatically when you first start Windows.

TIP

If Apache is running, the Monitor Apache Services icon appears as an arrow. If Apache is not running, the Monitor Apache Services icon appears as a square.

Installing and Running Internet Information Services on Windows

This section explains how to install and configure IIS on Windows operating systems. IIS is available with the Windows 2000, Windows XP, Windows Server 2003, and Windows Vista operating systems. Note that the steps for installing IIS on Windows Vista differ from the steps for installing IIS on the other Windows operations systems.

CAUTION

Do not perform these steps if you have already installed Apache as your Web server.

Installing and Controlling IIS on Windows 2000, Windows XP, and Windows Server 2003

Perform the following steps to install IIS on Windows 2000, Windows XP, or Windows Server 2003:

To install IIS on Windows 2000, Windows XP, or Windows Server 2003:

1. Open **Control Panel** from the **Start** menu.

2. If you are using Windows XP, click the **Switch to Classic View** link to display the Control Panel icons, if necessary.

3. Select the **Add or Remove Programs** icon. The Add or Remove Programs window opens.

4. In the Add or Remove Programs window, click **Add/Remove Windows Components**. The Windows Components Wizard window opens. The window lists components that can be installed with the Windows operating system. A selected check box indicates that a component will be installed, whereas a shaded check box indicates that only part of a component will be installed.

5. Scroll down the Components list and click the check box next to Internet Information Services (IIS). By default, IIS is only installed with the most common options, so the check box is shaded. If you want to select additional options for IIS, click the Details button. However, the default IIS installation options are all you need for this book, so click the **Next** button to begin installation.

6. During the installation process, you might be prompted for the location of your original Windows installation CD-ROM. The Windows Components Wizard displays a message when installation is complete. After installation is complete, click the **Finish** button to close the Windows Components Wizard.

7. If prompted, restart Windows.

8. Close the Add or Remove Programs window and Control Panel if you do not need to restart Windows.

The preceding steps install IIS as a service, so you do not normally need to start IIS yourself. To manually control the default Web site that is managed by IIS, you use the Internet Information Services window in Control Panel.

To manually control the default Web site with the Internet Information Services window:

1. Open Control Panel from the Start menu, and, if you are using Windows XP, switch to Classic view.

2. Use the **Administrative Tools** icon to open the Administrative Tools window.

3. Select **Internet Information Services**. The Internet Information Services window opens.

4. Click the plus sign next to the icon that represents your computer, and then click the plus sign next to the Web Sites folder, if necessary.

5. Click the **Default Web Site** icon. If the Default Web site is not currently running, the name of the icon changes to Default Web Site (Stopped).

6. Perform one of the following tasks to manually control the default Web site:

- To start the default Web site, select **Start** from the **Action** menu.
- To stop the default Web site, select **Stop** from the **Action** menu.
- To temporarily pause the default Web site, select **Pause** from the **Action** menu.

TIP
You can also use buttons on the IIS toolbar to start, stop, and pause a Web site.

Installing and Controlling IIS on Windows Vista

Perform the following steps to install IIS on Windows Vista:

To install IIS on Windows Vista:

1. Open **Control Panel** from the **Start** menu.
2. Display the Control Panel home page and then click **Programs**. The Programs window opens.
3. Under Programs and Features, click **Turn On or Off Windows Features**. If you see a warning dialog box, click **Continue**. The Windows Features dialog box opens. The window lists components that can be installed with the Windows operating system. (You might have to wait briefly before the list appears in the dialog box.) A selected check box indicates that a component is turned on, whereas a shaded check box indicates that only part of a component will be installed.
4. Scroll down the Components list and click the check box next to Internet Information Services. By default, IIS is only installed with the most common options, so the check box is shaded. If you want to select additional options for IIS, expand the features beneath Internet Information Services. However, the default IIS installation options are all you need for this book, so click the **OK** button to begin installation.
5. During the installation process, you might be prompted for the location of your original Windows installation CD-ROM. When installation is complete, the Windows Features dialog box closes and you return to Control Panel.
6. If prompted, restart Windows.
7. Close Control Panel if you do not need to restart Windows.

The preceding steps install IIS as a service, so you do not normally need to start IIS yourself. Perform the following steps to manually control the default Web site that is managed by IIS.

To manually control the default Web site with the Internet Information Services window:

1. Open the **Start** menu, right-click **Computer**, and then click **Manage**. The Computer Management dialog box opens.
2. In the Computer Management dialog box, expand **Services and Applications**, and then expand **Internet Information Services (IIS) Manager**.

3. Expand the icon that represents your computer, and then expand the Web Sites folder, if necessary.

4. Select the **Default Web Site** icon and the select **Start**, **Stop**, or **Restart** from the Actions panel.

Testing Your Web Server

For the typical user, the computer running the Web server and the local computer are two different computers. In that case, you open a file on the Web server by entering the domain name or IP address of a Web site in the local computer's browser. However, when developing a Web site, you need to be able to open your Web pages from a Web server that is running on your local computer. You can do this using *localhost*, which is the name that a local computer uses to refer to itself. Alternatively, you can access a Web server with *127.0.0.1*, which is the IP address that a local computer uses to refer to itself. For example, you can access a default Web page named index.html on your local computer by entering a URL of *http://localhost/index.html* or *http://localhost/*. Similarly, you can access the same Web page by entering a URL of *http://127.0.0.1/index.html* or *http://127.0.0.1/*.

By default, Apache serves Web pages from the /usr/local/apache2/htdocs directory on UNIX/ Linux, and from the C:\Program Files\Apache Software Foundation\Apache2.2\htdocs directory on Windows. This directory contains files that generate a default Web page based on your language. You can access Apache's default Web page with either *http://localhost/* or *http:// 127.0.0.1/*. The default directory from where IIS serves Web pages is C:\Inetpub\wwwroot. IIS does not create a default Web page. However, if you do not create a default Web page yourself, whenever you access *http://localhost/* or *http://127.0.0.1/*, IIS displays one Web page informing you that IIS is running and another Web page opened to the IIS online documentation page.

In the next exercise, you test your Web server with the *http://localhost/* and *http://127.0.0.1/* URLs.

To test your Web server:

1. Open your Web browser.

2. Type **http://localhost/** in the Address box and press **Enter**. You should see the default Web page for your server. If you installed IIS, you should see another Web page opened to the IIS online documentation page.

TIP

If you are using Firefox and cannot open the default Web page for your server by typing **http://localhost/**, then type **about:config** in the Address box and press **Enter**. A list of configuration settings appears along with a Filter box. Type **ntlm** in the Filter box, and then double-click the **network.automatic-ntlm-auth.trusted-uris** entry that appears in the list of configuration settings. In the Enter string value dialog box that appears, type **localhost** and click **OK**. Finally, restart Firefox.

3. Now type **http://127.0.0.1/** in the Address box, and press **Enter**. You should see the same page you saw in Step 2.

NOTE

The instructions in this appendix primarily use *http://localhost/*.

4.   Close your Web browser window.

In TCP/IP, a **port** represents the endpoint of a connection between a client and a server. Clients use a port number to identify a specific application on a Web server. Port numbers range from 0 to 65536, with ports 0 to 1024 being reserved for special purposes or well-known protocols. For example, port 80 is reserved for HTTP communications. This means that whenever you access a Web page such as *http://www.yahoo.com/*, you are really accessing it through port 80 on Yahoo's Web server. Although they are assigned by default to port 80, Apache and IIS can be configured to use any nonreserved port. If you do assign a Web server to a different port, you need to specify the port number in the URL by appending the port number with a colon to *localhost* or *127.0.0.1*. For example, to open the default Web page for a Web server that is configured to use port 8083, you can use either of the following URLs:

```
http://localhost:8083/
http://127.0.0.1:8083/
```

CAUTION

Two Web servers cannot share the same port. If you do have two Web servers configured to use the same port, the Web server that starts running first has exclusive access to the port. This means that if you install Apache and IIS on the same computer, you must configure one of the Web servers to use a port other than port 80.

Configuring Apache

To configure ports and other settings for Apache after installation, you must edit the httpd.conf file, located in the conf directory beneath the directory where you installed Apache. By default, this file is located in the /usr/local/apache2/conf directory for UNIX/Linux and in the C:\Program Files\Apache Software Foundation\Apache2.2\conf directory for Windows. In UNIX/Linux, you can edit the httpd.conf file with a text editor such as GNU Emacs. In Windows, you can quickly edit the httpd.conf file in Notepad or your default text editor by selecting the Edit the Apache httpd.conf Configuration File command, located in the Configure Apache Server folder in your Apache HTTP Server 2.2.4 folder under All Programs in your Start menu. Figure A-2 shows a portion of the httpd.conf file. The first lines shown in Figure A-2 configure Apache for the ports that it will use. Lines that begin with the pound sign (#) are informational comments that do not affect Apache's configuration. The lines without pound signs contain **directives**, which define information about how a program should be configured. The `Listen` directive in Figure A-2 configures Apache to use port 80.

After you edit and save the httpd.conf file, you must restart Apache for the changes to take effect.

NOTE

Although directives are case insensitive, keep in mind that the values you assign to them might be case sensitive. For example, in UNIX/Linux, directory names are case sensitive. This means that if you assign a directory name to a directive, it must use the correct letter case.

Figure A-2

httpd.conf

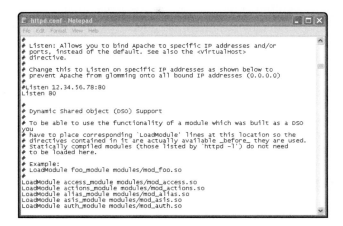

The `DocumentRoot` directive identifies the default directory from where Apache serves Web pages. The default document root is /usr/local/apache2/htdocs on UNIX/Linux systems and C:\Program Files\Apache Software Foundation\Apache2.2\htdocs on Windows systems. You can also use the `Alias` directive to identify other directories that Apache can use to serve Web pages. The syntax for the `Alias` directive is `Alias URL-path directory-path`. The `URL-path` identifies the alias that you will use to access the directory with your Web site's URL. For example, the following UNIX example defines an alias named specials for the /usr/local/WebPages/specials directory:

```
Alias /specials /usr/local/WebPages/specials
```

Here is a Windows example of the preceding `Alias` directive. Notice that the alias and the directory name include an ending forward slash and that the directory name is surrounded by quotation marks. Also notice that, even though this is a Windows example, it uses forward slashes (/). (Windows directories are usually referenced using backslashes.)

```
Alias /specials/ "C:/WebPages/specials/"
```

NOTE

The directory you specify for an alias must exist on your server.

The preceding `Alias` directives allow you to open files from the specials directory by appending the alias name to *localhost* or *127.0.0.1*. For example, to open a file named sales.html from the specials directory, you can use the URL *http://localhost/specials/sales.html* or *http://127.0.0.1/ specials/sales.html.*

Next, you add to the Apache httpd.conf file an `Alias` directive that points to the main directory where you will store the files you create with this book.

To modify the Apache httpd.conf file on UNIX/Linux systems:

1. Open the **httpd.conf** file from the **/usr/local/apache2/conf** directory or other directory where you installed Apache. Use any text editor such as GNU Emacs.

2. Add the following `Alias` directive to the end of the httpd.conf file. The new directive creates an alias for the /usr/local/course/0150-9 directory.

    Alias /JavaScript_Projects /usr/local/course/0150-9

3. Add the following `<Directory>` section to the end of the httpd.conf file. The statements in the `<Directory>` section allow users to open the files in the directory represented by the alias.

    ```
    <Directory "/usr/local/course/0150-9">
        Allow from all
    </Directory>
    ```

4. Save and close the **httpd.conf** file.

5. Use the following command to restart Apache (you might need to specify a different directory if you installed Apache in a location other than the default):

    /usr/local/apache2/bin/apachectl restart

To modify the Apache httpd.conf file on Windows systems:

1. Click **Start** and point to **All Programs**. Select the **Edit the Apache httpd.conf Configuration File** command, located in the **Configure Apache Server** folder in the **Apache HTTP Server 2.2.4** folder. The httpd.conf file opens in your default text editor, which is usually Notepad.

2. Add the following `Alias` directive immediately after the existing `Alias` directive. The new directive creates an alias for the C:\Course Technology\0150-9 directory.

    Alias /JavaScript_Projects/ "C:/Course Technology/0150-9/"

3. Add the following `<Directory>` section to the end of the httpd.conf file. The `Allow from all` statements in the `<Directory>` section allow users to open the files in the directory represented by the alias.

    ```
    <Directory "C:/Course Technology/0150-9/">
        Allow from all
    </Directory>
    ```

4. Save and close the **httpd.conf** file.

5. To restart Apache, click **Start**, point to **All Programs**, point to the **Apache HTTP Server 2.2.4** folder, point to the **Control Apache Server** folder, and then click the **Restart** command.

After you modify the httpd.conf file for your operating system and restart Apache, perform the following steps to test the new alias by opening in your Web server the ForestvilleFunding.html file you created in Chapter 1.

To test the `Alias` directive:

1.   Open your Web browser.

2.   Type the **http://localhost/JavaScript_Projects/Chapter.01/Chapter/ ForestvilleFunding.html** in the Address box, and press **Enter**. The Web page should open correctly in your Web browser. Note that the Web page opens from your Web server and not as a local file.

3.   Close your Web browser window.

Configuring Internet Information Services

You configure IIS with the Internet Information Services window. To open the Internet Information Services window, open Control Panel and switch to Classic View, if necessary. Select Administrative Tools, and then select Internet Information Services to display the Internet Information Services window. Within the Internet Information Services window, expand your computer name and the Web Sites folder. Then, click the Default Web Site icon, click the Action menu, and then click Properties. The Default Web Site Properties dialog box opens. This dialog box contains several tabs with various configuration options. The Web Site tab, shown in Figure A-3, allows you to select the default TCP/IP port.

Figure A-3

Default Web Site
Properties dialog box

NOTE

Depending on the options you selected during installation of IIS, your version of the Default Web Site Properties dialog box may not contain the same tabs and options shown in Figure A-3.

The Home Directory tab in the Default Web Site Properties dialog box allows you to specify the directory from where IIS serves Web pages. (The default directory is C:\Inetpub\wwwroot.) You can also specify a virtual directory that IIS can use to serve Web pages. After you create a virtual directory in IIS, you can use a Web browser to open any file in the virtual directory. The URL you type in the browser should follow this syntax: `http://localhost/directory/file` or `http://127.0.0.1/directory/file`. For example, if you create a virtual directory named *interests*, you can open a document named index.html by typing the following URL in a Web browser's Address box: *http://localhost/interests/index.html*.

NOTE

If you read the previous section on Apache configuration, you should recognize a virtual directory as being the IIS equivalent to an alias in Apache.

Next, you create a virtual directory in IIS that points to the main directory where you will store the files you create with this book.

To create a virtual directory in IIS:

1. Open Control Panel from the Start menu, switch to Classic View, if necessary, and then click the **Administrative Tools** icon. The Administrative Tools window opens.

2. Select **Internet Information Services**. The Internet Information Services window opens.

3. Click the plus sign next to the icon that represents your computer, and then click the plus sign next to the Web Sites folder, if necessary.

4. Click the **Default Web Site** icon, click **Action** on the menu bar, point to **New**, and then click **Virtual Directory**. The Virtual Directory Creation Wizard opens.

5. In the introductory dialog box of the Virtual Directory Creation Wizard, click the **Next** button to display the Virtual Directory Alias dialog box.

6. In the Virtual Directory Alias dialog box, type **JavaScript_Projects**, and then click the **Next** button. The Web Site Content Directory dialog box opens.

7. Type the path where you store your PHP projects. By default, this should be the C:\Course Technology\0150-9 directory. Click the **Next** button when you are finished. The Access Permissions dialog box opens.

8. Leave the options in the Access Permissions dialog box set to their default values, and click the **Next** button to display the final Virtual Direction Wizard Creation dialog box.

9. Click **Finish** to create the virtual directory, and then close the Internet Information Services window and Control Panel.

10. Open your Web browser to test the virtual directory. Type **http://localhost/ JavaScript_Projects/Chapter.01/Chapter/ForestvilleFunding.html** in the Address box, and press **Enter**. The Web page should open correctly in your Web browser. Note that the Web page opens from your Web server and not as a local file.

11. Close your Web browser window.

Installing PHP

This section explains how to install PHP on UNIX/Linux systems running Apache and Windows systems running either Apache or IIS. Before you install PHP, be certain to install and configure a Web server, as described in the previous section.

NOTE

For more information on how to install PHP, refer to the installation instructions in the online PHP manual at *http://www.php.net/manual/en/install.php*.

Installing PHP on UNIX and Linux Systems Running Apache

This section explains how to install and configure PHP from source code on UNIX and Linux systems running Apache.

CAUTION

Before installing PHP on UNIX and Linux systems, you might need to log in as the root user to ensure that you have the necessary permissions to perform administration tasks.

To install PHP from source code on UNIX and Linux systems running Apache:

1. Start your Web browser, and enter the Web address for the PHP download page: **http://www.php.net/downloads.php**. Download the compressed UNIX source file containing the most recent version of PHP. At the time of this writing, the most recent version is PHP 5.2.3 and the compressed UNIX source file is named php-5.2.3.tar.gz. Save the file to a temporary location such as your usr/src directory or another directory of your choice.

NOTE

If you download a different version of PHP, be sure to replace the "5.2.3" in the following steps with the correct version number.

2. Run the following `gunzip` command in the directory where you downloaded the compressed file. This command decompresses the php-5.2.3.tar.gz file into a tar file named php-5.2.3.tar within the same directory:

```
gunzip php-5.2.3.tar.gz
```

3. Run the following `tar` command, which extracts the files in the php-5.2.3.tar to a directory named php-5.2.3 within the current directory:

```
tar xvf php-5.2.3.tar
```

4.   Change to the php-5.2.3 directory:

cd php-5.2.3

5.   The php-5.2.3 directory contains a `configure` command that prepares your system for installation of PHP. You can specify a number of parameters when you run the `configure` command, including the `--prefix` parameter, which specifies the location to install PHP. One of the most common parameters is the `--apxs2=directory` parameter, which identifies the location of the Apache Extension Tool, which is necessary to associate PHP with Apache. You assign to the `--apxs2=directory` parameter the directory path containing the Apache Extension Tool, which is usually /usr/local/apache2/bin/apxs if you installed Apache in the default location. To run the `configure` command with the `with-apxs2=directory` parameter, enter the following, but be certain to enter the correct directory for the Apache Extension Tool if you installed Apache in another location:

./configure --with-apxs2=/usr/local/apache2/bin/apxs

TIP
For a complete list of parameters and syntax for the `configure` command, type `./configure --help`.

6.   After the configuration script finishes, compile the PHP source code by running the **make** command in the php-5.2.3 directory.

7.   Perform the installation by running the **make install** command in the php-5.2.3 directory.

8.   When installation is complete, you need to specify which configuration file you want to use with PHP. The PHP configuration file is named php.ini. The installation process creates two sample configuration files: php.ini-dist and php.ini-recommended. You need to copy one of these files to the usr/local/lib directory and rename it php.ini. The php.ini-dist file is intended for development environments, whereas the php.ini-recommended file is intended for production environments. Because you are using this book to learn how to develop Web sites with PHP, you will primarily use the php.ini-dist file. Run the following command to copy the php.ini-dist file to your usr/local/lib directory and rename it as php.ini:

cp php.ini-dist /usr/local/lib/php.ini

CAUTION
Be sure you understand the settings in the php.ini-recommended file before using it as your PHP configuration file in a production environment.

Installing PHP on Windows Running Apache or IIS

This section explains how to install PHP from binary format on Windows systems running either Apache or IIS.

To install PHP from binary format on Windows operating systems:

1. Start your Web browser, and enter the Web address for the PHP download page: **http://www.php.net/downloads.php**. Download the most recent Windows binary installer. At the time of this writing, the most recent version is the PHP 5.2.3 installer; the binary file for this installer is named php-5.2.3-installer.msi. Save the file to a temporary folder on your computer.

NOTE

If you download a different version of PHP, be sure to replace the "5.2.3" in the following steps with the correct version number. Also, note that the specific installation instructions may differ with other PHP versions.

2. Open **Windows Explorer** or **My Computer** and navigate to the folder where you downloaded the php-5.2.3-installer.msi installation file. Double-click the file to start the installation program. The Welcome screen of the installation wizard appears.

3. In the Welcome screen, click the **Next** button to proceed with installation. The License Agreement screen appears.

4. In the License Agreement screen, click the **I accept the terms in the License Agreement** button, and then click the **Next** button. The Destination Folder screen appears.

5. The Destination Folder screen allows you to change the folder where PHP will be installed. Change the destination folder if you need to, although in most cases you should accept the default value. Click the **Next** button to continue. The Web Server Setup screen appears.

6. In the Web Server Type screen, select the type of Web server that you want to use with PHP. You should select an Apache or IIS Web server. If you are using an Apache Web server, select the correct module for the version of Apache that you installed. For example, if you installed Apache 2.2.4, you should select **Apache 2.2.x Module**. If you are using an IIS Web server, then select **IIS ISAPI module**. Click the **Next** button to continue.

7. If you chose an Apache Web server, then the Apache Configuration Directory screen appears. If you did not select an Apache Web server, then skip to the next step. If you did select an Apache Web server, then in the Apache Configuration Directory screen, click the **Browse** button and select the folder where the httpd.conf file is stored (usually in a directory named \conf beneath the Apache installation directory). Click the **Next** button to continue. The Choose Items to Install screen appears.

8. In the Choose Items to Install screen, accept the default options and click the **Next** button to continue. The Ready to Install PHP screen appears.

9. In the Ready to Install PHP screen, click the **Install** button to begin installation. At the end of the installation process, you see a dialog box announcing that PHP was successfully installed. Click the last **Finish** button to exit installation.

10. Restart your Apache Web server. Use the following command to restart Apache on UNIX/Linux systems(although you might need to specify a different directory if you installed Apache in a location other than the default):

    /usr/local/apache2/bin/apachectl restart

    On Windows systems, restart Apache by clicking the **Start** button and pointing to **All Programs**. Select the **Restart** command, located in the **Control Apache Server** folder in the **Apache HTTP Server 2.2.4** folder.

Configuring Apache for PHP on UNIX/Linux Platforms

After you install PHP on UNIX/Linux platforms, you need to configure Apache to use it.

NOTE

You do not need to perform any additional steps if you installed PHP in a Windows environment.

To configure Apache for PHP on UNIX/Linux platforms:

1. Open the **httpd.conf** file from the **/usr/local/apache2/conf** directory or other directory where you installed Apache. Use any text editor such as GNU Emacs.

2. Search for the following LoadModule directive. If it does not exist, add it to the end of the file.

    LoadModule php5_module libexec/libphp5.so

3. Add the following AddType directive to the end of the file. This line configures Apache to use PHP to process files with an extension of .php.

    AddType application/x-httpd-php .php

4. Save and close the **httpd.conf** file.

5. Use the following command to restart Apache (although you might need to specify a different directory if you installed Apache in a location other than the default):

    /usr/local/apache2/bin/apachectl restart

Configuring PHP

You configure PHP by modifying the php.ini configuration file. For UNIX/Linux systems, you should have installed this file in the /usr/local/lib directory. On Windows systems, this file is installed automatically in your Program Files directory. You can edit the php.ini file with a text editor such as GNU Emacs for UNIX/Linux and Notepad in Windows. Figure A-4 shows a portion of the php.ini file that is used to configure resource limits, error handling, and logging. Lines that begin with a semicolon (;) are informational comments that do not affect PHP's configuration. The lines without semicolons contain **directives**, which define information about how a program should be configured.

Figure A-4

The php.ini configuration file

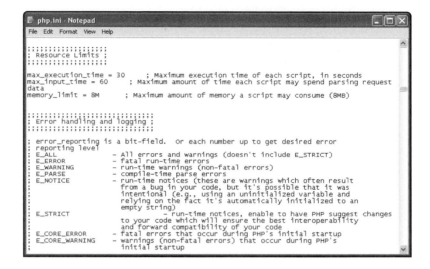

TIP

PHP reads the php.ini configuration file each time it processes a script. For this reason, you do not need to restart your Web server after modifying the configuration file.

Appendix B

Introduction to PHP

JavaScript and PHP are both referred to as **embedded scripting languages** because code for both languages is embedded within a Web page (either an HTML or XHTML document). You type this code directly into a Web page as a separate section. Although JavaScript code can be added to standard Web page documents that have an extension of .html, a Web page document containing PHP code must have an extension of .php. Whenever a request is made for a document with an extension of .php, the Web server sends the file to the scripting engine for processing. The scripting engine then processes any PHP code it encounters. Although PHP files use an extension of .php, they can contain the same HTML or XHTML elements you would find in a static Web page. The scripting engine ignores any non-PHP code and only processes any PHP code it finds within PHP code blocks. The Web server then returns the results of the PHP script along with any HTML or XHTML elements found in the PHP file to the client, where it is then rendered by the client's Web browser. In most cases, the results returned from a PHP script, such as database records, are usually formatted with HTML or XHTML elements. This means that PHP code is never sent to a client's Web browser; only the resulting Web page that is generated from the PHP code and HTML or XHTML elements found within the PHP file are returned to the client. Later in this appendix, you will see an example of a Web page that is returned to a client from a PHP file that contains both PHP code and XHTML elements. First, you need to learn about PHP code blocks.

NOTE

A PHP file does not need to contain any PHP code whatsoever. However, if this is the case with a file you are working on, you should name the file with an extension of .html to avoid the extra step of having the file processed by the scripting engine.

TIP

You can use whichever extension you want for your PHP scripts, provided that your Web server is configured to process the extensions you use with the scripting engine. However, .php is the default extension that most Web servers use to process PHP scripts.

Creating PHP Code Blocks

You write PHP scripts within **code declaration blocks**, which are separate sections within a Web page that are interpreted by the scripting engine. You can include as many code declaration blocks as you want within a document. The standard method of writing PHP code declaration blocks is to use the `<?php` and `?>` script delimiters. A **delimiter** is a character or sequence of characters used to mark the beginning and end of a code segment. When the scripting engine encounters the `<?php` and `?>` script delimiters, it processes any code between the delimiters as PHP. You need to use the following syntax in a document to tell the Web server that the statements that follow must be interpreted by the scripting engine:

```
<?php
statements;
?>
```

The following script contains a single statement that writes the text "Explore Africa!" to a Web browser window, using an `echo()` statement, which you will study shortly:

```
<?php
echo "Explore Africa!";
?>
```

Notice that the preceding statement ends in a semicolon. PHP, unlike JavaScript, requires you to end all statements with a semicolon.

Displaying Script Results

When you write a PHP script, you will often want to display the results of the script in the Web page that is returned as a response to a client. For example, you might want the Web page to display database records that the client requested or the result of a calculation that was processed by the PHP script. Recall that the scripting engine ignores any non-PHP code and only processes any PHP code it finds within PHP code blocks. The Web server then returns the results of the PHP script along with any HTML or XHTML elements found in the PHP file to the client, where it is rendered by the client's Web browser. To return to the client the results of any processing that occur within a PHP code block, you must use an `echo()` statement, which you've already seen, or a `print()` statement. The **echo()** and **print() statements** create new text on a Web page that is returned as a response to a client.

You might be thinking that the `echo()` and `print()` statements resemble functions because function names are usually followed by a set of parentheses. Actually, they are not functions but language constructs of the PHP programming language. A **programming language construct** is a built-in feature of a programming language. Both the `echo()` and `print()` statements are virtually identical, although the `print()` statement returns a value of 1 if it was successful, or a value of 0 if it was not successful. Keep in mind that you can use the exact same syntax with the `print()` statement that you use with the `echo()` statement. Next, you modify the PHPCodeBlocks.php document so it uses `print()` statements instead of `echo()` statements.

You should understand that the only reason to use the `echo()` and `print()` statements is to include the results of a PHP script within a Web page that is returned to a client. For example, you might want to return a new Web page based on information a user enters into a form for an online transaction and submits to a Web server. You can use a PHP script to process the submitted information and return a new Web page to the client that displays the sales total, order confirmation, and so on. If you simply want to display text in a Web page that is returned to the client, there is no need to use anything but standard XHTML elements.

If you want to pass multiple arguments to the echo() and print() statements, separate them with commas, just as with arguments passed to a function. In the following example, three text string arguments are passed to the echo() statement:

```php
<?php echo "Explore Africa, ", "South America, ",
    " and Australia!"; ?>
```

You can also use parentheses with the echo() and print() statements, in the same manner that you use them with functions, as follows:

```php
<?php echo("Explore Africa, ", "South America, ",
    " and Australia!";); ?>
```

Case Sensitivity in PHP

Unlike XHTML and JavaScript, programming language constructs in PHP are mostly case insensitive, although there are some exceptions. This means that you can use any of the following versions of the echo() statement without receiving an error message:

```php
<?php
echo "<p>Explore <strong>Africa</strong>, <br />";
Echo "<strong>South America</strong>, <br />";
ECHO " and <strong>Australia</strong>!</p>";
?>
```

CAUTION

Exceptions to PHP's case insensitivity include variable and constant names, which *are* case sensitive. You study variables and constants later in this appendix.

Adding Comments to a PHP Script

PHP supports the same two block comments as JavaScript: line comments and block comments. However, with PHP line comments, you can use either two slashes // or the pound symbol # before the text you want to use as a comment. The following code shows a PHP code block containing line and block comments. If a client requests a Web page containing the following script in a Web browser, the scripting engine ignores the text marked with comments.

```php
<?php
/*
This line is part of the block comment.
This line is also part of the block comment.
*/
```

```
echo "<h1>Comments Example</h1>";    // Line comments can follow
code statements
// This line comment takes up an entire line.
# This is another way of creating a line comment.
/* This is another way of creating
a block comment. */
?>
```

Using Variables

You must observe the following rules and conventions when naming a variable in PHP:

- Identifiers must begin with a dollar sign ($).
- You can use numbers or an underscore (_) in an identifier, but not as the first character after the dollar sign.
- You cannot include spaces in an identifier.
- Identifiers are case sensitive.

Unlike other types of PHP code, variable names are case sensitive. Therefore, the variable name $MyVariable is a completely different variable than one named $myvariable, $Myvariable, or $MYVARIABLE. If you receive an error when running a script, be sure that you are using the correct case when referring to any variables in your code.

When working with variables in PHP, you follow the same conventions that are used with JavaScript variables, with one important exception: in PHP, you must declare and initialize a variable in the same statement, using the following syntax:

```
$variable_name = value;
```

CAUTION
If you attempt to declare a variable without initializing it, you will receive an error.

The value you assign to a variable can be a literal string or a numeric value. For example, the following statement assigns the literal string "Don" to the variable $MyName:

```
$MyName = "Don";
```

Working with Data Types

PHP supports the six primitive data types described in Table B-1.

Data Type	Description
Integer numbers	Positive or negative numbers with no decimal places
Floating-point numbers	Positive or negative numbers with decimal places or numbers written using exponential notation
Boolean	A logical value of true or false
String	Text such as "Hello World"
NULL	An empty value, also referred to as a NULL value

Table B-1   Primitive PHP data types

NOTE

PHP also supports a "resource" data type, which is a special variable that holds a reference to an external resource, such as a database or XML file.

TIP

The term NULL refers to a data type as well as a value that can be assigned to a variable. Assigning the value NULL to a variable indicates that the variable does not contain a usable value. A variable with a value of NULL has a value assigned to it—null is really the value "no value." You assign the NULL value to a variable when you want to ensure that the variable does not contain any data. For instance, with the $SalesTotal variable you saw earlier, you may want to ensure that the variable does not contain any data before you use it to create another purchase order.

The PHP language also supports **reference**, or **composite**, data types, which can contain multiple values or complex types of information, as opposed to the single values stored in primitive data types. The two reference data types supported by the PHP language are arrays and objects.

TIP

Like JavaScript, PHP is a loosely-typed programming language.

Understanding Variable Scope

A variable's scope in PHP can be either global or local. A global variable is one that is declared outside a function and is available to all parts of your program. A local variable is declared inside a function and is only available within the function in which it is declared. Local variables cease to exist when the function ends. If you attempt to use a local variable outside the function in which it is declared, you receive an error message. With many programming languages, global variables are automatically available to all parts of your program, including functions. However, this is not the case in PHP. As an example, the output statement in the following script generates an error because $GlobalVariable is not recognized within the scope of the scopeExample() function:

```php
<?php
$GlobalVariable = "Global variable";
function scopeExample() {
    echo "<p>$GlobalVariable</p>"; // error message
}
scopeExample();
?>
```

In PHP, you must declare a global variable with the global keyword inside of a function definition for the variable to be available within the scope of that function. When you declare a global variable with the global keyword, you do not need to assign the variable a value, as you do when you declare a standard variable. Instead, within the declaration statement you only need to include the global keyword along with the name of the variable. The correct syntax for this is: global $variable_name;. The following code shows a modified version of the preceding script. This time, the code declares the global variable within the function, which allows the output message to print successfully.

```php
<?php
$GlobalVariable = "Global variable";
function scopeExample() {
    global $GlobalVariable;
    echo "<p>$GlobalVariable</p>";
}
scopeExample();
?>
```

Working with Operators, Functions, and Control Structures

The syntax for working with operators, functions, and control structures in PHP is virtually identical to JavaScript. To use operators, functions, and control structures in your PHP scripts, use the same syntax that is listed in Chapter 2, "Working with Data Types and Operators" and Chapter 3, "Functions, Events, and Control Structures."

Working with PHP Strings

Working with strings in PHP is very similar to working with strings in JavaScript, but with a few important differences, as described in this section.

Using String Operators

Up to this point, to print values from multiple literal strings and variables, you have sent them to the echo() and print() statements as multiple arguments separated by commas. For example, the following passes two literal strings and a variable to the echo() statement:

```
$Explorer = "Henry M. Stanley";
echo '<p>"Dr. Livingstone, I presume?", asked ',
        $Explorer,".</p>";
```

In PHP, you can also use two operators to combine strings. The first of these operators is the **concatenation operator** (.). The following code uses the concatenation operator to combine several string variables and literal strings, and assigns the new value to another variable:

```
$Destination = "Paris";
$Location = "France";
$Destination = "<p>" . $Destination . " is in "
        . $Location . ".</p>";
echo $Destination;
```

The combined value of the $Location variable and the literal strings that are assigned to the $Destination variable is "<p>Paris is in France.</p>".

You can also combine strings using the **concatenation assignment operator** (.=) to combine two strings. The following code combines two text strings, but without using the $Location variable:

```
$Destination = "<p>Paris";
$Destination .= " is in France.</p>";
echo $Destination;
```

Understanding Simple and Complex String Syntax

Values and variables can be combined in a literal string using simple or complex syntax. **Simple string syntax** allows you to use the value of a variable within a string by including the variable name inside a text string with double quotation marks. For example, the following code prints the text "Do you have any broccoli?" to the Web browser:

```
$Vegetable = "broccoli";
echo "<p>Do you have any $Vegetable?</p>";
```

TIP
Also recall that if you surround a variable name inside a text string with single quotation marks, the name of the variable prints.

When the PHP interpreter encounters a dollar sign with a text string, it attempts to evaluate any characters that follow the dollar sign as part of the variable name until it comes to a character that is not allowed in an identifier, such as a space. With the preceding example, the $Vegetable variable is interpreted correctly because the question mark is not a legal character for an identifier. However, consider the following version of the preceding code:

```
$Vegetable = "tomato";
echo "<p>Do you have any $Vegetables?</p>";
```

Because an 's' is appended to the `$Vegetable` variable name, the preceding `echo()` statement causes an error. This is because the PHP interpreter is attempting to locate a variable named `$Vegetables` (plural), which has not been declared. To make the preceding code work, you need to surround the variable name with curly braces { }, as shown in the following example. This type of structure, in which variables are placed within curly braces inside of a string, is called **complex string syntax**.

```
$Vegetable = "carrot";
echo "<p>Do you have any {$Vegetable}s?</p>";
```

The preceding `echo()` statement prints the text string "Do you have any carrots?". Complex string syntax is only recognized if the opening brace is immediately before or after a variable's dollar sign. The following version of the preceding code also works:

```
$Vegetable = "carrot";
echo "<p>Do you have any ${Vegetable}s?</p>";
```

However, if you place any characters between the opening brace and the dollar sign, the contents of the string are interpreted as literal values. For example, because the following code includes a space between the dollar sign and the opening brace, the `echo()` statement prints the text string "Do you have any { $Vegetable}s?":

```
$Vegetable = "carrot";
echo "<p>Do you have any { $Vegetable}s?</p>";
```

Parsing Strings

Table B-2 lists the functions you can use to count characters and words in a string.

Function	Description
str_word_count (*string*[, *format*])	Returns the number of words in a string
strcspn(*string1*, *string2*)	Returns the initial number of characters in one string that do not have matching values in another string
strlen(*string*)	Returns the number of characters in a string
strspn(*string1*, *string2*)	Returns the initial number of characters in one string that have matching values in another string
substr_count (*string*, *search_string*)	Returns the number of occurrences of a substring

Table B-2   PHP string counting functions

Finding and Extracting Characters and Substrings

To search for and extract characters and substrings in PHP, you use the functions listed in Table B-3.

Function	Description
stripos(*string*, *search_string*[, *start_position*])	Performs a case-insensitive search and returns the position of the first occurrence of one string in another string
stristr(*string*, *search_string*)	Performs a case-insensitive search for specified characters in a string and returns a substring from the first occurrence of the specified characters to the end of the string
strpos(*string*, *search_string*[, *start_position*])	Performs a case-sensitive search and returns the position of the first occurrence of one string in another string
strrchr(*string*, *character*)	Performs a case-sensitive search for specified characters in a string and returns a substring from the last occurrence of the specified characters to the end of the string
strripos(*string*, *search_string*[, *start_position*])	Performs a case-insensitive search and returns the position of the last occurrence of one string in another string
strrpos(*string*, *search_string*[, *start_position*])	Performs a case-sensitive search and returns the position of the last occurrence of one string in another string
strstr(*string*, *search_string*) or strchr(*string*, *search_string*)	Performs a case-sensitive search for specified characters in a string and returns a substring from the first occurrence of the specified characters to the end of the string
substr(*string*, *start_position*[, *length*])	Returns a portion of a string

Table B-3   PHP string search and extraction functions

There are two types of string search and extraction functions: functions that return a numeric position in a text string, and functions that return a character or substring. With the exception of the substr() function, all of the functions in Table B-3 return a value of false if the search string is not found. To use functions that return the numeric position in a text string, you need to understand that the position of characters in a text string begins with a value of 0, the same as with indexed array elements. For example, the strpos() function performs a case-sensitive search and returns the position of the first occurrence of one string in another string. You pass two arguments to the strpos() function: The first argument is the string you want to search, and the second argument contains the characters for which you want to search. If the search string is not found, the strpos() function returns a Boolean value of false. The following code uses the strpos() function to determine whether the $Email variable contains an @ character. Because the position of text strings begins with 0, the echo() statement returns a value of 9, even though the @ character is the tenth character in the string.

```
$Email = "president@whitehouse.gov";
echo strpos($Email, '@'); // returns 9
```

If you simply want to determine whether a character exists in a string, you need to keep in mind that PHP converts the Boolean values true and false to 1 and 0, respectively. However, these values are character positions within a string. For example, the following statement returns a value of 0 because "p" is the first character in the string:

```
$Email = "president@whitehouse.gov";
echo strpos($Email, 'p'); // returns 0
```

To determine whether the strpos() function (and other string functions) actually returns a Boolean false value and not a 0 representing the first character in a string, you must use the strict not equal operator (!==). The following example uses the strpos() function and the strict not equal operator to determine whether the $Email variable contains an @ character:

```
$Email = "president@whitehouse.gov";
if (strpos($Email, '@') !== FALSE)
        echo "<p>The e-mail address contains an @ character.</p>";
else
        echo "<p>The e-mail address does not contain an @ character.</p>";
```

Replacing Characters and Substrings

You can use the functions listed in Table B-4 to replace characters and substrings in PHP.

Function	Description
str_ireplace(*search_string*, *replacement_string*, *string*)	Performs a case-insensitive replacement of all occurrences of specified characters in a string
str_replace(*search_string*, *replacement_string*, *string*)	Performs a case-sensitive replacement of all occurrences of specified characters in a string
substr_replace(*string*, *replacement_string*, *start_position*[, *length*])	Replaces characters within a specified portion of a string

Table B-4   PHP string replacement functions

Comparing Strings

In addition to comparison operators, you can also use the functions listed in Table B-5 to compare strings in PHP.

Function	Description
strcasecmp(*string1, string2*)	Performs a case-insensitive comparison of two strings
strcmp(*string1, string2*)	Performs a case-sensitive comparison of two strings
strnatcasecmp(*string1, string2*)	Performs a case-insensitive natural order comparison of two strings, so that, for example, a set a strings would be ordered as Purchase1, Purchase2, Purchase3, Purchase4, Purchase5, Purchase6, Purchase7, Purchase8, Purchase9, Purchase10, Purchase11 (the way a human would naturally sort them), and not as Purchase1, Purchase10, Purchase11, Purchase2, Purchase3, Purchase4, Purchase5, Purchase6, Purchase7, Purchase8, Purchase9 (the way a computer would otherwise normally sort them)
strnatcmp(*string1, string2*)	Performs a case-sensitive natural order comparison of two strings
strncasecmp(*string1, string2, length*)	Performs a case-insensitive comparison of a specified number of characters within two strings
strncmp(*string1, string2, length*)	Performs a case-sensitive comparison of a specified number of characters within two strings
levenshtein(*string1, string2,*)	Returns the number of characters you need to change to make two strings the same
metaphone(*string*)	Determines a string's value as calculated by metaphone, which is an algorithm for indexing words by their sound, when pronounced in English
similar_text(*string1, string2[, float_percent]*)	Returns the number of characters that two strings have in common
soundex()	Determines a string's value as calculated by soundex, which is an algorithm for indexing words by their sound, when pronounced in English

Table B-5   PHP string comparison functions

Working with Arrays

The identifiers you use for an array name must follow the same rules as identifiers for variables: They must begin with a dollar sign, can include numbers or an underscore (but not as the first character after the dollar sign), cannot include spaces, and are case sensitive.

In PHP, you can create numerically indexed arrays and associative arrays. You create an indexed array using the array() construct or by using the array name and brackets. The array() construct uses the following syntax:

```
$array_name = array(values);
```

The following code uses the array() construct to create the $Provinces[] array:

```
$Provinces = array("Newfoundland and Labrador", "Prince Edward
Island", "Nova Scotia", "New Brunswick", "Quebec", "Ontario",
"Manitoba", "Saskatchewan", "Alberta", "British Columbia");
```

You access and modify values in a PHP array in the same fashion as you access and modify arrays in JavaScript. The following code assigns values to the first three elements in an array named $HospitalDepts[]:

```
$HospitalDepts = array(
    "Anesthesia",            // first element (0)
    "Molecular Biology",     // second element (1)
    "Neurology");            // third element (2)
```

After you have assigned a value to an array element, you can change it later, just as you can change other variables in a script. To change the first array element in the $HospitalDepts[] array from "Anesthesia" to "Anesthesiology," you use the following statement:

```
$HospitalDepts[0] = "Anesthesiology";
```

Manipulating Elements

This section describes the techniques for manipulating array elements.

Adding and Removing Elements from the Beginning of an Array

To add or remove elements from the beginning of an array, you need to use the array_shift() and array_unshift() functions. The array_shift() function removes the first element from the beginning of an array, whereas the array_unshift() function adds one or more elements to the beginning of an array. You pass to the array_shift() function the name of the array whose first element you want to remove. You pass to the array_unshift() function the name of an array followed by comma-separated values for each element you want to add. For example, the following code declares and initializes an array containing the names of the world's top-ranked golfers in 2005. The array_shift() function removes the first golfer, Ernie Els, from the top of the array and the array_unshift() function adds the two highest-ranked players, Tiger Woods and Vijay Singh, to the top of the array.

```
$TopGolfers = array(
    "Ernie Els",
    "Phil Mickelson",
    "Retief Goosen",
    "Padraig Harrington",
    "David Toms",
    "Sergio Garcia",
    "Adam Scott",
    "Stewart Cink");
array_shift($TopGolfers);
array_unshift($TopGolfers, "Tiger Woods", "Vijay Singh");
```

Adding and Removing Elements from the End of an Array

The easiest way to add additional elements to the end of an array is simply to use the array name and brackets syntax that you first saw in Chapter 3. For example, the first statement in the following code uses the `array()` construct to create the initial `$HospitalDepts[]` array. The second statement then adds a new value, "Pediatrics," as the fourth element of the array.

```
$HospitalDepts = array(
    "Anesthesia",
    "Molecular Biology",
    "Neurology");
$HospitalDepts[] = "Pediatrics";
```

You can also add and remove elements from the end of an array by using the `array_pop()` and `array_push()` functions. The `array_pop()` function removes the last element from the end of an array, whereas the `array_push()` function adds one or more elements to the end of an array. You pass to the `array_pop()` function the name of the array whose last element you want to remove. You pass to the `array_push()` function the name of an array followed by comma-separated values for each element you want to add. In the following example, the `array_pop()` function removes the last department, "Pediatrics," from the end of the array, and the `array_push()` function adds the two additional departments, "Psychiatry" and "Pulmonary Diseases," to the end of the array.

```
$HospitalDepts = array(
    "Anesthesia",
    "Molecular Biology",
    "Neurology",
    "Pediatrics");
array_pop($HospitalDepts);
array_push($HospitalDepts, "Psychiatry", "Pulmonary Diseases");
```

Adding and Removing Elements Within an Array

To add or remove elements anywhere else in an array, you need to use an array function. PHP includes numerous functions for working with arrays, including the `array_splice()` function, which adds or removes array elements. After adding or removing array elements, the `array_splice()` function also renumbers the indexes in the array. The syntax for the `array_splice()` function is `array_splice(array_name, start, characters_to_delete, values_to_insert);`. The *array_name* argument indicates the name of the array you want to modify. The *start* argument indicates the element within the array at which elements should be added or removed. The *characters_to_delete* argument is an integer value that indicates the number of elements to remove from the array, starting with the element indicated by the *start* argument. The *values_to_insert* argument represents the values you want to add as new elements to an array.

Removing Duplicate Elements

You might find it necessary to ensure that an array in a script does not contain duplicate values. For example, your script may use arrays of e-mail addresses, customer names, or sales items, each of which should contain unique elements. You can use the `array_unique()` function to remove duplicate elements from an array. You pass to the `array_unique()` function the name of the array from which you want to remove duplicate elements. As with the `array_values()` function, the `array_unique()` function does not operate directly on an array. Instead, it returns a new array with the renumbered indexes. For this reason, you need to write a statement that assigns the array that is returned from the `array_unique()` function to a new variable name or to the original array.

Manipulating Arrays

This section discusses how to sort, combine, and compare arrays.

Sorting Arrays

You sort arrays using the functions listed in Table B-6.

Function	Description
`array_multisort` `(array[, array, ...])`	Sorts multiple arrays or multidimensional arrays
`arsort(array[, SORT_REGULAR | SORT_NUMERIC | SORT_STRING])`	Performs a reverse sort of values in an associative array and maintains the existing keys
`asort(array[, SORT_REGULAR | SORT_NUMERIC | SORT_STRING])`	Sorts an associative array by value and maintains the existing keys
`krsort(array[, SORT_REGULAR | SORT_NUMERIC | SORT_STRING])`	Performs a reverse sort of an associative array by key
`ksort(array[, SORT_REGULAR | SORT_NUMERIC | SORT_STRING])`	Sorts an associative array by key
`natcasesort(array)`	Performs a case-sensitive natural order sort by value and maintains the existing indexes or keys
`natsort(array)`	Performs a natural order sort by value and maintains the existing indexes or keys
`rsort(array[, SORT_REGULAR | SORT_NUMERIC | SORT_STRING])`	Performs a reverse sort of values in an indexed array and renumbers the indexes
`sort(array[, SORT_REGULAR | SORT_NUMERIC | SORT_STRING])`	Sorts an indexed array by value and renumbers the indexes
`uk_sort(array[, comparison_function])`	Uses a comparison expression to sort an associative array by keys, maintaining the existing keys
`usort(array[, comparison_function])`	Uses a comparison expression to sort an indexed array by values, renumbering the indexes

Table B-6   Array sorting functions

Combining Arrays

If you want to combine arrays, you have two options. You can either append one array to another or merge the two arrays. To append one array to another, you use the addition (+) or the compound assignment operator (+=). Instead of appending one array to another, you can merge two or more arrays with the `array_merge()` function. The syntax for the `array_merge()` function is *new_array* = `array_merge($array1, $array2, $array3, ...)`;. The *$array2* array is appended to the *$array1* array, the *$array3* array is appended to the *$array2* array, and so on. If you use the `array_merge()` function with associative arrays, the keys in the array you are appending overwrite any duplicate keys in the array to which you are appending. With indexed arrays, all elements in one array are appended to another array and renumbered. The following statement demonstrates how to combine the associative `$ProvincialCapitals[]` and the `$TerritorialCapitals[]` arrays:

```
$CanadianCapitals = array_merge($ProvincialCapitals,
                $TerritorialCapitals);
```

Comparing Arrays

PHP includes several functions for comparing the contents of two or more arrays. Two of the most basic comparison functions are `array_diff()` and `array_intersect()`. The `array_diff()` function returns an array of elements that exist in one array but not in any other arrays to which it is compared. The syntax for the `array_diff()` function is *new_array* = `array_diff` `($array1, $array2, $array3, ...)`;. A new array is returned containing elements that occur in *$array1* but not in any of the other array arguments. Indexes are not renumbered in the new array.

The `array_intersect()` function returns an array of elements that exist in all of the arrays that are compared. The syntax for the `array_intersect()` function is *new_array* = `array_intersect($array1, $array2, $array3, ...)`;. As with the `array_diff()` function, keys and indexes are not renumbered in the new array, so you must use the `array_values()` function to renumber an indexed array.

Converting Between Strings and Arrays

You use the `str_split()` or `explode()` function to split a string into an indexed array. The `str_split()` function splits each character in a string into an array element, using the syntax *$array* = `str_split(string[, length])`;. The *length* argument represents the number of characters you want assigned to each array element. The `explode()` function splits a string into an indexed array at a specified separator. The syntax for the `explode()` function is *$array* = `explode(separators, string)`;. The following code demonstrates how to split the `$Presidents` string into an array named `$PresidentArray`:

```
$Presidents = "George W. Bush;William Clinton;George H.W.
Bush;Ronald Reagan;Jimmy Carter";
$PresidentArray = explode(";", $Presidents);
foreach ($PresidentArray as $President) {
    echo "$President<br />";
}
```

If the string does not contain the specified separators, the entire string is assigned to the first element of the array. The `explode()` function evaluates the characters in the *separator* argument as a substring. For example, a semicolon and a space separate each president's name in the following example. Therefore, the `explode()` function includes a semicolon and a space as the *separator* argument.

```php
$Presidents = "George W. Bush; William Clinton; George H.W. Bush;
Ronald Reagan; Jimmy Carter";
$PresidentArray = explode("; ", $Presidents);
foreach ($PresidentArray as $President) {
    echo "$President<br />";
}
```

NOTE

If you pass to the `explode()` function an empty string as the *separator* argument, the function returns a value of false.

The opposite of the `explode()` function is the `implode()` function, which combines an array's elements into a single string, separated by specified characters. The syntax for the `implode()` function is `$variable = implode(separators, array);`. The following example first creates an array named `$PresidentsArray`, then uses the `implode()` function to combine the array elements into the `$Presidents` variable, separated by a comma and a space:

```php
$PresidentsArray = array("George W. Bush", "William Clinton",
"George H.W. Bush", "Ronald Reagan", "Jimmy Carter");
$Presidents = implode(", ", $PresidentsArray);
echo $Presidents;
```

Handling Form Submissions

This section describes how to handle form submissions to a PHP script.

Using Autoglobals

PHP includes various predefined global arrays, called **autoglobals** or **superglobals**, which contain client, server, and environment information that you can use in your scripts. Table B-7 lists the PHP autoglobals.

Array	Description
`$_COOKIE`	An array of values passed to the current script as HTTP cookies
`$_ENV`	An array of environment information
`$_FILES`	An array of information about uploaded files
`$_GET`	An array of values from a form submitted with the GET method
`$_POST`	An array of values from a form submitted with the POST method
`$_REQUEST`	An array of all the elements found in the `$_COOKIE`, `$_GET`, and `$_POST` arrays
`$_SERVER`	An array of information about the Web server that served the current script
`$_SESSION`	An array of session variables that are available to the current script
`$GLOBALS`	An array of references to all variables that are defined with global scope

Table B-7   PHP autoglobals

The following statements print three elements of the `$_SERVER` autoglobal. The `$_SERVER["PHP_SELF"]` element prints the path and name of the current script, the `$_SERVER["SERVER_SOFTWARE"]` element prints the name of the server software that executed the script, and the `$_SERVER["SERVER_PROTOCOL"]` element prints the server protocol that was used to request the script.

```
echo "<p>The name of the current script is ",
     $_SERVER["PHP_SELF"], "<br />";
echo "This script was executed with the following server
software: ", $_SERVER["SERVER_SOFTWARE"], "<br />";
echo "This script was requested with the following server
protocol: ", $_SERVER["SERVER_PROTOCOL"], "</p>";
```

NOTE
The elements that are available with the `$_SERVER` autoglobal depend on the Web server that executes the PHP script. For more information on the `$_SERVER` autoglobal, see the online PHP documentation at *http://www.php.net/docs.php*.

Two of the most commonly used autoglobals are `$_GET` and `$_POST`, which allow you to access the values of forms that are submitted to a PHP script. The `$_GET` autoglobal contains values of forms that are submitted with the "get" method, while the `$_POST` autoglobal contains values of forms that are submitted with the "post" method. Which autoglobal you use depends on the value you assign to a `<form>` element's `method` attribute. The following code contains a typical form that uses the "get" method to submit the form to a script named ProcessOrder.php:

```
<form method="get" action="ProcessOrder.php">
<p>Name<br />
<input type="text" name="name" size="50" /><br />
```

```
Address<br />
<input type="text" name="address" size="50" /><br />
City, State, Zip<br />
<input type="text" name="city" size="38" />
<input type="text" name="state" size="2" maxlength="2" />
<input type="text" name="zip" size="5" maxlength="5" /><br />
E-Mail<br />
<input type="text" name="email" size="50" /></p>
<p><input type="reset" />
<input type="submit" /></p>
</form>
```

When you click a form's Submit button, each field on the form is submitted to the server as a name=value pair. When the "get" method is specified, the name portion of the name=value pair becomes the key of an element in the $_GET autoglobal and the value portion is assigned as the value of the element. Similarly, when the "post" method is specified, the name portion of the name=value pair becomes the key of an element in the $_POST autoglobal and the value portion is assigned as the value of the element. Upon submitting the preceding form to the ProcessOrder.php script, you can access the form fields with the following statements:

```
$_GET["name"]
$_GET["address"]
$_GET["city"]
$_GET["state"]
$_GET["zip"]
$_GET["email"]
```

Validating Submitted Data

You can validate data that is submitted from a form to a PHP script in essentially three ways:

- Use the isset() or empty() functions to ensure that a variable contains a value.
- Use the is_numeric() function to test whether a variable contains a numeric string.

Determining if Form Variables Contain Values

Both the isset() function and the empty() function can be used to determine if form variables contain values, but they do this in different ways. The isset() function determines whether a variable has been declared and initialized (or "set"), whereas the empty() function determines whether a variable is empty. You pass to both functions the name of the variable you want to check.

The following example contains a modified version of the script you saw in the previous section. The first script section uses the isset() function to determine whether the $_GET['height'] and $_GET['weight'] variables are set. If both variables are set, the script performs a body mass index calculation. In the form section of the example, if statements use the empty() function to determine whether the variables are empty. If they are not empty, their values are displayed in the text boxes. If the variables are empty, only the form displays.

```
<h1>Body Mass Index</h1><hr />
<?php
if (isset($_GET['height']) && isset($_GET['weight'])) {
    $BodyMass = $_GET['weight'] / ($_GET['height']
        * $_GET['height']) * 703;
    printf("<p>Your body mass index is %d.</p>", $BodyMass);
}
?>
<form action="BodyMassIndex.php" method="get"
enctype="application/x-www-form-urlencoded">
<p>Height: <input type="text" name="height" size="30"
value="<?php if (!empty($_GET['height']))
echo $_GET['height'] ?>" /> 
(Enter a height in inches)</p>
<p>Weight: <input type="text" name="weight"
size="30" value="<?php if
(!empty($_GET['weight'])) echo $_GET['weight']
?>" /> (Enter a weight in pounds)</p>
<p><input type="submit" value="Calculate" />
<input type="reset" value="Reset Form" /></p>
</form><hr />
```

Testing if Form Variables Contain Numeric Values

Even though the data that a PHP script receives from a form submission is usually in the form of a text string, the PHP scripting engine can usually perform the necessary type casting. This means that you do not need to explicitly convert form data to a specific data type. This is especially important when your script expects a numeric value that will be used in a calculation. For example, with the Body Mass Index script, PHP converts any numbers that are submitted from the form to a numeric format. However, you cannot be sure that a user will always enter a number into each text box. If a submitted form value must be numeric data, you should use an is_numeric() function to test the variable. The following example contains a modified version of the first script section from the previous example. This version contains a nested if statement that tests whether the $_GET['height'] and $_GET['weight'] variables are numeric after the first if statement checks to see whether they are set.

```
if (isset($_GET['height']) && isset($_GET['weight'])) {
        if (is_numeric($_GET['weight']) && is_numeric($_GET['height'])) {
                $BodyMass = $_GET['weight'] / ($_GET['height']
                    * $_GET['height']) * 703;
                printf("<p>Your body mass index is %d.</p>",
                $BodyMass);
        }
        else
                echo "<p>You must enter numeric values!</p>";
}
```

NOTE

You cannot use any other is_*() functions to test the data type of a form variable. If you want to ensure that a form variable is of a specific numeric data type, such as an integer, you should first use the is_numeric() function to test whether the variable is numeric, then cast the variable to the required data type.

Working with Files

In this section, you will learn how to read and store data in text files.

Opening and Closing File Streams

PHP includes several functions for reading data from a file. But before any of these functions can do their jobs, you must create a stream. A **stream** is a channel that is used for accessing a resource that you can read from and write to. For example, you might use a stream to access a file. The **input stream** reads data from a resource (such as a file), whereas the **output stream** writes data to a resource (again, such as a file). Using a file stream involves the following steps:

1. Open the file stream with the fopen() function.
2. Write data to or read data from the file stream.
3. Close the file stream with the fclose() function.

In the following sections, you first learn how to open and close file streams, and then you learn how to write and read data.

Opening a File Stream

When you use the echo() or print() functions to send data to an output stream, you only need to call each function for the data to be sent to the stream. With external files, such as text files, you must write code that opens and closes a handle to a file. A **handle** is a special type of variable that PHP uses to represent a resource such as a file. You use the fopen() function to open a handle to a file stream. The syntax for the fopen() function is $open_file = fopen("text file", "mode");. The $open_file variable is the handle that you can use to read and write data from and to the file. The mode argument can be one of several values that determine what you can do with the file after you open it.

Table B-8 lists the mode arguments that you can use with the fopen() function. Among other things, these arguments control the position of the file pointer. A **file pointer** is a special type of variable that refers to the currently selected line or character in a file. The file pointer is a way of keeping track of where you are in a file.

Argument	Description
a	Opens the specified file for writing only and places the file pointer at the end of the file; attempts to create the file if it doesn't exist
a+	Opens the specified file for reading and writing and places the file pointer at the end of the file; attempts to create the file if it doesn't exist
r	Opens the specified file for reading only and places the file pointer at the beginning of the file
r+	Opens the specified file for reading and writing and places the file pointer at the beginning of the file
w	Opens the specified file for writing only and deletes any existing content in the file; attempts to create the file if it doesn't exist
w+	Opens the specified file for reading and writing and deletes any existing content in the file; attempts to create the file if it doesn't exist
x	Creates and opens the specified file for writing only; returns false if the file already exists
x+	Creates and opens the specified file for reading and writing; returns false if the file already exists

Table B-8   Mode arguments of the `fopen()` function

The following statement shows how to use the `fopen()` function to open a handle to a file stream:

```
$BowlersFile = fopen("bowlers.txt", "r+");
```

Assume that the preceding statement opens a file that contains a list of people who have signed up for a bowling tournament. The `fopen()` function assigns the file to a handle named `$BowlersFile`. Notice that the function uses a *mode* argument of "r+", which opens the specified file for reading and writing and places the file pointer at the beginning of the file, before the first record. If you want to open a file and place the file pointer at the end of the file, you use a *mode* argument of `"a+"`, as shown in the following statement:

```
$BowlersFile = fopen("bowlers.txt", "a+");
```

Closing a File Stream

When you are finished working with a file stream, you use the statement `fclose($handle);` to ensure that the file doesn't keep taking up space in your computer's memory. The following code includes an `fclose()` statement:

```
$BowlersFile = fopen("bowlers.txt", "a");
$NewBowler = "Gosselin, Don\n";
fwrite($BowlersFile, $NewBowler);
fclose($BowlersFile);
```

Notice that the `fopen()` function in the preceding statement uses `"a"` as the *mode* argument. The *mode* argument of `"a"` opens the bowlers.txt file for writing only (or attempts to create it if it doesn't exist) and places the file pointer at the end of the file. The code also includes the `fwrite()` function, which writes a line to the open file. You learn about the `fwrite()` function in the next section.

Writing Data to Files

PHP supports two basic functions for writing data to text files: the `file_put_contents()` function and the `fwrite()` function. You study the more limited `file_put_contents()` function shortly, followed by the `fwrite()` function. But before you learn how to write data to text files, you need to understand how line breaks vary by operating systems.

Different operating systems use different escape sequences to identify the end of a line. UNIX/Linux platforms use the \n carriage return escape sequence to identify the end of a line, Macintosh platforms use \r to identify the end of a line, and Windows operating systems use both the \r carriage return escape sequence and the \n newline escape sequence to identify the end of a line. For example, to identify the end of a line on UNIX/Linux platforms, you append the \n carriage return escape sequence to the end of a line, as follows:

```
This is how you end a line on UNIX/Linux platforms.\n
```

The following statement demonstrates how to use both the \r carriage return escape sequence, and the \n newline escape sequence to identify the end of a line on Windows operating systems:

```
This is how you end a line on Windows operating systems.\r\n
```

If you do not use the correct end-of-line escape sequence, you may experience problems when working with text files on different platforms. For example, the following names of people registered for the bowling tournament end with the \n newline escape sequence, as required for UNIX/Linux operating systems:

```
Blair, Dennis\n
Hernandez, Louis\n
Miller, Erica\n
Morinaga, Scott\n
Picard, Raymond\n
```

The PHP file functions that you study in this chapter can usually accommodate any of these escape sequences and end lines in a text file appropriately, regardless of the operating system. For this reason, although the examples in this book use the \n newline escape sequence that is supported by UNIX/Linux operating systems, the PHP scripts you write will function correctly on any platform.

Writing an Entire File

The `file_put_contents()` function writes or appends a text string to a file. The syntax for the `file_put_contents()` function is `file_put_contents(filename, string[, options])` function. If the specified filename does not exist, it is created. However, if the specified filename does exist, any data it contains is overwritten. With the `file_put_contents()` function, you do not need to use the `fopen()` and `fclose()` function. Instead, you simply call the `file_put_contents()` function and pass to it the name of the file to which you want to write data along with a text string containing the data you want to write. For example, the following code builds a variable named `$TournamentBowlers` that contains the names of bowlers in the tournament separated by line breaks, along with a variable named `$BowlersFile` that contains the filename where the bowler names will be stored. The last statement passes the

$BowlersFile and the $TournamentBowlers variables to the file_put_contents()
function.

```
$TournamentBowlers = "Blair, Dennis\n";
$TournamentBowlers .= "Hernandez, Louis\n";
$TournamentBowlers .= "Miller, Erica\n";
$TournamentBowlers .= "Morinaga, Scott\n";
$TournamentBowlers .= "Picard, Raymond\n";
$BowlersFile = "bowlers.txt";
file_put_contents($BowlersFile, $TournamentBowlers);
```

The file_put_contents() function returns the number of bytes that were written to the file.
If no data was written to the file, the function returns a value of 0. You can use the return value
to determine whether data was successfully written to the file, as follows:

```
if (file_put_contents($BowlersFile, $TournamentBowlers) > 0)
    echo "<p>Data was successfully written to the
          $BowlersFile file.</p>";
else
    echo "<p>No data was written to the $BowlersFile file.</p>";
```

CAUTION
You can use an absolute or relative path with the filename you pass to the
file_put_contents() function. However, even though the function will create
a filename that does not exist, it will not create any directories that do not exist. If
you specify a nonexistent directory, you receive an error.

In addition to the filename and text string arguments, you can pass a third argument to the
file_put_contents() function that contains the FILE_USE_INCLUDE_PATH or the
FILE_APPEND constant. The FILE_USE_INCLUDE_PATH constant instructs PHP to search for the
specified filename in the path that is assigned to the include_path directive in your php.ini
configuration file. The FILE_APPEND constant instructs PHP to append data to any existing contents in the specified filename instead of overwriting it.

Reading Data from Files

PHP includes a number of different functions for reading data from text files. These functions can
be generally classified as functions that read an entire file or functions that read the contents of
a file incrementally. You study the functions that read an entire file first.

Reading an Entire File

Table B-9 lists the PHP functions that you can use to read the entire contents of a text file.

Function	Description
file (filename[, use_include_path])	Reads the contents of a file into an indexed array
file_get_contents filename[, use_include_path])	Reads the contents of a file into a string
fread($handle, length)	Reads the contents of a file into a string up to a maximum number of bytes
readfile (filename[, use_include_path])	Prints the contents of a file

Table B-9   PHP functions that read the entire contents of a text file

NOTE
You do not need to use the fopen() and fclose() functions with the functions listed in Table B-9.

The file_get_contents() function reads the entire contents of a file into a string. If you have a text file containing a single block of data (that is, not a collection of individual records), the file_get_contents() function can be useful. For example, assume a weather service uses a text file to store daily weather forecasts. The following code uses the file_put_contents() function to write the daily forecast for San Francisco to a text file named sfweather.txt:

```
$DailyForecast = "<p><strong>San Francisco daily weather forecast</strong>:
Today: Partly cloudy. Highs from the 60s to mid 70s. West winds 5 to 15 mph.
Tonight: Increasing clouds. Lows in the mid 40s to lower 50s. West winds
5 to 10 mph.</p>";
file_put_contents("sfweather.txt", $DailyForecast);
```

The following example uses the file_get_contents() function to read the contents of the sfweather.txt file into a string variable, which is then printed with an echo() statement:

```
$SFWeather = file_get_contents("sfweather.txt");
echo $SFWeather;
```

If you only want to print the contents of a text file, you do not need to use the file_get_contents() function to assign the contents of a file. Instead, use the readfile() function, which prints the contents of a text file along with the file size to a Web browser. For example, the following readfile() function accomplishes the same task as the file_get_contents() version you saw earlier:

```
readfile("sfweather.txt");
```

Appendix C
Processing XML

Extensible Markup Language, or **XML**, is a text-based format for defining and transmitting data between applications. The main benefit of XML is that it allows different applications running on different platforms to read and correctly interpret data that conforms to XML's rules. Like HTML, XML is based on SGML. Version 1.0 of XML achieved recommendation status by the W3C in 1998 and was still current at the time of this writing. Although XML is a markup language like HTML, it is not a replacement for HTML. However, HTML's successor, XHTML, is a combination of both HTML and XML. By itself, XML is primarily a way of defining and organizing data and does not include any of the display capabilities of HTML. The important thing to understand about XML is that it is now the de facto standard for defining and transmitting data across different applications and platforms, including the Internet.

In XML, a tag pair and the data it contains is referred to as an **element**. All elements must have an opening tag and a closing tag. The data contained within an element's opening and closing tags is referred to as its **content**. One concept that can be difficult to grasp is that XML does not specify any elements or attributes. Instead, you define your own elements and attributes to describe the data in your document. The following code is an example of an XML document that defines several elements used to describe the data associated with an automobile:

```
<auto>
     <make manufacturer="GM">Chevrolet</make>
     <model>Corvette</model>
     <year>1967</year>
     <color>Red</color>
</auto>
```

The preceding code is the most basic form of an XML document. In order for your XML documents to be properly structured, they must also include an XML declaration and adhere to XML's syntax rules. You study these requirements in the next few sections.

The XML Declaration

XML documents should begin with an **XML declaration**, which specifies the version of XML being used. You are not actually required to include an XML declaration because currently only one version of XML exists, version 1.0. However, it's good practice always to include the XML declaration because XML will almost certainly evolve into other versions that will contain features not found in version 1.0. Specifying the version with the XML declaration will help ensure that the application that is parsing your XML document will know which version to use.

You can use the following three properties with the XML declaration: version, standalone, and encoding. All of the properties are optional, but you should at least include the version property, which designates the XML version number (currently "1.0"). The following statement is an XML declaration that only includes the version property:

```
<?xml version="1.0"?>
```

NOTE
The XML declaration is not actually a tag but a processing instruction, which is a special statement that passes information to the application that is processing the XML document. You can easily recognize processing instructions because they begin with <? and end with ?>.

The encoding property of the XML declaration designates the language used by the XML document. Although English is the primary language used on the Web, it is certainly not the only one. To be a considerate resident of the international world of the Web, use the encoding property of the XML declaration to designate the character set for your XML document. English and many western European languages use the iso-8859-1 character set. Therefore, you should use the following XML declaration in your documents:

```
<?xml version="1.0" encoding="iso-8859-1"?>
```

The standalone="yes" attribute indicates that the document does not require a DTD in order to be rendered correctly. Unlike HTML, XML documents do not require a DTD to be rendered correctly. Because XML does not include predefined elements, it does not need a DTD to define them. However, some XML documents may benefit from a DTD, especially if multiple XML documents share the same elements. If your XML document requires a DTD, then you assign the standalone property a value of "no". However, if you are certain that your XML document will not require a DTD, then you assign the standalone property a value of "yes". For instance, you use the following XML declaration for any XML documents that do not require a DTD:

```
<?xml version="1.0" encoding="iso-8859-1" standalone="yes"?>
```

Parsing XML Documents

When you open in a browser an HTML document that is not written properly, such as a document that does not include the closing </html> tag, the browser simply ignores the error and renders the page anyway. In contrast, XML documents must adhere to strict rules. The most important of these rules is that all elements must be closed. When a document adheres to XML's syntax rules, it is said to be **well formed**. You will study XML's rules for writing well-formed documents in the next section.

TIP

The W3C actually uses the term *well formedness*, although grammatically it sounds strange, so this book uses the term *well formed*.

You use a program called a **parser** to check whether an XML document is well formed. There are two types of parsers: non-validating and validating. A non-validating parser simply checks whether an XML document is well formed, and if it is, displays its XML elements and data. A validating parser checks whether an XML document is well formed and also whether it conforms to an associated DTD. Firefox, Internet Explorer, and other browsers have the capability to act as non-validating parsers. For instance, if you open the automobile XML document in Firefox and the document is well-formed, then Firefox will correctly parse and display the document, as shown in Figure C-1.

Figure C-1

Well-formed XML
document in Firefox

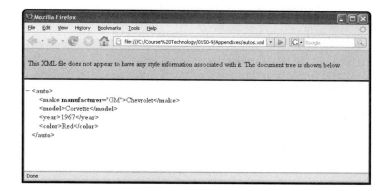

NOTE

The message at the top of the Web page in Figure C-1 indicates that the XML file does not contain any style information. To create formatted Web pages in XML, you must use **Extensible Stylesheet Language (XSL)**, which is a style sheet language for XML. Think of XSL as being roughly equal to the Cascading Style Sheets (CSS) you use with XHTML documents, although XSL is much more complex than CSS. For information on how to use XSL, refer to *XHTML* by Don Gosselin (the author of this book), published by Course Technology/Thomson Learning.

If an XML document is not well formed, then the parser displays an error message. For example, if the automobile XML document is missing the closing `</auto>` tag, then it is not well formed. In this case, a Web browser indicates the error, as shown in Figure C-2.

Appendix C

Figure C-2
XML document that is
not well formed in
Firefox

Writing Well-Formed Documents

One reason XML documents need to be well formed is to allow different applications to read the document's data easily. Most applications expect XML data to be structured according to specific rules, which allows the application to read data quickly without having to decipher the data structure.

In this section, you will study the rules for writing well-formed XML documents. The most important of these rules are:

- All XML documents must have a root element.
- XML is case sensitive.
- All XML elements must have closing tags.
- XML elements must be properly nested.
- Attribute values must appear within quotation marks.
- Empty elements must be closed.

These rules are explained in the following sections.

All XML Documents Must Have a Root Element

A **root element** contains all the other elements in a document. The <html>...</html> element is the root element for HTML documents, although most Web browsers do not require a document to include it. On the other hand, XML documents require a root element that you define yourself. For instance the root element for the XML automobile data document is the <auto> element. If you do not include a root element, then the XML document will not be well formed. For instance, the following version of the XML document containing the automobile data is not well formed because it is missing the <auto> root element:

```
<?xml version="1.0" encoding="iso-8859-1" standalone="yes"?>
<make>Chevrolet</make><model>Corvette</model>
<year>1967</year><color>Red</color>
```

XML is Case Sensitive

Unlike HTML tags, XML tags are case sensitive. For instance, in an HTML document it makes no difference whether the bold tag is uppercase or lowercase. Both of the following HTML statements will be rendered properly in a Web browser:

```
<B>This line is bold.</B>
<b>This line is also bold.</b>
```

You can even mix and match the cases tags in an HTML document, as in the following statements:

```
<B>This line is bold.</b>
<b>This line is also bold.</B>
```

With XML, however, you cannot mix the case of elements. For instance, if you have an opening tag named `<color>` that is all lowercase, you must also use lowercase letters for the closing tag, as follows:

```
<color>Red</color>
```

If you use a different case for an opening and closing tag, they will be treated as completely separate tags, resulting in a document that is not well formed. The following statement, for instance, is incorrect because the case of the closing tag does not match the case of the opening tag:

```
<color>Red</COLOR>
```

All XML Elements Must Have Closing Tags

As mentioned earlier, most Web browsers usually look the other way if the code in an HTML document is not properly structured and closing tags are missing. One common example is the paragraph element (`<p>`). The `<p>` element should be used to mark a block of text as a single paragraph by enclosing the text within a `<p>...</p>` tag pair, as follows:

```
<p>Sacramento is the capital of California.</p>
```

Many Web authors, however, do not follow this convention and simply place a `<p>` tag at the end of a block of text to create a new paragraph as follows:

```
Sacramento is the capital of California.<p>
```

One reason it is possible to omit closing tags is that Web browsers usually treat HTML documents as text that contains formatting elements. XML, however, is designed to organize data, not display it. As a result, instead of documents consisting of text that contains elements, as is the case with HTML, XML documents consist of elements that contain text. All elements must have a closing tag or the document will not be well formed. For instance, in the automobile data XML document you saw earlier, each element has a corresponding closing tag. The following version of the document is illegal because there are no corresponding closing tags for the `<make>`, `<model>`, `<year>`, and `<color>` elements:

```
<?xml version="1.0" encoding="iso-8859-1" standalone="yes"?>
<auto>
```

```
        <make>Chevrolet<model>Corvette
        <year>1967<color>Red
</auto>
```

TIP
You may have noticed that the XML declaration does not include a closing tag. This is because the XML declaration is not actually part of the document; it only declares the document as an XML document. For this reason, it does not require a closing tag.

XML Elements Must Be Properly Nested

Nesting refers to how elements are placed inside of other elements. For example, in the following code, the <i> element is nested within the <b> element, while the <b> element is nested within the <p> element:

```
<p><b><i>This paragraph is bold and italicized.</i></b></p>
```

In an HTML document, it makes no difference how the elements are nested. Examine the following HTML statement, which applies bold and italics to the text within a paragraph:

```
<p><b><i>This paragraph is bold and italicized.</b></p></i>
```

In the preceding code, the opening <i> element is nested within the <b> element, which in turn is nested within the <p> element. However, notice that the closing </i> element is outside of the closing </p> element. This <i> element is the innermost element. In XML, each innermost element must be closed before another element is closed. In the preceding statement, however, the <b> and <p> elements are closed before the <i> element is closed. Although the order in which elements are closed makes no difference in HTML, in XML, to be correct the statement must be written as follows:

```
<p><b><i>This paragraph is bold and italicized.</i></b></p>
```

As another example, consider the following version of the automobile data XML document. The code is not well formed because the <make> and <model> elements are not properly nested.

```
<?xml version="1.0" encoding="iso-8859-1" standalone="yes"?>
<auto>
        <make>Chevrolet
            <model>Corvette</make>
        </model>
        <year>1967</year><color>Red</color>
</auto>
```

In order for the preceding XML code to be well formed, the <model> element must close before the <make> element, as follows:

```
<?xml version="1.0" encoding="iso-8859-1" standalone="yes"?>
<auto>
```

```
    <make>Chevrolet
        <model>Corevette</model>
    </make>
    <year>1967</year><color>Red</color>
</auto>
```

Attribute Values Must Appear Within Quotation Marks

The value assigned to an attribute in an HTML document can be either contained in quotation marks or assigned directly to the attribute, provided there are no spaces in the value being assigned. For example, recall that a common HTML attribute is the src attribute of the image element (<img>). You assign to the src attribute the name of an image file that you want to display in your document. The following code shows two <img> elements. Even though the first element includes quotation marks around the value assigned to the src attribute, whereas the second element does not, both statements will function correctly.

```
<img src="dog.gif">Image of a dog</img>
<img src=cat.gif>Image of a cat</img>
```

With XML, you must place quotation marks around the values assigned to an attribute. An example is the company attribute of the <manufacturer> element you saw earlier in the automobile data XML document. You must include quotation marks around the value assigned to the company attribute using a statement similar to <manufacturer company="General Motors">. Omitting the quotation marks in the statement <manufacturer company=General Motors> results in a document that is not well formed.

CAUTION

You also cannot include an empty attribute in an element, meaning that you must assign a value to an attribute or exclude the attribute from the element. For instance, the statement <manufacturer company /> is incorrect because no value is being assigned to the company attribute.

Empty Elements Must Be Closed

A number of elements in HTML do not have corresponding ending tags, including the <hr> element, which inserts a horizontal rule into the document, and the <br> element, which inserts a line break. Elements that do not require an ending tag are called **empty elements**. They are called empty elements because you cannot use them as a tag pair to enclose text or other elements. You can create an empty element in an XML document by adding a single slash (/) before the tag's closing bracket to close the element. Most often, you use an empty element for an element that does not require content, such as an image. For instance, in the XML document of automobile data, you may create a <photo> element with a single attribute that stores the name of an image file. This image file contains a photograph of the automobile. An example of the <photo> empty element is shown in the following XML code:

```
<?xml version="1.0" standalone="yes"?>
<auto>
```

```
<photo image_name="corvette.jpg"/>
<make>Chevrolet</make><model>Corvette</model>
<year>1967</year><color>Red</color>
</auto>
```

Remember that the primary purpose of XML is to define and organize data. An empty image element like the one shown in the XML automobile document only provides the name of the associated image file—it does not display it. However, you can display an image from an XML document if you use XSL.

Index